Catechist Manual
Catechumenate
Year C

Bob Duggan • Carol Gura
Rita Ferrone • Gael Gensler
Steve Lanza • Donna Steffen
Maureen A. Kelly

RCL
Benziger

Allen, Texas

Contents

Authors:
Bob Duggan • Carol Gura
Rita Ferrone • Gael Gensler
Steve Lanza • Donna Steffen

Product Manager:
Maureen Kelly

Production Editor:
Becky Ivey

Book Design:
Barbara Mueller

Cover Design:
Karen McDonald

Nihil Obstat
Reverend George Smiga, S.T.D.
Censor Librorum

Imprimatur
† *Most Reverend Anthony Pilla*
Bishop of Cleveland

September 2, 1997

The Nihil Obstat and Imprimatur are official declarations that the material reviewed is free of doctrinal or moral error. No implication is contained therein that those granting the Nihil Obstat and Imprimatur agree with the contents, opinions, or statements expressed.

Send all inquiries to:
RCL Benziger
206 East Bethany Drive
Allen, Texas 75002-3804

Visit us at www.RCLBenziger.com

Toll free 877-275-4725
Fax   800-688-8356

Printed in the United States of America

12707 ISBN 978-0-7829-0761-2

6 7 8 9 10 11 • 13 12 11 10 09

Catechist's Manual:
Introduction

"According to the hopes of the Second Vatican Council, sacred scripture will then be a perpetual source of spiritual life, the chief instrument for handing down Christian doctrine, and the center of theological study."

(Pope Paul VI, Apostolic Constitution of the Roman Missal)

What you have before you is a great adventure. Each week the living God speaks to us—who could believe it?—a Word that turns the world upside down, calling us to conversion and newness of life. This manual is a companion to that process by which God reaches us and changes us through the gospel of Jesus Christ.

What is this resource, and who is it for?

The *Catechist's Manual* is a resource to help catechists involved in the Rite of Christian Initiation of Adults as they prepare to lead sessions with catechumens, candidates and their sponsors during the period of the catechumenate. It is the result of a collaborative effort by seven writers, all of whom have had extensive experience in various pastoral settings implementing the Rite. While this manual is intended primarily for catechists, it could conceivably be used also by homilists, especially those who are preaching to an assembly that is home to a catechetical group. Catechists who use this manual will find that in the Foundations in Faith series there is a corresponding resource for catechumens and candidates and their sponsors: the *Participant Book* to be used in conjunction with it.

Why a catechetical resource based on the Liturgy of the Word? This resource is based on the Liturgy of the Word celebrated at Sunday Mass, because the initiation process, as revised by the Second Vatican Council, clearly mandates that catechesis be wedded to the Word of God, experienced in the Sunday liturgy and the seasons of the church year. Catechumens and candidates become more familiar with the Christian way of life in the midst of the community of the church which proclaims, celebrates and reflects upon the gospel. By encountering the Word proclaimed in the community of faith, they truly meet the Word

who is Christ. The community also assists them in performing those acts of service and apostolic witness that show they take to heart the Word they hear (*RCIA*, 75-89).

The *Catechism of the Catholic Church* declares that the liturgy itself is the privileged place for catechesis (CCC, 1074). This declaration reflects the teaching of the Church as expressed in the *Introduction to the Lectionary* which insists that when the assembled people of God hear the Word proclaimed and reflect upon it they are made new in the promises of the covenant (*Lectionary for Mass: Introduction*, 7 & 8). In their "full, conscious and active participation in liturgical celebrations" the "true Christian spirit" is promoted and the Church lives up to its stature as "a chosen race, a royal priesthood, a holy nation, a redeemed people" (*SC*, 14). Thus, the liturgical cycle itself is catechetical.

According to the *Rite of Christian Initiation of Adults*, the catechumenate period requires "a suitable catechesis . . . provided by priests or deacons, or by catechists and others of the faithful, planned to be gradual and complete in its coverage, accommodated to the liturgical year, and solidly supported by celebrations of the word" (*RCIA*, 75.1). This "catechesis leads . . . to an appropriate acquaintance with dogmas and precepts but also to a profound sense of the mystery of salvation . . ." (RCIA, 75.1). The design of the *Catechist's Manual* takes its cue from this understanding of the relationship between liturgy and catechesis.

When do I use this book?

The period of the catechumenate, for which this resource is tailored, is an ongoing, year-round process. One enters the period of the catechumenate by celebrating the Rite of Acceptance (for catechumens) or the Rite of Welcome (for candidates). The period concludes with the Rite of Election. It is the longest of the four periods of initiation described in the *Rite of Christian Initiation of Adults*, and may last several years if necessary (*RCIA*, 76). There is a *Catechist's Manual* for each year of the lectionary cycle. There are separate resources for the Lenten period of Purification and Enlightenment, the inquiry period, or Precatechumenate, and the period between Easter and Pentecost, or Mystagogia.

Within the catechumenate period, this resource is used weekly on two occasions: after the dismissal, and at a subsequent session for catechesis. The rite asks that catechumens be "kindly dismissed" from the Sunday assembly after the homily (*RCIA*, 75.3), and usually the baptized but uncatechized candidates leave along with them. When they are dismissed, they go together with their catechist to a session called "dismissal catechesis," which lasts as long as the remainder of the liturgy. Then they reconvene with sponsors and others for another, longer catechetical session, which is somewhat different in style, either that same day or on a day later in the week. This second session is called "extended catechesis," because it takes more time than the dismissal session.

What is in this book?

The *Catechist's Manual* incorporates five basic sections that illuminate each Sunday, Holy Day and solemnity of the church year. The first three are found on the background pages titled *Understanding This Sunday*. The rest form the actual catechetical plan, and are found on the next two pages, titled *Session Plans*.

The Word in Liturgy

This section interprets the Sunday (or feast day) Word in light of its liturgical and seasonal context. While historical, critical and literary exegesis as well as other scholarly materials bearing on the Scriptures have been used in interpreting the readings, the main concern of this work has been to present the Word in a way that is faithful to its liturgical proclamation. In each liturgy the church combines several readings in such a way that they effectively interpret each other, and their meaning is heightened and focused by the seasons, feasts and fasts of the liturgical year. The interpretations of the readings offered here always bear these elements in mind.

The Word in Liturgy as much as possible weaves all four Scripture passages of the day (the first reading, the psalm, the second reading and the gospel text) into a coherent whole, and identifies one doctrinal theme which arises from all of them. On some occasions, especially during Ordinary Time, when the second reading is not thematically connected with the other texts, commentary on each of the readings is offered, and the doctrinal theme is selected from either the gospel or the second reading. With the help of the *Catholic Doctrine* section following, the catechist may then naturally proceed from cate-

chesis upon the Word to open up the riches of church teaching.

Catholic Doctrine

Given the identification of a particular doctrine in association with these particular Scripture readings, a summary of relevant Catholic teaching and understandings is then presented. The monuments of faith—Scripture itself, the writings of the Fathers of the Church, the prayer texts found in the Sacramentary and in the other ritual books, magisterial pronouncements found in papal writings and in conciliar documents, the work of theologians, the *sensus fidelium*, and writings of the saints—all have been employed to present this summary of Catholic teaching. This presentation is in keeping with the *Catechism of the Catholic Church*. The catechist will note that, where appropriate, reference is made both to the Catechism and to other documentary resources.

Catholic Culture

This section contains a brief collection of significant cultural artifacts that express the Catholic faith. Its content is related to either the readings of the day, the season of the liturgical year, the feast day or the doctrinal theme. It is not meant to be exhaustive, for the church is heir to a vast treasury of culture. It does, however, describe some notable Catholic works of art, architecture, hymnody, popular prayers and devotions, literature and the lives of the saints to enhance the understanding of that Sunday or feast day.

Dismissal Catechesis

This section is meant to be used by the catechist immediately after the catechumens and candidates are dismissed from the liturgical assembly and thus the material presented is fashioned for about a half hour time period. It consists of four parts: 1) "Getting Started," which proposes an action which will focus the attention of the group, 2) "First Impressions," which outlines a process or gives questions and activities to help the group share their experience of what just happened in the liturgy, 3) "Making Connections," which offers two or three sample questions or processes that elicit the link between the catechumens' and candidates' life experience and the day's liturgy, and 4) "Closing Prayer," which provides directions for a concluding prayer to the dismissal catechesis.

Extended Catechesis

This section always indicates a focus which relies upon the doctrinal theme identified in the *Word in Liturgy* and amplified in the *Catholic Doctrine* section. This focus may reiterate the theme or it may reformulate it in order that the catechetical process may flow with ease from the doctrine.

The material in this section is designed to be used in one of two ways: either immediately after the dismissal catechesis (after the catechumens and candidates are joined by their sponsors and friends and have shared some hospitality), or later in the week. (Please note: It is always used *after* the Sunday celebration, not *before*.)

The first part of this extended catechesis, "Gathering," reflects this dual usage and describes either the action which integrates the new participants (sponsors and friends) or the action which focuses the attention of the group later in the week as the Word is liturgically recalled and proclaimed. After this initial "Gathering," the extended catechesis consists of four parts: 1) "The Word," which describes a process using questions and activities connecting the Scripture with Christian living, 2) "Catholic Teaching," which proposes a user-friendly process to help participants assimilate the doctrine of the Church which flows from this Sunday or feast day, 3) "Putting Faith Into Practice," which outlines a process that links parts one and two with life and may include a tip on how to help participants decide to act according to what they have heard, and 4) "Prayer," which suggests a way to conclude this entire session using either a prayer text, a prayerful activity or one of the minor rites of the catechumenate.

How do I prepare to lead a session?

Prepare by first reading the Scriptures of the day, praying over them, reflecting upon them and hearing them in your own heart, with the needs of the particular catechumens and candidates of the parish in mind. Next, read the background page, *"Understanding This Sunday,"* noting significant insights that you want to remember from the Word, Doctrine, and Culture sections. You will want to have a copy of the *Catechism of the Catholic Church* nearby to consult when reading the Doctrine section.

Then read through both the *Dismissal Catechesis* and the *Extended Catechesis*, making note of any materials you will need to conduct the activities. Remember that the environment for catechesis is important, and requires attention and preparation. Suggestions are offered throughout the manual for how to set up the space where catechesis will take place. Visualize what you will do, and how you will do it. How will you need others to help you? Visualize what the participants will do and how they will do it. What will they need from you and others in order to do their part?

Read any prepared texts you plan to use (including scripts and prayer texts) aloud several times until you are comfortable with them, and can make eye contact easily while using them. If you feel ready to express the script or prayer in your own words, great! The texts in this book are intended to help you, not tie you down.

Many times the catechist is called upon to facilitate a discussion. Be aware that listening, drawing out responses, clarifying and summarizing are some of the most important things you do as a catechist. As you prepare, one of your goals should be to become so familiar with your catechetical plan that you are free to relax, listen and pay full attention to the participants as you facilitate their sharing in the course of the session.
One final note: If you are a first-time catechist, or unfamiliar

with the catechumenate, you owe it to yourself and to the people you serve to acquire some orientation and preparation beyond what is provided in this book. Your parish religious education director or pastor can help you to find an appropriate workshop or institute to attend in your diocese. Ongoing education and formation is desirable for everyone who ministers in the church, so you will be starting out on the right foot. The *Catechist's Manual* will then be of great assistance to you in your "on the job training."

May I adapt what is written here?

Absolutely. While every effort has been made so that the catechist may use this manual "as is" to facilitate a session, nevertheless, given the power of the Spirit and the special needs and character of one's own catechetical group, adaptation will certainly be required and is encouraged by the multi-faceted style in which this book is created. Throughout the catechetical plan, options are offered, and you are always free to substitute questions, activities and prayers of your own. The prayer context and the basic elements of the catechesis however (Word - Doctrine - Action) we do recommend that you keep. If any of these fundamental elements is missing, the participants will be shortchanged.

In the preparation of the manual the authors have attempted without manipulating the scriptures to choose a single doctrinal theme each week and also to present a comprehensive treatment of church teaching throughout the year. Catechists may choose to adapt this material to the needs of their own groups, including changing the doctrinal theme, but in doing so they should be careful to include a complete and comprehensive presentation of church teaching throughout the year. The analytical index of doctrinal themes (which appears on pages 300-301) is a tool to help you find whatever you may need to respond to particular questions and to insure this complete coverage.

What other books will I need?

You will need the ritual text, *The Rite of Christian Initiation of Adults*, which is referenced often in the *Catechist's Manual*, especially for prayers. (We have used the paragraph numbers from the U.S. edition.) You will need the *Lectionary for Mass*, from which to proclaim the readings. You will also want to have on hand the *Catechism of the Catholic Church*, an invaluable resource for assuring a sound presentation of Catholic doctrine. Participants will need the *Participant Book*, which contains many exercises to complement the plans included in this manual.

Excelsior!

Now you are ready to begin. As each Sunday unfolds, may it bring you lasting joy.

ADVENT
SEASON

First Sunday of Advent

The Word In Liturgy

Jeremiah 33:14-16
Psalm 25:4-5, 8-9, 10, 14
1 Thessalonians 3:12-4:2
Luke 21:25-28, 34-36

Each new liturgical year begins, on the first Sunday of Advent, not with looking back to our origins but with looking forward to our future. The liturgy invites us today to become a church of expectancy and hope, because we live in the light of a particular future. The coming of the Lord at the end of time is the theme of the First Sunday of Advent (Introduction to the Lectionary 11.1) and may be the focus of today's catechesis.

The gospel of Year C (Luke) describes the second coming of Christ, the Son of Man, in cosmic terms. Rather than present us with an image of servants facing a master's unexpected return home (Year B), or a householder guarding against a thief (Year A), Luke's gospel portrays a cosmos wracked with upheaval. The sun, moon and stars, the powers of the heavens, and the roaring sea will conspire to terrify whole nations and make individuals die of fright. Yet, at the same time, this passage breathes assurance that believers will not only endure these and any other disasters, but in the very midst of them will find their salvation revealed. The bold confidence proclaimed in Luke's gospel ("When these things begin to happen, stand up straight and raise your heads. . .") is distinctive.

In the midst of disaster, where does this confidence come from? The first reading, from the book of the prophet Jeremiah, offers the Christian assembly an important insight into this question, by drawing our attention to God's promise. As the prophet who spoke God's word of judgment in the midst of the complete destruction of Jerusalem, Jeremiah was no stranger to disaster. Yet his prophetic work also included some oracles of hope, of which the present reading is one. In it he tells of God's promise to raise up a "just shoot" to reign in the line of David, and of a time when the Lord God will rule over a Jerusalem fully restored and made whole ("they shall call her: 'the Lord our justice.'"). In the psalm we humbly ask God's guidance, full of expectation of divine kindness and faithfulness to the covenant.

In reading this oracle of Jeremiah, Christians have understood that the promise of a "just shoot" found its fulfillment in Jesus of Nazareth, a descendant of the family of King David, who was sent to inaugurate the reign of God and is the very embodiment of God's justice. Thus in the context of today's liturgy, Jeremiah's words lead us to recall the first coming of Christ as the fulfillment of God's promise. At the same time, the church believes that the full consummation of the future promised by God has not yet come about. We must rely on God's promise.

The second reading and the latter part of the gospel show us yet another source of confidence. We become anchored by living lives "pleasing to God," not allowing our spirits to become "bloated with indulgence and drunkenness and worldly cares," but using well the time we have, as St. Paul writes, to become more loving, "blameless and holy before our God." In this warm and affirming passage Paul acknowledges both the loving ways that the Thessalonians have already learned, and the fact that they "must learn to make still greater progress." The final words of the gospel put clearly before us the imperative of Advent: ". . .be on the watch. Pray constantly. . . to stand secure before the Son of Man."

Catholic Doctrine

"He will come again in glory."

This formulation from our Profession of Faith (the Nicene Creed) provides a doctrinal focus for the scriptures from the liturgy of the First Sunday of Advent. The kingdom of God is, as one theologian wrote, "already . . .not yet." In Jesus, the world has experienced the inauguration of the kingdom of God among us, although we believe that the fullness of that kingdom is something not yet experienced. We look forward to its final fulfillment at the end of time, when Christ comes again in glory.

In the midst of the Lord's Prayer, during the Communion Rite, the presider prays: "[Lord]. . . .In your mercy keep us free from sin and protect us from all anxiety as we wait in joyful hope for the coming of our Savior, Jesus Christ." Every Sunday we eat and drink the meal of the Lord joyfully waiting for his return in glory, our eyes fixed on the banquet set before us and, at the same time, on the fulfillment of God's promise in Jesus. Indeed, the prayer of today's Church gathered at the Eucharistic feast echoes the cry of early Christians (Revelation 1:4, 22:20) "maranatha" or "Come, Lord Jesus!" This ancient plea and hope finds expression in the words of Memorial Acclamation B, "Dying you destroyed our death, rising you restored our life. Lord Jesus, come in glory!"

The Second Vatican Council taught that far from promoting passivity, the expectation of "a new heaven and a new earth" (Revelation 21:1) should energize us. "The expectancy of a new earth should spur us on, for it is here that the body of a new human family grows, foreshadowing in some way the age which is yet to come. . . .When we have spread on earth the fruits of our nature and our enterprise . . . according to the command of the Lord and in his Spirit, we will find them once again, cleansed this time from the stain of sin, illuminated and transfigured, when Christ presents to his Father an eternal and universal kingdom. . ."(Pastoral Constitution on the Church in the Modern World, 23-24).

The Catechism of the Catholic Church examines the doctrine of Christ's return in several places. In its treatment of the Profession of Faith, (Article 7) the catechism stresses several key points. Catholics do not believe that the fulfillment of the destiny of creation and human beings will be brought about by material progress or human activity alone (secularism), but by God. Catholics reject any attempts to predict the end of the world (millenarianism) or to lessen in any way our responsibility for stewardship of this present world based on a future second coming of Christ. Catholics believe that we meet the glorified Lord upon the event of our death, as well as when his full glory is revealed to all the world at the end of time. (CCC 668-673, 675-676, 1041, 716, 1011.)

For further reading, consult the *Handbook of Catholic Theology*, which includes several articles on eschatology (the doctrine of the "last things"), including one focusing on "contemporary issues" (210-224).

Catholic Culture

In the four weeks of this season, we light Advent wreaths in church and in our homes. Consult the *Book of Blessings* (1509-1540), especially the introductory notes, for an explanation of the wreath and how it is used in the home. Similar material is found in *Catholic Household Blessings and Prayers* (108-112). Note the images of Jesus given in the prayer texts in both these sources.

The saints' days that we celebrate around the time of this first week are: Francis Xavier (Dec. 3), John Damascene (Dec. 4), Nicholas (Dec. 6) and Ambrose (Dec. 7). Many individuals and families delight in the use of specially designed Advent calendars to augment their prayer during this season.

The glorified Christ of the end times has been depicted in art throughout the centuries. For example, Byzantine mosaics of Christ the ruler of the world (Pantocreator) form an imposing backdrop to many eastern churches, and Michelangelo's painting of the Last Judgment on the apse of the Sistine Chapel presents a somber vision reflecting the spiritual and political crisis of his time. Music has also richly expressed Christian longings to meet the Lord who is coming, as in the African-American spiritual "Soon and Very Soon."

The contemporary American Catholic writer, Walker Percy, known for his novels about the end of the world, says of his work, "A serious novel about the destruction of the United States and the end of the world should perform the function of prophecy in reverse. The novelist writes about the coming end in order to warn about present ills and so avert the end.[H]e is like the canary that coal miners used to take down into the shaft to test the air. When the canary gets unhappy, utters plaintive cries, and collapses, it may be time for the miners to surface and think things over." ["Notes for a Novel About the End of the World," from *The Message in the Bottle* (New York: Farrar, Straus and Giroux, 1979)]

Notes

Dismissal Catechesis (30 min)

Getting Started

1. Prepare the space ahead of time with a circle of chairs around a table that has an advent wreath and, if possible, an icon of Christ the ruler of the world.

2. Invite the catechumens and candidates to gather in the circle.

3. Ask the candidates and catechumens to remain standing and face the center of the circle. Light the first candle, and sing the first verse of "O Come, O Come Emmanuel." After the lighting, this prayer may be prayed:

   O God, we praise you for your Son, Jesus Christ. He is Emmanuel, the hope of all peoples, the wisdom that teaches and guides us. He is the Savior of every nation. Open us to hear your Word. Kindle in our hearts your justice, as we await the day of the Lord and prepare to welcome the One who is coming. We ask this through Christ our Lord. Amen.

First Impressions

1. Invite the participants to describe the differences they notice in the church today. Explain the season of Advent in these words:

   The new liturgical year begins today with the season of Advent. Advent is a time of joyful anticipation that Christ's coming continues to pierce the gloom of our lives with the light of his presence.

2. Continue by asking the group to gather in pairs to discuss these questions: *In the Liturgy of the Word, what stands out for you? What gives you cause to stop and think?* Return the attention of the participants to the large group and draw out their responses to the questions. Summarize their insights in two or three sentences.

Making Connections

1. Ask the participants to name some of the images of chaos and destruction from today's readings. You may choose to record these on a poster board that is divided into two parts and is large enough for all to see. Then ask them to discuss the following in small groups: *What disasters and chaos have you experienced in your own life?*

2. Return their attention to the large group by asking the participants to name some of the promises made to those who trust in God. Record their responses on the other half of the newsprint. Here are some possibilities:

   "I will raise up for David, a just shoot."
   "Judah shall be safe, and Jerusalem shall dwell secure."
   "The Son of Man coming on a cloud in power and glory."

3. Once again, gather the participants in small groups to discuss the following: *How are these promises consoling as you face your own difficulties? How has God empowered*

you to stand up straight and raise your head in the midst of difficulty?

4. Invite the whole group to look at the two lists on the poster board. In the large group, ask them to offer any additional insights as to the meaning of these passages in their lives. Summarize their input.

Prayer

Conclude this segment by singing, once again, the next two verses from "O Come, O Come Emmanuel." Proclaim the text of the second reading (1 Thessalonians 3:12-4:2). Close with silence as the participants reflect on this passage.

Extended Catechesis

SESSION FOCUS: *The Second Coming of Christ*

Gathering

A. Sunday:

1. Greet and welcome the sponsors and team members as they arrive. Invite them to join the circle of catechumens and candidates. Ask everyone to spent a short time in silence before the lighted Advent wreath and/or the icon of Christ.

2. Invite the new arrivals to briefly share their reflections on the meaning of Advent and their impressions of today's liturgy.

3. Begin the prayer by inviting all to sing the Gathering Hymn used at today's liturgy. You will need songbooks for all those assembled. Proclaim the Gospel from Luke 21:25-28, 34-36. Close with this prayer or pray in your own words:

   God of the Promised One, you have restored your people through the coming of your Son on this earth, just as you said. Your Word became flesh, that we might have hope in the chaos and difficulties of our lives. We ask that the just shoot of David might grow in our hearts, that we might have the strength to stand upright as we face the perils on our journey toward initiation. Let us not be unduly concerned with worldly distractions. Keep us ever on watch for the coming of Christ into our lives every day. We pray all this in your holy name. Amen.

B. Weekday:

1. As the participants gather in the circle, greet and welcome each person. Ask everyone to spend a short time in silence as they reflect on the Advent Wreath and/or the icon of Christ.

2. Invite the participants to share briefly how the Lord brought them to this gathering.

3. Then pray this celebration of the Word, beginning by lighting one candle of the wreath, during the opening song.

- Song: Gathering Hymn from Sunday's liturgy
- First Reading: Jeremiah 33:14-16
- Sing Psalm 25
- Second Reading: 1 Thessalonians 3:12-4:2
- Silent reflection
- Gospel: Luke 21:25-28, 34-36
- Pray the prayer written above

The Word (30 min)

1. Using these or similar words, explain the background for the second reading.

   Paul exhorts the Thessalonians, reminding them to conduct themselves "in a way pleasing to God" because Christ will return soon, even if the exact time is not known. Jesus exhorts his disciples and us to be ready for the end times and to not lose ourselves in "drunkenness, excessive indulgence and worldly cares." Otherwise, the end will spring upon us like a trap. We find confidence by becoming more centered in using the time we have to become more blameless, loving, and holy before God.

2. In the large group, ask the participants to brainstorm how to live our lives in a way that is "pleasing to God." List these responses on large sheets of paper.

3. Proclaim the Gospel from Luke 21:25-28, 34-36 once again. Continue to explain the Sacred Scriptures in these words:

   There is a mix of emotions in these texts. There is tension, and there is joy. There is firm expectation, and there is an unspecified time. There is future glory and present power. There is faith, challenged by fear. The kingdom is already and not yet.

4. Call the attention of the participants to the final words of the gospel, *"be on the watch . . . pray constantly . . . stand secure before the Son of Man."* This is the meaning of Advent. In our own lives, we experience waiting with similar mixtures of emotions.

5. Ask the participants to use the worksheet contained in the Participant Book (page 4) or on the blackline handout to reflect on their own lives and when they had to wait patiently and be alert for something. When they have finished writing their story and answering the questions, invite them to share their responses with a partner.

Catholic Teaching (30 min)

1. Direct the participants to share their insights on the end of the world and the second coming in this manner:

   From your own experience of waiting, think about the way in which we all wait for the world to be more just, more loving and more peaceful. The anticipation of God's restoration of the earth is a basic human drive. While today's scriptures tell us not to be unduly concerned, and to pray as we wait, some people prefer to hold on to the belief that the end of this world is imminent. Some distrust the human heart's capacity for transformation. Some desire God's immediate judgment and justice to purge the cosmos of evil. Rather than try to predict the end of the world and Christ's second coming,

we are called to pray and be watchful, for Christ comes into our lives every day. This daily vigilance prepares us for the moment of our death when we will see Christ face to face and energizes us to look forward to the fulfillment of the kingdom of God, when Christ comes again in glory.

2. Ask the large group to offer their insights to these questions: *What are some contemporary incidents of predictions of the end of the world? Why are such predictions dangerous?*

3. Present the following points, regarding the second coming of Christ, to the group. Do this in your own words, or refer to the corresponding section of the Participant Book (page 5) or on the blackline handout. "The Church Says"

   - The kingdom of God is inaugurated by the first coming of Jesus, but it is not yet fully manifested. The seeds are planted and glimmers of the kingdom are perceived here and now of what will be seen fully at the end of time.
   - The expectation of the fullness of God's kingdom should energize us. As we wait, we are called to live lives that are blameless before the Lord, live in harmony with nature as wise stewards of the earth, and to proclaim with our lives and voices the saving action of Jesus who died and rose for us.
   - When we have spread on the earth the fruits of our work, we will find them cleansed , illuminated and transfigured, ready when Christ comes again to present this kingdom to the Father.

4. Gather the participants into small groups to discuss these questions: *What does the anticipation of Christ's second coming evoke in you? How will your life change as you expectantly watch and wait?*

5. Invite the participants to share a few of their insights in the large group.

Putting Faith Into Practice

1. Encourage the group to rethink their approach to Christmas preparations, using these words: *There is a great deal of hustle and bustle during this Advent season as Christians prepare to celebrate Christmas. While commercialism is rampant, there is much that is commendable in these weeks before Christmas. There are all sorts of glimmers of the kingdom yet to come.*

2. Invite the participants to offer suggestions that draw out these glimmers of the kingdom, from their own experiences and customs. Ask each person to decide one way they wish to prepare during this Advent season by writing their resolution in the Participant Book (page 5) or on the blackline handout, under the section titled, "I Want to Put My Faith Into Action by."

Prayer

Begin the closing prayer by inviting all to pause for a time of quiet and recollection. After an appropriate period of silence, extend your hands over the catechumens and candidates, and pray in your own words, using the prayer of blessing found in The Rite of Christian Initiation of Adults, # 97E. Follow the blessing by encouraging all to sing "The King of Glory" or another appropriate song.

Second Sunday of Advent

Understanding this Sunday:
Background for Catechesis

The Word In Liturgy

Baruch 5:1-9
Psalm 126:1-6
Philippians 1:4-6, 8-11
Luke 3:1-6

Paul's prayer that the community at Philippi grow in love and justice "up to the very day of Christ" continues to put before us the expectation of the final return of the Lord that appeared so strongly in the liturgy of the First Sunday of Advent. It also points clearly to the need for ongoing conversion in preparation to meet the Lord who is coming. Paul writes this warm and affectionate letter from prison, aware of the peril in which his own life stands, yet rejoicing in prayer "at the way you have all continually helped promote the gospel from the very first day."

A new note is sounded, however, in the joyful prediction of Israel's triumphant return to Jerusalem presented in the reading from Baruch: this passage offers a symbolic vision of the experience of salvation. From wherever they are scattered (west and east) but particularly from the place of exile (Babylon, in the east), the people of Israel return to their mother, the holy city, Jerusalem, like royalty, carried on thrones. Israel, who once was clad in the sackcloth and ashes of "mourning and misery," is now like a woman dressed in fine clothes: "the splendor of glory from God," and "a cloak of justice." She has a priestly role, wearing Aaron's "miter that displays the glory of the eternal name." God commands fragrant trees to shelter her from the sun and the ground to become level before her (echoing Isaiah 40), and he leads the procession himself, with justice and mercy personified as his retinue.

Who is to see this vision? In the passage itself, the spectators are two. Jerusalem is urged to see and welcome it, and "all the earth" will see it as well. The psalm likewise celebrates the fact that the return from exile experienced by the chosen people is good news shared openly with the rest of the world. The nations (those outside the people of Israel) see and are moved by the great things that God has done.

In today's gospel, Luke quotes Isaiah 40:3-5 (the same passage that Baruch has paraphrased) when describing the role of John the Baptist in preparing the way for Christ's coming. Anchored firmly in history, yet employing the rich symbolism of prophetic language, Luke's description of John the Baptist heightens our anticipation of this Lord whom John announces. Significantly, Luke adds a final sentence from Isaiah 52:10b: "All the earth will see the salvation of God." The coming of Jesus is an event of salvation that will be seen by all people. What we prepare for in Advent is of universal significance.

The focus of the word in today's liturgy is the prophetic promise of salvation (Baruch, Isaiah, John the Baptist). For the scattered people of God it will be an experience of being gathered; for the degraded and miserable it will mean honor and rescue; for all people it is offered through the mighty acts of God in history—particularly through the coming of Jesus, the Son of God, into the world.

Catholic Doctrine

"Through the prophets you taught [us] to hope for salvation."

Hope is the focus of today's catechesis. The prophets call us to live in hope, and their message gives form and substance to this hope. In Eucharistic Prayer IV we pray, "through the prophets you taught [us] to hope for salvation. Prophets do not function as fortunetellers. They do not always specify through their preaching the exact shape of the future. Rather, they educate our hope, which is to be placed in God alone.

This Sunday the promise of salvation, and therefore our hope, is given direction by the figure of John the Baptist. In the preface for Masses of John the Baptist, the Church addresses God, praying, "You chose John the Baptist from all the prophets to show the world its redeemer, the lamb of sacrifice." (*Roman Missal*, Preface 61). John the Baptist directs us to the object of our longing. He points the way to our hope.

In this vein, St. Augustine preached: God established a time for his promises and a time for their fulfillment. The time for promises was in the prophets, until John the Baptist . . . God, who is faithful, put himself in our debt, not by receiving anything but by promising so much. A promise was not sufficient for him; he chose to commit himself in writing as well . . . . He has promised [us] divinity, mortals immortality, sinners justification, the poor a rising to glory. . . . [B]ecause God's promises seemed impossible. . .God. . .established a mediator of his good faith, not a prince or angel or archangel, but his only Son. All this had therefore to be prophesied, foretold, and impressed on us as an event in the future, in order that we might wait for it in faith, not find it a sudden and dreadful reality. (Ps. 109, 1-3: CCL 40,1601-1603 and quoted in Liturgy of the Hours, Office of Readings, Wednesday, Second Week of Advent.)

God's promise of salvation, foretold by the prophets, forms our future in faith. In the preface for Advent I we pray to God, "when [Jesus] humbled himself to come among us. . .he fulfilled the plan you formed long ago and opened for us the way. . . .Now we watch for the day, hoping the salvation promised us will be ours" (*Roman Missal,* Preface I for Advent). The message of salvation, impressed upon us by the prophets, makes us who we are this Advent, a people who watch for the day, hoping God's promise will be ours.

See also the article on "Salvation," *Dictionary of Biblical Theology* (Xavier Leon-Dufour, ed.); the *Collegeville Pastoral Dictionary of Biblical Theology*, "Salvation," pp. 867-871; "Redemption/Redeemer," pp. 881-816, especially the pastoral-theological subsections in these articles; and *Encyclopedia of Catholicism*, "Salvation," pp. 1158-1159.

Catholic Culture

Artists frequently portray John the Baptist pointing, for his prophetic role is to point the way to Jesus. In the new world, John the Baptist is revered as the patron saint of Puerto Rico. Medieval cathedrals were deliberately designed to show the place of the prophets in the economy of salvation. The prophets, whose challenging words were associated with the chill north wind, were depicted on the north wall, while the wall to the south, associated with warmer and gentler climes, was reserved for depictions of the saints.

John the Baptist is traditionally considered the last of the Old Testament prophets and the first of the New Testament saints. For this reason, anyone who bears the name of an Old Testament figure (such as Adam, Ruth and Jacob) may consider the solemnity of the birth of John the Baptist (June 24) as their saint's day in the Christian calendar. There are only three births celebrated in the Christian calendar: Jesus, Mary and John the Baptist. For all other saints we celebrate the day of the saint's death as the saint's "birthday in heaven."

This week, on December 12 we will celebrate the feast of Our Lady of Guadalupe. During a time of violent clashes between the Iberian Christians of Europe and the Aztec Nahuatls of the Americas, Our Lady appeared to a poor peasant, Juan Diego, in Nahuatl. She exhorted Juan Diego to spread her message of love, compassion, and hospitality amid the violence of human sacrifice on the part of the Aztecs and judgment and condemnation on the part of the European missionaries. Her appearance marked the birth of the church in the Americas. There are times in our history that the violence and evil appears to be winning out over the hoped-for promise of salvation. It is at these times, when Mary appears to bolster our hope in God's salvation and to empower us to act in bringing about the salvation already won in Jesus.

Notes

Dismissal Catechesis (30 min)

Getting Started

1. Prepare the space ahead of time with a circle of chairs around the Advent wreath and, if possible, artwork depicting John the Baptist.

2. Invite the catechumens and candidates to gather in the circle.

3. As the first and second candles in the wreath are lit, sing "I Long For You," Balhoff, Ducote and Daigle (NALR, 1081). This prayer may then be prayed:

   O Come, O Come, Emmanuel, we sing in prayerful hope. O God of these Advent days, gather us together as sons and daughters of your promise. You chose John the Baptist to point the way to Jesus. You gave us the prophets of days gone by to show us the way of hope. You gave us Jesus, that all the earth and the peoples of the earth might see the salvation of God. As we gather today, renew our hope in this promise of salvation in Jesus. Open us to hear your Word made flesh and allow that Word to enter our hearts. We ask all this in the name of Jesus the Christ. Amen.

First Impressions

1. When the group is seated in the circle, invite them to spend a short time looking at the Advent Wreath and, if available, the picture of John the Baptist. As they sit in quiet reflection, repeat the following images from today's sacred scriptures. You may wish to play some instrumental music used in the liturgy as they reflect.

   "Take off your robe of mourning and misery"
   "Bear on your head the miter that displays the might of the glory of the eternal name"
   "For God is leading Israel in joy"
   "Those who sow in tears will reap with cries of joy"
   "I long for all of you with the affection of Christ Jesus"
   "The word of God came to John"
   "proclaiming a baptism of repentance"
   "A voice of one crying in the desert"

2. Ask the whole group this question: *What feelings and impressions well up within you as a result of the Liturgy of the Word?* Invite them to share in the large group.

Making Connections

1. Help the group recall the sense of the first reading from the liturgy in these words:

   Close your eyes and imagine with me the great procession of return from exile led by God. Two figures, "mercy" and "justice," accompany Yahweh in the retinue. Scattered from east to west the people are united as they move back to their home, the holy city, Jerusalem. Israel is dressed in her finest, "the splendor of glory from God." She is clothed in justice with the priestly 'miter that display the glory of the eternal name." This procession is

   a vision of the experience of salvation. All those who came before us, all who have passed on the faith to us—our families and friends are part of this ongoing, forever procession. Who in this procession are current-day figures of "mercy" and "justice" for you? How are these people clothed? Where is this procession leading?

2. Allow time for the participants to get in touch with their feelings as they imagine this procession. Gently, invite them to return to the present time and place. Ask them to share with one other person their responses to these questions: *What is your reaction as you imagined this vision of triumphal return? What about the vision gives you hope in the present day?* In the large group, invite some responses.

3. Survey the large group, asking them to quickly name some of the things for which they hope. When they have finished, distribute pieces of paper, asking them to write down their hopes.

Prayer

Create a litany of hope by asking participants to read aloud their expression of hope. Direct the group to respond, *"The Lord has done great things for us, we are filled with joy,"* after each hope is named. Conclude by singing or praying Psalm 126. Prepare copies of the psalm ahead and distribute them to the group before the prayer begins.

Extended Catechesis

SESSION FOCUS: *Hope for Salvation*

Gathering

A. Sunday:

1. Welcome sponsors and other team members as they arrive. Allow time for introductions. Invite them to join the circle of catechumens and candidates. Help the group center themselves by focusing on the lighted candles of the Advent wreath and/or the depiction of John the Baptist.

2. Begin by singing two verses of the gathering hymn used at today's liturgy. Ask one of the sponsors to proclaim the gospel from Luke 3:1-6. Conclude by singing or praying Psalm 126.

B. Weekday:

1. As the group gathers in the circle, greet and welcome each person. Allow time for introductions. Invite the participants to share something about their Advent journey this past week.

2. Begin with this celebration of the word.
   - Song: Gathering Hymn from Sunday's liturgy
   - Sign of the Cross, Greeting, and Lighting of Advent Wreath
   - First Reading: Baruch 5:1-9
   - Sing the Responsorial Psalm
   - Second Reading: Philippians 1:4-6, 8-11
   - Gospel: Luke 3:1-6
   - Pause in silence

The Word (30 min)

1. Gather the participants into small groups to begin a dialogue. Ask them to discuss these questions: *Which image in these scriptures did you find most compelling? Why? What do these passages say to your life?*

2. Share with the large group this background of the Gospel:

   The passage from the gospel of Luke hints at reversals. This is a thread that runs through Luke's narrative (1:53, 2:34, 6:24 and 16:25). God will lift up the lowly and fill them with good things, while the rich will be sent away empty. Every valley will be filled and every mountain and hill will be leveled. The winding ways will be straightened and the rough ways will be made smooth.

3. Invite the participants to recall their own journey, with its hills and valleys, by reflecting on the exercise in the Participant Book (page 6) or on the blackline handout. When they complete their journey, ask them to respond to the questions that follow. Invite each catechumen or candidate to share whatever they wish from their journey with their sponsor.

Catholic Teaching (30 min)

1. Call the attention of the participants back to the large group. Invite a few to share their responses to the last question on the reflection sheet, "Where do you find hope for your journey in these scriptures?"

2. Explain the church's teaching on hope for salvation, covering the following points:

   - Prophets exhort us to hope for salvation by giving form and substance to this hope. In the gospel, John the Baptist points to the object of our hope for salvation by preparing the way for Jesus.

   - God has promised us divinity, mortals immortality, sinners justification, the poor a rising to glory through the salvation won for us in Jesus. The era of prophecy (promise) ended with John the Baptist. These promises that seem so impossible are fulfilled with the Incarnation of Jesus, his only Son.

   - Through the promise of salvation, foretold by the prophets, and fulfilled in Jesus, our future in faith is formed. This message of salvation makes us who we are this Advent, a people who watch for the day, placing our hope in the fulfillment of God's promise in us.

   - The salvation for which we hope is the transformation and restoration of the entire universe. Thus, the process of salvation includes (but is not limited to) the transformation of unjust and oppressive social conditions. Whenever God's people or creation are denied their dignity or destroyed, God's salvation is needed and awaited. This ultimate restoration of all creation is effected by God's action in Jesus through the Holy Spirit.

3. In small groups, ask the participants to respond to these questions: *What global and local situations cry out for God's salvation? Where have you observed God at work in the world, restoring and reconciling some aspect of creation (this includes humankind) to its original*

harmony? What is your hope for salvation?

Putting Faith Into Practice

1. Ask all the participants to brainstorm ideas on how we can cooperate with God to bring about this total transformation and restoration of God's people and all of creation. List their ideas on a large poster board that all can read. Some examples include reconciling with alienated family members, working on specific environmental issues and advocating non-violence in conflict situations.

2. Ask the participants to look over the list and spend a few minutes in silence, during which they ask God to direct them to select an action as part of their Advent journey. Direct them to the Participant Book (page 7) or to the blackline handout and write their resolution in the section titled, "I Want to Put My Faith into Action by."

3. Describe the appearance of Our Lady of Guadalupe in the following manner:

   This week, on December 12 we will celebrate the feast of Our Lady of Guadalupe. During a time of violent clashes between the Iberian Christians of Europe and the Aztec Nahuatls of the Americas, Our Lady appeared to a poor peasant Juan Diego in Nahuatl. She exhorted Juan Diego to spread her message of love compassion and hospitality amidst the violence of human sacrifice on the part of the Aztecs and judgment and condemnation on the part of the European missionaries. Her appearance marked the birth of the church in the Americas. There are times in our history that the violence and evil appears to be winning out over the hoped-for promise of salvation. It is at these times that Mary appears to bolster our hope in God's salvation and to empower us to act in bringing about the salvation already won in Jesus.

Prayer

Close the session by asking the participants to name those global situations for which they wait with hope for God's salvation to transform. The response after each petition is, "Come, Lord Jesus, Come." Conclude by singing, "You Alone," Rory Cooney (NALR, 1984).

Third Sunday of Advent

Understanding this Sunday:
Background for Catechesis

The Word In Liturgy

Zephaniah 3:14-18a
Isaiah 12: 2-3, 4, 5-6
Philippians 4:4-7
Luke 3:10-18

St. John the Baptist, who was introduced as a prophet in last week's gospel ("the word of God came to John . . .") is one of the most compelling figures in the whole New Testament. A fierce ascetic chosen from the womb and later to die a martyr's death, he lived and preached in the desert. His baptism was one of repentance, and he prepared the way for Christ. In today's passage from Luke, we hear him speak in his own words.

Moved by John's prophetic preaching about God's coming judgment, people from all walks of life come forward asking, "What are we to do?" One Scripture scholar speculates that this question, asked frequently in Luke's gospel, is a ritual question asked by catechumens in the early church [*The Word We Celebrate*, Patricia Datchuck Sanchez, pp.268-269]. The baptizer responds in plain language, telling them to reform their lives in ordinary ways specific to their life situations. Moral conversion is a necessary preparation for the new era which begins with the coming of the Messiah. The moral virtues and how we acquire them may therefore be the doctrinal focus of today's catechesis.

The first and second readings provide a rich background against which to view moral conversion. The prophet Zephaniah speaks of the return of a sinful people to God as an event of mutual joy. The people rejoice when they are reconciled with God, and God rejoices over them. The following psalm is an exuberant canticle of Isaiah, praising God as "savior" and using the image of water as a focus of joy. (This psalm appears again in the Easter Vigil.) The second reading takes place in the context of a conflict between two women of the community at Philippi. St. Paul exhorts his quarreling followers to "rejoice in the Lord always," as well as to practice other virtues such as unselfishness and gratitude, in light of the nearness of the Lord. As we have seen in the readings throughout Advent, for the believer the expectation of Christ's coming is a cause for joy and renewed diligence in the moral life.

The third Sunday of Advent is known traditionally as "Gaudete Sunday." Gaudete is a Latin word meaning rejoice—an imperative taken from the readings of this day, especially the Pauline readings in all three years of the Lectionary cycle. The vigorously practical preaching of the fierce man of the desert, John, assures that we may not take this command to rejoice as a call for superficial cheeriness or an escape from necessary hard choices. On the other hand, the first and second reading, as well as the psalm, forbid us to imagine that the moral life is a set of grim duties. The call to moral conversion is an invitation to lasting joy.

Catholic Doctrine

Moral conversion prepares for the coming of Christ.

Human beings are created by God with an openness to truth and beauty, a sense of moral goodness, freedom and the inner voice of conscience. We long for the infinite and for happiness. (CCC 33) Even those people who have not accepted the good news in Jesus are capable of making distinctions between what is good and what is evil and acting accordingly.

Catholic teaching upholds that moral conversion is possible for all and needed by all. The final document issued by the Second Vatican Council, *Gaudium et Spes*, exhorts the world, "Let everyone consider it . . .[a] sacred duty to count social obligations among [one's] chief duties today and observe them as such. . . . This will be realized only if individuals and groups practice moral and social virtues and foster them in social living. Then. . .there will arise a new generation. . . the molders of a new humanity." (GS 30)

Thus the Council called for moral conversion. This conversion is accomplished in many ways through daily living. Gestures of reconciliation, concern for the poor, the exercise and defense of justice, the admission of one's faults, fraternal correction, and acceptance of suffering are outward signs of this moral conversion (CCC 1435). In other words, moral conversion takes time and practice but is accessible to all. The difference between an average piano player and a superb one is the virtuosity that comes with long practice fueled by innate skill and the desire to be truly good. Similarly, moral virtues acquired by human effort are fueled by the innate sensibility instilled in us by God and are the result of practicing goodness over time.

Catholic theology has long pointed to and explored the cardinal virtues as key elements that assist in moral conversion. Hence, the description of these virtues as "cardinal" (from the Latin cardo, or "hinge.") The cardinal virtues of prudence, justice, fortitude and temperance are central to the pursuit of the moral life. (CCC 1805)

Prudence, also described as "practical wisdom," enables its subject to discern specific actions that will best fulfill the requirements of authentic, virtuous living in particular situations. Justice disposes one to practice fairness in dealing with others. Fortitude enables a person to aim for the good in the face of contrary fears. Temperance helps the individual to maintain correct balance and appropriate limits in pursuing sensual pleasure. (*Encyclopedia of Catholicism*, "Cardinal Virtues," 227-228.) These cardinal virtues forge character and ultimately dispose the individual to communion with divine love (CCC 1810, 1804).

Consult Richard P. McBrien, *Catholicism, New Edition*, Winston Press, 1994 ("virtue" 926-28, "justice" 943-47, "temperance" 949-51, "fortitude" 951-52, and "prudence" 975-77). See also *Encyclopedia of Catholicism*, "habit, moral" 600.

Catholic Culture

Many Advent hymns express the joy of this Sunday as we wait in expectation of the Lord's coming. The most notable of these is "O Come, O Come Emmanuel." There is also "When the King Shall Come Again," whose ancient title is Gaudemus Pariter. "Awake, Awake, and Greet the New Morn," a contemporary hymn, expresses "rejoice, rejoice, take heart in the night." In some churches, rose-colored vestments or hangings indicate Gaudete (or joy) Sunday.

Christian art frequently portrays John the Baptist pointing with his finger, as an imperative to follow the One whose coming he announces and also as a demand for moral conversion.

The "O Antiphons" are a series of seven antiphons or short verses sung at the beginning and end of the psalms used in praying the Divine Office. The Divine Office, also called the Liturgy of the Hours, is the public prayer of the church for praising God and sanctifying the hours of the day. These antiphons all begin with the invocation "O" and are used at Vespers—Evening Prayer—from December 17-23. Taken from the prophetic and wisdom books of the Bible, the "O Antiphons" include these titles for Jesus, O Wisdom; O Lord of Lords; O Root of Jesse; O Key of David; O Radiant Dawn; O King of All Nations; and O Emmanuel (God with us).

Notes

Dismissal Catechesis (30 min)

Getting Started

1. Prepare the space ahead of time with a circle of chairs around a table, upon which is an Advent wreath. The cloth covering the table could be red-violet with a strip of mauve or pink on the top.

2. Invite the catechumens and candidates to join the circle. Begin the prayer by lighting three candles on the wreath as the group sings the Gathering Hymn used at today's liturgy. Invite the participants to center themselves and close their eyes, slowly praying this meditation:

You find yourself caught up in the crowd. The prophet Zephaniah is preaching, once again, in the center of the town. You are reluctant to follow. This prophet of doom and gloom has called for repentance for a long time. You admitted your pride and arrogance before Yahweh. You are tired of trying. Why isn't Yahweh keeping the covenant as promised? Somehow, you are shuffled along with the others in the crowd. Zephaniah's voice booms above the noise of the excited crowd "Sing aloud, O daughter Zion; shout, O Israel! / Rejoice and exult with all your heart, / O daughter Jerusalem! / The LORD has taken away the judgments against you, / he has turned away your enemies"(Zephaniah 3:14-15).

First Impressions

1. While the group is quiet, ask them to name the emotions experienced by those who heard the word of Zephaniah.

2. Gather them into small groups to discuss the following: *What is the overall tone of the liturgy today? What images in today's readings caused you joy?*

3. Proclaim the second reading from Philippians 4:4-7. Invite the small groups to share: *In this letter of Paul, what is the cause of our joy, even in times of trial?*

4. Ask the participants to share some of their responses with the large group. Summarize their input in a few sentences.

Making Connections

1. Ask the group to brainstorm possible situations that are cause for true joy. Note their responses on a poster board.

2. Invite them to return to their small groups to discuss: *When worried, troubled or indifferent, how can these negative feelings be transformed into authentic joy?*

3. Gather the insights from the small group discussions and create another list on poster board, called, REJOICE ALWAYS. Ask the participants to write their insights on turning negative experiences into cause for rejoicing on this list.

Prayer

Invite the group to reflect in quiet on the possibilities for "rejoicing always." During this quiet time, play "The Living Light," an instrumental piece from the C.D. *Vision: The Music of Hildegard Von Bingen*, Angel Records, 1994, or a piece that is appropriate. Invite the participants to create a Litany of Joy, by naming those things for which they are filled with joy. After each naming, the group response is: "Rejoice in the Lord always. I say it again, rejoice!" Or they may choose to sing "Rejoice In the Lord, Always."

Extended Catechesis

SESSION FOCUS: *Moral Conversion*

Gathering

A. Sunday:

1. Greet and warmly welcome the team members and additional participants as they arrive. Invite them to join the circle of candidates and catechumens. Allow time for introductions if the group does not yet know one another.

2. Spend a few moments in quiet as the participants focus on the lighted Advent wreath and the lists prepared by the catechumens and candidates during the Dismissal Session. Ask one of the candidates or catechumens to share a short summary of the sharing during the dismissal catechesis.

3. Begin the prayer by asking all to sing two verses of the Gathering Hymn used at today's liturgy. Provide song books in order that all may join the singing. Ask one of the sponsors to proclaim the gospel, Luke 3:10-18. Pray the psalm from Isaiah 12:2-3, 4, 5-6, pausing to sing "Rejoice in the Lord, Always" after each indicated set of verses.

B. Weekday:

1. As the group gathers in the circle pause and greet each participant. Allow a short time of silence as the participants think about the past few days. Ask them to share how these days have been a source of rejoicing. You may choose to refer the attention of the group to the lists prepared by the candidates and catechumens during the Dismissal Catechesis.

2. Pray this celebration of the Word.
   - Song: Gathering Hymn from Sunday's liturgy
   - First Reading: Zephaniah 3:14-18
   - Sing the psalm, Isaiah 12:2-6
   - Second Reading: Philippians 4:4-7
   - Silent reflection on the joyful expectancy with which we await the Lord's coming.
   - Gospel: Luke 3:10-18

The Word (30 min)

1. Begin with a story of a person you or another team member knows who is joyful in the midst of struggles.

2. Explain the second reading from Paul's letter to the Philippians 4:4-7 in these words:

A hallmark of the Advent season is Paul's emphatic "Rejoice always!" Originally this call to joy was directed at two women in the community, Evodia and Syntyche. They were ministers in the progressive church of Macedonia and had a disagreement that threatened the internal peace of the Christian community at Philippi. The section before today's passage referred directly to this issue. The letter seems to say, 'Life is too short to spend it on quarrels, set your priorities straight.' Paul's imperative to rejoice at all times is accomplished when we let go of petty differences and cultivate unselfishness, patience, gentleness and tolerance because the Lord is near.

4. Gather the participants into small groups and ask them to share their thoughts on these questions:
What is your reaction to the strife that was part of the early Christian community?
What does it take to transform our negative inner attitudes into a real sense of joy?

3. Share this background on the gospel with the participants:

John the Baptist offers his audience practical ways to reform their lives as they expectantly await the messiah. Three groups come to him with the question, "What should we do?" The response of John, and later Jesus, was to repent. The repentance they preached was not merely a matter of feeling sorry for one's sins and weaknesses, but it was a total transformation, that is, conversion. Conversion involves turning totally away from sin and wrongdoing toward God. John's practical advice to the crowd, tax collector and soldier (representing all walks of life) was to urge them to turn their lives around, both in attitude and in action. Radical conversion is cause for rejoicing always!

Catholic Teaching (30 min)

1. Ask the participants to turn to the exercises in their Participant Book (page 8) or on the blackline handout and reflect upon the changes that they need to make in their own conversion process.

2. Gather the participants into small groups and invite them to share their responses to the reflection.

OR . . .

Present the following teaching on moral conversion, making the following points:

• Moral conversion is possible for all and needed by all. The gospel challenges us to cultivate moral and social virtues. Virtues are acquired attitudes and behaviors motivated by the desire to live a morally good life.

• Moral conversion is accomplished through daily living. It is a total turning away from what is evil toward God and that which is perceived as good.

• The Catholic Church has taught that the cardinal virtues are key in the process of moral conversion. The cardinal virtues of prudence, justice, fortitude and temperance are key hinges in directing us to a humanly good way of life. However the theological virtues of faith, hope and love are necessary to bring us to full union with God.

OR . . .

Invite a member of the team to give a witness talk that illustrates how the cardinal virtues, cultivated both in attitudes and in actions brought about a moral conversion in their life.

Putting Faith Into Practice

1. Invite the participants to gather in pairs. Ask them to discuss this question: *How can I put into practice the virtue which I am most lacking?* Encourage them to be specific about a future action they wish to take on their personal journey of conversion.

2. This is a good week to explain the "O Antiphons" to the group. Use these or similar words:

The "O Antiphons" are a series of seven antiphons or short verses sung at the beginning and end of the psalms used in praying the Divine Office. The Divine Office, also called the Liturgy of the Hours, is the public prayer of the church for praising God and sanctifying the hours of the day. These antiphons all begin with the invocation "O" and are used at Vespers—Evening Prayer—from December 17-23. Taken from the prophetic and wisdom books of the Bible, the "O Antiphons" include these titles for Jesus, O Wisdom; O Lord of Lords; O Root of Jesse; O Key of David; O Radiant Dawn; O King of All Nations; and O Emmanuel (God with us).

Prayer

Ask the group to write on a piece of paper the virtue that they wish to cultivate. Direct them to place these papers on the table with the Advent wreath. As the prayer begins, burn incense as a sign of offering these desires of the heart to the Lord. Pray the Minor Exorcism 94-G. Close with the song "Our Prayers Rise Like Incense."

Fourth Sunday of Advent

Understanding this Sunday:
Background for Catechesis

The Word In Liturgy

Micah 5:1-4a
Psalm 80:2-3, 15-16, 18-19
Hebrews 10:5-10
Luke 1:39-45

As Advent draws to a close, the readings call our attention to the mystery of Christ's coming in the flesh. The reading from the prophet Micah compares the people of Israel waiting for divine deliverance to a woman in labor, giving birth to a child. The letter to the Hebrews takes special account of the importance of the body of Jesus. His body is accepted by the pre-existent savior as "prepared for me" by God's will. His body is obediently offered in sacrifice, surpassing all the sacrifices of the old covenant. Last of all, today's passage from Luke's gospel turns on the mystery of life taking shape in the womb of Mary.

Mary, pregnant with Jesus, goes in haste to see Elizabeth, who is also with child in unusual circumstances. The scene between the two women, honored in the tradition as "the Visitation," is both a human encounter and a moment of transcendent significance. When she sees Mary, Elizabeth is "filled with the Holy Spirit," and the baby within her "leaps for joy." Under the influence of this Spirit, she speaks a powerful truth, calling Mary "blessed" and her unborn child "my Lord." In its Advent context, this reading inspires awe for the mystery of Christ's coming in the flesh. Who is this woman, to be greeted thus? Who is the child of her womb, that even before his birth he inspires such prophetic utterances?

The prophet Micah, a vibrant preacher of social justice, takes special delight in announcing that the small and comparatively insignificant place of Bethlehem-Ephratha will be the place of origin of the king who will rule in the line of David and with the strength of God. This promised ruler will be not only king, but also—like David—shepherd of the people. Amid the chaos of frequent invasion, and a heritage of violent and self-willed rulers, Micah's prophecy that "he shall be peace" touches a profound longing in the human heart. Who can this ruler be who will shepherd the people on God's behalf, who will be peace? For the church the answer is clear: This promised one is Mary's child, the only-begotten Son of God.

Catholic Doctrine

The coming of Christ in the flesh

The four Sundays of Advent have progressed from the focus on the Second Coming of Christ to the coming of Christ proclaimed by John the Baptist to this Sunday's focus of the coming of Christ in human flesh. The long-awaited Messiah is born into the world through Mary. We pray, "the virgin mother bore him in her womb with love beyond all telling." (Advent Preface II)

Jesus the Christ is both human and divine. The humanity of Jesus is key to understanding his divinity. In the person of Jesus, God and humankind come together in perfect unity.

The Second Vatican Council, in the constitution on the Church, points out that Jesus fully reveals God to the world and reveals humankind to one another. In that human revelation, Jesus makes the divine call of all God's people clear. In the same document, the bishops of the world go on to state that Jesus' divinity does not diminish his humanity. But, in fact, "He worked with human hands, He thought with a human mind, He acted by human choices, and loved with a human heart." (#22)

St. Ambrose reflects on this Sunday's gospel scene of the Visitation and the significance of Christ's coming in the flesh:

Filled with God, where would [Mary] hasten but to the heights? The Holy Spirit does not proceed by slow, laborious efforts. Quickly, too, the blessings of her coming and the Lord's presence are made clear. . . .Notice the contrast and the choice of words. Elizabeth is the first to hear Mary's voice, but John is the first to be aware of grace. She hears with the ears of the body, but he leaps for joy at the meaning of the mystery. She is aware of Mary's presence, but he is aware of the Lord's. . . . The women speak of the grace they have received while the children are active in secret, unfolding the mystery of love with the help of their mothers, who prophesy by the spirit. . .

You are also blessed because you have heard and believed. A soul that believes both conceives and brings forth the Word of God and acknowledges his works. (Lib 2, 19. 22-23.26-27: CCL 14, 39-42)

It is not just Mary and Elizabeth in this gospel scene who visit one another. John and Jesus in the womb are also present. This raises a question for us. What role do the unborn play in our lives? The Church affirms the sacredness of life in the womb. John Paul II upholds this teaching in *Evangelium Vitae* (44.3) and cites the psalms in support of this (22:10-ll, 71:6, 139:13-14) and also refers to the Old Testament prophet, "Before I formed you in the womb I knew you, and before you were born I consecrated you" (Jeremiah 1:5). The pope writes, "Human life finds itself most vulnerable when it enters the world and when it leaves the realm of time to embark upon eternity." (VS 44.l).

Catholic Culture

The greeting of Elizabeth is enshrined in the Hail Mary and the Visitation is the second of five joyful mysteries of the Rosary. In praying the text of the Hail Mary, note that our two greatest vulnerabilities are either alluded to or directly mentioned: entrance into the world at birth ("fruit of your womb") and our departure from it ("at the hour of our death").

The much-loved story of the Visitation is frequently depicted in church art. One particularly famous example is found in the sculptures on the central portal of Reims Cathedral in France. The beautifully molded figures of Mary and Elizabeth, draped in garments reminiscent of ancient Greece and Rome, are considered by art historians to represent the high point of Gothic classicism.

Notes

Dismissal Catechesis (30 min)

Getting Started

1. Prepare the space ahead of time with a circle of chairs around a small table. On the table, arrange the Advent wreath and a piece of art depicting the Visitation of Mary to her older cousin Elizabeth.

2. Invite the catechumens and candidates to gather in the circle, pausing for quiet reflection as they look at the Visitation scene. Play an appropriate instrumental piece of music in the background, such as "Song to the Mother" from *Visions: The Music of Hildegard Von Bingen*, Angel Records, 1994.

3. While the song is playing, light the four Advent candles. Pray the Advent Preface II from the Sacramentary and proclaim the first reading, Micah 5:1-4a. Close with this prayer:

   O Wisdom, O Lord of Lords, O Root of Jesse, we long for your coming more fully into our world and into our hearts. You came in simplicity to offer the poor and alienated of our world a reason to hope. You came as our shepherd to guide us to follow God's will more perfectly. You came as ruler to bring peace into our violent and destructive world. O Key of David, restore us by your coming in flesh to dwell with your people. Amen.

First Impressions

1. To begin the discussion, name three images from today's readings that were important for you. These may include:

   "He shall stand firm and shepherd his flock by the strength of the Lord." (Micah 5:3)

   "By this will we have been consecrated through the offering of the Body of Jesus Christ, once for all." (Hebrews 10:10)

   "Most blessed are you among women and blessed is the fruit of your womb." (Luke 1:43)

2. Invite the group to add the images or phrases that appealed to them from today's passages.

3. Gather the participants into small groups to discuss: What did you find awe-inspiring about today's liturgy of the Word? How would you summarize the meaning of the Scriptures we heard proclaimed?

4. In the large group invite individuals to share their insights as to the meaning of these readings. Present two sentences summing up their comments.

Making Connections

1. Ask the group to brainstorm the descriptive images of the messiah found in the first reading from Micah 5:1-4. List their ideas on pieces of paper and place them on the floor around the center of the circle.

2. Invite them to think about these images and move into small groups to discuss: *What is the significance of this kind of messiah in your life? What other descriptive images would you add to those found in the first reading?* Instruct the participants to write their own images on additional pieces of paper and place these in the center of the circle.

Prayer

Begin the prayer with a short period of silence. Invite those present to begin a Prayer of Awe by praying aloud one of the descriptive images of the messiah in the center of the circle and following it with their own words of praise. For example, *Shepherd of strength, we praise you for coming into our lives.* Close with the group praying the 'Hail Mary."

Extended Catechesis

SESSION FOCUS: *The Word made flesh*

Gathering

A. Sunday:

1. Greet and warmly welcome the team members and additional participants as they arrive. Invite them to join the circle of candidates and catechumens. Allow time for introductions if the group does not yet know one another.

2. Spend some time in quiet, directing the participants to focus on the lighted Advent wreath, the scene of the Visitation and the pieces of paper with images of the messiah.

3. Begin the prayer by inviting all to sing "Hail Mary, Gentle Woman," Carey Landry (NALR, 1975). Pray in these or your own words:

   Loving and gracious God, you come to us in wonderful ways. We can hardly take in your coming to dwell among us in human flesh. We are heartened by your presence with us each day in the ordinary circumstances of our lives. We await with expectant hearts your coming once again at the end of time. We welcome your presence with us now as we reflect upon your Word and its meaning for us today. Be with us as we prepare more fully for your birth. Amen.

4. Ask one of the team members to proclaim the gospel from Luke 1:39-45.

B. Weekday:

1. As the group gathers in the circle pause and greet each person. Allow a short time of silence, asking them to think about the past few days. Invite a few to share: *What has this Advent experience helped you understand more clearly?*

2. Pray this celebration of the Word
   - Song: "Hail Mary, Gentle Woman," Carey Landry (NALR, 1975).
   - First Reading: Micah 5:1-4
   - Psalm 80 (sung or prayed, alternating right and left sides)
   - Gospel: Luke 1:39-45

- Silence
- Prayer (Use the prayer from the Gathering on Sunday)

The Word (30 min)

1. Ask one of the candidates or catechumens to share some of the images of the messiah gleaned from the Micah reading. (These are still on pieces of paper in the middle of the circle). Invite the team, sponsors and additional participants to add their own descriptive image of the messiah.

2. Engage the group by offering this presentation on the Gospel:

   Both Elizabeth and Mary learned of their unexpected pregnancies through a divine intermediary—an angel or messenger of God. Longed-for children are not new to the reader of the Scriptures. Think about Sarah's anticipation of the conception of Isaac and Hannah's longed-for son, Samuel. Miraculous births are signals from God that a purpose in God's plan of salvation is the destiny of the child. Both women were filled with the knowledge inspired by the Holy Spirit. Elizabeth speaks the truth of Mary's triple blessedness. (In the passage to follow Mary speaks her prayer of praise known as the Magnificat.) Mary is praised, "blessed are you among women, blessed is the fruit of your womb and blessed are you who believed." Mary and Elizabeth offer us a model of Advent spirituality, calling us to develop a constant attitude of faith and preparedness for the one who has come and will come again in glory.

3. Invite the participants to gather into small groups to discuss these questions:
   What challenges do these women present to you?
   What does Jesus' birth, from the womb of a woman, speak to your faith?

4. Ask the small groups to report a summary of their discussion to the large group. Invite everyone to turn to their Participant Book (page 11) or the blackline handout to the corresponding section and write one thing they wish to remember from this discussion.

Catholic Teaching (30 min)

1. Present the Catholic teaching on "the Word was made flesh," making sure to include the following points:

   - The long-awaited Messiah was born into the world through the Virgin Mary. In the power of the Holy Spirit, Elizabeth recognized the presence of the Lord in Mary's womb, as did John, who leapt in the womb of his mother.

   - Jesus the Christ is both human and divine. The humanity of Jesus is key to understanding his divinity. In the person of Jesus, God and humankind come together in perfect unity.

   - The Second Vatican Council, in the constitution on the Church, points out that Jesus fully reveals God to the world and reveals humankind to one another. In that human revelation, Jesus makes the divine call of all God's people clear.

   - In the same document, the bishops of the world go on to state that Jesus' divinity does not diminish his humanity. But, in fact, "He worked with human hands, He thought with a human mind, He acted by human choices, and loved with a human heart." (#22)

2. Ask the participants to discuss these questions in small groups: *What does Jesus coming in the flesh reveal about God? How have I recognized the presence of Jesus in others?* Invite them to share their stories of discovering Jesus present in their daily encounters with others.

3. In the large group, ask some participants to share their stories.

Putting Faith Into Practice

1. Direct the participants to turn the Participant Book (page 10) or the blackline handout and respond to the reflection and questions presented. Giving them sufficient time to respond, ask them to share their insights in pairs.

2. Explain that the second joyful mystery of the rosary is the Visitation. This may be a good opportunity to teach the group how to say the rosary and to explore its significance as a traditional prayer form of the church.

Prayer

Gather the group into a time of silence, followed by inviting them to sing the sixth and seventh verses of "O Come, O Come Emmanuel." Pray the Angelus found in any Catholic book of prayers. Close with the song, "Mary's Song," Michael Joncas (New Dawn Music, 1979).

CHRISTMAS SEASON

Christmas, Mass During The Day

Understanding this Feast:
Background for Catechesis

The Word In Liturgy

Isaiah 52:7-10
Psalm 98:1, 2-3, 3-4, 5-6
Hebrews 1:1-6
John 1:1-18 [or (short form) 1:1-5, 9-14]

The liturgical books provide four Mass formularies with which to celebrate the Solemnity of Christmas: a vigil Mass on Christmas Eve, and then one at midnight, at dawn, and during the day. Different historical factors and pieties are responsible for the development of each of these celebrations, but it is the Mass during the day that is the most ancient celebration. The perceptive observer will note that this original observance is focused less on the details of the historical event of Jesus' birth and more on the timeless meaning of the Incarnation for the believer. Consistent with this insight, we focus today especially on the reason behind the birth of the Word made flesh: "For our salvation." The wonderful truth of the Incarnation is that because of Christ's coming in human flesh, we can be drawn to the Father through him.

The first reading's joyful proclamation of "good news" is an announcement of Yahweh's return to Zion, a triumphant return from exile, which reveals God's salvation in the sight of the nations (Psalm 98). The image we are given is of a messenger bringing the news to Jerusalem that the God of Israel reigns over all peoples. In the midst of the "ruins of Jerusalem," the people experience the comfort of a God who has "redeemed Jerusalem" (v. 9). The scene is regal in scope: No focus on the homeless child in a manger, but a victorious King reclaiming his royal city. Psalm 98 echoes those same images, a joyful victory chant at God's triumph revealed before all people.

The Letter to the Hebrews stresses the revelatory character of the Incarnation, with God described as speaking to us in this, the final age, through the Son, the "reflection of God's glory." God spoke to our ancestors "in many and various ways" (v. 1), but now the superiority of God's full revelation is shown forth in Jesus, who has cleansed us from our sins. Once again, the meaning of the incarnation is described in terms of its redemptive impact on the human condition. Here, too, Christ is portrayed in royal splendor "at the right hand of the Majesty on high" (v. 3) rather than in the humble conditions of his birth.

The Prologue of John's Gospel has long been recognized as our most profound meditation on the meaning of the Incarnation. It proclaims the theme of God's self-disclosure in the Word made flesh, who comes as light in the darkness, the "glory as of a father's only son, full of grace and truth" (v. 14). This understanding of the Incarnation as God's self-disclosure in the human flesh of Jesus is a fundamental aspect of the Incarnation. In Jesus, we see divine love revealed as saving grace. The Son, who is "the reflection of God's glory and the exact imprint of God's very being" (Hebrews 1:3), is now proclaimed as the fulfillment of the ancient prophecy of "good news," a message that brings comfort and redemption to God's chosen people. The Church's doctrinal assertion of the divinity of Jesus becomes, in its liturgical proclamation, an experience of saving grace, the "power to become children of God" for all who have "received him" and "believed in his name." (v. 12).

Catholic Doctrine

For us men and for our salvation
He came down from heaven.

This feast celebrates the Incarnation. The eternal Word of God became flesh in Jesus. God's love is not distant but draws near to us, giving us the opportunity to become children of God. St. Augustine meditates, "For what greater grace could God have made to dawn on us than to make his only Son become the son of man, so that a son of man might in turn become son of God? . . .Ask if this were merited; ask for its reason, for it's justification, and see whether you will find any other answer but sheer grace." (Sermon 185: PL 38, 997-99.)

We did not merit the Incarnation by our own actions. This gift is given through the initiative of God. The Church proclaims, "In the wonder of the incarnation your eternal Word has brought to the eyes of faith a new and radiant vision of your glory. In him we see our God made visible and so are caught up in the love of the God we cannot see" (Preface for Christmas I).

Other prayer texts also express this gift of God: "[W]e recognize in Christ the revelation of your love. No eye can see his glory as our God, yet now he is seen as one like us. Christ is your Son before all ages, yet now he is born in time. He has come to lift up all things to himself, to restore unity to creation, and to lead [us] from exile into your heavenly kingdom" (Preface for Christmas II).

By an "utterly free decision," earth is wedded to heaven, we are reconciled to God and the gift of salvation is offered to the world. (CCC 50) For a theological reflection on "beholding the Christmas miracle all year long" see John Shea, *Starlight*, Crossroad, New York, 1992.

Catholic Culture

On the day after Christmas, December 26, the feast of the first martyr is celebrated, St. Stephen. The following day, December 27, the Church celebrates the feast of St. John, apostle and evangelist.

In the thirteenth century, St. Francis of Assisi popularized the use of figurines to depict the Christmas message. But as early as the fourth century, representations of the nativity of the Lord were painted as wall decorations depicting not only the infancy narrative accounts of Christ's birth but also the words of the prophets Isaiah and Habakkuk that the Messiah would be born in the midst of animals in a manger. (See *Book of Blessings*, 1541, for more background information and the blessing prayers over the manger scene.)

Some of the most beloved and well-known Christian hymns are those we sing on this feast and during this season: "Angels We Have Heard on High; Away in a Manger; Silent Night, Holy Night; Hark! The Herald Angels Sing." Their lyrics express the gift we have been given by God, for example, "Peace on earth and mercy mild, God and sinner reconciled, joyful all you nations, rise, join the triumph of the skies."

In spite of the commercialization of Christmas, the tradition of giving gifts at this feast symbolizes the gift of love given to us by God in Jesus.

Notes

Feast of the Holy Family

SUNDAY WITHIN THE OCTAVE OF CHRISTMAS

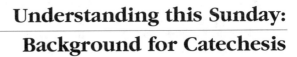

Understanding this Sunday:
Background for Catechesis

The Word In Liturgy

1 Samuel 1:20-22, 24-28
Psalm 84:2-3, 5-6, 9-10
1 John 3:1-2, 21-24
Luke 2:41-52

The Feast of the Holy Family is a modern addition to the universal calendar of the Roman Church (since 1921, when it was placed as the First Sunday after Epiphany). Like many feasts added in modern times, its emphasis tends to be more on a doctrinal theme than some specific action of God. Its contemporary character is also shown by the way it seeks to instruct and inspire through an obvious appeal to sentiment and emotion. The placement of Holy Family Sunday in the Christmas season is an even more recent adjustment to the calendar, stemming from the reform of 1969. Situated so closely to Christmas, today's celebration cannot help but resonate with overtones of the Incarnation. By highlighting the family as the context into which Jesus was born, today's liturgy reinforces the fact of his full humanity. Following a way of thinking common in the early centuries of the Church, we proclaim that the Word made flesh sanctifies everything that he has taken upon himself—our full human nature including, today, the reality of family life. The family, made holy by virtue of Jesus' life with Mary and Joseph, becomes a source of holiness for every Christian. Contemporary theology gives voice to this insight by teaching that the family is the "domestic church."

The Book of Sirach (also known as Ecclesiasticus) is part of the Wisdom literature, written most likely during the second century (circa 180 B.C.E.) in Jerusalem by Joshua Ben Sira, a member of the scribal class. Part of a larger section on family life, today's reading is considered by many scholars to be a commentary on the fourth commandment. The author's concern lies with the quality of relationships that must characterize family life. His suggestion that filial piety "will be credited to you against your sins" (v. 14) should be regarded

as a way of offering encouragement to the reader to show reverence and care for one's parents, not as a guarantee of divine forgiveness. However, the comment does support the sense of today's celebration that family life can be a source of holiness when lived in accord with God's will.

The reading from Colossians has been interpreted as part of an ancient baptismal catechesis (3:5-4:1). Paul's admonition to "put on love" is suggestive of the ritual clothing of the newly baptized in a white garment, an early Christian custom expressive of new life and holiness. Because of baptism, a Christian is recognized as "chosen . . . holy . . . beloved" (v. 12) and therefore one's behaviors and relationships must reflect those qualities. Paul's "household code," common in Greek philosophical writings of the day, is transformed into specifically Christian teaching by his insistence that family relationships be carried on "in the Lord" (vv. 18, 20). Thus, the reading links itself to a recognition of the family as a place where faith is found and holiness achieved.

Today's Gospel reading belongs to the specialized literary form known as "infancy narrative." The author's concern is not to supply historical details from Jesus' childhood, but to proclaim to the reader the theological truth of Jesus' identity as Messiah, Son of God and Savior. The reading builds to Jesus' climactic remark that it is his destiny to be in his Father's house (v. 49). Mary is presented as a model for all believers, pondering the meaning of these events—and of Jesus himself—in her heart. In the same way, catechumens grow in their faith step by step, contemplating the mystery of Christ; and, the members of a (holy) Christian family grow in discipleship by the ordinary lives they lead "in the Lord."

Catholic Doctrine

The family as the domestic Church.

On this feast of the Holy Family our attention as a Church inevitably is drawn to the role of the family. John Paul II, in an apostolic constitution, describes the family as a "domestic church" (FC 21) echoing the Second Vatican Council. In its dogmatic constitution on the Church, the Council declared, "From the marriage of Christians there comes the family in which new citizens of human society are born and, by the grace of the Holy Spirit in Baptism, those are made children of God so that the People of God may be perpetuated throughout the centuries. In what might be regarded as the domestic Church, the parents, by word and example, are the first heralds of the faith with regard to their children." (LG ll)

In the decree on the laity from the Council, the Church also contemplates the role of the family. "The mission of being the primary vital cell of society has been given to the family by God. This mission will be accomplished if the family, by the mutual affection of its members and by family prayer, presents itself as a domestic sanctuary of the church; if the whole family takes its part in the church's liturgical worship; if, finally, it offers active hospitality and practices justice and other good works for the benefit of all its sisters and brothers who suffer from want" (AA ll).

The Catechism continues this theme of the role of the family in society, teaching that the Christian family "is a communion of persons, a sign and image of the communion of the Father and the Son in the Holy Spirit. . . .[The family] is called to partake of the prayer and sacrifice of Christ. Daily prayer and the reading of the Word of God strengthen it in charity. The Christian family has an evangelizing and missionary task. (CCC 2205) Thus one is initiated into society through family life and the communion of love, moral values, faith and worship that is nurtured there.

The Prayer After Communion for this feast expresses this view of the role of Christian families, "Eternal Father, we want to live as Jesus, Mary, and Joseph, in peace with you and one another. May this communion strengthen us to face the trouble of life." (Roman Missal, Feast of the Holy Family)

There are many resources available to help families share their faith. See *We Pray*, M.J. Calnan and David Thomas, Thomas More Press, 1994; *We Are Family*, M.J. Calnan and David Thomas, Thomas More Press, 1994; and *Building Christian Families*, Mitch and Kathy Finley, Thomas More Press, 1996.

Catholic Culture

A considerable portion of *Catholic Household Blessings and Prayers* (all of Part Three) is devoted to blessings of family members, for example, prayers to bless the house, a blessing prayer for birthdays and the anniversary of baptism, blessings associated with children, and prayers for times of sickness. In all, there are more than forty such blessing prayers.

Many of the spiritual renewal movements and Catholic societies of this century (such as the Christian Family Movement, Marriage Encounter, the Holy Name Society and the Ladies Sodality) coalesce around the importance of the family in the Church and wider society. Each generation of Catholics seeks to foster and live the values embodied in our view of the family as a domestic Church.

Notes

Dismissal Catechesis (30 min)

Getting Started

1. Prepare the space ahead of time with a circle of chairs and a Christmas candle on the floor in the circle's center. An art piece, depicting the Holy Family, can also be placed near the candle.

2. Invite the catechumens and candidates to gather in a circle.

3. Ask all to join in singing Verse 1 of "Here I Am Lord," Dan Schutte (New Dawn Music, 1981) while lighting the Christmas candle. This prayer for families may be used, or you may wish to compose one that is similar.

Lord, Giver of Life, we are grateful for all those who have come before us in our families, those we have known and those ancestors whom we have never met or heard about. This lineage of parents, grandparents, great-grandparents and so many others has gifted us with life, faith and our family story. This story was chosen by You from all time. This tradition of holy parents is just another sign of your faithful love. May the threads of this story and the strands of tradition, which encircle our families, be cherished for generations to come. May we express our gratitude to You and to our ancestors by passing these rich traditions, this holiness and this story, on to the next generations. We bless and praise you, Heavenly Parent, who has been so generous with us, giving us a holy people to grow us in the faith. Amen.

First Impressions

1. To help focus the group upon the feast of the Holy Family and the Sacred Scriptures, invite them to begin by sharing their responses to the following question. How did your family impart values, a code of living, to you and your siblings? Share some ideas in the large group.

2. After explaining that this liturgy celebrates the Feast of the Holy Family, invite the participants to discuss this question: *What in the liturgy was of particular interest as you listened and participated?* If the group is large, gather into pairs or small groups.

Making Connections

1. To help the participants relate these readings to their lives, explain the following.

The first reading is part of the Wisdom literature, which taught the Israelites the way of life that flows from faithfulness to God. The large section on the family was considered to be an expansion of the meaning of the fourth commandment, 'Honor your father and mother.' In a similar fashion, the second reading to the Colossians was, in fact, instructions to the catechumens in the early church.

2. From these two readings, encourage the participants to recall and share: *What are some of the directives for family life and Christian holiness that are presented in these Scriptures?* Continue the discussion in the large group: *How do these instructions apply to our lives, our families today?*

3. Summarize the comments of the group in a few short phrases. Ask the group to silently recall the liturgy and the discussion. *What one thing do you want to pay more attention to, as a result of this session?* Allow time for them to write this in the corresponding section of the Participant Book.

Prayer

Psalm 128 is very short. Prepare copies of this psalm for each participant prior to the session and distribute them in preparation for the prayer. Begin the prayer by inviting all to sing verse two of "Here I Am Lord." Then invite all to stand and pray the psalm. Close with the Prayer after Communion, found in the Catholic Doctrine section of this session.

Extended Catechesis

SESSION FOCUS: *The family is the domestic church.*

Gathering

A. Sunday:

1. Extend a warm welcome to the sponsors, team and other participants as they join the circle, with the lighted Christmas candle and artwork of the Holy Family.

2. Invite the group to take time to recall their family of origins.

3. Allow a short time of silence, and then invite the group to pray a litany of thanks for all these ancestors represented here. Open the prayer with the response, "God of Life, We give thanks for . . ." Members of the group can name these family members, both living and dead, bringing them into the circle of prayer. Ask a team member to proclaim the gospel, Luke 2:41-52. Conclude with the Collect for the Feast of the Holy Family (Sacramentary).

B. Weekday:

1. Welcome and greet the participants as they arrive. Gather them in the circle of chairs with the lighted Christmas candle and the artwork of the Holy Family.

2. Invite the group to reflect and share how God has worked in their families over these past few days.

3. Lead the group in this celebration of the
   - Song: "Carol of the Mother," (Rory Cooney, NALR, 1977)
   - First Reading: 1 Samuel 1:20-22, 24-28
   - Psalm 84:2-3, 5-6, 9-10
   - Second Reading: 1 John 3:1-2, 21-24
   - Alleluia: Sung

- Gospel: Luke 2:41-52
- Silence
- Concluding Prayer: Collect for the Feast of the Holy Family

The Word (30 min)

1. In these or your own words, begin the discussion of the Word just proclaimed. The resource section "Understanding this Sunday" will be of help in your preparation.

   God speaks to the Israelites and to us today. Through the authority of God, parents are mutually responsible for imparting God's way of holiness to their children. Children, in turn, offer their honor, care and consideration to their parents. God's plan is that families live in right relationship with one another. To live in this way is to be faithful to God and obedient to God's plan.

2. Focus the discussion of the group on these or similar questions: *What would constitute right relationships for families today?* Make a list of ideas for right relationships as the participants brainstorm. Use a large poster to record their ideas. For example: forgive one another; treat family members with respect; listen to one another with compassion. Ask the participants to take a look at the ideas gleaned from the candidates and catechumens discussion on Paul's instructions for the early catechumens (these ideas from the dismissal session should be posted for everyone to see). Ask the large group: *How do these descriptions for holiness fit into family life today? What relevance do they have for the larger family of the faith community?*

3. After discussing this in the large group, gather into smaller groups and invite the participants to share a story from their family, which illustrates one of these virtues or qualities of holiness.

4. Continue to break open the Gospel story in these words.

   In this passage, Jesus, at the age of 12, declares his relationship with the Father. In the Temple he astonishes the teachers and religious leaders and stuns his parents. While he declares his work is that of the Father, he still needs the nurture and love of the Holy Family to grow in wisdom and grace—to grow into his Father's work.

5. Invite the participants to discuss the following in pairs: *What do you find puzzling/challenging about this gospel? How are you challenged, as was Mary, by that which is not understandable? What events or mysteries of life have you 'pondered in your heart'? What happened when you acted as Mary did?*

Catholic Teaching (30 min)

1. Share the Catholic teaching on the Family as the domestic Church in these or your own words.

   The family is the most basic unit of the Church. By reason of the communion among the members of the family under the loving guidance of God the Father, the Son and the Holy Spirit the family is recognized by the Catholic church as a domestic church—a sacred sanctuary of faith and worship. This intimacy with one another and with God is the way in which each family member is nurtured in the faith, grows in holiness, learns the way of forgiveness and extends justice and service to those in need.

2. Ask the participants to follow the directions in the Participant Book (page 16) or on the blackline handout, and draw their family tree, answering the questions indicated. When they have finished gather them into small groups to share their reflection and responses.

3. Refocus the attention of all to the large group and ask each small group to share a summary of their responses.

Putting Faith Into Practice

1. Invite the participants to continue their discussion in small groups with these questions: *From this reflection, how would you define what it means to be a domestic church today? How do single people/single parent families experience the notion of domestic church? How can families better support each other in this mission to holiness?*

2. In the large group, have the sponsors and catechists share some ways that prayer and traditions are celebrated in their families. Then encourage everyone to name specific actions they wish to take this week to better pass on the faith and live the holiness and values they treasure in the Participant Book (page 17) or on the blackline handout, under the section titled, "I Want To Put My Faith Into Action By."

Prayer

Close with a solemn blessing for families, taken from the *Catholic Household Blessings and Prayers, Part Three.* Have some of the resources available, including a list of parish ministries devoted to family, for candidates/catechumens to borrow and browse through. Offer to order any books on family prayer that they might wish to purchase.

Epiphany

The Word In Liturgy

Isaiah 60:1-6
Psalm 72:1-2, 7-8, 10-11, 12-13
Ephesians 3:2-3a, 5-6
Matthew 2:1-12

The Solemnity of the Epiphany has an extremely rich liturgical tradition, stemming from the earliest Christian centuries. In the churches of the East, this day has occupied a place of even greater prominence than Christmas. Rome has assimilated it into the Christmas season where, too often, many think of it only as a commemoration of the historical visit of the Magi to the newly born Christ child. However, the richer meaning of the feast is suggested by translating its name, *epiphania*, which means "revelation." Associated with this feast historically are several "revelations" of Christ: to the Magi, at his baptism in the Jordan, and at Cana in Galilee as he worked the first of his "signs." We draw attention today to the way in which this feast continues to unfold the Christmas mystery, highlighting the revelation of God's saving love in Jesus. We focus in a particular way on the universality of God's offer of salvation, symbolized by presence of the Gentiles, alluded to in all three readings.

The first reading reflects the joy felt by the inhabitants of Jerusalem after their return from exile. God's promise of deliverance has been fulfilled, and that saving act is like a beacon of light shining before the entire world, revealing the compassion and love of the Lord. It is that splendid act of mercy that has drawn even the Gentiles to the Holy City, proclaiming the praises of the Lord as they stream toward Jerusalem from every corner of the earth. The refrain to the responsorial psalm ("Lord, every nation on earth will adore you.") underscores this aspect of the reading as well.

Paul sees in his own ministry to the Gentiles a similar manifestation of God's gracious offer of salvation to all people. He calls it a "mystery" that the Gentiles have become "sharers in the promise" (v. 6), a mystery "made known to me by revelation" (v. 3). Nothing in Paul's background as a Pharisee, a strict observer of the Law, could have prepared him for such a startling revelation. Convinced as he had been of the privileged place of the Jewish people in God's plan of salvation, and remembering how fixated he was on the importance of a careful observance of the Law in order to be righteous in God's eyes, Paul writes now with wonder that Jew and Gentile alike are "members of the same body" (v. 6).

This same motif is echoed in the Gospel, where the Magi—foreigners—are drawn to the savior by the light of a star. These pagans, unschooled in the Law and ignorant of the prophets, nevertheless find the Christ and adore him. Matthew makes a point of contrasting their attitude with that of King Herod, the chief priests and scribes, and indeed "all Jerusalem" (v. 3). The Gentile astrologers who follow the light of the star are seen as the truly enlightened ones. "Enlightenment" in early Christian parlance referred to baptism. Catechumens preparing for baptism are in a unique position to appreciate the journey toward enlightenment represented in today's readings and lived out by them in their catechumenal process.

Catholic Doctrine

Christ is the light of all nations.

Reflecting on the mystery of the Church, the Second Vatican Council wrote, "Christ is the light of all nations; and it is, accordingly, the heartfelt desire of this sacred Council. . .that, by proclaiming his Gospel to every creature (cf. Mark 16:15), it may bring to all. . .that light of Christ which shines out visibly from the Church." (LG 1) The Church's self-understanding described in the dogmatic constitution on the church, *Lumen Gentium*, is embodied in today's feast, which proclaims that all people are attracted to and find salvation in the radiance of God's light. In *Lumen Gentium* Number 15-17, the bishops addressed the church's relationship with other Christians (15) and with non-Christians (16), emphasizing that the church's mandate from the Lord himself is ultimately to preach God's offer of salvation to the very ends of the earth (17). Epiphany means "showing forth" or "manifestation." In the context of the Christmas season, it is Jesus, the Word made flesh, who is shown as the light of all people (John 1:4).

The special preface for this day also reiterates: "Today you revealed in Christ your eternal plan of salvation and showed him as the light of all peoples" (Preface for Epiphany, *Roman Missal*). Several Eucharistic prayers also illuminate and carry forward this theme of universality, ". . .from age to age you [God] gather a people to yourself, so that from east to west a perfect offering may be made to the glory of your name" (Eucharistic Prayer III) and "You [God] have gathered us here around the table of your Son, in fellowship with the Virgin Mary, Mother of God, and all the saints. In that new world where the fullness of peace will be revealed, gather people of every race, language, and way of life to share in the one eternal banquet with Jesus Christ the Lord" (Eucharistic Prayer for Masses of Reconciliation II).

The church's missionary impulse derives from the conviction that all are meant to share in the banquet of God's love. The Council asserted, "The Church's essential nature is universal . . . preaching the Word of God and proclaiming the kingdom throughout the whole world." (AG 1).

St. Leo the Great preached: "The loving providence of God. . . decreed that all nations should be saved in Christ. . . .A promise had been made to the holy patriarch Abraham in regard to these nations. He was to have a countless progeny, born not from his body but from the seed of faith. His descendants are therefore compared with the array of the stars . . . Let the full number of the nations now take their place in the family of the patriarchs . . . Dear friends, now that we have received instruction in the revelation of God's grace, let us celebrate with spiritual joy the day of our first harvesting, of the first calling of the Gentiles . . . This came to be fulfilled . . . from the time when the star beckoned the three wise men out of their distant country and led them to recognize and adore the King of heaven and earth. The obedience of the star calls us to imitate its humble service: to be servants, as best we can, of the grace that invites all . . . to find Christ." (Sermo 3 in Epiphania Domini, 1-3,5: PL 54, 240-44, found in *Liturgy of the Hours*, Office of Readings for Epiphany.)

Catholic Culture

The Eastern Church adopted the feast of Christmas in the fourth century. Their celebration of Epiphany focused on the baptism of Christ, with a commemoration of the adoration of the wise men. The Western Church accepted the feast of Epiphany in the fifth century, and the three themes of the adoration of the wise men, the baptism of Christ, and his first miracle at Cana were adopted in whole or in part by the various local churches. (*Encyclopedia of Catholicism*, Epiphany article, 472).

The "twelve days of Christmas" are counted from December 25 to January 6, the day of Epiphany. In some cultures, children receive gifts on this day, a reminder of the wise men who brought gifts of gold, frankincense, and myrrh to Jesus. In Puerto Rico, for example, on the eve of January 6 ("Three Kings Day"), children fill shoes with hay for the camels and horses of the Magi. The next day the hay is gone, replaced with toys and candy. In Italy the "good witch" Befana (a derivation of the word Epiphany) leaves people surprises accompanied by Rudolfo, who threatens punishment to people who need encouragement to change for the better. Befana originally intended to join the Magi, but lost heart and so must now go in search of the Christ from house to house, seeing in everyone she meets the "light of all nations." (Mary Ellen Hynes, *Companion to the Calendar*, Liturgy Training Publications, 1993, pages 9-10.)

A Magus (singular of Magi) is not a king but an astrologer, that is, someone who scans the heavens for portents and knowledge of the universe. By as early as the third century in the East, Magi began to be identified with kings and were thought of as three in number. By the fifth century in the West, a tradition began of imagining one of the kings as black skinned. No names are given to the Magi in the Bible, but the names traditionally associated with them in the West are: Caspar, Balthasar, and Melchior. Their relics are said to rest in the Cologne Cathedral in Germany.

Notes

Dismissal Catechesis (30 min)

Getting Started

1. Prepare the space ahead of time with a circle of chairs around the Christmas creche, surrounded by several votive candles. Have the figures of the Magi at hand. You will need to have songbooks available for the prayer times.

2. With Christmas music playing softly in the background, invite catechumens and candidates to be seated in the circle.

3. Ask all to join in singing, "We Three Kings" as you light the votive candles. As the song continues, ask three different participants to place one of the magi figures into the creche. Continue the prayer in these words:

   O Light of Lights, you manifest your love to all the nations. In your coming, God's saving love is revealed from every corner of the earth. You have made us coheirs and sharers in the promise of salvation. Illuminate our minds and open our hearts that we might follow the way of the Magi. They persisted in their search, until they found you in the humblest of places. Let our search be as unrelenting, as was theirs. Enlighten us as we contemplate your Word today. Let us give homage to God who is all glory and light.

First Impressions

1. Invite the participants to share their insights into the following: *What did you find inspiring about the celebration of the Word today? What can you recall from the sacred scriptures that touched your heart?*

2. Ask the group to listen intently as you proclaim the second reading, Ephesians 3:2-3a,5-6 once again. Gathering them into small groups, ask them to discuss the following questions: *What is the "mystery" Paul speaks of in this reading? What do these phrases mean to you: coheir of the kingdom of God, members of the same body, and copartners in the promise?*

3. In the large group invite a few to share their understanding of these terms.

Making Connections

1. Explain to the group the background to this second reading in these words:

   Nothing in Paul's Jewish roots could have prepared him for the startling revelation that the Gentiles shared in the promise of salvation. As a strict observer of the law, Paul could only come to this knowledge through the revelation of the Holy Spirit. The fullness of God's epiphany (revelation) in Jesus continues to be made manifest in the apostles through the action of the Spirit. Paul is absolutely awed that Jew and Gentile, no longer enemies, are members of the same body of Christ. All differences and barriers have melted away!

2. Continue the discussion in the large group by asking: What differences and barriers continue to separate God's people, in spite of God's revelation that we are all sharers in the promise? Gather them into small groups to discuss: *What light can we bring to bear on situations of religious or racial intolerance? What action can we take to encourage open-mindedness when faced with such intolerance in our every day life?*

3. In the large group invite the small groups to write their actions for open-mindedness on a large poster board.

Prayer

Gather the participants for prayer by asking all to sing, "The Light Shines On," Carey Landry (NALR, 1985). Ask the participants to name those peoples and cultures who have been victimized by intolerance (the poster board will be a reminder) and after each naming, direct them to respond: *"Lord, every nation on earth will adore you."* Close with the last verse of the song.

Extended Catechesis

SESSION FOCUS: *Christ is the light of all nations.*

Gathering

A. Sunday:

1. Extend a warm welcome to the sponsors, team members and additional participants as they arrive. Invite them to join the circle and share their ideas about the meaning of this feast of the Epiphany with the catechumens and candidates.

2. Invite all to stand and sing the third verse of "Rise Up in Splendor," Daigle, Ducote and Ault (NALR, 1986) Then pray:

   O, God, you have revealed to us the greatness of your love through the birth of a small child, destined to become a light to the world. Grant us the ability to know this simple and great love in our lives. Open our hearts and minds to hear your word. Transform us that we might recognize your epiphany in our lives. We ask this in Christ's name, Jesus our Lord. Amen.

3. Continue with the proclamation of the gospel, Matthew 2:1-12. Close the prayer with a time of silence.

B. Weekday:

1. Welcome and greet each individual as he or she arrives. Encourage everyone to gather in the circle with the same centerpiece, described for the Dismissal Catechesis.

2. Ask the participants to share: *How has God revealed God's self to you in the ordinary events of these past few days?*

3. Lead this celebration of the Word:
- Song: "Rise Up in Splendor," verse three
- First Reading: Isaiah 60:1-6
- Quiet reflection on signs that the light of the Lord shines forth on all nations.
- Gospel: Matthew 2:1-12
- Close with the Singing of Psalm 72

The Word (30 min)

1. Invite the participants to close their eyes as you slowly read the following images from the Isaiah passage. Ask them to be aware of their reactions as they listen.

"Your light has come"
"the glory of the Lord shines upon you."
"over you appears his glory"
"Nations shall walk by your light"
"they all gather and come to you"
"your hearts shall throb and overflow"
"the wealth of the nations shall be brought to you"
"Caravans of camels shall fill you"
"All from Sheba shall come,
bearing gold and frankincense"

2. Explain that these images flow out of the joy felt by the Israelites because God's promised deliverance from their exile in Babylon has been fulfilled. Invite the participants to gather in small groups to discuss these questions: *What was your reaction as you listened to these images? What does this passage reveal about the nature of our God? When have you experienced the light of God's liberating love?*

3. Continue by presenting the background to the gospel in these or similar words:

The richness of this feast is expanded in the translation of epiphany to mean revelation. Think about all of the 'revelations' of Christ: to the Magi, at his baptism, at Cana and through all the signs and miracles during his ministry. These revelations unfold the depths of God's love for all peoples.

In the gospel, the astrologers were led to Jesus through a natural phenomenon, following the star. Matthew uses this to point to the fact that the Gentiles, who did not have the benefit of the Hebrew Scriptures, were open to the revelation of the birth of the king of the Jews. In contrast, Jewish leader, King Herod, did not recognize the kingly messiah even with the knowledge of the scriptures and the prophets. The determination of the Magi to find the Christ and adore him offers an example of the persistence needed by seekers today.

4. In small groups, ask the participants to share their insights on these questions: *Who were the enlightened ones in this gospel passage? What are some of the differences you can name between the Magi and Herod? Who are the "pagans" (Gentiles) of our world today?*

Catholic Teaching (30 min)

1. Explain the meaning of the church's teaching that "Christ is the light of all nations," by making the following points:

- This feast proclaims that all people are attracted to and find salvation in the radiance of God's light. In the context of this Christmas season, Jesus—the Word made flesh—is the light of all people. In other words, no one is excluded from God's offer of salvation in Jesus.

- All people are meant to share in the banquet of God's love. Thus, the Church's essential nature is universal.

- At the Second Vatican Council, the bishops of the world addressed the church's relationship with other Christians and with non-Christians in the constitution known as *Lumen Gentium* (Light of the Nations). In this document, the church understands herself as a sign and instrument of communion with God and of unity among all people.

- The Church stands at the service of Jesus' universal and reconciling mission to the world. Thus, the Church as the People of God, are called to give witness to this unity and reconciliation in the world, in which they work and raise their families.

2. Invite the participants into small groups to discuss these questions: *How has the light of Christ been visible to you as you journey toward initiation? How can you witness the light of Christ in your workplace? Among your family and friends?*

OR . . .

Ask the group to turn to the exercise in the Participant Book (page 18) or on the blackline handout to reflect on the power of the light of Christ in today's world. When they have finished, ask them to share their responses to the questions in small groups.

Putting Faith Into Practice

1. Encourage the participants to turn their attention to the large group. Ask them to brainstorm ways they can offer the light of Christ to others. Record their responses on a large poster board.

2. Invite them to reflect on one way they wish to put their faith into action by sharing the light of Christ. Direct them to write their resolution in the corresponding section of the Participant Book (page 19) or on the blackline handout.

3. Share with the group ways in which your parish is a "light to the nations" through ecumenical and interfaith activities and acts of service to those in need. You may choose to invite a person from one of these groups to share its mission with the participants.

Prayer

Gather the participants in silence, as you bring a Christ Candle into the center of the circle and light it. Have copies of Psalm 72, indicating antiphonal parts (left and right) prepared for each participant. Indicate the sides, left and right, of the group and ask all to stand and pray the psalm. Close by inviting all to sing, "You are the Voice," David Haas

Baptism of the Lord

The Word In Liturgy

Isaiah 40:1-5, 9-11
Psalm 104:1b-2, 3-4, 24-25, 27-28, 29-30
Titus 2:11-14; 3:4-7
Luke 3:15-16, 21-22

Today's celebration marks the end of the Christmas season. Since the scene at the Jordan is presented as the beginning of the public ministry of Jesus, today also serves as a "bridge" into Ordinary Time, which traces the historical unfolding of the ministry of Jesus through a continuous reading from the Gospel of Luke. Because we are still in the Christmas season, the theme of the Incarnation remains important in today's celebration. Even more prominent, and closely associated with last Sunday's celebration of the Epiphany, is the theme of the revelation of God's saving action in the person of Jesus. The gospel presents his baptism as the time when Jesus is revealed as God's Son, the beloved. But it is clear from the ensemble of readings selected for today that the Baptism of the Lord is also fundamental for our understanding of Christian baptism, the fulfillment of John's promise that "he will baptize you with the Holy Spirit and fire" (v. 16).

The text from Isaiah is one of the "Servant Songs," passages describing a chosen one who will deliver God's people from slavery by his suffering and death. Originally intended as a prophecy of consolation and hope for the Jewish people during the exile, these poems became messianic texts understood to speak metaphorically of the broader salvation that God would offer to the people in the midst of their moral slavery to sin. Christian tradition has found here allusions both to Jesus' ministry of reconciliation and to his redemptive suffering and death. This passage fits well with today's gospel, both because of its references to God's chosen servant, echoed

in Luke's voice from heaven, and because its imagery is so strongly suggestive of the redemptive ministry of Jesus described throughout the gospels.

That redemptive ministry is expressed in a more theological manner in the reading from Acts, an excerpt from a speech of Peter in which he reminds his listeners of how Jesus went about "healing all who were oppressed by the devil" (v. 38). The setting for Peter's sermon is the home of Cornelius, a pivotal scene in Luke's theology, because it revealed the divine will to call even the gentiles to salvation through faith in Jesus and baptism. Peter proclaims of Jesus, "God was with him," an affirmation that expresses powerfully the Christmas season's belief in the Incarnation and the basis for our Catholic belief in the efficacious power of Christian baptism.

Luke's description of the baptismal scene is striking in the way he underplays the actual water event at the hand of John. Instead, he highlights the prayer of Jesus, the descent of the Holy Spirit, and the heavenly voice proclaiming Jesus as God's beloved. These emphases are deliberate, revealing Jesus as a model for all believers. Catechumens seeking to be disciples of Jesus are presented with a vision of their own destiny, as they prepare in prayer for the waters of baptism, from which they will emerge as God's beloved, freed from sin, filled with the Spirit, consecrated to share in the mission of Jesus as foretold in the Servant Songs of Isaiah.

Catholic Doctrine

"We acknowledge one baptism for the forgiveness of sins." — *Nicene Creed*

On this Sunday we celebrate the Baptism of the Lord. It is fitting that we recall our own Christian baptism on this day as well. Jesus was baptized in the Jordan by John not because the Lord was sinful but because he wished to join himself to sinful humanity. It is also a sign of his self-emptying, ultimately achieved in his suffering and death on the cross. This gesture of self-emptying is made by Jesus and immediately afterwards all three synoptic accounts agree that the Spirit descended upon him. The Spirit who had hovered over the waters of the first creation descends on the Christ as a prelude of the new creation and the Father reveals Jesus as his beloved Son (CCC 1224).

Christian Baptism has two principal effects. One is purification from sin and the other is new birth in the Spirit.

By Baptism, all sins are forgiven. The original sin that taints this world, and all our personal sins are destroyed by the waters of Baptism (CCC 1263). The power of darkness is dispelled and for those reborn in this sacrament there is now nothing that would impede their entry into the kingdom of light. Thus baptism is described as the "door into life."

Baptism makes us a "new creation." (2 Cor 5:17) We are incorporated into Christ and become adopted children of God. We are joined as brothers and sisters to one another in the household of the faithful. Members of the Body of Christ, we become members of one another. From the womb of the baptismal font is born the one people of God which transcends all the natural or human limits of nations, cultures, races and sexes. "The one spirit baptizes us into the one body." (1 Cor 12:13)

Baptism is the sacrament of faith. But faith needs a community. The faith of the individual is supported and comes to maturity within the believing community, a community on a mission with Christ, "who was sent to bring to the poor the good news of salvation." (Preface for Baptism of the Lord, *Roman Missal*.) Born of the font, enlightened by Christ and growing in faith, believers walk as children of the light spreading the good news of salvation in their actions to assist the birth of the kingdom of God in this world.

In Baptism, the passover of the Lord becomes our own passover from death (sin) to life (grace). St. Ambrose writes, "See where you are baptized, see where Baptism comes from, if not from the cross. In him you are redeemed, in him you are saved." (De sacr. 2,2,6: PL 16, 444.)

Catholic Culture

Baptismal fonts come in varying shapes that suggest the different effects. For example, there are cross-shaped fonts suggesting that the one being baptized is joined to the death of the Lord on the cross, rounded fonts to suggest the womb of mother Church giving birth to God's adopted children; there are octagonal fonts to suggest the "eighth day" of the Resurrection and our new creation; square fonts to suggest that Baptism is the door to new life and rectangular fonts suggesting a tomb in which we die with Christ to sin.

When a new font is blessed, the Church prays:

Grant, O Lord, that the people who are reborn from this font
May fulfill in their actions what they pledge by their faith
And show by their lives what they begin by the power of
your grace. (*Book of Blessings*, 1101.)

A contemporary hymn (1971) relies on a translation of an ancient text from John of Damascus (700) to sing of baptism: "Come let us drink of that new river/Not from barren rock divinely poured,/But the fount of life that springs for ever/From the sacred body of our Lord." ("Come and Let Us Drink of That New River," Worship, GIA Publications, Inc., Chicago, 1986.) There are several distinctive African-American spirituals which sing of baptism, for example, "I've Just Come From the Fountain," and "Wade in the Water."

Christian history has often left architectural monuments to the values held most dearly by successive generations of believers. An inscription in the fourth century baptistry at St. John Lateran in Rome reads:

Here is born in Spirit-soaked fertility
a brood destined for another City,
begotten by God's blowing
and borne upon this torrent
by the Church, their virgin mother.
Reborn in these depths they reach for heaven's realm,
the born-but-once unknown by felicity.
This spring is life that floods the world,
the wounds of Christ its awesome source.
Sinner sink beneath this sacred surf
that swallows age and spits up youth.
Sinner here scour sin away down to innocence,
for they know no enmity who are by
one font, one Spirit, one faith made one.
Sinner shudder not at sin's kind and number,
for those born here are holy.

The great sixth-century baptistries of Ravenna, gleaming with their gold mosaics, proclaim the enormous theological and pastoral importance of Baptism in an era that had known first-hand the power of flourishing catechumenal communities. A thousand years later, long after the demise of the ancient catechumenate, the magnificent Renaissance baptistries of Pisa and Florence still preserved an awareness of Baptism's importance in communities where infant baptism was the norm.

Dismissal Catechesis (30 min)

Getting Started

1. Prepare the space ahead of time with a circle of chairs around a table. Upon the table place a large clear glass bowl of water. Next to the bowl place a Christ candle.

2. Invite the candidates and catechumens to gather in a circle as they arrive. Begin the prayer by inviting candidates and catechumens to sing, "Come to the Water," John B. Foley, SJ (New Dawn Music, 1978), verses one and two. You will need to have songbooks available for all the participants. Continue by praying Psalm 29.

First Impressions

1. In the large group, ask this question: *How do you connect this water symbol, in the center of our circle, with today's liturgy of the Word?*

2. When they have finished sharing some thoughts, continue by asking all to close their eyes and try to imagine themselves in the setting for today's second reading from the Acts of the Apostles. Use these or similar words:

   Relax and settle yourself, dismissing any thoughts or worries that are on your mind. Become aware of your heartbeat as you relax. Now that you are comfortable, imagine with me that you are back in time to the days of the early Christian community. You are a very strict Jew who believes in the resurrection of Jesus. Peter, himself baptized you on the day now known as Pentecost. All your life you guarded yourself and your family against false prophets and false gods. That was pretty difficult living. But somehow you lived your life keeping the covenant with the one true God. On that day of your baptism, you were on a business trip in Jerusalem and were absolutely transformed by the preaching of Peter. This Jesus who died and rose was indeed the messiah sent by God. But now you can't believe your ears. This Roman centurion, Cornelius, wants to join the followers of Jesus! How could this be since he is a gentile? You join the others in the courtyard of the house of Cornelius. Peter is beginning to speak now as you listen. . .

3. Proclaim the second reading, Acts 10:34-38.

4. Gather the participants into small groups, inviting them to discuss the following: *In the light of this meditation, what is your reaction to Peter's speech? How does God's revelation to the Gentiles connect with last Sunday's celebration of Epiphany? What does this speech tell you about baptism?*

Making Connections

1. Focus the attention of the participants' back to the large group. Invite all to think about Jesus' baptism in the light of all the scriptures in today's liturgy. Ask them to consider the effects of Jesus' baptism and their implications for us.

2. Then invite them to work in pairs, listing the implications of

baptism on pieces of paper, using the form: *Jesus' baptism revealed that _____, in my life this means that I_____.* This example will help clarify the process: *Jesus baptism revealed that God favored him, in my life this means that I too am God's chosen.* Prepare the pieces of paper ahead of time.

3. Ask the pairs to share their responses with the whole group and then direct them to post these responses around the meeting space.

Prayer

Invite the group to pray silently for those among them who are preparing for baptism. Pray the inscription found on the fourth century baptistry at St. John Lateran in Rome. The text is in the Catholic Culture section in the background piece for this week's session. Close by asking all to stand and sing verses three and four of "Come To the Water," *Glory and Praise,* p. 136.

Extended Catechesis

SESSION FOCUS: *The Meaning of Baptism*

Gathering

A. Sunday:

1. Greet and welcome the sponsors, team, and other participants as they join the group. Invite them to gather in the circle.

2. Begin the prayer by inviting all to stand and sing, "Come and Let Us Drink of That New River," (Worship, GIA Publications, 1986). Indicate to the group to be seated and in silence. Explain the significance of icons in these words:

   An icon is a religious image, painted in such a way that the image draws one into the painting. Some have described the experience of praying with an icon in this way, "As you look at the image of Christ or Mary, the image looks back at you." Icons are inspirational and sacred works of art, particularly in the Eastern Christian traditions. The large eyes, fixed in their gaze, dominate the images portrayed in an icon. An icon is prayer transformed into art. As you prayerfully look at this icon of Jesus' Baptism, allow the Father, Son and Spirit to look into your heart.

3. In silence, pass around the icon, *"The Baptism, the Theophany"* (17 century, Ukranian School). This can be found in *Festal Icons of the Lord,* Sr. M. Helen Weier (Collegeville: The Liturgical Press, 1977). As the group finishes praying in this manner, proclaim the gospel, Luke 3:15-16, 21-22.

B. Weekday:

1. As the participants arrive, warmly greet and invite everyone to join the circle.

2. Invite the group to briefly share how God has been revealed in their life these past few days.

3. Invite all to share in this celebration of the Word.
- Song: Gathering Hymn from Sunday's liturgy
- First Reading: Isaiah 40:1-5, 9-11
- Sing Psalm 104:1b-2, 3-4, 24-25, 27-28, 29-30
- Reflection: Using the script and process indicated in the Sunday gathering, provide an opportunity for everyone to pray with the icon of Jesus' baptism.
- Gospel: Luke 3:15-16, 21-22

The Word (30 min)

1. Invite the group to share their experience of praying with the icon and how that affected their hearing of the gospel.

2. When they have finished sharing, ask them to listen closely as you recall the following images from the first reading, Isaiah 40:1-5, 9-11.

"Prepare the way of the Lord!"
"The glory of the Lord shall be revealed."
"Cry out at the top of your voice."
"Like a shepherd he feeds his flock."
"In his arms he gathers the lambs."

3. Encourage the participants to discuss these questions in small groups: *What reactions do these images stir up from within you? How does this description parallel the life and mission of Jesus?*

4. Invite the participants to look at the pieces of paper that describe the implications of Jesus' baptism for all people. Present the background to the gospel, Luke 3:15-16, 21-22 in these or your own words:

In Luke's description of Jesus' baptism, he highlights the prayer of Jesus, the descent of the Holy Spirit and the heavenly voice proclaiming Jesus as God's beloved. Luke's baptismal scene presents Jesus as a model for all believers. In prayer, the believer is empowered by the Holy Spirit to live the life of a disciple. The disciple is one who like Jesus integrates faith with daily living. As Jesus fulfilled the description of the 'servant' in Isaiah—giving sight to the blind, bringing justice to all, releasing prisoners—the disciple will share in this same mission. Through prayer, empowered by God's favor and filled with the Holy Spirit, the baptized, like Jesus, will spread the light of the good news of salvation to all the nations.

5. Ask the group to turn to the exercise in the Participant Book (page 20) or on the blackline handout, and respond to the questions presented. When they have finished, direct them to write their own Baptismal Prayer on the same page.

Catholic Teaching (30 min)

1. Prepare a teaching on baptism, using the background information in the Catholic Doctrine section for this session. Be sure to include the following points.

- The effects of Christian baptism are twofold. Through baptism all sin is forgiven and the power of darkness is dispelled. In addition, baptism incorporates us into Christ, making us a new creation.

- As adopted children of God, we are in union with one another in the family of the faithful. "The one spirit baptizes us into the one body." (1 Corinthians 12:13)

- Through this sacrament of faith, the believing community becomes our support as we mature and carry on the mission of Christ.

- Baptism carries with it the responsibility to walk as children of the light spreading the good news of salvation in word and action as we work to bring about the kingdom of God in this world.

- Through baptism we experience the passing over from sin and death into the life of grace.

2. Invite the participants to gather in pairs. The sponsors and catechumens or candidates will want to be together. Ask the pairs to respond to these questions: *As you journey together in faith (both the baptized and those seeking baptism), what has baptism come to mean for you? In what concrete ways have you experienced the support and affirmation of the faith community?*

3. Encourage the pairs to share their Baptismal Prayers, when they have finished with the questions.

Putting Faith Into Practice

1. Invite a parishioner who was baptized at last year's Easter Vigil to join the group and witness as to what their baptism into this particular community of faith has meant to them over the past months.

2. Encourage the participants to raise any questions about baptism.

3. Invite each person to turn to the Participant Book (page 21) or on the blackline handout, and write one action they wish to take as they either journey toward initiation or as they renew their baptismal commitment.

Prayer

1. Gather the participants in silence in preparation for prayer. Pray in these words:

Jesus, Beloved of the Father, enliven in us the desire to fully live as your disciples. Teach us the way of prayer. Guide us with the presence of your empowering Spirit. Inspire us to bring the light of faith to the blind; the freedom of forgiveness to those who are imprisoned by hate; and your liberating love to those entrapped in the dungeons of addiction. May the baptismal waters become living waters that will quench our thirst for you and drench the dryness of our lives. Open us to the support and love of this faith community, as we journey to you, the fountain of life. Amen.

2. Close by asking the group to stand and pray Psalm 29 together. Be sure to have copies available for everyone.

LENTEN SEASON

Ash Wednesday

The Word In Liturgy

Joel 2:12-18
Psalm 51:3-4, 5-6, 12-13, 14, 17
2 Corinthians 5:20-6:2
Matthew 6:1-6, 16-18

The evolution of Lent as a time of preparation for Easter began as a very modest few days of preparation before the annual celebration of the Paschal Vigil. By the end of the fourth century, those days had expanded to a forty-day period of prayer and fasting that began on a Sunday, with an emphasis mainly on the preparation of catechumens for initiation at Easter.

In subsequent centuries, with the decline and virtual disappearance of the catechumenate, the focus of Lent shifted to those doing public penance in anticipation of being reconciled to the Eucharist for Easter. The public penitents had ashes placed on their heads as an outward sign of their mortification. When public penance disappeared, the custom grew up of all the faithful asking for penitential ashes at the start of Lent. At the beginning of the sixth century, the start of Lent was shifted from Sunday to the preceding Wednesday so that there would be exactly forty days of fasting (since Sundays were not observed as days of fast), and during the next two centuries a preparatory period of three weeks was added prior to Ash Wednesday. By the end of the eleventh century, Ash Wednesday was observed throughout Christendom, and by the thirteenth century even the Pope himself accepted ashes as part of the papal liturgy on Ash Wednesday.

Among the reforms of the Second Vatican Council was the elimination of the three weeks of preparation for Lent and the placement of the blessing and distribution of ashes within the Eucharistic liturgy rather than before the start of Mass (as it had been for centuries). The custom is retained of burning palm branches from Passion (Palm) Sunday of the previous year in order to obtain the ashes. Most importantly, the Council re-established the primary focus of Lent as a time

when the whole Church joins in penance not merely out of personal piety, but in order to help in preparing those to be initiated at Easter.

There is a considerable amount of scholarly disagreement as to when the Book of Joel was composed, but a date in the fourth or fifth century B.C. seems likely. The author writes at a time of devastation in Israel from locust plague and drought, which the prophet sees as a sign of divine judgment. He calls upon the people to repent and return to Yahweh. The Lord, for his part, is presented as "rich in kindness and relenting in punishment." The call to conversion of heart is extended to everyone in the community, even infants at the breast. And, the passage ends on a hopeful note, indicating that the Lord "took pity on his people." The reading's emphasis on conversion of heart is highlighted by the choice of Psalm 51, traditionally considered the great prayer of repentance of King David after his infidelity with Bathsheeba.

Paul's letter to the Corinthians offers a solid theological rationale for why we ought to reform our lives as Joel has suggested. Christ took on our sins by his death on the cross, so that "we might become the very holiness of God." This is the ultimate Good News of Paul's Gospel, that we have been "reconciled to God" in Christ. The urgency of our response to this grace of God is unmistakable in Paul's words: "Now is the acceptable time! Now is the day of salvation!"

The section of Matthew from which we read today has no direct parallels in other Gospels. This is the third part of the Sermon on the Mount, in which Jesus discusses almsgiving (vv. 2-4), prayer (vv. 5-8), and fasting (vv. 16-18), traditional acts of Jewish piety. The reading omits a section on the Lord's

Prayer (vv. 9-13) and forgiveness of sins (vv. 14-15). Jesus' emphasis is on the purity of one's interior dispositions, a way that he underlines the depth of conversion to which his disciples are called. He is not criticizing such acts of piety in themselves, nor is he speaking out against all public manifestations of piety. Rather, it is the ostentatious public display of one's personal piety that receives his negative critique. Presumably, this teaching was occasioned by perceived problems in certain Jewish circles, known to Matthew's community as well as in Jesus' day. But the advice that is offered is as important in our own time as it was for the first generations of believers.

SESSION PLAN: Ash Wednesday

Dismissal Catechesis (30 min)

Getting Started

1. Prepare the space ahead of time with a circle of chairs around a table with a purple cloth and a bowl of ashes in the center.

2. Invite the candidates and catechumens to sit in the circle and reflect on the ashes they have just received. Play soft instrumental music in the background.

3. Begin the session by singing the Gathering Hymn used at today's liturgy. Proclaim the first reading from Joel 2:12-18. Allow a period of quiet after the reading. Follow this with the following prayer:

God of our Longing, you have marked us with the sign of your cross. May this ashen cross be a reminder of your call, 'Return to me with all your hearts.' During these days of Lent, show us how to repent from our sinful ways. Teach us how to pray and offer you the work of our hands in a way that is fitting. Guide us as we act in love and justice for those in need. We ask that you receive our willing and repentant hearts through Jesus who suffered and died for our sake. Amen.

First Impressions

1. Ask the participants to share the following: *What did today's liturgy awaken in you? How do you understand the meaning of being signed with ashes?* Offer this brief explanation of the meaning of Ash Wednesday:

In the early church, those who needed forgiveness for grave sin (apostasy, murder and adultery), did public penance as a sign of repentance. Their return to the table and the community involved placing ashes on their heads as an outward sign of their mortification. When public penance disappeared, the custom grew of all the faithful asking for penitential ashes at the start of Lent. The palms of the previous year's Palm Sunday are burned to obtain the ashes. These are blessed and placed on the forehead of the faithful in the sign of a cross with the words (here use the form used at your parish liturgy).

2. Help the participants recall some of the key images from the readings used at the liturgy by asking: *What images and ideas do you recall from today's readings?* As the images

are named, ask the individual to print that image on a large poster or paper. Prepare your own list prior to the session and add to those named by the group when they seem finished. Ask them to gather into small groups to discuss: *How would you summarize the meaning of today's scriptures? What did you find confusing?* Invite the small groups to present their responses in the large gathering.

3. Explain the scriptures in these words:

This penitential theme flows throughout all of the scriptures used at today's liturgy. The first reading from the Book of Joel is a call for conversion of heart for all of the community. Paul offers a theological reason for reforming our lives in the second letter to the Corinthians. Paul urges and exhorts us, "Now is the acceptable time! Now is the day of salvation." The passage from the gospel of Matthew flows from the previous section in which Jesus emphasizes the purity of one's interior disposition for conversion. Thus, it follows that this section of the gospel continues to criticize public displays of personal piety, urging the follower of Jesus to perform acts of prayer, fasting and almsgiving in private.

Making Connections

1. Invite the participants to gather in small groups to discuss: *How do our interior motives affect our spiritual practices? From Matthew's gospel, what does God require of us as we journey toward conversion?*

2. Ask the participants to share their insights in the large group. When they have finished, invite them to brainstorm some of the ways they can make their penitential journey this Lent more authentic. You may choose to record their ideas on a large poster or paper. Summarize their discussion and pause, asking everyone to think of one action they will take this Lent.

Prayer

Allow a brief period of silence for each person to make their resolution. Proclaim the gospel, Matthew 6:1-6, 16-18. Ask the group to write their resolution on a slip of paper and place it on the table with the ashes as an offering to God. Close by praying Psalm 51 together. Copies of the psalm will need to be available for each person.

First Sunday of Lent

The Word In Liturgy

Deuteronomy 26:4-10
Psalm 91:1-2, 10-11, 12-13, 14-15
Romans 10:8-13
Luke 4:1-13

To understand the readings this Sunday it is necessary to recall the place of divine election in salvation history. The greater part of the Old Testament concerns God's actions in relation to the people of Israel, whom God chooses from among all peoples to reveal divine goodness. The people of Israel, unlike their neighbors, believed that God was revealed not primarily through the cycles of nature, but rather through God's free actions in history. Israel's consciousness of being God's elect was not based on pride or a sense that they had merited God's favor, but simply on their repeated experience of God's faithfulness to them. A small and insignificant people compared to the flourishing civilizations around them, Israel marveled at God's favor given freely to them and regarded it as a wonder and a sign. This is the people who are bidden by the first reading from Deuteronomy to bring the first fruits of their harvest to the Lord, and in doing so, to confess God's goodness. Considered by many to be one of the most ancient and important passages of the Pentateuch, this creedal statement recalls God's special favor to Israel in the events of its history. It is the people's own acknowledgment of the election that lay at the very center of their existence.

Today's second reading from Romans, also thought to be a very early confession of faith, emphasizes both belief in the heart and the importance of speaking one's faith aloud. Jesus Christ and his resurrection stand at the center of this faith. What the children of Israel found in the covenant with Abraham and the events of the Exodus, Christians find in the person of Christ and his passover from death to life—the substance of their common identity as a people.

An account of Jesus' temptations in the desert appears in all the synoptic gospels and is taken from one common source by both Matthew and Luke. In Luke's gospel, the devil's power amounts to a separate kingdom, in tension with the kingdom of God. Throughout Jesus' public ministry, and finally at the cross, the conflict between the kingdom of God and the kingdom of the devil continues to be revealed in Luke.

The temptations Luke describes would have recalled to his gentile audience the three great temptations: love of pleasure, love of riches, and love of power. More fundamental to the story, however, is its Jewish background, which is found in the Israelite experience of wandering forty years in the desert after the deliverance from Egypt. There they were tested by physical hunger, the lure of idolatry, and the temptation to test God. Led into the desert by the Spirit for forty days, Jesus experiences the very same temptations but responds to each of them out of his deep fidelity to God. He answers the devil's proposals with the words of Deuteronomy, that passionate work revealing the heart of the Mosaic covenant. He chooses to rely on God's word, to worship God alone, and to trust God humbly. By responding in this fashion, Jesus reverses the human unfaithfulness that has ever been part of the story of God's dealing with those whom he chooses and becomes the exemplar of the right response to God's election.

On this day when the church celebrates the election of catechumens, it is appropriate to reflect on the mystery of God's election, seen in the chosen people, epitomized in Jesus, and lived out continually by the believing and confessing church.

Catholic Doctrine

Divine Election

The starting point for a Catholic understanding of divine election is with Hebrew scriptures and Israel's own view on being set apart that is contained in those sacred pages. This point has already been emphasized in the previous section, but it bears repetition. It is God who does the choosing. Israel is not elected or set apart because of any intrinsic characteristics as a people. The choosing comes about because God is totally and absolutely gracious—in spite of the repeated refusal of humans to turn away from sin.

Israel experienced this divine election in the historical events of a loving God who again and again pursued this wayward and insignificant people. As expressed in the Old Testament, the purpose of this special election as the Chosen People is not for their own sake but for the sake of manifesting God's grace, glory and power to the whole world.

Jesus Christ stands at the apex of this historical unfolding of God's divine election. The New Testament scriptures attest that Jesus is God's elect. The Greek term for "elect" is applied to Jesus by the gospel of John (1:34, although many versions translate this as "Son of God rather than elect of God), and by Luke in both the transfiguration and crucifixion scenes (9:35, "chosen Son" and 23:35, "chosen one"). Elect is also a term used by Peter (1 Peter 2:4,6). "What God has done in his chosen one, Jesus, has decisive significance. It is the occasion either for the founding of steadfast faith in those who believe or for the downfall of those who refuse to believe." (*On the Rite of Election*, Rita Ferrone, Liturgy Training Publications, Chicago, 1994, p. 49.)

Jesus, in his humble submission to the will of the Father and the plan of God, exemplifies for us the right response to divine election. On this Sunday, when the Church celebrates God's election of catechumens, we always read from a gospel account of the temptation of Jesus. His forty days in the desert echo Israel's testing for forty years. These gospel accounts tell of Jesus' unswerving trust and worship of his loving Father.

God acts, God chooses, and in so doing, human pride is confounded. So, too, the pride of Satan is overturned. The entire life of Jesus, his ministry, his suffering and death, all point to God and God alone whose reign is overtaking this world. For in Christ, the faithful are gathered up, given membership in this kingdom and presented to God in a new and everlasting covenant.

Therefore, Catholic teaching emphasizes that the Church inherits Israel's election. While we still regard the Jewish people as "chosen" (for how could God go back on his promise?), nevertheless divine providence and grace are opened up in a new way by the coming of Christ. The Second Vatican Council chose to describe the Church as the "People of God." The Council proclaimed, "Christ instituted this new covenant, namely the new covenant in his blood (cf. 1 Cor 11:25); he called a race made up of Jews and Gentiles which would be one . . . and this race would be the new People of God (*Lumen Gentium*, 21 November 1964, n. 9).

Thus, the Church proclaims in prayer at the Easter Vigil, "Lord God, in the new covenant you shed light on the miracles you worked in ancient times: the Red Sea is a symbol of our baptism, and the nation you freed from slavery is a sign of your Christian people. May every nation share in the faith and privilege of Israel and come to new birth in the Holy Spirit." (Easter Vigil, Prayers After the Readings, n. 26, *Roman Missal*.)

Catholic Culture

"Desert" experiences are a well-known feature of the spiritual life, regarded as a time of spiritual testing. The desert fathers and mothers (late third and fourth centuries in Egypt and Palestine) were forerunners of monastic and hermetic life. The wisdom of Anthony of Egypt, Macarius of Egypt, Mother Sarah and Mother Syneletia still enriches the Church today and is collected and contained in the Sayings of the Elders (*Encyclopedia of Catholicism*, "Desert Fathers and Mothers," p. 411).

Giovanni Bellini's oil painting (late 1400) of St. Francis in the desert (Frick collection, New York), plays on the themes of the saint's encounter with God and the formation of identity in the wilderness experience.

Hymns such as "The Church's One Foundation" ("Elect from every nation, Yet one o'er all the earth . . .") and "Church of God" ("Church of God, chosen people, sing your praise . . .") celebrate the election of the Church by God (found in the hymnal *Gather Comprehensive*, GIA Publications, Chicago, 1994, nos. 661 and 664).

Notes

Dismissal Catechesis (30 min)

Getting Started

1. Prepare the space ahead of time with a desert-scape for the center of the circle. This might be a wide flat pottery dish filled with sand, rocks and some scrubby, cactus-like plants.

2. Invite the catechumens and candidates to gather in the circle and silently pause to take in the desert scene.

3. Pray in these or your own words:

   God of graciousness, you gather us today from the desert of our own lives. This time of Lent begins today, and we welcome this holy season for we are in need of time away for prayer. Our lives are so full and satiated that we crave the fasting that will empty and purify our hearts. We have been generously gifted and seek ways to share our talents and treasure with those in need. Prayer, fasting and almsgiving mark this season as we are marked with the ashen sign of your cross. Grace us to live the penitential spirit of these Lenten days in your wide embrace. Through Jesus, who walks this desert journey with us, we pray. Amen.

First Impressions

1. If the candidates and catechumens were present for the Rite of Election, invite the group to share what they noticed about the ritual. In your own words explain the significance of the rite and the special place the elect now have in the community, reminding them that they, too, will share that place when they are ready.

2. Survey the group, asking: *What did you notice that was different about the church today?* This would be a good opportunity to offer some information about the symbols that point to the Lenten season in your parish.

3. Ask the group to gather in small groups to discuss their experience of the liturgy of the Word. One or two of these questions may be of help: *What is the significance of the desert in the gospel? What emotions did the scriptures evoke in you this morning? What phrases or images from these readings have stayed with you? Why are these important to you?*

Making Connections

1. Explain the significance of 'desert' experiences in spiritual life. You may wish to refer to one of the desert Fathers or Mothers of the third century as an example of those who went out into the desert to pray and fast as a time for spiritual testing. *The Encyclopedia of Catholicism* and the references in the Catholic Culture section of Understanding This Sunday will be of help.

2. Invite the group to discuss one of the following questions: *What have you experienced in your own life that may be called a desert experience, that is, a time of spiritual testing?* After they have responded, describe a time when this has happened in your own life. Then ask the group: *How can we understand spiritual testing as a blessing from God?*

3. Take a few moments to summarize the ideas of the group. Then call for a period of silence asking the each participant to choose one thing they wish to put into practice from today's session.

Prayer

Using the sung response, "**Be with me Lord when I am in trouble, be with me Lord, I pray**" (Marty Haugen), pray Psalm 91 with the participants. Lead the psalm prayer slowly praying the verses and inviting the group to sing the refrain between the verses.

Extended Catechesis

SESSION FOCUS: *We are God's chosen people.*

Gathering

A. Sunday:

1. Extend a welcome to the sponsors and other participants as they join the circle.

2. Call for a time of silence, asking the group to reflect upon the desert-scape centerpiece and the meaning of Lent.

3. Then pray in these or your own words:

   God of Moses and Miriam, you brought your chosen people out of the bondage of slavery in Egypt. Be with us this day as we remember with gratitude all those ways you have set us free.

   God of the prophets you promised to set your people free from the captivity of Babylon. Be with us this day as we recall your fulfillment of these promises through Jesus, your Son.

   God of Joseph and Mary, through their 'yes,' you offered your only Son, Jesus, to redeem us from the bondage of sin and death. Be with us this day as we gratefully acknowledge your covenant with us through his death.

   God of the desert Fathers and Mothers, you continually purify us as a church, through the spiritual renewal of these monastic ancestors. Be with us this day as we ask you to purify us and make us worthy to be sharers in this covenant of love.

   For your constant presence in re-creating us as your holy people, we are filled with thanks and awe. Amen.

4. Proclaim the gospel, Luke 4:1-13. Invite the group to pause in silent reflection.

B. Weekday:

1. As the group gathers in the circle, greet and welcome each person. Allow a time of quiet reflection on the desert-scape centerpiece. Ask the group to share what things they observed this week that were reminders of Lent.

2. Lead this celebration of the Word:
   - Song: "Church of God" or "The Church's One Foundation"
   - First Reading: Deuteronomy 26:4-10
   - Psalm 91:1-2, 10-11, 12-13, 14-15
   - Second Reading: Romans 10:8-13
   - Gospel: Luke 4:1-13

- Period of Silence for reflection upon the Word
- Concluding Prayer: You may wish to use the suggested prayer above (A.)

The Word (30 min)

1. Set the stage by leading the group in the following meditation. Begin by asking them to settle into a comfortable position. Continue, using the script below, making sure to pause as it seems appropriate and move through the meditation slowly and prayerfully.

As you relax become aware of your breathing. Breathing in deeply, allow yourself to gradually move inward. Continue to relax as you enter into the depths of your being.

Imagine yourself, struggling for forty years, wandering in circles in the desert. At first you were glad to be freed from the slavery of the Egyptians, but now, you are just sick and tired. You have seen the older people die, many births and marriages. You have all but forgotten why you left. The harshness of the desert has replaced the severity of slavery. In fact, a whole new generation is ready to enter the promised land. As you enter the promised land, God prepares your heart and reminds you that it was all worthwhile. Allow God to move within your heart now.

Pause for an appropriate period, then invite the group to gradually and gently return to this room. Remaining quiet repeat the passage from Deuteronomy 26:4-10, with emphasis on God's faithfulness to the chosen, the elect.

2. Gather the participants into small groups and ask them to discuss the following questions: *What would you have felt if you were one of those entering the promised land? What did it mean to be the chosen race? Have you ever felt like you were special or chosen by God?* Talk about this experience in your group.

3. Using the information on The Word in Liturgy contained in the Understanding this Sunday section, explain the temptations of Jesus as an indication of God's favor upon him. Use these or similar words:

After acknowledging the Sonship of Jesus, at the baptism in the Jordan, God indicated that Jesus is favored, that is, chosen. From this experience of favor, Jesus is propelled into the desert by the Spirit. In the desert, Jesus experienced the same temptations—physical hunger, the lure of idolatry and the drive to test God—as did the Israelites in the desert. Yet, Jesus' response was motivated out of his deep fidelity to God. In humble trust and authentic worship, Jesus relied upon God's word, quoting Deuteronomy. Jesus overcame these three temptations making it possible for us to reverse our unfaithfulness.

4. Read, once again, the gospel, Luke 4:1-13. Ask the participants to reflect upon the temptations of Jesus, using the worksheet in the corresponding section of the Participant Book, to further discover the meaning of this gospel in their lives. After allowing sufficient time to reflect upon the questions, encourage them to share their insights in their small group.

Catholic Teaching (30 min)

1. Help the participants understand the church's teaching on Divine Election through your own summary of the Catholic Doctrine section found in Understanding This Sunday. These points contain the heart of that teaching:

- Through God's graciousness the Israelites were chosen, that is, set apart from all other nations.
- Jesus was the chosen and favored Son of God. Through steadfast faith and humble submission to God's will, Jesus modeled for us the right response of the chosen—even when tempted.
- Thus, God's providential love and grace is opened for all people through the coming of Christ.
- The Second Vatican Council emphasized this notion of election, describing the church as the People of God.
- The covenant between God and the Israelites is now extended to all people, making Jew and Gentile one, the chosen People of God.
- In celebrating the Rite of Election, on the first Sunday of Lent, we proclaim this special relationship with God and respond by living our lives for God's glory for the sake of the world.

OR…Ask them to turn to the Participant Book (page 4) or the blackline handout, and read the section, "The Church Says."

OR…You might choose to select a person, who was baptized last Easter, and arrange to have that person witness to the group. Ask him or her to share the experience of receiving God's favor at their baptism and how that was lived out over the past year.

2. After completing either of these options, invite all to react to this church teaching in the large group by brainstorming the signs of 'being chosen' that they have experienced. Record their examples on a newsprint, large enough for all to see.

3. Explain that the traditional Lenten responses to Divine election is prayer, fasting and almsgiving using these words:

Prayer unites with God and opens us to change. When we fast we are emptied to receive God and know our hunger for God. In giving alms we are connected to the human family by sharing our gifts with those in need.

Putting Faith Into Practice

1. Ask the participants to gather in pairs to choose a way in which they will respond to God this Lent. Direct the group to turn to the Participant Book (page 25) or the blackline handout, to write their Lenten resolves.

2. Suggest a communal project for the sharing of talent and treasure which encompasses your parish efforts. Offer times for specific communal prayer events in the parish for this group to plan to attend.

Prayer

Call the group to silence. After sufficient time, ask in prayer for the courage and strength to grow in faithfulness in these or words of your own choosing.

Gracious God, we desire with all our hearts to follow the example of Jesus in our response to your Divine favor. You bless our lives in so many ways. You are faithful to us in times of need and distress. You chose us to be your people. Grant us the courage to respond to your great love with open hearts. Grant us the wisdom to know your will in all we do. Grant us the ability to trust that, no matter many times we fail, you are waiting for our return with open arms. Help us to change our lives in order that all might see in us the power of your grace and your love. Amen.

Second Sunday of Lent

Understanding this Sunday:
Background for Catechesis

The Word In Liturgy

Genesis 15:5-12, 17-18
Psalm 27:1, 7-8, 8-9, 13-14
Philippians 3:17-4:1 [or 3:20-4:1]
Luke 9:28b-36

The nature of the Lenten season as a time of preparation for (or renewal of) baptism is quite obvious in the themes prominent in today's readings. Both the first and third readings portray a mystical encounter with God in prayer. From ancient times, prayer (along with fasting and almsgiving) has been a primary means of accomplishing the "work" of Lent. Abraham's prayer results in a solemn covenant with the Lord, just as the prayer of catechumens ultimately leads to their baptismal covenant. The baptismal covenant is understood as a relationship with God in which we experience ourselves as "chosen" (the title given to Jesus on the mountain) and "transformed" (an image Paul uses in today's letter to the Philippians). This is the hope of catechumens: that their lives will be transformed as they encounter God in the baptismal covenant and become God's "chosen," destined for glory.

The reading from Genesis describes in cultic terms a time of mystical prayer in which God forges a covenant with Abraham, promising him both land and progeny. These promises seemed impossible in human terms, yet Abraham puts his faith in the Lord nonetheless. In a graphic description of an ancient ritual used to seal a sacred covenant, Abraham falls into a kind of trance and sees the Lord's presence symbolized by the blazing torch passing between the split carcasses. The vision represents a departure from the usual custom of the time, in which both parties to a covenant stood between the sacrificial offerings to swear their oaths. Here, God alone does so, indicating the unconditional nature of the Lord's decision to enter into relationship with (and fulfill the promises to) Abraham and his descendants.

In his letter to the community at Philippi, Paul is concerned about the many attempts being made, both by Judaizers and by gnostic sympathizers, to dissuade his converts from a steadfast allegiance to Christ. He holds up the example of his own life, and he reminds them how their baptism has united them to Christ, in whom they must "stand firm." Paul is concerned over both behaviors and beliefs that he saw as contrary to Christian faith. His solution to both concerns is to urge the Philippians to remain firm in their baptismal covenant, keeping their gaze fixed on their "citizenship in heaven," from which will come their savior, the Lord Jesus Christ.

Luke's version of the transfiguration differs from the other synoptic accounts in minor ways that reflect his particular understanding of Jesus and his mission. The setting is a special time of prayer, always a sign in Luke that something important is about to take place. In the larger context of the Gospel, this scene occurs just after Peter's confession of faith and between the two predictions of the Passion. Jesus is portrayed speaking with Moses (representing the Law) and Elijah (the Prophets) about his "passage" (the Greek word is "exodus"), by which Luke understands the suffering, death and resurrection Jesus was about to undergo in Jerusalem. The message of the voice from heaven is clearly directed to the early Christian community, affirming that Jesus is God's Son, the Chosen One, and insisting that they "listen to him," in similar times of prayer. Coming to know Jesus in this way involves a recognition of his messianic, divine identity, as well as a willingness to follow him along the path of suffering to glory. Catechumens will surely hear this admonition in a particular way in light of their eventual sacramental immersion into the death-resurrection of Christ. The focus of today's catechetical session is on the kind of deep, transformative prayer that will bring them to that kind of personal knowledge of Jesus and that will prepare them for discipleship that involves suffering as well as glory.

Catholic Doctrine

Contemplative Prayer

Every Ash Wednesday the Church proclaims the same gospel pericope (Matthew 6, 1-6, 16-18) detailing Jesus' teaching on prayer, fasting and almsgiving. These three religious activities help set the tone for the observance of the Lenten season as a preparation for or remembrance of baptism. The first reading and the gospel for this Sunday of the season portray two symbolic occurrences of prayer, the trance or vision of Abraham and the mountaintop transfiguration of Jesus as he is praying.

There are three basic types of prayer: spoken, meditative and contemplative. Spoken prayer uses words that are recited or sung. Examples are the Lord's Prayer, the Hail Mary, litanies, liturgical texts and so on. Meditative prayer may begin with spoken prayer but then employs an imaginative reflective process that focuses the wandering mind in order to draw the one praying into a more affective mode. An example is guided meditation. Contemplative prayer may begin with meditation, but then it moves further away from the self and into a more complete union with God. There is, eventually, a deep wordlessness, an inner silence, a "letting go." (*Encyclopedia of Catholicism*, "Prayer," pps 1037-1041.)

While this type of prayer can be worked toward, it is ultimately a gift. It is less a method and more something into which one is drawn. It is not so much an activity as a stillness and a way of being. (CCC 2713) Contemplative prayer arises from a longing for God as the object of one's love and is almost always therefore described as a union with God.

Great mystics such as St. Teresa of Jesus and St. John of the Cross struggled to attain this gift and maintained that a simplified form of contemplation is the birthright of every Christian believer. Teresa's gift to the church community was a description of contemplative prayer in her well-known work, *The Interior Castle*. Inasmuch as God calls to the heart of every Christian, the inner gaze of faith through contemplation is open to every believer (CCC 2699).

Richard J. Foster advises that contemplative prayer is an outgrowth of those who have exercised their "spiritual muscles" and who know something about "the landscape of the spirit." This type of prayer indicates a maturing of faith.

Its signals are found in a continuing desire for intimacy with God, the willingness to forgive others even at great personal cost, a sense that God alone can satisfy the longings of the heart, and humility about one's own spiritual accomplishments. (Richard J. Foster, *Prayer*, HarperSanFrancisco, 1992, pg 156.)

Catholic Culture

The Carmelites are a contemporary contemplative religious order whose origins can be traced to about the year 1200 when a group of lay hermits established a community at Mount Carmel dedicated to a following of Jesus in solitude. From the beginning, they engaged in devotion to Mary, and they became known as the Brothers of Our Lady of Mount Carmel. Two of the best known members are considered great teachers of mystical prayer: St. Teresa of Avila and St. John of the Cross. In modern times, Edith Stein and Titus Brandsma, both executed in Nazi concentration camps, attest to the continuing vibrancy of the Carmelite charism. (*Encyclopedia of Catholicism*, "Carmelite order," pps 228-29).

St. Bruno founded the Carthusian religious order in 1084, dedicated to the pursuit of God in silence and solitude. St. John of the Cross almost departed the Carmelites to become a Carthusian until St. Teresa persuaded him otherwise. The only Carthusian monastery established in North America is located in Arlington, Vermont: the Charterhouse of the Transfiguration (*Encyclopedia of Catholicism*, "Carthusian order," pp 232-33).

Catholic piety reflecting a more contemplative form of prayer includes retreat experiences, prayer before the Blessed Sacrament and perpetual adoration. Thomas Aquinas crafted the lyrics to a hymn that has come to be used in exposition of the Blessed Sacrament, and its fifth verse expresses the mysticism inherent in contemplative prayer: "Come, adore this wondrous presence; bow to Christ, the source of grace! Here is kept the ancient promise of God's earthly dwelling place! *Sight is blind before God's glory, faith alone may see his face*!" (Pange Lingua, St. Thomas Aquinas, 1227-1274, tr. James D. Quinn, S.J., 1969 found in *Order for the Solemn Exposition of the Holy Eucharist,* The Liturgical Press, Collegeville, Minnesota, 1993, pgs. 102-03.)

Notes

Dismissal Catechesis (30 min)

Getting Started

1. Prepare the space ahead of time with a circle of chairs around a table. Have an icon of the Transfiguration and a candle on the table.

2. Invite the candidates and catechumens to gather and be seated quietly within the circle. Then light the candle and pray in these or similar words:

   Good and gracious God, you gave the disciples a glimpse of your Son filled with light. Enlighten our minds and hearts with the word you want us to hear this day that we, too, may be filled with your light. We ask this through Christ our Lord. Amen.

First Impressions

1. Invite the participants to reflect for a moment on the images they heard in today's scripture. Ask them to name these images aloud.

2. Then gather the participants into pairs to discuss these questions: *What feelings do these images evoke in you? Which image stays with you and why?*

3. Elicit responses from each pair. Then ask the large group: *What might the feelings of Peter, James and John have been at Jesus' transfiguration?* Summarize the discussion in a few sentences, emphasizing the apostles' experience of awe.

Making Connections

1. Ask participants to recall their own experiences of awe, for example, seeing a sunset, a birth of a child, children playing, or hearing a symphony. Invite the group to share their experiences in pairs.

2. Continue the conversation in pairs with this question: *Have you ever thought of those experiences of awe as prayer or as a time you felt connected to God?* Then invite the pairs to respond in the large group. Remaining in the large group, ask: *What was the ongoing effect of these awe-filled experiences?*

3. Ask participants to note something they want to remember from this sharing. Take a moment of quiet for this reflection.

Prayer

Invite everyone to sit comfortably, to close their eyes and to take several deep breaths. In a slow, quiet manner direct them to inhale saying silently *"Jesus,"* and to exhale, saying silently, *"fill me with light."* Repeat this five or six times and then stop. After a few minutes, say, *"Amen."* Invite them to open their eyes.

Extended Catechesis

SESSION FOCUS: *Contemplative Prayer*

Gathering

A. Sunday:

1. Welcome the sponsors, team members and additional participants.

2. After asking everyone to sit in groups of four, in a few sentences summarize the sharing from the dismissal session.

3. Invite everyone into a moment of silence. Pray in these or similar words:

   God, quiet us to hear and see you. Slow us down. Create space in us for you. We pray in Jesus' name. Amen.

4. Invite the group to imagine themselves on the mountain with Jesus. Proclaim the Gospel, Luke 9:28b-36.

B. Weekday:

1. Welcome and greet the participants as they arrive. Invite all to gather in the circle around the table with the lighted candle and the icon of the Transfiguration.

2. Have them name aloud an experience of awe they have had since Sunday.

3. Lead this celebration of the Word.

   - Song: "Jerusalem, My Destiny"
   - Greeting, sign of the cross.
   - First Reading: Genesis 15:5-12, 17-18
   - Sing: Psalm 27, The Lord is my light and my salvation
   - Gospel Luke 9:28b-36
   - Silence
   - Concluding Prayer: You may wish to use the prayer above (A).

The Word (30 min)

1. Explain the background of the gospel, in these words:

   The Gospel of the Transfiguration is always used on the second Sunday of Lent. Scholars believe that the transfiguration may have been a post-resurrection experience. The Gospel writers all put it before Jesus goes to Jerusalem for his passion and death. During Lent the already baptized are renewing the meaning of their baptism in Christ. Those who will be baptized this Easter are using this Lenten time to prepare for their baptism in Christ. The transfigured Jesus, filled with light with white clothing is an image of who we are as the baptized in Christ.

   Ask the participants to reflect on this image of the enlightened Christ in connection with baptism by turning to the corresponding section of the Participant Book.

2. Invite the participants to continue to imagine the impact that seeing Jesus transfigured had on Peter, James, and John. Ask participants to share in their small groups: *What powerful experience of God have you had?* These experiences may be described in the corresponding section of the Participant Book.

3. Then invite some large group sharing of the powerful experiences. Make the following observations:

- Peter wanted to do something immediately

- We often have difficulty staying with a powerful experience of God, and find ways to move away from them.

4. Gathering them into small groups, ask these questions: *How did you respond to your powerful experiences of God? Did these experiences create a further longing for God in you?* Encourage the small groups to share this sense of longing. Then ask, *How do you attempt to fill this longing with other things? How do you create a space for God to fill you?*

Catholic Teaching (30 min)

1. Talk about contemplative prayer in these or similar words. Consult the Catholic Doctrine section for more background.

There are many ways of experiencing God, and many ways of praying. Prayer is a way of communicating with God and may include talking and/or listening. Prayer can be communal or individual. Prayer may be expressed in one's own words, or in specific formulas.

Contemplative prayer is a specific form of prayer that has long been part of the Catholic tradition. Contemplative prayer is a prayer of the heart, of quiet, of listening. In contemplative prayer one sits in quiet and creates space for God to speak or fill. Teresa of Avila (of Jesus) wrote "The Interior Castle," which describes contemplative prayer as a place where the person comes to closer union with God.

There is no right or wrong way to pray. The best form of prayer is what most helps the person develop a closer relationship with God.

2. Invite the participants to raise questions about contemplative prayer. Then ask them to think about their own experiences of contemplative prayer. Allow some time for sharing their insights about contemplative prayer.

OR...

Invite someone from the parish who frequently engages in contemplative prayer to share their experience of contemplative prayer.

You may wish to invite the group to explore contemplative prayer further, using question No. 3 in the Participant Book (page 26) or on the blackline handout.

OR...

Instead of holding this session, gather for an evening of contemplative prayer at a nearby retreat center, if available. The exercises from one of Anthony de Mello's books will be helpful in planning this evening. As a conclusion to the evening, be sure to gather for a period of reflection on the contemplative prayer experience.

Putting Faith Into Practice

State that becoming quiet is a challenge in today's busy and noisy world but is necessary to pray contemplatively. Ask participants to think about their schedule for the coming week. In quiet, ask them to choose a time they will create a space of quiet to pray contemplatively for ten minutes. Invite them to share this resolution in their small group. Participants may want to write this in the Participant Book (page 27) or on the blackline handout.

Prayer

Invite everyone to sit comfortably, to close their eyes and to take several deep breaths, inhaling and exhaling slowly. In a slow, quiet manner direct them to inhale saying silently, *Be still* and to exhale saying silently, *Know that I am God.* Repeat this five or six times, each time getting softer and then stop. Allow for a few minutes of silence and then say, *Amen* . Invite them to open their eyes. Encourage them to pray in this manner during their chosen time this week.

Third Sunday of Lent

Understanding this Sunday:
Background for Catechesis

The Word In Liturgy

Exodus 3:1-8a, 13-15
Psalm 103:1-2, 3-4, 6-7, 8, 11
1 Corinthians 10:1-6, 10-12
Luke 13:1-9

On the first two Sundays of Lent, all three years of the lectionary cycle focus on important events in the life of Jesus: the temptation in the desert (Lent 1) and the transfiguration (Lent 2). However, for the next three Sundays, each year has its own particular focus. This year, C, looks at penance and reconciliation. Today's readings reveal a God who is merciful and forgiving, patiently calling us to conversion. Next week the focus is on the experience of reconciliation, expressed in the story of the prodigal son; and, on the fifth Sunday, the readings point to the new life made possible for us because of God's forgiveness, symbolized in Jesus' words to the woman caught in adultery.

Today's reading from the book of Exodus is one of the most widely known and one of the most important passages in the entire Bible. In this pivotal section, God reveals the divine name to the Jewish people in the person of Moses, a privilege previously denied even to the patriarch Jacob (Gen. 32:30). Despite the enigmatic character of that name ("I am who am"), God is identified as one who is filled with compassion ("I have witnessed the affliction of my people"). God is further revealed as the very one who has acted in the history of the people time and again ("God of your ancestors . . . Abraham . . . Isaac . . . Jacob"), who now wishes to "come down to rescue," and who will remain with the people "for all generations." The psalm, with its refrain ("The Lord is kind and merciful"), captures the collective experience of the Jewish people whose God constantly rescued and forgave them.

In Paul's letter to the Christian community at Corinth, he is addressing a number of problems that had arisen since his departure. Perhaps because of gnostic influences, a misunderstanding of Paul's teaching on justification by faith, or just from moral laxity, some of the Corinthians had become presumptuous, thinking that the sacraments (especially baptism and eucharist) guaranteed their salvation, regardless of their behavior. In a passage that shows clearly his rabbinic training, Paul interprets the events of the Exodus as prefiguring the Christian experience: the passage through the sea foreshadowed baptism, and the manna was a type of the eucharist. But the point that Paul wants to make is that these spiritual realities did not keep the Israelites from being "struck down in the desert" because of their sinfulness. Paul is reminding the Corinthians that, despite the salvation they have experienced in the sacraments, they must undergo constant conversion, lest they perish like the Israelites of old.

The stern warning of Paul is balanced by today's gospel, in which Jesus tells the parable of the fig tree, both to stress the urgency of repentance, and to remind his hearers of how patient God has been while calling us to conversion. The fig tree, long a symbol of God's chosen people (Hosea 9:10, Jeremiah 8:13), is not cut down, as would have been the usual practice after being barren for three years. Instead, it gets extra care for one more year and another chance to "bear fruit." Jesus' call to repentance was central to his preaching and to his ministry. The "good news" of that call is that ours is a God who does forgive, in fact who welcomes our repentance and who sends a savior to offer us personally the gift of reconciliation.

Catholic Doctrine

"The Lord is kind and merciful."—God's nature revealed.

Catholicism, like Judaism, believes that something of the nature of God has been revealed to us through God's actions in history, chronicled in the pages of sacred scripture. For example, God discloses the divine name to Moses, saying, "I am who am." This is not exactly a name. And yet how does one identify utter mystery? A burning bush that does not burn up is the phenomenon that attracts Moses. A name that is not a name discloses and reveals a God who is mystery and compassion. This God is faithful to the promises first made to Abraham, Isaac and Jacob and will save their descendants from slavery and bondage (CCC 203 and 205-06).

In Jesus we find the full revelation of a God who is merciful and forgiving. The very name Jesus, means "God saves" in Hebrew. In delivering Israel from slavery into the promised land, God not only brought them out of Egypt but also saves his people from sin. All salvation history is recapitulated in Jesus. Indeed, the only Son of God, the Savior, epitomizes divine mercy and kindness (CCC 430-31)

Today's gospel contains a parable illustrating the kindness and mercy of God. Jesus himself has been described as "the parable of God" among us. His teaching and preaching, his life and death, point to the loving God who "is always ready to forgive" even though "time and time again" the covenant was broken. God does not abandon sinners. The Church proclaims the mercy of God, praying, "through your Son, Jesus our Lord, you bound yourself even more closely to the human family by a bond that can never be broken." (Preface, Eucharistic Prayer for Masses of Reconciliation I, *Roman Missal.*)

Indeed, every time the Church gathers to celebrate, it is gathered by the loving kindness of God and frequently recalls this initiative of God in the Introductory Rites. Thus, the Penitential Rite of the Mass is less focused on our sinfulness and need for penance and more directed toward a proclamation of the mercy, love, and newness of life achieved for us through the Lord Jesus.

In Chapter Six of his second encyclical letter, *Dives in Misercordia* (Rich in Mercy), Pope John Paul II examines the present-day need for God's mercy. Contemporary advances in science and technology have greatly contributed to the advancement of the human condition and yet, in spite of this progress, there also exists "unease and a sense of powerlessness, (10.3)" and a "feeling of being under threat (11.1)." The Pope asserts that what is most needed in contemporary society is a greater awareness of God's mercy.

Catholic Culture

This week many communities begin celebrating the Scrutinies for the elect, that is, those who are preparing for baptism. In the Scrutiny celebrations the Church prays that the elect be delivered from evil. These rituals proclaim the healing mercy of God in Christ even as they seek to strengthen the elect on their spiritual journey. In the Scrutinies, the Church is acting in fidelity to God's nature as revealed in the ministry of Jesus.

Many Catholics are taught the Jesus prayer, which expresses the loving stance of God toward us: "Lord Jesus Christ, Son of the living God, have mercy on me, a sinner."

The figure of the burning bush has often been used by artists as an Old Testament type of the virginity of Mary. A painting, for example, by Nicolas Froment (1476) in Aix-en-Provence Cathedral, shows Moses taking off his shoes, surrounded by his sheep with an angel standing in front of him. But in the upper part of the picture there is a burning bush with the virgin and child seated on it. The child Jesus holds a mirror, another symbol of Mary (Peter and Linda Murray, *The Oxford Companion to Christian Art and Architecture*, Oxford University Press, New York, 1996, pg 69).

Notes

Dismissal Catechesis (30 min)

Getting Started

1. Prepare the space ahead of time. Place a barren-looking potted plant and a candle in the center of the table, which is covered with a purple cloth to provide a Lenten atmosphere.

2. Gather participants in a circle and invite everyone into a moment of silence. Then sing the refrain of the Psalm response "The Lord is kind and merciful" several times.

First Impressions

1. If catechumens and candidates were present for the celebration of the scrutiny, invite them to share their experience of the ritual. If year A readings were used, refer to the Manual for Purification and Enlightenment.

2. Help the group recall the liturgy of the Word. Begin by mentioning the gathering hymn and these images from the scriptures.

   Moses standing before the burning bush

   God saying, "I am who am."

   The owner of the vineyard fertilizes and cultivates the barren tree.

3. Invite the participants to share in pairs: *How did God touch you through the liturgy of the Word today? What image of God was particularly meaningful?*

4. Invite them to come back together as a large group and share their responses. Encourage each pair to share. Comment briefly. Then summarize the variety of responses.

Making Connections

1. Remaining in the large group, invite the participants to discuss: *What does today's liturgy say about who God is? What specific word or phrase expresses this?* Highlight these responses by quoting the particular scripture references from today's readings.

2. Continue by asking them to notice if these descriptions of God are true to their experience of God or if these descriptions invite them to a new image. As they respond be sure to encourage a free flow of ideas. Then ask the participants to share a personal experience of God that portrays this quality. Briefly summarize the main points stated.

3. Conclude by asking each participant to choose the quality of God that most expresses who God is for them. Tell participants that these qualities will be used in the prayer.

Prayer

Invite everyone into a moment of silence. Create a litany of prayer in the following manner. Ask each person to name a particular quality of God. The same quality may be used more than once. Move around the circle beginning with yourself, and then to your right, using this formula, **"God, you are . . . (quality of God) . . . "** All respond: **"Be with us."**

Extended Catechesis

SESSION FOCUS: *God is kind and merciful.*

Gathering

A. Sunday:

1. Extend a welcome to sponsors, team members and additional participants. Invite them sit in small groups. Spend a moment in silence. Ask a catechumen or candidate to briefly state the focus of the sharing during the dismissal catechesis.

2. Then invite the participants to think about the significance of the barren plant in the center. Ask to share their thoughts in the small groups. Begin the prayer by asking all to join in singing Psalm 103, or a version of the refrain *The Lord is kind and merciful.* Proclaim the Gospel, Luke 13:1-9. Allow a short time of silence.

B. Weekday:

1. Greet and welcome each participant as they arrive. Invite them to gather in the circle around the barren plant.

2. Ask each person to share their experience of God over the last few days.

3. Lead this Celebration of the Word.

   - Silence
   - First Reading: Exodus 3:1-8a. 13-15
   - Psalm: Sing psalm 103 with refrain: The Lord is kind and merciful
   - Gospel: Luke 13:1-9
   - Silence
   - Prayer:
     God you are the one who is all things to us. You truly are kind and merciful. Let us take this understanding into all the fibers of our being. Reveal your love and mercy more fully to us. For you are our God, now and forever. Amen.

The Word (30 min)

1. Explain that there is a both a contrast and a connection between the images of God portrayed in today's scriptures. Include the following points:

   - the God of the Exodus reading is the one who is (I am who am)
   - is as elusive as the smoke in the burning bush
   - is the holy one before whom shoes are removed
   - and the one who is personal and caring enough to be aware of suffering and leads the Israelites to freedom.

2. Then ask the group: *Which of these images reminds you of your experience of God?*

3. Explain that today's gospel in these or your own words:

   This gospel is a parable. Parables often have a unique twist at the end. In this parable the owner of the vineyard

*does not cut down the barren fig tree (a traditional
symbol of Israel), instead he nurtures it into growth.
This is a reminder to all hearers of the urgency of
repentance and how patient God has been while calling
us to conversion.*

Proclaim the Gospel again. Ask the participants to discuss:
*How is your life like that of a barren fig tree? Who is this
God, Jesus portrays? From this parable, what can we say
about God's mercy, patience and love?*

4. Continue the sharing in small groups, asking: *In what ways
is your life like the barren fig tree?*

In the large group invite participants to name the insights
from their discussion. From these comments, lead into the
following teaching.

Catholic Teaching (30 min)

1. Ask participants to reflect back on their lives and think about
how they came to have a sense of God who is kindness and
mercy. To help in this reflection, ask them to turn to the
Participant Book (page 28) or the blackline handout, and
answer the questions. When they have finished, ask them to
share their responses in the large group.

2. Using the section on Catholic doctrine develop a
presentation on God's mercy and kindness, making the
following points:

- The burning bush in the first reading discloses and
  reveals God who is mystery and compassion.

- The very name Jesus means God saves in Hebrew.
  Jesus, the only Son of God epitomizes divine mercy
  and kindness.

- Jesus, the parable of God among us, reveals the loving
  God whose always stands ready to forgive, through his
  teaching, life and death.

- When the church gathers at liturgy, the community is
  gathered by Gods loving kindness. Even the Penitential
  Rite of the Mass is directed toward a proclamation of
  the mercy, love and newness of life achieved for us
  through Jesus.

- Pope John Paul II asserts in his encyclical letter, *Rich in
  Mercy,* that what is most needed in contemporary society
  is a greater awareness of God's mercy.

OR . . .

Continue by sharing:

*God reveals God's self to us in ways we can understand.
God is revealed through people and ordinary circumstances. Jesus*

Share your own experience of coming to know God's mercy.
Emphasize that the qualities of God's kindness and mercy
are central to the faith of the Catholic church.

Putting Faith Into Practice

1. Invite participants to answer these questions in their small
groups: *How has knowledge of God's kindness and mercy
been helpful in cultivating your faith? How would this
understanding of the nature of God nurture situations
in the world which cry out for God's mercy?*

2. Direct the participants to consider one way in which you can
help yourself or another experience the kindness and mercy
of God. Ask them to write this decision in the Participant
Book (page 29) or on the blackline handout.

Prayer

Gather the group in silent reflection and prayer that they
might have the courage to spread the Good News of Gods
mercy this week. Invite all to sing the refrain of Psalm 103:
The Lord is kind and merciful. Pray Minor Exorcism E as
described in the ritual text. Close by singing the refrain of
Psalm 103 again.

Fourth Sunday of Lent

Understanding this Sunday:
Background for Catechesis

The Word In Liturgy

Joshua 5:9a, 10-12
Psalm 34: 2-3, 4-5, 6-7
2 Corinthians 5:17-21
Luke 15:1-3, 11-32

Today the Church's Lenten catechesis on conversion is carried one step further. Last week's readings drew our attention to the God of mercy and forgiveness who patiently calls us to conversion. Today's scripture texts focus our attention on our human response: the experience of conversion, which constitutes our acceptance of God's offer of forgiveness. Next week, in the story of the woman caught in adultery, we will see an image of how God's forgiveness opens up for us a new life. This Sunday was called "Laetare Sunday" in the old Latin liturgy, from the opening words of the Entrance Antiphon. That text is still preserved in today's Mass formulary, and the rubrics still allow the wearing of rose vestments today as a sign that a pause in the rigors of penance may be appropriate at this stage of the Lenten journey. A mood of festive celebration, in fact, still resonates in the scripture texts of the day.

The Book of Joshua describes the conquest of Canaan at the hands of Joshua, Moses' successor as leader of the tribes of Israel. The "disgrace" that has been removed from the people is most probably a reference to their slavery in Egypt, now ended as they establish themselves in the Promised Land. The setting for this scene is a period of rest before the siege of Jericho. The Passover meal that is described marks an end to the people's need for manna, the miraculous food God provided during their desert wanderings. The responsorial psalm refrain ("Taste and see the goodness of the Lord") highlights the meal motif—clearly a eucharistic reference when sung in the context of our liturgy.

The reading from Paul today comes from a longer section in which he is discussing his apostolic ministry, a ministry founded on the conversion experience that made him an "ambassador" for Christ. For Paul, the experience of conversion is like a "new creation" that remakes a person "in Christ." The intensity of his personal feelings shows through in his words, "We entreat you...be reconciled to God." For Paul, the consequence of conversion is the same for all Christians: They must share with others the reconciliation they have experienced in Christ. The strange-sounding phrase, that "God made Christ to be sin," is a reference to Christ's sacrifice on the cross in expiation for our sins. In Paul's theology, it was Jesus' embrace of our sinful human condition that has made it possible for us to "become the righteousness of God."

The parable of the Prodigal Son is an extremely dense tale, rich with many layers of meaning. It offers at one time a phenomenology of the process of conversion, a powerful and even shocking image of the unconditional nature of God's forgiving love even before we repent, and a sharp rebuke of the self-righteous attitudes typified in the older brother. Each of the three figures in the story carries an important message for us today, just as they did for Jesus' contemporaries and for the community of Luke. Read against the backdrop of today's first reading, the parable becomes a story of how the "disgrace" of the son's slavery is rolled back. Like the ancient Israelites celebrating the Passover meal in the Promised Land, the son is offered a festive meal with which to celebrate his reconciliation. The early Christian community of Luke would surely have understood that authentic conversion leads to the eucharistic table.

Catholic Doctrine

Conversion

As the Church prepares to enter into the Lenten season, the faithful are marked with the sign of the cross, the sign of redemption, with ashes and are admonished, "Turn away from sin and be faithful to the gospel!" (Ash Wednesday Mass, *Roman Missal*.) Even though the baptized have been freed from sin through the suffering, death and resurrection of Jesus and in Lent recall their salvation, everyone who has been initiated still experiences the weakness of the human condition and concupiscence, the inclination to sin. (CCC 1426)

The newness of life received by those who are baptized can help overcome this inclination toward sin. This is the "turning away from sin" referred to in the Ash Wednesday ritual of signing with ashes. Such a turning may require a lifelong struggle, and the changes entailed are described as conversion.

Jesus begins his public ministry with the call to repent and believe in the good news (Matthew 4:17 and Mark 1:15). Jesus preaches conversion. The imperative to change one's life in accord with the life of God is not simply meant for those who are hearing the gospel for the first time in preparation for baptism. Catholic theology has always recognized conversion as an ongoing reality after one's baptism. (CCC 1428)

In pondering the mystery of the Church, the fathers of Vatican II explained: "The Church, . . . clasping sinners to her bosom, at once holy and always in need of purification, follows constantly the path of penance and renewal." Thus, the Church may "reveal in the world, faithfully, however darkly, the mystery of her Lord until, in the consummation, it shall be manifested in full light." (*Lumen Gentium*, Dogmatic Constitution on the Church, 21 November 1964, Vatican II, n. 8).

Conversion is not only an individual task but is an invitation for communities and groups to pursue, since sinfulness and the tendency toward sin can also be experienced within, imbedded in and practiced by those communities and groups. John Paul II has devoted a significant portion of his apostolic exhortation "Reconciliation and Penance" (2 December 1984, n. 16) to an exposition of the social aspects of sin and the resulting need for conversion by groups. Understanding the need for both individual and communal reconciliation, the Church prays during Lent to God: "Each year you give us this joyful season when we prepare to celebrate the paschal mystery with mind and heart renewed . . . . As we recall the great events that gave us new life in Christ, you bring the image of your Son to perfection within us." (Preface, Lent I, *Roman Missal*.)

The inner conversion called for by Jesus and for which all constantly strive is expressed eventually in outward signs and gestures. The radical reorienting of one's life issues forth in good works. This is given expression in the Lenten prayer of the Church to the God who pursues us with mercy and forgiveness, "You give us a spirit of loving reverence for you, our Father, and of willing service to our neighbor." (Preface, Lent I, *Roman Missal*.)

Catholic Culture

Christians have cherished down through the ages the autobiographical work of St. Augustine, *The Confessions*, which detail his journey away from sin and toward God. In 1948, Thomas Merton told the story of his journey to Catholic faith and monastic life in his autobiography, *The Seven Storey Mountain*. The book was a bestseller and continues to inspire readers today. Contemporary movies, such as *Romero* and *Dead Man Walking*, have also tackled the subject of conversion.

The parable of the prodigal son has been brought to life countless times by artists. Durer's masterful etching "Son amid the Swine" shows the son kneeling in prayer at the trough surrounded by the pigs (c. 1496). Bartolome Esteban Murillo depicted this parable in six memorable scenes (c. 1675) (Peter and Linda Murray, *Oxford Companion to Christian Art and Architecture*, Oxford University Press, New York, 1996, pps 370 & 409).

During the Vietnam war, American POWs copied in secret portions of the Bible, since books were denied to them except for Christmas day. They used toilet tissue for paper, wire for pens, and ashes for ink. The passages they recorded were the Lost Sheep, and the most famous of all Jesus' parables: the Prodigal Son (Mark Link, *Path Through Scripture*, Thomas More, Allen, Texas, 1987, p. 137).

Notes

Dismissal Catechesis (30 min)

Getting Started

1. Prepare the space ahead of time with circle of chairs around a table with a purple cloth, candle, and place for the lectionary. If you have an art piece of the Prodigal Son available, this too may be displayed on the table.

2. Invite the candidates and catechumens to gather in the circle of chairs and to stand and sing the refrain of the Entrance Hymn, used in today's liturgy, as you light the candle. Invite all to be seated and pray in these or similar words:

   God of compassion, we rejoice in your Word, Jesus, who reconciles us to you. Like our ancestors, we have wandered far in the desert, searching for your promised one, Jesus. Remove our disgrace and turn us around, leading us ever closer to the long-awaited Easter feast. Nourish us with the food of your holy scriptures and open us to receive and rejoice in the Word this day. We bless and praise you, for you are our God, now and forever. Amen.

3. Ask the participants to silently reflect upon this past week in the light of what they observed at today's liturgy of the Word.

First Impressions

1. If catechumens and candidates were present for the celebration of the scrutiny, invite them to share their experience of the ritual. If year A readings were used, refer to the Manual for Purification and Enlightenment.

2. Ask the participants to close their eyes and allow these images from today's scriptures to touch their minds and hearts. Slowly and prayerfully offer the following images:

   "they ate of the produce of the land"
   "the yield of the land of Canaan"
   "taste and see how good the Lord is"
   "anyone in Christ is a new creation"
   "be reconciled to God"
   "he ran out to meet him and threw his arms around his neck"
   "let us eat and celebrate"

3. In the large group ask: *What image from these scriptures particularly touched you?* Listen to several responses.

4. Gather the participants into small groups, asking them to continue the sharing with these questions: *How would you describe the God of these readings?*

Making Connections

1. Remind the group that last week's gospel told of a God who is kind and merciful. Invite a few to share their insights as to the God of this week's readings. Guide the discussion toward the group's acknowledgment of God's open forgiveness.

2. While remaining in the small groups invite all to discuss: *What stance do we need to take to accept God's gift of forgiveness? What is the effectiveness of God's forgiveness upon our lives?* When the discussion seems to be concluding, field some insights from the small group discussion. As they respond, record the significance of God's forgiveness on newsprint, large enough for all to read.

Prayer

Encourage the participants to spend some time silently reflecting upon the effects of God's forgiveness on our lives. Ask everyone to respond to the praying of Psalm 34 by singing, **"Taste and see, taste and see, the goodness of the Lord"** as you pray verses 2-3, 4-5, and 6-7.

Extended Catechesis

SESSION FOCUS: *Conversion*

Gathering

A. Sunday:

1. Welcome the sponsors, team members and additional participants as they arrive. Encourage them to join the candidates and catechumens in the circle.

2. If an art piece of the Prodigal Son is available, ask the participants to reflect upon it and offer any comments to the group. Invite the new arrivals to share the images that touched them from the liturgy today.

3. Invite all to stand and sing the Gathering Hymn from today's liturgy. You will need to have song books available for everyone. Pray in these or your own words:

   God who is all forgiving and loving, enter our lives and change them. Heal and free us that we might prepare to celebrate this Easter feast with hearts renewed. Turn our hatred into love; our struggles into serenity; our discouragement into hope and our fears into faith. In You we can change and grow into a people, ready and willing to be Your ambassadors of love to a world in need. Grant us this conversion, through the death and resurrection of Jesus. Amen.

4. Proclaim the Gospel, Luke 15:1-3, 11-32. Allow for a time of silent reflection after this proclamation.

B. Weekday:

1. Welcome and greet the participants as they arrive. As they join the circle, encourage them to spend some time looking at the art piece of the Prodigal Son, if one is available to you.

2. Invite the group to recall the experience of God's forgiveness which they might have noticed since Sunday.

3. Lead this celebration of the Word.
- Song: "Change Our Hearts", Rory Cooney (NALR, 1984)
- First Reading: Joshua 5:9a,10-12
- Psalm 34: Sing, "Taste and See," James Moore (GIA, 1983)
- Second Reading: 2 Corinthians 5:17-21
- Gospel: Luke 15:1-3, 11-32
- Silence

The Word (30 min)

1. Share this presentation of the background to the readings:

In the first reading from the Book of Joshua, the tribes of Israel celebrate the Passover meal. Their disgrace—slavery in Egypt and wanderings in the desert—has ended. As they settle themselves in the long sought Promised Land, the miraculous manna is no longer needed instead they enjoy the produce of the land. Their lives are forever changed from wandering nomadic tribes to a settled, agricultural people.

In Paul's first letter to the Corinthians a similar transformation is observable. The shift from life before and after Christ is described by Paul. The baptized Corinthians are in Christ and thus a new creation. For Paul to be 'in Christ' is to be radically and continually transformed in the life of faith. This is not just a matter of becoming a better person. But it is a total conversion made possible by God who reconciled all of humankind to God's self through Christ.

This radical transformation is very beautifully illustrated in the gospel account of the son, who is empowered to change his whole life, because of the waiting forgiveness, the open-armed reconciliation of the father. Notice that while the son might have rehearsed his speech of repentance, before he could open his mouth, the father accepted him.

2. Ask one of the sponsors to proclaim the gospel, Luke 15:1-3, 11-32 once again. Invite the participants to gather into small groups to discuss these questions: *How might the Israelites felt about their radical change of lifestyle? Have you ever experienced a similar change? What does being 'in Christ' mean for your life? What in the parable of the Prodigal Son reminds you of God's reconciling love?*

3. As the participants conclude their discussions, invite them to share some insights with the large group. Ask the whole group to turn to the Participant Book (page 30) or the blackline handout to reflect on the transformative power of God's forgiveness.

Catholic Teaching (30 min)

1. Ask a few participants to share the transformative power of God's forgiveness or offer your own witness of that power in your own life.

2. Present the Church's teaching on conversion, making the following points:

- Lent is a time of conversion. Conversion means a *metanoia,* a change in direction, a radical turning around.

- We began the season with the Ash Wednesday reading from Joel, in which we are told to "return to me (God) with all your heart." The signing with the ashes signifies our willingness to turn away from sin.

- Conversion marks the entire Christian life. This radical call to repent and believe is not simply meant for those about to be baptized, but for all the baptized.

- Conversion is not only an individual task but is an invitation for communities and groups to pursue.

3. In the large group, ask the participants to reflect upon Paul's challenge to become ambassadors of God's reconciliation to the world. Ask this question of the group: *How does our continual transformation make us ambassadors?* As they respond record their insights on newsprint, large enough for everyone to read.

Putting Faith Into Practice

1. Invite everyone to look at the list they have compiled. In small groups ask them to continue the share this question: *How has your ongoing conversion process led you to reach out to others?* Encourage each person to share his or her stories of how conversion has empowered them to be God's ambassadors.

2. When this discussion is concluded, focus the attention of the participants back to the large group. Invite a parishioner who is involved in an outreach ministry to share their story of involvement, focusing upon the continual need for conversion as they minister.

3. Ask participants to reflect on and share in pairs where they sense God is leading them to a change of heart—to conversion. Based on this sharing, ask each pair to write an intercession to be used in the closing prayer. This formula will be of help, *God of forgiveness and unconditional love, change my heart that I might* _____.

The participants may want to write their insights in the Participant Book (page 31) or on the blackline handout.

Prayer

1. Begin the prayer by inviting all to stand and sing the last verse of, "Change Our Hearts." Ask all to be seated as you direct them to pray their petitions aloud. Ask all to respond to each intercession, *"Loving God, hear our prayer."*

2. Conclude by praying,

Loving God, change our hearts, our minds and our lives, through the power of your reconciling love. In Jesus, we are reconciled to you and to one another. Let us grow in our faith with a willingness to be transformed in love. We are your willing ambassadors to the world. Prepare and transform us as we seek your divine will. All this we ask in Jesus' name. Amen.

Fifth Sunday of Lent

Understanding this Sunday:
Background for Catechesis

The Word In Liturgy

Isaiah 43:16-21
Psalm 126:1-2, 2-3, 4-5, 6
Philippians 3:8-14
John 8:1-11

Today's readings conclude a unit of three weeks in year C of the lectionary that have been dealing with the theme of reconciliation. Next week, Passion Sunday, the readings of all three years once again have a single focus on the Passion of Jesus.

Today's first reading is from the section of Isaiah (cc 40-55) called the Book of Consolation, written to encourage the Israelites during their exile in Babylon. With imagery that hearkens back to the story of the exodus from Egypt, as well as to the creation story of Genesis, the author exhorts his fellow Jews to trust that God will continue to come to their aid, to rescue them and to forgive their transgressions. They are to be mindful of the history of God's kindnesses, not to dwell on their past sins. Rather, they are to anticipate the "new thing" that God is about to do on their behalf. In the midst of their shame and guilt, in the face of their doubts over whether or not Yahweh had given up on them, the oracle asserts that they are still "my chosen people, the people whom I formed for myself." (vv. 20-21) In the refrain to today's responsorial psalm, we sing out what must surely have been the Israelites' reaction to this prophecy: "The Lord has done great things for us; we are filled with joy."

The powerfully emotional and personal section of Paul's letter to the Philippians that we read today serves as an example of one who has heeded the message proclaimed in today's first reading. Paul describes himself as "forgetting what lies behind and straining forward to what lies ahead" (v 13), which is exactly what the passage from Isaiah urged the ancient Israelites to do. So decisive has been Paul's experience of forgiveness in Jesus Christ that he looks upon his entire previous life as so much "rubbish" when compared to "the righteousness from God" (v 9) that he has found "through faith in Christ." (v 9) In the final section of the passage, Paul makes it clear that he knows he has not yet "arrived" at perfection (a rebuttal of gnostic enthusiasts who claimed to be "perfect" already?). Rather, he presses on to the goal, the "heavenly call of God" (v 14).

In the gospel today we are given a story that illustrates in moving fashion the divine love that unconditionally forgives our past sins, freeing us to lead an new life of grace. The scribes and Pharisees who bring the adulterous woman to Jesus personify the harsh judgment of the Law. John further ascribes to them duplicitous motives underlying their self-righteous behavior. The response of Jesus is brilliant. Without condoning her sin, Jesus reveals the hypocrisy of her accusers and at the same time restores to her a sense of self-worth. For the early Christian community of the evangelist, Jesus' admonition to go and sin no more would surely have been suggestive of the "born-again" life of the believer who has found in the baptismal waters a whole new way of living. She leaves her encounter with Jesus reconciled to God, to her community and to herself.

Catholic Doctrine

Reconciliation

God's love for us is complete and unconditional and from this abundance flows the forgiveness of our sins. It is in Jesus that this divine love is shown fully. The Church prays:

> *God of power and might,*
> *we praise you through your Son, Jesus Christ,*
> *who comes in your name.*
> *He is the word that brings salvation.*
> *He is the hand you stretch out to sinners.*
> *He is the way that leads to your peace.*
>
> *God our Father,*
> *we had wandered far from you,*
> *but through your Son you have brought us back.*
> *You gave him up to death*
> *so that we might turn again to you*
> *and find our way to one another.*
>
> *Therefore we celebrate the reconciliation*
> *Christ has gained for us.*
> (Eucharistic Prayer for Masses of Reconciliation II,
> *Roman Missal*)

Jesus' public ministry began with a call for repentance. He forgave sins. Jesus ate and drank with sinners, a remarkable gesture that graphically illustrates the reconciling nature of his mission. His suffering, death and resurrection represent not only his own passover into new life but our passover with him. Jesus himself is the primordial sacrament of reconciliation. This gift is given to the Church, which by its activities becomes in the world a sign of conversion.

The victory of Jesus Christ over sin is first actualized for believers in baptism where our fallen nature is crucified with Christ so that we might be freed from the slavery of sin and rise with Christ to live with God (Romans 6:4-10). "For this reason the Church proclaims its faith in the one Baptism for the forgiveness of sins." (Rite of Penance, Congregation for Divine Worship, 1973, n. 2.) We are claimed for Christ in baptism and are incorporated into the Church, his body. Thus we are made members of this ecclesial communion and belong to one another (CCC 1267).

Those who fall into sin after baptism experience the forgiveness of God in the sacrament of Reconciliation. The healing effected by the celebration of this sacrament also restores one's relationship with the Church. To be reconciled to God means to also be reconciled with God's Church (CCC 1440 & 1445).

Reconciliation does not mean merely being detached from sin. The healing brought about by the sacrament and the forgiveness experienced in reconciliation works a real change in the person. With the remission of sins, there is, at the same time, the sanctification and renewal of the inner person. "This is finally expressed in a renewed and more fervent sharing of the Lord's table . . ." where those who have been reconciled grow in their friendship with Christ and celebrate the unconditional love of God. (Rite of Penance, 6d and CCC 1395)

Catholic Culture

Catholics come to know God's forgiveness apart from the formal sacraments of Baptism, Reconciliation and Eucharist, in daily praying the Lord's Prayer ("forgive us our trespasses as we forgive those who trespass against us") and in works of mercy. In the daily examination of conscience or review of one's actions and thoughts, and in the heart-felt recitation of the Act of Contrition, we experience the loving forgiveness of God. One form of the Act of Contrition given in the rite is:

> *Lord Jesus Christ,*
> *you are the Lamb of God;*
> *you take away the sins of the world.*
> *Through the grace of the Holy Spirit*
> *restore me to friendship with your Father,*
> *cleanse me from every stain of sin*
> *in the blood you shed for me,*
> *and raise me to new life*
> *for the glory of your name.*
> (Rite of Penance, n 91)

In the penitential season of Lent many communities celebrate the rite of reconciliation in a group setting. In this context, opportunities are then made available for penitents to individually confess their sins to a priest.

Notes

Dismissal Catechesis (30 min)

Getting Started

1. Prepare the space ahead of time with a circle of chairs around a table. Place a purple cloth, a candle and a glass container with oil on the table.

2. Invite the candidates and catechumens to gather in the circle and stand around the table. Light the candle and pray in these words:

God of power and awe, console us with your mercy which has no limits. You are in our midst, opening your reconciling embrace to everyone. Guide us in our journey of conversion during this Lenten season. Inspire us to hear your Word and discover in it the truth of your unconditional forgiveness. All this we ask in the name of Jesus. Amen.

3. Indicate to the group that they may be seated.

First Impressions

1. If the catechumens and candidates were present for the celebration of the Scrutiny, invite them to share their experience of the ritual. If Year A readings were used, refer to the manual for Purification and Enlightenment.

2. Lead the group in a meditation on today's gospel story of the adulterous woman. Begin by asking them to find a comfortable sitting position. Continue the meditation, using the script below. Be sure to take your time and pause as they follow the scene you are about to recount.

Relax and breathe deeply as you move into the enter of your being. Become aware of your heartbeat and allow its rhythm to quiet and relax you even more deeply. You move into the depths of your imagination, where the Holy Spirit directs you in the meditation. Allow the Spirit of God to work in you.

It is early morning in Jerusalem. As you make your way through the old city to make purchases at the market, you notice a crowd begin to gather. There is a great commotion. One of those itinerant rabbis is teaching the crowd. But some religious leaders break through the crowd of eager listeners, dragging a woman and thrusting her before the rabbi. Your curiosity gets the best of you and you ease your way to the fringes of the crowd to watch and listen. Not one to get involved you are careful not to attract any attention. These religious leaders mean business! They are demanding that this woman caught in adultery be judged by the rabbi, whose name appears to be Jesus. You watch their actions, listen to the tone of their voices and see the fury in their faces. You feel . . . .

The one they call Jesus, turns his attention to the woman. You see his eyes. His whole demeanor is permeated by . . .

You follow his gaze as the woman lifts her face to meet Jesus' gaze. As you watch from the edge of the crowd you are filled with . . . . When the teacher stoops to write in the sand, the scene swiftly changes. The religious leaders turn on the heels and leave. You wonder . . . The woman pulls herself to a standing position. As her frightened body straightens up, you hear this Jesus say, "Go and sin no more!" You are stunned. As you wander home in a daze you think . . . .

Pause for a time as people gently return to the gathering space.

3. After the participants have finished their meditation, ask them: *What did you experience as you observed the scene?* Listen to several responses and continue by asking, What can you now say about the nature of God after entering into this healing story?

Making Connections

1. Continue the dialogue on the gospel in small groups of less than four. These questions or something similar will be of help: *What do the actions and words of Jesus in this gospel say to your life? If God is this generous in granting forgiveness to the repentant sinner, what attitudes are we challenged to develop as we observe the hurtful and unjust actions of others?*

2. After some time of sharing, gather everyone back to the large group. Invite the participants to share examples of the difference between wrongdoing in secret versus "getting caught." Ask them to offer their insights to this question: *What does this gospel teach us about this issue?*

Prayer

Invite everyone to stand quietly in the circle and face the lighted candle. After a few minutes of silence, ask them to bow their heads as you extend your hands and pray the Minor Exorcism, 94-J, from the ritual text. If the group includes baptized candidates, adapt the prayer to reflect this.

Extended Catechesis

SESSION FOCUS: *Reconciliation*

Gathering

A. Sunday:

1. Extend a welcome to the sponsors team members and additional participants as they join the group.

2. Begin the session with the following prayer in the circle around the table. Invite all to join in singing, "Save Us, O Lord," Bob Dufford (New Dawn Music, 1981). Invite a team member to proclaim the Gospel, John 8:1-11. After a few minutes of silence pray the Eucharistic Prayer for Masses of Reconciliation II, found in the Catholic Doctrine section of Understanding This Sunday.

B. Weekday:

   1. Invite the candidates and catachumens to gather in a circle around the table with the lighted candle and the glass container of oil.

   2. Allow a time of quiet and ask the participants to share how God has led them to a change of heart over the past week.

- Lead this celebration of the Word.
- Song: "Save Us, O Lord"
- First Reading: Isaiah 43:16-21
- Silence
- Gospel John 8:1-11
- Eucharistic Prayer for the Masses of Reconciliation II, found in the Catholic Doctrine section of Understanding This Sunday.

The Word (30 min)

1. Invite the participants to name the ideas and images that came to mind as they heard the Sacred Scripture proclaimed. These may be recorded on newsprint large enough for everyone to read.

2. Offer this background to the first reading in these or similar words:

Known as the Book of Consolation, chapters 40-55 of the Book of Isaiah offers hope and encouragement to the exiled Jews. In the passage for this Sunday's reading, Isaiah 43:16-21, the author encourages his people to trust that God will continue to come to their aid, to rescue them and to forgive their transgressions. Their focus needs to be on the story of God's kindness—not on their past sins. The anticipation of this passage is heightened for all readers as God promises a "new thing" is about to occur. God declares to everyone, "now it springs forth, do you not perceive it?" In the midst of shame, guilt and self-doubt, we trust God's promise.

3. In small groups, ask the group to discuss this passage, with these questions as a catalyst: *What new thing does God seem to be doing in your life, as you journey toward initiation? What is the history of God's kindness and mercy in your experience and in your observation of other Christians on this faith journey?*

4. Draw the attention of the participants back to the large group as you offer this background information on the gospel.

The story of the woman caught in adultery illustrates the divine love that unconditionally forgives our past sins, freeing us to lead a new life of grace. That is the "something new" that God continues to do in our lives as we journey through failures, conversions, repentance and new life over and over again in this life of faith. Notice that Jesus does not condone her sin in forgiving her. Instead he challenges her to a sin no more, to live anew. Notice the contrast between the attitude of the religious leaders and the woman.

5. Direct the group to turn to the Participant Book (page 32) or the blackline handout, and reflect upon the Examination of Heart, following the directions and taking time to prayerfully contemplate.

Catholic Teaching (30 min)

1. Reassemble as a large group. Solicit all the words, phrases and emotions the participants associate with the word reconciliation. Record these on poster board or paper large enough for everyone to see.

2. Present the Catholic teaching on reconciliation, being sure to cover the following points.

- Jesus began his public ministry by calling all to repentance. Throughout his ministry he offers us example after example of the reconciling nature of his mission.
- God's love for us is unconditional and complete. We do not earn God's love. We do not earn God's forgiveness. God extends this offer of love and forgiveness to all who will accept it.
- Through the life of Jesus, God extends the offer of reconciliation. This reconciliation is actualized as we are healed, set free and forgiven.
- The sacrament of Reconciliation is offered to those who fall into sin after Baptism. The healing effected by this sacrament also restores one's relationship with the Church. To be reconciled to God means to also be reconciled with God's Church.

OR . . .

You may choose to invite the group to read through and discuss the concepts found in the Participant Book (page 33) or on the blackline handout in the section entitled, The Church Says.

Putting Faith Into Practice

Offer this simple explanation of a daily examination of conscience:

A good habit that has been part of the Catholic tradition is known as a daily examination of conscience. This is a review of the day and your response to God and others. These elements are included in this reconciling prayer.

Begin with a prayer for God's presence and guidance.

In quiet, review your day from beginning to the present moment.

Think about those people and situations for which you are grateful.

Recall those moments of weakness, for which you seek God's healing, forgiveness and release.

In quiet of your heart ask God to change you, do something new in you.

Trust that God is indeed reconciling you.

Close with an Act of Contrition, found in most books of Catholic prayers.

Prayer

Gather the group and invite a period of silence. Play some simple, instrumental music, that is in keeping with the theme of this session. Pray together the Prayer from the Rite of Penance, found in the Participant Book (page 33) or on the blackline handout.

Palm Sunday of the Lord's Passion

Understanding this Sunday:
Background for Catechesis

The Word In Liturgy

Isaiah 50:4-7
Psalm 22:7-8, 16-17, 18-19, 22-23
Philippians 2:6-11
Luke 22:14-23:56 [or 23:1-49]

We celebrate the entire Paschal Mystery of Jesus (i.e., his suffering, death and resurrection) every time we gather for Eucharist. At certain times, however, one particular dimension of that single reality is focused upon more prominently than others in a given liturgical celebration. The many celebrations of Holy Week, starting with today's, exemplify how the liturgy is able to celebrate the entire Paschal Mystery, even while commemorating one or another historical moment of its unfolding. Today, our focus is first on the Lord's triumphal entrance into Jerusalem, and then on the events of his passion and death. Nonetheless, we also celebrate his resurrection, as we recognize in the breaking of the bread the presence of the Risen One in our midst.

The second part of the Book of Isaiah, written during the exile in Babylon, was intended as a word of consolation and hope to the Jewish people in a time of severe national trial. Particularly in the so-called Songs of the Servant, the author attempts to make sense out of the suffering which Israel was undergoing. Many scholars believe that the unnamed servant represents Israel (although there may have been an individual whose actual experience became in these poems a metaphor for the nation's suffering). Today's reading is from the third of the Servant Songs. The servant's sufferings, graphically portrayed here, are ultimately seen as redemptive. It is little wonder that the early Christian community identified Jesus with the servant, and even shaped their narrative of his passion and death in light of the descriptions found here. The gospels describe Jesus quoting from today's responsorial psalm as he hung on the cross. Although today's psalm refrain ("My God, my God, why have you abandoned me?")—taken from the psalm's opening verse—expresses utter desolation, the later

verses that are used today show that the prayer is ultimately one of unshaken trust in God's deliverance.

Our second reading today is believed to be an early Christian hymn incorporated by Paul into his letter to the Philippians. Some have seen it as a Christian equivalent to Isaiah's Servant Songs. In any event, it contains a magnificent theology of divine abandonment in the incarnation, an abandonment that includes even an embrace of suffering and death. That self-emptying of the godhead is redemptive, as is seen in the resurrection of Jesus and in his exaltation at God's right hand. This is a crucial feature of Paul's theology, in which he stresses time and again that our being "in the Lord" is salvific. Because of our union with his dying, we know also his rising. It is our union with Christ that, for Paul, transforms the meaning of all human suffering.

While the other readings are the same every year, the gospel reading changes in each lectionary cycle. In year C we read from Luke's account of the passion. Despite the many similarities of all of the passion accounts, each evangelist tells the story in ways that reflect his particular concerns. One of the distinctive features of Luke's account is his deliberate effort to stress the paradigmatic nature of Jesus' suffering and death. Luke is the only evangelist to record the words of Jesus, "Do this in remembrance of me." (v 19) And, Luke shows that Jesus is the model for his disciples to follow by describing the death of the first martyr, Stephen, in terms clearly intended to evoke the pattern of Jesus' death. For Luke, as for Paul, our experience of suffering and death can only be understood in light of the meaning of the suffering and death of Jesus.

Catholic Doctrine

The meaning of suffering.

For the five weeks of the Lenten season the Church prepares by works of love and self-sacrifice to celebrate the Lord's paschal mystery, his suffering, death and resurrection. Today's feast celebrates how the Messiah accomplished our salvation through this passover from death to new life. Following Christ in faith, the Church professes that if we are united with the Lord in his suffering on the cross, we too will share in his resurrection and new life. From that union is derived the Christian understanding of pain and suffering.

Sickness, pain and suffering are burdens shared by everyone to greater or lesser degrees. In the light of faith, these burdens are given significance. For St. Paul, the passover effected by the suffering, death and resurrection of Jesus is the basic pattern of all redemption. He goes so far as to say that believers must be ready to fill up what is lacking in Christ's sufferings for the salvation of the world (Colossians 1:24).

In an ancient homily given by St. Gregory Nazianzen, this bishop of the early Church urges, ". . .we must sacrifice ourselves to God, each day and in everything we do, accepting all that happens to us for the sake of the Word, imitating his passion by our sufferings, and honoring his blood by shedding our own. We must be ready to be crucified." (Oratio 45, 23-24: PG 36, 654-655, found in Liturgy of the Hours, Office of Readings for Saturday, Fifth Week of Lent).

St. Paul reminds the Corinthian community that believers continually carry within their own bodies the dying of Jesus, "so that in our bodies the life of Jesus may also be revealed." (2 Corinthians 4:10) The dying of Jesus that the apostle urges that we embrace may be more than a metaphor. Dietrich Bonhoeffer, reflected on discipleship, "When Christ calls a person, He bids them to come and die." (*Cost of Discipleship*, 1953). This Christian pastor was executed by the Nazis shortly before the liberation of the concentration camp where he was imprisoned.

Affirming the value and significance of human suffering does not mean, however, that we are not to fight against illness or do nothing to alleviate conditions of misery, suffering and pain. Jesus, in his earthly ministry had compassion on those who were sick and worked miracles of healing. As disciples who continue the ministry of Jesus, we owe those who are suffering as much physical relief and spiritual comfort as we can possibly provide.

The celebration of the sacrament of Anointing of the Sick with its laying on of hands and anointing with holy oil seeks to help the ones suffering to see in their sickness the suffering of Christ. Those who are sick receive in this sacrament the strength to unite themselves more closely to the passion of Jesus. Thus, the sick participate in the saving work of Jesus, who, as the Lamb of God, the Suffering Servant, embodies the compassion of God.

Catholic Culture

Salvator Mundi (from Latin, "Savior of the World"), is a devotional image that shows Christ blessing. In some of these images he is shown with an orb in his left hand. The orb represents both the world, and in its roundness, the wholeness of healing. This subject shows Christ as sometimes crowned with thorns. (Peter and Linda Murray, *The Oxford Companion to Christian Art and Architecture*, Oxford University Press, New York, 1996, pg 467-68.)

Mother Teresa of Calcutta and the religious order she leads, the Missionaries of Charity, exemplify the voluntary embrace of suffering and the Church's solidarity with those who are neglected, in pain and dying. Some other congregations founded to work with the sick are the Sisters of the Holy Cross, Sisters of Mary of the Presentation and the Sisters of Mercy.

Contemporary authors who have written on suffering from a Christian perspective range from C.S. Lewis *(A Grief Observed* and *The Problem of Pain)* to Henri Nouwen *(A Letter of Consolation and In Memoriam)*.

The stigmata (from Latin for "marks") are bodily signs of Christ's passion. St. Paul refers to carrying the "marks" of the Lord Jesus (Galatians 6:17). The most notable stigmatic was St. Francis of Assisi, who experienced the wound marks of Jesus in 1224, two years before his death. Stigmata may be visible or, as in the case of St. Catherine of Sienna, invisible. Rarely does the Church accept as authentic a case of the stigmata, and has not attempted to define how they occur.

Notes

Dismissal Catechesis (30 min)

Getting Started

1. Prepare the space ahead of time with a circle of chairs around a table arranged with palm branches and a large cross or the icon "Salvator Mundi"—Savior of the World (described in the Catholic Culture section for this session).

2. Pray with the group, beginning with the Gathering Hymn used at today's liturgy. Continue by prayerful reading of the second reading, Philippians 2:6-11, which is an early Christian hymn. After allowing a period of silence to reflect upon this reading, close in these or similar words:

   Jesus the Christ, you emptied yourself to take on the form of humankind, humbling yourself even to your death on the cross. May this cross be a sign for all generations of your triumph over evil, suffering, sin and death. Lift us out of our own apathy today. Unite us with your passion that we might truly recognize you in our own suffering. Raise us out of our desolation that we might rejoice with triumphal "hosannas" as we walk with you every day of our life. Amen.

First Impressions

1. Invite the whole group to respond: *What was different about the church and the liturgy today?*

2. In small groups ask the participants to discuss the following questions: *What did you find significant in these scriptures? What did you find compelling about Paul's hymn? What did you find surprising about it?*

3. After listening to some of the responses from the small group discussion, continue by asking the meaning of the terms listed below. Add to their ideas as needed.

   Palms – Sacramental, used at the palm Sunday liturgy to commemorate the triumphal entrance of Christ into Jerusalem.

   Suffering servant – An Old Testament title attributed to Jesus, who was our suffering messiah.

   Paschal mystery – The term used to denote the redemptive power of Jesus' suffering, death and resurrection.

   Passion of Jesus – The entire scope of the sufferings of Christ as told in all four gospels.

   Triumph of the cross – The phrase used to describe the paradox that this sign of execution and torture became the means by which humankind was set free from sin and death.

   Crucifix – A cross upon which is the broken body of Christ.

Making Connections

1. Return the attention of the group to the paradox of the passion of Jesus in these words:

   In this early Christian hymn, Paul expresses the theology of Jesus passion. Through the humiliation of the cross, God exults Jesus above all creation. The paradox is that Jesus' suffering and death leads to his triumph over sin, death and suffering.

2. In small groups, invite the participants to discuss these questions: *What other paradoxes do you see in these scripture passages and in the passion of Jesus? What paradoxes have you experienced in your own life?*

3. Ask the participants to share some of their insights with the large group. Summarize the discussion and invite the group to think of one thing they wish to remember from this session. Allow for a time of quiet and then proceed with the prayer.

Prayer

1. Pray the following litany asking the participants to respond, **"O God, our God, do not abandon us."** The prayer leader, selected from among the team members, will pray the following:

   Let us turn to Christ as we pray: O God, help us put on the attitude of Christ,
   Take the sorrows of our lives and transform them with your joy . . . Response
   Take the chaos of our lives and transform them with your calm . . . Response
   Take the humiliations we have experiences and transform them with your glory . . . Response
   Take the adversities of our lives and transform them with your strength . . . Response
   Take our mourning and weeping and transform them with your consolation . . . Response
   O God, Our God, rouse us to willingly empty ourselves that we might be filled with the glory of the Risen One. Amen.

Extended Catechesis

SESSION FOCUS: *The meaning of suffering*

Gathering

A. Sunday:

1. Greet and welcome the sponsors, other spiritual companions, and team members as they arrive. Invite them to join the circle of catechumens and candidates. Ask them to spend a short time in silence as they contemplate the palms and cross or icon.

2. Ask the new arrivals to share their reflections on the meaning of Palm Sunday and the effect of this liturgy upon them.

3. Begin the prayer by singing the "Gloria." Read the gospel, Luke 19:28-40, and allow a time of silence before continuing. Close with Psalm 22 read antiphonally, that is, alternating right and left sides of the room for every three to four verses.

B. Weekday:

1. As the group gathers in the circle, greet and welcome each person. Allow a time of quiet as the participants reflect upon the psalm and the cross or icon. Invite all to share the impact of this past celebration of Palm Sunday upon their lives this past week.

2. Then pray this celebration of the Word.
   - Song: "Gloria"
   - Sign of the Cross and Greeting
   - Prayer:

     O God, you conquered the power of death through the suffering, death and resurrection of Jesus. Unfold the story of saving grace in our lives as we continue our journey of faith leading to eternal life. We ask this through Christ our Lord who lives and reigns with you and the Holy Spirit, one God, forever and ever. Amen.
   - Reading: Isaiah 50:4-7
   - Psalm 22 Prayed antiphonally—left side alternating with right side (Prepare a copy indicating the procedure prior to the session
   - Proclamation of the Passion: Luke 22:14-23:56
   - Silence

The Word (30 min)

1. Draw from the large group some images contained in the Passion narrative, for example, Jesus praying on the Mount of Olives, Peter's denial, by asking: *What about the passion of Jesus moved you?* As these images are named, write them on pieces of paper and add them to the center of the circle.

2. Explain the first reading in these or similar words, using the Word section from the background for this week.

   In this section of the Book of Isaiah, known as the Songs of the Servant, the writer graphically portrays the servant's suffering. The early Christian community identified Jesus with the servant and shaped the narrative of his passion and death in the light of the descriptions found here. This unnamed servant found in Isaiah may be an individual or may represent the nation of Israel and her sufferings under the Babylonian exile.

3. Invite the participants to gather in small groups to discuss: *How does this passage rouse you and even liberate you from your own experiences of suffering? How does it sharpen your sense of the need for forgiveness?*

4. Continue to explore the Passion narrative in these or similar words:

   Luke's passion narrative stresses the innocence of Jesus, showing him to be the suffering servant whose is innocently martyred for our sake. In this account the reader is drawn into the passion as a participant in the work of salvation. Those who suffer with Jesus are also assured a share of his glory.

5. Direct the participants to the reflective exercise in the Participant Book (page 34) or on the blackline handout. Allow them time to reflect and write their thoughts and reactions. These can be shared later in the week between the sponsors and candidates or catechumens.

Catholic Teaching (30 min)

1. Call the group's attention back to the large gathering and ask them to respond to this question: *What did you learn from the reflection on the passion? Take a few responses from the participants.*

2. Use the Catholic Doctrine section of Understanding this Sunday to discuss the meaning of suffering. Make the following points:

- The church teaches that when we unite our suffering to the passion of Jesus and his death on the cross, we too will share in his resurrection and new life.

- Sickness, pain and suffering are part of the human condition. The significance of these trials are explained by Paul, who states that believers fill up what is lacking in Christ's suffering for the salvation of the world.

- While affirming the value and significance of human suffering, we continue to fight and offer compassion as we attempt to alleviate the human conditions of suffering and pain.

- The sacrament of Anointing of the Sick is a celebration of the healing power of God, present in the faith community. Those who are ill receive the strength to unite their pain to the passion of Jesus and to participate in the saving work of Jesus, through this sacrament.

3. Invite the participants into small groups to discuss the following questions: *What cross of suffering do you carry? How can this pain be transformed by Jesus' pattern of redemption? As a result of this session, what new insights do you have as to the meaning of suffering? How has your own suffering led you to reach out in compassion to others who suffer?*

Putting Faith Into Practice

1. Inform the participants about some of the groups in your parish or local area that help the poor, the sick or the lonely. Ask them how they are already working with these groups. Offer additional information and specific details on how to get involved. You may choose to have pamphlets and lists of these charity and justice groups available for the participants to read. Encourage their involvement as part of the journey of initiation, by inviting them to write one action they will take on behalf of those who suffer in the Participant Book (page 35) or on the blackline handout.

2. Advocate that everyone participate in the Triduum. Explain the meaning of Holy Thursday, Good Friday and the Easter Vigil and give them a schedule of the parish gatherings on these days. Invite the catechumens and candidates to gather for the dismissal catechesis on Holy Thursday and Good Friday.

Prayer

Begin with a short time of quiet before the cross or icon. Proclaim the second reading from Philippians 2:6-11. Pray for those who are suffering by asking the group to name some of the people or groups in your area or in the world who are suffering today. After each naming, allow for a silent pause. Conclude with this prayer:

Jesus, we unite the suffering and pain of these people we have named to your passion and death. Carry them in your embrace of compassion and lift them in power of your resurrection. We also pray for ourselves, as we struggle with our own sorrows. Help us to willingly take up our crosses as did Simon, that we might follow you to the hill of Golgotha and rise with you in the glory of your resurrection. For this we pray with the confidence and the assurance of faith. Amen.

Holy Thursday

Understanding this Feast:
Background for Catechesis

The Word In Liturgy

Exodus 12:1-8, 11-14
Psalm 116:12-13, 15-16, 17-18
1 Corinthians 11:23-26
John 13:1-15

The General Norms for the Liturgical Year and the Calendar (Washington: USCC, 1976), revised as part of the liturgical reform mandated by the Second Vatican Council, emphasizes the unity of "the Easter triduum of the passion and resurrection of Christ [which is] the culmination of the entire liturgical year." (#18). "The Easter triduum begins with the evening Mass of the Lord's Supper, reaches its high point in the Easter Vigil, and closes with evening prayer on Easter Sunday." (#19) A sense of the unity of these days is found early on in the Church, as is evident from a letter of St. Ambrose (d. 397) regarding the celebration of Easter: "We must observe both the days of the passion and resurrection, so that there may be a day of woe and a day of joy, a fast-day and a feast-day . . . This is the holy Triduum . . . during which Christ suffered, was buried and rose again." [Letter 23, in J. P. Migne, Patrologie latine, 16, col. 1030. Cited in Days of the Lord, vol. 3, p. 3. (Collegeville: Liturgical Press, 1993)] At the time of Ambrose, the three days were considered to be Friday, Saturday and Sunday. But by the seventh century, a liturgical celebration had been added on Holy Thursday and the Triduum was considered to start with the Mass of the Lord's Supper.

The liturgy of Holy Thursday allows the symbolic action of washing feet to take place after the homily, but it is important not to see this merely as an historical re-enactment of Jesus' action, any more than this or any other Eucharist is just a re-enactment of the Last Supper. Rather, the liturgy is a commemoration of Jesus' passion, death and resurrection within the context of a ritual meal. Our theology of the liturgy holds that the saving reality of Christ's entire Paschal Mystery is actualized in the celebration, not that one discrete moment of his life is rendered present, as if in a kind of liturgical

"passion play." This understanding of how today's celebration is a "memorial" of the Lord's death and resurrection is rooted in the Jewish understanding of "zikkaron" (memorial or "anamnesis" in Greek). One of the best examples of this practice is found in the Passover meal, a memorial of the events of the Exodus which in some real way rendered the saving power of the Lord present in every age. Today's reading from Exodus describing the origins of the Passover meal even concludes by saying, "This day shall be a memorial feast for you." The reading is taken from the narrative of the tenth plague, into which the sacred author has inserted traditional material describing the rituals which Israel was to observe in remembrance of the events of their liberation from Pharaoh.

The psalm refrain is taken from 1 Corinthians ("Our blessing cup is a communion with the blood of Christ")—an appropriate choice given the content of today's second reading. In this part of 1 Corinthians, Paul is emphasizing the traditional nature ("I received . . . I handed on") of the teaching which the Corinthians were given about the origins and meaning of the eucharistic ritual. Paul's assertion that "every time" they perform this ritual they "proclaim the death of the Lord until he comes" is an excellent example of the continuity of the Jewish notion of zikkaron with our Christian understanding of how the Eucharist is a "memorial" of the Lord's saving death and resurrection, rendered present to us in every Eucharist.

The Gospel helps us to understand how every liturgical commemoration also contains an implicit ethical imperative. Jesus tells his disciples that they "must wash each other's feet" and that what he has done is meant as an example for them to follow. Every ritual celebration that is done "in memory of"

Jesus—whether it contains his proclamation of the Gospel, a repetition of his classic actions of taking . . . blessing . . . breaking . . . sharing, or a symbolic washing of feet—because it renders present again in our day the saving reality of the event, also requires that we live in conformity with its meaning, lest we engage in the ritual without authenticity. That is why the foundational stories in the Gospels are always so important—because in them are embedded the deep meanings that lie behind the ritual memorials we celebrate.

This helps us to see the key role played by today's Johannine text, which some scholars feel functions as an equivalent to the "institution narrative" missing in John but found in all the other Gospels. The meanings that are contained in this story are about self-emptying service for the sake of others, redemptive identification with the lowly as a "suffering servant," discipleship as willingness to share the mission and ministry of Jesus, and a host of other themes that make up the dense content of today's feast.

Notes

SESSION PLAN: Holy Thursday

Dismissal Catechesis

Getting Started

1. Prepare the environment ahead of time with special care. On a table in the center of a circle of chairs place a white cloth, a large pitcher with water, bowl and towel.

2. Ask the candidates and catechumens to gather in the circle and quietly reflect upon their experience of the liturgy of the Word.

3. Pray in these or similar words:

   Gracious God, you gather us for this great feast of your love. From the time of the first Passover, we continue to gather as we remember your saving power. Jesus, our Passover Lamb, taught us the meaning of eucharist as he washed the feet of his disciples. We ask that we might be encouraged to serve one another, following the example of Jesus. Open us to hear your word as we gather this evening of the Lord's Supper. Amen.

First Impressions

1. Ask participants to find one or two words that describe what they observed or felt during the liturgy of the Word this evening. Write these words on poster board or paper, large enough for everyone to read.

2. In the large group continue the discussion by asking: *What did you notice that was different or new to you at this evening's celebration?* Take the time to allow the participants to ask questions about the various liturgical actions that they experienced at your parish liturgy, for example, washing of the feet, renewal of priesthood, ringing of bells.

3. Using the information found in Understanding Today's Feast, explain that this evening's Mass is the beginning of the Easter Triduum—the three days.

Making Connections

1. Offer the following explanation of this feast:

   This liturgy is a commemoration of Jesus' passion, death and resurrection within the context of a ritual meal. Just as the Passover meal is a memorial of the Exodus event, each Eucharist is a memorial of the Lord's saving death and resurrection. The gospel John 13:1-15 also contains an imperative that all who partake of this meal—all who would profess to follow Jesus—must wash one another's feet.

2. Ask the participants to gather into small groups to discuss: *What does the action of Jesus—washing the feet of his disciples—mean for you? What is the challenge of Jesus' action for you?*

3. In the large group gather a few insights from the small group discussion. Tell the group about some of the service activities—foot washing—that take place in your parish.

Prayer

1. Invite the group to join in singing the "Servant Song," Rory Cooney (NALR, 1987). Ask each participant to think about an action they wish to serve others following the call of Jesus. These can be written on pieces of paper, folded and placed in the empty bowl on the table. Close leading Psalm 116 in the following manner—Pray verses 12-13, 15-16 and 17-18 and invite the participants to sing "Our Blessing Cup," Michael Joncas (NALR, 1979), as a response.

Good Friday

The Word In Liturgy

Isaiah 52:13-53:12
Psalm 31:2, 6, 12-13, 15-16, 17, 25
Hebrews 4:14-16; 5:7-9
John 18:1-19:42

The Triduum is a single feast, and each day's liturgy celebrates the entire Paschal Mystery (see the Word in Liturgy for Holy Thursday for a full explanation). This is true of Good Friday, although our attention today is certainly focused on the events that transpired on the day of the Lord's passion and death as a way of understanding and celebrating their meaning in the larger context of the whole Triduum. Today's liturgy consists of three parts: Liturgy of the Word, Veneration of the Cross and Communion. The history of these distinct segments is quite diverse, but the most ancient element of the Roman tradition is certainly the Liturgy of the Word with its proclamation of the narrative of the Passion at its heart. The veneration of the Cross was first celebrated in Jerusalem after the discovery of the True Cross, and only later incorporated into liturgies elsewhere in the Christian world. Reception of Communion on this day was sometimes observed and sometimes not, depending on differences of time and locale.

The text from Isaiah is the fourth Servant Song, one of a series of poems celebrating a mysterious figure whose vicarious suffering for the people is ultimately redemptive. Christian tradition has from the beginning seen in this text a remarkable foreshadowing of the suffering and death of Jesus. Its influence on the formulation of the Gospel accounts of the passion has long been noted by scholars. It would be hard to overstate the influence of this text on Christian understanding of the meaning of Christ's death. The graphic descriptions of the physical sufferings of the Servant make the text a natural selection to accompany today's Gospel reading. But even more to the point are its interpretation of the meaning of the Servant's death: "... he gives his life as an offering for sin ... my servant shall justify many ... he shall take away the sins

of many." The redemptive nature of the Servant's fate is suggested by the author's allusion to the Jewish custom of sacrificing a lamb for the sins of the community ("like a lamb led to the slaughter"). It is important to note also that the text contains its share of expressions which Christian tradition has seen as allusions to the resurrection ("He shall be raised high and greatly exalted ... he shall see the light in fullness of days"). Reflective of this, the responsorial psalm proclaims a vision of deep trust in God ("Father, I put my life in your hands"), peace and confident praise in God's ultimate vindication ("you will redeem me, O Lord, O faithful God").

In contrast to Isaiah's unnamed Servant, the reading from Hebrews boldly proclaims the name of him from whom our deliverance has come: "Jesus, the Son of God." The text alludes clearly to the human sufferings of Jesus ("with loud cries and tears ... from what he suffered"), but it is also unequivocal in its insistence that "perfected, he became the source of eternal salvation for all who obey him." Written to a Jewish Christian community in danger of lapsing from their Christian faith, the letter is straightforward in its insistence that "we must hold fast to our profession of faith" if we are to be saved. For a community undergoing the trials of persecution and the temptation to defect, the author has reassuring words of encouragement, urging his readers to "confidently approach the throne of grace to receive mercy and favor and to find help in time of need."

John's account of the passion is strikingly different from that of the synoptics. Throughout his Gospel, John portrays Jesus as eager for his "hour" to come. When the time does come, Jesus is shown not merely to submit to his fate, but rather to be master of his destiny, freely ascending the cross as if it were a royal throne from which he will rule. The theological themes so carefully woven throughout the earlier chapters of the Gospel all come together in the passion narrative. Jesus is revealed to be a true king, as the prescription over his head will proclaim and as Pilate is forced to acknowledge; the new passover lamb willingly offers his life for sinners, just as the lamb is being sacrificed in the Temple; from the cross he gives his mother, the new Eve, to his followers in the person of the beloved disciple; and also from the cross, he breathes forth his spirit in death as if in a new creation of the world, just as the blood and water flowing from his side are seen as the source of the Church's sacramental life. The Johannine account of the passion seems ideally suited for Good Friday, when the Church celebrates not only the dying of Jesus but also his glorious triumph in the resurrection and sending of the Spirit.

Notes

SESSION PLAN: Good Friday

Dismissal Catechesis (30 min)

Getting Started

1. Prepare the space ahead of time with a circle of chairs around a table. The table should have a red cloth upon which is a cross (not a crucifix) and a candle.

2. Invite the candidates and catechumens to stand in a circle around the table.

3. Begin the prayer by lighting the candle. Pray the words of the Entrance Antiphon for Good Friday:

   "We should glory in the cross of our Lord Jesus Christ, for he is our salvation, our life and our resurrection; through him we are saved and made free."

First Impressions

1. Invite the participants to spend several minutes seated in silence as they look at the centerpiece. Invite them to share their thoughts and feelings by asking: What did this experience of the liturgy evoke in you.

2. Ask them to continue their reflection by sharing in small groups: *What did you observe about today's liturgy? What images, words and actions were particularly meaningful for you?*

Making Connections

1. Ask the participants to name some of the people involved in the Passion of Our Lord. Write these on a large poster board. Ask each person to choose one of these people. Direct a prayerful meditation on the Passion in these words:

   Allow yourself to enter the Passion of Jesus through the mind and heart of this person. As you watch Jesus being tried, mocked, and sentenced to death like a criminal, what do you observe?

   You continue to follow this man Jesus as he walks the hill to the place of crucifixion. What are you feeling as you watch?

   You are at the foot of the cross as he speaks and eventually dies. What is happening in the quiet of your hear? What are your fears?

   Jesus has died and is being taken from the cross. What questions would you ask the character you chose? What would you change in the story of the passion if you could? Why?

2. Gather the participants into small groups, inviting them to share their experience of the Passion of Jesus through the eyes of one of the people in the account.

3. Continue with the participants in small groups asking them to think about an action they can take or a change they wish to make in their lives in response to Jesus' passion and death. These ideas can be shared in the groups.

Prayer

1. Invite everyone to enter into a time of prayer. Begin by asking them to join in singing, "Jesus Remember Me," J. Berthier (Taize, 1982). Hold up the cross. Invite the group to reflect silently on the great love Jesus has for each person.

2. Once again ask everyone to sing: "Jesus Remember Me." Take the cross to each person. Encourage each one to reverence the cross: hold the cross or bow to it or kiss it.

3. After several minutes encourage the participants to sing: "Jesus Remember Me."

EASTER SEASON

Easter Sunday

Understanding this Sunday:
Background for Catechesis

The Word In Liturgy

Acts 10:34a, 37-43
Psalm 118:1-2, 16-17, 22-23
Colossians 3:1-4 or 1 Corinthians 5:6b-8
John 20:1-9

"This is the day the Lord has made. . ." Psalm 118 rings out in the church on this day of days that celebrates the resurrection. From beginning to end, the liturgy is imbued with paschal, baptismal joy. The liturgy may begin with a blessing and sprinkling of water, or, in the United States, include a renewal of baptismal promises and sprinkling with water after the homily. A sequence praising the risen Christ, our paschal lamb, is sung or recited prior to the gospel reading: "Christ indeed from death is risen, our new life obtaining. . ."

Peter's preaching in the first reading, from the Acts of the Apostles, presents the entire scope of the life, death, and resurrection of Jesus and its meaning for the world. Beginning with John the Baptist, Peter recounts the essential story of Jesus' coming, preaching, overthrow of the powers of evil, his passion, death, and resurrection, and the forgiveness of sins that results from these events. He speaks as one of the chosen witnesses who ate and drank with Jesus after his resurrection, thus emphasizing the real, physical nature of the resurrection.

In its context in Acts, Peter's speech is momentous. It provokes an outpouring of the Holy Spirit upon its hearers. Peter delivers it to Gentiles gathered in the home of Cornelius, who is a virtuous and devout non-Jew. In the context of its Easter Sunday proclamation, the passage retains its urgency and eruptive power. It both announces the whole message of the good news of Jesus, centering on his resurrection, and states the universal import of that message in the good news of forgiveness of sins for Jew and Gentile alike.

The two alternative epistle readings of the day declare that the resurrection is the foundation of new life for those who believe. Paul reminds the Colossians that they have died and have been raised up (in Greek, 'co-raised') in the company of Christ—a reference to their baptism—and urges them to live accordingly.

The passage from First Corinthians draws its imagery from the Jewish practice of sweeping the house before Passover to assure that no yeast remained in it. Yeast, a mysterious living thing spoken of figuratively as a corrupting influence, was thought unsuitable in bread made for sacrifices. Unleavened bread, on the other hand, was a metaphor for purity and holiness. The context of the passage is Paul's pastoral response to a conflict caused by a case of incest tolerated by some in the community. Paul will have no accommodation with "corruption and wickedness," but expects the community to sweep its house clean in order to truly celebrate (live) Christ's Passover.

The gospel passage from John tells the story of the resurrection in terms more personal than those of Peter's speech in Acts. Set in the darkness of Mary Magdalene's early morning pilgrimage to the tomb, the gospel is an account of several lights dawning: daybreak itself, the disciples' discovery that the tomb is empty and their dawning awareness of what that fact meant, and finally, the beloved disciple's coming to believe that Jesus has been raised from the dead.

Most striking in this account is the role of the beloved disciple (assumed in the tradition to be John). Having heard the story of Mary, he outruns Peter to the tomb, yet allows Peter to enter first. Both enter the tomb, but the beloved disciple alone is described as believing. Why is John the first to reach the tomb and to believe? The simplest explanation is the most likely one: the author of John's gospel wished to show the power of love to put the believer in touch with the truth of the resurrection. The figures of Peter and John are not in competition with one another. The beloved disciple however, because of his love for Jesus, comes more quickly to discern and to believe that Jesus is risen.

The empty tomb, though important, is not the sole basis for Christian belief in the resurrection. The grave could have been robbed of its corpse, as indeed Mary first assumed. John's account, like that of the Synoptics, shows that the disciples did not expect the resurrection, and found it hard to believe until the risen Lord himself appeared to them (for "they did not yet understand the scriptures. . ."). Crucial to their faith in the resurrection were their subsequent personal encounters with the risen Christ, encounters described in various ways in the gospels proclaimed throughout the Easter season. Thus we have, alongside the positive proclamation of Acts, a gospel account today that only begins to unfold the meaning of the event of the resurrection in the lives of those who witnessed it.

The mystery of the resurrection, celebrated every Sunday, and par excellence at Easter, may be the doctrinal focus of today's catechesis.

Catholic Doctrine

"On the third day he rose again, in fulfillment of the scriptures. . ."

The unconditional and overwhelming love of God for us made visible in the incarnation does not disappear and fade with the death of Jesus on the cross. Indeed, that passionate love of God for us is enthroned upon the cross, which becomes the pulpit of God's truth. That message of divine love is deepened in the death and entombment of Jesus. That love transcends the tomb in the resurrection of Jesus from the dead. The Church exults: "Jesus Christ broke the chains of death and rose triumphant from the grave!" (Easter Vigil, Exsultet, *Roman Missal*.)

The chains of death are truly broken. Just as the divine nature took on our humanity (in all things but sin), so too the resurrection of Jesus was accomplished in a real human body. The Risen Lord is not a ghost who returns to haunt the disciples, nor some sort of resuscitated corpse (CCC 645). The resurrection of Jesus is a passing over from death into a new life, a new existence. The Church sings: "Exult, all creation around God's throne! Jesus Christ, our King, is risen! Sound the trumpet of salvation!" (Exsultet).

The resurrection is a glorious mystery that deserves a full-throated "alleluia" from every believer. And yet this wonderful gift from God to us comes at a price that Jesus is willing to pay (CCC 649). It is continuous with the mystery of the cross. Jesus Christ is the Crucified, Risen Lord, in whose resurrected body wound marks are visible. The Church gives thanks: "This is our passover feast, when Christ, the true Lamb is slain, whose blood consecrates the homes of all believers!" (Exsultet).

That Jesus rose from the dead is an actual, historical event and not a psychological or spiritual experience of the disciples (CCC 643). This is not some myth or wish-fulfillment on their part, or ours. Those first disciples witnessed something totally unexpected and surprising and which they only gradually understood. And in understanding it, they were willing to be martyred in telling the good news of the resurrection. The Church proclaims: "What good would life have been to us, had Christ not come as our Redeemer?" (Exsultet).

The implications for us believers is that by the resurrection God ratifies Jesus' whole life and teaching (CCC 651). Baptized into his death by our plunging beneath the waters of the font, we rise as adopted children of God whose inheritance is the resurrection. Even now we taste the promise of new, risen life in the Eucharist. The Church glories in this mystery: "Christians everywhere, washed clean of sin and freed from all defilement, are restored to grace and grow together in holiness!" (Exsultet).

Catholic Culture

The reason we celebrate the Lord's day on Sunday, not Saturday, is that "on the first day of the week" Jesus was raised from the dead. Sunday is resurrection day. Sunday is also the eschatological "eighth day." After the seven days of creation, the eighth day represents the day of redemption, the day of the "new creation." This symbolism of the number eight has inspired eight-sided tombs, fonts, baptisteries and church buildings. For example, the city of Chur, Switzerland, which was a major city of the Roman Empire and was Christianized in that empire's dying days, boasts numerous fountains and water troughs—all of which are eight-sided.

In the northern hemisphere, signs of spring and new life in nature help us to celebrate the resurrection of Jesus. The early Church fathers saw springtime as "the sacrament of the resurrection."

The custom of wearing Easter clothes descends from the clothing of the newly baptized with fine, new white garments.

Dismissal Catechesis (30 min)

Getting Started

1. Prepare the space ahead of time with a circle of chairs around a table. On the table place a lit Paschal Candle and a large bowl of water, along with some spring flowers.

2. Invite the candidates and catechumens to gather in the circle.

3. Have copies of the Exsultet from the Easter Vigil available for all. Invite all to stand and pray the Exsultet to express the joy of Easter.

First Impressions

1. Help the group reflect upon their experience of the liturgy with these or similar questions. This discussion can take place with the whole group.

   What did you feel and see as you entered the church today?

   How did the music set the tone for the celebration?

   What was your reaction to the sprinkling rite? The communal renewal of the baptismal promises?

2. Remaining in the large group, invite all to offer their initial ideas about the meaning of "resurrection." These or similar words may be of help in starting the discussion.

   The word resurrection is used several times throughout today's scriptures. What does the word mean for you?

   Jot their ideas on a poster board or paper, large enough for all to see.

Making Connections

1. To help the participants discover the implications of these scriptural texts for their lives, explain the context for the reading from Acts 10:34-43 in these or similar words:

   Peter's speech in the reading from Acts, contains the Good News of Jesus. This Good News is the basic teaching of our faith. This Good News includes all people.

2. Gathering the participants into small groups, invite them to look at the text of Peter's speech. Have copies of this passage available for everyone. Each small group can list, on the large poster board or paper, those elements of the speech that would be Good News for us all. These lists can be displayed around the room.

3. Invite each small group to name one message of Good News from the speech and explain why it is Good News for us today.

Prayer

Pray Psalm 118 in the following manner: with the entire psalm copied for each participants, pray the psalm verse by verse, with each person proclaiming a verse. Move around the circle until the psalm is completed. Invite the remainder of the participants to add their own verse that expresses their joy at this Good News of Jesus' resurrection.

Extended Catechesis

SESSION FOCUS: *The Resurrection of Jesus*

Gathering

A. Sunday:

1. Take the time to welcome the sponsors and team to the circle. Keep the same centerpiece, lighted Paschal candle, bowl of water and spring flowers.

2. Ask the participants to look at the Good News from Peter's speech, listed in the dismissal catechesis. Invite the newcomers to add to the list.

3. Pray in these or your own words:

   O Light of lights, Risen Jesus, enter our hearts with your Good News. Enlighten our minds to understand that you have overcome death by your own dying and rising. Melt our frozen hearts with this Easter fire, that in our hearts of flesh we might come to believe that you forgive even our sins. Help us to see your presence everywhere as the first light of dawn beams upon our clouded vision. O, Radiant Light, be in our midst as we gather to more clearly hear your Word of Life. Amen.

   Proclaim the Gospel of John 20:1-9. Invite a time of silence to ponder the Word. Close by inviting everyone to sing the Closing Hymn from today's liturgy.

B. Weekday:

1. Welcome and greet the participants as they arrive. Invite them to gather in the circle with the same centerpiece as the Dismissal Catechesis.

2. Ask everyone to reflect on the last few days. Listen as they respond to this question: *How has the Good News of Jesus' resurrection been a reality in your life?*

3. Lead this celebration of the Word.

   - Gathering Song: "Jesus Christ is Risen Today"
   - First Reading: Acts 10:34a, 37-43
   - Psalm 118: This is the day the Lord has made!
   - Second Reading: Colossians 3:1-4 or 1 Corinthians 5:6b-8 (use the passage that is proclaimed in your parish)
   - Gospel: John 20:1-9
   - Silent reflection
   - Closing prayer: Collect for the Easter Feast

The Word (30 min)

1. To help the group understand the sense of power of the resurrection, begin with this meditation on Mary Magdalene.

   Guide the participants to make themselves comfortable, by closing their eyes and relaxing. Give them time to become aware of their breathing and their heartbeat. Then move into this imaginative reflection.

   It is still dark, when, no longer able to find peace, I come to the place where Jesus was buried. My heart catches in my throat. The large stone is rolled back. In panic, I search the tomb, but find it empty. Where have they taken my Lord? Frightened, I rush to tell the men—Peter and John. I hurry them back to the place of burial and they too see that the tomb is empty. The burial cloth is lying there. Why did they uncover him? John comes running and looks into the empty tomb. In its emptiness he seems to see something. What does he see?

2. Allow a short time for the participants to gather into groups of four and share their insights into the resurrection from this meditation. This question may be a helpful beginning: *In looking at the resurrection through the eyes of Mary of Magdalene, what power and emotion does the meditation evoke in you?*

1. In these or your own words explain the context of the Sacred Scriptures just proclaimed. The background material found in Understanding this Sunday will be helpful.

   The resurrection is experienced through the witness of those who arrived at the empty tomb and in the preaching of Peter in the house of Cornelius. Jesus, rising from death, overthrows the powers of evil, sin and death in our lives. The power of this event is very real, both for the early followers of Jesus and us. This Good News is for all people, for all times. Yet it took, even those who saw the empty tomb, a while for them to understand its full impact upon our salvation.

4. Invite the participants to look around at the newsprint with the lists of Good News gleaned from the second reading from Acts. Remaining in the small groups ask the participants to discuss one of the following questions: *What was it that helped the early followers of Jesus believe that he had truly risen? What part did their love for Jesus play in the apostles' understanding of the empty tomb?*

Catholic Teaching (30 min)

1. Ask the participants to turn to the Participant Book (page 38) or the blackline handout, and reflect on the resurrection. Allow them enough to respond to the questions which follow. When they have had sufficient time to respond, gather them into small groups to share their insights.

2. Explore the connection between Easter and baptism by preparing a short teaching taken from the Catholic Doctrine section of Understanding this Sunday. Include the following points:

   - Understanding the full implications of the resurrection takes time. This is the heart of the Christian's journey of faith.

   - The Good News of the resurrection and its meaning for our lives is meant to be shared today, just as it was proclaimed in the early church.

   - As we are baptized into the death of Jesus by being plunged into the baptismal waters, we rise as adopted children of God whose inheritance is the resurrection.

   - The risen life of Christ is tasted and savored in the Eucharist.

Putting Faith Into Practice

Invite the participants to take a period of time alone to write their story of how they have come to see the power of the resurrection in their own lives. This may be written in the Participant Book (page 39) or on the blackline handout. You may wish to share a story from your own life to help their understanding. These may be shared later in the week between catechumens or candidates and their sponsor.

Prayer

Close with the Preface for Easter and an Easter hymn that expresses our joy and thanksgiving.

Second Sunday of Easter

The Word In Liturgy

Acts 5:12-16
Psalm 118:2-4, 13-15, 22-24
Revelation 1:9-11a, 12-13, 17-19
John 20:19-31

Following an ancient tradition, the church regards the eight days from the Paschal feast to the Second Sunday of Easter as a single unit of celebration (an octave). On the Second Sunday of Easter the church sings again Psalm 118, the psalm for Easter day, which proclaims: *"This is the day the Lord has made..."* The preface for Easter day is prayed again on the Second Sunday as well: "We praise you with greater joy than ever *on this Easter day...*," even though that day, by secular reckoning, is already a week behind us. All the prayers of the liturgy and the tone of the celebration are unmistakably full of joy as the church comes to the close of the octave of its greatest feast. The readings are to be understood in this spirit.

Throughout the Easter season, the first reading of the liturgy is taken from the Acts of the Apostles in order to illuminate the mystery of the church as it developed from its beginnings at Pentecost. Today's passage is a summary of the early Christian community's growth and success in the exercise of its gifts, particularly gifts of healing, and the faith with which the apostles are met as they go about their mission.

The apocalyptic visions contained in the book of Revelation supply the content of the second readings for year C. Today's passage centers on a vision of "one like a Son of Man" (Christ) who is revealed to be Lord of all. In a phrase reminiscent of the service of light at the opening of the Easter Vigil, this "one who lives" is identified as: "the First and the Last."

The gospel for today is constant in all three years of the Lectionary. It is a story of mission, forgiveness, and faith. The risen Lord appears to his followers on the evening of the resurrection, when they are gathered behind locked doors,

afraid. He speaks a greeting of "peace" and at once commissions them to continue his own saving work: "As the Father has sent me, so I send you." As God breathed on the waters at creation, so Jesus now breathes on the disciples in this scene and gives them the Spirit, with an immediate creative effect. In the giving of the Spirit, Jesus imparts a particular power for reconciliation: "If you forgive sins they are forgiven; if you hold them bound they are held bound." Just as the earthly Jesus exercised a power to forgive sins, now his followers are given that power in the Spirit.

The liturgy places a somewhat greater accent however on the latter part of the gospel narrative. At this point in the chronology of the story, the disciples are eight days away from resurrection — exactly where the church is today on the Second Sunday of Easter. The story unfolds of the apostle Thomas, who, obdurately insisting that he will never believe that the Lord is risen unless he sees and touches his wounds, is confronted by the resurrected Jesus and comes to a profound articulation of faith: He calls Jesus, "My Lord and my God." At the end of the passage, the words of Jesus seem to speak directly to us. We have not seen as Thomas did, but are called upon to believe.

The focus of today's catechesis may therefore be upon faith: the faith of the early Christian community described in Acts, the faith of John whose vision reveals to him the full scope of the risen Christ's reign, the faith of doubting Thomas who finally sees and believes, and the faith of generations of believers who have not seen the risen Lord but who rely on the word of the original witnesses to the resurrection.

Catholic Doctrine

"Blessed are those who have not seen, but have believed."

Faith invites us into a relationship of love, for "God is love" (1 John 4:8 referred to in CCC 221). The hidden, triune God is fully revealed in Jesus Christ, who embodies divine love and who communicates that love to us by his life and mission and by his suffering, death and resurrection. That divine love is freely given, and our free response is how Catholic teaching describes "faith." (CCC 142 & 166). The gift of faith is, therefore, a relationship wherein we trust the truth of that which has been revealed in Jesus Christ, handed down by those first witnesses, and afterwards, from generation to generation in the church.

Old Testament scriptures speak of faith in terms of one's personal obedience to the Word of God. There are several Hebrew words for faith, all of which refer to something "solid" or "trustworthy," to which we pledge our loyalty. Our word "amen" comes from a Hebrew word for faith *(aman)*. From this perspective, faith is understood as "I believe you," a relationship of trust.

New Testament scriptures continue this understanding of faith and add to it. The Greek verb *pisteuein* means not only "to trust" or "show confidence in" but also "to accept as true." St. Paul thus writes about the "obedience of faith" (Romans 1:5, 16:26) and in a variety of places he summarizes the content of his preaching on the faith (Romans 10:9-10; 4:24-25). For Paul, faith is not just an interior reality, believing in the heart, but also confessing with one's lips. In other words, the experience of faith includes doctrinal content, "the faith" *(Encyclopedia of Catholicism*, p 513).

It is through the community that the individual first receives the gift of faith from God. Faith comes through "hearing" and depends on witnesses who hand it on, who "speak it." By the action of the Holy Spirit tongues are loosened to tell the good news and ears are opened to hear what is told (CCC 153).

A heritage of faith is entrusted to the whole church (CCC 84). The Catholic genius understands this sacred deposit, this inheritance, as contained in both Scripture and Tradition. Indeed, the development of the New Testament shows the process of the living Tradition at work (CCC 83). The function of authoritative church teaching is to explain and guard this "deposit of faith" (1 Tim. 6:20).

Our relationship to God in faith can be shaken. We experience evil, suffering and injustice in this world, and we question God, we doubt, and we struggle in our belief (CCC 164). In times of doubt and struggle, individuals can turn to the community of faith for support.

Through Baptism we are born within, nourished by and are members of a living tradition handed down from the time of the apostles to the present day, in a pilgrim church walking by the light of faith. St. Augustine, bishop and teacher, preached to the newly-baptized:

> . . . [Y]ou. . . are the new offspring of the Church, gift of the Father, proof of Mother Church's fruitfulness. . . You are walking now by faith, still on pilgrimage [to] the Lord; but he to whom your steps are directed is himself the sure and certain way for you. . . This is the octave of your birth. Today is fulfilled in you the sign of faith. . . (found in Liturgy of the Hours, Sunday within the Octave of Easter, Office of Readings)

Catholic Culture

The Act of Faith is a traditional Catholic prayer that expresses both in its address ("my God") that faith is both a relationship and, in its body ("I firmly believe that. . ."), that faith has a content. It also expresses trust in the truth of what is revealed and held in faith. The text is:

> O my God,
> I firmly believe that you are one God in three divine Persons,
> Father, Son and Holy Spirit.
> I believe that your divine Son became man and died for our sins,
> and that he will come to judge
> the living and the dead.
> I believe these and all the truths which the holy Catholic Church teaches,
> because you revealed them,
> who can neither deceive nor be deceived.

The Alpha and Omega traced in the wax of the Paschal Candle, cf. Revelation.
Wounds of the Lord (traditionally 5) are an object of devotion; certain saints participate in Christ's suffering through "the stigmata."
"Peace be with you," is the bishop's greeting in the liturgy.
Today's gospel is understood by Catholics as the foundation for the Sacrament of Penance.

Notes

Dismissal Catechesis (30 min)

Getting Started

1. Prepare the space ahead of time with a circle of chairs around a table. On the table place a white cloth, the Christ candle, and the lectionary. At the base of the table place an Easter bouquet of spring flowers.

2. Invite the candidates and catechumens to be seated in the circle. Light the Christ candle and invite all to stand and pray with arms extended upward as did the early Christians. Encourage the group to sing Alleluia several times. Pray in these or similar words:

   O God, we gather on this first day of the week and recall the wonders of your marvelous works. Breathe your Spirit upon us. Give us the grace to recognize the Risen Christ who stands among us. Guide us to understand your Word that our lives might reflect the joy of the resurrection. Teach us to live as a community of believers. We pray, through Christ, our risen Lord. Amen.

First Impressions

1. Lead the group sharing by asking: *What signs of Easter did you hear and see at today's liturgy of the Word? What about the scriptures touched you?*

2. In small groups ask the participants to discuss the following questions:

   What did you find significant in these scriptures?

   What did you find compelling about Paul's hymn?

   What did you find surprising about it?

3. Then slowly and prayerfully ask the participants to close their eyes as you recall these images from the scriptures:

   Many signs and wonders occurred among the people.

   More and more believers were continually added to the Lord.

   The stone which the builders rejected has become the cornerstone.

   Write on a scroll what you now see

   Peace be with you

   Put your hand into my side

   Through this faith you may have life in his name

4. Invite the participants to gather in small groups to share: *What about these readings is cause for joy?*

Making Connections

1. Explain a little about the Easter season in these words:

   The joyous season of Easter continues for seven weeks. Over this time the church celebrates the significance of the resurrection for the life of the church and for all people over the ages. In this first scripture passage from the Acts of the Apostles describes the growth of the early church
   and the power of the resurrection in the daily lives of the baptized.

2. Invite the group to gather in pairs to discuss these questions: *What was the power of the resurrection in the life of the early church? How is the resurrection event still a powerful force in the life of believers today? What signs of the resurrection do you see in your ordinary living?* Direct the pairs to write one effect of the resurrection that they have observed on a 3x5 card.

3. Focus the attention of the pairs back to the large group and ask a few participants to share one way that they have seen the power of the resurrection at work today. When they have shared a few insights, ask them to pass the cards to their right.

Prayer

1. Begin the prayer by inviting all to quietly reflect upon the sign of the resurrection named on the card which they have received. Initiate a Litany of Joy by directing the group to respond to each naming with the prayer, **Give thanks for God's love is everlasting.** Invite participants to move around the circle prayerfully reading the sign of the resurrection named on their card. Then pray:

   Gracious God, we are grateful for these signs of the resurrection in our midst. This season of Easter, may the joy of your saving victory be ever in our hearts. This truly is the day that you have made, let us give thanks and rejoice. Amen.

2. Close by inviting all to stand and raise their hands as they sing the Alleluia.

Extended Catechesis

SESSION FOCUS: *Faith*

Gathering

A. Sunday:

1. Warmly welcome the sponsors, team members and additional participants as they arrive. Invite them to join the circle around the lighted Christ candle.

2. Ask a catechumen or candidate to give a brief summary of the dismissal sharing.

3. Begin the prayer by asking all to stand and sing the first two verses of "We Walk By Faith," Marty Haugen (GIA, 1984). Continue by praying the words of St. Augustine found in the Catholic Doctrine section in Understanding This Sunday. Invite a sponsor to proclaim the gospel, John 20:19-31. Close with the third verse of "We Walk By Faith."

B. Weekday:

1. Greet and welcome the participants as they arrive. Invite them to gather in the circle around the lighted Christ candle and flowers.

2. Ask participants to share their observations of the joys of the resurrection over the past few days. The candidates and catechumens may also offer a brief summary of the dismissal catechesis.

3. Lead this celebration of the Word.
- Song: "We Walk By Faith" (first two verses)
- First Reading: Acts 5:12-16
- Sing: Psalm 118
- Second Reading: Revelation 1:9-11a, 12-13, 17-19
- Sing: Alleluia
- Gospel: John 20:19-31
- Silence

The Word (30 min)

1. Explain the background to the readings in these words:

During the Easter season the first reading of the liturgy is taken from the Acts of the Apostles to help us understand the development of the early church. This passage is significant in that it celebrates the growth of the community of faith by recounting the gifts of healing and faith so evident as the apostles carried on the mission of Christ. In the second reading from the Book of Revelation the focus is the vision of the Risen One like the Son of Man, clothed in glory. Our hope is in the sovereignty of the risen Lord over all, who takes away all our fear. The gospel is the story of mission, forgiveness and faith. The breath of God over the waters at creation is now breathed upon the apostles, gathered behind locked doors. Thus, the Spirit is breathed out upon the early church, accompanied by the power of reconciliation. With the appearance of the risen Jesus and his greeting of peace, the apostles' fear is transformed by the gift of faith. The profound articulation of faith in the person of Thomas My Lord and my God, draws the believer into the transforming resurrection event. For Jesus seems to speak directly to us today: Blest are they who have not seen and have believed.

2. Invite the participants to gather into small groups to discuss these questions: *Which of the characters can you most identify with and why? What fears were transformed into faith in these passages? How is the presence of the resurrected Jesus a source of profound peace for the early believers?*

3. Ask the participants to turn to the Participant Book (page 40) or the blackline handout and respond to the reflection questions. When they seem to be finished, invite them to share their insights from this reflection in pairs. Sponsors and candidates or catechumens will want to be together.

Catholic Teaching (30 min)

1. Focus the attention of the participants back to the large group. Ask them to name the ideas that come to mind when they hear the word, faith. List these on a poster board or paper large enough for everyone to read.

2. Present the Catholic teaching on faith, making sure to include these points:

- Faith invites us into a living relationship with God, who communicates love to us through the life, death, and resurrection of Christ in the Holy Spirit.

- Faith goes beyond knowledge or statements of truths taught by the Catholic Church. Because of this relationship of love, we trust the truth of what has been revealed in Jesus Christ and handed down to us by the first witnesses and afterwards through the church.

- Through the community the individual first receives the gift of faith from God. We hear and depend on witnesses who share the Good News of the dying and rising of Jesus to grow in faith.

- While our relationship to God in faith can be shaken by trials, suffering and injustices and we may experience doubt, we have a community of faith to turn to for support. The opposite of faith is fear. We can come to the Lord and to the community of believers to transform our fears into an even deeper faith.

- Through Baptism we are born within, nourished by and become members of a living tradition of faith, handed down from the apostles to the present day. We walk by the light of faith, which is the gracious and free gift of our loving God.

3. Ask the participants to gather into small groups and share their insights to these questions: *What message do you hear for your own life of faith through the doubts expressed by Thomas? What has caused you to doubt? How did the gift of faith transform you and help you grow?.*

OR. . .

Invite a member of the parish to witness to faith in times of doubt and trials. When the witness is offered, invite the participants to share similar stories of faith.

Putting Faith Into Practice

1. Invite the participants to think of a time when their faith was supported through the actions of the church community and share that in the group.

2. Gathering them into pairs ask the participants to think of one way they could support another's faith during a time of struggle over the next week. Encourage them to write this action in the Participant Book (page 41) or on the blackline handout.

Prayer

Invite everyone to silently reflect upon their resolve to support another in faith this week and pray for the help of the Risen Jesus in this mission. Then pray Blessing F as indicated in the *Rite of Christian Initiation of Adults #97*, making necessary adaptations when candidates are present. Invite all to stand and raise their hands as did the early Christians praying together, **Let us proclaim our joy in the Risen Christ singing: Alleluia.** Invite all to join in singing the last verse of "We Walk By Faith."

Third Sunday of Easter

Understanding this Sunday:
Background for Catechesis

The Word In Liturgy

Acts 5:27-32, 40b-41
Psalm 30:2, 4, 5-6, 11-12, 13
Revelation 5:11-14
John 21:1-19

The readings of the Third Sunday of Easter in all three years of the lectionary cycle tell of a meal with the resurrected Jesus. This Sunday is, therefore, a privileged time for catechesis on the Eucharist. In each year, specific themes within this general subject come to light. In today's gospel reading, for example, the breakfast that the disciples share with Jesus on the beach is prefaced by a story that is symbolic of the call to discipleship (the great catch of fish), and it is followed by a dialogue between Jesus and Peter concerning love and mission. Both illuminate the relationship of Eucharist to mission, which may be the focus of today's catechesis.

The passage begins with failure. The disciples have spent the night fishing and caught nothing. When Jesus appears and tells them where to cast their nets however, they haul 153 fish into their boat (the reason for this precise number is lost to us, except that it is obviously large). When one recalls that at the beginning of John's gospel the call of the disciples to share in the mission of Jesus was described in terms of catching fish, the symbolism of this event at the end of John's gospel becomes clear. In the presence and under the direction of the risen Lord, the disciples can undertake their evangelizing mission with new and unparalleled fruitfulness.

The meal that follows literally brings the fruit of the combined work of Jesus and his followers to the table ("Bring some of the fish you have caught . . . Come and have your meal."), and in a gesture of humble service, Jesus prepares the meal himself. Though the story tells that the Beloved Disciple, and through him Peter, recognized Jesus while they were still at sea, in the meal itself this knowledge is revealed to be general ("No one dared to question him, for they knew

it was the Lord.")

The meal finished, the narrative goes on to speak about feeding in yet another way. In response to Peter's three-fold profession of love for him, Jesus asks this disciple who three times betrayed him during his passion to "Feed my sheep." Again the story issues an imperative to mission—this time in the form of a pastoral ministry modeled on Jesus' own role as shepherd. Finally, Peter is warned that as a faithful servant he will experience suffering, which the Johannine editor tells us will amount to martyrdom. When Peter is called to follow the Master, he is being asked to give his very life.

The theme of suffering in service of mission is repeated in each of the first two readings, which speak of trials and perse-cution in an exultant tone. The apostles in Acts are hauled into court for having preached the name of Jesus in defiance of the Sanhedrin, a powerful juridical body that ruled in the Jewish community at that time and had condemned Jesus. Not only do the disciples show no fear in the face of this dangerous opposition, they positively rejoice that they have been ill-treated "for the sake of the name" of Jesus. Their mission goes on in spite of persecution.

The book of Revelation recounts several apocalyptic visions that present the triumph of the suffering Christ. The present passage takes place inside the court of heaven in the presence God, at a kind of heavenly liturgy in which an angel asks who is worthy to open the scroll that is sealed with seven seals, which contains the purposes of God. At first it appears that no one is worthy. But then the response of all present—first those in the heavenly court (the four living creatures, the elders, and the angels), next all creation (on earth as well as in heaven)—is to sing out that the slain Lamb is worthy. Their cry becomes a chorus of praise for the slain Lamb, an image which evokes the redemptive paschal sacrifice of Christ. It is precisely the Christ who suffered who is worthy to open up for all the eternal purposes of God. The scene is one of suffering transformed into glory. Christ's suffering makes possible the fulfillment of his mission.

Catholic Doctrine

Eucharist and Mission

Discipleship does not turn in upon itself. By its nature, Christian discipleship is a following of Jesus who calls us to join him in carrying the cross and witnessing to the good news of the kingdom of God. Discipleship thus leads to the Eucharist, the meal of the sacrifice of Jesus and, in turn, this meal leads us to evangelize.

Catholics believe that the Eucharist is the foundational sacrament which makes us who we are as a Church. The Second Vatican Council describes the Eucharist as "the source and summit of the Christian life" (*Lumen Gentium*, 21 November 1964, n 11). Those who join together in the celebration of the Eucharist not only offer to God the sacrifice of Christ but offer themselves and their lives in union with the Savior (*Sacrosanctum Concilium*, 4 December 1963, n 48). Indeed, it is our Catholic understanding of this sacrament that it brings to perfection all the gifts offered and all the sacrifices made by us for the kingdom of God. (CCC 1350)

The meal of the Lord also strengthens believers for the mission of Christ. It increases our love for the poor and unfortunate, those whom we are called to serve (CCC 1397). It renews within us our baptismal inheritance (CCC 1392). The very name we Catholics give to the whole celebration of the Eucharistic liturgy, the Mass (derived from the Latin, *missa*, "be sent"), indicates the thrust of this sacrifice. Nourished by it we go forth to spend our lives in service as bread broken and a cup poured out for the life of the world (CCC 1332). Pope Paul VI, issuing his encyclical letter on evangelization, reminds the Church of the connection between the celebration of the sacraments and our efforts to spread the good news. He admonishes us to live "the sacraments as true sacraments of faith—and not to receive them passively or to undergo them." (*Evangelii Nuntiandi*, Paul VI, 8 December 1975, n 47).

As followers of Jesus we are led to the meal which is the source and summit of our Christian life. And in partaking of this sacrifice by which God gives himself to us, we are enjoined to do the same for our brothers and sisters in need, to "go in peace to love and serve the Lord."

Catholic Culture

The fish is a symbol of Christ and of a Christian (from the Greek word for "fish," ichthus). ICHTHUS was an acronym used by early Christians and stood for "Jesus Christ, Son of God, Savior" (*Iesous Christos theou uios soter*). The Lamb, carrying the banner of triumph, sometimes marked with a cross, is an Easter image representing the crucified, risen Lord.

In 1951, director Mervin LeRoy made a film of the popular novel *Quo Vadis* by the Polish author Henryk Sienkiewicz (1896). As Peter is fleeing the persecutions of Nero, Jesus appears to him and the disciple asks "Lord, where are you going?" Jesus replies, "To Rome, to be crucified a second time." Peter returns to Rome to be martyred. This legend is preserved in a small church on the Via Appia Antica near the catacombs of St. Sebastian. In it is a replica shown to visitors of a stone supposedly impressed with Christ's footprints. (*Rome*, Knopf Guides, Alfred A. Knopf, Inc., 1994, p 324-25.)

The descriptions of the four living creatures in the Book of Revelation (Rev. 4:7) have become symbols associated with the four evangelists (from the Greek, "proclaimer of good news"). The figures are: a man (Matthew), a lion (Mark), an ox (Luke), and an eagle (John). These images can be found in mosaics and stained glass, in illuminated manuscripts, and on pulpits, the doors of churches, and the covers of gospel books.

Notes

Dismissal Catechesis (30 min)

Getting Started

1. Prepare the space ahead of time with a circle of chairs around a table. On the table place a white cloth, a Christ candle and if possible, one of the symbols for Jesus mentioned in the Catholic Culture section at the beginning of this session. Place spring flowers at the base of the table.

2. Invite the candidates and catechumens to gather in the circle and quietly reflect upon the centerpiece.

3. Begin the prayer by inviting all to stand and sing several Alleluias. Pray in these words adapted from the Evening Prayer of the Liturgy of the Hours for this day.

   God of heaven, God of truth, a people once in darkness has listened to your Word and followed your Son as he rose from the tomb. Hear the prayer of this newborn people and strengthen your Church to answer your call to mission. May we rise and come forth into the light of day to stand in your presence until eternity dawns. We ask this through Christ our Lord. Amen.

4. Conclude by inviting all to once again sing several alleluias.

First Impressions

1. Invite everyone to reflect on the liturgy of the Word, just experienced. Then ask the participants to name one thing that stayed with them from this celebration.

2. Call the group to relax, close their eyes and to become quiet, within. Lead them through a guided imagery meditation on the Gospel. Read these words slowly and prayerfully:

   Continue to relax and become aware of your breathing. As you breathe in imagine the breath of Jesus' peace entering your being. Continue breathing in and out as you move deep within yourself. Enter today's gospel by imagining with me that you are out on the lake in the early morning air. A bit sleepy, you are frustrated since you have been fishing all night and have caught nothing. This onlooker on the shore speaks to one of your companions telling your friend to cast the net on the other side of the boat. When the nets bulge with fish, you are _____. You are so caught up in hauling the net that you are surprised to see Peter leap into the water and splash to the shore. You think _____. When you pull your boat up to the sandy beach you realize the Risen Lord is preparing a breakfast of fish and bread for the whole group. You are feeling _____, as you share in this meal.

3. Gently bring the group back to the room. Invite them to gather in small groups to share their insights on the meditation. Ask, *What emotions did you experience during this meditation? What new insights did you gain about the resurrection as you entered this scene from the gospel? What is the significance of the shared meal?*

Making Connections

1. While the small groups are still together continue the discussion by asking: *When have you experienced similar emotions in your own life? How did Jesus make his presence known to you?*

2. In the large group share your own story of how Jesus made his presence known during a time of failure in your life. When you have finished this witness, invite the large group to share a few ideas about ways that they might grow in their awareness of Jesus presence.

3. Invite participants to reflect on how they might make the presence of Jesus known to another person at work or in their family during the next week.

Prayer

Invite the group to pray Psalm 30 together. If possible, ask them to sing the psalm refrain, *"I will praise you Lord for you have rescued me,"* while you pray the verses. Close by inviting all to stand and sing several Alleluias.

Extended Catechesis

SESSION FOCUS: *Eucharist calls us to mission.*

Gathering

A. Sunday:

1. Welcome and greet the sponsors, team members, and additional participants as they arrive. Invite them to join the circle and reflect quietly on the centerpiece. If you have used one of the symbols mentioned in the Catholic Culture section, ask the new arrivals about the meaning of this symbol.

2. Ask a catechumen/candidate to briefly summarize the sharing at the dismissal session. Encourage the other participants to share their observations from the liturgy.

3. Begin the prayer by inviting all to sing, "You Are Our Living Bread," Michael Joncas (New Dawn Music, 1983). Invite all to imagine themselves at the Sea of Galilee in the early morning after fishing all night. Proclaim the Gospel from the lectionary. Allow for a few moments of silence.

B. Weekday:

1. Welcome and greet the participants as they arrive and ask them to gather in the circle of chairs around the same centerpiece. If you have used one of the symbols mentioned in the Catholic Culture section, ask the participants to share their sense of the meaning of this symbol.

2. Invite participants to recall one person through whom they experienced the presence of the risen Christ since Sunday. Invite a brief sharing in the large group.

3. Lead this celebration of the Word.
- Song: Gathering Hymn from Sunday's liturgy
- First Reading: Acts 5:27-32b, 40-41
- Sing: Psalm 30
- Second Reading: Revelation 5:11-14
- Sing: Alleluia
- Gospel: John 21:1-19
- Sing: "You Are the Living Bread"

The Word (30 min)

1. In the large group, ask the participants to share which part of John's Gospel passage catches their attention.

2. Explain the background for the gospel in these words:

Beginning with the failure to catch any fish, Jesus appears to the disciples and tells them where to cast their nets. They haul 153 fish into the boat. This passage recalls the beginning of John's gospel call of the disciples to share in the mission of Jesus. In the presence and under the direction of the risen Lord, the disciples can undertake their evangelizing mission with new and unparalleled fruitfulness.

The meal brings the combined fruit of the work of Jesus and his followers to the table, to be shared by all. Repeating the servant attitude of the true disciple, Jesus prepares the meal.

At the conclusion of the meal, the gospel narrative speaks about feeding in another way. Three times Jesus responds to Peters three-fold profession of love by saying, **Feed my sheep.** *Thus, once again, Jesus models the role of the minister in the likeness of the shepherd. This narrative ends with the warning that the disciple (Peter) will suffer. This link to the suffering of the followers of Jesus is made in both the first reading from Acts and the second reading from Revelation. The Lamb that was slain is worthy and his suffering is transformed into glory as Christ fulfills his mission of redemption. Likewise, the disciples faced dangers and opposition as they carry on the mission of Jesus in the early church.*

3. Ask the participants to turn to the Participant Book (page 42) or the blackline handout and reflect upon the mission of the disciple. When they have finished, gather them into small groups to share their insights from this reflection.

Catholic Teaching (30 min)

1. Share the teaching of the church that Eucharist leads us to mission, making sure to cover these points:

- Discipleship calls to join in carrying the cross and witnessing the Good News of Jesus saving death and resurrection.

- Eucharist invites those who join together in the meal of the Body and Blood of the Lord to join themselves in offering the sacrifice of Christ to God.

- The meal of the Eucharist strengthens believers for the mission of Christ to the world.

- Nourished by the Eucharist, we go forth to spend our lives in service as bread broken and the cup poured out for the life of the world.

2. Ask participants in what ways they see the church as already being bread for the world, and what ways the church is called further to be bread for the world. Ask them to share this in their small groups. In the large group, invite them to share their insights. Record these on poster board or paper, writing large enough for all to read. Connect these examples with any particular situations in your city, parish or in the world today.

OR. . .

Instead of gathering for this session, invite the group to work together to a soup kitchen or a homeless shelter for an evening. When you return provide adequate time for the participants to share their experiences and insights.

Putting Faith Into Practice

Gather in the large group and ask the participants to name a concrete way they sense the Spirit is prompting them to feed others, speak out, or live out the mission of Jesus. In small groups invite them to share this action and their commitment to do it during the week. Participants may want to write their mission in the Participant Book (page 343) or on the blackline handout.

Prayer

Open the prayer by inviting all to join in singing the Closing Hymn from Sunday's liturgy. Invite all to share one thing they wish to do to carry on the mission of Jesus. As they share have soft music playing in the background. Conclude this sharing by praying:

God, you have called us to share in the mission of the Risen Jesus. You have inspired us to take action as true disciples. Empower us to meet the needs of those who hunger for you in our families, our workplaces and our communities. May the breath of your Holy Spirit give us the courage and the wisdom to take your Good News to the ends of the earth. We pray this in the name of this same Jesus, our brother. Amen.

Fourth Sunday of Easter

Understanding this Sunday:
Background for Catechesis

The Word In Liturgy

Acts 13:14, 43-52
Psalm 100:1-2, 3, 5
Revelation 7:9, 14b-17
John 10:27-30

The Fourth Sunday of Easter is known as Good Shepherd Sunday. The readings in all three years of the lectionary cycle employ the images of sheep and shepherd to explore the relationship between Jesus and those who belong to him. The gospel passage for year C highlights the gift of eternal life given to the sheep, and establishes the connection between Jesus the good shepherd, and God the Father.

The first reading concerns one episode in Paul's first missionary journey. The passage recounts how the good news was welcomed by some in the Jewish community at Antioch, but greeted with jealousy and rejection by others. Although the conflict between the apostles and those who reject their message culminates in the announcement that the good news will be preached to the gentiles, Paul's explanation shows that the mission to the gentiles is part of God's foreordained plan, and not caused by Jewish rejection. Upon leaving that area, Paul and Barnabas "shook the dust from their feet"—a cleansing gesture common to Jews in leaving foreign territory, which Jesus told his first disciples to practice when they are rejected (Luke 9:5; 10:11)—yet the passage ends on a positive note. Those in Antioch who persist in their newfound faith are full of joy and the Holy Spirit. These humble believers come to mind as we sing the refrain of the responsorial psalm: "We are his people, the sheep of his flock."

Written in the context of a community suffering persecution during the reign of the Roman emperor Domitian (89-96 AD), the book of Revelation contains several apocalyptic visions of consolation that would have been received with great joy by contemporary listeners. In today's passage, the "great trial" referred to is the period of tribulation at the end of the world, yet the "tears" and "hunger and thirst" that will be wiped away by God are also present realities for the first hearers of this message. The white robes, palm branches and flowing water recall features of the Jewish festival of Tabernacles, as well as Christian baptism. Christ, the Lamb who will shepherd this white-robed throng, is here depicted on a throne and thus identified with God.

The brief passage from the tenth chapter of John's gospel is remarkable first of all for its promise of eternal life. Not only safe pasture, guidance, and protection are given to the sheep, they are promised unending life. The providential care of Jesus is expressed by the image of the sheep being held safely in the hand of the shepherd. Yet because this image is accompanied by a promise of eternal life, it points beyond human commitment and caring to a divine gift. Jesus goes on to say that the sheep have been given to him from the Father's hand, from which no one can snatch them (recall Wis. 3:1). The final statement of the passage, "The Father and I are one," makes explicit that the ground of Jesus' promise to give life to the sheep and protect them forever from destruction lies in his oneness with God. This is the second remarkable feature of the passage. Important in many early controversies about the Trinity, these words have resounded in the church throughout the centuries as an affirmation of the divinity of Christ.

Catholic Doctrine

The Divinity of Christ

The Church gradually articulated its understanding of who Jesus Christ is, often in response to heretical movements. For example, Arius, a priest from Alexandria (d. 336), provoked the first great controversy over Christ's identity. He claimed that Christ was not divine in the same sense that God the Father was. He asserted that Jesus was the highest of all creatures but still a created being with a beginning.

The Council of Nicea (325), employing terms from Greek philosophy, taught that Christ is not created but "of the same substance" *(homoousios)* as the Father (CCC 242). St. Athanasius joined the debate as the great defender of Nicene orthodoxy. Then, in the latter part of the fourth century the Cappadocians St. Basil of Caesarea (d. 379), St. Gregory of Nyssa (d. 394) and St. Gregory of Nazianzus (d. 390) furthered Christological understanding by brilliantly articulating Trinitarian teaching: there is one God, who exists in three equal Persons.

The Trinity is described as the most fundamental and essential teaching (CCC 234) in the whole articulation of "the hierarchy of the truths about faith" (General Catechetical Directory, 43). These early Fathers rendered an invaluable service in the evolving understanding of the divinity of Christ by providing a standardized vocabulary regarding God the Father, Son and Holy Spirit, clearly distinguishing between "particular person" *(hypostasis)* and "common substance or nature" *(ousia)*.

After the Arian controversy, Eunomius (d. 394) claimed that since God the Father is unbegotten and that the Son is begotten they do not therefore share the same essence. Gregory of Nanzianzus fired back that no one can define the essence of God's nature as Eunomius tried to do ("unbegotten"). Even the term "Father" fails to define God's hidden essence. "Father," rather, names the relationship between God and Christ. In other words, in defining the divine Persons indirect and oblique language is used: "God the Father comes from no one; God the Son comes from the Father; God the Spirit comes from the Father through the Son." *(Encyclopedia of Catholicism*, "God," p 568.) God's essence is a mystery in the strict sense. Logic and reason alone cannot grasp this hidden mystery without it being revealed by God through faith (CCC 237).

At about the same time, St. Augustine (d. 430) also added to the Church's understanding of the Trinity. Whereas the Cappodocians' starting point focused on the distinct relations within the Trinity, Augustine began by focusing on the unity of the divine substance common to all three Persons of the Trinity. He employed analogies such as the images of lover-beloved-love and memory-understanding-will, illustrating how the same substance could be internally differentiated without dividing that substance. Loving and knowing are distinct operations of the soul, but there is only one soul which does this (Encyclopedia of Catholicism, "God," p 569).

Augustine's thought was extremely influential in the West and influenced St. Thomas Aquinas (d. 1274) who provided a comprehensive treatment of the faith using principles of the ancient Greek philosopher, Aristotle.

At liturgy, the Church prays what we believe about the Trinity using terms developed by our forebears in faith. We proclaim of Christ that he is "begotten, not made, one in Being with the Father" (Order of Mass, Profession of Faith, *Roman Missal*). God has been revealed to us by Jesus as the Father not only because God is our Creator but because of the unique relationship between the Son and the Father (CCC 240).

Catholic Culture

Early Christian art often decorated tombs with images of Christ the Good Shepherd, for example the drawing of a shepherd and his sheep etched on a tomb in the catacombs of St. Callistus in Rome. The Good Shepherd is associated with the resurrection because of today's gospel passage.

The bishop of a diocese is known as the "chief shepherd" of the local church. His crosier, or staff, is modeled on a shepherd's crook.

Sofia Cavaletti, Italian scripture scholar and pioneer of early childhood religious education based on the principles of Maria Montessori, calls the method she developed the "Catechesis of the Good Shepherd." Through her research she discovered that the parable of the Good Shepherd is of central importance and inexhaustible interest to the young child. Today, centers for the Catechesis of the Good Shepherd exist in many countries around the world.

In our Catholic practice, we acknowledge the divinity of Christ by giving him worship, as contrasted with the saints whom we honor. The prayer at Mass for the mingling of the water and wine expresses our longing to share in the divinity of Christ, "By the mystery of this water and wine may we come to share in the divinity of Christ, who humbled himself to share in our humanity." (Order of Mass, Preparation of the Altar and Gifts, *Roman Missal*).

Notes

Dismissal Catechesis (30 min)

Getting Started

1. Prepare the space ahead of time with a circle of chairs. On a table in the center of the circle have a picture, a statue or icon of Jesus, the Good Shepherd and a Christ candle.

2. Invite the candidates and catechumens to be seated and enter into a period of silence as you pass the picture, statue or icon around the circle.

3. Ask everyone to join in singing the refrain to Psalm 100, "**We are His people; the sheep of his flock**", as you light the Christ candle. Pray in the words adapted for the Evening Prayer for the fourth Sunday of Easter in the Liturgy of the Hours:

   God of our Lord Jesus Christ, though your people walk in the valley of darkness, no evil should they fear; for they follow in faith the call of the shepherd whom you have sent for their hope and strength. Attune our minds to the sound of his voice, lead our steps in the path he has shown, that we may know the strength of his outstretched arm and enjoy the light of your presence for ever. We ask this in the name of Jesus the Lord. Amen.

First Impressions

1. Ask the group to spend a few moments in silence recalling today's liturgy of the Word. Invite them to name all the words, phrases and images which they can recall from the scriptures and the gathering hymn. List these on a poster board or paper large enough for all to read. Ask one participant to prayerfully read the list aloud while the rest of the group listens prayerfully.

2. Gather them into small groups and ask each group to select one of these phrases and discuss: What does the image of this phrase mean to you?

3. Focus the attention of the participants back to the large group. Explain the significance of this fourth Sunday of Easter in these words:

   The fourth Sunday of Easter is often referred to as Good Shepherd Sunday. The readings in all three years of the lectionary cycle use the images of sheep and shepherd to explore the relationship between Jesus and those who belong to him.

4. Invite the participants to return to their small groups and ask them to discuss: *What is your response to the image of sheep and shepherd used in today's scriptures? What do these images tell you about your relationship to the Lord?*

Making Connections

1. In the large group invite everyone to share their thoughts on the relationship imaged in the gospel. On a large poster board or paper, record the qualities of the Good Shepherd as they emerge from the sharing.

2. Then ask the participants to share one of these questions in their small groups. These may be posted on a large paper or on an overhead, in order that the groups can determine their choice. *How can I model the qualities of the Good Shepherd in my own relationships? For whom do I show the concern of a 'good shepherd'? What changes are called for as I try to follow the Good Shepherd?*

3. While remaining in the small groups, ask the participants to decide on one action they feel called to pursue in imitation of the Good Shepherd.

Prayer

Close by asking all to stand and sing the refrain of Psalm 100 after each verse is prayed.

Extended Catechesis

SESSION FOCUS: *The Divinity of Christ*

Gathering

A. Sunday:

1. Welcome the sponsors, team members and additional participants as they arrive. Invite all to join the circle around the centerpiece.

2. After a short time of silence during which the participants have an opportunity to reflect on the art piece of the Good Shepherd, invite the new arrivals to share their insights into the images in today's readings. The newsprint listing all the images from the Dismissal Catechesis will be of help.

3. Begin the prayer by inviting all to stand and join in singing the Gathering Hymn used in today's liturgy. Then pray in these words:

   Jesus, Good Shepherd, here us as we gather today. We seek your consolation and protection as we follow you in this our journey of conversion. You are God. You are our Shepherd. You are our Savior. Bless this time together as we seek to understand your Word. Gather us as your flock and bring us to your promised kingdom. Amen.

4. Ask one of the team members to proclaim the gospel, John 10:27-30. Invite the group to remain silent, reflecting upon the Good News just heard.

B. Weekday:

1. Offer a warm welcome as you greet each arrival. Invite all to gather in the circle around the same centerpiece as described in the Dismissal Catechesis.

2. As the group centers their thoughts in silence, ask them to reflect upon their experiences of God these past few days. Ask them to share: *How did you perceive the presence of the Good Shepherd in the ordinary circumstances of your life?*

3. Lead this celebration of the Word :
- Song: Gathering Hymn from Sunday's liturgy
- First Reading: Acts 13:14, 43-52
- Silence
- Sung Alleluia
- Gospel: John 10:27-30
- Sung Alleluia

The Word (30 min)

1. Introduce the background for the first reading from the Book of Acts in these words:

Today's first reading, one episode of Paul's first missionary journey, describes how the good news was welcomed by some and rejected by others. Paul preached not only to the Jews but also to the Gentiles (non-Jews). Jealousy and anger resulted. The message is no less important today. Consider who might be jealous or angry today because certain outcasts or sinners are hearing the good news and accepting faith.

Invite the participants to share these questions in pairs. The sponsors and candidates or catechumens will want to be together. *What are some causes for jealousy and anger in faith communities even today? Is your community/parish inclusive?*

2. Continue the background explanation in these words:

Paul and Barnabas spoke fearlessly, convinced that they were vehicles of bringing salvation to the ends of the earth. When Paul and Barnabas were expelled from the area, they shook the dust from their feet and filled with the holy Spirit went joyfully to other towns and villages. Every person is invited to accept the good news of salvation and every person is free to respond. Gathering the participants in the same pairs ask them to discuss: What is your reaction to the actions of Paul and Barnabas? Have you ever experienced something similar?

3. Explain the background to the gospel in these words:

In this passage, Jesus is responding to the demand to prove whether or not he is the messiah. The concluding line clearly states that Jesus and the Father are one. Just prior to this passage, in John 10: 7 and 11, Jesus states, "I am the gate of the sheepfold and I am the good shepherd." Then this passage includes that powerful statement Jesus makes that those who are part of the flock shall have eternal life. The power of Jesus' promise to give life to the sheep and protect them forever from destruction lies in his oneness with God.

Ask the participants to turn to the Participant Book (page 44) or the blackline handout to reflect on the message of this gospel.

Catholic Teaching (30 min)

1. Open a discussion in the large group, inviting all to share their sense of the gospel verse, "the Father and I are one." Encourage them to share any additional insights they received through their reflection.

2. Share the church's teaching on the divinity of Christ making sure to include these points:

- In the early Church, controversy arose regarding the identity of Jesus Christ. Arius claimed that Christ was not divine in the same sense that God the Father was divine. The Council of Nicea in 325 declare Arius' teaching to be heresy (contrary to the doctrine of the faith) and declared the Trinity, one God and three persons to be the most fundamental and essential truth of the faith.

- The Trinity is the most fundamental and essential teaching. In the later part of the fourth century Saints Basil of Caesarea, Gregory of Nyssa and Gregory of Nazianzus furthered our understanding about Christ in their articulation of the Church's teaching on the Trinity. The church teaches that there is one God, who exists in three equal Persons.

- In the strictest sense God's essence is a mystery, not understood by logic and reason, but grasped through the revelation of God through faith.

- The church holds that Jesus is truly and fully God and fully human. As God, Jesus is begotten from the Father.

3. Gather the participants into small groups, asking them to discuss: What is your understanding the Divinity of Christ? How does this teaching—that Jesus is truly God—affect your life?

Putting Faith Into Practice

1. In the small groups invite the participants to discuss: *What does the image of a God who is a Good Shepherd evoke in you? How can you respond to this protection, care and guidance offered by the Good Shepherd? How can you shepherd others?*

2. Ask the participants to focus their attention in the large group and invite their insights from the discussion. From the input of the group on the responses that might be made, ask each person to choose one action they will take this week. They may write this in the Participant Book (page 45) or on the blackline handout.

Prayer

1. Begin the prayer by asking everyone to stand. Ask the sponsors and team members to stand behind the catechumens and candidates and to place a hand on their shoulders. Invite them to bow their heads in prayer. After a few minutes of quiet prayer, pray aloud in these or similar words:

God of power and might, you sent your only Son, Jesus Christ, to be our Savior and Shepherd. Fill the hearts of these candidates and catechumens with a deep desire to always belong to your flock. Keep them always in your love. Strengthen them in times of temptation. Give them your Spirit to guide them as they strive to follow the Good Shepherd. We pray in the name of Jesus, the Lord, who lives and reigns with you and the Holy Spirit, one God forever and ever. Amen.

2. Invite everyone to join in singing, "Shepherd Me, O God."

Fifth Sunday of Easter

The Word In Liturgy

Acts 14:21-27
Psalm 145:8-9, 10-11, 12-13
Revelation 21:1-5a
John 13:31-33a, 34-35

Throughout the Easter season, the readings can lead us to meditate upon various aspects of Christian life understood in light of the resurrection. The events surrounding the birth of new Christian communities described in Acts, for example, illustrate some essential elements of life in the Spirit of the Resurrected Christ. These communities are founded on the preaching of the apostles, and continually encouraged by them. They are structured communities of faith and prayer, helped by people such as the elders mentioned in today's reading. And the life of these communities is marked by love and joy and the attraction of new members.

The readings from the book of Revelation in this season can likewise be seen as meditations on Easter themes in the Christian life. In these readings we have been introduced to a living Christ who stands at the center of all things in heaven and earth, the Easter Christ—bearing the marks of his passion, yet reigning and receiving the worship of the whole universe. In these readings we have seen the destiny of those who persevere in faith: they are clothed in white, delivered from sorrow, shepherded by the Lamb, and refreshed with streams of water. And today the book of Revelation invites us into a vision of new heavens, a new earth, and a new Jerusalem. Not only is the Easter Christian one who hopes for personal salvation; Easter faith reaches out to embrace the hope for a renewed cosmos, and a holy city, a new Jerusalem.

Today's gospel reading is from the "farewell discourse" that Jesus makes to his disciples once the train of events leading to his crucifixion has begun. Yet as Jesus speaks, it becomes clear that the evangelist has told the story in such a way that we do not merely hear the earthly Jesus speaking to his band of followers, but we hear the resurrected Lord speaking to his disciples through all the ages. Where the synoptic gospels place the account of the institution of the Eucharist as the memorial of Jesus, John's gospel situates Jesus' new commandment: "Love one another." The command to love is made specific: the disciples' love must be like the love that the exalted Jesus bears for them. Thus their love becomes a memorial and a sign of Jesus, even as the Eucharist is celebrated in imitation of and in memory of Jesus. It is the way that all will know that these are his disciples.

The fundamental quality of Jesus' commandment of love, therefore, may be the occasion for even deeper insight into the first two readings of this Sunday. What is the Easter life of the first Christian communities founded by the apostles, if not a life permeated by this love that is a memorial and a sign of the love of Jesus? What is this new Jerusalem for which every Christian longs, if not the city where the love between God and humanity may be fully realized? What are these new heavens and new earth seen by John, if not the promise of a world transfigured by the love of God poured out in Jesus Christ? The Easter season is a time for meditating on the Christian life in light of the resurrection. Today's catechesis may therefore be on the quality of love that animates the church: a love that is an effective sign of the living Jesus, present in our midst.

Catholic Doctrine

The New Commandment: Love One Another

The covenant made by God with the people of Israel was given expression through the Law of Moses. This Law symbolized the way God kept faith with the people and, in turn, the way they would keep faith with God. It not only expressed how people related to God but how they were to relate to each other, that is, it structured relationships within the community. For example, lying, stealing and adultery were forbidden by the ten commandments. Also, the way in which clans and families could go about exacting revenge was regulated so that the people would not forever be involved in blood feuds, tearing the social fabric completely apart. The code of behavior stipulated by the law of the old covenant was therefore seen not only as a challenge and an obligation but as a great gift to the whole community.

On this Sunday we celebrate the new commandment, the law of love, that Jesus gives us, his disciples. This law of love is not unknown to the old covenant. It is recorded in Deuteronomy (love God wholly and completely, 6:5) and in Leviticus (love your neighbor as yourself, 19:18). This new commandment of Jesus is new in that not only does he put these two injunctions together to express how the whole law is summed up, but Jesus, in his own person, by his life, his mission and his own sacrifice incarnates this command. In other words, while based in this heritage of the old covenant, this command of Jesus is "new" in that through the incarnation and redemption of the Son of God it is given to the Church to be lived as a law of grace, a law of love, a law of freedom (CCC 1972).

This new law of Jesus and the gospel does not negate the old law but perfects it and opens us believers to the full potential of that first covenant (CCC 1968). And while the shape of the new law can be discerned in the New Testament scriptures, it is not codified in a series of prescriptions so much as brought to life by the action of the Holy Spirit in the life of the Church. As St. Paul writes, we "put on" the new person of Christ in baptism. In the same way, the new commandment of love is etched upon our hearts by not only pondering scripture but by partaking of the living tradition of discipleship in a church formed by the outpouring of the Spirit in Christ. In that way we "put on" love as the inner disposition of the garment of believers.

This new commandment to love is given explicit form by the example of Jesus who teaches his disciples to love as he himself loved them. Not only did he show them this love through the years of their mission together but he symbolized this love (reported in the verses just prior to this Sunday's gospel passage) by washing their feet, and later by dying on the cross. Eucharist, as presented in John's gospel, is thus the meal which symbolizes our following in the way of love, the way of service and sacrifice for one another.

In reflecting on the new law of love given in Christ, St. Augustine wrote, "This love is the gift of the Lord who said: *as I have loved you, you also must love one another*. His object in loving us, then, was to enable us to love each other. By loving us himself, our mighty head has linked us all together as members of his own body, bound to one another by the tender bond of love." (Tract. 65, 1-3: CCL 36, 490-492 found in Liturgy of the Hours, Fourth Week of Easter, Thursday Office of Readings).

Catholic Culture

At the Evening Mass of the Lord's Supper the Church not only proclaims the last supper passage from John's gospel (John 13: 1-15) but then in a ritual action enshrines the teaching of this scripture. The action is called, in Latin, the "mandatum," (commandment) from "Mandatum novum do vobis" or "I give you a new commandment."

In 1633, St. Vincent de Paul and Louise de Marillac founded a religious community of women, the Daughters of Charity, who were not cloistered and who therefore able to work directly among the poor. In 1809 St. Elizabeth Ann Seton, the first American ever to be canonized, brought this community to the United States and eventually created from it a new community, the Sisters of Charity (*Encyclopedia of Catholicism*, p. 394).

Notes

Dismissal Catechesis (30 min)

Getting Started

1. Prepare the space ahead of time with a circle of chairs around a table. On the table place a white cloth, a Christ Candle, and a bouquet of flowers.

2. Invite the candidates and catechumens to spend few minutes in quiet.

3. Begin the prayer by singing an "Alleluia" refrain. Pray in these or similar words:

   God of our lives, you who have loved us from the beginning, continue to form us as a people of love and service. Make our hearts wide and generous that the world may benefit from what we hear in your Word. We ask this in the name of your Son and our brother Jesus. Amen.

   Conclude by inviting all to once again sing the Alleluia refrain.

First Impressions

1. Ask the participants to share about one element of today's liturgy of the word that really touched them.

2. Reread the second reading from the Book of Revelation (21:1-5). At the conclusion of the reading pose the following questions: *What are the strongest images for you in the reading? What areas of your own life does the reading speak to? What hopes do the reading raise for you?* Have the group share and discuss their responses.

Making Connections

1. Use the participants' comments to move into making connections. Make the following points in your own words:

   - This reading reflects the themes of a people who believe in the resurrection, e.g., hope, healing and newness.

   - Easter faith has to do with reaching out to realize hope for a renewed world.

   - It is the living Christ who is our center and hope.

2. Ask participants to spend a few minutes thinking about the various situations they find themselves in every day . Ask them to identify one area where there is a lack of hope, or where they or others are longing for change. Invite them to make a decision about doing something in or for that situation.

Prayer

Invite each participant to pray aloud for the needs and wants of their family and friends and the needs and wants of the world. At the conclusion, pray in these or similar words: *God we bring our needs and wants before you. Bless us and those we pray for and with. Stay with us that we may be made new. We ask this in the name of your Son and our brother, Jesus.*

Extended Catechesis

SESSION FOCUS: *The Law of Love*

Gathering

A. Sunday:

1. Welcome and greet the sponsors, team members and additional participants as they arrive.

2. Ask a catechumen or candidate to share the highlights of the dismissal session. Encourage the other participants to share their observations from the liturgy.

3. Begin the prayer by inviting all to sing "Ubi Caritas" (Taize) or another appropriate song. Ask participants to recall ways they have been recipients of God's love in the past week. Proclaim the gospel from the lectionary.

B. Weekday:

1. 1. Welcome and greet participants as they arrive. When they are settled, ask them to recall ways they have been recipients of God's love in the past week.

2. Lead this celebration of the Word

   - Song: Gathering hymn from Sunday's Liturgy
   - First Reading: Acts 14:21-27
   - Sing Psalm 145
   - Second Reading: Revelation 21:1-5a
   - Sing Alleluia
   - Gospel: John 13, 31-33a, 34-35

The Word (30 min)

1. Begin with some background on today's gospel. Use these or similar words:

   Today's gospel reading is from the "farewell discourse" that Jesus makes to his disciples once the train of events leading to his crucifixion has begun. Yet as Jesus speaks, it becomes clear that the evangelist has told the story in such a way that we do not merely hear the earthly Jesus speaking to his band of followers, but we hear the resurrected Lord speaking to his disciples through all the ages. Where the synoptic gospels place the account of the institution of the Eucharist as the memorial of Jesus, John's gospel situates Jesus' new commandment: "Love one another." The command to love is made specific: the disciples' love must be like the love that the exalted Jesus bears for them. Thus their love becomes a memorial and a sign of Jesus, even as the Eucharist is celebrated in imitation of and in memory of Jesus. It is the way that all will know that these are his disciples.

2. Have participants move into small groups. Give each group a large sheet of paper and a marker. Instruct them to brainstorm all the ways that outsiders would know that your parishioners are disciples of Jesus. Then ask the sponsors and other team members in each small group to use the large sheet of paper to write what they want the catechu-

mens and candidates to "remember" as they continue their journey of faith.

3. While the sponsors are completing this task, ask the catechumens and candidates to record their responses to the following questions: *Christ has first loved us, and asks us to become a fuller part of him in loving one another. State what you need from God to truly love all people. Name the people who have truly loved you. Next to their names write down the feelings or qualities their love evoked in you. How were you changed by their love? Let yourself feel Christ's love for you. How are you changed by this love?* When the sponsors have finished have a representative from each group read their text of remembrance to the catechumens and candidates.

4. Proclaim the gospel again. Invite the group to silently reflect on how in their daily life the people they interact with are recipients of their love.

Catholic Teaching (30 min)

1. Begin this section by asking participants to divide into three to four groups . Catechumens and candidates should be in each group. Assign each group a "LAW CONTEXT," e.g., family laws, traffic laws, tax laws, sport laws. Give them 10 minutes to list laws of love in each context and then share their responses with the whole group. From their sharing, ask them to identify common characteristics of laws of love.

2. To begin a focus on the Catholic teaching on love Summarize their sharing, being sure to include the following points:

   • Laws of love are based on relationships of trust.

   • Laws of love look toward the common good.

3. Have participants read "The Church Says" in the Participant Book (page 47) or on the blackline handout.

OR. . .

Use these or similar words: *The Law of Moses structured relationships in society. For example, lying, stealing and adultery were forbidden by the ten commandments. The law of love is also found in the old covenant. In Deuteronomy 6:5 people are told to love God wholly and completely, and in Leviticus 19:18 people are exhorted to love your neighbor as yourself. Jesus calls the commandment to love a "new" commandment. The new law of Jesus opens believers to the full potential of that first covenant. The new commandment of love is etched upon your hearts not only by pondering scripture, but by partaking of the living tradition of discipleship through the outpouring of the Spirit in Christ. This commandment is also new because it derives its meaning from example and love of Jesus. He showed us this love through his examples in the many events of his life, by washing the disciples' feet, and later by dying on the cross. Eucharist, as presented in John's gospel, is the meal which symbolizes our following in the way of love, the way of service and sacrifice for one another. Loving one another is the sign by which we are known as Christ's disciples.*

The gift of God's love empowers us to love. The command

and the gift of love is not only for ourselves but for the building up of the community. It is meant to set people free, to support one another, and to enhance the world we live in together. Love recognizes that there is great power when the community works together to bring love into the world. Love has the power to transform the pain and isolation people experience in the world. In the history of the church, great examples of love abound.

4. Refer to Catholic Culture for some concrete examples of men and women who lived lives of love for others. Examples of parish organizations or parishioners can give concrete expression of the community's power to bring love into the world.

Putting Faith Into Practice

With the group reflect on the following questions:

How do you hear yourself called to live the law of love in your home, in workplace, in neighborhood, in society? What are the obstacles? What would be the blessings?

Prayer

Invite the sponsors to lay their hands on the catechumens and candidates for a prayer of exorcism using these or similar words;

All-powerful God,
you revealed the power of your love to us through the raising of your Son from the dead. Not even the darkness of death could overcome your love for the world. We pray for these candidates and catechumens who present themselves to you.

In the name of your Son, our Lord Jesus Christ, and in the power of the Holy Spirit, we ask you to remove from them the barriers to love. Free them from that which keeps them from recognizing and accepting your love, from memories that bind them, and from hesitancy to reach out in love.

Strengthen in them your gifts of faith, hope and love. May they come to live as apostles, witnesses of your love for all people.

We ask this through Christ our Lord. Amen.

Sixth Sunday of Easter

The Word In Liturgy

Acts 15:1-2, 22-29
Psalm 67:2-3, 5, 6, 8
Revelation 21:10-14, 22-23
John 14:23-29

Several times during the Easter season we have heard of the controversy created by God's gift to Gentiles of faith in the Lord Jesus. What was initially an entirely Jewish body of disciples only gradually was persuaded—by signs and wonders and painstaking discernment—to fully accept gentiles into the messianic community of the church. Today's reading from the Acts of the Apostles presents the final decision reached by the church's leadership in Jerusalem and received by the Gentile community at Antioch.

The shortened form of the story that appears here ought to be understood in context of the longer passage from which it is taken. The full account shows a collegial process which involved the whole church in deliberation, and required listening to the stories of God's deeds among the gentile converts. Luke makes clear that the decision to accept the gentiles was not handed down from "on high" or derived from abstract principles. Rather, a divine-human collaboration involving many people and the Holy Spirit led to the decision. The process was not complete until the local church sent back emissaries to Jerusalem "in peace," showing that the teaching had been accepted. Thus, Luke's account is important because it sets forth a model of decision-making in the early church.

To appreciate the significance of the new Jerusalem, spoken of in the second reading, recall the importance of the city of Jerusalem for the Jewish people. The Temple in Jerusalem was the place where God dwelt, and Jerusalem was therefore the center of national worship. Not a shrine apart from human habitation, but a bustling city bursting with life, Jerusalem was made holy because of God's presence within it. When the Book of Revelation was written, the temple and the city of

Jerusalem had been completely destroyed. The new city appearing from heaven as the pure gift of God is therefore especially poignant. It is not a vision of mere rebuilding with bricks and mortar, however, but a presentation of the fulfillment of the ultimate goal of human life: union with God. Rich with symbolism, the new Jerusalem is a perfect cube, like the holy of holies in the Temple. With its twelve gates (signifying the twelve tribes of Israel, the twelve apostles, and fullness generally), and its illumination from within by the divine presence, it symbolizes all the beauty and perfection of the Church.

The gospel reading from John continues the farewell discourse of Jesus. Ideally situated in the liturgical year to anticipate the coming feasts of Ascension and Pentecost, the reading tells both of Jesus' immanent departure and his promise of the Paraclete. Central to the passage are the words of Jesus concerning the peace that he gives to his disciples. Peace is his farewell, and his gift to them—a peace that the world cannot give. More than a simple word of greeting, this peace will be a token of Jesus' abiding presence even as he leaves them, just as the Spirit, or Paraclete, will provide for the disciples those things which Jesus did for them in his lifetime (taught, led, etc.). Thus, a full picture emerges of a community of disciples who will be cared for and not abandoned even when Jesus departs from them. They are promised a divine indwelling, the gift of peace, and the Paraclete to guide them.

The phrase "If you loved me. . ." does not suggest that the disciples do not love Jesus, but challenges them to a generous rather than a possessive love. As the church nears Pentecost, which can be a time of leave-taking and transition within the catechumenate (as the neophytes take their rightful place among the faithful), Jesus' words speak to the experience of separation and letting go. His promise of peace speaks in every age to the troubled heart of the human person, as well as to common life of the faithful and indeed to the whole world in which we live.

Catholic Doctrine

Peace

Pope John XXIII wrote his encyclical, *Pacem in Terris*, in 1963, and it was published two months before his death. One theme in this encyclical is that to achieve peace in a world bristling with weapons of mass destruction will require a concerted effort by all nations. This papal encyclical was the first to be addressed to even those outside the church, to men and women of good will.

Pope John's message, and the Catholic understanding of peace, begin with Jesus farewell gift to his disciples. Jesus speaks the word "peace" in the context of a biblical understanding of "shalom." The Hebrew 'shalom," found in the Old Testament, means much more than the absence of war or maintaining a balance of power. "Shalom" means the well-being of daily life, a total harmony with nature, God and self. It issues forth from justice and is experienced in a fruitful land and people, who have plentiful food, and dwell in security, free from fear. "Shalom" is the sum of all the benefits of God's presence with his people. Jesus gives this gift of peace in the widest sense possible. Peace is the fruit of the covenant between God and believers. Those who follow the light of Jesus as disciples walk the paths of peace and know from his teaching that "blessed are the peacemakers." (Matthew 5:9)

Since its inception, the church has been aware of the grave potential for evil inherent in waging war. Only under certain rigorously defined conditions does the church allow for the possibility of legitimate defense by military force (see CCC 2309). Even in the waging of war, human beings are subject to the moral law (CCC 2312), and crimes committed during wartime are always to be condemned. In our own day, the church has recognized the terrifying potential of modern weapons of destruction. Genocide and indiscriminate destruction of whole cities or areas with their inhabitants are condemned by the church (CCC 2313-4).

The 1983 Pastoral Letter of the U.S. bishops on peace (*The Challenge of Peace: God's Promise and Our Response*) outlines a program for pursuing peace in our time. It includes the reduction of nuclear weapons and conventional arms, education within parish communities about peace, and personal commitment to prayer for peace. *The Catechism of the Catholic Church* affirms the value of those who witness to the dangers of violence (CCC 2306), and insists that citizens and governments must work to avoid war (CCC 2308) and the injustices, envy and pride that threaten peace and lead to war (CCC 2317).

In the words of *The Challenge of Peace*, "peacemaking is not an optional commitment. It is a requirement of our faith. We are called to be peacemakers, not by some movement of the moment, but by our Lord Jesus. The content and context of our peacemaking is set not by some political agenda or ideological program, but by the teaching of his Church." (Summary, *The Challenge of Peace: God's Promise and Our Response*; NCCB, May 3, 1983; p 9).

Catholic Culture

The hymn "I Want to Walk as a Child of the Light" (Kathleen Thomerson) links the image of the new Jerusalem with Christ's indwelling: ". . . The Lamb is the light of the city of God. Shine in my heart, Lord Jesus."

There are many individuals and groups in the church that cherish a deep commitment to peace. For example, *Pax Christi* is an international Catholic association devoted to promoting world peace. Commitment to complete non-violence (pacifism) is practiced by the Catholic Worker movement, founded by Dorothy Day.

Thomas Merton, Trappist monk and author who wrote extensively the contemplative life and peace, had this to say about Mahatma Gandhi: ". . . Gandhi recognized, as no other world leader of our time has done, the necessity to be free from the pressures, the exorbitant and tyrannical demands of a society that is violent because it is essentially greedy, lustful and cruel. . . . He recognized the impossibility of being a peaceful and non-violent man if one submits passively to the insatiable requirements of a society maddened by overstimulation and obsessed with the demons of noise, voyeurism and speed." (*Seeds of Destruction*, New York: Farrar, Straus and Giroux, 1964, p. 232).

The much-loved prayer of St. Francis of Assisi (d. 1226), known as the "Peace Prayer," begins: "Lord, make me an instrument of your peace. . . "

Notes

Dismissal Catechesis (30 min)

Getting Started

1. Prepare the space ahead of time with a circle of chairs. Arrange the center of the circle with symbols of peace and violence. For example, scattered around a white potted Easter lily have a few headlines from the newspaper and magazines.

2. Invite the candidates and the catechumens into the circle with the John Michael Talbot version of the Peace Prayer playing in the background. When all have been seated, pray in these or similar words:

   Spirit of Peace, dwell with us today as we gather in your name. You have been sent to counsel, guide and direct our lives and the life of the church. Come, Holy Spirit and fill our hearts with your peace. Light the fire of love in us that we might become signs of your peace for the sake of the world. In your peace renew the face of the earth. Create in us a willingness to become your instruments of peace, for this we pray. Amen.

3. Invite everyone to offer their comments on the centerpiece of news clippings. Allow a time of silence for the group to think about the struggle for peace in our world.

First Impressions

1. Ask the catechumens and candidates to share their first reactions when they hear the word "peace." List these on a poster board or paper that is visible to all.

2. In these or your own words, explain that the gospel for today concerns Jesus' farewell gift of peace.

   The peace Jesus speaks of is not just about the absence of chaos or war, but has multiple meanings.

3. In the large group invite all to indicate what the Word of God in today's liturgy offers to help us understand the fullness of Jesus' gift of peace. As they respond to all these symbols, put the phrases and ideas on the paper or poster board. These sheets can be posted on the wall.

4. In small groups, request that the participants respond to the following questions, concerning today's liturgical experience. What about today's liturgy and the church setting gave you a sense of peace? What images from the Scripture were especially meaningful for you? Why was this so?

Making Connections

1. While remaining in the small groups, invite the participants to delve further into the meaning of peace in their lives. Ask all to recall a time when they felt deep peace. *What were the circumstances? The setting? What was the cause of your peace?* Now help the group shift focus by asking them to remember a time of confusion and inner turmoil. *What were the circumstances? The setting? What was the cause of your lack of peace?*

2. In these same groups, examine the source of peace with one of these questions: *What made the difference between peace and chaos in your life? How do you move from confusion to peace when confronted with a difficult choice? What is your source of true peace and harmony?*

3. Turn the attention of the smaller groups back to the larger gathering and invite a few responses as to the source of peace. Then summarize the session, while individuals have an opportunity to decide what they wish to remember from this gathering.

Prayer

Close this session with the Prayer of St. Francis. A copy of this can be found in the Remembrance Book.

Extended Catechesis

SESSION FOCUS: *Peace*

Gathering

A. Sunday:

1. Welcome all the participants and invite them to join in the circle. Offer a period of silence for all to look at the newsprint and the centerpiece.

2. Begin the time of prayer by asking everyone to join in singing the Gathering Hymn from today's liturgy. Ask one of the sponsors to proclaim the Gospel from, John 14:23-29. Encourage the group to reflect on their hope for peace today. Invite them to create a spontaneous Litany of Peace by praying their prayer for peace aloud, using the formula, "I long to see Your peace in. . ." After the petitions have concluded pray Psalm 67 as a concluding prayer of thanks. You will need to have copies for each participants.

B. Weekday:

1. Welcome and greet the participants as they arrive. Invite everyone to gather in the circle and reflect on the thoughts displayed in the center.

2. Ask a few participants to share the signs of Jesus' gift of peace that they have observed in these past few days.

3. Lead this celebration of the Word.

   - Opening Song: "Peace Prayer," John Foley (New Dawn Music, 1976).
   - First Reading: Acts 15:1-2, 22-29
   - Psalm 67:2-3, 5, 6, 8
   - Second Reading: Revelation 21:10-14, 22-23
   - Gospel: John 14:23-29
   - Pause for a time of silent reflection

The Word (30 min)

1. Invite all share their usual manner of expressing farewell when they will be gone for a long period. Ask them to share the emotions experienced during such a time. Explain that this was precisely the setting for today's gospel.

2. Assist the group in understanding the gospel in these or your own words.

Jesus is offering a farewell discourse to his friends and followers in the gospel. His farewell is peace, not just a greeting or a good wish, but a peace that will take real shape in the abiding presence of the Holy Spirit. This presence is a continuation of the actions and promises of Jesus for the disciples, in spite of the fact of his leaving. Jesus' departure, then, is not abandonment, but a new, indwelling presence, yielding the gift of peace.

3. In small groups of four or less, invite those present to share: *What does the presence of the Holy Spirit mean in your life? How have you experienced the peace of the Spirit? How has the gift of peace been made real in your experience of the Spirit?*

4. Move further into the meaning of the scriptures by explaining the second reading from Revelation in these or similar words.

The city of Jerusalem was very important to the people of Israel and remains so even today. A bustling city, Jerusalem was the center of their worship. Jerusalem was made holy because of God's presence within it. Revelation, written after the complete destruction of the temple and the city of Jerusalem, speaks of the new Jerusalem which God will restore. Thus, the new Jerusalem symbolized the fulfillment of the ultimate goal of human life: union with God. This vision of the new Jerusalem presented in the second reading is vital for the life of the church today. The vision of the new Jerusalem offers a parallel to the Kingdom of God, preached by Jesus. Both are characterized by the fullness of peace. A peace which is freely given as we move toward this vision of a new Jerusalem through the abiding presence of the Spirit.

5. Offer a period of time for the participants to dream of their vision of the kingdom of God, the new Jerusalem by asking them to turn to the Participant Book (page 48) or the blackline handout. When they have had an opportunity to respond to the questions, ask them to share one thing from their reflection in the small groups of four or fewer.

Catholic Teaching (30 min)

1. Expand on the notion of peace, using the information contained in the Catholic Doctrine section found in Understanding This Sunday. These points would be important in your presentation:

   • The Hebrew word, "shalom" means the well-being of daily life, a total harmony with nature, God and self.

   • Peace flows out of the covenant between God and all people. This peace frees us for authentic, holistic living—life rooted in right relationships and harmony. Jesus' gift of peace is the sum of all the benefits of God's presence with God's people.

   • This is the understanding of peace that the encyclical letter, *Pacem in Terris*, issued in 1963 by Pope John XXIII, envisioned. In this papal letter, the church upholds the 'astonishing' order in the universe, which is the source of human dignity. This dignity of the human person is the basis for a wide variety of rights and duties.

2. Working in the small groups, invite the discussion to center around the church's teaching on peace. The following questions may prove helpful for this discussion.

   What is the link between this expanded notion of peace and human dignity? What are some of the rights and duties of the human person in seeking peace? In your life, how has inner peace and harmony helped you understand the dignity of others?

Putting Faith Into Practice

1. Remaining in the small groups continue the discussion in the following manner. *Called, as followers of Jesus, to be peacemakers, how can we bring about this peaceable kingdom? What some specific ways can we work for the human dignity of all persons?* Invite the small groups to report on their discussions. Record some of the responses on a large sheet of paper or poster board. With the help of the group, summarize and prioritize some of the specific suggestions.

2. Invite a member of a parish or diocesan peace and justice organization to speak, informing the participants of the ways the parish or diocese is already working toward peace. (Someone from the local chapter of Pax Christi could also be of help.) The group could also share their suggestions for bring about a parish focused on peace.

Prayer

Begin the prayer by asking everyone to quietly think about the insights they have gained from this session. Then invite a member of the team to proclaim the Beatitudes (Matthew 5:1-12). Pause and then invite all to name those places and people in the world, the community, the parish where human dignity and right relationship are in need of peace. Ask the group to respond: **"Lord, make me an instrument of your peace."** Close with the song, "I Want to Walk as a Child of the Light," by Kathleen Thomerson.

Seventh Sunday of Easter

Understanding this Sunday:
Background for Catechesis

The Word In Liturgy

Acts 7:55-60
Psalm 97:1-2, 6-7, 9
Revelation 22:12-14, 16-17, 20
John 17:20-26

The account of Stephen's martyrdom in Acts serves two of Luke's theological purposes. First, it models the death of Stephen, the first Christian martyr, upon that of Jesus. Stephen, like Jesus, is accused of blasphemy and betrayed by false witnesses, enrages his persecutors by speaking of the coming Son of Man, commends his spirit to the Lord, and forgives those who put him to death. These parallels strongly suggest that those who believe in Jesus will indeed conform to the pattern of his death, as the early community struggled against persecution. Second, the narrative of the stoning of Stephen introduces Saul in an uncompromisingly villainous role.

Stephen's magnificent, Spirit-filled vision of Jesus standing at the right hand of God possesses a subtle significance: rather than being seated, the Son of Man is standing, which is a position of an advocate at a trial. Stephen has had no fair trial. His human enemies have perjured themselves and wrought his execution as a mob without the sentencing of the Sanhedrin. But before God, who alone judges justly, Stephen finds his true advocate and bears witness to him.

This eschatological vision of the Son of Man at the right hand of God anticipates somewhat the Christ who is proclaimed in the second reading. Taken from the epilogue to the Book of Revelation, in which John sums up the message of this entire work, today's passage announces Jesus whose reign is all-encompassing, and who will come in judgment. In one brief, evocative passage, almost all the major themes that we experience today in the Easter Vigil come into play: clean robes, paradise, word, light, life-giving water, the wedding feast. Most dazzling of all are the epithets for Christ himself, who is Alpha and Omega (the first and last letters of the Greek alphabet, suggesting the fullness of the Word made flesh), who identifies himself with king David (God's anointed, whose kingdom was promised to endure forever), and who is the Morning Star (regarded by the ancients as a symbol of power). As we come to the end of the Easter season, this reading from the book of Revelation reminds us of the great scope of all that has been celebrated in the great fifty days.

Today's passage from John's gospel is the last section of the majestic prayer which concludes Jesus' farewell discourse at the Last Supper. The form of this discourse, culminating in prayer, is reminiscent of the book of Deuteronomy in which Moses turns to address God at the end of his exhortations to the people. Here, in a section which has a marked future orientation, Jesus prays for unity among all those who will someday come to faith through the words of his disciples. The unity for which Jesus prays is to be like the unity of the Father with Jesus himself. Two features of it are especially noteworthy. First, this unity finds its origin in God; the very fact that Jesus prays for it suggests that it is not available through human striving or natural associations alone. Second, it cannot be a purely spiritual unity, for it must be enough in evidence that it will confront the world with a powerful truth: "So shall the world know that you sent me, and that you loved them as you loved me."

The prayer concludes with a covenant motif of indwelling. At the conclusion of the covenant with Moses, God promises to dwell within the midst of the people by his mysterious presence in the ark of the covenant that they are to carry with them. Here, the indwelling is accomplished by Jesus himself living in those who believe.

Catholic Doctrine

Christian Unity

Ecumenism is the movement to achieve unity among all the Christian churches. The word in English derives from biblical Greek, *oikoumene*, "the whole inhabited earth." In obedience to the prayer of Jesus proclaimed in this Sunday's gospel passage ("that they may all be one"), Christians of many churches have worked throughout this century to manifest greater unity.

The Catholic Church teaches that unity is a gift given to the Church by Christ (CCC 820). Its source is the Trinity, the union of God, one in three (CCC 813). The gift of unity does not mean uniformity. From its beginning, the Church has been characterized by a great diversity and liveliness. Yet for various reasons, including human sinfulness, the one church of Jesus Christ has experienced deep divisions and separations (schisms) which weaken our witness in the world. The Second Vatican Council teaches that none of the churches are exempt from taking responsibility for the scandal of this separated condition (UR 1).

The drive toward ecumenism began early in this century by non-Catholic Christians and was embraced by the Catholic Church in the years prior to the Second Vatican Council. In 1949, the Holy Office issued an instruction endorsing Catholic participation in conferences whose aim was the promotion of ecumenism. Subsequently, Catholic observers attended meetings of the World Council of Churches, and Protestant and Orthodox observers were invited and attended the Vatican II. Indeed, ecumenism was one of the four principal goals of the Second Vatican Council. With the publication of the Decree on Ecumenism in 1964 (*Unitatis Redintegratio*) the Catholic Church became irrevocably committed to ecumenism.

Does the Catholic Church believe, therefore, that all churches are equal and the differences between them unimportant? By no means. The Constitution on the Church affirmed that the church of Jesus Christ "subsists in the Catholic Church" (LG 8) and that all means of salvation have been given to the Catholic Church by Christ, even though we do not always live by them as we should. In the Catholic view, non-Catholic churches are objectively wounded by not having certain elements, such as the Petrine ministry, apostolic succession, valid sacraments, or profession of the one faith received from the apostles.

Nevertheless, the Council's Decree on Ecumenism states clearly that many of the significant elements which build up and give life to the household of God can and do exist "outside the visible boundaries of the Catholic Church" (UR 3). These endowments are, for example, the written Word of God, the life of grace, faith, hope and love, and interior gifts of the Spirit (CCC 819, cf. UR 3). Those who are born into separated communities are not personally responsible for the sin of separation. All who have been justified by faith in baptism are incorporated into Christ, are brothers and sisters to us, and are rightly called "Christian" (UR 3). Indeed, salvation can be experienced in Christian churches and communities outside the Catholic Church (UR 3).

The ecumenical movement has impelled Catholics, Orthodox and Protestants to join together in prayer, good works, study and dialogue. Official dialogues among the churches have resulted in consensus in many areas of theological controversy, and in clarity about issues which continue to divide the Christians. Scholarship, especially in biblical and historical studies, has benefited from ecumenical cooperation. In an ecumenical spirit, the Catholic church promotes collaboration among Christian churches in works of mercy, social justice, and world peace. The Church characterizes public prayer for unity between Christians as the soul of the whole ecumenical movement, meriting the name "spiritual ecumenism" (UR 8).

In 1995, John Paul II issued an encyclical letter, *Ut Unum Sint*, in which he makes his own contribution to the ecumenical movement. Common prayer, spiritual renewal and conversion will result in one family, in that Christians will cease seeing each other as enemies or strangers and instead as "brothers and sisters" (UUS, 42.1). He urges us to be authentic disciples, true to the prayer of Jesus that we all may be one.

Catholic Culture

The Week of Prayer for Christian Unity, begun in the Anglican Communion in 1908, is celebrated by Catholics (and other Christian churches) in January and in some countries around Pentecost. Lewis Thomas Wattson, who began this week of prayer, also founded with Lurana Mary White a Franciscan community called the Society of the Atonement, in Graymoor, New York. In 1909, they and fifteen followers were received into the Roman Catholic church. The Society of the Atonement continues to promote Christian Unity through the Week of Prayer, publications, and the work of their members.

Pope John XXIII was regarded as a strong advocate for ecumenism, and the council he convened (Vatican II) did much to promote church unity. Rumor has it that his dying words were "ut unum sint" (that they may be one).

At the opening of the Easter Vigil, the wax of the paschal candle—a symbol of Christ—is etched with an Alpha and an Omega, recalling today's reading from Revelation.

Dismissal Catechesis (30 min)

Getting Started

1. Prepare the space ahead of time with a circle of chairs. On the table place a white cloth with a Christ candle. At the base of the table have Easter or spring flowers.

2. Invite the candidates and catechumens to stand quietly in a circle.

3. Light the Christ candle. Lead them in prayer singing the hymn "Christ Be Beside Me" or praying the prayer of St. Patrick.

   Christ be with me, Christ within me,
   Christ behind me, Christ before me,
   Christ beside me, Christ to win me.
   Christ to comfort and restore me,
   Christ beneath me, Christ above me,
   Christ in quiet, Christ in danger,
   Christ in Hearts of all that love me,
   Christ in the mouth of friend and stranger.

First Impressions

1. Explain to the group that the Ascension of our Lord into heaven has just been celebrated and next Sunday is the celebration of Pentecost.

2. Invite all to silence. Recall the Liturgy of the Word using words and phrases from the songs, prayers, Scripture readings and homily. After a few quiet moments, ask them to share in small groups: *What did you hear or experienced at the liturgy. What was the mood of the Liturgy? What in the scriptures was challenging?*

3. Following their sharing, elicit responses and comments from the whole group. Summarize the discussion in a few sentences. Ask everyone to quietly recall one thing they wish to remember from the scriptures today.

Making Connections

1. Proclaim the first reading, Acts 7:55-60. After a few moments of quiet, ask this question in the large group: *What did you hear in this reading"?*

2. Offer this information about Stephen:

   Stephen's death is offered in this passage with several similarities to the death of Jesus. He, like Jesus is accused of blasphemy, betrayed by false witnesses, enrages his persecutors by speaking of the coming Son or Man, commends his spirit to the Lord, and forgives those who put him to death. This first Christian martyr—one who his put to death for religious convictions—suffered a terrible death, stoning, to bear witness to Jesus.

3. Invite the group to gather in small groups to discuss: *What does it means to be a disciple of Jesus Christ. In what ways do Christians today experience persecution and/or suffering? What does this powerful witness of Stephen say to you as a follower of Jesus?*

4. In the large group, ask the participants to share their insights on the last question. When they have finished, summarize their responses. Conclude by asking all to silently think about their willingness to suffer for the sake of following Jesus.

Prayer

Move into the prayer while the participants are reflecting on their commitment to Jesus. Begin the prayer by inviting the participants name people, living and dead, who are examples of discipleship for them. Ask them to respond to each name with, "Glory and praise to you, Lord Jesus Christ."

Extended Catechesis

SESSION FOCUS: *Christian Unity*

Gathering

A. Sunday:

1. Welcome and greet the sponsors, team members, and additional participants as they arrive. Encourage them to join the circle.

2. Ask the new arrivals to share their experience of the liturgy. Encourage one of the candidates or catechumens to share one thing they remember from the Dismissal Catechesis.

3. Begin the prayer by asking everyone to stand and sing the first two verses of "We Are Many Parts." Pray in these or similar words:

   Risen Jesus, you call us to be one with you and the Father. From the moment of creation you ordered all things by embracing all that you made. We give you thanks for you have joined us to yourself through your death and resurrection. We praise you for you have joined all of humankind together, as the family of God. We celebrate for we are one with you in the Father through the Holy Spirit. Amen.

4. Proclaim the Gospel John 17:20-26 and invite all to sing the last verse of "We Are Many Parts."

B. Weekday:

1. Warmly welcome and greet the participants as they arrive. Invite them to gather in the circle.

2. Encourage one of the candidates or catechumens to share one thing they remember from the Dismissal Catechesis. Invite the participants to share an experience of their struggle to live out their call as a follower of Jesus during these past few days.

3. Lead this celebration of the Word
- Song: Gathering Hymn from Sunday's Liturgy.
- First Reading: Acts:7:55-60
- Silence
- Second Reading: Revelation 22:12-14, 16-17
- Silence
- Sing the Alleluia
- Gospel John 17:20-26
- Sing the Alleluia

The Word (30 min)

1. Present this background to the gospel, John 17:20-26.

This passage is the last section of the majestic prayer that concludes Jesus' farewell discourse at the Last Supper. Jesus' prayer for unity is a reminder of Moses' address to God at the end of his exhortations to the Israelites. It is Jesus' desire that all will know this intimate unity that exists between the Father and Jesus. This unity originates in God, rather than from human striving. This is not purely a spiritual unity. It is a unity which is tangible. Such unity comes with the gift of faith and living such faith. Just as God promised Moses that God would dwell in the midst of the people by his mysterious presence in the ark of the covenant that they carry with them; so, too, Jesus lives in those who believe.

2. Invite the participants to gather in small groups and share their responses to these questions: *What does Jesus' vision of unity evoke in you? How would you explain the phrase, "That all may be one"?*

3. Ask the participants to turn to the Participant Book (page 50) or the blackline handoutto reflect on the unity of all in God. When they have finished invite them to gather in pairs to share their insights. The sponsors and candidates or catechumens will wand to share together.

4. In the large group ask the participants to share one they have for hope for unity.

Catholic Teaching (30 min)

1. Prepare two large pieces of paper with a line down the middle of each. At the top of one paper, write 'unity.' At the top of the other write, 'uniformity.' On the left side of each piece of paper, have participants list as many words or phrases that they can think of that describe the word at the top of the page. On the right side, describe what results from each. In groups of four or five, discuss unity, uniformity and conformity. In what ways do today's scripture passage have an impact on our understanding of these words?

2. Use Understanding this Sunday to lead a discussion on ecumenism. The focus is to strive to name ways in which we are in union rather than emphasize that which divides. Invite representatives of two or three other Christian churches to speak about John 17:20-26. Continue the discussion, emphasizing the need for openness and dialogue among all Christian churches. Name efforts of collaboration that already exist, such as establishing shelters for the homeless, food programs, homes abused women and children as well as joint worship services for peace, Thanksgiving, and Easter Sunrise services. Inform the participants of ecumenical dialogues that are taking place in your diocese. The week of January 18-15 has been designated as a special time of prayer for Christian unity.

3. Explain that the emphasis of Jesus' prayer is unity, not uniformity. The unity described in John's Gospel today is not conformity determined by human beings. Unity exists in diversity. What unites us is faith in the promise of Jesus Christ that "all may be one."

Putting Faith Into Practice

Invite everyone to quietly reflect on this session. Share with the group an insight or affirmation or challenge. Invite them to take time each day this week to reflect and/or to journal on how their actions for the day supported or brought about unity. Ask them to pray every day for those who think and act differently and for the gift of tolerance.

Prayer

Invite them to join hands in a circle as you prayerfully proclaim John 17:20-26. Sing again "We Are Many Parts."

Pentecost

The Word In Liturgy

Acts 2:1-11
Psalm 104:1, 24, 29-30, 31, 34
1 Corinthians 12:3b-7, 12-13
John 20:19-23

Today's feast of Pentecost celebrates the sending of the Spirit upon the church. It is the last Sunday of Easter, and brings the season to a close. The liturgical year honors the chronology of Luke by placing our celebration of the Spirit's descent fifty days after the Resurrection. The Christian Pentecost in Luke coincides with the Jewish feast of Weeks, fifty days after Passover, which was a festival of the harvest, and later became a commemoration of the giving of the Law. Against this background, Luke's presentation of the Pentecost event calls our attention both to the way in which the descent of the Spirit resembles the theophany at Mount Sinai (fire, sound, and word), and to the effects of Pentecost as the "harvest" of the Paschal Mystery.

The liturgy does not bind itself to Luke's chronological unfolding of the events of Easter in every respect, however. All the readings from Acts that have been proclaimed in previous Sundays of the Easter season are about events that took place *after* Pentecost. In other words, the effects of Pentecost have been the subject of our reflection and our celebration *throughout* the fifty days of Easter. In today's gospel passage from John, read every year on Pentecost, Jesus gives the Spirit on the evening of Easter day itself. Thus, in a certain sense, the liturgy draws the whole fifty days of Easter into one.

The first reading tells in very few words the story of the Spirit's descent and how it was manifested: a loud sound (like wind), tongues (like fire) coming to rest on each disciple, and bold proclamation of the Good News thereafter by the disciples. Glossolalia, a form of ecstatic speech-like babbling known in the ancient world and attested to in the New Testament, here

is presented as intelligible speech, understood by listeners from around the world as communication in their own languages. By naming the geographic origins of all the diaspora Jews living in Jerusalem at the time of Pentecost, Luke paints a vivid symbolic picture of the worldwide proclamation of God's great works.

The psalm reminds us of the role of the Spirit in creation, and the dependence of all earthly things on the Spirit of God for life and sustenance. The second reading develops the theme of the Spirit's diverse but united gifts. First making the point that the Holy Spirit mediates the believer's confession of faith in the exalted Lord, Paul goes on to explain that the multiplicity of gifts in the church is united by their source—the Spirit—and that indeed the body of people that is the church is also diverse and yet one because of baptism and the Spirit.

The gospel passage, introduced by the description of the disciples gathered in fear behind locked doors, draws our attention to the reversal of their fear to joy and their transformation from frightened followers to apostolic witnesses ("apostle" means "one sent"). At the heart of this change is the presence of the risen Lord, the command to go forth, and the giving of the Spirit. In a gesture that recalls God's act of creation, Jesus gives the Spirit by the action of breathing on the disciples. His imparting of the Spirit is from his own wounded and risen body. The giving of the Spirit is thus a new act of creation, by the crucified and glorified Christ. Last of all, as in Luke's gospel, reconciliation is central to the mission entrusted to them and enabled by the Spirit.

Catholic Doctrine

The gifts of the Spirit and the Sacrament of Confirmation

On this Sunday which closes the fifty days of the Easter Season, the conferral of the Holy Spirit upon the gathered apostles and Mary is celebrated by the Church. The Sacrament of Confirmation perpetuates this grace by which new members of the Church, in the context of their initiation journey, are sealed with the gift of the Spirit. The purpose of this sealing is to strengthen them so they may witness to Christ (as did the first apostles). This faithful witness builds up the body of Christ in love. Catholic teaching emphasizes that just as those who are baptized, those confirmed are so marked with the special character or seal of the Lord that this sacrament cannot be repeated (Rite of Confirmation, 2).

There are, admittedly, differing practices within the Catholic Church in the timing or sequence of celebrating this sacrament of initiation. For those who are baptized as infants, this sacrament is sometimes delayed until after reception of first Eucharist. For those who are baptized as adults, this sacrament is immediately celebrated, after which those who are newly baptized and confirmed then approach the table of the Lord to celebrate first Eucharist. But whenever this sacrament is celebrated, it completes baptismal grace (CCC 1285).

The Spirit is received at Baptism. Subsequently, one is strengthened in the gifts of the Spirit at Confirmation, and is thereby is enriched for the task of witnessing to the faith, and is more closely bound to Christ (*Lumen Gentium*, ll).

Both the Old and New Testaments refer to the Spirit. The Spirit is described as descending upon Jesus, the Messiah, at his own baptism in the Jordan by John (Matthew 3:13-17 and John 1:33-34). But the fullness of the Holy Spirit was not meant for only the Messiah but for the entire people claimed for God by Jesus. More than once, Jesus promised that this outpouring of the Spirit (Luke 12:12; John 3:5-8; 7:37-39; l6:7-15; Acts 1:8) would be the gift he would send to his Church.

In the early history of the Church, the laying on of hands was recognized as the origin of the sacrament of Confirmation. An anointing with chrism (perfumed oil) on the forehead was soon added to the laying on of hands. A "Christian" is one who is "anointed."

In scriptural symbolism, anointing with oil is a sign of joy and abundance. It cleanses, as before and after a bath and makes limber (the anointing of wrestlers and athletes). In the ancient world it is also a sign of healing, whereby bruises and wounds are soothed. In those ancient times it was also a cosmetic applied to improve beauty. Anointing in the sacrament of Confirmation has all these meanings (CCC 1293-94). Thus, those who are Confirmed are strengthened by the Spirit so their lives may share more completely in the mission of the Savior, Jesus(CCC 1294), and give off the aroma of Christ (2 Corinthians 2:15).

St. Ambrose admonished those confirmed, "Guard what you have received. God the Father has marked you with his sign; Christ the Lord has confirmed you and has placed his pledge, the Spirit, in your hearts." (De myst. 7, 42: PL 16, 402-403).

Catholic Culture

The minister of Confirmation prays in these words for the gifts of the Spirit to be given:

> *All-powerful God, Father of our Lord Jesus Christ,*
> *by water and the Holy Spirit*
> *you freed your sons and daughters from sin*
> *and gave them new life.*
> *Send your Holy Spirit upon them*
> *to be their helper and guide.*
> *Give them the spirit of wisdom and understanding,*
> *the spirit of right judgment and courage,*
> *the spirit of knowledge and reverence.*
> *Fill them with the spirit of wonder and awe in*
> *your presence. . .*
> (Rite of Confirmation, 25.)

Since the New Testament reports that the Spirit descended upon Jesus as a dove (Mark l:10 for example), artists have depicted the Holy Spirit, the Church, the Christian soul and the gifts of the Spirit as doves. The symbol of the dove is common in catacombs and on early Christian sarcophagi. Certain depictions of the saints employ doves to represent the inspiration of the Spirit. (*The Oxford Companion to Christian Art and Architecture*, "Dove," p. 144).

The Catholic Charismatic renewal, a movement which emphasizes the gifts of the Spirit in the lives of the faithful, has enriched the church in recent decades. Glossolalia, or "speaking in tongues," is a phenomenon that can be heard today in charismatic prayer meetings.

Pentecost Sunday is the last Sunday of the Easter season, during which the Paschal candle has been kept in the sanctuary, lighted, during the liturgy. The candle is taken from the sanctuary at the end of the Mass of Pentecost (sometimes in procession), and placed in the church's baptistry, where it remains for the rest of the year.

Notes

Dismissal Catechesis (30 min)

Getting Started

1. Prepare the space ahead of time with a circle of chairs, a candle, and the lectionary in a significant place. Use a red cloth as a background for the setting.

2. Welcome the group into the circle. Share with them that the church uses red on Pentecost as a symbol of fire and that Pentecost marks the end of the Easter season.

3. Begin the session by slowly re-reading the gospel. As the gospel is re-read, ask the group to imagine themselves in the locked room with the disciples as Jesus comes into their midst. After the reading, spend some time in silence.

First Impressions

Ask the group to share a word, phrase, or image that impressed them from the reading.

Making Connections

1. Having shared that, invite participants to reflect back on their life in the time since Easter and recall what has happened to them that may have made the image, word, or phrase stand out for them. Have them share that with one other person in the group.

2. Tell the group that Pentecost is a great opportunity to reflect on the significance of the Holy Spirit in our lives and in the world. Connect their first impressions to the gospel and their lives, with the gift of the Holy Spirit. Bring out that the Holy Spirit is the great hope for our lives and for the world. Because of the life, death and resurrection of Christ, the Spirit now comes to us in our daily lives, even when we are behind "locked doors." Even in our deepest moments of fear, loss, alienation, separation, Christ comes to us in the Holy Spirit and proclaims peace. Because of this peace there is an experience of healing and hope for the future.

3. Invite the group to respond to the following questions:

   As Christ comes to you, where in your life, do you seek peace or to be made a new creation? How are you being called to be an ambassador for peace?

Prayer

As a closing, a song may be sung or played. Suggestions: the opening or closing song of the liturgy, "Veni Sancte Spiritus" (Taize) or "Send Us Your Spirit" (D. Haas, GIA).

Or pray the following adapted Alternative Opening Prayer of the Liturgy for Pentecost:

Let us pray in the Spirit who dwells within us.

God of light, from whom every good gift comes send your Spirit into our lives with the power of a mighty wind, and by the flame of your wisdom open the horizons of our minds.

Loosen our tongues to sing your praise in words beyond the power of speech, for without your Spirit we could never raise our voices in words of peace or announce the truth that Jesus is Lord, who lives and reigns with you and the Holy Spirit, one God, for ever and ever.
Amen.

Extended Catechesis

SESSION FOCUS: *The Gifts of the Spirit and the Sacrament of Confirmation*

Gathering

A. Sunday:

1. Prepare a festive space with music, candles, and a red background for the lectionary.

2. Extend a welcome to the sponsors and other participants as they join the group.

3. Begin with a quiet reflection, a singing of Veni Sancte Spiritus and the opening prayer adapted from the Preface for Mass during the Day of Pentecost:

   Almighty and powerful God, we do well always and everywhere to give you thanks. Today you send your Holy Spirit on those marked to be your children by sharing the life of your only Son, and you brought the paschal mystery to its completion. Today we celebrate the great beginning of your church when the Holy Spirit made known to all peoples the one true God, and created from the many languages one voice to profess one faith the joy of the resurrection, and the hope of the coming of your kingdom in Christ's name.

4. Using several readers re-read the gospel and first reading as follows:

   Reader 1: *On the evening of that first day of the week, even though the disciples had locked the doors of the place where they were for fear of the Jews, Jesus came and stood before them.*

   Reader 2: *"Peace be with you," Jesus said.*

   Reader 1: *He then showed them his hands and his side.*

   Reader 2: *"Peace be with you. As the Father has sent me, so I send you."*

   Reader 3: *Then he breathed on them and said:*

   Reader 2: *"Receive the Holy Spirit. If you forgive a man or women's sins, they are forgiven them; if you hold them bound, they are held bound."*

   Reader 3: *At the sight of the Lord the disciples rejoiced!*
   Pause

   Reader 1: *When the day of Pentecost came it found the disciples of Jesus gathered in one place.*

Reader 2: *Suddenly from up in the sky there came a noise like a strong, driving wind which was heard all through the house where they were seated.*

Reader 3: *Tongues as of fire appeared which parted and came to rest on each of them. All were filled with the Holy Spirit.*

Reader 2: *They began to express themselves in foreign tongues and make bold proclamation as the Spirit prompted them.*

Reader 1: *Staying in Jerusalem at the time were devout Jews of every nation under heaven. These heard the sound, and assembled in a large crowd.*

Reader 2: *They were much confused because each one heard the disciples speaking in his or her own language. The whole occurrence astonished them.*

Reader 3: *"Are not all of these men and women who are speaking Galileans? How is it that each of us hears them in our native tongue?"*

Reader 2: *"There are even visitors from Rome. . . all Jews, or those who have come over to Judaism, yet each of us hears them speaking in our own tongue about the marvels God has accomplished."*

Reader 1: *The Word of God!*

Silence

B. Weekday:

1. As the group gathers, greet and welcome each person.

2. Begin as in the Sunday session above with the prayer and reading.

The Word (30 min)

1. After the opening prayer and reading, ask the participants first to share one feeling they had during the reading. When they have finished with the sharing of feelings, ask them to share one thought they had during the reading, and finally one question that the feast and reading raise for them today. Instruct the group to stay with the topic of feelings, thoughts and questions as each comes up. As they are sharing, have someone note each response on a large sheet of paper or blackboard.

2. In these or similar words bring out the significance of the coming of the Holy Spirit to the people of Israel. *Israel hoped for the day when God in the power of the Spirit would reign in the world and bring an end to their experiences of oppression and exile. As it says in the Prophet Ezekiel: "O my people! I will put my spirit in you that you may live" (Ezekiel 37.14). As a people, Israel looked forward to this day, the Lord's day.*

3. Invite the participants to break into small groups and discuss the following questions from the Participants Book (page 52) or the blackline handout. After the group discussion, surface at random, reactions from the different groups.

   What does the gift of the Holy Spirit mean for us as a people—today?

   Where are the places in your neighborhood, city, state or

world that cry out for the spirit?

Where in your own life do you need to break through to a new horizon of the power of the Spirit?

Catholic Teaching (30 min)

1. Begin by singing "Veni Sancte Spiritus" (Taize) or another appropriate hymn to the Holy Spirit.

2. Present the church's teaching on Confirmation. Include the following points:

   • The sacrament of Confirmation is a sealing of baptism.

   • The sacrament of Confirmation is an initiation sacrament.

   • The Spirit is received at Baptism and at Confirmation the gifts of the Spirit are strengthened.

   • In confirmation there is a laying on of hands and an anointing with oil.

3. Use the following activities to help the participants integrate the points being made:

   • Ask the participants to move into small groups. Have cards with a gift of the spirit (wisdom, understanding, counsel, fortitude, knowledge, piety, fear of the Lord) written on each card. Distribute one card to each group and ask them to think about a person they know who exhibits this gift. Have them share their stories in the group and come up with a list of behaviors that exemplify that gift.

   • Explore the group's human experience of oil. Ask them to list all the kinds of oil they use in their daily life and what purpose each serves. Using their responses talk about the meaning of being anointed with oil in the sacrament of confirmation.

   • Read "The Church Says" in the Participant Book (page 53) or on the blackline handout.

Putting Faith Into Practice

Invite the participants to quietly reflect on their personal lives. Use the following questions as a guide: *How are you being called to respond to what has been presented in this session? What support do you need from the community to answer this call?* After a brief reflection period, ask them to share their responses in a small group.

Prayer

Together pray the following prayer:

   Leader: *Come, Holy Spirit, fill the hearts of your faithful.*

   Response: *And kindle in them the fire of your love.*

   Leader: *Send forth your Spirit and they shall be created.*

   Response: *And you will renew the face of the earth.*

   Leader: *Lord, by the light of the Holy Spirit, you have taught the hearts of your faithful. In the same Spirit help us to relish what is right and always rejoice in your consolation. We ask this through Christ our Lord.*

ORDINARY TIME

Second Sunday in Ordinary Time

The Word In Liturgy

Isaiah 62:1-5
Psalm 96:1-2, 2-3, 7-8, 9-10
1 Corinthians 12:4-11
John 2:1-11

The Second Sunday in Ordinary Time functions in the liturgical cycle as a kind of bridge, linking what has gone before with what is to come. Last Sunday's celebration of the Baptism of the Lord marked the close of the Christmas season, and began the first week of Ordinary Time. On this Sunday, in each year of the lectionary cycle, the Gospel is taken from John rather than the respective synoptic Gospel read throughout the remainder of Ordinary Time. Today's reading from John also completes a triad of "epiphany" texts (the "revelation" of Jesus to the Magi, at his baptism, and now at Cana) read in recent weeks. The Cana miracle is described by John as the "first" of Jesus' signs, and so it is a fitting beginning to Ordinary Time (although, as we will see next week, the gospel text read on the Third Sunday always has one of the synoptics' version of the beginning of Jesus' ministry). Introducing catechumens and candidates to the logic of the lectionary at the beginning of a major season can help to orient them and deepen their understanding of how the Church reads the scriptures in the framework of the liturgical cycle.

Today's reading comes from the third section (cc 56-66) of the Book of Isaiah, written in the turbulent years after Israel's return from exile in Babylon. The prophet writes to reassure the Jewish people at a time of national disillusionment and, for many, growing skepticism that Jerusalem would ever regain its previous splendor. Using images evocative of Yahweh's long history of rescuing Israel from dire straits, the prophet renews God's promise to restore Jerusalem to a place of honor and prestige among the nations. The familiar description of Israel as Yahweh's spouse is used to reassure the people that God's love is faithful and unbroken. The passage's rich marital imagery is certainly the reason why this text was

chosen to be read together with today's Gospel. In the responsorial psalm we have a classic expression of praise and thanksgiving on the lips of those who have experienced firsthand the saving deeds of the Lord.

Today and for the next six weeks of Ordinary Time, a semi-continuous reading will cover chapters 12, 13 and 15 from First Corinthians. In today's text, Paul is addressing the difficulties that had arisen in that community over the exercise of charismatic gifts. Arrogance and competition over whose gifts were more important threatened to divide the community. Paul is intent on showing that all of the gifts come from the one Spirit and are intended to build up the Body of Christ in a climate of harmony and mutual acceptance. Paul does not question the reality of the miraculous gifts that were apparently so manifest in the Corinthian community. But he does insist that all of these gifts were given "for the common good" (v 7), rather than to inflate any individual.

In today's reading from John, we hear the miracle at Cana described as the "first" of Jesus' signs which "revealed his glory" and as a result of which "his disciples believed in him" (v 11). In this brief allusion, we are given a clue to the highly symbolic nature of John's Gospel in general and of Jesus' miracles in particular. In John, no aspect of the narrative is casual; each detail points to a larger meaning, always connected to the Gospel's ultimate purpose: "so that you [the hearer of the Gospel] may come to believe that Jesus is the Messiah, the Son of God, and that through believing you may have life in his name." (20:31) The miracle of Cana, then, is about Jesus being revealed as the Messiah, the Holy One, in the midst of our ordinary human experience (e.g., at a marriage), transforming our "secular" reality into the fine wine of God's grace. Scholars debate how much John's Gospel intends any explicit sacramental reference here and elsewhere. But it is easy to see why this passage has been used by the Church over the centuries to deepen our understanding of how, in marriage, the action of Christ transforms the love of Christian spouses into a graced reality (i.e., a sacrament).

Catholic Doctrine

The Sacrament of Marriage

Love is our origin. Love is our constant calling. Love is our fulfillment in heaven. Everything the Catholic Church teaches about marriage begins with this proclamation. As a church, we know that in varying forms throughout history and in widely varying cultures, men and women have married one another in love.

Marriage is not simply a human institution, but is part of God's plan in creation (CCC 1603). The Old Testament scriptures speak eloquently about marriage and the love of a husband and wife for one another. With the coming of Christ, however, God in Jesus raised the marital covenant between baptized persons to the dignity of a sacrament (CCC 1601). This Sunday's gospel account reports how Jesus works his first sign, changing water into wine, at a wedding feast. By his presence at the wedding at Cana, the Church understands that Jesus confirmed the innate goodness of love in marriage. Thus, marriage becomes an effective sign of Christ's presence (CCC 1613).

In the eyes of the Church, what is this sacrament? Marriage between two baptized persons (a man and a woman who freely enter into a permanent, loving and faithful covenant with one another) shares in the fruitful love and unity that exists between Christ and the Church. Husband and wife assist each other in attaining holiness of life and in the rearing of children. Therefore, they have their own special place, their own gift and vocation, among the people of God (Rite of Marriage, Congregation of Rites, 19 March 1969, n. 1).

This sacrament is not a contract, but a covenant. Freely entered into, the marriage covenant cannot be dissolved until death because it is a total self-giving, one person to the other. Jesus himself taught this truth as determined by God (Matthew 19:6). The covenant between husband and wife in marriage is integrated into God's loving, covenant relationship with his people (CCC 1640). Jesus gives those who are married the ability to live up to the demands and expectations of marriage precisely through the gift of the sacrament (CCC 1650).

John Paul II, taking up themes taught by the Second Vatican Council, elaborates on the characteristics of conjugal love. In his apostolic exhortation, *Familiaris Consortio* (22 November 1981), he further clarifies the teaching of the Council, describing the love between husband and wife as involving a totality of body, instinct, power, emotion, and aspiration of the spirit and will, aiming at a deeply personal unity which goes beyond union in one flesh to encompass the formation of one heart and soul (FC, 19). This is, in part, offered as a rationale which demands the indissolubility of marriage

(CCC 1643). The Council itself had stipulated that along with the mutual self-giving of the two partners, the other purpose of marriage is procreation and the rearing of children (*Gaudium et Spes*, 7 December 1965, n 48).

However, since a valid marriage depends upon the free will of a husband and wife to truly enter into the sacrament, if the necessary freedom is lacking the Church can declare the union null. This declaration of nullity is commonly called an annulment (CCC 1629). This declaration is not effected through a civil divorce, but through a Church process. While some may consider the annulment process lengthy and intrusive, its purpose is to protect marriage as a symbol of God's unbreakable and loving fidelity to us (CCC 1647).

Thus the Church prays, "Father. . . By this sacrament your grace unites man and woman in an unbreakable bond of love and peace. You have designed the chaste love of husband and wife for the increase both of the human family and of your own family born in baptism. You are the loving Father of the world of nature; you are the loving Father of the new creation of grace. In Christian marriage you bring together the two orders of creation: nature's gift of children enriches the world and your grace enriches also your Church." (*Roman Missal*, Preface for Marriage I.)

Catholic Culture

Marriage is the only sacrament of the seven which is ordinarily administered by lay people. In the Latin rite, the sacrament is understood to be mutually conferred by the spouses upon one another. The priest or deacon witnesses the wedding, but the couple actually do the deed. In the eastern rite Catholic churches, the priest or bishop is the minister of the sacrament. He crowns the bridegroom and bride, to symbolize their covenant of love.

Programs of preparation for marriage, and for strengthening and enriching marriages, abound in the church. The *Book of Blessings* also indicates the high regard the church places on this sacrament and on the institution of marriage, listing blessings for a married couple on their anniversary and on other occasions, (n. 90), for an engaged couple (n. 95), for parents before and after childbirth (n. 236), for parents after a miscarriage (n. 279), for parents and an adopted child (n. 302).

Norwegian Catholic author Sigrid Undset (1882-1949), who won the Nobel Prize in 1928, wrote *Kristen Lavrensdatter*, a three-volume epic of a woman's life and faith, set in medieval Norway. Kristen's marriage plays a central role in the novel, which enjoyed great popularity among generations of Catholic readers and has never been out of print since its first publication in 1927.

Dismissal Catechesis (30 min)

Getting Started

1. For the center of the circle this week, leave the space empty, except for a lit candle.

2. Invited the candidates and catechumens to gather in the circle of chairs. Have instrumental music playing in the background as they are seated.

3. Pray Psalm 96, asking all to respond, "Sing to the Lord a new song, sing to the Lord all the earth." Pause between every two or three verses.

First Impressions

1. Encourage a general discussion of the observations of the group as they entered the church today. Try one of these questions: *What did you notice about the church environment today? Why were there no special decorations or symbols?* Explain that the Christmas season ended last week and that this time of the church year is known as Ordinary Time.

2. Invite the participants to share some of the images and symbols they can recall from the readings in this week's Liturgy of the Word. As they name these symbols and images, particularly from the first reading from Isaiah, print these on large pieces of paper and place them in the center of the circle.

3. Ask the group to share in pairs: *What feelings did these passages evoke in you? As you listened to the Word of God, what caused you to want to praise God?*

Making Connections

1. Turn the focus of the group to remember a time when they were disillusioned or disappointed in their relationship with their family, friends or with God. Invite them to share this time with another person in the group.

2. When they have finished, ask the group to recall what happened to change their disappointment and disillusionment into a feeling of joy or happiness. Direct the pairs to share, once again, using these questions to guide the discussion: *What caused the reversal? In hindsight, do you think was God at work to bring about this change? How do you understand God's faithfulness in your life?*

3. Summarize the discussion of the group and invite all to write down one thing they wish to remember from this session.

Prayer

- Song: "Sing a New Song" (Schutte), verse 1.
- Pause to recall those gifts from God for which we are all thankful.
- Invite the participants to name these aloud. After each naming, all respond: *"We are filled with gratitude for your gifts, O God."*
- Song: "Sing a New Song" (verses 2 and 3).

Extended Catechesis

SESSION FOCUS: *The Sacrament of Marriage*

Gathering

A. Sunday:

1. With the candle still lit and the printed papers, naming the images in the Scriptures still in the center of the circle, welcome the sponsors and team members into the circle. (If your gathering is in another space bring the candle and printed papers to the extended session)

2. Ask for quiet. Proclaim the gospel (John 2:1-11) and pray this reflection:

It is ordinary time, O Lord. . .
No fasting or feasting, just common, plain time.
Days drifting into nights, then dawning new days again.
Time for brushing teeth, feeding babies, changing the oil. . .
Plenty good time for cozy reading by the fire.
Time for dishes and dusting, fixing leaky faucets
Plenty good time for dunking doughnuts in hot, black coffee.
Ordinary time is your time to do your extraordinary miracles. . .
Changing
Water into wine, into ice, into snow;
Tears into laughter, into hugs, into full-blown kisses on the mouth.
Let us notice your ways of keeping ordinary time.
Help us keep time with You.

B. Weekday:

1. Use the same centerpiece as described in A.

2. Begin with the reflection in Gathering A to focus the group.
- First Reading: Isaiah 62:1-5
- Silent reflection
- Gospel: John 2:1-11
- Silent Reflection

The Word (30 min)

1. Refocus the attention of the group on the reflection on Ordinary Time asking: *What is this period in the liturgical year called Ordinary Time? Why do we need a break from feasting and fasting? How are your spiritual rhythms in sync with the liturgical rhythms?* Give some examples. This can be a general discussion, unless the group is too large and needs to be divided into smaller segments. Explain that Ordinary Time starts at the beginning of Jesus' ministry. This week, John's gospel tells the story of the miracle at Cana that was the 'first' of Jesus' signs. The lectionary will proceed next week to offer one of the synoptic gospel passages on the beginning of Jesus' ministry.

2. Invite the group to offer their thoughts on the scriptural images that are written and scattered in the center of the circle. Then, ask them to share their initial impressions of the scriptural passages. *What was particularly comforting about these readings? What phrases caught your attention?*

3. In these or your own words, summarize the Word in Liturgy section of Understanding This Sunday, focusing on the faithful and unbroken love of God.

   God's promise to restore Jerusalem to a place of honor among the nations is the focus of the first reading from Isaiah. The writer used the imagery of the marriage of God to Israel, after their return from the Babylonian exile, to indicate the tender love God has for the chosen people. This same love, which ideally exists in the marriage covenant, is further held in God's embrace when Jesus chose to revealed his glory by the miracle at Cana, a wedding feast. Through the lens of the gospel it is evident that Christ who had the power to change water into wine, also had the power to transform the ordinary love of spouses into a graced reality.

4. Gathering the participants into small groups, invite them to turn to the Participant Book (page 52) or to the blackline handout and complete the reflection on marriage and respond to the questions. After sufficient time for personal reflection, invite all to share in groupings of four, using the questions provided as a basis for their discussion.

5. Invite the small groups to share one thing from their discussion of the readings. Give them an opportunity to write in their Participant Book (page 53) or on the blackline handout those insights they wish to remember.

Catholic Teaching (30 min)

1. Summarize the teachings of the church on marriage, using the Catholic Doctrine section found in Understanding This Sunday. These points will need to be included.

   - Marriage is a covenant of love between the spouses, implying a total self-giving of one spouse to the other.

   - The sacrament of marriage continually offers God's grace, that is the power of God's love, Jesus presence and the energy of the Spirit, to sustain the covenant of love between spouses.

   - The love between husband and wife involves a totality of body, instinct, power, emotion and aspiration of the spirit and will aiming at a deeply personal unity which goes beyond union in one flesh to encompass the formation of one heart and soul.

   - This union of heart and soul is possible because of the union of love between God and God's people, gained for all in the life, death and resurrection of Jesus and sustained by the presence and power of the Holy Spirit.

2. Invite the group to gather into groups of four to discuss one or two of the following questions: *What examples of total self-giving can you name among married couples with whom you are acquainted? If you are married, when have you experienced God's grace help you and your spouse through a difficult time? How would you describe this 'union of heart and soul' spoken of by Pope John Paul II? What is your understanding of the difference between a contract and a covenant.*

3. After allowing a few of the small groups to share a summary of their discussion, open the group to a discussion of annulments, if that fits the needs of your participants. You may wish to ask a parish priest or a member of your diocesan tribunal to present the basis teaching of the church on annulments and be available after the session for further questions with those who wish to remain.

Putting Faith Into Practice

1. Several opportunities exist to help partners sustain and improve their marriage. If Marriage Encounter is available in your area, explain the essence of this couple's retreat to the group. It is essentially an opportunity for healthy marriages to better their relationship by teaching them how to communicate, particularly in expressing feelings and love between the spouses. Retrouville is another opportunity for couples to improve communication and spirituality when they are experiencing difficulties in their marriage.

2. Introduce the participants to prayers of blessing for ordinary and extraordinary occasions that occur in a marital relationship. Have available a copy of the *Book of Blessings* and Ed Hays' *Prayers for a Domestic Church* (Forest of Peace Books) for the group to peruse as samples of such prayers.

Prayer

To bring the session to a close, use the Preface for Marriage I as a prayer and close with the Prayer of Blessing found in RCIA #97 C, as you and the sponsors extend your hands over the group.

Third Sunday in Ordinary Time

Understanding this Sunday:

Background for Catechesis

The Word In Liturgy

Nehemiah 8:2-4, 5-6, 8-10
Psalm 19:8, 9, 10, 15
1 Corinthians 12:12-30 [or 12:12-14, 27]
Luke 1:1-4; 4:14-21

Following the return of the Jewish people to Jerusalem after their exile in Babylon, the task of rebuilding the nation was an imposing one: Not only were the temple and the holy city in ruins, but the religious fabric of society and the people's fidelity to the Mosaic Covenant were also in considerable disarray. Today's first reading comes from that era of rebuilding and reflects what was undoubtedly a pivotal event in the process of reconstituting the people's religious identity. In this text from Nehemiah we see what an important role the proclamation of the sacred scriptures played in renewing Israel's Covenant with Yahweh. The description is clearly meant to evoke a cultic setting (scholars point out that the description reflects later liturgical practice, both in the temple and the synagogue). As the Book of the Law is solemnly read, the people stand for the proclamation, hear an explanation of the reading, give their assent ("Amen, Amen") and then offer worship, recommitting themselves to the Covenant. The structural similarities of this description with our own order of worship in the Christian dispensation are remarkable.

The brilliance of Paul both as a theologian and as a pastoral leader is clearly evident in today's reading, a continuation from that of last week. In a single passage he skillfully interweaves solid teaching of Christian doctrine with sound pastoral advice. Paul is addressing the critical issue of the divisions that threatened to tear asunder the Corinthian community. But his pastoral admonitions about the behaviors the Corinthians must adopt are embedded in and flow from his reflections on the profound unity that Christians enjoy by virtue of their being members of a single body, with Christ as the head. Scholars still debate whether Paul was influenced more by Jewish thought, by gnosticism or by Greek philosophy in his use of the metaphor of the body. What is clear, however,

is that Paul has developed in a profound way the notion of the body as an image of the Christian community. The body's harmonious interrelationships among its various parts implies the mutual acceptance and support of one another's charisms that is required if the community is to function in a healthy manner. Pursuing this reflection on the orderly arrangement of parts in a body leads Paul, in the final section of the reading, to draw attention to how the various ministries of the church are ordered.

There are two quite distinct parts to the gospel reading: first, the literary introduction to Luke's two-volume history (Luke-Acts); and, second, the scene in chapter four that depicts the programmatic beginning of Jesus' ministry. Luke's deliberate adoption of familiar Greek literary convention in the composition of the formal preface to his work invites a reflection on the type of literature we are dealing with in his gospel. He makes it clear that he is writing for a previously evangelized audience, as they seek to understand more deeply and to be reassured of the reliability of the events already proclaimed to them. Catechumens and candidates will be able to identify with Theophilus, the named recipient of the work (and perhaps a wealthy patron of the author?), knowing that Luke says his aim is to catechize rather than to evangelize. In the second part of the reading we are offered a glimpse of how first-century Jews proclaimed the scriptures in the synagogue and of how Jesus himself interpreted the sacred text's meaning for his own ministry. Jesus' statement that the ancient prophecies of Isaiah were being fulfilled in his ministry is consistent with our own understanding of the word of scripture as living and active. The doctrinal focus of today's catechesis may therefore be on Sacred Scripture, that outstanding means by which God's living word is made present in every generation.

Catholic Doctrine

Sacred Scripture

God communicates to us by using words. Just as the hidden, eternal Word of God is made visible to us through the incarnation of Jesus, so too, the message of God is made intelligible to us through our human language (CCC 101).

Although there are many words which together constitute scripture, Catholic reverence for Scripture begins in the belief that there is only one single Word communicated by God to us (CCC 102). This one Word is Jesus Christ (Hebrews 1:1-3). St Augustine taught, "that it is one and the same Utterance that resounds in the mouths of all the sacred writers, since he who was in the beginning God with God has no need of separate syllables; for he is not subject to time." (En. in Ps. 103, 4,1: PL 37, 1378.) We humans need many syllables and words to express ourselves, but God's message to us is singular and personal, expressed in the person of Jesus.

Two important Catholic notions follow from this understanding of the personal revelation of God. First, since there is only one Word "spoken," then both Scripture and Tradition come from the same source. In other words, the divine self-revelation of the eternal Word is the source for both the Tradition of the Church and Scripture (CCC 80). Indeed, all things of this world were made through the Word (John 1:1-3 cited in CCC 291). Second, since the contents of the Bible are not merely human words, we do not treat the Bible as just any book, but as that which reveals to us the Word of God. We Catholics not only hold it in honor but we venerate Scripture as we venerate the Lord's Body (CCC 103).

We venerate Scripture because these sacred pages were composed through the agency of the Holy Spirit. Its authors were divinely inspired (CCC 105). The inspired books of the Bible teach the truth as God intends it to be revealed: firmly, faithfully and without error (*Dei Verbum*, 18 November 1965, n. 11).

This inspired and authoritative collection nourishes and challenges us as we follow Jesus. The Second Vatican Council thus directed that the treasure found in scripture be further opened up to the faithful "so that a richer fare may be provided . . .at the table of God's word" (*Sacrosanctum Concilium*, n. 51). Access to Scripture by all the faithful is emphatically encouraged by the Council (*Dei Verbum*, n. 22).

Catholics esteem every ministry of the Word, from the homily, to other forms of pastoral preaching, catechetics and instruction. All these ministerial activities seek to understand and apply the truth of God's revelation to our lives. They derive from the well-spring of the Word found in Scripture (*Dei Verbum*, n. 24). Indeed, in examining the life of the laity, the Council asserted that even through individual meditation on the Word of God one can discern the will of the divine and act accordingly (*Apostolicam Actuositatem*, 18 November 1965, n. 4).

Catechumens aptly exemplify our posture toward Scripture. Sunday after Sunday they are called to conversion by Scripture. They share with the whole community "at the table of God's Word" (RCIA no. 60). The teaching of St. Bonaventure applies not only to catechumens but to those who, fully initiated, continue to attend to the Word. He wrote, "The outcome or the fruit of reading holy Scripture is by no means negligible: it is the fullness of eternal happiness. In order to achieve this, we must study holy Scripture carefully, and teach it and listen to it. . ." (St. Bonaventure, *Prologus: Opera omnia* 5, 201-202 found in Liturgy of the Hours, Monday, Fifth Week Ordinary Time, Office of Readings).

Catholic Culture

Lectio divina (Latin for "divine reading") is a communal form of meditative reading of scripture which has its roots in the Monastic tradition. The Rule of St. Benedict assigned such reading for as much as two to three hours daily. Eventually, lectio divina expanded beyond Scripture itself to include biblical commentaries, writings of the Fathers of the church and works dealing with the spiritual and moral life (*Encyclopedia of Catholicism*, p. 762).

The Liturgy of the Hours, once celebrated by clergy and religious only, is now also celebrated by lay people as a result of the Second Vatican Council. This body of prayers, Scripture readings, intercessions and texts from the Fathers of the Church is prayed throughout the day and could be considered a form of lectio divina.

The New Testament scriptures were enthroned at every session of Vatican II as a "witness" to the proceedings. The book, a precious, hand-illuminated work of the renaissance, was made for the Duke of Urbino, and acquired by the Vatican by Pope Alexander VII (1655-1667). [Council Daybook (Vatican II, Sessions 1 and 2), Floyd Anderson, ed. NCWC, Washington, DC, 1965, p. 220]

Notes

Dismissal Catechesis (30 min)

Getting Started

1. Prepare the space ahead of time. Use a green cloth for the table in the center and have a candle ready.

2. Invite the catechumens and candidate to be seated quietly within a circle.

3. Light a candle and pray in these or similar words: *"Gracious God, you have revealed your word to us. Your word is always near to us. Open our minds to hear your word, our mouths to speak your word and our hearts to cherish your word. Amen."*

First Impressions

1. Take a few minutes to reflect on the Liturgy of the Word just celebrated.

2. Ask participants to silently recall words or phrases from the songs, prayers, scripture readings and homily.

3. Invite the catechumens and candidates to name a feeling, a thought, or phrase from the Liturgy of the Word that was particularly important to them today. In the large group draw out from them what the feeling, thought or phrase says to them about their own faith journey.

Making Connections

1. Invite discussion about their experience of the Scriptures by alluding to the gospel reference to Theophilus (a very early catechumen). Open the discussion with one or two of the following questions: *When were you first aware of the Scriptures? How comfortable are you with reading scripture on your own? Do you have a favorite Scripture story?*

2. Today's first reading and Gospel speak of the importance of the Bible. Ask them to recall their own Rite of Acceptance or Welcome and the ritual that was used to hand over the Word to them. Emphasize the importance of the Scriptures to their own formation. Continue the discussion by asking why they think the Bible was important to people in the past and how it is important to them and us today.

3. Mention questions that they might have about the Bible. Draw out terms used, such as: Sacred Scripture, Old and New Testaments, Hebrew Scripture, Christian Scripture, Torah, Gospels, epistles, psalms. Explain these terms if they are unfamiliar with them.

Prayer

Invite them to recall the person who introduced them to scripture. Pause for a few moments in silence to thank God for the person who has introduced them to this wonderful book. Close with the prayer *"Glory to the Father and to the Son and to the Holy Spirit, as it was in the beginning, is now, and will be forever. Amen."*

Extended Catechesis

SESSION FOCUS: *Sacred Scripture*

Gathering

A. Sunday:
Welcome sponsors, other team members and spouses. Invite them to form small groups. After a few minutes of quiet, proclaim the reading from Nehemiah and pause. Continue with the proclamation of the Gospel reading from Luke.

B. Weekday:
Welcome everyone. Begin with a Celebration of the Word such as:
- Song: Use the opening song from Sunday's liturgy.
- Sign of the Cross and Greeting
- Reading: Nehemiah 8:2-4, 5-6, 8-10
- Quiet
- Alleluia
- Gospel: Luke 1:1-4; 4:14-21

The Word (30 min)

1. Use these words from Understanding This Sunday's material to situate Nehemiah's passage.

   The Israelites have returned to Jerusalem after the Babylonian exile not only to find the temple in ruins, but also their adherence to the Mosaic Covenant to be very strained. Ezra, the prophet, reminds the people of the importance of God's Word. The people weep in response to his words. Perhaps they had forgotten their story; the story that made them the people of God.

2. In small groups, discuss how stories help us to know who we are. Use the following questions as a guide: *Does your family have a group of stories that are told and retold at family gatherings? If so share one of them with the group along with what you think the story tells people to about the family. What would happen if that story never got told again, if it were forgotten?*

3. Emphasize that when we forget the stories we forget important aspects of who we are as a person or as a family. Make the parallel with Scriptures. Without these stories we forget that we are the people of God.

4. Reread the gospel and invite the participants to name what their response would have been if they had been present in the synagogue of Nazareth when Jesus proclaimed that today the Scriptures were fulfilled in their hearing. Explore what they would have heard when Jesus proclaimed a year of favor from the Lord. What does it mean for us today?

5. Summarize the discussion.

Catholic Teaching (30 min)

1. Explore the meaning of the word 'bible'—a collection of books. Describe how the Bible came to be written down. Be clear that it is not a chronological nor historical book, though it contains events of history. The authors of the books were divinely inspired. They teach the truth as God intends it to be revealed: firmly, faithfully and without error. Be clear that divine inspiration does not mean that God dictated verbatim the words to be written. Consult paragraph 11 of *Dei Verbum*, a document from the Second Vatican Council.

2. View a video such as Introduction to the Scriptures from the series, **Echoes of Faith**, RCL Enterprises, or *How the Bible Came to Be*, from the **Scripture From Scratch** series, Franciscan Communications. Discuss the insights gained from the video.

OR . . .

3. Clarify the importance of Scripture for Catholics. Use these or similar words:

    God communicates to us by using words. God's message to us is singular and personal, expressed in the person of Jesus, who is the Word of God. Since there is only one Word "spoken," Scripture and Tradition come from the same source. Because the contents of the Bible are not merely human, but come from God, we venerate it. The Bible reveals to us the Word of God. We believe that Jesus is truly present in the Word proclaimed in the Liturgy, as stated in paragraph 7 of the Constitution on Sacred Liturgy. Thus, catechumens and candidates are fed on the Word of God and nourished by it to go forth to live the Word which has taken root within them.

OR . . .

4. Read The Church Says in the Participant Book (page 59) or on the blackline handout.

5. Have ready several translations of today's Gospel passage, Luke 1:1-4; 4:14-21. Share how these translations are different. Briefly explain what biblical scholarship offers us and that each translation has something to give to us.

Putting Faith Into Practice

1. Discuss the importance of reading the Bible as a means to help us understand how we are to live today.

2. Share with the groups some examples of liturgical celebrations based on the Word, such as the Liturgy of the Hours, the Wake Service from the Order of Christian Funerals, and a Liturgy of the Word described in the Book of Blessings.

3. Encourage daily reading of the Bible. Suggest reading the Gospel or the Psalm of the day. Tell them how to find out about the Scripture readings of the day.

Prayer

Invite everyone to stand. Have the sponsors face their catechumen or candidate and place a hand on their shoulder. Celebrate a Minor Exorcism, using RCIA #94 H. The prayer will need to be adapted if candidates are present.

Fourth Sunday in Ordinary Time

Understanding this Sunday:

Background for Catechesis

The Word In Liturgy

Jeremiah 1:4-5, 17-19
Psalm 71:1-4, 5-6, 15, 17
1 Corinthians 12:31-13:13 [or 13:4-13]
Luke 4:21-30

In this early period of the season called "Ordinary Time," our first reading and Gospel deal with the beginning of the prophetic ministry of Jeremiah and of Jesus. The passage from the opening of the Book of Jeremiah is a classic example of how the Jewish scriptures describe God's call of an individual to be a prophet. The divine initiative is highlighted ("Before I formed you . . . before you were born," [v 5]); and the nature of the prophet's ministry is anticipated, both its universal aspect (" . . . a prophet to the nations," [v 5]), as well as the resistance he will encounter (" . . . they will fight against you," [v 19]). The prophet is reassured that God will protect him from his enemies and enable him to carry out his mandate. Today's reading does not include the prophet's response, and this tends to focus our attention even more on God's role in the encounter. Two important themes from the Jeremiah reading will reappear in today's Gospel: the mission of the prophet to the nations, and the inevitability of resistance to his ministry. The psalm expresses the sentiments of one who encounters opposition but trusts deeply in God's protection. One can envision both Jeremiah and Jesus praying this psalm at different points in their respective careers.

Today's text from 1 Corinthians picks up where last week's ended. The opening verse of today's reading reminds us of the larger context for this passage: Paul's concern over rivalries within the community, apparently centered on whose charismatic gifts were more important. Paul introduces his famous hymn about charity with the promise that he will show them a "more excellent way," (v 31) i.e., a superior charism. Some scholars believe that the hymn which follows was borrowed by Paul from another source. Paul inserts it here to reinforce his admonition that the most critical need in the Corinthian community is for jealousies and contentions to cease and to be replaced by mutual acceptance and love.

Last week we read the first half of the story of Jesus in the synagogue at Nazareth. Today, in the second half of that story, the focus is on the angry reaction of Jesus' audience to his claim that in his ministry he is fulfilling the messianic prophecy of Isaiah. In the face of their resistance and rejection, Jesus points to the stories of Elijah and Elisha who also brought God's saving message to the Gentiles. Commentators point out that in this passage Luke is antici-pating a fundamental theme of his Gospel and a basic truth about the prophetic ministry (both for Jesus and for the early Church). In reaching out to those most desperately in need of salvation (the Gentiles), Jesus would encounter resistance from his fellow Jews, but he would persevere and would continue steadfastly "on his way" (v 30). Luke intends for this example of Jesus to be followed by Jesus' disciples as well. Preaching to the outcast and steadfast perseverance in the face of opposition are fundamental to the Christian's baptismal call as a prophet, which may be the focus of today's catechesis.

Catholic Doctrine

Our Identity as Prophets

As described in the Hebrew scriptures, a prophet is one who speaks the word of God. Prophets played a remarkable role in Israel's history. In times when Israel's faith was compromised or undermined, it erupted with new force through the word of the prophets. The prophet saw life from the perspective of God and preached accordingly. In that sense the prophet could be said to "speak for" or on the behalf of God (*The Collegeville Pastoral Dictionary of Theology*, p. 784). Old Testament prophets frequently "enacted" their prophecies and warned the people of the consequences of their activities. They also formed the people in the hope of God's salvation and the promise of redemption (CCC 64). Some examples of Old Testament prophets are: Moses, Elijah, Amos, Hosea, Isaiah, and Jeremiah.

Although it does not describe his entire identity, Jesus functions as a prophet. In Old Testament times, those who were called and set apart for a special lifelong task by God (priests, kings, and some prophets) were anointed. The term *Christ*, from the Greek translation of the Hebrew word "messiah," which means "anointed," indicates the prophetic mission of Jesus in that some prophets were anointed for their task. Because Jesus fulfills God's message of love and concern for the world he was anointed for his mission as priest, prophet and king (CCC 436).

By baptism believers share in the mission of Jesus. The newly baptized are anointed and the Church prays:

> *God the Father of our Lord Jesus Christ has freed you from sin and given you a new birth by water and the Holy Spirit, and welcomed you into his holy people. He now anoints you with the chrism of salvation. As Christ was anointed Priest, Prophet, and King, so may you live always as a member of his body, sharing everlasting life.* (Rite of Infant Baptism, n 98.)

But as the prayer indicates, this share in the identity of Christ as prophet, is given to the entire people claimed for Christ by this sacrament. The Second Vatican Council teaches, "The holy People of God shares also in Christ's prophetic office: it spreads abroad a living witness to him, especially by a life of faith and love . . ." (*Lumen Gentium*, n. 12).

Catholics believe that our baptismal identity in Christ as prophets empowers us to spread the good news, as Jesus commanded (Matthew 28:18-20). Indeed, the Council is emphatic, proclaiming that the Church is "*driven* by the Holy Spirit to do her part for the full realization of the plan of God, who has constituted Christ as the source of salvation for the whole world" (*Lumen Gentium*, n. 17, emphasis added).

Thus those who are baptized are not prophets in the sense of Old Testament prophets. That age ended with John the Baptist. A new age is inaugurated in Christ who commands us to be prophets of the gospel, going to the ends of the earth with this good news.

Those of us who share in Christ's identity and mission knowingly accept the task of witnessing to and spreading the gospel in spite of the hardships it may entail. It is with this understanding that prior to their baptism as infants and prior to adults being welcomed into the catechumenate, the first ritual action the Church celebrates is their being signed with the cross.

Catholic Culture

St. Therese of Lisieux (the "Little Flower") and St. Francis Xavier are the patron saints of the missions. Therese, a Carmelite nun, was given the name Therese of the Child Jesus and the Holy Face (1873-97). She died of tuberculosis but not before she had completed an autobiography detailing not so much the events of her life as the action of God's loving grace in those events—in spite of the great suffering she experienced. Francis, a Jesuit priest (1506-52), undertook missionary work in India and Japan. He died while attempting to enter China to begin more missionary efforts there. (*Encyclopedia of Catholicism*, "Therese of Lisieux," and "Francis Xavier," p. 1251 and 543.)

Contemporary examples of people who embody a positive response to their own share in Christ's prophetic identity are Dorothy Day (1897-1980) and Archbishop Oscar Romero (1917-1980). Day, a convert to Catholicism, founded the Catholic Worker movement in the United States, embraced voluntary poverty, opened a house of hospitality and a farm commune. Romero, as bishop of San Salvador, preached against the violence occasioned by attempts at land reform and publicly condemned human rights abuses. He was assassinated while celebrating Mass on March 24, 1980. (*Encyclopedia of Catholicism*, "Day, Dorothy M." and "Romero, Oscar Arnulfo" p. 395 and 1137.)

Notes

SESSION PLAN: Fourth Sunday in Ordinary Time

Dismissal Catechesis (30 min)

Getting Started

1. Gather in a circle around a center table with a cloth, candle, oil of catechumens, and place for the lectionary.

2. Invite all into a moment of silence. Ask everyone to picture God forming them in their mother's womb for a special purpose.

3. Pray: *God, you formed us in our mothers' wombs. You know us well, and you appoint us to speak your word to others in our world. Let your word deepen in us. Speak your word to us now in our time together. We ask this through Christ our Savior. Amen.*

First Impressions

Ask participants: *What one image from today's hymns or scriptures do you remember?* Then ask them to choose one image that appeals to them and talk about this in pairs. Invite each pair to give a summary in the large group. Briefly highlight the variety of responses.

Making Connections

1. State as an introduction: *Today's readings present Jeremiah's call to be a prophet and Jesus beginning to live his ministry as a prophet. Prophets hear God's word spoken within them.* Ask the participants: *What word did God speak in your heart in today's liturgy?* Invite some reflection, and then a sharing in pairs. Elicit some large group sharing. Comment on their responses.

2. Recall the moments of Jeremiah's call:

   *God said that God formed Jeremiah in the womb,
   God knew Jeremiah even before this,
   and that before Jeremiah was born God dedicated him.*

   Ask the participants: *What is your own sense of how God has formed you, known you, dedicated you?* After this sharing invite some large group response. Facilitate the conversation.

3. Ask the participants: *What do you want to remember from todays word or sharing?* Go around the circle for this sharing.

Prayer

1. Invite the participants: *Place your hands on your hearts as a gesture to acknowledge that you have been formed by God and are dedicated by God.* Pause for a moment of silence.

2. Ask: *As you sit with your hands on your heart, what do you want to pray God for?* Invite this sharing in the large group. Summarize their words in a prayer.

3. Sing the Psalm refrain from the liturgy (Psalm 71) or Lord, You Have the Words (Psalm 19).

Extended Catechesis

SESSION FOCUS: *The Christian Call to Prophecy.*

Gathering

A. Sunday:

1. Welcome all who are gathered. Ask people to sit in small groups.
2. Briefly summarize the sharing during the dismissal.
3. Invite everyone into a few minutes of silence. Proclaim the Gospel, Luke 4:21-30.
4. If a priest or deacon is able to be present, celebrate an anointing with the oil of catechumens . Begin with a brief explanation: *The church anoints catechumens with oil, called the oil of catechumens. The Christian call to live as a prophet is difficult. The oil of chrism used in baptism and in confirmation conveys our sense of a special role of being a prophet and living the Christian faith. This anointing with the oil of catechumens, however, is a strengthening to live courageously as a Christian while preparing for baptism.*
5. Celebrate the anointing with the oil of catechumens as in the ritual text #102 and #103.

B. Weekday:

1. As the group gathers in a circle, greet and welcome each person.
2. Going around the circle, ask the participants: How have you spoken God's word to someone since Sunday?
3. Lead a celebration of the Word with an anointing with the oil of catechumens if a priest or deacon is able to be present.

   • Sign of the Cross, Greeting, Invitation to hear God's word
   • First Reading: Jeremiah 1:4-5, 17-19
   • Sing: Psalm 71
   • Silence
   • Gospel: Luke 4:21-30
   • Silence
   • Homily: Use the explanation of the anointing with the oil of catechumens as in A. SUNDAY.
   • Anointing with the oil of catechumens as in the ritual text #102 and #103.

The Word (30 min)

1. Give input on the Gospel:
   Today's Gospel is a continuation of last Sunday's ,when we heard that Jesus claimed in his hometown of Nazareth that the prophetic words of Isaiah are fulfilled in him. Today's passage goes on to speak of the response of indignation of the townspeople to the point of literally throwing him out of town.

2. Then ask the participants: *When have you experienced speaking the truth and feeling the rejection or scorn of others? What was this like for you?* Participants may use the corresponding section of the Participant Book to help with this reflection. Ask for a few moments of silence, invite sharing in small groups. When they are finished, ask each group to share a response with the large group.

2. Give more input on the Gospel.
   Luke continues to assert that Jesus has come for all people, including the Gentiles as represented by Elijah and Elisha.

   Ask the participants to discuss one of the following questions: *What words of Jesus do you find difficult to hear? What people or groups of people do you find hard to include?* Participants may use the Participant Book (page 60) or the blackline handout, for this reflection. Then invite some sharing in small groups.

3. Ask each small group to give a brief summary of their sharing in the large group. Make connections from their comments to today's Gospel. State the following:

   This Gospel cuts into Christian experience in two ways. First, disciples of Christ at times are called to speak the truth in various situations. Second, God continues to challenge Christians beyond our own limited view of situations and people.

   In small groups, ask participants to discuss: *Which of these two ways do you sense God is speaking to you today in this gospel? Are you being called to speak the truth in some way? Or are you being called to see someone or some situation with new eyes?*

Catholic Teaching (30 min)

1. Present a teaching about prophets. Consult the Catholic Doctrine section.

   Prophets hear God's word within themselves, and know they are called to speak this word to others. Prophets did not tell the future. However, God's word at times stated that unless people changed their lives, there would be a negative result. Prophets knew themselves called by God, as in todays reading from Jeremiah. The prominent prophets in the Christian Bible are Jeremiah, Isaiah, Ezekiel, and Daniel. Because prophets were usually speaking a difficult truth, they often were not received well. Jeremiah was even thrown in a pit. Christians are called to speak a prophetic voice. The Church continues to make statements for human rights, including Rerum Novarum, Pacem in Terris, and the U.S. Peace Pastoral.

2. Ask for some response in the large group to the following questions: *Who are some people you know who have spoken Gods word to the world? Think of people in your family, in your city or neighborhood, or people you know about nationally or internationally. What is the word this person spoke? What is the effect of this word? What happened to the person speaking it?*

Comment on their examples, and include your own:
- Cesar Chavez, who spoke for the rights of the United Farm Workers
- Martin Luther King, Jr., though not of the Catholic community, speaking for racial equality
- Dorothy Day working with and for the poor;
- Jean Vanier, involved with L'Arche community; and Oscar Romero, Bishop of El Salvador, killed as a result of standing with the poor.

OR . . .

Have participants use the reflection questions in the corresponding section of the Participant Book about their personal call to be a prophet.

Putting Faith Into Practice

Ask the participants: *What is the word of God you have heard within and know needs to be spoken? What is the word you are willing to speak this week?* After a moment of reflection or writing in the Participant Book (page 61) or on the blackline handout, invite them to share their response in the small group.

OR . . .

Before ending your session, have participants write a letter about a specific issue to an elected official, corporation, etc., making a statement for human rights.

Prayer

Invite participants to touch the lips of another in their small group during this prayer.

Pray: *O God, you have created, formed, and appointed us to speak your word of truth and justice for others. Open our lips. Put your word in our mouths. Give us the strength we need to live as Jesus calls us. Help us stand and walk straight. Empower us with your love and truth. We ask this in the name of Jesus. Amen.*

Fifth Sunday in Ordinary Time

The Word In Liturgy

Isaiah 6:1-2a, 3-8
Psalm 138:1-2, 2-3, 4-5, 7-8
1 Corinthians 15:1-11 [or 15:3-8, 11]
Luke 5:1-11

Today's first reading, from the Book of Isaiah, describes the prophet's mystical encounter with Yahweh, in which he experienced a divine call to be the Lord's prophet. The text is a classic expression of the human person's encounter with what has been called the *mysterium tremendum et fascinans* (Rudolf Otto), the Absolute Mystery of God, which we find both terrifying and seductively attractive ("Woe is me . . . Here I am; send me!"). The vision of Isaiah is a revelation of the awesome majesty of the infinite God, yet it also discloses a divinity in relationship with human creatures who wishes those creatures to know something of the divine person. The unknowable One offers a glimpse of his divine Being, and in turn directs the prophet to speak to the people God's own words. This scene captures in powerful fashion the conviction shared by both Judaism and Christianity that we are privileged recipients of the divine self-disclosure we term "revelation," and that this revelation is passed on to us through the medium of human messengers. ("Whom shall I send?") Psalm 138 and the refrain chosen for today ("In the sight of the angels I will sing your praises Lord") highlight the appropriate response of Isaiah (and us) to the theophany: praise and thanksgiving. In the context of the Liturgy of the Word, this response reaffirms our belief that the Word of God proclaimed in our midst is a continuing encounter with divine revelation.

One of the issues Paul needed to address with the Corinthian church was the truth of Christ's resurrection. Apparently gnostic sympathizers within the community were downplaying or even dismissing the bodily resurrection of Jesus, and Paul immediately saw how such teaching undercut Christian faith. He chooses very carefully words that stress the authenticity of the message they had received at his hand: "proclaimed . . . received . . . handed on . . . " In addition, he makes a point of his own authority as an apostle ("by the grace of God"), as well as the reliability of the entire apostolic witness ("then to all the apostles") to the truth of the resurrection. In addressing this early attack on the integrity of Christian faith, Paul illustrates how from the earliest period the Christian community relied on the apostolic college to guarantee fidelity to the truth of the Gospel and to pass on God's revelation in unadulterated form. What is at stake, as far as Paul is concerned, is nothing less than their salvation ("the good news through which also you are being saved, if you hold firmly to the message . . .").

In describing the call of Peter, Luke draws on Mark's earlier version as well as other sources. The miraculous catch of fish described on this occasion is found in John's Gospel after the resurrection, not before as here. Instead of Peter receiving an abrupt call from a virtual stranger, Luke has already told of Jesus' cure of Simon Peter's mother-in-law. Here he describes Jesus as having preached "the word of God" (v. 1) from Peter's boat prior to directing him to set out into "deep water" for a catch (an image perhaps intended for the encouragement of Luke's community in their efforts to spread the Gospel). Luke is making the point that Christian mission flows from hearing the word of God and from having received Jesus's call to discipleship. The final phrase of the reading ("they left everything and followed Jesus") is an important Lucan theme, i.e., that discipleship requires the willingness to renounce everything for the sake of the Gospel.

The sharing of divine revelation commissioned in the call of the prophet (Isaiah) and the call of the first disciples (Luke), as well as Paul's emphasis upon the faithful handing on of the truth he received (1 Corinthians), suggest that the concept

of *tradition* may be an appropriate focus for doctrinal catechesis today.

Catholic Doctrine

Tradition

Jesus, a human person, the Son of God, called other persons, his disciples, to follow him in preaching the gospel, the good news of the kingdom of God to the world. Peter and the others accepted his invitation to follow him and, witnessing his life and mission over a number of years saw Jesus, their teacher and master go to the cross, after which they experienced him risen from the dead. They fervently preached Jesus as the Crucified, Risen One, the Savior of the world and the definitive revelation of God, until they themselves were martyred. They preached orally, passing on the good news of Jesus' life, his works and the significance of his resurrected life, under the direction of the Holy Spirit. Eventually they transmitted the good news in writing, either themselves or those associated with them (CCC 76).

The revelation of God to us is not merely a long-ago event that focuses on the role of those first apostles. We Catholics believe that while nothing essential is added to the content of revelation, nevertheless we continues even today to deepen our understanding of that unique revelation. As the Second Vatican Council teaches, the God who spoke in the past "continues to converse" with the Church (*Dei Verbum*, 18 November 1965, n. 8).

There are two ways in which this continuing conversation takes place, through Scripture and Tradition. In an earlier Doctrine section (Third Sunday Ordinary Time), mention was made of Tradition, in that both it and Scripture issue forth from the divine self-revelation of God. But what exactly does the Catholic Church mean by "Tradition?"

In discerning the significance of the good news of Jesus Christ for today's world, the Church has not been set adrift. We believe that the teaching authority of the original apostles has been handed on to their successors, the bishops (CCC 77). Through their teaching, the living gospel is preserved and the truth of that good news is made present to us now.

We have inherited from the apostles the *depositum fidei*, the sacred deposit of the faith, contained in Scripture and Tradition (CCC 84). Tradition, handed on down through the ages in the Church is "everything that serves to make the People of God live their lives in holiness and increase their faith. In this way the Church, in her doctrine, life and worship, perpetuates and transmits to every generation all that she herself is, all that she believes" (*Dei Verbum*, n. 8).

Therefore, Tradition is characterized as both a process and as having a content. Its process is made up of the teaching, life

and worship of the Church by which the truth of revelation is handed on to successive generations. Its content comprises the whole life of the Church which furthers holiness, that is, all that the Church is and believes. (*Encyclopedia of Catholicism*, "Tradition," p. 1261).

St. Irenaeus (d. ca. 202) witnesses to this notion of the living body of the Church which hands on the message of salvation in an unbroken succession. He wrote in the second century:

> True knowledge is the teaching of the Apostles. . .passed down through the succession of bishops in charge of the church. . . which has come down to our own time, safeguarded, without. . . addition or subtraction. . . avoiding danger and blasphemy; and the special gift of love, which is more precious than knowledge, more glorious than prophecy, and which surpasses all other spiritual gifts. (*Adversus Haereses*, IV.xxxiii.8, found in *The Christian Theology Reader*, Alister E. McGrath, ed., Blackwell Publishers, Inc., Cambridge, Massachusetts, 1995, p. 260.)

Scripture and Tradition, which serve to transmit revelation, build up the living body of the Church as it cherishes and practices the love of God.

Catholic Culture

The installation liturgy for a pastor expresses how a particular ministry should serve the living body of the Church and its sacred deposit of faith. At that liturgy, the new pastor makes a Profession of Faith whose text (the Apostle's Creed) can be recited along with the entire body of the faithful. Then the pastor continues with a statement called the "Oath of Fidelity," praying, in part, "With firm faith I also believe everything contained in God's word, written or *handed down in tradition* and proposed by the Church, whether by way of solemn judgment or through the ordinary and universal magisterium, as divinely revealed and calling for faith." (*"Rescript from an Audience of His Holiness Containing Formulas for the Profession of Faith and the Oath of Fidelity,"* AAS v. 81, 1989, p. 1189. Emphasis added.)

The presentation of the Creed and the Lord's Prayer to catechumens takes place during the period of Purification and Enlightenment (or, for pastoral reasons, during the period of the Catechumenate). We believe these texts express the heart of the Church's faith and prayer (RCIA, n 147). These treasures are handed on orally (the word "tradition" comes from the Latin for "handed down" or "handed over") and the elect listen and "receive" them.

Dismissal Catechesis (30 min)

Getting Started

1. Prepare the center table with a lighted incense coal, a container of incense, a lighted candle, and place for the lectionary. Gather in a circle of chairs around the table.

2. Invite participants into a moment of silent prayer. Then pray in these or similar words:

   God, You have given us Jesus the Christ to speak your word to us, and you invite us, his followers to speak your word. Help us now to hear your word in our hearts and in one another. We pray in the name of Jesus. Amen.

First Impressions

1. Note: Because today's first reading and Gospel have the sense of God's invitation to hand on God's word to others, today's liturgy lends itself to the Presentation of the Creed. If the Creed is presented to the elect by the community, then this section would begin with the elect sharing their experience of being presented with the Creed. Discussion on how faith is transmitted, the many ways they have received their faith and also hand it on to others, and the living tradition of faith would replace some or all of the dismissal session described below.

2. State that today's scripture readings are filled with striking images. Ask participants to state aloud an image they recall from the scriptures or hymns. Note the variety of the images. State that the words in the call of Isaiah, "Holy, Holy, Holy" have become part of our liturgy.

Making Connections

1. Ask participants to recall a time when they experienced God as awesome, powerful, or majestic. Then ask them to remember how they felt during this experience. Invite them to share this experience and their feelings in pairs. Then invite some large group response.

2. Recall that last week the scriptures told of Jeremiah's call to be a prophet. Todays scripture presents both the call of Isaiah and of Peter, James, and John. Ask participants to recall a time they experienced being called by God. Invite a sharing of these moments. Explore with them some of the elements of the call, e.g., their feelings of fear or excitement, willingness, or timing. Ask them to talk about the way in which they responded.

3. Invite participants to choose a word that describes their experience of call. Go around the circle and name this word.

Prayer

Ask participants to hold their hands open with palms up in front of them as a sign of wanting to open to Gods call. Ask them each to name something they need and want to pray for to enable them to follow Gods call. Then pray: *God we bring before you our desire to respond to your call, and our needs. We are grateful for your call. Make us your faithful followers, now and forever. Amen.*

Extended Catechesis

SESSION FOCUS: *Tradition*

Gathering

A. Sunday:

1. Welcome all who have gathered. Ask everyone to sit in small groups.

2. Briefly summarize the dismissal sharing.

3. Invite everyone into a moment of quiet. Sing the refrain of Psalm 138 used at the liturgy. Proclaim the Gospel.

B. Weekday:

1. Welcome all the participants into the circle. Ask participants to go around the circle and respond to this question: *Since Sunday how have you shared who God is with someone either through a word or action?* Then lead a celebration of the Word.

   - Gathering Hymn: Here I am, Lord vs. 1,2
   - Sign of the Cross, Greeting
   - First Reading: Isaiah 6:1-2a,3-8
   - Sing: Psalm 138:1-2, 2-3, 4-5, 7-8
   - Second Reading: 1 Corinthians 15:1-11
   - Sing: Alleluia
   - Gospel: Luke 5:1-11
   - Silence
   - Hymn: Here I am, Lord vs. 3

The Word (30 min)

1. Give input about the Gospel using the following points:

   - Today's Gospel passage is near the beginning of Jesus ministry.
   - Jesus uses something that was part of the life experience of Peter—fishing—to get his attention.
   - Both Isaiah and Peter felt unworthy to be called to speak Gods word.

   Gather the participants into pairs and ask them to discuss this questions: *How have you been called to speak God's word? How did you feel to be called by God to do this?* When the groups are finished, invite some general sharing of this experience in the large group.

2. Make the following points:
   - Both Isaiah and Peter felt humbled.
   - Being humble means being who one is, not more or less, and comes from "humus," of the earth. When humble we know that we are human and belong to God.
   - Isaiah portrays a great, powerful God. Peter recognizes Jesus greatness in the great catch of fish.
   - For God, Isaiah's and Peter's humanity is not a problem.

   Ask participants to reflect on this question: *What effect does feeling humbled have on the actual doing of God's work?* Refer participants to the reflection in the Participants Book (page 62) or on the blackline handout. Then invite some large group response. In the discussion highlight the sense that it is God who makes things happen, not us. Through human actions and words it is God's grace that is acting.

3. State the following:

   The church's mission is to bring God's saving work to all people. This mission is symbolized in Luke's gospel through Jesus call to Peter to go out and fish for others. Ask participants to be alert to other aspects of Peter's call as you proclaim the Gospel again. Proclaim the Gospel. Invite participants to name what they hear. Include the following points:
   - God uses people to continue God's work.
   - God calls people through real experiences to be part of God's work.
   - The gospel provides the wonderful metaphor of catching people.
   - The response of leaving everything, of total commitment.

Catholic Teaching (30 min)

1. State the following: *The Bible contains stories of different peoples' experiences of who God is. God today continues to reveal who he is to people through various human experiences.* Ask participants to reflect on the following question: *What are some of the ways you experience God in your life?* Encourage the Catholics to think beyond their experiences of Sacraments and Mass. Refer participants to the reflection exercise in the Participant Book (page 62) or on the blackline handout. Then invite some large group sharing.

2. Provide some input on revelation including the following points:
   - Revelation literally means an unveiling of who God is.
   - We experience God in human experiences, through people, and in nature.
   - In Biblical times God's revelation occurred through creation, theophanies, dreams, prophecy, and historical events.
   - Jesus is the fullest revelation of who God is.

   - Revelation will be completed with the Second Coming of the Lord.
   - Revelation includes both scripture and tradition.
   - Revelation is a living, dynamic process as well as a body of content.
   - The church clarifies the revelation that is meant for the entire church community through its teaching. Individuals may have private revelations that are not meant for the whole church.

3. In the large group, ask participants to respond to these questions: *What are some truths contained in the church's revelation? What are the ways the church hands on this revelation?* Include scripture, liturgy, and ministry if not stated by participants. Then ask: *What are some examples of private revelation that are not meant for the entire church?*

4. Emphasize that God's revelation is meant for all people, even people we might naturally feel some distaste for. Then ask: *Which groups of people is the church called to take God's word?* Describe real ways this might happen.

OR . . .

Use the reflection in the Participant Book (page 62) or on the blackline handout to enable participants to understand more about revelation.

Putting Faith Into Practice

State that: *God uses humans, such as Peter and us, to continue the process of deepening our understanding of what has been revealed in Christ.* Ask the participants to reflect on the following question: *What is one way you are able to help another, someone you know or someone who is outside of your normal sphere of living, to experience who God is before next Sunday?* Participants may wish to write this action in the Participant book (page 63) or on the blackline handout. Then invite them to share in pairs this action they commit themselves to this week.

Prayer

Light the incense coal. Ask participants to reflect on this question: *What is your prayer or intercession for what you need from God to bring an experience of who God is to another?* Going around the circle, invite each participant to take a piece of incense, and put it on the coal while praying their prayer in silence or aloud. Conclude by singing one verse of "Here I am, Lord."

Sixth Sunday in Ordinary Time

Understanding this Sunday:
Background for Catechesis

The Word In Liturgy

Jeremiah 17:5-8
Psalm 1:1-2, 3, 4, 6
1 Corinthians 15:12, 16-20
Luke 6:17, 20-26

The prophet Jeremiah preached at a point of great moral decay in the Jewish people's history, warning them of impending disaster if they did not repent of their sins and renew their fidelity to the covenant with Yahweh. Of particular concern to Jeremiah was the manner in which the kings of Israel were making alliances with various pagan nations. In Jeremiah's eyes, seeking security through reliance on the military might of their neighbors was tantamount to placing faith in the pagan gods of those nations. Today's reading reflects a rhetorical style typical of wisdom sayings, in which blessings and curses are juxtaposed to emphasize the only viable path to true happiness: reliance on God alone. The lush imagery associated with a desert oasis, contrasted with the stark picture of a "lava waste, a salt and empty earth," would have evoked powerful associations in the mind of Jeremiah's contemporaries. In the background of this passage is a similar text from Deuteronomy, in which the author makes explicit his appeal and what is ultimately at stake in Israel's choice: "I have set before you life and death, the blessing and the curse. Choose life, then, that you and your descendants may live." (30:19) The selection of Psalm 1 today is an obvious one, given that scholars feel its composition was inspired by this very section from Jeremiah. The psalm refrain ("Happy are they who trust in the Lord") underlines the common theme found in both the first reading and today's Gospel.

Paul devotes all of Chapter 15 of his first letter to the Corinthians to a consideration of Christ's resurrection. In today's passage, we are given a clue as to why this topic has drawn his attention. Apparently, some in the community were under the influence of gnosticism and other currents of Greek philosophy that negated the body in favor of a belief in the immortality of the soul. These were saying "there is no resurrection of the dead" (v. 12). Paul argues the case against them forcefully, using a relentless logic that leads inexorably to the conclusion that those who hold such views are "the most pitiable of men" (v. 19). Using negative language, Paul nonetheless is able to end by making a strong positive assertion: "Christ has been raised from the dead," (v. 20), thereby showing that in fact we have been saved from our sins. It is worth noting that here Paul ties our deliverance from sin not to Jesus' death, but to the resurrection.

The lectionary invites us to reflect on Luke's Sermon on the Plain for the next three weeks. Equivalent to Matthew's Sermon on the Mount, Luke's version of the "beatitudes" contains many unique elements which reveal his theological vision. Luke is more direct and immediate than Matthew: no mention of "poor in spirit" here; it is the poor who are blessed. No hungering for righteousness; it is those who are hungry who will be filled. Notable also are the reversals that are promised: those undergoing trials now will be blessed later. The addition of corresponding woes further highlights the notion of a future of blessedness which awaits Jesus' disciples. In Luke, the sermon is preached to the disciples, thus placing added emphasis on Luke's concern with the theme of discipleship, its requirements and its rewards. For the Christian community of Luke, already struggling for survival in the era of persecutions, these words of reassurance were critical. Not only would their ultimate fate involve a reversal of fortunes; they would enjoy a blessedness that more than compensated for their present sufferings. We who hear the word today are likewise reminded of our vocation to beatitude, which may be the doctrinal focus of today's catechesis.

Catholic Doctrine

Our Vocation to Beatitude

In reaching "beatitude" the believer achieves the final good that fulfills spiritual beings in grace. Catholic teaching asserts that this final good is God, who is the end point of our natural ways of knowing and loving. Although this end is achieved through our natural human desire to know and to love, ultimately beatitude is a gift given by God.

In other words, we all want to live happily. That desire originates with God who places it within our hearts. Throughout life we pursue happiness, a pursuit that God alone will satisfy. We believe that the desire for happiness has been placed within us in order to draw us to the Source that will fulfill it. (CCC 1718)

The scriptural beatitudes recorded in the gospel (this Sunday's text and Matthew 5:3-12) constitute the heart of Jesus' preaching and they give further shape to the promises made by God to the chosen people since the time of Abraham. Indeed, the beatitudes enunciated by Jesus fulfill those promises by locating them no longer in a territory but in the realm of the kingdom of heaven. (CCC 1716)

Thus, the promise of the good news of Jesus Christ is that people can and will share in the life of God. By human knowing and loving it is possible to attain a full share in the intimate communion of knowing and loving between Father, Son and Holy Spirit which constitutes the life of the Trinity. Attaining this full share in the life of the Trinity is not possible without assistance from God.

The Catholic perspective regarding this assistance, therefore, is that God's grace builds on a human nature which is intrinsically oriented toward the final happiness of union with the divine. The transcendent blessedness of knowing and loving God is itself a gift from God. So, while the desire for this beatitude rests within our human nature, it also surpasses our understanding and abilities. The grace which disposes us to seek divine joy is entirely the free gift of our gracious God. (CCC 1722)

The beatitudes reveal the ultimate goal of the human person and of our acts: to enter into the full communion of the love of God. This vocation is offered by God to each individual and to the Church as a whole. (CCC 1719)

This fulfillment of the pilgrimage of God's people is described by St. Augustine in his work, *The City of God*: "There we shall rest and see, we shall see and love, we shall love and praise. Behold what will be at the end without end. For what other end do we have, if not to reach the kingdom which has no end?" (De civ. Dei 22, 30, 5: PL 41, 804) God has put us in this world to know, to love and to serve God, and so, come to the blessedness of the beatific vision, to the experience of paradise. In beatitude, we enter into the glory of Christ and the surpassing happiness of the life of the Trinity. (CCC 1721)

The promise of beatitude confronts believers with decisive moral choices and teaches us that true human happiness is not found in worldly wealth, comfort, power, science, and art, however good these realities may be. In God alone, the source of every good thing and of all love, our true human happiness and joy is found. (CCC 1723)

Thus, the beatific vision is one particular way of describing heaven. It is the perfect fulfillment of God's gracious self-communication to those who accept it, and it results in the most intimate union with the divine, where we will see God face to face. The Church prays, "Father . . . [t]hrough all eternity you live in unapproachable light. Source of life and goodness, you have created all things, to fill your creatures with every blessing and lead [us] all . . . to the joyful vision of your light." (*Roman Missal*, Eucharistic Prayer IV.)

Catholic Culture

Dante Alighieri (1265-1321), an Italian, wrote the *Divine Comedy*, a poem in three parts *(Inferno, Purgatorio, Paradiso)*. Hell is described as an abyss of nine descending circles of various punishments. The poem tells the story of an individual's journey through the circles of hell, up the mount of purgatory, through the spheres of heaven, until the vision of God is attained. Dante draws on various images and metaphors of pilgrimage and journey to finally describe the great crystal rose (another image) in which are situated all of the elect of God, those saved. His descriptions greatly influenced the Christian imagination in the West. Art, poetry and even theology has drawn on his portrayal of the human quest for beatitude.

In 1880, Auguste Rodin drew upon Dante's *Divine Comedy* in sculpting a work titled "The Gates of Hell."

Notes

Dismissal Catechesis (30 min)

Getting Started

Gather the group in a circle with a candle and the lectionary in a prominent place. Invite the group to silence, light the candle, and begin with the following prayer (adapted from the Opening Prayer of the liturgy) or a similar prayer:

Lord, God, you promised to remain for ever with those who do what is just and right. Help us to know how we are to live, to be faithful to your word made known through Jesus Christ, and to always live in your presence. We ask this through Christ our Lord. Amen.

First Impressions

1. Reread the gospel and then invite the group to reflect on the following questions in small groups or with one other person: *Have you ever had an experience of being ostracized, insulted, rejected, or misunderstood? Describe the experience. What feelings did you have at the time? How was the experience resolved?*

2. Return the attention of small groups and pairs back to the large group. Invite the participants to share any comments or responses. Continue the discussion with the following questions: *Was there anything in the scriptures you heard today that is still unclear? What new understandings did you gain from reflecting on the gospel? Was there anything in the liturgy that struck you or perplexed you?*

Making Connections

1. Share with the group the background of the gospel passage referring to the Word in Liturgy. Focus on the significance the gospel would have had for the community known to Luke, who at the time the gospel was written would have been experiencing persecution. This gospel would have offered consolation that God would not forget them.

2. To help the participants connect these scriptures to their own lives, explore with the group how sometimes our faith in God's presence is challenged. Faithfulness to God or even to our commitment to the church is challenged in the workplace, by our neighborhoods, by a family member or even from within ourselves. Invite the group to share their experiences of being challenged or rejected for their faith. Ask for them to respond to the following question as a large group: *What do you need in your life or from this community to live faithfully and trusting in God?*

Prayer

Rite of Blessing (adapted from RCIA #97 D)

God our Father,
you have sent your only Son, Jesus Christ,
to free the world from falsehood.

Give to your catechumens and candidates fullness of understanding,
unwavering faith, and a firm grasp of your truth.

Let them grow ever stronger in faith,
and the courage to profess their faith.

We ask this through Christ our Lord.
Amen.

Extended Catechesis

SESSION FOCUS: *Our Vocation to Beatitude*

Gathering

A. Sunday:

Welcome catechumens, sponsors, and team members. Invite everyone into a circle. Ask the group to name one thing that makes them happy.

B. Weekday:

If you are gathering later in the week for extended catechesis, begin with a Celebration of the Word similar to the one below.

- Gathering Hymn
- Greeting and Gathering Prayer
- Read Jeremiah 17:5-8
- Sing the Responsorial Psalm
- Read 1 Corinthians 15:12, 16-20
- Sing the Gospel Acclamation
- Read Luke 6:17, 20-26
- Pray using a prayer text from the Preface for the Sundays in Ordinary Time.

The Word (30 min)

1. Using the information from the Word in Liturgy section, bring out that the Sunday readings offer to us both consolation and challenge. Offering consolation the readings remind us that even in the midst of chaos and trial God is present to us. The challenge is to rely on God alone.

   Invite the group to reflect on the following question in small groups: *How do the Jeremiah reading and the Gospel console you, affirm you, and/or challenge you personally?* Reconvene the large group and invite any comments or responses.

2. Note the following points for the group: that Israel's choice between dependence on military might or reliance on God was a choice between life or death, and that for the disciples their choice was to follow Christ knowing that it might lead to persecution. Point out to the group that like Israel and like the disciples we can believe that God's desire is for us to live a truly blessed life but it often requires a dying to some things in our life in order to find life.

Invite the group to reflect on the following questions in small groups: *Describe what a truly blessed life would be for you. How would it be the same and different from your current life? If this is something you desire what choices do you need to make now about how you live your life?* List them. After the small group discussion ask several people to share their responses.

Catholic Teaching (30 min)

1. Note to the group that the readings today invite us to look at the meaning of beatitude for our lives and as the hope expressed by the church for all believers. In these or similar words present the following points about the life of beatitude. The beatitudes expressed in the scriptures give a foundation for the Church's hope in the fulfillment of God's promise for true happiness. Using the Doctrine section develop with the group the meaning of beatitude, the hope expressed in this teaching, and the consequences for our lives as Christians. Be sure to emphasize to the group that God's desire is that we attain true happiness and goodness in our life and that the attainment of this goal is not just a matter of a strong will on our part. Instead, God, through grace, helps us in our lives to achieve happiness. Ultimately, true joy comes when we enter into full communion with the love of God.

2. Develop with the group an understanding of the vision of hope that is presented. Explain that the vision also extends a challenge to the believer who is called to live a life in accordance with Gospel. The challenge is to hear the voice of God over the world's voice offering happiness in ways contrary to the gospel.

Ask the participants to make a list of suggestions that our culture makes for achieving true happiness. Have them make another list of what they believe to be true happiness offered by God. Ask them to be as concrete as possible and encourage them to surface the subtle suggestions culture presents about true happiness. At the end of the discussion and preparing of lists ask representatives of the group to share their lists with the larger group.

3. At the conclusion of presenting Catholic teaching, share with the group the story of St. Augustine and his work, The City of God as mentioned in the Catholic Doctrine section. Explain to the group that the church looks forward to the fulfillment of the pilgrimage of God's people on earth. This is our greatest hope in the future blessings of God for all people.

Putting Faith Into Practice

In small groups ask them to respond to the following question and then invite some of the participants to share their responses with the larger group. *These readings are addressed to us not only as individuals but as the church, as the people of God. How are we, as a people, as the church, called to respond to the word proclaimed in the readings, through the discussions, and in the Catholic teaching?*

Prayer

Invite the group to gather themselves for prayer. Give them a few moments to get settled while you prepare the prayer environment. After an appropriate period of silence, extend your hands over the catehcumens and candidates, sponsors, and team members. Pray in your own words for the wisdom and courage to live the spirit of the beatitudes. Conclude by singing together "Blest Are They."

Seventh Sunday in Ordinary Time

Understanding this Sunday:

Background for Catechesis

The Word In Liturgy

1 Samuel 26:2, 7-9, 12-13, 22-23
Psalm 103:1-2, 3-4, 8, 10, 12-13
1 Corinthians 15:45-49
Luke 6:27-38

The story told in today's first reading reveals several important motifs from the sacred history of Israel: Saul's mean-spirited jealousy of the more popular David stands in stark contrast to the younger man's respectful attitude toward the king. David's respect is founded on the fact that, for all of his faults, Saul is nonetheless the Lord's anointed. The lesson to be learned here is that the monarchy is of divine origin, and commands respectful obedience, even when the king's actions are worthy of condemnation. The narrative also makes a point of saying that the deep sleep of Saul and his soldiers was induced by the Lord, thus highlighting how Yahweh is guiding the destiny and fortunes of David. David's personal qualities are ideal: He does not take advantage of the king's vulnerability, but rather offers forgiveness toward the very one who was persecuting him. This is precisely the behavior that Jesus urges in today's Gospel. The responsorial refrain ("The Lord is kind and merciful") and today's psalm both remind us that it is the Lord's prior forgiveness toward us which is the origin of our own capacity to forgive others.

We have been following Paul's discussion of the resurrection (Christ's and our own) for the last two weeks, and we have seen that he is addressing very specific pastoral problems that had arisen in the Corinthian church. Scholars can infer from Paul's "answers" the "questions" that had arisen within the community. It is obvious that Paul is deeply concerned over the harmful influence of gnosticism, with its dualistic view of the body as evil, and its belief that salvation requires an escape from the body into some purely spiritual realm. Paul insists that the resurrection of Christ's body is a vindication of the opposite—the goodness of our bodies and their ultimate destiny to be resurrected with Christ in heaven. In today's reading, Paul is refuting a widely known gnostic commentary of Philo on the Book of Genesis, which saw there two arche-

typal Adams, one which was heavenly (Genesis 1) and one which was earthly, fallen (Genesis 2). Using this framework of two Adams, Paul asserts that the second Adam was Christ, not the fallen Adam of Genesis 2. And, just as we resemble the first Adam (i.e., the physical Adam described in both Genesis 1 & 2) in our earthly existence, so we are destined to resemble the second Adam (i.e., Christ) in his heavenly existence (i.e., in his resurrected body). This means that our bodies are destined for glory with Christ, not something to be despised and shed as a condition of true salvation.

Today's Gospel reading is a continuation of Jesus' Sermon on the Plain. After last week's blessings and woes (vv. 20-26), Luke here offers teachings (vv. 27-38) and then next week, illustrative parables (vv. 39-45) . This section of teachings first sets out a general principle (vv. 27-28) regarding love of enemies, and then applies it in the context of one's enemies, followed by a comparison of how one operates in the context of one's friendships. The basis of this ethic is clearly articulated as being God's treatment of us (v. 36). Then, there is a final admonition against being judgmental of others. Both the newness and the significance of this teaching of Jesus are important to note. Here he is going well beyond the conventional wisdom—both secular and religious—of his day, insisting that this revolutionary ethic was rooted in the standard God has set in our regard by acting mercifully and extending to us undeserved forgiveness. Little wonder that this passage has so often been pointed to as containing the core of the Good News preached by Jesus. His entire ministry— and ultimately his death— modeled for his disciples the centrality of this unearned gift of love and forgiveness in the divine plan of salvation. Jesus' teaching on love of enemies may therefore be the focus of today's catechesis.

Catholic Doctrine

Love of Enemies

In Greek, there are three words to denote types of love, *eros* (sexual love), *philia* (friendly affection), and *agape* (preferential love). *Agape* is the term used in the New Testament in referring to the unlimited love of God who is love itself. Love (*agape*) is to bind together and distinguish the Christian community (1 Corinthians 12:13). Jesus makes love of God and neighbor the new and greatest commandment which sums up all the other commandments (Matthew 22:37-40 and Mark 12:29-31). In this Sunday's gospel text and elsewhere (for example, Matthew 5:44) the evangelists report that Jesus also explicitly extends this commandment to include love for one's enemies.

Jesus sacrificed himself for us while we were estranged from God. St. Paul relates to the Romans that Christ died for us sinners while we were yet God's enemies. Thus, Jesus asks of us to live as he himself lived, loving our enemies (CCC 1825).

Simply put, seen from this perspective, the new commandment of Jesus has no fixed boundaries. As disciples of Jesus who follow his teachings, we are to love God and love all people. To love all means to love those close by us, our neighbors, those far off, sinners, and those whom we consider "enemies." Loving without boundaries binds everything together in harmony (CCC 1844).

St. Thomas Aquinas examines the virtue of charity, or love, in his *Summa Theologiae*. Through the practice of love, we participate in the life of the triune God, even though as humans we love imperfectly. Enemies and sinners are loved for God's sake. (ST 2-2.23.1) Indeed, everything in life, the pursuit of all immediate and particular goods and all of the intellectual and moral virtues that direct these pursuits, can be brought under the activity of charity, which completes and perfects them by ordering them to their source, God.

Pope John Paul II's encyclical letter, the focus of which is the mercy of God, extols the spiritual transformation which comes about when one's whole lifestyle attempts to communicate divine mercy and love. He writes, "It consists in the constant discovery and persevering practice of *love as a unifying and also elevating power* despite all difficulties of a psychological or social nature: it is a question, in fact, of a *merciful* love which, by its essence is a creative love. . . .Love is never a unilateral act or process. . . .in reality the one who gives is always also a beneficiary." (John Paul II, *Dives in Misericordia*, 1980, n. 14.2)

John Paul II has also written an encyclical letter to celebrate the twenty-fifth anniversary of the Second Vatican Council's decree on missionary activity. In *Redemptoris Missio*, the Pope presents a theology of mission and a pastoral vision intended to direct the Church's energies in evangelization. He writes, "The Kingdom aims at transforming human relationships; it grows gradually as people slowly learn to love, forgive and serve one another. . . .The Kingdom's nature, therefore, is one of communion among all human beings— with one another and with God." (John Paul II, RM, December 7, 1990, n. 15.1)

To love one's enemies requires the deepest acceptance of the liberating grace of God who delivers us from sin and evil. Catholic teaching emphasizes that this deliverance is achieved by God's actions throughout history, but most especially in the passion of Jesus.

Violence and hate were directed to Jesus. Those who put him to death saw him as "the enemy" and they mocked and shunned him. Yet, in this dark hour, the sacrifice of Christ became the font from which forgiveness of sins flowed forth from God (CCC 1851). At that moment Jesus forgave his "enemies."

Catholic Culture

The faith community of *San Egidio* in Rome has a tradition of weekly sung evening prayer after members of the group have assisted the poor in soup kitchens throughout the city. As more and more Italians have joined in this movement, the renown of the community has spread and leaders from both Eastern Europe and North Africa have asked for members of *San Egidio* to establish centers in countries experiencing civil war, to pray for reconciliation between enemies.

Catholic tradition gives to St. Augustine (d. 430) the title of *Doctor Caritatis*, Doctor of Charity, because he was the first significant early Christian writer to propose a systematic account of the theology of this virtue, charity.

Notes

Dismissal Catechesis (30 min)

Getting Started

1. Prior to the gathering, prepare the center of the circle with a collage of newspaper or magazine photos of people who have met their enemies and have extended their embrace. Some of these might include: Pope John Paul II's meeting with Ali Agca, who attempted to assassinate him; the son of Martin Luther King Jr. encountering his father's assassin; Serbs and Croats embracing after the Bosnian war; Cardinal Bernadin's meeting with the man who falsely accused him of sexual abuse, etc.

2. Invite the catechumens and candidates to gather in the circle of chairs. Ask them to look at the collage and share some of their reactions.

3. Pray in these or similar words:

   Jesus of eternal love you command us, "Love your enemies." But our hearts are stalled and frozen in rage and pain. Your answer, "I will make your hearts of stone into hearts of flesh."
   We pray that you soften the edges of our angry hearts.
   Caught between pain and pardon, we step out to forgive, but you demand even more. You call us to love even as our heavenly Father loves us.
   Help us to see the image of Divine Love in the face of our enemies.
   Make of us channels of this love even among those who have done us harm.
   For this grace to see and understand, we rely upon you, Lord of Love. Amen.

First Impressions

1. Call the group to remember the readings from this week's liturgy and ask them to share their responses to them. *What about these passages did you find disturbing? What caused confusion or skepticism for you?*

2. Help the group understand the circumstances and emotion of the first reading by offering this short reflection.

   David, anointed to be the next King of Israel, is pursued by the jealous and raging King Saul. After several attempts on his life, David fled to the desert. Saul and his troops gave chase. While they were encamped for the night, all fell into a divinely induced sleep. David and his men crept into the tent of his enemy. Even though the men urged David to kill Saul, and God had presumably offered him the opportunity; David spared Saul's life.

3. Ask the participants to discuss the following in pairs: *Why did David refuse to kill Saul? Contrast the largeness of heart in David with the smallness of heart found in Saul. What makes it possible for David to love his enemy?*

Making Connections

1. Invite the pairs to share their discussions by preparing a two-column poster. They can list the characteristics of the two men under these headings. LARGENESS OF HEART and SMALLNESS OF HEART.

2. Ask the large group to share their own examples of stories of 'Davids' and 'Sauls' that they may have encountered.

3. Summarize the group's discussion and invite all to write in the Participant Book (page 66) or on the blackline handout one idea they wish to remember from this morning's discussion.

Prayer

Invite the participants to name their enemies and pray for them by spontaneously creating a Litany of Love. Begin in this manner: *Let us pray for those who have hurt us. . . . Allow the group to call out several names (first names only). Let us pray for those who refuse to understand and accept us. . . . Let us pray for those who have hurt members of our families. . . . Let us pray for those who have spoken ill of us behind our backs. . . . Let us pray for those who have not allowed us to be who we are. . . . Let us pray for ourselves for all the times we, whether knowingly or unknowingly, have caused another's pain or sorrow.*

Extended Catechesis

SESSION FOCUS: *Love of enemies*

Gathering

A. Sunday:

1. Welcome the sponsors and team-members into the circle by greeting each one as they enter the room. Invite all to reflect upon the collage in the center of the circle and think of one person who has been hurtful in their lives. With this person in mind, proclaim the gospel (Luke 6:28-38). Allow a short period of silence for these words of Jesus to permeate the depths of everyone's heart. Then pray in this or a similar manner:

   Loving God, it is only in turning to you that I will ever have the grace to 'turn the other cheek' to my enemies. It is only in reliance upon your love that I will ever be capable of loving my enemies. For you are the source of love, mercy and forgiveness. Let me love as you have loved me. Let me let go of hurt and pain and replace them with the joy of knowing that you have created all people in love and you love us in spite of our petty human faults and arguing. All this we ask in the name of Jesus, who loved us enough to die for our sins. Amen.

B. Weekday:

1. Prepare a liturgy of the Word in pattern similar to that described below.

   - Song: Ubi Caritas
   - First Reading: 1 Samuel 26:2, 7-9, 12-13, 22-23
   - Psalm 103: Pray all verses antiphonally, that is, alternates from left to right

- Gospel: Luke 6:27-38
- Silence

The Word (30 min)

1. After a time of silence to absorb the implications of these scriptures invite some initial reactions to this teaching of Jesus. Ask these questions of the whole group, and invite just a short, first impression: *What effect do these words of Jesus cause within your heart? What are some ways you might be tempted to dismiss the depth of love called for by this gospel?*

2. Explore this Word further by summarizing the Word in Liturgy, found in Understanding this Sunday.

   Jesus challenges his followers, even today, to counter the norms of our culture and go beyond the acceptable mode of behavior. He calls us to love even our enemies; he challenges us to the core. We can no longer keep an account of wrongdoing in our relationships, only loving those who are worthy of our love. We can no longer be content with forgiving those who have hurt us. Instead we are challenged to love all people, especially our enemies, freely and without measuring the deservedness of the other. God has loved the world unconditionally, and we are called to do the same. Christians are to break the cycle of maliciousness and violence by a choice to love.

3. Invite all to spend time reflecting on this challenge of the gospel with the help of the exercise in the Participant Book (page 66) or on the blackline handout.

4. Have the group share in pairs (sponsor/catechumen, sponsor/candidate) whatever they wish from their responses.

Catholic Teaching (30 min)

1. Refocus the attention of all back to the large group. Ask them to quickly name those ideas that come to mind when you say the word 'love.' Explain the different kinds of love, using the Catholic Doctrine section of Understanding this Sunday to as a help. Emphasize that "agape" love is without condition or limits. This is the love called for by the gospel. This is the love required of those who wish to follow Jesus.

2. Further summarize the teaching of the church on love in these or your own words:

   Both David and Jesus are examples of how we are challenged to love our enemies. In the center of the circle we have modern day examples of people who go beyond the measure of our society to love.

3. Ask the participants to think of other examples of people who have loved their enemies.

   Continue with the Church's teaching.

   The love Jesus commands has no boundaries. Pope John Paul II explains that this practice of preserving love is both a unifying force and a powerful means of transformation in our lives. To love one's enemies requires the deepest acceptance of the liberating grace of God who delivers us from sin and evil. Catholic teaching emphasizes that God's actions throughout history, but most especially the passion of Jesus, achieve this deliverance. Thus, we are capable of loving our enemies when we abandon

our pain to God's mercy and rely upon God's grace to infuse us with divine love.

4. Allow some time for questions and further discussion of this topic as needed by the group.

Putting Faith Into Practice

1. It would be fitting to take this opportunity to describe the practice of Healing of Memories as a way of letting go of anger and hurt in relationships and moving toward love. Begin this meditative prayer by explaining this prayer form. The book, *Healing Life's Hurts*, by Dennis and Matthew Linn (Paulist Press) will be helpful.

   Christ heals our memories from the hurts and pain of broken relationships and walks with us through these shadows into the bright light of surrender to God's love. In this prayer, we invite Christ to show us the source of pain, as we recall the circumstances and feelings of a particular moment of injustice or hurt. We ask for the grace to see God working even during this painful encounter. We invite God to heal us and love us into forgiveness. In the presence of Christ we pray to be relieved of our negative feelings, fears and hurts; to look for goodness present in the situation; and to see our enemies as God sees them.

2. Invite all into a prayerful meditation with instrumental music playing in the background as you begin. During this prayer, pause often to allow the religious imagination to take each individual to that space where God is calling.

3. Continue with this meditation:

   Recall a person who has unjustly hurt you. Who is your enemy? Remember when this relationship began to be painful for you. What happened? What did you feel at the time? What words were spoken? What actions did you find most painful?

   Now invite Jesus to enter this same scene as you recall it once again. Tell Jesus exactly how hurt you feel. Tell him other times you felt this way with this same person. Tell him all that has happened since and how you feel right now.

   Jesus takes your hand and consoles you. He helps you to see your enemy in a different way . . . through Jesus' eyes. You discover and understand the pain of your enemy . . . his or her feelings. You see the weaknesses and the strengths of this person who has been your enemy. You see a warm light bathe this person. The light extends out to you. Jesus enfolds you both in the warmth of his love. Allow yourself to rest there for a while.

   As you re-enter this room, remain silent and write some of your feelings toward this person now. Use your Participant Book (page 67) or the blackline handout to note your insights. Know you can return to the scene of pain, in the presence of Christ any time that you feel the need.

   Allow quiet time for the participants to write their thoughts.

Prayer

Close with a prayer of gratitude repeating Psalm 103, this time inviting all to respond: "Bless the Lord all my soul," as you pray a few verses at a time.

Eighth Sunday in Ordinary Time

Understanding this Sunday:

Background for Catechesis

The Word In Liturgy

Sirach 27:4-7
Psalm 92:2-3, 13-14, 15-16
1 Corinthians 15:54-58
Luke 6:39-45

The Book of Sirach comes from the tradition of Jewish Wisdom literature, Israel's attempt to confront the cultural challenge of its pagan neighbors with its own version of divinely inspired guidance. More than mere philosophical musings, this literature is concerned with teaching the basis of moral behavior that is in accord with the designs of Israel's God. The current passage, obviously chosen to support today's Gospel reading, is part of a larger section on the dangers to integrity and friendship. Specifically, it is part of a commentary on the eighth commandment, against lying. The advice is clear and obvious: one's speech is a sure guide that reveals the inner character of the person. One who is desirous of the moral life is well advised to avoid the company of a person whose speech betrays a corrupt heart. This instruction is a practical application of an important insight into the necessary connection between a person's behavior and the moral values by which one ought to live. The psalm echoes this wisdom and takes up explicitly the theme of today's Gospel, that by a person's fruits you shall know their inner character. It does this by a focus on the just person who "flourishes" in God's courts and bears fruit even in old age.

We conclude today the series of readings from 1 Corinthians which has been proclaimed for the past six weeks. The present passage also concludes Paul's treatment from chapter 15 of various implications of the Christ's resurrection. This passage is extremely dense, as Paul references in summary form a number of his key teachings. Quoting from Isaiah 25:8 and Hosea 13:14, he insists that in Jesus' resurrection the ancient promise has been fulfilled that death will be destroyed. Even more, death—seen as punishment for sin—has been overcome in Jesus' resurrection. With an implicit allusion to

his teachings in Galatians ("sin gets it power from the law"), Paul affirms that Christ's resurrection has brought to the Christian freedom from sin, the law and death. Yet, he still admonishes his converts regarding the importance of their behavior (". . . engaged in the work of the Lord"). Against the gnostic teaching that claimed Christians have already "arrived" at salvation, Paul nuances such understandings: We experience the power of the resurrection "already" at work in our lives ("God who has given us the victory"); but, its full realization has "not yet" come upon us, and so we must continue to be attentive to how we conduct ourselves ("be steadfast and persevering").

We saw in last week's commentary that Luke divides the Sermon on the Plain into three parts: blessings and woes (Ordinary Time 6), teachings (Ordinary Time 7) and parables (today). There are three parables, but today's reading stops short of the third. The first has to do with blindness, the second is about trees bearing fruit, and the third uses the image of building a house on solid foundations. The warning against one "who listens but does not act" (v. 49) that is contained in the third parable is important: It alerts us that Luke wants his audience—those who are listening to his account of Jesus' Sermon on the Plain—to act on it. In their own way, the previous two parables also make the same point about the importance of Jesus' disciples living exemplary lives in accord with his teaching. The admonition about blindness is important for those whose example will influence others. Otherwise, one risks the catastrophe of falling into a ditch, or the absurdity of an unnoticed plank hanging from one's eye. Catholic moral theology has always insisted that the basis of Christian morality is the teaching and example of Jesus. Luke extends responsibility for Jesus' teaching and example to the next—and to every successive—generation of Christians who must show others the way by listening to Jesus and putting his words into action. Because of the clear connection between today's gospel and the moral life of Christians, this Sunday opens naturally to a consideration of the principles of Catholic morality, which may be the doctrinal focus of today's catechesis.

Catholic Doctrine

Principles of Catholic Morality

Catholic teaching insists that God speaks to our hearts, that his law is written within us and that is possible for us together, informed by Scripture, tradition and the teaching authority of the Church, to discern this law. Deep within one's conscience, God's voice echoes, calling us to love and do good and to avoid evil. The Catholic perspective on conscience is that we do not, on our own, invent this inner voice, but that we are drawn to obey it (CCC 1776).

Precisely because we are free to choose either good or evil, we are moral subjects. When, in freedom, a person acts deliberately, that individual is the author of his actions. Those actions can be morally evaluated as either right or wrong (CCC 1749).

Traditional Catholic teaching emphasizes that the determination of the morality of a human act depends on three things: the object, the intention, and the circumstances. Some acts, in and of themselves, are always intrinsically evil, for example blasphemy and perjury, murder and adultery (CCC 1756). In other words, murder is always the unjustified killing of an innocent human being. But sometimes killing, while never characterized as a "good thing," may have less moral culpability, as when, for example, it is unintentional or accidental.

Catholic moral theology holds that for an action to be judged as morally good, all three things (the object itself, the intention and the circumstances) must be good. For this reason, a good intention cannot transform an intrinsically bad behavior into something which is good. St. Thomas Aquinas asserted, "An evil action cannot be justified by reference to a good intention." (St. Thomas Aquinas, *Dec. praec.* 6) In other words, the end does not justify the means (CCC1753).

Thus, there are objective norms of morality available to us which express the rational order of good and evil. These objective norms are attested to by our conscience. (CCC 1751)

Conscience enables us to act responsibly. It is that reasoned judgment by which a person recognizes the moral quality of a concrete action that is going to be performed, is currently being performed or has been performed (CCC 1778). Newman has written, "[Conscience] is a messenger of him, who, both in nature and in grace, speaks to us behind a veil, and teaches and rules us by his representatives . . ." (John Henry Cardinal Newman, "Letter to the Duke of Norfolk," V,

in *Certain Difficulties felt by Anglicans in Catholic Teaching II*, Longmans Green, London, 1885, p. 248)

Catholics believe that the "inner voice" of conscience must be informed. Church teaching assists us in that formation of conscience. Through good preaching, sound religious education, an understanding of scripture, spiritual direction, the witness and example of other Christians and the authoritative teaching of the Church, conscience is formed. This formation is a life-long project where we prudently sift through our experience and the signs of the times, seek competent advice, and with the help of the Holy Spirit educate our conscience. (CCC 1785)

The purpose of educating one's conscience is to propel the believer further along on the path of right and to help one avoid sin. Sin offends against reason, truth and right conscience. Catholic teaching makes the distinction between mortal and venial sin. Grave sin destroys the relationship we have with God in Christ through baptism and is therefore called "mortal." Mortal sin must meet three conditions: the object is grave matter and it is committed with full knowledge and deliberate consent. (CCC1857) Venial sin does not irrevocably rupture one's relationship with God. It is defined as either having a less serious matter, or when it does, the sin is committed without full knowledge or complete consent. (CCC 1862)

Catholic Culture

The "examination of conscience" is a Catholic practice that dates from the earliest centuries of Christianity. It is a type of prayer wherein a review of one's life takes place based on gospel values. Egyptian monasticism practiced a form of this prayer. Examination of conscience was furthered in the practice of the Church when Celtic monks, in the sixth century, popularized private forms of the sacrament of reconciliation (confession). As founder of the Society of Jesus, the Jesuits, St. Ignatius Loyola (1491-1556), through his *Spiritual Exercises* and the *Constitutions* of the Society, furthered the practice of examination of conscience. Jesuit spirituality seeks to encourage the individual and the whole Jesuit community to discern God in the fabric of life, prayer and ministry.

In the days before the Second Vatican Council, just about every sin was considered, in the popular mind, as mortal or grave. The Council restored our Catholic understanding that when the church says mortal it means just that: deadly.

Dismissal Catechesis (30 min)

Getting Started

Invite everyone to be seated quietly within the circle. Light a candle and pray in these or similar words:

"O God, creator of all life and source of all goodness, you gave your only Son, Jesus Christ as a model of your unending love. Mold us in the likeness of Christ as witnesses of the Gospel. Strengthen us in the service of others in a world hungering for peace and justice. We ask this through Jesus Christ who lives and reigns with you in union with the holy Spirit, one God forever and ever. Amen."

First Impressions

1. Invite everyone to sit quietly for a few minutes to reflect on the Liturgy of the Word just celebrated. Encourage them to jot down in the Participant Book (page 68) or on the blackline handout or on a sheet of paper, words and phrases that touched them in the liturgy, or the mood of today's liturgy.

2. Share in small groups of two or three. After a few minutes, collect the responses on a large sheet of paper or chalkboard. Synthesize the responses.

3. In the large group, ask if there are questions or points of clarification about today's liturgy. Record these.

Making Connections

1. To connect these scriptures to our daily lives, invite the catechumens and candidates to name the proverbs found in the first reading from Sirach. Point out that first three proverbs repeat the message and the fourth proverb states bluntly not to praise anyone until you have heard them speak. Discuss the point of the proverbs.

2. Apply the directive of the proverb to today's world. Name the many ways, such as telephone, printed word, e-mail, in which words are communicated and for what purpose. In what situations would these proverbs challenge or console the speaker? In what situations would these proverbs challenge or console the listener or the audience?

3. Spend a few minutes in quiet reflection or journaling on what these proverbs say to each of us personally about how we use or abuse the gift of speech. Encourage participants to reflect on specific examples. Invite them to share in pairs.

Prayer

Pray together the responsorial psalm from today's liturgy. Psalm 92: 2-3,13-16.

Extended Catechesis

SESSION FOCUS: *Conscience*

Gathering

A. Sunday:

Welcome everyone. Invite them to be seated in groups of three or four. Remind them that we are in the presence of God who has invited us to this time and place. After a few minutes of silence proclaim Sirach 27:4-7. Allow time for quiet reflection, then proclaim the Gospel, Luke 6:39-49. After a few minutes continue with the Word.

B. Weekday:

Welcome everyone. Begin with a Celebration of the Word such as:

- Sign of the Cross and Opening Prayer:
- Reading: Sirach 27:4-7
- Quiet
- Alleluia
- Gospel Luke 6:39-45
- Alleluia

The Word (30 min)

1. Introduce the session with some background on today's Gospel. Use these or similar words:

Today's gospel concludes Luke's Sermon on the Plain. Three parables comprise this section and the third, which is included here for the purpose of the discussion, is not part of today's proclamation. This section of Luke's Gospel provides us with proverbial sayings of Jesus.

Invite them in groups to discuss the images found in the Gospel. One image has to do with blindness; the blind can't lead the blind. Another is students are not greater than their teachers; but when the students finish the course of studies, they are on par with their teachers.

2. The most developed sayings of Jesus in today's Gospel include the contrast between a splinter with a beam, a good tree with a decayed tree and house built upon a solid foundation and a house with no foundation. The contrast described in the first of these examples is between the minute and the extensive. Elicit examples of seeing the minute in our neighbor and not seeing the foundational faults in our own lives. Be prepared to offer a few examples of your own.

3. Note the image of good trees producing good fruit and decaying trees producing no fruit. Trees are known by the fruit they produce. A person's values are readily known through their words and deeds. Have the group cite examples from public figures or from personal experience.

4. Explore the third image of building a house on a solid foundation or building a house without a foundation. This clearly is a message that listening to the Sermon on the Plain is not enough. A believer must also act on the message. Elicit examples of saying, "Yes, Lord, I believe your words, but I have no actions or deeds to back up my 'yes.'"

5. Invite them to name which image they would choose to have framed in their homes, and share the reason for their choice.

Catholic Teaching (30 min)

1. Begin this segment by asking the question: *What does it mean to you to say, "Someone leads a good moral life?"* After several minutes of sharing, list on a large sheet of paper or chalkboard, words or phrases from their sharing. Explain that the basis of Christian morality is the teaching and example of Jesus. Compare how what Jesus taught, including the great commandment and the beatitudes, is similar or different from what is on their list.

2. Explain the background on conscience in these or similar words:

   Formation of conscience is essential to living a moral life. We do not, on our own, invent our conscience. It is formed by the values of the communities we live in and commit ourselves to. God speaks to our hearts in many ways. God's law is written within us and it is possible for us together, informed by Scripture, tradition and the teaching authority of the Church, to discern God's law and because of our conscience (a knowing with)to lead a moral life. A Christian conscience (a conscience informed by the message and mission of Jesus) enables us to make choices to follow the teachings and example of Jesus However, at times we do make choices to turn away from the promptings of our conscience. . . ." Freely choosing to turn away from the teachings and example of Jesus is an immoral act, or sin.

3. Note that conscience enables us to act responsibly. To choose to act irresponsibly or to choose to not act responsibly constitutes sin. Cite examples of such choices, such as the decision to cheat on taxes, to not help the poor, the homeless, the hungry, to gossip, to destroy another's reputation by spreading half-truths. Ask the group to explore the impact that conscience has on such decisions.

4. Describe the conditions necessary for mortal sin. Include that free will, full knowledge and a grave act must all three be present to constitute mortal sin. Feeling guilty does not determine whether an act is sinful or not. Feelings in themselves are neither right nor wrong.

5. Be sure to emphasize the great love God has for us, in that Jesus Christ has redeemed us all from sin. All sin can be forgiven if the person is truly sorry and has a firm resolve to try not to commit that sin again.

6. As an alternative to numbers 2 - 6, you may show the video, *"Catholic Morality,"* from the *Echoes of Faith* series, and pursue the questions provided in the video discussion guide.

Putting Faith Into Practice

1. Explain the Catholic practice of examination of conscience. Explore how the great commandment, the beatitudes and the ten commandments form the basis of an examination of conscience. Such examination of conscience includes not only acts done, but also acts not done. A daily examination of conscience leads us to give thanks and praise to God for good that we do and to ask forgiveness for the sins that we commit. Refer to the Participant Book(page 69) or to the blackline handout.

2. Share with the group an example or two of a prepared examination of conscience, such as are found in the Rite of Penance, the Catholic Update, titled "Examining Your Conscience Today" (#0477), and the Oregon Catholic Press Hymnal.

Prayer

Invite the catechumens and candidates to stand in a circle. Sponsors and team members stand behind and place a hand on the shoulder of their catechumen or candidate. Adapt and celebrate Minor Exorcism D, found in RCIA #94. Conclude with a song, such as "We Are Called" (Haas) or "Anthem" (Conry) or "City of God" (Schutte).

Good and gracious God, take all my liberty. I give to you my memory, my understanding, my entire being. Everything I have and own has been given to me by you, my God. To you, I freely return it. Your will is all that I desire. Grant me the grace to love you along; then I am rich and I ask for nothing more. Amen.
(Paraphrase of prayer of St. Ignatius of Loyola, Founder of the Society of Jesus, the Jesuits)

Ninth Sunday in Ordinary Time

Understanding this Sunday:
Background for Catechesis

The Word In Liturgy

1 Kings 8:41-43
Psalm 117:1-2
Galatians 1:1-2, 6-10
Luke 7:1-10

The First and Second Book of Kings contain accounts of Israel's history from the death of King David to the destruction of the Temple and the beginning of the Exile. The compilation of this material in its present form was done well after the events in question, so that the final editor was able to weave a coherent theological perspective into the entire work. That perspective is basically the same as the other deuteronomistic authors who stressed that fidelity to the Covenant brought success to the nation and infidelity inevitably meant divine punishment. The section read today is an excerpt from a long prayer ascribed to Solomon at the dedication of the Temple. In this part, he prays that foreigners who are attracted to Yahweh will find a receptive hearing and, for the glory of the Lord's name, will be granted their petitions. The reading was chosen because of the story of the centurion in today's Gospel, which so clearly seems to be the deepest fulfillment of Solomon's prayer. The psalm is an expression of the praise that is brought to Yahweh by the gentiles, while the refrain ("Go out to all the world, and tell the Good News") focuses on the Christian mission to bring the Gospel to all nations.

This week the lectionary begins a six-week series of readings from Paul's Letter to the Galatians. A brief introduction to the situation which prompted this letter could help the catechumens and candidates to understand it better over the coming weeks. Paul is writing to a group of churches he had founded in Asia Minor after having received word that the so-called "Judaizers" were following him, attacking his credibility and "correcting" his version of the Good News. The Judaizers held that in order to be saved one must not only put faith in Christ, but must also observe the Mosaic Law (e.g., circumcision, dietary restrictions, and so forth). Paul here defends himself

against certain personal attacks, insisting that his apostolic mission is authentic and that he was not trying to curry favor with a watered down version of the Gospel. His tone is stern to the Galatians who had so quickly strayed from Paul's teaching. Paul's defense of his version of the Gospel is strong, and his contempt for the Judaizers is quite evident.

Today's Gospel follows immediately upon the conclusion of the Sermon on the Plain. Luke's narrative has introduced us to the Lord through his preached word. Now, over the next three weeks, we will read of three key encounters of the Lord (with the centurion, the widow of Naim, and with the sinful woman in the house of the Pharisee) which reveal who he is by what he does. In the mighty deeds of power which he performs, Jesus is shown to be ushering in the messianic age. The cure of the servant of the centurion has a number of details worth noting. The centurion is a model of faith that can be emulated by every subsequent generation of believers, in that, like us, he does not at any point see the Lord face to face. Instead, he sends two separate delegations: first, the Jews and then others who will speak on his behalf. He only knows of Jesus through the witness of others--through the words and works that have been reported to him—yet he comes to faith. The healing power of Christ is still mediated by a community of believers who witness to his words and works among us. And, that healing still requires a response of faith on our part. In the Sacrament of Anointing of the Sick, the community of the Church continues to intercede with the Lord for healing. And, in that sacrament we also continue to seek faith on the part of those who are to be cured and those who pray for them.

Catholic Doctrine

The Sacrament of Anointing of the Sick

As presented in this Sunday's reading from the Gospel of Luke, Jesus is sent by a loving God to be a healer and physician of all our ills, addressing both our physical illnesses and our sinful condition (CCC 1503).

Sickness is a reminder of our human frailty, limitations, and mortality. It can lead a person to despair, or it can be an opportunity to renew faith in the God who will not abandon us and who has, in Jesus, suffered indignities, pain and torture unto death. Sickness is not a punishment from God. The Son of God has made our pain his own (cf. Matthew 8:17 and Isaiah 53:4). The Lamb of God, sacrificed on our behalf, takes away the sin of the world. By the mystery of his own suffering and death, Jesus gives new meaning to our own illness and suffering whose earthly reality is transformed by the Lord (CCC 1505).

While Jesus did not heal everyone who was sick throughout the world during his three years of public ministry, he has commanded us believers to follow him, take up our own cross, and in compassion tend to the needs of those around us who are hurting, in pain and sick. We are to care for those who are sick and pray for those who are ill, accompanying them by our intercessions (CCC 1509).

From the earliest times, the Church has attested to a rite of anointing for those who are sick and this prayerful action has been considered a sacrament (James 5:14-15). Bishops and priests pray over, lay hands upon and anoint those who are sick with holy oil, and in this way, the whole range of care by the Church community for those who are sick is signified. Prior to the Second Vatican Council this anointing of the sick was celebrated for only those who were perceived to be in immediate danger of death. The Council taught that this sacrament was not only for those who were in immediate danger of death but any who experienced the difficulty of sickness, debilitation, or old age (*Sacrosanctum Concilium*, 4 December 1963, n. 73).

As Catholics, we believe that through this sacrament of anointing, the sick are strengthened and through the grace of God they are given peace and courage. They are united to the passion and suffering of Christ on the cross and their own suffering can thereby acquire a transforming power. It is always a communal celebration. Even if this sacrament is celebrated by a priest alone with the sick one, the communion of saints, the whole household of the faithful, is present in prayer, consoling the one who is sick.

Thus, the Church earnestly prays, "Father, your Son accepted our sufferings to teach us the virtue of patience in human illness. Hear the prayers we offer for our sick brothers and sisters. May all who suffer pain, illness or disease realize that they are chosen to be saints, and know that they are joined to Christ in his suffering for the salvation of the world. . ." (*Roman Missal*, Masses and Prayers for Various Needs and Occasions, For the Sick, n. 32).

Catholic Culture

The anointing during the Sacrament of Anointing of the Sick is done on the forehead and the palms of the hands using the ritual words, "Through this holy anointing, may the Lord in his love and mercy help you with the grace of the Holy Spirit. Amen. May the Lord who frees you from sin save you and raise you up. Amen." (Rite of Anointing and Pastoral Care of the Sick, n. 25.)

Imago Pietatis, "image of pity", is from the Latin (in Italian, "pieta"), a devotional image depicting Christ, recumbent, dead of his wounds. Jesus is shown by various artists as supported by God the Father, or by his mother Mary, or by Mary and John or by angels. One of the most beloved examples is Michaelangelo's Pieta, in St. Peter's basilica, Rome. (*The Oxford Companion to Christian Art and Architecture*, Peter and Linda Murray, "Imago Pietatis," p. 239.)

The Sienese painter Domenico di Bartolo (c.1400-47) executed a series of frescos for the receiving ward (the Pillegrinaio) of the Sienese hospital of Santa Maria della Scala. They depict scenes dealing with the charitable, civic and medical functions of the hospital and are today prized for their great detail and thus what they betray of the practices of the times. It is interesting to note that in one of the frescos the "care" given to the sick person is a washing of the feet that looks amazingly like that of Christ who "took a towel" and washed the feet of his disciples at the Last Supper (John 13:4) The bowl painted in that fresco is still in the possession of the hospital and is on display. (Hartt, *History of Italian Renaissance Art*, p. 362)

Notes

Dismissal Catechesis (30 min)

Getting Started

1. Prepare the space with a vessel of oil (if possible, use your parish's vessel of oil for anointing the sick), a lighted candle, and a place for the lectionary on the center table. Gather in a circle of chairs.

2. Invite everyone into a moment of silence. Pray in these or similar words: *Jesus, like the centurion we believe that you heal and save through your word. Speak your word to us now. Let us hear your words with faith. We ask this in your name. Amen.*

First Impressions

1. Recall briefly the gathering hymn, and a phrase or two from each of the readings. Invite the participants to share in pairs a word, phrase or image that stands out for them today.

2. Have them come back together as a large group and share their responses. Make brief comments. Then summarize the variety of responses.

Making Connections

1. Ask the participants to notice any way they felt moved during the liturgy, or what they heard God saying to them for their life today. Have them share this in pairs for several minutes. Then invite some sharing in the large group.

2. Invite participants to become aware of times they have asked Jesus for healing for someone else. Ask them how they felt, and whether they expected Jesus would do this. Invite conversation around the sense of believing that Jesus not only can heal but does heal. Also ask if they have ever experienced someone else praying for their own healing. Invite them to name their feelings around the experience of praying for healing.

3. Conclude by asking each participant to name something they want to take with them from today's liturgy. Go around the circle.

Prayer

State that this prayer will lift up those they know who need healing. Invite them to call out names of people, possibly including themselves, in need of healing. Then pray: *Jesus, as the centurion did, we pray in faith asking that you bring healing to our sisters and brothers whom we have named. Let them know of your presence and care. We pray knowing that you will hear and answer us. Amen.*

Extended Catechesis

SESSION FOCUS:
The Sacrament of Anointing of the Sick

Gathering

A. Sunday:

Welcome sponsors, spouses, fiancees, and team members. Have them sit in groups of four with two sponsor/catechumen or sponsor/candidate pairs in a group. Additional persons also form groups of four. Spend a moment in silence. Ask a catechumen or candidate to briefly summarize the sharing from the dismissal catechesis.

After a moment of quiet, sing the refrain from either "Jesus, Heal Us," or today's Psalm 117 used at Mass. Invite participants to sense the centurion's emotions in sending his servant to Jesus. Proclaim the Gospel from the lectionary.

B. Weekday:

Prepare the environment as in the dismissal session. Ask each person to briefly name a way they have put their belief in Jesus since Sunday. Go around the circle. Then conduct this Celebration of the Word or use your own design.

- Sing: Jesus, Heal Us or another appropriate hymn
- The Sign of the Cross, Invitation to listen to God's word
- Proclaim: 1 Kings 8:41-43
- Sing: Psalm 117
- Proclaim Luke 7:1-10
- Silence
- Concluding Prayer: *Gracious God, you desire healing and wholeness for your people. Deepen our faith in the healing power of Jesus, the Christ. We pray in the name of Jesus. Amen.*

The Word (30 min)

1. State that the Centurion, who is not a Jew, out of respect for Jesus sent his servants to Jesus rather than approaching him directly. Note that this is one of only two Gospel passages that state that Jesus is amazed. Ask participants to name a time when they felt amazed at another person's faith. Invite them to share this in their group of four.

2. Recall for the participants that in the reading from the first book of Kings, Solomon is praying for the foreigner. Say that Luke, too, by including this story of the centurion's faith, is saying to the church of his day that Jesus has come for all people, and indeed, people who are outside the community may have stronger faith than those within it. Invite the participants to listen once more to the Gospel, and to note the words or meanings they sense God is speaking to them today. Proclaim the Gospel. Invite the sharing in the small groups. Then ask for some brief naming of these words or meanings in the large group.

3. Invite the participants to name the connection they sense between faith and healing. Invite large group discussion. Note that in Mark 6:5-6 Jesus says he could not do any healing because of the lack of faith. Include an awareness that healing is God's action, and faith opens the person to this action of God. Then ask participants to name God's invitation to them today through this Gospel. Have them share this in the small groups.

Catholic Teaching (30 min)

1. Ask participants to recall a time they or someone in their family were sick, how they felt, and who reached out to them in kindness and prayer. Invite some sharing in the large group. State some of the church's view of sickness as not a punishment from God, but often a critical time when a person can either move toward despair and hopelessness, or toward a closer relationship with God.

2. Talk about sickness as a time of special need when acts of kindness and presence are needed and appreciated. State that the Catholic church as a praying community reaches out to people in a time of sickness. Note that the church has a whole book entitled the *Pastoral Care of the Sick* which includes various prayer forms of ministering to someone who is ill. Ask participants to talk about ways the parish reaches out to the sick in the community.

3. State that the Sacrament of Anointing of the Sick is grounded in Christ's healing of those who were ill, the healings at the hands of the apostles noted in scripture, and the Church's long tradition of praying for, laying hands on, and anointing those who were ill. Ask if any of the participants have personally experienced this Sacrament or been present when the Sacrament of Anointing of the Sick was celebrated. Elicit their experience of aspects of the Sacrament and weave in information. Note that the healing involved in the sacrament is both spiritual and physical. Bring forth the awareness that over the centuries the laity of the church continued to anoint and pray for the sick, and that many people in the church today are involved in ministry to the sick. Hold the vessel of oil as you talk about the sacrament's former name of Extreme Unction, a last "oiling" or anointing in preparation for death. Note that Vatican Council II restored the earlier practice of anointing for healing and strengthening of a sick person. Point out that no sacrament is celebrated for someone who has just died. Talk about the common use of oil as a healing ointment, e.g., hand lotion or a salve. Note the same root of the word "salve" and "salvation." See the Catholic Doctrine section for more information.

4. Ask any participants who have been part of the Sacrament of the Sick either as one of the sick, or as part of the praying community, to speak of what this experience meant for them. State that the preferred way of celebrating all the sacraments is in the context of community, and note the parish's times of celebrating this sacrament at a Mass. State that family members and friends are encouraged to be present when this sacrament is celebrated in a home or hospital. Mention the specific words of the Sacrament, and the anointing done on the forehead and hands.

Putting Faith Into Practice

Invite participants to talk in their groups about ways they can extend prayer and other forms of support to the sick of the community. The group may choose an action to do together, such as visiting a nursing home, or taking food to a family with an ill member. Ask them to name something they will do this week.

Prayer

Ask participants to hold their hands with palms up in openness to God and bring before God the names of people they know who are ill and want to hold in prayer. After this naming, sing the refrain of "Jesus, Heal Us" or "Lord, hear our prayer."

Tenth Sunday in Ordinary Time

Understanding this Sunday:
Background for Catechesis

The Word In Liturgy

1 Kings 17:17-24
Psalm 30:2, 4, 5-6, 11, 12, 13
Galatians 1:11-19
Luke 7:11-17

This story is part of a larger collection of material on Elijah (and Elisha) which has been incorporated into the deuteronomic history of First Kings. In the perspective of the deuteronomic writers, it was very important to demonstrate that the events of Israel's history—indeed, of all history—were guided by Yahweh, especially by the Word of God uttered through the prophets. The background of the story has Elijah fleeing for his life from King Ahab and Queen Jezebel, and the widow of Zarephath offering to shelter the man of God. When the widow's son dies, she is at first convinced that the prophet's presence was responsible for his death. But after the son has been restored to life, she gives testimony to the power of God at work in the prophet's word. The power of God is the real theological point of this narrative, a point underlined time and again in many other tales of the miraculous power at work through the prophets.

Psalm 30 is a prayer of praise and thanksgiving by one whom Yahweh has rescued from the brink of disaster. Its reference to being "brought up from the nether world" makes this text a perfect complement to the theme of resurrection from the dead found in the first reading and the Gospel—a theme which provides the doctrinal focus for today's catechesis.

We reviewed last week the general situation that prompted Paul to write this letter to the churches of Galatia. Here, we have a remarkable passage in which Paul passionately defends himself from the accusations of the Judaizers who questioned his apostolic credentials. Paul points out that his call is the result of a divine intervention ("by a revelation

from Jesus Christ"), and not of human origin. In language reminiscent of a classic description of a prophetic call ("set me apart before I was born and called me by his favor"), Paul insists that he bears the stamp of divine approval on his ministry. His visit to Jerusalem was consultative, not an effort to receive permission from that community for his ministry among the Gentiles. Establishing his credentials in this manner is crucial for what is to follow, for Paul will quickly insist that the Galatians follow his teaching as authentic and reject the efforts of the Judaizers who wish to convince them that they must embrace the Mosaic Law in order to be saved.

Luke generally follows the outline of Mark's Gospel in telling his story. Today's passage describing the miraculous act of raising the widow's son from the dead is found only in Luke however, and it is the second of six units that Luke has inserted at this point into Mark's framework. (Last week's story of the cure of the centurion's servant was the first.) Luke's account is clearly meant to recall the similar stories of Elijah (today's first reading) and Elisha (2 Kings 4:18-37). But Luke's literary touch is unique: His focus is on Jesus' compassion for the woman who, as a widow, would surely have faced disaster with the death of an only son. The miracle happens without ritual or fanfare—there is simply the word of Jesus, and the boy is restored to life. Also of interest to Luke is the reaction of the crowd that exclaims, "God has visited his people." The notion of divine visitation is always, for Luke, an experience of grace.

Catholic Doctrine

Resurrection of the Body

Both the Apostles' Creed and the Nicene Creed proclaim belief in a triune God—Father, Son and Holy Spirit—and in the last part of the text conclude with the assertion that the dead will rise on the last day to life everlasting. Thus, the God who creates, who saves and who sanctifies will not abandon us to the tomb and darkness but ensures the resurrection of the dead. The work of the Trinity for each of us who are redeemed does not stop with our physical death. In other words, the last word in the story of our life is not uttered by the figure of death but by the triumphant Christ who has risen and who offers us new and eternal life (CCC 988-89).

Belief in the resurrection of the body is not an article of faith that has developed over the Christian centuries. Rather, it has been an element of the proclamation from the beginning (CCC 991). Without an informed understanding of the resurrection, revealed in Jesus' rising from the tomb, the first apostles would never have had the courage to witness to the faith. Indeed, what faith would they have witnessed to without the resurrection of Jesus and the firm assurance in the Lord that we too will share in the new life of the One who promises us "I am the resurrection and the life?" (John 11:25)

Even prior to the new covenant established in Christ, God's faithful people, Israel, held some notion of the promise of risen life. While the Sadducee party denied resurrected life, the Pharisees and many others in Jesus' day believed that God would raise them from death. In the face of the Sadducees' denial, Jesus strongly preached the promise of resurrection (CCC 993).

Those who eat and drink the body and blood of the Lord will be raised up on the last day by Christ, who even now in this life offers us a sign and pledge of resurrection by restoring some who have died to life again.

Belief in our own bodily resurrection with Jesus has been proclaimed from the earliest times of the Church. Yet, lack of comprehension and opposition has met this teaching on our bodily resurrection. Perhaps opposition lies not so much in that we believe we will be transformed (worms are transformed into butterflies), but that we believe our bodies, too, will rise to new life (CCC 996).

The Catholic Church believes and prays, "In [Christ] the world is saved, [we are] reborn, and the dead rise again to life." (*Roman Missal*, Preface for Christian Death III) The resurrection to new life offered to believers is accomplished in Jesus, the Crucified, Risen One. The transformation that occurs, our corruptible bodies changed into glorified bodies, takes place in and through the One who saves us by his own passion, death and resurrection (CCC 999).

The resurrection of the body, the promise to believers, cannot totally be explained. We can pray it, we can proclaim it, we can begin to understand it in faith, but ultimately, the community of the faithful experiences it (even if faintly) because we already experience the Risen Lord and his life among us. The Risen Christ is hidden and yet powerfully animates his Church. United with him in baptism, are feet are already set on the path of new life in Christ (CCC 1003). The very dignity of our bodies lies in the promise already at work in us (CCC 1004).

Catholic Culture

The reverence with which Catholics honor the mortal remains of those who have died indicates in a powerful way the hope we have of resurrection. Catholic funerals include many gestures to bless and honor the body. Whether the bodies of the deceased are buried or entombed, or cremated and placed in the earth or in a burial niche, our respectful treatment of them gives expression to our belief that these "temples of the Holy Spirit" (1 Cor. 6:19) await the resurrection of the dead.

Early Christians marked graves with the initials RIP (Latin for "rest in peace') denoting their belief in the resurrection of the body. The grave was place of resting or sleeping in peace until the time when Christ would call forth those who had died believing in him.

The last judgment is a favorite subject of artists. The earliest known Italian example is a wall painting in Sant'Angelo in Formis, near Capua (eleventh century). Two of the most famous depictions are Signorelli's "Hell" found in the chapel of San Brizio in Orvieto where the devils are shown for the first time as humans with vividly rotting flesh (1499) and Michelangelo's vision of the last judgment in the Sistine Chapel (1536-41) which imagines Christ as a Jupiter figure almost as if throwing thunderbolts instead of rendering judgment (*The Oxford Companion to Christian Art and Architecture*, pp. 261-62). These images testify to the Church's belief in our bodily resurrection.

Notes

Dismissal Catechesis (30 min)

Getting Started

1. On the center table have a lighted candle and a place for the lectionary. Gather in a circle of chairs.

2. Invite everyone to sit in silence, and say: *Become aware of your breathing, sensing God's breath of life in your body. Take a few deep breaths in and out.* Pause for a moment.

3. Pray: *Gracious and life-giving God, you raised the son of the widow of Naim and the son of the widow with whom Elijah stayed back to life. Breathe more fully in us. May our breath remind us of your presence within us. You are the author and source of all life. We pray to you, who live and reign, now and forever. Amen.*

First Impressions

Recall a few phrases from the gathering hymn, the raising to life of the widow's son by Elijah, and the raising of the widow's son in Naim by Jesus. Invite the participants to share in pairs: *What touched you at today's liturgy?* Then have each pair share a summary in the large group. Comment on the variety of responses.

Making Connections

1. Invite participants to discuss the following questions in the large group: *When was someone you loved, a family member or friend, dying, and you prayed for healing? How did you experience God at this time?*

2. Then ask participants to discuss this question: *In what ways have you seen God bring someone else or yourself more alive in human spirit?* Discuss ways our spirits can be dead and come back to life.

3. In conclusion, ask participants to share their response to this question with another person: *In what way do you sense God speaking to you through today's word?* Then invite large group sharing. Highlight from their responses ways God is present and calls forth life.

Prayer

1. Lead into prayer with these words: *Let us open ourselves to the God who brought us to life.*

    Pray, God of the living and of the dead, we belong to you in life and in death. Keep us in your care. Give us what we need to live in you. We pray in the name of Jesus. Amen.

Extended Catechesis

SESSION FOCUS: *Resurrection of the Body*

Gathering

A. Sunday:

1. Welcome sponsors and other participants.

2. Ask participants to sit in pairs. Ask a catechumen or candidate to summarize the dismissal sharing.

3. Invite all into a moment of silent prayer. Sing the refrain of Psalm 30 sung at the liturgy. Pray: *Lord Jesus, you desire full life for each one of us. Open us ever more to the life you offer. Amen.* Proclaim the Gospel.

B. Weekday:

1. Welcome everyone. Invite participants to go around the circle and respond to this question: In what way have you cared for your body since last Sunday?

2. Invite everyone to spend a moment of silent prayer in this way: *Let yourself feel the various parts of your body from your head, to your shoulders and back, to your legs and feet. Notice any pains, tension, or tightness. Feel your body in the chair. Become aware of your breathing in and out.* Then lead a celebration of the Word.

    - Hymn: We Shall Rise Again (Young), verses 1 and 5
    - Sign of the Cross, Greeting
    - First Reading: 1 Kings 17:17-24
    - Sing: Psalm 30 (or one used at the previous Sunday liturgy)
    - Alleluia
    - Gospel: Luke 7:11-17
    - Silence
    - Hymn: O Breathe on Me, O Breath of God

The Word (30 min)

1. Introduce the Gospel with these points:

    - *Both Elijah and Jesus brought the son of a widow back to life.*

    - *Luke probably used a widow in his story, because he continually showed God's reign was for the poor and oppressed. A widow was not able to make it on her own in Jewish society.*

    - *Luke portrays Jesus acting out of compassion.*

    - *Elijah is also putting to rest the widow's concern that her son's death is in response to some evil she may have done.*

Tell participants you will proclaim the Gospel again and give this direction: *Listen for a word or phrase that stands out to you.* Then proclaim the Gospel. Ask the participants to simply call out the word or phrase. After this occurs, highlight the many powerful images in the Gospel.

2. Make these points about the Gospel:

- *Today's passage includes for the first time in Luke's gospel someone referring to Jesus as the Lord, which suggests that he is the messiah.*

- *In Luke 7:22 Jesus responds to John the Baptist's question about whether he is the messiah by noting signs, including that of raising the dead.*

Then ask the participants to reflect on this question: *In what way have you felt dead, and had God bring you back to life?* Participants may use the reflection in the Participant Book (page 72) or on the blackline handout. Then invite them to share their reflection in pairs. When they are finished, elicit some large group response.

3. State: *God's action is always evidenced by signs of life, either large or subtle.*

Ask participants to name aloud a response to this question: *What signs of God's life do you see in the church?* Think more broadly than liturgical or even parish ministries. Allow some time for discussion in the large group.

Catholic Teaching (30 min)

1. Lead into the teaching on the resurrection of the body with the following exercise: *Visualize how you see yourself at the end of the world. Do you picture yourself with a body, and if so, with your present body or one from a different age? Also think of seeing relatives and friends who have died.* Invite them to share some of their images.

2. Talk about the Church's belief in the resurrection of the body using the following words or your own:

The church believes in the resurrection of the body at the end of time. This belief is stated in the Nicene Creed. In the Old Testament time just prior to Christ's coming, some Jewish people were beginning to believe in the resurrection of the body. The church views a human person as having both a body and soul. In the second creation story in Genesis, God is pictured as breathing life into Adam formed of the clay of the earth. This life breath is part of the person from the time of birth until death.

The belief in the resurrection of the body shows that the church values the body. The body is an integral part of the person, not just a vehicle for the spiritual self. 1 Corinthians 3:16-17 states that the body is a temple of the Holy Spirit. The Church reverences and incenses the body of the deceased person as part of the rite of

Christian funerals.

The resurrected body of the widow's son are different than Jesus' resurrected body, for he will die again. Qualities of Jesus' resurrected body include that he could pass through closed doors or wall, yet he ate and still had the marks of his wounds. No one knows exactly what the resurrected state will be like. Paul brings together the understanding of Christ's resurrection and the resurrection of all people in 1 Corinthians 15.

3. Ask participants to discuss the following question in the large group: *What does this belief in the resurrection of the body tells you about who God is?* Draw out an awareness that God is truly and continually a God who brings about wholeness and life.

OR . . .

Use the reflection in the Participant Book (page 72) or on the blackline handout.

Putting Faith Into Practice

Ask participants to reflect on these questions: *In what specific way is God inviting you to greater care and respect for your body? What concrete actions of care for your body will you commit to doing this week?* Allow time for sharing in pairs. Participants may record this action in the Participant Book (page 73) or on the blackline handout.

Prayer

Pass the candle around, and simply invite each person to state his or her name. While a person holds the candle all pray in silence and reverence for this person and for what he or she needs to be more fully alive in Christ. Then pray blessing C as stated in the ritual text #97. Close with singing "Amazing Grace," Vs. 1 and 5.

Eleventh Sunday in Ordinary Time

Understanding this Sunday:

Background for Catechesis

The Word In Liturgy

2 Samuel 12:7-10, 13
Psalm 32:1-2, 5, 7, 11
Galatians 2:16, 19-21
Luke 7:36-8:3 [or 7:36-50, short form]

Today's first reading comes from the court history of David. We read only the concluding section of a much longer narrative, a tale which is certainly one of the masterpieces of biblical literature. David has lusted after the wife of Uriah, one of his lieutenants, and impregnated her. To cover their wrongdoing, he arranges the death of Uriah; but the prophet Nathan confronts the king with his sin, provoking David's moral outrage by the clever telling of a parable of covetous greed, and only then revealing that the parable was actually about the king's own sinful actions. Our reading describes the confrontation between the prophet and David at that point. Nathan reveals that David's deepest betrayal lies in the fact that Yahweh had chosen him as the anointed one, entrusted with the welfare of the people. In the face of David's admission of guilt ("I have sinned against the Lord"), Nathan pronounces the Lord's forgiveness and reduces his sentence ("you shall not die"). One might have expected Psalm 51 (traditionally considered to be David's prayer of repentance) to be today's responsorial psalm. However, Psalm 32 is equally appropriate, stressing as it does God's forgiveness of the one who confesses guilt.

Although today's text from Galatians is part of our semi-continuous reading from previous weeks, it fits nicely with the themes of divine mercy and forgiveness found in the other two readings today. In this section of the letter, Paul is developing the central thesis of his apostolic ministry: that salvation comes to us as a free gift through faith in Jesus Christ, and not as a result of our observance of the prescriptions of the

Mosaic Law. Furthermore, salvation has come to us because of the death of Jesus for our sins, a saving death to which we have been sacramentally joined ("I have been crucified with Christ") and which has mediated for us God's forgiving love. The experience of that forgiving love—what theologians call justification—is pure grace ("God's gracious gift"), and it cannot be earned by our human efforts at following the Law. It can only be accepted, and that act of acceptance—what theologians call faith—is required on our part in order for the subjective side of salvation to be accomplished ("I still live my human life, but it is a life of faith in the Son of God").

Luke's story of the woman forgiven by Jesus while at table in the house of Simon the Pharisee is an eloquent expression of the core experience of Jesus' ministry: He brings in his person God's offer of unconditional forgiveness and, at table, restores to sinners the integrity they had lost by their sin. The scene includes an action and a parable, with the latter explaining the former. Jesus shows that he forgives the woman's sins by accepting her act of hospitality, even before he pronounces the words of his forgiveness. And, as his parable explains, her love, in turn, is great because she has been forgiven much. Luke's story matches perfectly the Pauline doctrine of justification alluded to earlier: In the face of a divine offer of saving love, the woman is saved by her faith in Jesus (i.e., by her acceptance of his offer of love). It is this same experience of divine grace in the form of forgiving love that we ritualize in the Sacrament of Penance.

Catholic Doctrine

Sacrament of Reconciliation

The Church desires "that the baptized who have sinned should acknowledge their sins against God and their neighbor and have heartfelt repentance for them, and it tries to prepare them to celebrate the sacrament of penance." (Rite of Penance, Decree, Congregation for Divine Worship, 2 December 1973) Sin harms our relationship with God, indeed mortal sin has deadly effects on that relationship. Sin not only offends against God, it damages our communion with the Church. Thus, in the Sacrament of Reconciliation one's relationship to God is renewed or restored and one is reconciled to the Church (CCC 1440).

God alone forgives sin. Yet the Second Vatican Council describes Jesus as the "one mediator" between humanity and God whose mission of reconciliation is entrusted to the Church (LG 8).

Thus Catholic teaching professes that Christ instituted the sacrament of Reconciliation and imparts to bishops and priests his own authority to forgive sins and reconcile sinners to the Church (1446, 48). We believe that this sacrament, on the part of the penitent, consists of three components: contrition, confession of sins, and satisfaction.

Contrition means that the penitent experiences genuine sorrow for the sins committed and is moved by this sorrow to not only.celebrate the sacrament but also to resolve not to sin again (CCC 1451). Confession means the actual disclosure of the sins, admitting them to the priest, taking responsibility for them in that disclosure. This is accomplished privately and what is revealed remains sealed. The priest cannot under any circumstances reveal or make use of what has been confessed (CCC 1455, 1467). Satisfaction means that having been raised up from sin by the celebration of the sacrament, the penitent then recovers full spiritual health in doing something more to make amends for sinning. This satisfaction (also called penance) may consist of prayer, works of mercy, the service of neighbor or voluntary self-denial and sacrifice (CCC 1460).

According to the law of the Church, "after having attained the age of discretion, each of the faithful is bound by an obligation faithfully to confess serious sins at least once a year" (CCC, 989) that is, provided that grave or mortal sin has been committed. Also, anyone who is aware of having committed a mortal sin may not receive Holy Communion without first celebrating the sacrament of Reconciliation (CCC, 916). Children must go first to the sacrament of Reconciliation before celebrating Holy Communion for the first time (CCC, 914).

Because of the various realities involved in this sacrament, it goes by various names. In addition to being called the sacrament of Reconciliation, it is also called the sacrament of conversion, the sacrament of penance, the sacrament of confession, and the sacrament of forgiveness. This variety of names suggests the significance and complexity of the mystery which is expressed and experienced by this sacrament which continues the healing ministry of Jesus.

The official formula used by the priest in the sacrament to express the healing which takes place in Reconciliation emphasizes what we believe: God alone forgives sins, God reconciles us to himself through Jesus Christ, and the Church carries on this ministry which effects pardon and peace to those who so desperately need and desire it. The Church prays:

> God, the Father of mercies,
> through the death and resurrection of his Son
> has reconciled the world to himself
> and sent the Holy Spirit among us
> for the forgiveness of sins;
> through the ministry of the Church
> may God give you pardon and peace,
> and I absolve you from your sins
> in the name of the Father, and of the Son,
> and of the Holy Spirit.
> (RP, 46)

Catholic Culture

Catholics relate all sorts of stories of pre-Vatican II experiences in the confessional box. Still more rigorous was the practice of penance in the early Church, when the process of reconciliation for sinners who committed grave sin (idolatry, murder, adultery) entailed a public discipline and could last for years. This practice was known as the Order of Penitents. In the seventh century, Irish missionaries introduced to Continental Europe the practice of "private" penance, which did not require such prolonged and public completion of penitential practices as experienced in the Order of Penitents. From then on, the sacramental practice has been performed privately between priest and penitent.

The Second Vatican Council, in its reform of sacraments, emphasized their communal nature. One form of the celebration of Reconciliation places it within a Liturgy of the Word which includes an examination of conscience and the praise of God's mercy. But the actual confessing of sin follows privately.

Notes

Dismissal Catechesis (30 min)

Getting Started

1. In preparation for this time, make certain that there is an environment of hospitality in this room, enough chairs for all participants, arranged in a manner conducive to communal prayer and conversation. Prepare a place of prominence for the lectionary, with a candle nearby. You may also like to include some flowers or plants of the season.

2. When everyone is seated, invite the group to silence. Place the lectionary in a prominent place and light a candle. Call the group to prayer:

   O God of mercy, we praise you for your great love for us. Help us to persevere in our faith in you through our love for one another. May your word come alive within us. We ask this in Christ's name. Amen.

First Impressions

1. In these or similar words, invite participants to recall today's first reading: *Today's first reading comes from the court history of David. We read only the concluding section of a much longer narrative, a tale which is certainly on of the masterpieces of biblical literature. David has lusted after the wife of Uriah, one of his lieutenants, and impregnated her. To cover their wrongdoing, he arranges the death of Uriah; but the prophet Nathan confronts the king with his sin, provoking David's moral outrage by the clever telling of a parable of a covetous greed, and only then revealing that the parable was actually about the king's own sinful actions. Our reading describes the confrontation between the prophet and David at that point. Nathan reveals that David's deepest betrayal lies in the fact that Yahweh had chosen him as the anointed one, entrusted with the welfare of the people. In the face of David's admission of guilt ("I have sinned against the Lord"), Nathan pronounces the Lord's forgiveness and reduces his sentence ("You shall not die").*

2. Now invite participants to close their eyes and picture the story in their mind's eye. After a few moments, ask them to recall a time when they may have felt as David must have felt: (speak these words slowly and quietly as participants silently reflect) *perhaps you felt guilty . . . maybe you were embarrassed and wanted no one to know what you had done...you may even have thought no one could ever forgive you . . . perhaps you were ashamed.*

3. Continuing in the reflective silence, ask participants to recall three people who have generously forgiven them. After a minute or two, encourage them to take just a moment to thank God (in silence) for the kindness of these people who have forgiven them.

Making Connections

1. To help individuals connect these scriptures to daily life, remind them that as God forgave David in the Old Testament story, and the woman in the gospel, so God mercifully forgives us. Just as David admitted his wrong and as the woman acknowledged her sin, so too we are called to admit our sinfulness and seek forgiveness.

2. For discussion, ask the group: *What is it that gets in our way when we need to admit that we have done wrong? Why is it so difficult to ask for forgiveness?*

3. For a closing reflection invite participants to consider: *Is there any in your life that you need to forgive or that you need to seek forgiveness from? How difficult would it be to be reconciled? What is keeping you from resolving this?* (During this time, softly play the song, "Cleanse Us, O Lord," by David Haas, GIA Publications).

Prayer

Conclude this segment with this prayer from the Penitential Rite for the Second Sunday of Lent. (RCIA)

Lord of infinite compassion and steadfast love, your sons and daughters stand before you in humility and trust.
Look with compassion on us as we acknowledge our sinfulness.
Stretch out your hand to save us and raise us up.
Do not allow the power of darkness to triumph over us, but keep us free from sin as members of Christ's body, and sheep of your own flock.
We ask this through our Lord Jesus Christ, your Son, who lives and reigns with you and the Holy Spirit, one God, for ever and ever. Amen.

Extended Catechesis

SESSION FOCUS: *God's merciful forgiveness*

Gathering

A. Sunday:

Welcome the sponsors, other spiritual companions and team members to the expanded circle. Ask the participants to list some of the ways that we can show we are sorry when we are seeking forgiveness. These responses can be recorded on a sheet of paper large enough for all to see.

B. Weekday:

If you are gathering later during the week to engage in the extended catechesis, begin with a Celebration of the Word such as the one below.

- Gathering Hymn
- Sign of the Cross and Greeting
- Read 2 Samuel 12:7-10, 13
- Sing the Responsorial Psalm

- Read Galatians 2:16, 19-21
- Sing the Gospel Acclamation
- Read the Gospel, Luke 7:36-8:3 [or 7:36-50, short form]
- Pray using prayer text from the Preface for Sundays in Ordinary Time

The Word (30 min)

1. Referring to the Word in Liturgy section draw out that the Old Testament and gospel stories emphasize God's great love for us even when we sin. Reflect on how David's sin was an affront to God and to the people of Israel who put great trust in David's kingship. In the gospel the Pharisees indicted the woman and challenged Jesus for associating with her. In each story both David and the woman acknowledge their sin in word or in action and seek repentance. The Lord God received David's sincere contrition and forgave him. Jesus received the woman's generosity and set her free from her sin. Forgiveness restored the relationships between God, David and the community of Israel. Through Jesus' forgiveness of the woman, her relationship with the community was restored.

2. Invite the group to reflect on the following question in their small groups: *Who are the great sinners in our culture today? How would you respond if you were invited to a dinner where a great sinner was present?* After the small group discussion, ask for general responses from the large group.

3. In a large group ask them to respond to the following question: *What do these readings have to say to us, as a people and as church, about sin and about forgiveness?*

Catholic Teaching (30 min)

1. Before beginning an explanation of the Sacrament of Reconciliation ask the participants to move into groups of two and respond to the following questions.

    Describe a time in your life when it was difficult to forgive someone. What effect did this experience have on your relationship with one another? What is required for us to forgive one another?

    Explore by asking the large group the difficulty they experience forgiving people and the effect it has on relationships. List the elements that they believe are required for there to be reconciliation.

2. Building upon their responses and using the Catholic Doctrine section give a brief presentation on the significance of the Sacrament of Reconciliation for the church. In the presentation talk about the effect of sin on our relationships with God and with each other and how God desires us to be reconciled with one another.

3. Again building on their list of the important elements for forgiveness and reconciliation develop with the group the three components which are necessary on the part of the penitent for forgiveness of sin: contrition, confession of sins, and satisfaction. These three components are described in the Catholic Doctrine section.

4. To help the participants understand the sacrament invite a priest to come to the session. Ask the priest to share his experience of the sacrament, the importance of it for his own life, and how a person celebrates the sacrament. In addition to a priest invite a neophyte or ask a sponsor to share his or her experience of the sacrament, what it means, and how it has helped with his or her spiritual life.

5. Invite the group to share their questions, concerns, reactions regarding the sacrament of reconciliation.

Putting Faith Into Practice

Ask the group to respond to the following questions:
Reflect on the place of forgiveness and reconciliation in your life. Given the message of the scriptures and the church's teaching, how are you affirmed and or challenged?

Prayer

As a closing either sing or read the responsorial psalm. Close with the following blessing:

May the Lord bless us and keep us. May God's face shine upon us and be gracious to us. May God look upon us with kindness and give us peace.

May almighty God bless us in the name of the Father, and the Son, and the Holy Spirit.
Amen.

Twelfth Sunday in Ordinary Time

The Word In Liturgy

Zechariah 12:10-11; 13:1
Psalm 63:2, 3-4, 5-6, 8-9
Galatians 3:26-29
Luke 9:18-24

Today's first reading was evidently chosen to correlate with the first prediction of Jesus' passion narrated in the Gospel. The background to this passage is uncertain. The Book of Zechariah seems to be a compilation of several sources, the latter half of the book from which this section is taken most likely coming from the third or fourth century B.C. The overall theme of this section is one of reassurance to Israel that deliverance will come, but only at the price of suffering. An unnamed figure, reminiscent of the Suffering Servant of Deutero-Isaiah, is described as being "thrust through," undergoing a death which results in a "spirit of grace" being poured out on the inhabitants of Jerusalem. It is little wonder that this messianic, eschatological passage would have been used extensively (the latter part of Zechariah is cited or alluded to at least thirty-nine times) by various New Testament writers to help understand the Christ event.

Paul, in his letter to the Galatians, continues to unfold the consequences of his teaching that we are saved by faith in Jesus Christ, not adherence to the Mosaic Law. Here, he points to the radical equality we enjoy as baptized members of Christ, an equality superseding all other distinctions ("Jew or Greek, slave or freeman, male or female") that tend to separate us one from another. It is by faith in Christ that we are made "descendants of Abraham," and so it is not necessary to undergo the ritual requirements of the Law (e.g., circumcision) in order to "inherit all that was promised."

Paul's allusion to the fact that the baptized have "clothed yourselves with [Christ]" might be a reference to an actual donning of a baptismal garment, much as the pagan cults often clothed initiates in the garment of the god. Or, it may simply follow the familiar Jewish usage of clothing as a metaphor for putting on a whole new moral/religious perspective.

The setting for the scene depicted in today's Gospel is while "Jesus was praying," always a signal in Luke that something important is about to happen. In fact, for Luke as for the other Gospel writers, the disciples' explicit acknowledgment of Jesus' messianic identity is a decisive turning point in his ministry. The prediction of his passion is linked to this event as a clear indication that the disciples of the Messiah will surely share in his destiny of redemptive suffering. Luke has added "each day" to Mark's version of Jesus' admonition that his disciples must take up their cross to follow him. Scholars see this change as a shift from Mark's earlier perception that suffering will come as part of the last days, to Luke's later awareness that suffering is an integral part of the Christian life on an ongoing basis. Concerned as he is throughout his Gospel with the meaning and cost of discipleship, Luke is careful to note this detail that a share in the redemptive cross of Christ will always be a part of the life of the disciple.

Catholic Doctrine

The Cross in the Life of Jesus' Followers

With an assassination attempt that put him in the hospital and with later surgery in his life due to a fall, John Paul II is no stranger to the phenomenon of human suffering. Like many Christians, he chooses to see in that suffering our share in the cross of Jesus Christ. He has written that with the passion of Christ all human suffering finds itself in a new situation. Indeed, the Pope preaches to the world that in bringing about the redemption through suffering, Christ has raised human suffering to the level of the redemption. (*Salvifici Doloris*, 11 February 1984, n. 19)

Thus, every believer can, in suffering, become a sharer in the redemptive suffering of Christ. The Church understands that there is a virtue in consciously uniting one's own suffering to the passion of Jesus. The paschal mystery consists of Christ's passion, death and resurrection. The first portion of that mystery centers in the image of Christ crucified, that is, it focuses on the image of the cross. John Paul II writes, "[Jesus] dies nailed to a cross. But if at the same time in this *weakness* there is accomplished His *lifting up*, confirmed by the power of the resurrection, then this means that the weakness of all human sufferings are capable of being infused with the same power of God manifested in Christ's cross." (SD 23)

The cross, therefore, becomes for us believers a dual symbol. In it we·behold the horror of deliberately inflicted human suffering, that is, torture unto death. At the same time, given that the redemption of the world takes place through the cross of Christ and that as members of his body, the Church, we can unite our sufferings to his redemptive suffering, the cross becomes a sign of the ultimate victory of God. What was the executioner's instrument has become the throne upon which Jesus is lifted up in glory (John 12:27-32).

In this vein, St. Andrew of Crete, a bishop of the early Church, exults, "Therefore, the cross is something wonderfully great and honorable. It is because through the cross the many noble acts of Christ found their consummation—very man indeed, for both his miracles and his sufferings were fully rewarded with victory. The cross is honorable because it is both the sign of God's suffering and the trophy of his victory." (*Oratio 10 in Exaltatione sanctae crucis*: PG 97, 1018-19. 1022-23 found in Liturgy of the Hours, vol. IV, Office of Readings for Triumph of the Cross, p. 1390.)

This holy cross of Jesus, which is at once a horror and an honor, enables John Paul II to create a new term, the gospel of suffering. He movingly writes about Jesus who transforms our suffering and in that transformation points that hurting person to a place close to the Lord himself. "*It is He*—as the interior Master and Gude—*who reveals* to the suffering brother and sister this *wonderful interchange*, situated at the very heart of the mystery of Redemption. Suffering is, in itself, an experience of evil. But Christ has made suffering the firmest basis of the definitive good. By His suffering on the cross, Christ reached the very roots of evil, of sin and death. He conquered the author of evil, Satan, and his permanent rebellion against the Creator. To the suffering brother and sister, Christ *discloses* and gradually reveals *the horizons of the kingdom of God:* the horizons of a world converted to the Creator, of a world free from sin, a world being built on the saving power of love." (SD 26) Through the very heart of the experience of suffering, we know that we are led into the kingdom of God, for suffering cannot be transformed and changed from the outside, but only from within the very depths of a person through the Spirit. Thus, we believe that the way in which followers of Jesus pick up their cross and follow the Master is a matter of the heart, the interior spirit and love.

Catholic Culture

Our baptism into the cross of Jesus figures prominently in Catholic liturgical practice and devotion. Upon entering and leaving church, Catholics sign themselves the sign of the cross using holy water. At the start of every Mass, we sign ourselves. At the Rite of Acceptance, the sign of the cross is marked upon catechumens. At the beginning of the Rite of Infant Baptism, the baby is signed with the cross by parents and Godparents. At the Rite of Reception of the Bishop in the Cathedral Church, the ordinary kisses the cross at the doors of the church. In all of these gestures, we acknowledge the primacy of this symbol and our acceptance of the "gospel of suffering."

St. John of the Cross, through his mystical prayer and writings, and St. Francis of Assisi, through the stigmata (bearing in his own body the wounds of Christ) which he received near the end of his life, attest to the power of this symbol in our Christian life. All of ascetical theology is an attempt to develop an understanding of how growth in holiness is related to a progressive embrace of the suffering and dying of Jesus in our own lives.

Notes

Dismissal Catechesis (30 min)

Getting Started

1. In the circle's center place a lighted candle and a crucifix or an art piece of the crucified Jesus. Invite the candidates and catechumens to join the circle, greeting each person as they arrive.

2. Help the group recall the Liturgy of the Word by opening with the Gathering Hymn used at today's liturgy. You will need to have hymnals available for all to join in the singing. Follow with a time of silence, during which key lines from the day's Sacred Scriptures are read. Pause between the reading of the following verses. *"And they shall look on him whom they have thrust through, and they shall grieve over him as one grieves over a first-born."* (Zechariah 12:10) *"My soul clings fast to you; your right hand upholds me."* (Psalm 63:9) *"For through faith you are all children of God in Christ Jesus."* (Galatians 3:26) *"Then he said to all, "If anyone wishes to come after me, he must deny himself and take up his cross daily and follow me."* (Luke 9:23) *"Whoever loses his life for my sake will save it."* (Luke 9:24)

First Impressions

1. Following the reflective time to recall the Liturgy of the Word, invite the group to name their initial reactions to these passages, by using the following questions: What did you find startling about these readings? *What was comforting? What lines or phrases from the readings do you want to remember?*

2. Ask the participants to share in small groups their sense of what it means to be a follower of Jesus. After allowing enough time for discussion, listen to and list their ideas in the larger group. The list can be on pieces of paper that have "A follower of Jesus_____" pre-printed on them. The participants can fill in the blanks, writing large enough for everyone to see, and display these strips around the room.

Making Connections

1. Invite the participants to gather in small groups and imagine that they are part of the gospel story. This script will be of help.

Imagine yourself in the dusty outskirts of Bethsaida late in the day. Exhilarated by the feeding of the multitudes that afternoon, you want to find the Master and share your excitement. After a little searching one of the twelve discovers him in prayer. A little reluctant at first, you gather at his side with the rest of the group. He startles you out of your reverie with the question, "Who do the crowds say I am?" You hedge, not wanting to make a mistake. But Peter gets it right. "The Messiah of God," he exclaims. Jesus asks you all to keep this knowledge to yourselves. Then he goes on to explain that, "the Son of

Man must suffer greatly°" You are troubled. This suffering Messiah of God will die. Your mind is whirling with confusion. As the Master continues, "If anyone wishes to come after me, he must deny himself and take up his cross daily and follow me," you become very uncomfortable. You leave walking into the darkening shadows of night, puzzled and frightened.

2. Allow this meditation to sink into the hearts of those present. Then, invite them to gather into groups of four or less to share their experience of the gospel. *What is your reaction to being part of the gospel scene? What emotions did you experience? Now, how do you understand the words of Jesus: "The Son of Man must suffer greatly"?*

Prayer

Close with the "Prayer before the Crucifix:"

Look down upon me, good and gentle Jesus while before Your face I humbly kneel and, with burning soul, pray and beseech You to fix deep in my heart lively sentiments of faith, hope, and charity; true contrition for my sins, and a firm purpose of amendment.

While I contemplate, with great love and tender pity, Your five most precious wounds, pondering over them within me and calling to mind the words which David, Your prophet, said of You, my Jesus:

"They have pierced my hands and my feet, they have numbered all my bones." Amen.

Extended Catechesis

SESSION FOCUS: *Bearing Our Cross*

Gathering

A. Sunday:

1. Welcome the sponsors and team members into the circle. Invite all to pause for a time to reflect on the art piece or the crucifix in the center of the circle.

2. Begin by gesturing all to stand and bow to the cross. Proclaim the gospel reading (Luke 9:18-24). Then pray Psalm 63 together. Have copies of this short psalm available for all.

B. Weekday:

1. Prepare a short Celebration of the Word in the following manner:

   - Song: "You are Near" (Schutte) (stand)
   - Sign of the Cross: All sign themselves and bow to the cross
   - First Reading: Zechariah 12:10-11; 13:1 (seated)
   - Psalm: Sing "I Long for You, O Lord"
   - Second Reading: Galatians 3:26-29
   - Gospel: Luke 9:18-24
   - Silent Reflection

The Word (30 min)

1. Invite the participants to offer their general impressions of the meanings of such terms as: messiah . . . suffering servant . . . take up your cross . . . lose your life. You may wish to jot these down on a large paper or poster board. Ask them to look at the pieces of paper around the room, regarding the meaning of discipleship. Now invite all to discuss the relationship between suffering and discipleship, asking: How does the follower of Jesus (the disciple) integrate suffering and the cross into his or her life?

2. Present the heart of the scriptural texts to the group in these or your own words. For further help read the Word in Liturgy section, found in Understanding This Sunday.

In the first passage, from Zechariah, the spirit of grace and petition will be poured upon the people of Israel with the death of the one who had been thrust through or pierced. The prophet points out that contemplation of the suffering servant would inspire mourning as for an only son. This passage assured the Israelites that their deliverance would indeed come, but only at the price of suffering.

Paul assures the Galatians that we have been saved and made one by faith in Jesus. Baptized into Christ, clothed with Christ, the believer is united with God in a way that goes beyond all other relationships. The believer has the privilege of becoming a child of God and an heir to the kingdom. This victory, described by Paul, was won through the redemptive suffering of the messiah of God, Jesus.

Because the followers of Jesus had misconceptions about the nature of his messianic call, Jesus has to correct their false notion of messiahship. The authentic understanding of Jesus as the Messiah of God is that he is the suffering servant who will suffer and die for our redemption. Luke goes further by emphasizing that suffering is an integral part of the Christian life, for those who would clothe themselves with Christ and follow him.

3. Invite the group to gather into small groups. Ask them to discuss *two* or more of the following questions. You may want to have all the questions displayed so that the groups can make their selection. *What is the connection between our salvation and the need for a suffering messiah? Have you experienced the spirit of grace and petition through your own suffering? How would you describe the relationship of being a child of God? What makes us all one and equal? How do you understand Jesus' command that the disciple must take up the cross daily? Who do you say that Jesus is?*

Catholic Teaching (30 min)

1. Following this discussion, request the attention of the whole group as you describe the Church's teaching on redemptive suffering. These points will need to be included in your presentation:

- Suffering is not desirable, but it is often a path to conversion and grace.

- As we seek to follow Jesus, we will encounter day-to-day struggles and sufferings.

- We all share in the redemptive suffering of Christ on the cross when we suffer.

- Through the cross, the suffering servant saved us from evil, sin and death. In this way the cross became the sign of the ultimate victory of God.

- As we take up this cross—life's struggles, pain and sorrows—with a willing heart, we share in the victory.

- As children of God, we share in the intimate relationship of the first-born son, who suffered and triumphed, died and rose again. Through Jesus we are given the grace to bear our cross daily, for in him we too will triumph and be lifted up.

2. Invite the participants to reflect upon their own crosses, using the material provided in the Participant Book (page 76) or on the blackline handout. When they have had time to write their story and answer the questions, ask them to share whatever they wish from this exercise with a partner.

Putting Faith Into Practice

You may wish to present a short account of the life of St. John of the Cross. In preparation, *The Classics of Western Spirituality* (Paulist Press) offers selected writings in John of the Cross, edited by Kieran Kavanaugh, O.C.D. Some relevant facts include:

John, a member of the Carmelite order, was a mystic, poet and writer during the late Middle Ages in Spain. He is also recognized today as a Doctor of the Church. His many writings describe a process of integration into the mystery of Jesus suffering, death and resurrection. His writings outline three phases of the spiritual journey. In the first stage, John describes the joys and exultation of first conversion through which the gifts of creation lead the disciple into deeper appreciation and love of God. The purification and desolation of what John calls the "Dark Nights" follow this: the dark night of the senses and the dark night of the soul. Because much of John's work describes the detachment and suffering of this period—hence his connection with the cross of Christ— he is called John of the Cross. All of John's life led to a final stage of transcendence and union with Christ, which is complete union with God. John is relevant even today, for the power of his body of writing lies in its authentic renewal of the soul.

Prayer

Have everyone stand and make the sign of the cross. Invite the group to pray. Read St. John of the Cross's prayer, "Stanzas of the Soul," found in the Participant Book (page 77) or on the blackline handout.

Thirteenth Sunday in Ordinary Time

Understanding this Sunday:
Background for Catechesis

The Word In Liturgy

1 Kings 19:16b, 19-21
Psalm 16:1-2, 5, 7-8, 9-10, 11
Galatians 5:1, 13-18
Luke 9:51-62

This section of the Book of Kings narrates the flight of Elijah into the wilderness, a place of testing and encounter with God. The Lord tells Elijah to anoint Elisha as his successor, a command that is unique in prophetic literature. The cloak thrown over Elisha would have been recognized as the distinctive hairskin garment of the prophet. The overall impact of this story of Yahweh's command to recruit Elisha is to reassure the Jewish people that God's word will continue to be spoken in their midst. Prophecy is guaranteed by the divine initiative, not by any human decision or effort. The twelve yoke of oxen indicates that Elisha was fairly prosperous. It is not entirely clear, however, what the meaning is of the exchange between him and Elijah regarding his farewell to his parents. But the act of slaughtering the oxen and burning his plowing equipment certainly is an expressive indication of his decision to pursue wholeheartedly his new vocation as a prophet. His choice of the Lord as his inheritance is picked up on in today's psalm refrain and put on our lips as a hopeful sign of our commitment to our own calling as disciples: ("You are my inheritance, Lord").

Chapter five of Galatians marks the beginning of that section of Paul's letter in which he offers a whole series of exhortations. Paul's opening expression is key here: "It was for liberty that Christ freed us." Freedom for Paul is both a present gift ("Christ freed us"—perfect tense in Greek) as well as the goal of our Christian life ("for liberty"—dative of purpose). True Christian freedom is liberation from the Law ("the yoke of slavery") and its demands which bring sin, from the tyranny of the flesh that wars against the spirit, and ultimately from death itself. The liberty for which we have been set free is in the final analysis a freedom to love. That is why Paul admon-

ishes the Galatians to stop "biting and tearing one another to pieces." Conscious of the licentious lifestyles that had previously characterized some of his Gentile converts, Paul is quick to point out that this freedom does not mean giving "free rein" to physical cravings. In this connection, we should not misread the contrast between spirit and flesh to which Paul alludes. He is not suggesting an opposition between our physical being and our spiritual selves. Flesh, as Paul uses the term, refers to any aspect of our being, whether physical or at the level of our human choice, that is in opposition to God's plan for us. To live in true freedom is to live in harmony with God's will, "guided by the spirit."

In the literary plan of Luke's Gospel, the geography of Jesus' ministry takes on deep theological significance. In today's reading we see the important point at which Jesus "firmly resolved" to set out for Jerusalem. And, as scholars have noted, for the next 10 chapters Luke no longer follows the plan of Mark's Gospel, but instead describes Jesus' journey to his ultimate destiny in Jerusalem. All along the way, he instructs his followers in the meaning of true discipleship. We see in this reading that the disciple must be willing to encounter rejection ("the Samaritans would not welcome him"), poverty ("nowhere to lay his head"), sacrifice of one's previous priorities ("come away and proclaim the Kingdom of God"), and a decisive break with one's entire past.

This Sunday's teaching of St. Paul on freedom, as well as the break from the past narrated in the first reading and gospel, suggest today's doctrinal focus on Christian freedom.

Catholic Doctrine

For Freedom Christ Has Set Us Free

Jesus Christ is our liberator. Through his cross and resurrection the Savior has freed us from the tyranny of sin and the power of death (CCC 1741). Jesus invites us into communion with the truth, which makes us free (John 8:32). Christian freedom therefore is far from an abstract philosophical ideal. It is the result of a historical event: the victorious death of Jesus; and it is conveyed by union with the person of Christ, experienced in baptism.

The church teaches that human freedom is part of the original order of God's good creation (CCC 1730). It is one of the ways in which the human person resembles the Creator. In God's design, the gift of freedom makes it possible for the person to respond to God willingly—not as a slave, but as a beloved daughter or son. The human choice to sin and turn away from God is therefore a profound abuse of the gift of freedom.

The Catholic viewpoint on freedom cannot be discussed without also referring to the responsibility which is ours to direct our actions toward the good that God holds out to us. We have been created as rational beings who are able to initiate and control our own actions. This dignity, bestowed upon us by our Creator, means that we have the capability to learn and grow, to make decisions and act accordingly—as opposed to being driven by blind impulses and passions.

The Second Vatican Council noted that in modern times people prize freedom and eagerly strive for it. But it is often cherished improperly, as if it gives total autonomy and license to an individual (GS 17). Nothing could be further from the truth of the gospel and Catholic teaching on the freedom we have in Christ. Catholic moral theology holds that freedom is not authentic unless it is in the service of what is good and just (CCC 1733). Choosing to do otherwise, to disobey and do evil, abuses the freedom we have in Christ and leads to the "slavery of sin" (Romans 6:17). Thus, the freedom we are given in Christ is a freedom to act responsibly.

Responsibility for one's actions however can be diminished by ignorance, inadvertence, duress, fear, habit, drugs and psychological factors (CCC 1735). For human freedom has been weakened by sin and it is only with God's grace that we are able to strive for what is right and good, giving to our actions their full and proper relationship to the divine plan (GS 17). Christ redeems us from the sin which held us in bondage and for freedom's sake has set us free. St. Paul proclaims that already we "share in the glorious freedom of the children of God." (Romans 8:21)

The grace of Christ is not the rival to our freedom, but its necessary complement. When we act in accord with a sense of the true and the good that God has put in our heart, we believe that we actually grow in inner freedom. Through the workings of this grace the Holy Spirit educates our hearts and our spiritual freedom expands, making us true collaborators in God's work in the Church and in the world (CCC 1742).

The Second Vatican Council spoke about freedom in connection with religious liberty, emphatically stating that one of the "key truths in Catholic teaching. . .is that [our] response to God by faith ought to be free, and that therefore nobody is to be forced to embrace the faith against [one's] will. The act of faith is of its very nature a free act." (*Dignitatis Humanae*, 7 December 1965, n. 10) Consequently, we are bound to God in conscience, but not coerced. Humans are guided by their own judgments and enjoy the freedom to do so, a truth most fully manifested in Jesus Christ (DH, n. 11).

Catholic Culture

What gives direction to freedom in the life of a Christian is love. St. Augustine (d. 430) recognized this truth in his oft-quoted maxim: *"Ama, et fac quod vis."* ("Love, and do what you will.")

The *Spiritual Exercises* of St. Ignatius Loyola (d. 1556) aim at increasing the freedom of the one who makes them. They stress a freedom from inordinate attachments and choosing to follow the way of Christ in all our decisions and actions. In his "rules for thinking with the Church," St. Ignatius cautioned, ". . .in our discourse we ought not to emphasize the doctrine that would destroy free will. We may therefore speak of faith and grace. . . But. . .it must not be done in such a way that good works or free will suffer any detriment or be considered worthless." (*The Spiritual Exercises of St. Ignatius*, trs. Anthony Mottola, Image Books, Garden City, 1964, p 141).

Liberation Theology is the name of a social and theological movement, begun in Latin America in the late 1960s. It uses the experience of the poor and oppressed as a starting point for theological reflection. Notable Catholic liberation theologians are Gustavo Gutierrez of Peru, Leonardo Boff of Brazil, and Jon Sobrino of El Salvador. The movement was confirmed by two documents of the Vatican Congregation for the Doctrine of the Faith: "Instruction on Certain Aspects of the 'Theology of Liberation'" (1984) and "Instruction on Christian Freedom and Liberation" (1986).

Notes

Dismissal Catechesis (30 min)

Getting Started

1. Prepare the space ahead of time.

2. Invite the catechumens and candidates to be seated quietly within the circle. Light a candle and pray in these or similar words:

   God, creator of all life, you call us to walk in the light of Jesus as your sons and daughters. Take away the doubt and despair that weigh us down. Fill us with hope of living in eternal light. We ask this through Jesus Christ our Lord, who lives and reigns with you in union with the Holy Spirit one God forever and ever. Amen.

First Impressions

1. Give participants a few minutes to reflect on the Liturgy of the Word just celebrated. Briefly recall a few words and phrases from the Liturgy. Elicit additional words and phrases from the candidates and catechumens. Ask them to summarize these words and phrases. Be prepared to help them do this.

2. Ask if any of the words or phrases which surfaced made them uncomfortable or confused them.

3. What did they hear as the message of this liturgy? Who would be comforted by this message? Who would be challenged by it?

Making Connections

1. Proclaim the first reading, 1 Kings 19:16b, 19-21. Review with the group that Elijah, the prophet, has been sent by God to anoint Elisha as his successor. The symbol of Elijah throwing his cloak, probably the distinctive, hairskin garment of a prophet, over Elisha would have been a great challenge to Elisha. Elisha is obviously wealthy, since he has 12 yoke of oxen, and he is well established in his profession. Discuss not only his surprise at this turn of events but also Elisha's response to his call.

2. Reflect on the word 'vocation'—a call that each one is given by God. One's vocation demands a wholehearted response and often involves great sacrifice. Have ready a sheet of paper with the following questions: *Have there been times when, like Elisha, they were asked to let go of everything? In the Lord's prayer, we pray, "Thy will be done on earth as it is in heaven." What does it mean to do God's will? How do we know God's will? Is there a cost to doing God's will; if, yes, what is the cost? What are we promised if we do God's will?* Invite everyone to spend some time in quiet reflecting or journaling on these questions. After a while, invite anyone who wants to do so, to summarize their reflection or journaling.

Prayer

Invite everyone to pray in silence for a few moments asking God for whatever they need in order to do God's will

Extended Catechesis

SESSION FOCUS: *Christian Freedom*

Gathering

A. Sunday:

Welcome everyone and invite them to be seated. Play or sing the song, "Jerusalem, My Destiny" (Cooney). Proclaim the gospel: Luke 9:51-62.

B. Weekday:

1. Welcome everyone. Begin with a Celebration of the Word such as:
   - Song: "Jerusalem, My Destiny" (Cooney)
   - Sign of the Cross and Greeting:
   - Reading: Galatians 5:1, 13-18
   - Quiet
   - Alleluia
   - Gospel: Luke 9:51-62
   - Alleluia

The Word (30 min)

1. Explain that early Christianity was sometimes referred to as 'The Way.' Invite participants to discuss:

   What does it mean to say Christianity is a way of life?

   What's involved in such a way of life?

   What are the costs and what are the rewards of living a Christian way of life?

2. Discuss the passage from Luke, paying particular attention to Jesus' resolve to set out for Jerusalem. From this point on in Luke's Gospel, Jesus' journey leads to Jerusalem which becomes the place of his death and resurrection. Along the way, he instructs his followers in the meaning of true discipleship. Ask the question: *What does that mean for his disciples? What does that mean for us?* Allow for some quiet time before asking them to share in pairs. After some time of sharing, draw out comments, insights or clarifications.

3. Focus the discussion on the challenge that every person who claims to be Christian struggles to keep Christ as the center of life and to make Christ's way his or her own. Everyone will live Christianity in a different way but Christ must be recognized in all these ways.

4. St. Paul's letter also addresses this challenge to live as Christ has directed. Paul directs the Galatians to put themselves at one another's service. Paul speaks of freedom to embrace to law of Christ, not that we have been freed to indulge the flesh. Stress that for Paul the contrast between spirit and

flesh is the challenge to live in harmony with God's will, "guided by the spirit," not to choose the flesh, which is anything in opposition to God's plan for us. Discuss in groups of three or four, what they understand by Paul's words that " we have been called to live in freedom, not to take on the yoke of slavery." After some time, gather feedback from the groups. Conclude with the point that Paul was making that we are set free to love.

Catholic Teaching (30 min)

1. Begin this segment with this or a similar introduction: *God created us rational beings. We have an intellect and free will. Free will is not a license to do anything we want. In today's world, freedom is often sometimes understood as "I am free to do anything I want, when I want to do it, how I want to do it and nobody is going to tell me what to do. After all, it's a free world."* Ask participants to reflect quietly about what impact such a notion of freedom has on our lives and world today. After a few minutes invite their responses.

2. Use the sections **Understanding This Sunday** and **Catholic Doctrine** as background to presenting the idea that freedom involves responsibility. Make the following points:

   - Freedom is only authentic when it is in service for what is good and just.

   - It involves actions and decisions for the common good of all, not just of the individual.

   - Choosing to act against the common good abuses the freedom we have in Christ and leads to the "slavery of sin."

   Elicit examples of such abuse from the group. Be ready with examples of your own, such as:

   - Money is not evil, but when the accumulation of money leads to greed, cheating, lying or exploitation of others, then it is evil.

   - Material things are good, but when they lead to excess or materialism, consumerism, denying others the essentials of life so that one can have more, then they are evil.

   Continue the discussion on what is each person's responsibility for their actions and decisions. Talk about what would lessen one's responsibility.

   - The Church stresses the responsibility we have in all of our decisions and actions to progress in virtue and pursue the good.

3. In small groups discuss further St. Paul's letter to the Galatians. Use the following questions: *What would happen if all laws but the great law were abolished? Would the great law of love of God and love of neighbor be enough to guide us as disciples of Jesus?* After some time, gather feedback from the groups. Invite the participants to summarize what they have learned about Christian Freedom.

Putting Faith Into Practice

1. Discuss the freedom of religion. No one can be forced to embrace faith. Faith is a gift and each person must choose to accept faith freely. God calls us to serve the divine plan in spirit and truth. We are bound to God in conscience but not coerced.

2. Invite the participants to spend some time this week reflecting on Christian freedom and the responsibility such freedom demands. They might name people such as Martin Luther King, Mahatma Gandhi, Archbishop Oscar Romero, and others who exercised great freedom and responsibility.

3. Encourage them to reflect on their decision to explore the Catholic faith. Is it a decision made freely or do they experience some coercion?

Prayer

Invite everyone to stand and to pray the responsorial psalm, Psalm 16: 1-2, 5, 7-8, 9-10, 11.

God, all faith is a gift from you. As I continue on this journey of faith, help my faith to deepen each and every day. I desire to understand and love you more and more each day. Take away the doubts that cause me to hesitate on this journey or turn away from you. I rely on your promise to never forget me, and the reminder that you have carved me in the palm of your hand.

Fourteenth Sunday in Ordinary Time

Understanding this Sunday:

Background for Catechesis

The Word In Liturgy

Isaiah 66:10-14c
Psalm 66:1-3, 4-5, 6-7, 16, 20
Galatians 6:14-18
Luke 10:1-12, 17-20 [or 10:1-9]

The third section of the Book of Isaiah, from which our first reading is taken, was written following Israel's return from exile, at a time when the Jewish people were both joyful at their restoration and in need of encouragement to sustain them in the task of rebuilding their entire society. In this passage we are presented with some of the most tender and moving imagery to be found anywhere in the sacred scriptures. Jerusalem is depicted as a nursing mother, fondling her infant. Further on, it is Yahweh who is identified as offering that maternal comfort to the people. The image of a river—always a sign of prosperity in that desert region—is used to convey the promise of great prosperity that the Lord will bring upon the people. It is significant to note that the "wealth of the nations" will flow into Jerusalem, perhaps a hint of the universalist perspective that foresaw an eventual gathering of even the pagan nations around the Lord's Temple in Jerusalem. That inclusive vision of universal salvation is underlined in the refrain to today's psalm ("Let all the earth cry out with joy") as well as in several of the selected verses ("Sing joyfully to God, all you on earth . . . let all on earth worship").

We end our series of readings from Galatians today with Paul's conclusion to the letter. While his opponents, the Judaizers, may have been boasting of circumcision as a sign of their favor with God, Paul will "never boast of anything but the cross." Indeed, he bears "the brand marks of Jesus" in his body, a probable allusion to the many beatings he received as part of his apostolic ministry (see 2 Cor 11:23-27). For Paul, all that matters is that a person has become a new creation, a process that happens through faith in Christ, not through

observance of the Law ("It matters nothing whether one is circumcised or not"). After all of the strong, even harsh, words that he has written, Paul ends on a conciliatory yet clear note, wishing "peace and mercy on all who follow this rule of life." The rule of life in question, of course, is not the Mosaic Law but the Gospel as Paul has preached it and in this letter defended it once again. To all of his hearers who have received his teaching with open hearts and minds, he prays a final blessing, that the "favor of our Lord Jesus Christ [may] be with your spirit."

Just as Jerusalem in the first reading serves as an image of salvation for all peoples, so in Luke's Gospel the Holy City toward which Jesus journeys plays an important symbolic role as the place of salvation for all people. In today's description of the sending out of the seventy (some texts read seventy-two) on mission, Luke is clearly associating the missionary activity of his own community with a mandate from the Lord himself. The number in Jewish tradition is representative of the nations, another way that Luke expresses the legitimacy of his community's focus on evangelizing the Gentiles. The Lord tells the disciples that "the harvest is rich." Harvest, of course, was an eschatological symbol, evocative of the Day of the Lord, when the promise of salvation would be fulfilled. Little wonder that the disciples are portrayed as jubilant at the successes they have encountered. To a missionary community under siege as was Luke's, that image of eschatological success was an important source of comfort and encouragement. Luke wanted to remind his hearers that their work of evangelization is the Lord's work, and that it is sure to succeed as long as they are faithful to his mandate.

Catholic Doctrine

The Church Exists in order to Evangelize

The Second Vatican Council affirmed the centrality of evangelization in the life of the Church in *Ad Gentes* (7 December 1965). But it was Paul VI who wrote in the most detailed and concrete way about evangelization. This pope promulgated his encyclical letter on evangelization to commemorate the tenth anniversary of the closing of the Second Vatican Council. His first point is clear: Jesus Christ is the first evangelizer. He is the good news of God, to the point of perfection and to his own self-sacrifice, proclaiming the kingdom or dominion of God and the happiness of those who are joined to this kingdom. This happiness is paradoxical, however, because the world rejects the things which make up this kingdom. (*Evangelii Nuntiandi*, 8 December 1975, n. 7)

It is the vocation of the Church to continue spreading the good news of Jesus and follow in the footsteps of the Twelve who were commanded by the Lord to carry the gospel to all, engaging in the ministry of preaching, teaching and healing. Indeed, Paul VI characterizes evangelization as the "deepest identity" of the Church. (EN 14)

Born through the evangelizing efforts of Jesus, the Church, in turn engages in self-evangelization and the evangelization of the world. The purpose of both this internal and external evangelization is conversion, to make of all of the world and everyone in it that "new creation" (Revelation 21:5). For, if the gospel is proclaimed and accepted, then humanity's judgment, determining values, points of interest, lines of thought, sources of inspiration and models of life which are contrary to the good news will be upset and reformed. (EN 19) In other words, what is being evangelized is culture, not superficially but radically and vitally, to its depth. Paul VI notes, "The split between the Gospel and culture is without doubt the drama of our time, just as it was of other times. Therefore every effort must be made to ensure a full evangelization of culture, or more correctly of cultures. They have to be regenerated by an encounter with the Gospel. But this encounter will not take place if the Gospel is not proclaimed." (EN 20)

The first way in which members of the Church evangelize is by the witness of their lives. Why we live as we do should cause others to notice and inquire. All Christians are called to this type of witness. But this is only an initial kind of evangelizing. There is also the need for explicit, public and unequivocal proclamation of Jesus Christ. "There is no true evangelization if the name, the teaching, the life, the promises, the Kingdom and the mystery of Jesus of Nazareth, the Son of God are not proclaimed." (EN 22)

The content of this proclamation is, in a nutshell, that God loves us, redeems us in Jesus, frees us from sin, promises us eternal life, and that the Word of God has relevance to our lives here and now as we await the fulfillment of the kingdom. This content is expressed and conveyed by a variety of means which include personal example, preaching, catechetics, the use of mass media, individual contact, through Word and Sacrament, and through popular piety and devotion. Thus, Catholic evangelizing efforts are comprehensive, woven directly into all facets of life and our activities.

John Paul II has further developed the Church's understanding of evangelization. Indeed, as Christianity prepares to enter its third millennium, he frequently preaches on the need for a "new evangelization." He writes, "The process of insertion into peoples' cultures is a lengthy one. It is not a matter of purely external adaptation, for inculturation 'means the intimate transformation of authentic cultural values through their integration in Christianity and the insertion of Christianity in the various human cultures.' The process is thus a profound and all-embracing one, which involves the Christian message and also the Church's reflection and practice. But at the same time it is a difficult process, for it must in no way compromise the distinctiveness and integrity of the Christian faith." (John Paul II, *Redemptoris Missio*, 7 December 1990, n. 52.2)

Catholic Culture

The patron saints of foreign missions are St. Francis Xavier and St. Therese of Lisieux. (See the Catholic Culture section for the Fourth Sunday in Ordinary Time.)

In the earliest period of the Church, monks frequently carried forth missionary efforts. Certain bishops are remembered as "apostles" to their respective regions because of their work in evangelizing, such as St. Augustine to England, St. Patrick to Ireland, St. Boniface to Germany, and Sts. Cyril and Methodius to the Slavic people. (Encyclopedia of Catholicism, p. 871) John Paul II has written an encyclical commemorating the eleven-hundredth anniversary of the evangelization of the Slavs by Sts. Cyril and Methodius, *Alavorum Apostolii* (2 June 1985).

Japanese novelist Shusako Endo has written a variety of novels. Two of them deal with the early evangelization efforts in Japan. The *Samurai* grapples with the failure of initial missionary efforts in the sixteenth century. *Silence* (1976) is about the Japanese Catholic martyrs. It is of this latter work that Graham Greene writes, "In my opinion one of the finest novels of our time."

Notes

Dismissal Catechesis (30 min)

Getting Started

Before Mass, prepare the meeting space with a prayer environment and a place for the lectionary. Gather the group in a circle and begin with the following praise from the Responsorial Psalm:

Shout joyfully to God, all you on earth,
sing praise to the glory of God's name;
proclaim God's glorious praise.

Say to God, "How tremendous are your deeds!"

First Impressions

1. Invite the group to recall the readings and the homily from the liturgy. You might need to recite a few phrases from the readings in order to help the group recall the scripture texts. Note to the group that the readings speak about God's blessing upon two communities and how it inspired them to share this good news.

2. Explain that as a people, we all are called to reflect on the good news in our lives. Ask the group to respond to the following question: *If you were sent out by the Lord, what is the good news you would share about your life?* Invite responses and comments from the group.

Making Connections

1. Share briefly the background to the Old Testament and the gospel reading, explaining the reasons for Israel's rejoicing and for the disciples enthusiasm for the mission. Explain that Israel had been sent into exile from Jerusalem, their holy city, for many years. They thought they had been abandoned by God. Now, returning to Jerusalem, they rejoiced at the words of the prophet proclaiming that God would never forget them. Good news!

2. For the disciples, their experience of Jesus revealed a God who came to the people to heal them, to set them free, and to bring new life. Having known this love of God through their intimacy with Jesus, the disciples now desired to go out and proclaim the news that God was with the people. Good news!

3. Ask the group to respond to the following questions: *What message of God's love have you heard in your own life? How are you discovering you want to share this good news with others?* Invite any responses or comment from the group.

Prayer

For prayer, invite the group to give thanks for those people in their lives who have been good news for them, people who have brought them the good news of God's love to them. After offering prayers of thanksgiving, you might want to close with a song of your choosing or one of the following: the closing song of the liturgy, "Sing to the Mountains" (Bob Dufford, Glory and Praise), or "Sing a New Song" (D. Schutte, New Dawn Music).

Extended Catechesis

SESSION FOCUS:
The Church Exists in Order to Evangelize.

Gathering

A. Sunday:
Welcome sponsors and team members to the extended circle. Ask each person to share one bit of good news from their past week.

B. Weekday:
If you gather during the week for extended catechesis, be sure to begin with a Celebration of the Word, such as the following:

- Gathering Hymn
- Greeting and Gathering Prayer
- Read Isaiah 66:10-14
- Sing the Responsorial Psalm
- Read Galatians 6:14-18
- Sing the Gospel Acclamation
- Read Luke 10:1-12, 17-20 or Luke 10:1-9
- Conclude with a prayer text from the Preface for the Sundays in Ordinary Time

The Word (30 min)

1. The Old Testament and the gospel give us the witness of Israel and Jesus' disciples proclaiming God's goodness to the people. For Israel, the good news was that they were returning to Jerusalem. For the disciples, the good news brought healing, freedom, and hope. Ask the participants to break into small groups or pairs to discuss the following questions: *Where in the world, in your neighborhood, in your city, do people hunger to hear the good news? What is the good news the world hungers to hear today?* Afterward, invite any responses or comments to be shared with the large group.

2. Using the Word in Liturgy section, give some of the social-historical circumstances behind the Reading, be sure to explain in these or similar words what the experience of exile would have meant for the people. *Aside from the destruction of their sacred temple and thousands of people dying, they were taken into slavery, oppressed, families were separated, and much more. This was an experience of being forgotten and abandoned by God. It was through the voices of the prophets that the people came to believe and have hope once more in God as their salvation.*

During the time of Jesus, the Jews were once more the victims of occupation, this time under the Romans. Although the Romans were more generous to their subjects, the incidence of oppression still existed. These were not good times for those who were poor. They needed to bear the burden of sickness, oppressive taxes, and death. Jesus' words and deeds of healing and exorcism gave hope to the people. The disciples were sent to continue this work of Jesus.

3. Explain that we have inherited all this good news, that God is with us, and continues to bring good news to us, healing us, setting people free, and offering hope in what can be for some in the world, an experience of hopelessness.

4. The gospel states that the disciples were sent as lambs among the wolves. In other words, the good news would not always be well received. There were obstacles and resistance among some of the people to the good news. Invite the group to reflect on and respond to the following question: *As you reflected on the good news the world hungers to hear today, what are some of the obstacles and resistance to hearing and receiving it?*

Catholic Teaching (30 min)

1. Today's gospel is about evangelization. To evangelize means to proclaim the good news, the gospel of Jesus Christ. As the disciples were sent, so the Church is sent to evangelize, that is, to proclaim the good news of Jesus Christ. Using the Catholic Doctrine section, highlight that the mission of every Christian is to evangelize. Explore with the group the ways that we as Christians evangelize through the witness of our lives and words we speak.

2. It is important to point out that we are called to bring the good news of Christ into many parts of our world today. Places such as our inner cities, our neighborhoods, schools, and even in out parish, need to hear the good news that brings hope.

3. Each of us evangelizes out of our own gifts. We need to discover the gifts we have, be willing to respond to the call of God to proclaim the good news, and to share our gifts with those who hunger for a word of hope. Invite participants to work in pairs. Have each person tell the other person what gifts they see in the other that could be used to bring good news to others.

4. Share with the group stories of people who have been evangelizers in the church in your area. You might want to share who the people are that brought Catholic Christianity to your city or state.

Putting Faith Into Practice

Invite the group to reflect in silence on the following questions: *What concrete ways can you identify in which you can evangelize in your work place, in your neighborhood, and in your community? What apprehensions, questions, and hesitations do you have?* Invite any responses or comments to be shared with the group.

Prayer

Close with a prayer of your own composition or the following:

Let us pray,

Almighty God, all the earth rejoices and cries out to you with joy. You save your people and set them free. You fulfill your promises and we proclaim your good news to all the world. Guide our feet in your ways, inspire our hearts and minds to give witness to your love, fill us with your courage to proclaim the good news of your Son, Jesus Christ.

We ask this through Christ, our Lord. Amen.

Fifteenth Sunday in Ordinary Time

The Word In Liturgy

Deuteronomy 30:10-14
Psalm 69:14, 17, 30-31, 33-34, 36, 37
Colossians 1:15-20
Luke 10:25-37

The rhetorical format of the Book of Deuteronomy is that of a farewell address uttered by Moses at the end of his life, prior to the Israelites entering into the Promised Land. Scholars recognize in the book the compilation of many ancient materials, as well as the original handiwork of the deuteronomic author(s). This passage seems to fit a liturgical context, perhaps a ceremony of Covenant renewal. Most scholars would ascribe it to the time of the exile, meant to bolster the faith and commitment of the people as they look forward to a "return to the Lord"—not only by a renewed spiritual commitment to the Covenant, but also in the antici-pated physical return to Jerusalem. The author's words are meant to reassure the Jewish people that God has not abandoned them: The Lord's word is not "too mysterious and remote;" rather, it is "very near to you." Neither is observance of the demands of the Covenant an impossibly difficult task: Yahweh's Law is "already in your mouths and in your hearts." We Christians have sometimes been guilty of an indiscrimi-nate portrayal of the Jews' attitude to the Law as legalistic. Jesus certainly charged some of his contemporaries with that fault. But we see in this passage how the vision of the deutero-nomic school was that of a deeply internalized embrace of God's Law out of a sense of love, not mere compliance from a sense of duty. Today's psalm refrain ("Turn to the Lord in your need, and you will live,") is a fitting summary of Deuteronomy's emphasis on internalizing the Law as a way of staying close to the Lord.

We begin today a four week series of readings from the Letter to the Colossians. Like the Galatian community, Colossae was also experiencing difficulty due to individuals who were spreading opinions contrary to authentic Christian faith. The author writes to correct those views and to urge the community to remain faithful to the teaching they had received. The first issue that is addressed is Christ's sovereignty over all of the angels and other powers of the universe. Our reading today is the text of an early hymn, no doubt used here to bolster the author's point regarding the absolute supe-riority of Christ over every cosmic power. The hymn, identi-fying Christ with the late Jewish personification of Wisdom, ascribes to him a role in both creation and redemption. It concludes with a recognition of "the blood of his cross" as the instrument through which Christ has achieved reconciliation and peace.

Jesus' commandment to love God and neighbor appears in Luke's Gospel as an answer given by a questioning lawyer who wished to know the way to eternal life. In Mark and Matthew it is Jesus himself who answers a question by giving the commandment. Scholars recognize the origin of the two commandments in texts from Deuteronomy and Leviticus, but still debate whether their linkage is original to Jesus. Regardless of that issue, it is clear that the two-fold command of love is at the core of Jesus' teaching. Luke's use of Jesus' journey to Jerusalem as the setting for this and other instruc-tions on the meaning of discipleship serves to underline the importance of this teaching. In the parable of the Good Samaritan, Jesus invites his hearers to take love of neighbor to an entirely new level by a surprising suggestion as to how inclusive must be our sense of who qualifies as our "neighbor."

Catholic Doctrine

Love of Neighbor

Scripture records that Jesus preached to the crowds saying that he did not come to abolish the Law but to fulfill it. Catholic teaching on Jesus' relationship to the Jewish religious Law is that the Son of God came and fulfills it (Matthew 5:17). He shows the power of the Spirit at work in the letter of the Law (CCC 2054).

While Jesus, as a teacher and interpreter of the Law, is not necessarily unique in summing up all the commandments into one great commandment, nevertheless, the "great commandment" which Jesus preaches is powerful in the way in which it combines two injunctions, that is, the command to love God with one's whole self and love one's neighbor as oneself. The Decalogue, the ten commandments, must be interpreted in the light of this single commandment. Jesus proclaimed that all of the Law and the prophets as well hang on this two-fold, yet single command. (CCC 2055)

Jesus himself perfects exemplifies how we are to follow this great commandment to love God and love our neighbor. Truly, the Lord manifests the fulfillment of God's Law and in his life, his ministry and his suffering and death we are invited to rediscover the law of love. (CCC 2053) Disciples of Jesus are invited to follow this law of love which encompasses both God and neighbor.

The Catechism of the Catholic Church divides its treatment of the Ten Commandments into two chapters. The first chapter focuses on the first three commandments (love God with your whole self). The second chapter focuses on commandments four through ten (love your neighbor as yourself). In this division of the Decalogue, a sense of the genius of Jesus' preaching on the great commandment is vividly perceived.

Catholic tradition also holds out to us the works of mercy, those charitable acts by which we help our neighbor in spiritual and bodily necessity. The spiritual works of mercy are: admonishing the sinner, instructing the ignorant, counseling the doubtful, comforting the sorrowful, bearing wrongs patiently, forgiving all injuries and praying for the living and dead. The corporal (or bodily) works of mercy are: feeding the hungry, giving drink to the thirsty, clothing the naked, visiting the imprisoned, sheltering the homeless, visiting the sick and burying the dead. Of all these works of mercy, giving alms to the poor is one of the chief witnesses to fraternal love and at the same time a work of justice pleasing to God. (CCC 2447)

Our Catholic understanding is that these spiritual and corporal works of mercy are prime actions that help us realize the love of neighbor which Jesus enjoined upon his followers. These actions, when rendered to another believer, help build up the body of Christ, and when show to non-believers help to evangelize them.

The Second Vatican Council teaches, "works of charity have become much more urgent and worldwide, now that means of communication are more rapid, distance between [people] has been more or less conquered, people in every part of the globe have become as members of a single family. Charitable actions today can and should reach all [people] and all needs. Whenever [people] are to be found who are in want of food and drink, of clothing, housing, medicine, work, education, the means necessary for leading a truly human life, wherever there are [people] racked with misfortune or illness, [those] suffering exile or imprisonment, Christian charity should go in search of them and find them out, comfort them with devoted care and give them the helps that will relieve their needs." (*Apostolicam Actuositatem*, 18 November 1965, n. 8)

The Council went on to teach that not only the effects of evil but their very causes should be addressed by the faithful. In meeting the needs of our hurting brothers and sisters, we are ultimately serving Christ, who has made himself the object of our attention, for when we show this charity to the least, we show it to Jesus. (Matthew 25:40)

Catholic Culture

St. Martin of Tours (317-397) was born in Hungary where his father was stationed with the Roman army. He wished to become a catechumen but his father forebade it and forced him to enter the army at an early age. Sent as a soldier to Amiens in 338, legend has it that upon meeting a naked beggar, he cut his fur cloak in two and offered half to the nearly frozen man. The next night a vision was granted to Martin of Christ wearing the half-cloak, saying, "Martin, who is only a catechumen, covered me with his cloak." This forms the basis of traditional iconography of St. Martin and the beggar. A mosaic depicting Martin offering a crown is found in St. Apollinare Nuovo, Ravenna and dates from the sixth century. (*The Oxford Companion to Christian Art and Architecture*, pps. 308-09)

St. Brigid of Ireland (d. 525), along with Sts. Patrick and Columba, is a patron saint of Ireland. Born near Kildare, she founded a double monastery of women and men. For long centuries (until the Church placed convents under the jurisdiction of men) the monastery at Kildare was led by a double line of abbesses and abbot-bishops. It was a bustling center of artists and educators which offered the liberal arts and religious studies, famous throughout Europe. Kildare was a major influence in the spread of Christianity and produced scholars, artists, educators and missionaries.

Dismissal Catechesis (30 min)

Getting Started

1. Prepare the center of the circle with a lighted candle and an art piece depicting St. Martin of Tours.

2. After greeting the participants, focus their attention on the depiction of St. Martin and tell them the story of his offering his cloak to the freezing beggar. (Note the summary in the Catholic Culture section found in Understanding This Sunday.)

3. Invite the group to listen to the John Michael Talbot version of "St. Teresa's Prayer," (Christ has no body now but yours).

First Impressions

1. In the large group, invite the participants to share their impressions of the meaning of the Greatest Commandments, from the perspective of their experience of today's liturgy.

2. Invite them to gather in pairs and discuss the following questions: *What about the scripture passages and the prayers today touched your heart? Upon listening to God's Word, what motivates you to live out your commitment to the Lord?*

3. Ask the pairs to offer an insight from their discussion.

Making Connections

1. Survey the group, asking if anyone knows of a person whose life exemplifies the Commandment of Love. Invite them to describe this person, specifically naming the loving characteristics. Note these attributes on a poster, on which you have drawn a stick figure of a person. Write the characteristic near an appropriate body part, for example, write, 'a good listener' near the ear of the stick person.

2. Continue by inviting stories of these loving people, noting their characteristics. When the group seems finished, allow for time to reflect upon the attributes of a loving person.

3. Complete the session by summarizing the discussion and inviting everyone to name one attribute or attitude they wish to develop. These can be written in the Participant Book (page 83) or on the blackline handout., under "I want to put my faith into action by:"

Prayer

Conclude by celebrating a Minor Exorcism, found in the RCIA, #94 E.

Extended Catechesis

SESSION FOCUS: *Love of Neighbor*

Gathering

A. Sunday:

1. Welcome and greet the sponsors and team members as they arrive. When they have joined the circle, invite one of the catechumens or candidates to share a little about the life of St. Martin of Tours. Invite the participants to share stories of other saints who are noted for their love of neighbor.

2. Open the prayer by standing to sing the hymn, "We are Many Parts" (Haugen), verses 1 and 2. Have copies of the second reading from Colossians 1:15-20 prepared prior to the session. Invite all to pray this Christological Hymn as they remain standing. Proclaim the gospel: Luke 10: 25-37. In a prayer of petition, ask the participants to pray for a 'neighbor' who is in need, while all respond, "Lord, Hear our Prayer." Close with the third verse of the song, "We are Many Parts."

B. Weekday:

1. Keep the same centerpiece, a lighted candle and an art piece depicting St. Martin of Tours. Retell the story of St. Martin and his concern for his 'neighbor.' Ask members of the group to name other saints noted for their charity to all people.

2. Proceed to proclaim the Word through this liturgy.
   - Song: "We are Many Parts" (Haugen)
   - First Reading: Deuteronomy 30:10-14
   - Psalm 69:14, 17, 30-31, 33-34, 36, 37
   - Gospel: Luke 10:25-37
   - Silence
   - Closing Prayer, spoken together: Colossians 1:15-20 (Have copies available for all)

The Word (30 min)

1. Ask the participants to share stories from the recent news accounts, where individuals demonstrated love for neighbor. Bring out the poster of the stick person, created by the catechumens and candidates. Summarize some of the qualities named on the poster.

2. Develop a general discussion around the difficulties and obstacles we experience in loving our neighbor, especially the stranger.

3. Present the background of the scriptures in these or your own words.

The passage from Deuteronomy is part of a Covenant renewal ceremony among the exiled people of Israel. The writer is assuring the people that God has not abandoned them. They are to observe the demands of the Covenant with their whole heart and soul. This means that Yahweh's law is not just an external practice, but it is an inspiring and motivating way of life that comes from within.

Jesus reiterates this covenant-attitude regarding the Two Great Commandments: Love of God and love of neighbor as yourself is the heart of the intimate relationship which God desires. This two-fold command of love is at the core of Jesus' teaching. He takes the meaning of love of neighbor to a new level, shattering stereotypical modes of behavior, both then and now. For Jesus, neighbor goes beyond acquaintances, countrymen or like-minded individuals. His parable of the good Samaritan (a foreigner resented by the Jews), expands the scope of this commandment. For Jesus, the word neighbor is all inclusive, embracing the stranger, foreigner and the detestable.

4. Gather participants into small groups, asking them to discuss one or more of the following:

How did Jesus fulfill the Law of the Hebrew people in his teaching? What was shocking to the lawyer, who was aware of the two-fold commandment of love? How is this shocking for you? How can we transform keeping the commandments externally to an action of love flowing from within?

Catholic Teaching (30 min)

1. Present the Spiritual and Corporal Works of Mercy (see the Participant Book (page 82) or the blackline handout.) Explain that these are part of the Catholic tradition, going beyond and putting 'flesh' on the commandments 4-10.

2. Invite all to reflect on the Works of Mercy through the exercise found in the Participant Book (page 82) or on the blackline handout.

3. Ask the sponsors/catechumen and sponsor/candidate pairs to share whatever they wish from their reflection on the Works of Mercy.

Putting Faith Into Practice

Prepare a short presentation on a contemporary individual who has modeled love of neighbor. One such person is Dorothy Day. Here are a few highlights of her contribution.

Dorothy Day was a contemporary (1897-1980) who lived the Parable of the Good Samaritan. As a young woman she lived in a cheap apartment, having dropped out of college, church, marriage and, basically, out of life. While the rise of communism inspired her, it held nothing for her soul. It was only when she found "a church of the poor" and "the folly of the cross" in the Catholic church that she saw more clearly her mission in life. After her conversion she began to publish the Catholic Worker, a penny newspaper to comfort and counsel poor people like herself. She took the works of mercy seriously, opening soup kitchens and hospitality houses to feed, clothe and give shelter to those in need. One thing led her to another. When the war broke out she persisted in a radical pacifist posture, landing her in jail many times. Her witness was "living simply so that others could simply life." The Catholic Worker Movement has spread and is thriving today, with Hospitality Houses all over the world. She is an icon of the Good Samaritan.

For further reading consult, Chittister, Joan, *A Passion for Life: Fragments of the Face of God*, (Maryknoll, NY: Orbis Books), 1996, pp. 59-63.

Prayer

Close with the prayer in remembrance of Dorothy Day, found in the Participant Book (page 83) or on the blackline handout.

O God, you have given us our senses that we might hear, see, touch, feel and smell the wonders of creation. Bless us so that we might use these senses to better hear your Word in order to put it into practice in our daily lives. Help us to bring the Good News of Jesus Christ to those who have been pushed aside by society. May we, like Martha and Mary, become both hearers and doers of the Gospel message. We ask this through Jesus Christ, our brother, who lives and reigns with you and the Holy Spirit, one God forever and ever. Amen.

Sixteenth Sunday in Ordinary Time

Understanding this Sunday:

Background for Catechesis

The Word In Liturgy

Genesis 18:1-10a
Psalm 15:2-3, 3-4, 5
Colossians 1:24-28
Luke 10:38-42

Today's reading from the Book of Genesis is part of a whole cycle of stories concerning Abraham. The intent of these stories is to contrast the failure of the "first creation" in the sin of Adam with the success of the "second creation" in the obedience of Abraham. Today's reading, a tale of hospitality in which Abraham unwittingly entertains the Lord himself, is evidently chosen to go with the Gospel story of hospitality, in which Martha and Mary welcome the Lord Jesus into their home. The narrative is elusive in its description of the divine visitor, at one point saying it was "the Lord" who appeared to Abraham and at another describing "three men" who appear at the entrance of his tent. Abraham offers the customary oriental hospitality—quite lavish by our standards—and the divine visitors in return make the promise of offspring to the elderly man and his wife Sarah. Folk tales such as this, in which an act of hospitality turns out to be an encounter with a divine figure, were rather commonplace in the culture of the day. However, the author of Genesis has skillfully woven this conventional story into a larger framework that is meant to reveal God's commitment to the covenant forged with the Jewish people in the person of their patriarch, Abraham. Today's responsorial psalm does not have an obvious connection with the first reading. Its choice, perhaps, was governed by its focus on the qualities of one who "does justice" and consequently lives "in the presence of the Lord," surely an apt description of Abraham.

The opening section of the letter to the Colossians offers various teachings of Paul designed to refute the false teachers who were proselytizing among the Gentile converts at Colossae. Mindful of the personal attacks leveled against his credibility, the author points out the divine commission given

to Paul, as well as how he has shown his fidelity through endurance of trials for the sake of preaching the Gospel. A negative comparison with his detractors is probably intended. The divine commission was "to preach among you his word in its fullness." The result of that preaching, if the word is accepted in its fullness, is to make the hearers of the Gospel message "complete in Christ." Among the Gentile community in Colossae, the prevalence of various mystery religions can certainly be assumed. Those cults taught that access to divine mysteries could be obtained in secret cultic celebrations, and that those rituals guaranteed the initiate a form of salvation which made them "complete." For the Christian believer, salvation is presented here as a result of accepting the preached word, "that mystery hidden . . . but now revealed." The somewhat shocking expression about "what is lacking in the sufferings of Christ" is not a denial of the sufficiency of Christ's redemptive act. Rather, it refers to the temporal nature of our participation in the mystery of Christ's saving death, a participation that necessarily implies a "completion" of the Christ event in us over time. The focus of today's catechetical session picks up on the foundational nature of the preached word and on the necessary response on our part—to be a hearer of the "full measure of wisdom" contained in that word.

Commentators have often interpreted today's Gospel as a discussion about the relative merits of the contemplative life versus the active life. In fact, this story is the second illustration that Luke gives to explain the meaning of the "great commandment" to love God and neighbor, the first being the parable of the Good Samaritan. Active compassion for one's neighbor (10:29-37, last week) and receptive hearing of the word of God (10:38-42, this week) are each highlighted as ways of fulfilling the one great commandment that Jesus has given at 10:27. In today's passage, Martha's anxiety is chastised, and the honor that Jesus gives to Mary, saying that "she has chosen the better part," is clearly the point of this story. The most important aspect of hospitality, surprisingly, is not what is given to, but what is received from the guest. Listening to Jesus is crucial to receiving him.

Catholic Doctrine

Hearers of the Word

God communicates divine love to us in words and deeds. His words proclaimed his message and his deeds professed and gave proof to that message (*Dei Verbum*, 18 November 1965, n 2). Thus, "it follows that the interpreter of sacred Scriptures, if he is to ascertain what God has wished to communicate to us, should carefully search out the meaning which the sacred writers really had in mind, that meaning which God had thought well to manifest through the medium of their words" (DV, 12). Thus, God's Word, as attested in Scripture, is not a dry word limited to the printed page or to the spoken proclamation. It is a living Word whose intimate truth is revealed in Jesus Christ through his life, his ministry, his suffering, death and resurrection.

The Second Vatican Council sought to open the riches of Scripture to the faithful, to support, encourage and invigorate them in their following of the eternal Word. The Council preached, "It follows that all the preaching of the Church, as indeed the entire Christian religion, should be nourished and ruled by Sacred Scripture. In the sacred books the Father who is in heaven comes lovingly to meet his children, and talks with them." (DV, 21)

Indeed, the Church venerates the Scriptures as it venerates the Lord's Body. The instructions given in the Lectionary indicate, "In the readings, explained by the homily, God is speaking to his people, opening up to them the mystery of redemption and salvation, and nourishing their spirit; Christ is present to the faithful through his own word. . . .The liturgy itself inculcates the great reverence to be shown toward the reading of the gospel, setting it off from the other readings by special marks of honor. . . .The people, who by their acclamations acknowledge and confess Christ present and speaking to them, stand as they listen to it. Marks of reverence are given to the Book of the Gospels itself." (*General Instruction of the Roman Missal*, n 33 & 35) Catholics, therefore, see themselves as receiving nourishment from the one table of God's Word and Christ's Body (CCC 103).

Bible study has exploded throughout the Catholic world since Vatican II. Catechetical endeavors, small faith communities, and parish programs have all enthusiastically embraced the study of sacred Scripture. So, too, has the process of Christian initiation of adults. In the early Church, catechumens were called "hearers of the Word" because of the centrality of the Word to their time of formation for entering into the sacramental life of the church.

The very fact of scripture's expanded use in the Sunday Mass has furthered an appreciation of the Word of God. The Council, in encouraging bible study and in expanding the Sunday readings from two selections to three quoted St. Jerome, saying, "Ignorance of the Scriptures is ignorance of Christ." (DV, 25) In the Introduction to the Lectionary, the Church insists, "Whenever, therefore, the Church, gathered by the Holy Spirit for liturgical celebration, announces and proclaims the word of God, it has the experience of being a new people in whom the covenant made in the past is fulfilled. Baptism and confirmation in the Spirit have made all the faithful messengers of God's word because of the grace of hearing they have received. They must therefore be the bearers of the same word in the Church and in the world, at least by the witness of their way of life." (*Lectionary for Mass: Introduction*, revised 1981, n. 7) To hear the Word of God and believe is to bear the Word of God in witness.

Catholic Culture

Every blessing found in the *Book of Blessings* is accompanied by a Liturgy of the Word such that if the blessing does not take place within a Mass appropriate Scriptures set the context for the ritual action of the blessing. All the rites of the Church and its sacramental celebrations follow this structure, indicated by the Council, so that in every ritual action, the Word of God is proclaimed, heard and followed.

The formation of the canon of scripture has a complex history. One immediate clue to its complexity is the fact that Catholic bibles include 46 books in the Old Testament, whereas Protestant and Jewish bibles contain only 39 (although they organize them differently). The Catholic canon includes all the books of the Septuagint, a Greek translation from Alexandria that was current at the time of Christ. The Protestant reformers followed instead a collection in Hebrew from Palestine. Current scholarship has lessened the tension of this controversy however, and many Protestant bibles today contain the seven books included in the Catholic bible in a special section called "apocrypha."

Baron Friedrich von Hugel (1852-1925), theologian and biblical exegete championed the cause of modern scientific biblical study within the Catholic Church. He was a popular and renowned spiritual director and influenced English religious life who was also associated with Modernists Alfred Loisy and Gorge Tyrrell but was not himself condemned because of his lay status and eminent social position.

Dismissal Catechesis (30 min)

Getting Started

1. Prepare the space ahead of time.

2. Invite the catechumens and candidates to be seated quietly within the circle. Light a candle and pray in these or similar words:

   O God, creator of the whole universe, you have given us The Word, your son, Jesus Christ. May we be open to hear the word spoken to us that it may take root in our minds and in our hearts so that the words we speak and the deeds we do will lead others to know, love and serve you. We ask this in the name of Jesus the Lord. Amen.

First Impressions

Give everyone paper or instruct them to turn to the Participant Book for this Sunday (page 84-85) or the blackline handout. Invite them to close their eyes and to recall the Liturgy of the Word just celebrated. After a few minutes ask them to jot down words or phrases they heard in the liturgy. Ask them to jot down any comments or questions they have regarding the liturgy. Invite them to summarize the message they heard proclaimed today. After a few minutes, ask them to share as much as they choose with another person. Then invite anyone who wishes to share insights and comments with the whole group to do so. Summarize the sharing.

Making Connections

1. To help individuals to connect these scriptures to daily life, on a chalkboard or a large piece of paper for all to see, list some of the ways we receive messages. Have each person indicate which way they most prefer and least prefer to receive messages. Discuss the reasons for their choices.

2. Ask them to think about the most important message they ever received. What was the message? How was the message delivered and by whom? What was their response to the message and to the messenger? After a few minutes, invite them to share their story with a partner. When they have had some time to share, ask them to recap briefly for the large group their response to the message and the messenger.

3. Briefly summarize today's readings, in these or similar words: *Abraham and Sarah invited strangers, God's messenger into their home, and received a promise of a son in their old age. Paul reveals the message of God, the mystery of Christ to the holy ones. At the feet of Jesus, Mary listens to his words and is told that she has chosen the better part.* Ask participants to pair up and discuss a time when they received 'a message.' If so, did they recognize the message and the messenger. What was their response to the message, to the messenger, in their own life?

Prayer

Invite everyone to sit quietly, to close their eyes and to take several deep breaths. Lead them by asking them to imagine themselves in a very beautiful place, just sitting quietly. In the distance, they see Jesus coming toward them. He approaches and quietly sits down beside them. What would Jesus say to them? What would they say to Jesus. After several minutes of quiet continue by saying Jesus says good-bye, stands up and walks away. Invite them to return to this room and to open their eyes.

Extended Catechesis

SESSION FOCUS: *Hearers of the Word.*

Gathering

A. Sunday:

Welcome everyone. Invite them to gather in a circle around the candle and sing either "Send Us As Your Blessing, Lord" (Christopher Walker, Oregon Catholic Press, 1987) or "We Have Been Told." (David Haas, GIA Publications, 1983). Proclaim the gospel: Luke 10:38-42.

B. Weekday:

Welcome everyone. Begin with a Celebration of the Word, such as:

- Song: "We Have Been Told"
- Sign of the Cross and Greeting
- Reading: Genesis 18:1-10a
- Quiet
- Reading: Colossians 1:24-28
- Alleluia
- Gospel Luke 10:38-42
- Alleluia

The Word (30 min)

1. Have everyone sit in small groups. Begin the discussion on the topic of hospitality: *How is a new person in your workplace made to feel welcome? Describe the welcome given to a new member of the family such as a baby or a new in-law. How does the neighborhood welcome a new family from another culture?* After some time in the groups, elicit key elements of hospitality.

2. Proclaim Genesis 18:1-10a again. Describe the hospitality of Abraham and Sarah, Martha and Mary. How does it compare with the key elements of hospitality they named? Discuss the importance of hospitality, particularly the hospitality offered to the stranger, who is the Lord.

3. Continue the discussion with the promise made to Abraham and Sarah that next year by this same time, they would have

a son. This begins the fulfillment of the covenant made to Abraham, that his descendants would be more numerous than the stars. Just as Abraham and Sarah did not recognize the stranger, so, too, we do not recognize the presence of God in the people we meet day after day. Martha and Mary challenge us to practice hospitality not merely as doing something for someone but taking the time to listen to our neighbor. Time is often the greatest gift we can give to another. Giving time is integral to hospitality.

4. Proclaim Colossians 1:24-28 again. Recall for the groups that Paul is refuting the false teachers who were proselytizing among the Gentile converts. At the time of Paul, there existed numerous mystery religions which taught that access to divine mysteries could be obtained in secret cultic celebrations, and such rituals guaranteed the initiate a form of salvation which made them "complete." Paul states that our participation in the mystery of Christ's saving death takes place over time and requires that we become hearers and doers of the Word.

Catholic Teaching (30 min)

1. The goal of today's session is to inform the catechumens and candidates understanding of "The Word" and its place in their lives and in our worship.

2. Ask two or three parishioners who serve as lectors to speak to the group about their understanding of the Word they proclaim; why the Word is proclaimed, not just read, and its importance in the worship and the lives of the people gathered.

3. Share that the Israelites thought of The Word as the manifestation of God. In "The Word" God is revealed and present. The Word is always dynamic. To hear The Word demanded a response. Further the discussion using the background found in the Catholic Doctrine section.

4. Explain the development of the Lectionary. Include the organization of the three-year cycle; that it includes readings from the Old Testament Scriptures, the Psalms, the letters, Acts of the Apostles, Revelation and the Gospels. If possible, share excerpts from the Introduction to the Lectionary. Show them several other ritual books and the way in which Scripture is present.

5. Mention that beginning with Pope Pius XII, including the Second Vatican Council and Pope Paul VI (*Introduction to the Roman Missal*), and up to the present (*Catechism of the Catholic Church*), the church has re-emphasized that Scripture is to be the foundation of all theological study. There has been, therefore, an explosion of bible study groups, faith communities based on scripture, and revised catechetical materials which include Scripture passages. The Word, God's revelation and presence, not only is the source of our formation but also the summit to which we are called to be witnesses and doers.

Putting Faith Into Practice

Invite the participants to quietly reflect on their personal lives. Use the following questions as a guide: *How are you being called to respond to what has been presented in this session? What support do you need from the community to answer this call?* After a brief reflection period, ask them to share their responses in a small group.

Prayer

Invite everyone to stand in a circle. Celebrate Minor Exorcism H (found in RCIA #94). Adapt it if both catechumens and candidates are present. Sing: "Take the Word of God With You."

O God, you have given us our senses that we might hear, see, touch, feel and smell the wonders of creation. Bless us so that we might use these senses to better hear your Word in order to put it into practice in our daily lives. Help us to bring the Good News of Jesus Christ to those who have been pushed aside by society. May we, like Martha and Mary, become both hearers and doers of the Gospel message. We ask this through Jesus Christ, our brother, who lives and reigns with you and the Holy Spirit, one God forever and ever. Amen.

Seventeenth Sunday in Ordinary Time

Understanding this Sunday:
Background for Catechesis

The Word In Liturgy

Genesis 18:20-32
Psalm 138:1-2, 2-3, 6-7, 7-8
Colossians 2:12-14
Luke 11:1-13

Today's reading from Genesis picks up where last week's left off. After the departure of the mysterious strangers from his tent, Abraham finds himself walking with the Lord, bargaining over the fate of Sodom and Gomorrah. The scene should strike a chord with the attentive reader: Adam had been destined to walk in the garden with God, but lost that privilege by his sin. Now Abraham, by virtue of God's promise, is accorded the great gift lost by Adam. The two walk together in intimate exchange, not as equals, but surely in respectful mutuality. Abraham seeks to know the Lord better, to understand his mind and will. The appearance may suggest the haggling at an oriental bazaar, but at a deeper level Abraham is coming to a better knowledge of the Lord with whom he is walking. He is not necessarily trying to change God's mind, just to understand whether God's justice would allow the just to perish together with the wicked. As an image of what our prayer should be like, the passage is a gold mine of insights. In Psalm 138 we find a song of praise and thanksgiving for God's deliverance (perhaps from the exile). Its choice is surely guided by the first reading's portrayal of a God willing to relent in punishment and spare the wicked if only a handful can be found who are faithful.

Today's selection from Colossians is taken from the final part of the teaching section of the letter. After presenting the truth proclaimed by Paul's ministry, the author now deals with errors that were being spread in the community. Those errors had to do with the claim that Gentile converts must observe certain prescriptions of the Mosaic Law (e.g., dietary restrictions and circumcision) in order to appease the powers that held sway over the cosmos. Presenting baptism as a type of circumcision, the author insists on the "power of God" at

work in that sacrament, a power that gave them "new life in company with Christ." That power is far superior to the so-called powers of this world, as is revealed by the fact that through it God has "pardoned all our sins." An interesting image, whose origin is not entirely clear, is used in this regard: God has canceled the bond against us, "snatching it up and nailing it to the cross." While the reference is not clear, the image expresses powerfully the decisive forgiveness that has come to us through Christ's sacrificial death on the cross. The following verse, not part of today's reading, further underlines the victory won by Christ's cross by using an image familiar to the Roman world, that of a military triumphal procession: "despoiling the principalities and the powers, he made a public spectacle of them, leading them away in triumph by it." (v. 15)

It was the custom in Jesus' day that a rabbi give to his followers a distinctive way of praying, by which their unique identity could be identified and fostered. Luke describes Jesus as being at prayer when his disciples ask for "their" special prayer. Scholars have long commented on the importance of the way that Jesus addresses God as "Abba," a word equivalent to our "daddy." In that intimate address to Yahweh, so unusual among Jesus' contemporaries, we see the heart of the filial consciousness of Jesus. Luke has five petitions that follow, each one well documented elsewhere in the Gospel as characteristic of Jesus' way of acting. Most likely, each of the petitions in its original form was highly eschatological; Luke has made them more relevant to the daily life of the Christian. Luke then adds three parables that illustrate Jesus' teaching on the prayer of petition. Our reading, however, covers only the first two.

Catholic Doctrine

The Lord's Prayer: Summary of the Gospel

The fundamental importance that the Catholic Church places on the prayer Jesus taught his disciples is reflected in *The Catechism of the Catholic Church*. A major portion of the section on Christian Prayer is dedicated to illuminating the text of the Lord's Prayer. One-hundred and six paragraphs are given over to an explanation of this prayer (CCC 2759-2865). On this particular Sunday, our doctrine section will focus on how the Lord's Prayer aptly sums up the gospel message in prayer.

St. Augustine asserted that when comparing the text of the Lord's Prayer to all the other prayers contained in scripture there cannot be found anything in those other prayers that is not in the Lord's Prayer. While the psalms are the mainstay of the prayers given voice by the people of God (especially in the Liturgy of the Hours), the themes of the psalms flow together into the petitions of the Lord's Prayer (CCC 2762).

Indeed, we believe that all of the scriptures, whether from the Law, the Prophets or the Psalms, are fulfilled in Christ. When one refers to the "good news" of God, the point of reference is the person of Jesus Christ. Christ is the eternal Word of God who in his person, his ministry and his teaching brings to the world the gospel of Life. The initial proclamation of the gospel is recorded for us by St. Matthew in the Sermon on the Mount, and the text of Jesus' prayer to the Father is found in the center of this teaching. (Note: While this Sunday's gospel passage comes from Luke's gospel, which also has a version of the Lord's Prayer, the Church, in its liturgical tradition makes use of the seven petitions preserved in Matthew's text.)

St. Thomas Aquinas points out, "The Lord's prayer is the most perfect of prayers. . . .In it we ask not only for all the things we can rightly desire, but also in the sequence that they should be desired. This prayer not only teaches us to ask for things, but also in what order we should desire them." (STh II-II,83,9) Thus, while the Sermon on the Mount is teaching for life, the text of the Our Father is prayer for life. In both instances, the spirit of Jesus animates the church, through teaching and through prayer.

In what way is this prayer text a summary of the good news? Why do we believe that it is unique and fundamental?

It comes from the mouth of Jesus himself, he who is the eternal Word of God among us. As the incarnate Word, he understands in his human heart the needs of our own hearts and gives us the means to express our innermost longings through this text. In one sense, we have many needs, many prayers that we address to God. But God has only One prayer (if you will) for us, Jesus Christ (CCC 2765). He is the very model of Christian prayer. Our own life of prayer is based in his example.

The text of the Our Father is not merely words strung together, such that when we pray them we recite them automatically. We have also been given, along with these words and the teachings of Jesus, the Holy Spirit. In that Spirit we are adopted as sons and daughter of the Most High and therefore we can correctly address God as "Abba," or Father (2766).

From the very beginning, this text has not only been revered but prayed as a gift from Christ to the members of his body, the Church. Initially, Christian communities prayed this prayer three times daily (stipulated in the *Didache* 8,2,3; the title comes from the Greek for "teaching" as in "the teaching of the apostles"). This practice replaced the "Eighteen Benedictions" which was a custom of Jewish piety (CCC 2767). It is truly the prayer of the Church community, evident in the very first word Jesus gives us in this prayer, not "my" Father, but "our" Father. Even when spoken alone by an individual, this prayer on the lips of Jesus' followers refers the believer to the larger community, the Church. One is offering petitions on behalf of the entire body of believers (CCC 2768).

The liturgical practice of the Church places this prayer within the major hours of the Divine Office (the Liturgy of the Hours). At Mass, after the Eucharistic Prayer and before the Communion Rite, this prayer of the Lord is always offered by the community. Always, as believers attend the eschatological banquet, the words of the Lord who taught us to pray and await the fullness of the kingdom are on our lips and in our hearts.

Catholic Culture

This prayer is recited by the faithful at Morning Prayer and Evening Prayer (Liturgy of the Hours). Thus, Catholics pray this prayer and the beginning and the eve of each day. The prayer dedicates and closes the day, appealing to "Our Father."

The Elect, in the Period of Purification and Enlightenment (and sometimes anticipated during the Catechumenate stage of the RCIA process), first hear the prayer of the Our Father handed on to them by the community of the faithful. It is handed on through the proclamation of the Gospel.

The Lord's Prayer also figures prominently in the recitation of the Rosary.

Notes

Dismissal Catechesis (30 min)

Getting Started

1. Prepare the space with a lighted candle and a place for the lectionary on a table in the center. Gather in a circle of chairs.

2. Invite everyone to share a time of silence. Ask everyone to open their hands in a gesture of prayer. Pray:

   God, you love us with the love of a father and mother. You want us to bring our needs to you with trust that you will give us all that is necessary. Deepen our trust in you. Help us hear your word in our hearts and souls. We ask this in the name of Jesus. Amen.

First Impressions

1. Note: Today's Liturgy of the Word lends itself to the community's presentation of the Lord's Prayer. If this presentation occurs at Mass, then in the dismissal session give an opportunity for the participants to express their experience of this rite. Otherwise, proceed with the following session.

2. Recall briefly the gathering hymn, Abraham's asking God over and over to save the city if there are even fewer innocent people, Jesus giving the disciples a prayer, and then talking about asking God for what is needed. Invite participants to go around the circle and respond to this question: *What image or phrase from today's liturgy stays with you?*

Making Connections

1. Ask participants to respond to discuss the following in pairs: *Choose one image that speaks to you and state what you hear God is saying to you personally.* Then have each pair share some insights with the large group. Facilitate the conversation, inviting further discussion from personal experience.

2. Relate the Genesis reading—portraying Abraham with a close enough relationship with God to dialogue a fourth and a fifth time for what he wanted—to the gospel which includes this prayer Christ taught, and examples of a God who easily responds to prayer. Ask participants to share their response to these questions in pairs: *When was a time you asked God for something with persistence? What does praying persistently say about who God is for you?* After the sharing, elicit responses in the large group.

3. Conclude by asking participants to state aloud their response to this question: *What is something you want to ask God for today?*

Prayer

Hand out printed copies of the Lord's Prayer for those who do not know it. Pray together the Lord's Prayer.

Extended Catechesis

SESSION FOCUS:
The Lord's Prayer: Summary of the Gospel

Gathering

A. Sunday:

1. Welcome sponsors and other participants. Have them sit in small groups.

2. Invite them into a moment in silence. Ask a catechumen or candidate to state briefly the focus of the sharing during the dismissal catechesis.

3. After a moment of quiet, sing Psalm 138 or the psalm used at today's Mass. Pray, *Lord, our God, out of his own prayer, Jesus taught us to pray. We know the words. Teach us to pray this prayer in the depths of our being. We ask this in the name of Jesus. Amen.* Proclaim the Gospel Luke 11:1-13.

B. Weekday:

1. Greet and welcome the participants as you gather in a circle.

2. Ask participants to respond aloud to this question: In what way have you experienced your dependence on God to give what is needed since Sunday?

3. Then lead this Celebration of the Word.
   - Hymn: You Are All We Have
   - Sign of the Cross, Greeting
   - First Reading: Genesis 18:20-32
   - Sing Psalm 138
   - Pause
   - Gospel: Luke 11:1-13
   - Silence
   - Pray the prayer in A. Sunday

The Word (30 min)

1. Introduce today's Gospel with the following points:
   - This passage occurs when Jesus is making his journey to Jerusalem.
   - Disciples were used to asking their teacher to show them how to pray.
   - Jesus himself had just finished praying when asked how to pray.

Invite the participants to do the following: *Choose one line of the Lord's Prayer that feels like your prayer today. Speak this line aloud as we go around the room. Repetition is okay.*

2. Then ask participants to talk in their small groups about their experience of the Lord's Prayer: *What parts of the prayer do you most like? What parts do you find challenging?* Note that some of the catechumens might not be familiar with the prayer, and may find themselves more in a listening posture. Then invite a summary from each of the small groups to be given aloud.

3. Proclaim the Gospel again, telling the participants: Listen especially to the additional statements about prayer after the Lord's Prayer. Ask the participants to share their response to this question in the large group: *What do these statements say about what God is like?*

   Make the following points:

   - Abraham had a close relationship with God that allowed him to be comfortable enough to make one request then another of God.

   - The word Jesus used for Father, Abba, is more like Daddy. A child trusts and is dependent on Daddy and Mommy. Invite those who wish to do the following: *Imagine yourself being held in God's arms as a child being held by a loving parent. What do you like or dislike about this image?* See the Participant Book (page 86) or the blackline handout for this reflection. Then invite some response in the large group.

4. Ask participants to reflect on these questions: *How do you let yourself depend on God? How do you try to control your life yourself. How have you been letting God be more in control of your life?* The Participant Book (page 86) or the blackline handout has an exercise for this reflection. Invite the participants to discuss their responses in their small groups. Ask for some large group sharing to lead into the following teaching.

Catholic Teaching (30 min)

1. Ask the participants this question: *What are the significant things prayed for in the Lord's Prayer?* Put these on paper or poster board. Include the intention of God's reign coming about, God's giving of daily sustenance, forgiveness, and protection from evil.

2. Talk about the Lord's Prayer in these or your own words.

   The Lord's Prayer contains a summary of the life of a disciple, of living as a Christian. Disciples allow themselves to be dependent on God, whose name is truly holy or hallowed. Disciples know God is the source and fullness of life, and God loves them and will truly give what is good and needed. Disciples live life in a close relationship with God. It is through the Holy Spirit that we

are able to address God as Abba. In praying the Lord's Prayer all who are disciples enter into filial relationship with God and share in the mission of Christ to bring about God's reign. In the early church Christians prayed the Lord's Prayer three times a day.

In Matthew's gospel the Lord's Prayer has more intentions stated than in Luke's gospel. These elements include both the present time and circumstances as well as the fullness of time and God's ultimate victory. These elements (refer to paper or poster board) involve all dimensions of the life of a disciple. Even when prayed alone, the prayer is communal, using the plural pronoun us.

3. Ask the participants this question: *What are the effects of praying this prayer on the person and on the community?* Invite some discussion. State: If this prayer is truly prayed from the heart it will cause us to truly engage in life as disciples.

OR . . .

Use the reflection in the Participant Book (page 86) or on the blackline handout.

Putting Faith Into Practice

Invite participants to reflect on this question: *In what way is God inviting you to more truly and faithfully pray this prayer?* Participants may write their response in the Participant Book (page 87) or on the blackline handout. Have them share their commitment to this action in small groups.

Prayer

Invite all to pray in the following way: *Let us stand with hands extended upward and pray the Lord's Prayer together slowly and meaningfully.* Pray the Lord's Prayer.

Eighteenth Sunday in Ordinary Time

Understanding this Sunday:
Background for Catechesis

The Word In Liturgy

Ecclesiastes 1:2; 2:21-23
Psalm 90:3-4, 5-6, 12-13, 14, 17
Colossians 3:1-5, 9-11
Luke 12:13-21

The Book of Ecclesiastes is part of the Wisdom literature of the Bible. Little is known of its origins or authorship, although the text is piously attributed to Solomon, presumably because of his reputation as Israel's greatest sage. Most probably, the book dates to a late stage of the Jewish biblical tradition. The author's thesis ("All things are vanity") runs contrary to other sections of the Jewish scriptures that had discerned a divine justice at work in the world. Rather than assert that good is always rewarded and evil punished—as the Deuteronomists had; or, as many Wisdom authors held, that the wise person can discern the rules of the universe and learn to live in accord with them in order to assure a measure of earthly success—the author of Ecclesiastes is convinced of the ultimate futility of human life and effort. Despite the author's pessimism, the book does contain a strong faith in the Lord and advises the reader to trust in God alone for security. The section we read today is cast in the first person as a form of royal testament, spoken in the voice of Solomon. The king looks back on his life at its end and sees that much of what he accomplished will pass to another and can easily be undone. When read in connection with today's Gospel, this text underlines the transitory nature of human wealth and accomplishment. The text fairly cries out to be completed with the words of the Gospel that advise "growing rich in the sight of God" rather than for oneself. The choice of Psalm 95 as our responsorial psalm is probably governed by its emphasis on listening to God's voice: ("If today you hear his voice, harden not your hearts"). The task of the sage in Israel was, above all, to hear God's voice and to help others do so as well.

This last of our four weeks of readings from Colossians is taken from the opening part of the hortatory section of the letter. The author warns and admonishes his hearers to put aside all of the trappings of their "old way" of life that preceded their conversion. Using traditional lists of what should be avoided, the author emphasizes the Pauline focus on Christ's risen life, in which the believer already shares by virtue of baptism ("you have been raised up in company with Christ"). One can legitimately make a connection between the perspective of this reading and the theme of detachment from worldly wealth found in today's Gospel and first reading. The admonition to "be intent on things above rather than on things of earth," would quite rightly reject an excessive attachment to material possessions such as Jesus condemns in the Gospel.

This week and next the lectionary provides us with an extensive section from Luke's Gospel in which he deals with the issue of material possessions. The larger context of this discourse is Jesus' journey to Jerusalem, during which he instructs his followers on the requirements of discipleship. Luke first offers the core of Jesus' teaching about avoiding greed (vv. 13-15), followed by an illustrative parable (more accurately, an example story) in which he drives home the point that greed only blocks one from acquiring what is really importance, i.e., a deeper relationship with God ("rich in the sight of God").

Catholic Doctrine

The Tenth Commandment

The traditional catechetical formulation of the tenth commandment ("you shall not covet your neighbor's goods") concerns the unjust desiring of another's property. Moral handbooks of the past century tended to treat the subject of property in an isolated fashion instead of placing the issue in the larger scope of God's plan of creation and salvation. Thus, in the past, property was seen as an unconditional right, as if it were a value in and of itself. But the earlier viewpoint of the Fathers of the Church saw property more in the context of stewardship in service of God and Christian love.

The social encyclicals of the popes uphold this latter viewpoint and the social function of property within the universal purpose of all created things. Material possessions are thus to be understood as placed within the universal dominion of God who owns all things and who is the common Creator of all people. "Property is of instrumental character, subordinated to the development of the human person, the needs of the community and the promotion of God's creative design." (C. Henry Peschke, S.V.D., *Christian Ethics*, vol. 2, C. Goodliffe Neale, Dublin, 1978, p. 513.).

The tenth commandment forbids greed and all of the violence, disorder and injustice arising from this desire to amass property beyond what one truly needs or deserves. Greed also goes by the name of avarice, which is the passion for wealth, riches and power (CCC 2536). The tenth commandment also forbids against envy (CCC 2538). Envy, the feeling of resentment over another's goods, can lead to the worst crimes. Indeed, the Book of Wisdom speaks of the devil's envy as the way in which death entered the world (Wisdom 2:24).

Both avarice and envy are considered "deadly" or capital sins because they, in turn, lead to other sins and vices. There are seven deadly sins: pride, avarice, envy, wrath, lust, gluttony and sloth. Sinning creates a proclivity to sin by the very repetition of action—in other words sin can become habitual, trapping one into a pattern of behavior. These seven deadly sins can thus spawn a host of other sins.

Both St. Augustine and St. John Chrysostom saw envy as one of the worst of all sins. From it are derived hatred, detraction, calumny, joy in the misfortune of another and displeasure caused by another's property (CCC 2539). St. John Chrysostom writes, "We fight one another, and envy arms us against one another. . . . If everyone strives to unsettle the Body of Christ, where shall we end up? We are engaged in making Christ's Body a corpse. . . We declare ourselves members of one and the same organism, yet we devour one another like beasts." (*Hom. in 2 Cor.* 27, 3-4: PG 61, 588)

Jesus preaches a poverty of the heart and sets an example for his disciples to renounce property and goods for the sake of the kingdom. Our Catholic tradition calls this "detachment." True happiness will be found and fulfilled in the vision and beatitude of God (CCC 2548). Believers own property in this world and amass a reasonable amount of wealth in order to insure for the future. At the same time, Catholics strive to mortify their cravings and, cooperating with divine grace, prevail over the seductions of pleasure and power. The Second Vatican Council exults, "For the spirit of poverty and charity is the glory and witness of the Church of Christ." (GS, 88)

Catholic Culture

Popular culture has long been fascinated by the Catholic notion of the "deadly sins." A recent movie entitled "Seven," for example, is a gruesome depiction of seven murders based on the seven deadly sins.

The seven deadly sins rarely are depicted in art individually. Sometimes they are represented in conjunction with the virtues. A painted tabletop by Bosch found in Madrid at the Prado does show the seven deadly sins alone. Giotto depicts some of the seven in the Arena Chapel frescoes. (*The Oxford Companion to Christian Art and Architecture*, p. 133)

Notes

Dismissal Catechesis (30 min)

Getting Started

1. Prepare the space with a cloth, lighted candle, and place for the lectionary on the center table. Gather in a circle of chairs.

2. Invite participants into a moment of silent prayer. Pray: *"God, you are the source of our lives. We belong to you. You give our lives meaning. Open us today to hear your words that lead to fuller life in you. We ask this in the name of Jesus." Amen.*

First Impressions

Recall images from today's liturgy of the Word: the gathering hymn, The words "Vanity of vanities" from Ecclesiastes, the statement in Colossians of our life being hidden with Christ in God, and Jesus telling us, "Avoid greed in all its forms." After a moment of reflection, invite the participants to go around the circle and share something from the liturgy that was meaningful for them.

Making Connections

1. Ask participants to discuss in pairs: *What was God saying personally in the liturgy today?* When they are finished, invite each pair to express some of their sharing in the large group.

2. State: *Vanity means a vapor that quickly vanishes.* The superlative expression "vanity of vanities!" is associated with possessions. In pairs ask the participants to discuss: *What feelings arise in you as you hear this expression? Then ask: What feelings arise in you when you hear the image in Colossians of our life being hidden with Christ in God, and the exhortation to set our hearts on what pertains to God?*

   In the large group ask the participants to discuss this question: *How difficult is it for you to set your heart on what pertains to God, on a scale of 1 to 10, with 10 being nearly impossible?* Facilitate the conversation, inviting comments from each of the participants. Then ask this question: *What in the church, in our culture, or in the family helps or hinders us from responding to God's invitation today?*

   In conclusion, ask participants: *In the form of a phrase or sentence, what is one thing you want to take with them from today's liturgy and sharing?* Go around the circle for this naming.

Prayer

1. Pray: *God, through your invitation we have heard and named your message to us today. You invite us to live our lives by values that will bring about true and lasting happiness. Fill our hearts with desire for you and the gifts that you offer. We pray through Christ our Lord. Amen.*

Extended Catechesis

SESSION FOCUS:
The Tenth Commandment and the Seven Deadly Sins

Gathering

A. Sunday:

1. Welcome sponsors and other participants into the circle. Have them form small groups.

2. Invite everyone into a moment of silence.

3. Ask a catechumen or candidate to summarize the content of the dismissal catechesis.

4. Sing: Blest Are They. Proclaim the Gospel, Luke 12:13-21.

B. Weekday:

1. As the group gathers in the circle, greet and welcome each person.

2. Ask participants to respond in the large group to the following question: *Since Sunday, when have you experienced the pull to have more money or more or better possessions?*

3. Lead this Celebration of the Word.

   - Hymn: Blest Are They
   - Sign of the Cross, Greeting
   - First Reading: Ecclesiastes 1:2; 2:21-23
   - Sing: Psalm 90
   - Second Reading: Colossians 3:1-5, 9-11
   - Sing: Alleluia
   - Gospel: Luke 12:13-21

   - Pray: *God, once again you gather us and we hear your word. You invite us to set our hearts on you rather than on possessions and things of this world. Speak your word deep within our hearts. Let our hearts true joy be the gifts that you offer. We ask this in Jesus name. Amen.*

The Word (30 min)

1. Introduce the gospel with these points:

- *This passage from Luke is part of Jesus' teaching to form disciples as Jesus is making his way to Jerusalem.*

- *The setting of the gospel is: Jesus is asked to make a determination about an inheritance, and chooses not to get involved in material concerns.*

- *Jesus then states very clearly his concern with greed both in a direct statement and in a parable.*

Ask participants to reflect on these questions: *How have you experienced greed trying to gain a hold on you? What choices have you made to go along with greed? What choices have you made against the pull of greed?* They may wish to write their responses in the Participant Book (page 88) or on the blackline handout.. When the groups are finished, ask the large group this question: *What are you noticing about greed?*

2. State this point: *Today's three readings together give a view about life in which we are either directed toward life with Christ or toward values honored by the world.* Invite participants to discuss this question in small groups: *How does the world and the culture in which we live support and encourage greed?* Then elicit from the groups and compile on paper or poster board the many ways greed is encouraged by the surrounding culture. Comment on how strongly the surrounding environment pressures us to seek more and better possessions.

3. State the following: *Today's gospel identifies getting rich for oneself as the opposite of growing rich in God's eyes.* Invite participants to reflect on these questions: *What does it mean to grow rich before God? How are you already growing rich before God? How is God inviting you to take a next step in growing rich in God's ways?* Participants may write this reflection in the Participant Book (page 88) or on the blackline handout.. After some time for reflection, invite
a sharing in small groups. Then elicit some large group response.

Catholic Teaching (30 min)

1. Present this teaching in these or your own words. Consult the Catholic Doctrine section.

The avoidance of greed is the content of the tenth commandment found in Exodus 20:17, You shall not covet your neighbor's house. You shall not covet your neighbor's wife, nor his male or female slave, nor his ox or ass, nor anything else that belongs to him. Greed is an inordinate desire for possessions. Possessions in them-selves are not bad. Greed involves an attachment to possessions. The church has named greed as one of the deadly or capital sins, because it can take over and direct a person's life.

2. In the large group ask the participants to respond to these questions: *What other vices can direct a person's life? What effects of these vices have you seen in people you know?* List the vices on paper or poster board as they are named.

State the following: *The other capital or deadly sins are pride, envy, wrath, lust, gluttony, and sloth. Each of these vices involves a way of being rather than simply doing an action. The church's naming of these sins as deadly gives a clue as to their potential harmfulness. Though these tendencies may all be present in a person, usually a person is more prone to one or another of them.*

3. Make the following point: *The church, the community of believers, is meant to be a support to grow in freedom from sin.* Ask participants to discuss this question: *How does the church, both locally and in the broader sense, provide help to choose God's values rather than letting these sins gain a foothold?* Include examples of spiritual opportunities, prayer, education, and collaboration with other members of the church in various arenas. *Colossians 3:1-5, 9-11 says that in baptism the sinful nature dies and is hidden, and a new person emerges. Living with Christ involves a giving of one's heart over to God.*

OR . . .

Participants may use the reflection in the Participant Book (page 88) or on the blackline handout..

Putting Faith Into Practice

Ask participants to reflect on these questions: *In what concrete way is God asking you to set your heart on God's ways? What action will you undertake this week?* State that: *This action may serve as an antidote to one of the seven sinful tendencies. For example, if the tendency is greed, then choose an action of material generosity.* Participants may write this action in the Participant Book (page 89) or on the blackline handout.. After reflecting, invite participants to share this action in their small groups

Prayer

1. Ask participants to pray for a few minutes in their small groups in whatever way they choose for the particular helps they need to turn away from these seven areas of sin.

2. Then sing: "Blest Are They."

3. Celebrate Minor Exorcism D as indicated in the ritual text (RCIA #92) When candidates are present, adapt language to reflect their baptismal status.

Nineteenth Sunday in Ordinary Time

Understanding this Sunday:

Background for Catechesis

The Word In Liturgy

Wisdom 18:6-9
Psalm 33:1, 12, 18-19, 20-22
Hebrews 11:1-2, 8-19 [or 11:1-2, 8-12]
Luke 12:32-48 [or 12:35-40]

The Book of Wisdom, written in the century before the birth of Jesus at Alexandria (one of the great centers of learning in the ancient world) aimed to strengthen the faith of the Jewish community living in the diaspora. Today's passage comes from the second part of the book (cc. 11-19), a lengthy midrash (homily) on Israel's history in which the author reflects on God's abiding presence and constant saving action among the people. This section deals with the events of the first Passover, Israel's escape from Egypt. The reading was no doubt chosen because of how it portrays the Israelites who "awaited the salvation of the just . . ." That attitude of watchful readiness is precisely the attitude commended by Jesus in today's Gospel. Psalm 33 forms a fitting response to this lesson in its reference to those who "hope for his kindness" and whose "soul waits for the Lord."

Our second reading for the next four weeks will be taken from the Letter to the Hebrews, chapters 11 and 12. Hebrews is more like a theological essay that an epistle. Most likely written to shore up a Jewish-Christian community that had grown lax in its faith, the heart of the argument of the letter is the superiority of Jesus' priesthood and sacrifice over that of the Old Covenant. The author also emphasizes that believers must remain strong and faithful during their earthly pilgrimage as they look forward to their heavenly reward. The section from which we read today is about faith and endurance, and at this point the author holds up the example of Abraham as a model to be followed. The discussion of Abraham's faith here is more a description than a careful theological analysis. In

fact, what is described is very closely aligned with our understanding of Christian hope (which is the focus of today's catechesis), as well as faith. Although the similarity was not deliberately intended, this reading fits nicely with the Gospel theme of watchfulness "concerning what we hope for." The examples given are of those who faithfully waited for the fulfillment of God's promise "from afar . . . searching for a better, a heavenly home."

We continue to read from the section of Luke's Gospel in which he arranges his material as a travel narrative. Jesus is on a journey to Jerusalem, where he will encounter his death/destiny and there receive ultimate vindication in the glory of his resurrection. Along the way, Jesus instructs his followers about the meaning of true discipleship. Luke, of course, is concerned to tell the story in a way that will help his own (and our!) community to live more faithfully as disciples of Jesus during this time between his resurrection and his final coming. A first section (vv. 32-34 [omitted in the short version of the reading]) deals with the disciples' attitude towards wealth, which should be characterized by detachment and generosity towards the poor. Then, in the concluding section (vv. 35-48 [35-40 in the short version]), Jesus teaches that his disciples must be watchful and ready for the master's return. The eschatological context reflects Luke's concern that his community live in light of the expected final coming. The concluding parable about not abusing one's stewardship is a further reinforcement of the idea that watchfulness (and appropriate behavior) are essential for the faithful disciple.

Catholic Doctrine

Christian Hope

It was St. Paul in his letter to the Corinthians that grouped the realities of faith, hope and love together (1 Cor 13:13). Earlier this liturgical year we examined "faith" and in that connection examined the three theological virtues (faith, hope and charity). We also examined "hope" but not from the perspective of the theological virtues (rather, in the context of the Advent Season). Now we take up the doctrinal theme of Christian hope from the perspective of Catholic teaching on the theological virtues.

The *Catechism* treats of "hope" in two places, as a theological virtue and in its exposition on the first commandment. To understand this key concept, let us first explore the theological virtues. These are distinguished from human virtue in that faith, hope and love are gifts instilled by God and orient us toward union with the Trinity. They are, if you will, the highest of virtues. Faith, hope and love are the firm foundation of the correct moral life precisely because they have their origin in the Triune God (CCC 1812-13). While they are given to us by God, they can, however, be perfected in the exercise of our Christian life or squandered by our neglect.

Hope is that steadfast orientation toward ultimate union with the divine. It is by hope that we desire heaven and have the firm conviction that with divine help we will attain to the promises of God offered to us and fulfilled in Christ (CCC 1817). In difficult and painful times, indeed, in the "dark night of the soul" (as St. John of the Cross has written) it is hope which sustains us and keeps us from being discouraged (CCC 1818).

The forerunner of our Christian hope is Abraham, who in faith believed in the promises of God. Faith is related to hope and seen by some theologians as preceding hope because to hope in something requires a goal—which can only be illuminated by faith in something, that something being the promises of God. Such was our forebear in faith, Abraham, who believed in the promise of God and whose hope was fulfilled in Isaac (CCC 1819).

Christian hope is centered in the person of Jesus, his preaching, especially the beatitudes as they outline for us the path that takes us through difficulties in this life to the life which awaits us on high. Hope is also a weapon in the war against evil, our breastplate (see 1 Thessalonians 5:8). Hope is nourished and sustained in prayer, especially the prayer that Jesus taught us wherein we express our longing for the coming kingdom, here yet not fully (CCC 1820).

When the catechism examines the first commandment, it also talks about hope and the sins against this virtue, namely, despair and presumption. In despair, one loses the sense that salvation is possible and promised by God. Presumption means that one understands oneself as capable of achieving salvation without God or that one assumes God will save one without true conversion or radical orientation toward the divine. The first commandment clearly emphasizes that love of God be total, that there is no other god in whom we place our fidelity or trust. This includes either placing ourselves in the god of despair or the god of ourselves.

St. Teresa of Avila has written, "Hope, O my soul, hope. You know neither the day nor the hour. Watch carefully, for everything passes quickly, even though your impatience makes doubtful what is certain, and turns a very short time into a long one. Dream that the more you struggle, the more you prove the love that you bear your God, and the more you will rejoice one day with your Beloved, in a happiness and rapture that can never end." (*Exclamaciones del alma a Dios* 15:3)

At Mass, as the Communion Rite begins, the community prays the Lord's Prayer and concludes, saying, "Deliver us, Lord, from every evil, and grant us peace in our day. In your mercy keep us free from sin and protect us from all anxiety as we wait in joyful hope for the coming of our Savior, Jesus Christ." (*Roman Missal*, Order of Mass, Communion Rite) The theological virtue of hope, a gift from God, allows us to place ourselves in the joyful expectation of the fullness of the kingdom, tasted in the meal of the Eucharist.

Catholic Culture

In Christian iconography, the anchor is the sign of hope (Heb 6:19-20) and is found inscribed on artwork in the catacombs. Some anchors also have horizontal bars so that they incorporate a cross.

St. Monica, the mother of St. Augustine, prayed and wept for him through the years of his dissolute living before his conversion. Through her resolute hope in God, Augustine was converted to Christianity. Nonetheless, there is no patron saint for the hopeful, perhaps because those who evidence this virtue are already directly disposed toward the divine because they are cooperating with this gift from above. However, the patron saint of "hopeless cases" (or, more appropriately, desperate situations) is St. Jude.

Notes

Dismissal Catechesis (30 min)

Getting Started

1. Arrange the center of the circle with some symbols of hope: a picture of an anchor, evergreen boughs, and flowers. Or, if you can find the icon of Christ the Giver of Life, use that as a focal point.

2. Greet everyone and invite them into the circle. Have instrumental music, with a hopeful theme, playing in the background. Allow a few moments for the group to sit in silence and collect their thoughts.

3. Use the words of St. Teresa of Avila as an opening prayer:

   "Hope, O my soul, hope. You know neither the day nor the hour. Watch carefully, for everything passes quickly, even though your impatience makes doubtful what is certain, and turns a very short time into a long one. Dream that the more you struggle, the more you prove the love that you bear your God, and the more you will rejoice one day with your Beloved, in a happiness and rapture that can never end." (Exclamaciones del alma a Dios 15:3)

First Impressions

1. Help the group to recall the today's liturgy of the Word by using key lines from the passages to trigger their memory: *"the people awaited the salvation of the just . . ."* (Wisdom 18:7) *"Our soul waits for the Lord, who is our help and shield."* (Psalm 33:20) *"Faith is the realization of what is hoped for and evidence of things not seen."* (Hebrews 11:1) *"Do not be afraid any longer, little flock, for your Father is pleased to give you the kingdom."* (Luke 12:32)

2. Invite them to discuss the following: *What about today's scripture stands out for you? How do the passages relate to your life? What line, image or insight do you want to remember from these scriptures? Why is this important to you?*

Making Connections

1. Tell the story about the atheist who fell off a cliff.

   An atheist fell off a cliff. As he tumbled downward, he caught hold of the branch of a small tree. There he hung between heaven above and the rocks a thousand feet below, knowing he wasn't going to be able to hold on much longer.

   Then an idea came to him, "God!" he shouted with all his might.

   Silence! No one responded.

   "God!" he shouted again, "If you exist, save me and I promise I shall believe in you and teach others to believe."

Silence again! Then he almost let go of the branch in shock as he heard a mighty Voice booming across the canyon. "That's what they all say when they are in trouble."

"No, God, no!" he shouted out, more hopeful now. "I am not like the others. Why, I have already begun to believe, don't you see, having heard your Voice for myself. Now all you have to do is save me and I shall proclaim your name to the ends of the earth."

"Very well," said the Voice. "I shall save you. Let go of that branch."

"Let go of the branch?" yelled the distraught man. "Do you think I'm crazy?"

2. Ask the participants to gather into smaller groupings of four or less. These questions will be helpful for their discussion: *What is the story saying about 'letting go? When have you experienced the hopelessness of 'hanging over the edge of a cliff'? How do we find hope in these times?*

3. Ask the small groups to share some of their insights in the larger group. Summarize their discussion. Invite them to write one conclusion about hope in the Participant Book (page 91) or on the blackline handout, under the section entitled, 'I Want to Remember.'

Prayer

Pray Psalm 33 a few verses at a time, asking the group to respond: "May your kindness, Lord, be upon us; we have put our hope in you."

Extended Catechesis

SESSION FOCUS: *Christian Hope*

Gathering

A. Sunday:

1. Greet the team and the sponsors as they arrive. Offer a warm welcome to join the circle. Use the same instrumental music to help the group quiet down and focus on the centerpiece.

2. Begin the prayer time with the Gathering Song used at today's liturgy. Then proclaim the second reading from Hebrews 11:1-2, 8-19, explaining beforehand that this is the story of Abraham, told to the Jewish–Christian community to enliven their hope and endurance. Abraham, a model of faith to this community, is likewise a model for us. Close the prayer in these or similar words:

   Jesus, you have raised up Abraham, for us to understand the need for hope, endurance and total faith in God. We have confronted the impossible in our own lives, as did Sarah and Abraham. Plant your gift of hope deep within our hearts, that we might follow God's call, as did these ancestral parents. For this we pray, that we might surrender our lives totally into your hands. Amen.

B. Weekday:

1. Prepare a liturgy of the Word using the following scriptural passages from the past Sunday.

   - Song: "Trust in the Lord" (O'Connor), verse 1
   - Reading: Hebrews 11:1-2, 8-19 [or 11:1-2, 8-12]
   - Response: "Trust in the Lord," verses 2 and 3
   - Gospel: Luke 12:32-48 [or 12:35-40]
   - Silence

The Word (30 min)

1. Invite the participants to share their definition of 'hope.' Record these words and phrases on a poster board large enough for everyone to see.

2. With the help of the "Word in Liturgy" section found in "Understanding this Sunday," prepare a presentation on the readings, such as:

   The first reading, taken from the Book of Wisdom, is a homily that recalls for the Israelites the blessings of their exodus redemption. As promised, Yahweh preserved the chosen people, secured their freedom and assured their fruitfulness. By celebrating the Passover every year, the Jews are reminded to wait and trust in the faithfulness of the God who saves.

   Likewise, the second reading recounts the story of Abraham and Sarah's hope in their God to fulfill the promise of progeny—'as numerous as the stars.' The author of Hebrews brings this to mind for the Jewish-Christian community that had grown lax in faith. In this theological essay, the emphasis is on the need for believers to remain strong and faithful during their earthly pilgrimage as they look forward to their heavenly reward.

   In the passage from Luke's Gospel, Jesus instructs his followers about the meaning of true discipleship. The disciple must assume a posture of detachment from wealth and generosity towards the poor. In the concluding section, Jesus teaches that his disciples must be watchful and ready for their master's return. Thus, preparedness, vigilance and responsible stewardship characterize the disciple. Our hope for the treasure of heaven lies in these attitudes.

3. Ask the participants to discuss one or more of these questions in small groups: *How is the Passover event an inspiration of hope to Christians and Jews throughout history? How would you describe the kind of hope it took for Abraham and Sarah to move to a new land, to believe the promise of children and to sacrifice Isaac? How does the gospel inspire hope in you?*

Catholic Teaching (30 min)

1. Explain the Catholic teaching on hope in these or your own words.

   Hope is steadfast orientation toward ultimate union with the divine. It is by hope that we desire heaven and have the firm conviction that with divine help we will attain the promises of the treasure reserved for us in heaven. A theological virtue, hope is a gift freely given to us by God that is nourished by prayer and practice. To sin against hope is either to despair, in which case the sense of salvation by God is lost, or, to be presumptuous, in which case one asserts that salvation can be won without God and without conversion.

2. Invite the group to brainstorm a list of what they hope for in God through the person of Jesus, in the power of the Holy Spirit. Record their ideas on a poster large enough for everyone to read.

Putting Faith Into Practice

1. Ask the group to read the story of hope in the Participant Book (page 90) or on the blackline handout, and to write their own story of hope. Allow enough time for this activity. You may choose to play instrumental music softly in the background.

2. Invite the catechumens and candidates to pair with their sponsors to share their stories of hope.

3. When they have finished, refer back to the list and ask these questions of the large group: *How is it that we can hope that God will do these good things in our lives? How do we grow in hope?*

Prayer

As a concluding prayer, invite the group to pray a spontaneous Litany of Hope from the needs on the poster board and any additional needs. The response to each prayer for hope can be, "Lord, we place our hope in you." Conclude the prayer with the conclusion of the Lord's Prayer, *"Deliver us, Lord, from every evil, and grant us peace in our day. In your mercy keep us free from sin and protect us from all anxiety as we wait in joyful hope for the coming of our Savior, Jesus Christ."* (*Roman Missal*, Order of Mass, Communion Rite)

Blest Be the Lord

—hopeless situation; God came through?

Twentieth Sunday in Ordinary Time

Understanding this Sunday:

Background for Catechesis

The Word In Liturgy

Jeremiah 38:4-6, 8-10
Psalm 40:2, 3, 4, 18
Hebrews 12:1-4
Luke 12:49-53

The prophet Jeremiah's mission to preach repentance to the Israelites often brought him into direct conflict with the powerful elite of his day. At a time when Judah was a subject state of the much more powerful Babylon, the weak King Zedekiah was convinced by various leaders of the people to form an alliance with Babylon's enemies and offer armed resistance. Jeremiah strenuously objected and predicted doom if the King did not change his plans. The prophet insisted that instead of revolt, repentance of their sinful ways was the only way out of their difficulties. Seeing how his preaching was demoralizing the army, the princes accused Jeremiah of treason and convinced the King to give him over into their hands. Today's reading describes his fate: First, he was lowered into a cistern and left to die. And then, at the hand of a foreigner who interceded on his behalf with the King, Jeremiah was finally rescued. The responsorial psalm chosen for today might well have come from the lips of the embattled prophet ("The Lord . . . drew me out of the pit of destruction, out of the mud . . ."). Jewish tradition might well regard the psalm as an image of the prophet's ordeal; our Christian eyes also recognize a foreshadowing of Christ's resurrection in the psalm's image of being drawn out of the pit.

In last week's reading from Hebrews, we were introduced to the heroes of old, offered by the author as examples of faith. In chapter twelve, he refers back to that "cloud of witnesses," but the imagery now shifts to a sports arena. Those ancient heroes are the spectators watching the race being run in the arena. It is the same race that they have already completed, a race that the readers of the letter are still running. The author exhorts his readers to keep their eyes fixed on the example of

Jesus, "who inspires and perfects our faith." Jesus, too, has completed the race and is now seated "at the right of the throne of God," just as winning athletes were often offered a seat beside the emperor. The point of all of this imagery is to encourage the faltering recipients of the letter to persevere in their Christian faith, no matter what the obstacles they may face (". . . do not grow despondent or abandon the struggle"). They are told to remember that Jesus "endured the opposition of sinners;" hence, they should not be surprised or discouraged if they, too, meet with resistance.

The theme of opposition between good and evil appears in all three readings today. Luke continues his travel narrative, in which he has Jesus instructing his followers on what they should expect (and what is expected of them) as his disciples. In today's reading Jesus uses the images of fire and baptism to express the ultimate struggle that he knows awaits him in Jerusalem. Fire was a symbol of purification (Luke 3:16-17) as well as of judgment (Revelation 20:10). Luke describes the descent of the Spirit at Pentecost as appearing like tongues of fire upon the disciples. Clearly, it is not only Jesus who will have to face the refining fires of the end time. His disciples, too, will be "immersed" (i.e., "baptized") in the bath of suffering, just as was Jesus. To illustrate this, and perhaps to recognize the reality already being lived by those in his community, Luke further describes the kind of opposition and division that is inevitable for those who cast their lot with Jesus, the messiah bound for suffering and death in Jerusalem.

Catholic Doctrine

The Conflict Between Good and Evil—The Two Ways

While there are similar elements in the creation account of Hebrew scriptures and the pagan Near Eastern creation mythologies, the Old Testament places a very different emphasis on the balance between good and evil as God brings forth creation. For example, in the Babylonian creation myth, the *Enuma Elish*, two gods battle, the good god, Marduk, and the evil monster-god, Tiamat. Marduk wins and in winning chaos is controlled and good triumphs and the cosmic order that had been threatened is restored. In the Genesis creation account it is clear that God alone creates and is solely responsible for all goodness. There was no battle between and good god and an evil god or force. Israel came to understand that the creator-God is One and the people expressed this monotheistic faith in the scriptures.

The Catholic theology of creation has its foundation in this understanding and has three basic points. The first is that we have affirmed from the earliest times that God created *ex nihilo* or, "out of nothing." This means that there was not some sort of pre-existent material, but that everything in creation owes its existence to God. Even though there is evil in the world, someday God will overcome it. The second point is that God created the world good. This is a refrain echoed in the Genesis account (1:1-2:4) and that therefore evil is not the result of God. Through our human freedom, somehow evil entered the world after God created it. The third point is that since creation is the handiwork of God, we humans can come to know God through it by the efforts of our reason (although the fullness of revelation is found in Jesus Christ).

Thus, Scripture and Catholic theology attests that good and evil are not equal principles, with equal force. God is more powerful than evil. We know that in Christ, God triumphs over evil. And yet, evil does exist.

The Church, from the earliest times, therefore, has referred to the "two ways." An ancient book of basic instructions for catechumens, the *Didache* (from the Greek for "teaching"), insists in its opening lines, "There are two ways, one of life and one of death: and great is the difference between the two ways. The way of life is this: first, you shall love God, who created you; second, your neighbor as yourself." (*Didache* 1:1)

The way of Christ is the path believers take which leads to life. A contrary way leads to death and destruction. (CCC 1696)

John Paul II promulgated an encyclical devoted to this message of the two ways, in which he speaks of the culture of life and the culture of death. The gospel and the Church that proclaims this good news promotes and preaches a culture of life based in Jesus Christ. He writes:

"Today this proclamation is especially pressing because of the extraordinary increase and gravity of threats to the life of individuals and peoples, especially where life is weak and defenseless. In addition to the ancient scourges of poverty, hunger, endemic diseases, violence and war, new threats are emerging on an alarmingly vast scale.

The Second Vatican Council, in a passage which retains all its relevance today, forcefully condemned a number of crimes and attacks against human life . . . I repeat that condemnation . . . 'Whatever is opposed to life itself such as any type of murder, genocide, abortion, euthanasia or willful self-destruction; whatever violates the integrity of the human person such as mutilation, torments inflicted on body or mind, attempts to coerce the will itself; whatever insults human dignity such as subhuman living conditions, arbitrary imprisonment, deportation, slavery, prostitution, the selling of women and children; as well as disgraceful working conditions . . . all these things are infamies indeed.'" (Evangelium Vitae 25 March 1995, n. 3.2-3.3)

The point of reference for every Christian who promotes and seeks the culture of life is Jesus Christ who himself is "the way, the truth and the life" (John 14:16). By loving Christ every Christian draws closer to the Lord and is able to pursue the good work which God has begun in us. (CCC 1698)

Catholic Culture

There is an icon titled "The Image 'Not Made by Human Hands.'" It consists of a cross contained within a circle which itself is contained in a square. This highly centralized yet expanding pattern symbolizes the "orderly and beneficent entry of the Transcendent. . .into the earthly reality. . . ." In the middle of this pattern is the face of Christ, with hair combed in waves, a profound gaze, painted in shades of white, gold, brown and ochre. The entire icon is an expression of Creation and Redemption and proclaims that "in Christ everything that exists has become light." (Maria G. Muzj, *Transfiguration: Introduction to the Contemplation of Icons*, trs. K.D. Whitehead, St. Paul Books & Media, Boston, 1987, p. 16)

The mystic Julian of Norwich (1342-1416) writes, "I often wondered why, through the great prescient wisdom of God, the beginning of sin was not prevented. For then it seemed to me that all would have been well . . . . But Jesus, who in this vision informed me about everything needful to me, answered with these words and said: Sin is necessary, but all will be well, and all will be well, and every kind of thing will be well." (quoted in Edmund Colledge, OSA and James Walsh, S.J., ed. *Julian of Norwich: Showings*, Paulist Press, NY, 1978, p 224-25)

Dismissal Catechesis (30 min)

Getting Started

1. Prior to the session find one of the icons (or some similar art piece): "The Image 'Not Made by Human Hands,'" "The Descent Into Hell," or "St. Joan of Arc." Have this, with a bouquet of fresh flowers, in the center of the circle.

2. Invite the catechumens and candidates to join the circle, asking them to take some quiet time to look at the icon or art piece. Ask them to share the connection they see between the image and today's readings.

First Impressions

1. Invite the participants to name some of the images they can recall from today's Liturgy of the Word, including the Gathering Hymn and the Collect. These can be recorded on a poster or paper. Be sure to write large enough for all to see.

2. Gathering them into groups of no more than four, ask these or similar questions: *What did you find disturbing in these scriptural passages? Why? How would you describe the conflicts presented in the three readings? What did you find consoling?*

Making Connections

1. Explain that Jeremiah was punished for preaching repentance to the leaders of his day who wanted armed revolt. When he told the weak king of God's punishment if he did not change his plans, Jeremiah was accused of treason.

2. Continue the small group sharing with further questions: *Have you ever found yourself in Jeremiah's dilemma? When faced with a choice of life over death; evil over good; difficult virtue or the easy way out, how have you responded? Having heard this passage, would you do anything different in the future?*

3. Invite the smaller groups to share some of their insights with the whole group. Summarize their input and ask the participants to decide on one small action they can take this week, as a choice for life over death. This can be shared or written in the Participant Book (page 93) or on the blackline handout.

Prayer

Close with Psalm 40. This can be prayed, alternating from the right to the left side every three or four verses. For this prayer, all will need copies of the entire psalm.

Extended Catechesis

SESSION FOCUS: *The Two Ways*

Gathering

A. Sunday:

1. Welcome the sponsors, godparents and team members into the circle. After a period of silence, during which they have time to ponder the icon or art piece, ask for their reactions and insights. Ask them to notice the images printed on the poster or paper, gleaned from today's readings. Invite them to add more images to the list or to comment on the ones listed.

2. Proclaim the gospel: Luke 12:49-53.

3. Pray in the following manner:

Jesus, you have triumphed over death, sin and evil. You know the evil and suffering present in our world today. We believe in your loving zeal, which is present with us even today—a zeal so strong, you spoke of it as 'igniting a fire on earth.' Send your fire of love on us now. Rain down your love. Spark us with your fervor for life. Let your goodness, once again, triumph over the evil of the world today. Fire us up to be your instruments for goodness, life and joy in the places where we live and work. Help us be your presence of goodness wherever we may be. This we ask in your name. Amen.

B. Weekday:

1. Create a short Celebration of the Word, using the format below:

   - Gathering Hymn (from today's liturgy)
   - Opening Prayer or Collect (20 Sunday of Ordinary Time)
   - First reading: Jeremiah 38:4-6, 8-10
   - Pause
   - Second reading: Hebrews 12:1-4
   - Pause
   - Gospel: Luke 12:49-53
   - Pause

The Word (30 min)

1. Present some summary of the background to the second reading in these or your own words.

In the struggle for victory of good over evil, the followers of Jesus were and are still today, supported by a 'cloud of witnesses.' This image is presented in the letter to the Hebrews as a means of encouragement to the readers in the race to victory in Jesus. Rather than discouragement or despondency or the temptation to give up the race, the disciple is challenged to persevere no matter what evil, persecution or obstacles he or she might face.

2. Invite the participants to gather in to smaller groups of four to discuss this reading. These or similar questions will help spark the discussion: *What evils do we face in today's world as we try to follow Jesus? What practical actions can we take to 'keep our eyes fixed on Jesus?'*

3. Explain the background for the gospel, using the information found in "The Word in Liturgy" for this session. These or similar words may be used.

Jesus' presence and teaching brought division to the world in which he lived. As Jeremiah's opposition to the leaders of his time landed him in the pit, so Jesus' challenge to the leaders of his time got him nailed to the cross. The image of fire, which is part of this gospel, is a symbol of purification. The fire, through which God's intervention among God's people is signified, will purify the world of death and evil through the actions and teaching of Jesus. As disciples, we are called to be both purified in the fire and to be a fire for the world, that is, to purify it. As disciples we too will be immersed (baptized) in the bath of suffering, the crucible of fire. Our decision to follow Christ is one that will cause division, when we are challenged to make choices for life and goodness.

4. Using the exercise found in the Participant Book (page 92) or on the blackline handout, ask the group to reflect and respond to the questions.

Catholic Teaching (30 min)

1. Ask the participants to share one response from their reflection.

2. After listening to several responses, summarize the insights of the group.

3. Proceed to expand the Church's teaching on the conflict between good and evil in these or similar words.

The church has long recognized the need for decisive choices in the life of the believer. The fundamental alternatives that the believer faces are sometimes called "The Two Ways"— the way of life, and the way of death. The path of Christ is the believer's choice for life over death; for good over evil. This path can lead to suffering and division. Yet, the church guides the follower of Jesus to the way of life: first, you shall love God, who created you; second, your neighbor as yourself.

While evil, pain and suffering exist in our world, we believe that God created the world good. Evil is not the result of God, but of our human freedom which allowed evil to enter the world which God created. In Jesus victory over evil, we are challenged to follow in his way, his truth and his life.

4. Invite the participants to discuss this teaching in small groups: *How do we deal with the evil we see in the daily world of our lives? Where do we find the strength to do what is right, even when it defies human authority?*

Putting Faith Into Practice

1. Present the story of St. Joan of Arc, as a model of choosing good, and following God's voice, even in the face of death. Here are a few points to include. Further information can be found in, *A Passion for Life: Fragments of the Face of God* by Joan Chittister (Orbis Books).

Joan, a simple peasant girl in France at the height of the Hundred Years War, listened to the voices in her head to follow God's will. She saw and experienced the way in which the foreign invaders oppressed the poor of her land. Through her persistence she led an army, saved her king and saved her country from foreign invasion by the English. But her British captors condemned and burned her alive, accusing her of being a witch and a heretic. This girl, who at the encouragement of the French clergy, risked her life to follow the voice of God within her, was accused and burned by another church court of bishops. Joan was a woman with a conscience who dared to threaten the status quo of her day.

2. If there is time, engage the group in a general discussion of how today's disciple might be challenged to threaten the status quo.

Prayer

Close the session with the celebration of a Minor Exorcism, RCIA #94 B.

Twenty-first Sunday in Ordinary Time

Understanding this Sunday:

Background for Catechesis

The Word In Liturgy

Isaiah 66:18-21
Psalm 117:1, 2
Hebrews 12:5-7, 11-13
Luke 13:22-30

Scholars generally date the third part of the Book of Isaiah (cc. 56-66) to the time after the return from exile. Among the concerns of the author(s) of this book are a desire to overcome the narrow particularism found especially in certain priestly circles and to hold up a vision of universal salvation where even the pagan nations will be welcomed in the house of the Lord. The section we read today describes an incredible assembly of people from every corner of the earth, streaming to Jerusalem where all—Jew and Gentile alike—will join in worship at the Temple ("They shall . . .bring their offering to the house of the Lord"). Even more startling is the Lord's promise to include Gentiles among those who minister in the Temple: "Some of these I will take as priests and Levites." The prophet's vision is eschatological, a dream of a world transformed by the action of a God whose glory consists in receiving praise and worship from all peoples ("They shall come and see my glory"). The refrain of the responsorial psalm ("Go out to all the world and tell the Good News") is a fitting complement to the prophet's description of how messengers will be sent to gather the nations.

Last week's reading from Hebrews used the image of a race to encourage the recipients of the letter to persevere in their Christian faith. This week, the image that is used is of a father disciplining a child in order to make the child strong and healthy. The notion of salutary discipline was familiar, both from the Greek culture's athletic experience, referred to

earlier, and from the Jews' experience of rabbinic training. In this passage the author suggests that the sufferings and hardships the Christian community is undergoing are God's way of providing the necessary discipline to strengthen their faith. The author quotes from the Book of Proverbs in vv 5-6. Then, by way of commentary on that text, he urges the Hebrews to endure their discipline gracefully, to correct their lax ways, and they will find that the discipline of the Lord "brings forth the fruit of peace and justice to those who are trained in its school."

In the Gospel Luke once again emphasizes that Jesus is teaching as he is "making his way to Jerusalem." Contemporary Jewish apocalyptic speculation foresaw numerous reversals of fortune in the final age. Here, a question is posed to Jesus about who will be saved, and he takes the opportunity to warn his fellow Jews against assuming that their status as children of Abraham guarantees them anything. The possibility is real of being excluded from the kingdom. Jesus reiterates the prophetic stance heard earlier in our first reading, namely that Gentiles from the four corners of the earth will stream to God's the eschatological banquet and find a place at table. But in sobering terms he adds the implied judgment in his closing dictum ("Some who are last will be first and some who are first will be last.") that the presence of the Gentiles at table may go hand in hand with an exclusion of those in his audience.

Catholic Doctrine

Final Judgment

Jesus has ascended to the Father and sits at the right hand of the Most High in glory. Both the Apostles' Creed and the Nicene Creed proclaim our belief that Christ will come again to this world to judge both the living and the dead. Catholic teaching refers to this as the final or last judgment. Till then we live in the age of the Spirit and of witness, as we await in hope for this second coming and Christ's definitive judgment on the nations and the world.

The Church teaches there are two moments of judgment. At one's death, God judges the moral quality of one's total life, how one has chosen fundamentally to either cooperate with God's grace or how one has chosen to reject God's grace. Accordingly, judgment is rendered and the person is assigned to either heaven, purgatory or hell. This immediate judging after one's death is called the particular judgment. Justin (d. 165) and Irenaeus (d. 200) both argued for a particular judgment and this theological question was discussed at the Second Council of Lyons (1274). Pope Benedict XII in his decree *Benedictus Deus* (1336) resolutely affirmed the notion of a particular judgment. The Second Vatican Council reaffirmed this teaching, "Before the judgment seat of God an account of [one's] own life will be rendered to each one according as [that person] has done either good or evil." (GS, 17)

What, then, is the difference between particular judgment and the final judgment? While the former concerns the individual and reflects our belief in the immortality of the soul (whether in heaven or hell), the latter looks to that end-time when Christ will come again bringing the fullness of the kingdom of God. At this end-time, Christ who is the Lord of eternal life will pass definitive judgment on the works and hearts of all people, nations and times (CCC 679). It is by his cross that Jesus has been given the right to judge, and yet, as the gospel affirms, the Son of God did not come in order to judge but to save and to give life (John 3:17; 5:26).

So, how does Christ judge? The form of judgment is a revelation from the Lord who is the fullness of God's revelation among us. Each person will be revealed in this judgment, and thus the judging has already been achieved by the way in which one lived.

The final or last judgment also constitutes God's final word on all of history. Jesus Christ, who is the living Word of God, will reveal God's glorious triumph over evil and at the same time manifest the ultimate meaning of the whole work of creation. Then, all will be revealed concerning the way divine providence has led everything to this completion. God's plan will come to fruition and all will know that love truly is stronger than death and that the last word in all things belongs to God (CCC 1040).

The meaning of the last judgment for believers is an urgent call to conversion, to make the best use of the time available. The Church, in this regard, speaks of holy fear, that feeling which commits us to the justice of God's kingdom and pursuing the way of life in Christ rather than the way of death (CCC 1041).

An early father of the Church, St. Cyprian, Bishop of Carthage (d. 258), writes, "Oh what a day that will be, and how great when it comes, dearest brethren! when the Lord begins to survey his people and to recognize by examining with divine knowledge the merits of each individual! to cast into hell evildoers. . .and indeed, to present to us the reward of faith and devotion! What will be that glory, and how great the joy of being admitted to the sight of God! to be so honored as to receive the joy of eternal light and salvation in the presence of Christ. . .to greet Abraham, and Isaac, and Jacob, and all the patriarchs, apostles, prophets, and martyrs! to rejoice with the just and with the friends of God in the kingdom of heaven!" ("Letter of Cyprian to the People of Thibar," in William A. Jurgens, *The Faith of the Early Fathers*, v. 1, The Liturgical Press, Collegeville, MN, p. 231; CSEL, v.3, pt. 3, 58, 10)

Catholic Culture

Michelangelo's "Last Judgment," a gigantic fresco that appears on the back wall of the Sistine Chapel, totally overpowers the altar table in front of it. The artist broke with traditional representations of the last judgment which were characterized by hierarchy and compartmentalization wherein even the dead were dressed according to their station. Michelangelo, instead, presents a unified scene, without compartments, without thrones or ranking. The nude figures swirl in a clockwork motion (a kind of wheel of fortune). Figures of souls rise from their graves, gravitate around the center, Christ, and sink downward to hell. The dead show no joy, only dread in the judgment taking place. Some look dazed, some without hope, and some look upward in awe. Some of the figures soar upward as if pulled by divine attraction. Other figures are fought over by demons who drag them down.

As a child, Michelangelo must surely have contemplated the last judgment scenes in his home city, Florence, the mosaic ceiling of the Cathedral baptistry and Orcagna's frescoes in the Church of Santa Croce. (Frederick Hartt, *History of Italian Renaissance Art*, 4th ed., Harry N. Abrams, Inc., Publishers, 1994, p. 631-33)

Notes

Dismissal Catechesis (30 min)

Getting Started

1. Prepare the space ahead of time.

   Invite everyone to be seated in a circle around the table. Light a candle. Pray in these or similar words:

   "O Loving God, you are all holy and wise. You have the words of everlasting life. Transform us that we will recognize you in our brothers and sisters. Make us firm in our commitment to make you known to the ends of the world. We ask this through Christ our Lord. Amen."

First Impressions

1. Ask the candidates and catechumens to sit quietly for a few minutes reflecting on the Liturgy of the Word just celebrated.

2. Draw from the group any words or phrases that touched them. Draw out also if there were words or phrases that perplexed them. List these on paper or chalkboard.

3. Invite them to reflect on the mood of today's readings. Discuss their experience of the mood and what might have prompted their response.

Making Connections

1. State that most of us live our lives as if there is always a tomorrow. Each evening when we retire we expect to rise in the morning. When things or events seem to go wrong, we expect them to get better.

2. Proclaim Hebrews 12:5-7, 11-13. Lead a discussion naming the images contained in the passage. What is the message of the letter to the Hebrews? Consult Understanding This Sunday for help in articulating this message.

3. Ask participants to think about and discuss the different forms of discipline we use in our lives facilitate the discussion by using some of the following questions: *What is the importance of discipline for us? Why is it so difficult to discipline ourselves? What helps us to keep to the task? What type of goals help us not to lose heart? What causes us to lose heart? How does the letter to the Hebrews encourage us to be faithful?* Lead the group in summarizing the key points.

Prayer

Spend a few minutes quietly reflecting on the importance of self-discipline. Invite everyone to speak to the Lord in the quiet of their hearts, asking for the help needed to be strong, courageous and faithful. Sing or play the song "You Are Mine," by David Haas.

Extended Catechesis

SESSION FOCUS: *Final Judgment*

Gathering

A. Sunday:
Welcome everyone and ask them to be seated in a circle around the table with the lighted candle. Proclaim Isaiah 66:18-21. Allow for some silence; proclaim Luke 13:22-30 followed by some more silence.

B. Weekday:
Welcome everyone. Begin with a Celebration of the Word, such as:

- Song: "Seek Ye First"
- Prayer: Opening Prayer from 21st Sunday in Ordinary Time
- Reading: Isaiah: 66:18-21
- Quiet
- Alleluia
- Gospel Luke 13:22-30
- Alleluia

The Word (30 min)

1. In pairs, discuss these readings, using these or similar questions: *Christ came to save all peoples, but are we willing to accept that people of other cultures and other religions such as Muslim, Hindu, and others will also be in heaven? What is required of a person in order to gain eternal salvation? What is this narrow door that Jesus speaks about?* After a few minutes, gather feedback in the large group.

2. Situate the passage from Isaiah for the participants. Include the following points:

   - Sometime after the return from the Babylonian exile.

   - The leaders, priests and Levites, seem to have a narrow view of who will be welcomed into the house of the Lord.

   - They consider themselves the chosen people because of the covenant made between God and Abraham. The others are pagan and surely not welcomed into God's house. Isaiah, the prophet, is warning them that these very pagans of which they speak and others of whom they don't even know will offer sacrifices acceptable to God and will be welcomed into house of God.

   - Some will even be accepted before the chosen people.

   Ask members of the group to share their response to your input.

3. Review the gospel with the participants: *In the Gospel, Jesus is making his way to Jerusalem and is stopped along the way. In response to the question of who will be saved, Jesus warns his fellow Jews that their status as children of Abraham does not guarantee them anything.*

Ask participants to consider how they might have responded to such a warning. Discuss the paradox Jesus states at the conclusion of this passage.

4. Refer back to the questions in point one. Describe those who Jesus says will be welcomed at the heavenly banquet. *What is the message of these scripture passages? Whom do they console? Whom do they challenge?*

Catholic Teaching (30 min)

1. Begin this section by showing a picture of Michelangelo's "Last Judgment." If possible, provide several copies of it for the participants. Discuss what is found in this gigantic fresco.

2. Explain that the Apostles Creed and the Nicene Creed both proclaim that Jesus, who has ascended to the Father and sits at the right hand of God, will come again to judge both the living and the dead. This article of the creed speaks about the end of the world, which will be at a time that no one knows or can predict. Discuss briefly psychics who claim to know the exact time the world will be destroyed. Though they can be very adamant in their predictions and interpret all events in light of such a prediction, no one knows when the world will end.

3. Explain that the Church teaches there are two moments of judgment: A particular judgment which is at the end of one's earthly life and the final judgment which is at the end of the world when Christ will come again bringing the fullness of the kingdom of God.

4. Explain particular judgment. Note that such a judgment is the revealing of one's total life and is determined by the way in which one lived. It is a judgment of how one either cooperated with God's grace or how one rejected God's grace. Accordingly, judgment is rendered and the person is assigned to either heaven, hell or a time of purification in purgatory before entering heaven. The teaching regarding particular judgment has been part of the church's belief since the second century and was reaffirmed by the Second Vatican Council in the early 1960s.

5. Explain final judgment. This judgment constitutes God's final word on all history. Jesus Christ, who is the living word of God, will reveal God's glorious triumph over evil and at the same time manifest the ultimate meaning of the whole of creation. God's plan will come to fruition and all will know that love truly is stronger than death and that the last word in all things belongs to God.

6. Invite them in pairs to name insights gained about the church's teaching on either final or particular judgment. Surface any questions or concerns that the catechumens and candidates have.

Putting Faith Into Practice

Note that the idea of particular judgment for believers is an urgent call to conversion, which is a life-long process of moving from self-centeredness to God and to being centered on others. The knowledge of particular and final judgments urges every believer to pursue the way of life in Christ rather than the way of death. Ask the participants to take time this week to step back from the busyness of life and name their priorities. Use the remaining time to initiate a reflection on the following questions (note that this reflection may continue during the coming week): *What in your life requires reordering to a more Christ-like way of living? What do you need to change? How do you plan to achieve such a change? Be specific.* Choose one aspect or dimension of your life to change. Pray for the grace to change.

Prayer

Invite the catechumens and candidates to stand in a circle. Ask the sponsors to stand behind their catechumen or candidate and place their hands on that person's shoulders, as the following prayer is prayed. Celebrate Blessing D from the *Rite of Christian Initiation of Adults*, #97. This would also be a good Sunday on which to do an anointing with the oil of catechumens, if a priest or deacon is available (RCIA #98).

Most loving God, you desire that all people will be one with you in heaven for all eternity. Help each of us to live each day according to your desire. When we forget what your desire is, send a gentle reminder that heaven is for all eternity. Grant that when each of us comes to the end of our earthly life, you will find us ready to meet you face to face. Bless us with perseverance, acceptance, and patience each and every day of our lives.

Twenty-second Sunday in Ordinary Time

The Word In Liturgy

Sirach 3:17-18, 20, 28-29
Psalm 68: 4-5, 6-7, 10-11
Hebrews 12:18-19, 22-24a
Luke 14:1, 7-14

The Book of Sirach was written in Hebrew at the start of the second century B.C.E., at a time when the "wisdom" of Israel's pagan neighbors was the envy of the entire world. The author is a sage, well traveled and well versed in the many cultures and philosophies of his day which might seem quite attractive to his Jewish countrymen. He writes his own book of reflections on the Torah, on the wisdom of the nations, and on God's ways in the world, in order to convince his countrymen of the superiority of relying on the wisdom of Yahweh over any other source of guidance. In this section, the author offers fatherly advice regarding humility and warns against a prideful attitude ("Humble yourself the more, the greater you are"). The final verse contains a proverb about how concern for the poor can "atone for sin." The text is thus linked to today's gospel reading, not only by its teaching on self-effacing humility, but also by the example of care for the poor, which is commended by Jesus. The refrain of the responsorial psalm further underlines the liturgy's attention to the poor today: ("God, in your goodness, you have made a home for the poor.")

We conclude today our four week series of readings from the letter to the Hebrews. The author of the letter is concerned to convince his hearers that they must not falter in their Christian faith, that a return to Judaism would be foolish and futile. Here, he stresses the superiority of the Christian dispensation over that of its Jewish precursor. The mention of the "untouchable mountain and a blazing fire" is a reference to the account in the Book of Exodus of Moses receiving the Law on Mount Sinai. Earlier, in chapter three, the author had compared Moses and Jesus and shown the superiority of Christ. After this somewhat negative comparison, the author goes on to stress the blessings of their new Christian faith: that they have "drawn near" to the heavenly Jerusalem. As those born again in baptism ("the assembly of the first-born enrolled in heaven"), Christians have already experienced union with the saints and angels because they have drawn near to "Jesus, the mediator of a new covenant."

Sociological studies of ancient Judaism have recently deepened our understanding of Jesus' social milieu in significant ways. Scholars have in particular highlighted the importance of dining protocols for establishing and maintaining social hierarchies. These studies offer helpful insights into why Luke so often describes the table fellowship of Jesus, taking pains to point out his custom of welcoming at table the poor and outcast. The jockeying for position at table which Jesus castigates in today's reading would have been judged reprehensible by many of Jesus contemporaries. However, Jesus goes beyond a lesson in etiquette here when he suggests that welcoming the poor and outcast to table is linked to the final judgment. That apocalyptic reference puts the entire scene into the context of Jesus' proclamation of the Kingdom of God which, he has shown, is already a present reality in his person and in his mission to bring the Good News to those judged least deserving of it by his pious contemporaries. Throughout his ministry, Jesus shows a "preferential option" for the poor. Luke obviously felt that this example of Jesus was (or should be) normative for every Christian community.

Catholic Doctrine

Preferential Option for the Poor

In our Catholic teaching, the purpose of society is to ensure a proper framework to promote the conditions for both associations and individuals to obtain what is their due, given their nature and vocation. Social justice relies, therefore, on the notion of the "common good," which is defined as the "the sum total of social conditions which allow people, either as groups or as individuals, to reach their fulfillment more fully and easily." (GS, 26) Thus, the common good concerns all. And, that concern focuses on making accessible to each those basic things that provide a genuine human life: food, clothing, housing, health, work, education, culture, suitable information, the right to establish a family, privacy, and so on. (CCC 1908)

It is within this context of the Catholic social teaching and our understanding of the common good, combined with the Church's reflection on the good news of Jesus Christ that a preferential option for the poor has been articulated. We believe that God blesses those who help the poor and that there is a definite gospel imperative for us to act for when the "poor have the good news preached to them" it is a sign of the presence of Christ (Mt 11:5; Lk 4:8). A love of the poor has been a constant hallmark of the Church's tradition. As one of the fathers of the Church has vigorously insisted, "Not to enable the poor to share in our goods is to steal from them and deprive them of life. The goods we possess are not ours, but theirs." (St. John Chrysostom, *Homiliae in Lazarum* 2,5: PG 48, 992D)

While love for the poor is a gospel hallmark and has been present in the tradition from the earliest times, the Church only relatively recently articulated this concern as expressed in the language of a "preferential option." This theme arose particularly in the Church of Latin America, as Catholics there grappled with massive injustices and oppressive social conditions. The situation gave rise to liberation theology. Since the early 1970s, this notion of a preferential option for the poor has found its way into the vocabulary of papal and curial writings.

Material deprivation, unjust oppression, physical and psychological illness and death—all the many forms of human misery—have elicited the compassion of Jesus and the concern of the Church. This concern of the Church for the poor is not only directed to helping each individual but also is directed to addressing the social causes of inequality, deprivation and misery. "Hence, those who are oppressed by poverty are the object of a *preferential love* on the part of the Church which, since her origin and in spite of the failings of many of her members, has not ceased to work for their relief, defense, and liberation through numerous works of charity which remain indispensable always and everywhere." (Congregation for the Doctrine of the Faith, instruction, *Libertatis conscientia*, 22 March 1986, n. 68)

Special attention to the needs of the poor and for the causes of poverty is seen, therefore, as a moral obligation for individual Christians, for the Church, and for society. Within the framework of the common good, Catholics believe that there is a systematically weighted concern to be responsive to the needs of the poor. In their pastoral letter on Catholic social teaching, Economic Justice for All, the bishops of the United States have developed at length the basis for this teaching and its implications for U.S. economic policy.

Concern for the poor is expressed in the prayer of the Church gathered at the table of the Lord, "[Father,] open our eyes to the needs of all; inspire us with words and deeds to comfort those who labor and are burdened; keep our service of others faithful to the example and command of Christ. Let your Church be a living witness to truth and freedom, to justice and peace, that all people may be lifted up by the hope of a world made new." (*Roman Missal*, Eucharistic Prayer for Masses for Various Needs and Occasions IV: Jesus, the Compassion of God)

Catholic Culture

St. Rose of Lima (1586-1617) is the first canonized saint of the Americas. She is the patron saint of South America and the Philippines. Her reputation was that of a mystic with extraordinary gifts, who took as her model St. Catherine of Siena, living a reclusive life and practicing extreme mortification and penance. Early on, however, when her mother chided her for caring for the poor and sick at home, St. Rose of Lima responded, "When we serve the poor and the sick, we serve Jesus. We must not fail to help our neighbors, because in them we serve Jesus." (P. Hansen, *Vita mirabilis*, Louvain, 1668)

St. Anthony of Padua (1191-1231) was a Franciscan friar and renowned preacher who was accorded the title "Doctor of the Church." An Italian, he began as a missionary to North Africa but returned home due to illness. Back in Italy, his renown grew as a preacher and scholar and he eventually was given permission by Francis to teach theology to the friars. For a time he pursued this teaching mission in southern France. His sermons are marked by a concern for social problems. This concern is reflected in the practice today of St. Anthony's Bread, contributions from which assist the relief of the poor.

Notes

Dismissal Catechesis (30 min)

Getting Started

Be sure that the meeting space is prepared before Mass begins with a prayer environment and a place for the lectionary. Gather the group in a circle and place the lectionary in a prominent place. Begin with a prayer of your own composition or the following:

Let us remind ourselves of God's presence.

Lord God, your creation reveals the magnitude of your love for us. We thank you for our lives, and for the gift of your love made known to us through our brothers and sisters. Teach us humility and gratitude as we stand before you and wonders of creation. We ask this through Christ our Lord. Amen.

First Impressions

1. Recall for the group the Old Testament and Gospel readings. Point out that one of the primary messages of the two readings is about humility. The gospel says, "Everyone who exalts himself should be humbled and he who humbles himself shall be exalted."

2. Ask the group to respond to the following questions: *When you were growing up, what did it mean to be humble? What does humility mean for you today?* Continue with a discussion of the meaning of humility.

Making Connections

1. Building on the group's comments in First Impressions, develop the meaning of humility as presented in the scriptures. Point out that humility is not about defacing oneself or putting oneself down. Instead humility has to do with how we, the created, stand before God, our creator. Humility is the virtue that acknowledges God as our creator, that creation is a gift, and that the goods of creation were intended for all to receive. We are called by God to respond to this gift of God in our life's words and actions. Humility is openness to God. If we are consumed with our own self-worth than we cannot hear God's call and the danger is to believe we do not need God in our lives. Our response to the gift is unselfishness and gratitude.

2. Ask the participants to reflect as a large group on the following questions: *Why could humility be described as counter-cultural? What does humility look like when it is lived out in actions? What is the challenge of the gospel for you?*

Prayer

Conclude the session with a prayer using the following adapted Alternative Opening Prayer of the Liturgy for the Sunday or in similar words:

In closing, let us pray for the openness of humility as we stand before our God.

*Lord God of power and might,
nothing is good which is against your will,
and all is of value which comes from your hand.
Place in our hearts a desire to please you
and fill our minds with insight into love,
so that every thought may grow in wisdom
and all our efforts may be filled with your peace.*

We ask this through Christ our Lord. Amen.

Extended Catechesis

SESSION FOCUS: *Preferential Option for the Poor*

Gathering

A. Sunday:

Gather the participants into a circle. Welcome any new members. Invite the group into silence and begin with the following prayer taken from the Opening Prayer of the liturgy.

Let us pray:

Almighty God, every good thing comes from you. Fill our hearts with love for you, increase our faith, and by your constant care protect the good you have given us. We ask this through Christ our Lord. Amen.

B. Weekday:

If you gather during the week for extended catechesis, be sure to begin with a Celebration of the Word using the following or similar format:

- Gathering Hymn
- Greeting and Gathering Prayer
- Read Sirach 3:17-18, 20, 28-29
- Sing the Responsorial Psalm
- Read Hebrews 12:18-19, 22-24a
- Sing the Gospel Acclamation
- Read Luke 14:1, 7-14
- Pray using a prayer text from the Preface for the Sundays in Ordinary Time

The Word (30 min)

1. Referring to the Word in Liturgy section, focus on the gospel commentary. As the commentary points out, Luke often uses stories about Jesus being invited to meals or eating a meal. In this story, Jesus uses the opportunity to teach that "welcoming the poor and outcast to table is linked to the final judgment." (See Word in Liturgy section). In small groups invite the participants to reflect on the following question: *What does this reading mean for us as a people, as the Church?* After the small group discussion ask the group to share some of their responses with the large group.

2. The gospel reading points to the fact that the early followers of Jesus understood that they were to care for the poor and the outcasts. This powerful message is handed down to the Church today and is often articulated in the Church's preferential option for the poor. As a large group ask the participants to name those people in the world today, in their neighborhoods, and in the parish who might be considered the poor and outcasts in our culture.

Catholic Teaching (30 min)

1. An important element of today's gospel relates to Jesus' inclusion of the poor and the outcasts in the culture of his time. Using the Catholic Doctrine section present the Church's teaching on its preferential option for the poor. Explain that the Church does not neglect its concern for all people but it has a special concern to care for those in societies that are least cared for, who are often the silenced and neglected in our world.

2. With the group clarify the distinction between spiritual poverty and physical poverty. Ask the group to define and describe the results of physical poverty. List them on a piece of newsprint. Ask the group to list the various ways society responds to the poor and the outcasts in our world. Include services, programs, and attitudes.

3. Present to the group some of the Church's teachings regarding a response to the poor. Discuss with them ways the teachings are currently and could be put into action in our world. Share with the group any specific ways the local church is responding to the poor, such as St. Vincent De Paul Society, soup kitchens, Catholic Charities, parish programs.

Putting Faith Into Practice

1. Invite the group to reflect on the following question in small groups or pairs: *How do they hear themselves individually and as a group called to respond to the Church's preferential option for the poor?* Allow time for individuals to share their responses with the large group.

2. This is an appropriate time to invite a guest from the parish who is actively involved in ministry to the poor. Ask the guest to tell about how they became involved in the ministry as well as what the ministry involves.

Prayer

1. Give the participants a few moments to center themselves. Once all are settled, continue with the words of Pope John Paul II as a meditation.

"In the faces of the poor, I see the face of Christ. In the life of the poor I see reflected the life of Christ. In turn, the poor and those discriminated against identify more easily with Christ, for in him they discover one of their own . . . "

Jesus said that in the final analysis he will identify himself with the disinherited—the sick, the imprisoned, the hungry, the lonely—who have been given a helping hand.

Keep Jesus Christ in your hearts and you will recognize his face in every human being. You will want to help him out in all his needs: the needs of your brothers and sisters. This is the way we prepare ourselves to meet Jesus, when he will come again, on the last day, as the Judge of the living and the dead."

(Taken from *A Justice Prayer Book: Reflections on the Scriptures*, Thoughts on social justice by Pope John Paul II, Campaign for Human Development, 1982, p 17-18. The following speeches were quoted: Manila, February 1981; Puebla, Mexico, January 1979; New York City, homily, October 1979.)

2. Conclude with the following blessing:

May the Lord enlighten us with the truth of the gospel,
May we come to recognize Christ's face in every human being,
May we be strengthened with courage to work for justice.

We ask this through Christ our Lord. Amen.

Twenty-third Sunday in Ordinary Time

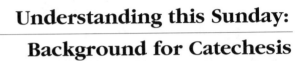
The Word In Liturgy

Wisdom 9:13-18b
Psalm 90:3-4, 5-6, 12-13, 14-17
Philemon 9-10, 12-17
Luke 14:25-33

Anyone who for the sake of following Christ is detached from family, renounces all possessions, and willingly endures daily the path to crucifixion is in a very particular condition: That person has nothing to lose. That person is free. If one did not know the love of God or the amazing life-giving power of the gospel, such self-renunciation would seem absurd, foolish, and indeed, impossible. Only having known Christ and the power of his resurrection, and having heard God's free, redeeming Word, can make such behavior intelligible, desirable, and possible.

Set in the context of a previous story in which worldly entanglements kept those invited to the feast of the kingdom from attending, today's gospel passage proclaims a radical message that detachment is a fundamental characteristic of the disciple. (To "hate" here is a Semitic expression that, while harsh, does not indicate an emotion, but means a state of detachment.) At the same time, the two short parables at the close of the passage serve to emphasize that discipleship is a clear-headed plan that should not be undertaken without care and thought as to its consequences. Detachment does not mean that the disciple must withdraw into some other-worldly haze. Rather, one must know the cost of undertaking the particular way of life that leads to the freedom of God's children, and be prepared to pay its price. One might expect that such advice would be reserved for a few select disciples, but in fact, the passage is addressed to the multitude. What is being described is not the path of an elite group, but is the common call to discipleship addressed to everyone who follows Jesus.

The first reading and psalm, in their praise of wisdom, and expressions of longing for wisdom, echo the gospel's call for a fair assessment of what is truly important in life. "Teach us to number our days aright," the psalmist cries out; the very transience of human life provokes a deep desire for wisdom. Yet wisdom is difficult to attain. The first reading, from the book of Wisdom, written in Alexandria at about 60 B.C. by a well-educated, sophisticated Hellenistic Jew, frankly acknowledges that many obstacles stand in the way of acquiring wisdom. Only with "your holy spirit" is it possible to become truly wise.

By the standards of his time, the apostle Paul would be regarded as exceptionally foolish for his words in today's second reading. Slavery was a long-established and completely accepted institution in the ancient world, and the slave was considered property. In spite of the fact that some slaves were talented, and educated, and occasionally rose to influence through their masters, the social gulf between the slave and the free person remained an unbridgeable chasm. For Paul to harbor Philemon's runaway slave, Onesimus, and foster his conversion, was daring. To instruct Philemon, as Paul does at the close of his letter to "accept and know Onesimus as a beloved brother in the Lord," and "accept him as you would accept me," is no less than amazing. It is of one piece with Paul's understanding of the radical change in relationships wrought by the love that is ours in Christ. While Paul did not crusade for change of the *institution* of slavery, his words and example in this very personal letter aim to effect a change of heart that is no less radical.

Several radical messages are interwoven in today's readings: Wisdom can only be gained through the help of God's spirit, love reconfigures our relationships, and detachment is the pre-requisite for true freedom in following Christ. Self-renunciation, a strong and challenging theme in today's gospel, may be the focus of today's catechesis.

Catholic Doctrine

Self-Renunciation as Requirement for Discipleship

In following Jesus as his disciples we are provided an example of self-emptying in the Lord himself who obeyed his heavenly Father to the point of suffering and dying upon the cross. On his way to Jerusalem and the cross, Jesus pointedly instructs his disciples (this Sunday's gospel) to be sure and count the cost of following him. The cost of following Jesus is to put the calculation of the kingdom of God before all else, including our most precious possession—our very self.

Another aspect of self-renunciation is detachment. In the spiritual life, detachment requires the necessary mastery of self so that both our inner core, the ego, (our dearest possession) and all our other "possessions" of family, primary groups and physical goods do not end up possessing us. As disciples of Jesus, the priority of the kingdom of God comes first (CCC 2544).

The Second Vatican Council cites St. Paul's letter to the Corinthians (1 Cor 7:31), observing that "[a]ll the faithful are invited and obliged to holiness and the perfection of their own state of life. Accordingly let all of them see that they direct their affections rightly, lest they be hindered in their pursuit of perfect love by the use of worldly things and by an adherence to riches which is contrary to the spirit of evangelical poverty, following the apostle's advice: Let those who use this world not fix their abode in it, for the form of this world is passing away. . ." (LG, 42) Worldly things, including our very selves, must be used in light of the absolute priority of the kingdom.

The Beatitudes of Jesus urge us to the practice of self-renunciation and to let go of our attachments to the things of this world ("blessed are the poor"). In a sense, the Beatitudes reveal a higher order of happiness and grace, of beauty and peace that cannot be found in worldly goods and status (CCC 2546).

In our Catholic tradition, the Church has connected renunciation and discipleship in the discipline of priestly celibacy. In addition, there are those who freely embrace the evangelical counsels of Christ by taking vows of poverty, chastity and obedience as a way of witnessing to the world the priority of the kingdom of God. The consecrated life upholds for all the faithful the need to renounce self in following Jesus. The Second Vatican Council rejoices that within the Church there are "many men and women who pursue more closely the Savior's self-emptying and show it forth more clearly, by undertaking poverty with the freedom of God's [children], and renouncing their own will: they subject themselves to man for the love of God, thus going beyond what is of precept in the matter of perfection, so as to conform themselves more fully to the obedient Christ." (LG, 42)

Those who are on this more narrow path encourage those of us who are not in following the spirit of the Beatitudes, for they bear witness that the world cannot be transfigured and offered to God without the renunciation of self. Another way to say this is that in the pursuit of the spiritual life, we who follow Jesus as his disciples, are invited into the task of self-transcendence. Alone, we cannot do this, but cooperating with the grace of God made possible by the sacrifice of Jesus, we are gathered "into the one body of Christ, a living sacrifice of praise." (*Roman Missal*, Eucharistic Prayer IV)

Catholic Culture

Prior to making baptismal vows, one renounces Satan, all his works, and all his empty promises. While this is not renunciation of self per se, it certainly does symbolize liturgically that turning away from the one who would take us down the path of adherence to self, possessions and status, all for their own sake.

Clerical celibacy is a form of self-renuciation in which the good of marriage is given up for the sake of service to the kingdom. Members of religious communities give up the private ownership of goods as well, and place themselves at the service of their communities and the people of God through the vow of obedience.

In Christian family life, self-renunciation is practiced whenever the needs of others are placed first out of love. Care for children and the elderly always includes an element of self-renunciation, as does the mutual love of husband and wife. When practiced in a Christian spirit, these acts are united with the love of Christ and give witness to the gospel.

Notes

Dismissal Catechesis (30 min)

Getting Started

1. Prepare a natural arrangement, suggestive of the fall season (nuts, apples, leaves, mums . . .) for the center of the circle.

2. Invite the catechumens and candidates to enter the circle. Begin the session by praying together the Serenity Prayer:

   God grant me the serenity to accept what I cannot change, the courage to change what I can, and the wisdom to know the difference.

First Impressions

1. Help the group recall today's scriptures by inviting them to silence. When they are quiet, play soft instrumental music and prayerfully read some of the phrases and images taken from the readings. Some quotes might be: "Show your deeds to your servants, your glory to their children." (Psalm 90:15) "who can conceive what the Lord intends?" (Wisdom 9:13) "you had given Wisdom and sent your spirit from on high." (Wisdom 9:17) "welcome him as you would welcome me." (Philemon 17) "everyone of you who does not renounce all his possessions cannot be my disciple." (Luke 14:33)

2. Invite the group to share these questions in smaller groups of 3 or 4. *What did you find inspiring and encouraging in these passages? What in them is challenging and difficult? What word or phrase sums up the meaning of these passages?*

3. Take time in the large group to listen to each person's short summary as to the meaning of these passages. Record these on an overhead or on paper, writing large enough for all to read.

Making Connections

1. Ask the participants to think about their normal weekday routines. As they get ready for the day, ask them: *What is generally running through your mind? What kinds of issues, problems, thoughts pre-occupy you during the course of the day? What is on your mind as you try to fall asleep at night?* As they finish sharing their responses, repeat the Serenity Prayer.

2. Based upon the passages for today's liturgy, ask the participants to share in the small groups: *What does the Sacred Scripture teach us about these preoccupations?* Ask that they make a list of the insights found in these scriptures. They may need to have the passages at hand for their discussion.

3. When the groups have finished their discussion, invite them to share their lists with the whole group. Summarize these insights, using poster board or a large sheet of paper to create one group list.

Prayer

1. Pray this litany of surrender, asking the group to respond: *"Fill us at daybreak with your love, that all our days we may sing for joy."* (Psalm 90:14)

   In all our anxious moments, O God . . .
   In our relationships with friends and co-workers, O God . . .
   In problems to be solved and work to be done, O God . . .
   In our suffering and pain, O God . . .
   In our simple pleasures, O God . . .
   In the laughter and tears of our families, O God . . .
   In all our fears and failures, O God . . .
   In the anguish of our world, O God . . .
   (The Participants may wish to add to this litany)

2. Close with the Serenity Prayer

Extended Catechesis

SESSION FOCUS: *Self-renunciation*

Gathering

A. Sunday:
Begin the Prayer with a song, "I Lift Up My Soul," Tim Manion, or something with a similar theme. Celebrate the Minor Exorcism found in RCIA #94 H (adapted if necessary to reflect the presence of baptized candidates).

B. Weekday:
Prepare a Liturgy of the Word, similar to the one outlined below.

- Song: "I Lift Up My Soul" (Manion)
- First Reading: Wisdom 9:13-18b
- Silence
- Gospel: Luke 14:25-33
- Quiet reflection with instrumental music softly playing

The Word (30 min)

1. Recall the two parables found in today's gospel. Invite the large group to share their insights regarding these parables.

2. Further the development of today's gospel message in these or your own words.

   The gospel from Luke challenges the crowd, not just the disciples. This is a signal for everyone to listen to its message. In this reading and the first passage from the Book of Wisdom we are reminded to assess what is truly important in life. For the follower of Jesus nothing is to be more important than Christ is. To know the Risen Lord and to make Christ our priority is the radical message for anyone thinking of being baptized or initiated into the Catholic community. This will mean detaching ourselves, which is, renouncing anything that comes between Christ and us. These two readings from Wisdom and Luke require us to be clear about the cost of following Jesus. The word 'hate' is a Semitic expression, implying detachment. Thus, to hate one's family did not mean animosity but detachment, as in forgoing the comfortable security of family ties to be focused on God.

3. Invite the participants to gather into small groups to discuss one or two of the following questions. These may be posted on an overhead, in order that the small groups might choose their area of interest. *What familial and worldly entanglements might prevent union with God? What is the challenge of this gospel for those on the journey of initiation into the Catholic community? How has the Spirit inspired and supported you in your journey of discipleship? How would you describe the committed disciple in today's world?*

Catholic Teaching (30 min)

1. Invite the large group to listen to a further explanation of the meaning of self-renunciation as requirement for discipleship. Prepare a short input in these or similar words, using the background material found in the Catholic Doctrine section in, "Understanding This Sunday."

Self-renunciation involves both placing our first priority on our relationship with God and detaching ourselves from those possessions and relationship which distract us from following Jesus wholeheartedly. As followers of Jesus the kingdom of God is our first concern. All else that preoccupies our life, including our own ego, must be put aside—surrendered—for the sake of union with God. Thus, self-renunciation can lead to an inner freedom to live for God's kingdom. Only in Christ and the power of the resurrection can the power of self-renunciation become a possibility for which we long.

2. Encourage the small groups to discuss these questions: *What are some of the detours and distractions in our commitment to Christ? How are these overcome? How can we foster this single-hearted love for God and God's kingdom as we pursue this journey of conversion?*

Putting Faith Into Practice

1. Describe for the group a little about the life of Julian of Norwich. The following will be helpful. For further resources look to, Joan Nuth's *Wisdom's Daughter* (Crossroad) and *Praying with Julian of Norwich* by Gloria Durka (St. Mary's Press).

The English mystic Julian of Norwich was an anchoress during the tumultuous period of the latter twelfth century. An anchoress was a person dedicated to a life of strict solitude and penance—praying, writing, studying and fasting, without ever leaving home. This solitary vocation as an anchoress was not unusual during these medieval times. An example of total self-renunciation, Julian had a deep desire to come closer to the passion of Christ. She is said to have prayed for three 'wounds'—contrition, compassion and longing with her whole will for God. When she became ill and near death at the early age of 31, Julian had 16 dramatic revelations of the love of God, which she called 'showings' in her writings. Julian was the first woman of letters in the English language. Her profound theological writings, based upon her visions and her feminine-inspired spirituality are a great contribution for contemporary disciples.

2. Pointing out the reflection from the writings of Julian of Norwich, found in the Participant Book (page 98) or on the blackline handout, invite the group to think about her commitment and respond to the questions indicated. When they have completed this exercise, ask them to share some insights with the large group.

Prayer

1. Have copies of these two prayers prepared ahead of this session. Invite the participants to silence and then encourage them to pray:

2. Julian of Norwich and Teresa of Avila share the same conviction that God alone suffices. Let us pray with them for the grace of self-renunciation:

(Julian)
God, of your goodness,
give me yourself,
for you are enough for me, and
I can ask for nothing . . . less
which can pay you full worship.
And if I ask for anything . . . less
always I am in want;
but only in you do I have everything. (*Showings*, p. 184)

(Teresa)
Let nothing disturb you,
nothing cause you fear;
All things pass
God is unchanging.
Patience obtains all:
Whoever has God
Needs nothing else,
God alone suffices. (*Saints for All Seasons*, p. 128)

Twenty-fourth Sunday in Ordinary Time

Understanding this Sunday:

Background for Catechesis

The Word In Liturgy

Exodus 32:7-11, 13-14
Psalm 51:3-4, 12-13, 17, 19
1 Timothy 1:12-17
Luke 15:1-32 [or 15:1-10]

The incident of worship of the golden calf, which we hear about in today's first reading, makes a crucial theological point in the unfolding of the book of Exodus: The relationship of the people with God is characterized *at its heart* by rebellion on the people's part, and forgiveness on the part of God. The people turn to an idol to replace God even before Moses comes down from the mountaintop! Their resistance to God is presented as something patent, reflexive; they are "a stiff-necked people." But through the intercession of Moses, and remembering the covenant with the patriarchs, God relents and forgives even this flagrant violation of their relationship.

Although the first letter to Timothy may have been composed by someone other than Paul himself, it is generally agreed that much of the material it contains reflects Paul's ideas and, in some cases, Paul's own words. Today's passage emphasizes the extreme seriousness of Paul's sins, as proof of the great truth that "Jesus Christ came into the world to save sinners" (v. 15). As an avid persecutor of Christians, Paul did indeed come to Christ with blood on his hands. Paul admits his guilt fully and glorifies God the more for the mercy he has received. Remembering his own sin guards against pride, arouses gratitude, and serves as an example that no one—no matter how grave their sin—stands outside the mercy of God.

Setting the context for today's gospel is the complaint by some of the religious leaders that Jesus welcomes sinners and—making the scandal complete—eats with them. The short form contains two parables: the lost sheep and the lost coin. The long form also includes the parable of the prodigal son, which was read on the fourth Sunday of Lent. All three illustrate God's solicitude in searching for sinners, and the shared joy that accompanies their return to safety (their complete

reconciliation to God). But the parable of the prodigal son most of all penetrates the leaders' objection, by its sensitive and incisive treatment of the elder brother. Ideally, therefore, the long form of the gospel should be read, for the greater depth the third parable introduces.

The lost sheep and the lost coin are parallel stories (the second unique to Luke): one image of God is male (the shepherd), the other female (the woman whose coin is lost). In both, great care is taken to find what is lost. The tenderness of the shepherd, expressed in the detail of taking the sheep on his shoulders, further indicates the loving nature of the search. Each parable concludes with a joyful communal celebration. The celebration is not an afterthought, but an integral part of the lesson of the parables. The reconciliation of the lost is naturally portrayed not as an exercise of grim duty, but as something that delights the heart of God—and can be expected to delight the friends of God as well. This theme is carried through the parable of the prodigal son as well, which, in rich detail, elaborates all of these features.

Yet this last parable brings a new twist, by probing the reaction of the elder brother. When the elder brother's jealousy keeps him away from the feast, the father likewise goes out to him, and in the ensuing conversation, the depth of the elder son's alienation is revealed. The elder son is alienated from his brother: he calls him not "my brother" but "that son of yours" (a point on which the father gently corrects him); he exaggerates the younger son's crimes, inventing "loose women" that were never mentioned before; and most poignant of all, he reveals that he is alienated from his father. "All these years I slaved for you," he says. Son though he was, sharing in all that his father has, nevertheless in his heart he felt himself to be a slave. The religious leaders, seeing sinners enter the kingdom ahead of those who have kept the law, are plainly depicted in this character of the elder brother. The father's response is instructive. He is generous with the elder, but will not abandon the younger. All are invited to the feast.

The church continues to welcome and rejoice over the reconciliation of sinners, the lost, and the alienated. The focus of today's catechesis may therefore be on the church's outreach, and its continual mission to welcome the alienated home to the feast of God's love.

Catholic Doctrine

The Church's Ministry of Reconciliation

The church's ministry of reconciliation is basic to its life, given that the church's founder, Jesus, came to restore us to God the Father and thus engaged in a ministry of reconciliation. He is imagined as the physician who provides the healing necessary for us to be made right with God. Jesus healed those who were not only bodily sick but also who were sick spiritually (CCC 1503). In the incarnation of Jesus, the initiative of divine love, seeks out every single human being, to bring us back and welcome us to our true home with God (CCC 605).

This mission of Jesus continues in the church, whom the early Fathers envisioned as the safe boat by which we navigate this unsafe world and a type of Noah's Ark which saves us. Those who are scattered, those who are far off, those who are led astray are invited back to the church and rediscover unity and salvation (CCC 845).

The Second Vatican Council, referring to Christ who was sent to heal the contrite of heart, goes on to reflect, "Similarly, the Church encompasses with her love all those who are afflicted by human misery and she recognizes in those who are poor and who suffer, the image of her poor and suffering founder . . . .The Church, however, clasping sinners to her bosom, at once holy and always in need of purification, follows constantly the path of penance and renewal." (LG, 8)

This way of imaging our ecclesial mission is not limited to the Sacrament of Reconciliation, but rather, encompasses an attitude, an outlook, and the entire range of activities by which the People of God minister to those who are hurting, alienated and marginalized, within and outside the Catholic Church. There are many different forms of alienation and bitterness, within families, between groups and races, between whole peoples. Individuals are alienated from the Church itself. Efforts to heal, to bring together, to reconcile properly belong to the Church whose founder preached the parable of the prodigal son. Thus, we believe that "The whole Church, as a priestly people, acts in different ways in the work of reconciliation which has been entrusted to it by the Lord." (*Rite of Penance*, n 8)

In his encyclical *Dives in Misericordia* (Rich in Mercy), John Paul II emphasizes, "If Paul VI more than once indicated the 'civilization of love' as the goal toward which all efforts in the cultural and social fields as well as in the economic and political fields should tend, it must be added that this good will never be reached if in our thinking and acting concerning the vast and complex spheres of human

society we stop at the criterion of 'an eye for an eye, a tooth for a tooth' and do not try to transform it in its essence, by complementing it with another spirit. . . .the realization of this task is precisely the mission of the Church in the modern world. Society can become ever more human only if we introduced into the many-sided setting of interpersonal and social relationships, not merely justice, but also that 'merciful love' which constitutes the messianic message of the gospel." (DM, 14.7)

John Paul II has also written, "In intimate connection with Christ's mission, one can therefore sum up the church's mission, rich and complex as it is, as being her central task of reconciling people: with God, with themselves, with neighbor, with the whole of creation; and this in a permanent manner since. . . 'the church is also by her nature always reconciling.'" (*Reconciliatio et Paenitentia*, Apostolic Exhortation, 2 December 1984, n. 8) In other words, the good news message of Jesus and the mission of the Church is directed less toward the found and the saved, and more toward those who desperately need it, the lost and the scattered.

Catholic Culture

A charming story regarding the life of St. Francis of Assisi (d. 1226) is found in the "Legend of the Wolf of Gubbio". St. Francis effected reconciliation between the wolf and the townspeople. It is depicted in a tempera panel (1437) from the high altar of San Francesco in Borgo San Sepolcro now in the National Gallery of Art, London. The saint is shown bending down, holding the extended paw of the wolf and reaching with his other hand toward the townspeople who are gathered behind him. As shown in their eyes and postures, the townspeople are apprehensive and cautious. (*Welch, Art and Society in Italy 1350-1500*, Oxford University Press, NY, 1997, p 110)

In 1994, Catholic film maker Frank Moynihan (*billy budd films*) produced a short animated film of the poem "The Prodigal Son" by the African-American poet and statesman, James Weldon Johnson (1871-1938). Johnson sought to emulate the deep, resonant voices of black preachers in a series of poems called "God's Trombones," of which "The Prodigal Son" is one. The famous line "Young man, young man, your arm's too short to box with God," is taken from Johnson's poem. The movie, which uses clay animation, was filmed in Capetown, South Africa.

In the late 1970's a Bostonian Catholic, Mary Gordon, wrote a best selling novel detailing her journey of reconciliation with her mother titled *Final Payments*.

Dismissal Catechesis (30 min)

Getting Started

1. Prepare the space ahead of time.

2. Invite the catechumens and candidates to stand in a circle around the table. Light a candle. Sing Psalm 51: "Be merciful, O Lord," or use the alternate opening prayer from the Sacramentary for the Twenty-Fourth Sunday in Ordinary Time.

First Impressions

1. Invite everyone to write down on paper words or phrases from the liturgy. Ask them to further reflect what their words or phrases mean to them; what feelings did the liturgy stir within them. Have them choose a partner and share their reflection.

2. Reassemble the group, asking for responses from the group. Summarize the responses.

Making Connections

1. Begin with reflection on the experience of the Israelites turning to worship the golden calf. Explain that the Israelites had been freed from the slavery of the Egyptians by a loving and protecting God. They are on their way to a land flowing with milk and honey which this God had promised to them. Yet here they are turning to the worship of a golden calf, an idol to replace God, before Moses even returns from the mountaintop. Discuss the following question with the group: *Are you surprised by the actions of the Israelites? Why or why not?*

2. Remind the participants that the golden calf is an idol, a false god. Ask the question: *What are the modern-day golden calves or idols, that our world, our society, place before us to worship?* List their responses on poster board or chalkboard. Continue with other questions: *How do we respond to these idols? How do we recognize them? What idols do we have in our own lives that cause us to turn away from a loving and caring God?*

3. Point out that God's response to the Israelites was to relent. Ask the group to sit in silence for a few minutes and reflect on a God who relents.

Prayer

Ask each catechumen and candidate to write their own prayer to God addressing the times they have turned to other "gods."

Extended Catechesis

SESSION FOCUS:
The Church's Ministry of Reconciliaation

Gathering

A. Sunday:

Welcome the sponsors, other team members and other companions.

Give them each a sheet of paper or ask them to turn to the Participant Book (page 100) or the blackline handout, and ask them to write how they experienced reconciliation as a child; as a young person and now. Invite them to share in pairs. After a few minutes, ask them to name the elements of reconciliation. List these on paper or on a chalkboard.

B. Weekday:

Welcome everyone. Begin with a Celebration of the Word, such as:

- Song: "Amazing Grace"
- Sign of the Cross and Greeting
- Reading: Exodus: 32:7-11, 13-14
- Quiet
- Reading: 1 Timothy 1:12-17
- Alleluia
- Gospel Luke 15:1-32
- Alleluia

The Word (30 min)

1. Proclaim Exodus 32:7-11, 13-14, unless you have used Gathering B. Using the section The Word in Liturgy as background, describe the relationship between God and the Israelites. Stress the following points:

- The rebellion on the part of the people and forgiveness on the part of God.

- This resistance to worshipping only one God is presented as instinctive; they are a "stiff-necked" people.

- Through Moses' intercession and remembering the covenant established with Abraham, God relents and forgives even this appalling violation of their relationship.

- Ask the participants to pair and to share their response to the question: *Discuss ways in which we are the "stiff-necked" people who frequently return to former ways rather than change our ways of doing things even when we know better.* Ask for responses from the pairs.

2. Read 1 Timothy 1:12-17, Explain in these or similar words: *Paul, formerly Saul, had been a persecutor of Christians. He came to Christ with blood on his hands. Paul admits his guilt and gives thanks and praise to God for the mercy he has received. Paul attests to the truth that Jesus Christ came into the world to save sinners. Recounting his own sins guards against pride, incites gratitude and serves as an example that no one stands outside the mercy of God. There is no sin that God will not forgive.* Discuss in pairs: *Why is it that we sometimes think that there are some sins that just can't be forgiven. Name the sins that are difficult for us to forgive.*

3. Read Luke 15:1-32, (Even though verses 11-32 are optional, do include them.) Explain in these or similar words: *Great care is taken to find what is lost. Each search concludes with a celebration when the lost is found. The celebration extends outside to include the community. Whether it's the shepherd or the woman or the father, each depicts the joy of God when one who is lost is found. The elder son refuses to come to the celebration. The dialogue with the father reveals the extent of his alienation. The father reaches out to bring him in but the son refuses to accept. The father wants both sons to come to the party but will not choose one over the other. Each son is free to respond to the father's invitation.* Ask the participants to discuss in pairs experiences when they have been either the prodigal son or the elder son.

Catholic Teaching (30 min)

1. Have two parishioners describe for the group ways in which they experienced reconciliation when they were children. Have two other parishioners describe for the group ways in which they experienced reconciliation as young people. Have two more parishioners describe ways in which they experience reconciliation today. In pairs, name the elements of reconciliation described in the stories. Compare these elements with those already listed on the poster paper, chalkboard, Participant Book (page 100) or on the blackline handout. Summarize the essential elements of reconciliation. Be sure to include: willingness to reach out, ability to name what separates people, recognition of one's own participation in the alienation, desire to be healed and to change one's behavior or attitude.

2. Ask the parishioners to describe ways in which the parish reaches out to: people who have been hurt by the Church, outcasts in the town or village, minorities. Describe the ways the parish is inclusive.

3. Conclude the session by summarizing the Church's ministry of reconciliation: *In the incarnation of Jesus, the initiative of divine love seeks out every single human being to bring us back and welcome us to our true home with God. There are many forms of alienation and bitterness within families, between groups and races, between whole peoples, and between individuals. Efforts to heal, to bring together, to reconcile, properly belong to the Church whose founder preached the parable of the prodigal son. The message of John Paul II in* **Reconciliatio et Paenitentis, Apostolic Exhortation** *(2 December 1984) states that the good news message of Jesus and the mission of the Church is directed less toward the found and the saved, and more toward the lost and the scattered.*

Putting Faith Into Practice

1. Ask participants to spend a few minutes each day this week focusing on the questions: *With whom do I need to be reconciled and how will such reconciliation be achieved?*

2. Challenge them to seek out someone with whom they need to be reconciled and, if possible, to initiate such reconciliation.

Prayer

Form a circle around the lighted candle. Ask sponsors and team members to step behind the candidates and catechumens and to place a hand on their shoulder. Celebrate an adapted Minor Exorcism, RCIA #94 K. Sing: "Amazing Grace."

God of our lives, we pray for direction and steadfastness. Take away the darkness that sometimes overshadows us. Grant us faith that knows no limits, hope that never fails, and love that embraces all. Guide us to know your will and fill us with a desire to conform our wills to yours.

(Paraphrase of prayer of St. Francis of Assisi)

Twenty-fifth Sunday in Ordinary Time

Understanding this Sunday:

Background for Catechesis

The Word In Liturgy

Amos 8:4-7
Psalm 113:1-2, 4-6, 7-8
1 Timothy 2:1-8
Luke 16:1-13 [or 16:10-13]

Today is the first of two Sundays in which we hear readings from the prophet Amos, who preached God's word in the northern kingdom of Israel before its destruction in 721 B.C. by the Assyrian invasion. His message was simple but biting: Through the events of history, divine judgment was being visited upon Israel for having abandoned the ways of justice and mercy so central to the covenant. The people are in a crisis, although they do not know it. The purpose of Amos' preaching is to shake them into an awareness of their true situation before God.

Today's passage is a harsh indictment of the greed and corruption common at the time. The reading highlights the damage done to the poor by the rapacious business practices of the rich. The poor are "bought" and "sold;" they are aggressively exploited by the wicked. The Mosaic law fixed the measure of the ephah and regulated the cycle of commerce and labor by the Sabbath and the cycles of the moon. The law was for the benefit of all, but it especially benefited the poor, who were more likely to suffer from being cheated, and for whom the relentless burdens of work would become intolerable without Sabbath rest. In Amos' description, the wicked chafe at these restrictions, and do their best to subvert them. The Lord pledges never to forget their crimes — a sure promise of judgment.

Today's reading from 1 Timothy centers on the theme of prayer. Prayer for all people is the obligation of Christians, and those in authority are to be a special focus of prayer because of the role they play in securing the peace and well-being of the whole community. Such prayer is oriented toward the salvation of all, which is here linked to knowledge of the truth. Lifting of one's hands—palms open and facing upward—is a gesture of prayer common to Judaism,

Christianity, and paganism.

Today's gospel from Luke is taken from a passage addressed to Jesus' disciples, not his opponents, and so is meant to state a positive message rather than launch a polemic. Although rather complicated in its details, the passage contains a coherent message which is in fact quite straightforward. The wily manager of the rich man's estate shows initiative when faced with a crisis (confrontation with his master, and loss of his job). The coming of the Messiah is likewise a crisis. The implicit question that is raised is: What are those who encounter the good news going to do about it? Will they be resourceful? Will they respond?

Throughout Luke's work, the way in which people use possessions reveals their character, their response to the good news, and ultimately their destiny. Today's passage enjoins the disciples to use their possessions (which ultimately belong to God and so are not their own anyway) to secure their everlasting reward (the one thing that will be theirs truly). They are asked to be faithful in a small thing (use of this world's goods) so as to be entrusted with a great thing (eternal life with God). When their worldly goods run out (death), they will have secured a place in heaven by having given generously to the poor and thus pleased God. Last of all, the passage warns that money can become an idol that competes with God for the worshipful allegiance of the human person. Each person must choose a single master. A decision is upon us.

Money, possessions, the goods of this world are all of crucial importance in how we live out our faith. Are we aware of our true situation before God? In the face of the crisis which the coming of God in Christ represents, will we be resourceful? When faced with the choice of a single master, what will we decide?

Catholic Doctrine

Social Justice: Part I

On the Twenty-Second Sunday in Ordinary Time we examined the Church's social justice teaching from the viewpoint of the preferential option for the poor. On the Thirty-Third Sunday we will treat the notion of kingdom justice from the point of view of the end of the liturgical year and the impending feast of Christ the King. On this Sunday and next Sunday we treat some general doctrinal issues regarding social justice based on the gospel texts, official documents and related resources.

Each of us, as we are born into this world, are not equipped with everything we need in order to develop bodily or spiritually. We need each other. Differences in individuals are due to age, physical abilities, intellect, moral aptitude, the benefit of social commerce and the distribution of wealth (GS 29). Thus, while we are all equally valuable, created in the image and likeness of God, our innate personal gifts are not distributed equally and we are not born into the same social situation and opportunities.

The Catholic position on these differences is that this is part of God's plan. God builds these differences into us so that we are required to receive from others what we need both bodily and spiritually to flourish. Differences among us encourage and oblige persons to practice generosity, kindness, sharing of goods. On a larger scale, these differences foster the mutual enrichment of cultures (CCC 1937).

In traditional Catholic moral theology, based in Thomas Aquinas, justice is understood as "the strong and firm will to give each person their due" (ST 2-2.58.1). Each should be given what they are due, and fairness is required in all our mutual agreements and exchanges. For example, the relationship between owners and employees, and between sellers and buyers should be characterized as just. Justice may lead to laws against unfair monopolies, or to laws upholding truth in advertising, or to laws ensuring a just wage, safe working conditions, and reasonable working hours.

St. Catherine of Siena, writes from the perspective of God, proclaiming, ". . .I have given many gifts and graces, both spiritual and temporal, with such diversity that I have not given everything to one single person. . . .I have willed that one should need another and that all should be my ministers in distributing the graces and gifts they have received from me." (Catherine of Siena, *Dialogues*, I,7)

Thus, the purpose of justice is, ultimately, to protect the dignity of persons and our rights which flow from this dignity. The very differences among us, given our abilities, our situations and our station in life, demand and encourage that love of one another that is the distinctive hallmark of the gospel of Jesus (CCC 1946). In loving one another, we are giving ourselves to kingdom values and to the God who is our Creator and author of that kingdom.

Catholic Culture

Les Miserables enjoys considerable popularity today due to the hit musical version which premiered on the London stage and later moved to Broadway and from there throughout the world. At its heart, this novel by the French Catholic, Victor Hugo, details the gulf between the classes and the great social and economic differences due to accidents of birth—and yet how some who are poor and have nothing are more honorable and just than those who are rich and have everything. In the novel, Marius says, "A creditor is worse than a master; for a master owns only your person, a creditor owns your dignity and can belabor that." (Victor Hugo, "Marius," *Les Miserables*, 1862, 5.2, trs., Charles E. Wilbour)

St. John Capistrano (1386-1456) is the patron saint of jurists, perhaps because before joining the Observant Franciscans in 1415 he studied law and served as a magistrate. After joining the order, he tirelessly promoted monastic reform in the Franciscan order and elsewhere.

Notes

Dismissal Catechesis (30 min)

Getting Started

1. Prepare the space ahead of time.

2. Gather the catechumens and candidates into a circle around a prayer centerpiece. Pray the following prayer or one of your own composition:

   God, our Creator, we come together today to reflect on your word. We pray that our hearts may be open to your teaching, as taught in the Gospel through the gift of your son, Jesus Christ. We ask this through Christ our Lord. Amen.

First Impressions

1. Invite the group to silent reflection. Help them to remember the liturgy by prayerfully repeating lines and phrases from the gathering hymn, the psalm, the first, second and gospel readings, and the homily. When finished, allow a minute of continued silence, and then ask the participants to share in pairs. The following questions may be helpful: *What clearly stands out for you from the liturgy? What came to mind as you listened to the readings?*

2. Focus the group's attention to the large group. Offer an opportunity for the individuals or pairs to share any comments or responses. Continue the discussion in the large group with the following questions: *What in the liturgy did you find exciting or surprising? Did anything cause you to stop and think? Did you find anything confusing or unclear?*

Making Connections

1. Using the Word in Liturgy section reflect with the group on the cultural-historical background at the time of the prophet Amos. Bring out that the words of Amos were a harsh indictment of the corrupt merchants whose business practices inflicted injustice and oppressed the poor. In response to the Amos passage, ask the group to reflect on the following questions: *Have they ever had an experience when they thought they were being cheated or treated unjustly? Describe the feelings. Was there anyone there to defend them?*

2. Help the group to understand the meaning of justice from the scriptures. This can be found in the Word in Liturgy section. Connect the scriptures with the events of the modern world by bringing out that there can be a tendency today to brush off the powerful words of Amos as irrelevant. Ask the participants to reflect in small groups on the following questions: *With a biblical understanding of justice, who cries out for justice in our world today? Name the people, places, and situations.* Offer each small group an opportunity to share their responses with the large group. In the large group discuss: *How do you hear yourself called to respond to the words of Amos?*

Prayer

Conclude the session by inviting the group to offer prayers of petition that reflect a concern for justice. Close with the song, "Let Justice Roll Like a River" (Marty Haugen, 1991, GIA Publications)

Extended Catechesis

SESSION FOCUS: *Social Justice*

Gathering

A. Sunday:

Invite the participants to gather. Welcome any new people. Ask each person to share a social issue that is particularly meaningful to them.

B. Weekday:

If you are gathering later in the week for extended catechesis, begin with a Celebration of the Word such as the one below.

- Gathering Hymn
- Greeting and Gathering Prayer
- Read Amos 8:4-7
- Sing the Responsorial Psalm
- Read 1 Timothy 2:1-8
- Sing the Gospel Acclamation
- Read Luke 16:1-13, [or 16:10-13]
- Pray using a prayer text from the Preface for the Sundays in Ordinary Time

The Word (30 min)

1. Explore the background for these readings using the Word in Liturgy section and focusing on the following points. In the first reading Amos speaks out against those engaged in trade and business for not protecting the poor and for not acting with justice. It was the responsibility of everyone in the covenant community of Israel to see that all people, but especially the poor, were treated with justice. Underlying this conviction was the belief that the goods of the earth were given by God for the common possession of all the people. The very existence of the poor was an indictment of Israel's infidelity to God.

   Invite the participants in small groups to reflect on the following question: *In light of the readings and the homily, what do these readings have to say to us as a people, as a nation, as the church?* After the small group discussion, invite each small group to share their ideas.

2. Continue to explore the gospel's theme of justice. Bring out how the disciples are challenged to weigh the importance of money, possessions, and the goods of this world in living out their faith. They are warned that money can become an idol, competing with God, and often attained at the price of poverty for another. Invite the participants to discuss the following question in small groups and then elicit some

general responses from the larger group: *How do the readings challenge you personally? How do they challenge our culture? Are they threatening or hopeful?*

Catholic Teaching (30 min)

1. The Catholic Church is committed to working for social justice. This Sunday provides an opportunity to explore the meaning of social justice and the its distinction from works of charity. Referring to the Catholic Doctrine section develop the foundation for understanding the Church's work for social justice. Be sure to point out that the pursuit of social justice is based in a biblical understanding of the covenant. As a result, the work for justice places the institutional church in the center of concern for the poor and the outcasts of society. Invite the group to respond as a large group on the following questions: *What do you think is the place of the church's involvement in defending the poor or working for justice in our society or in the world? What guidelines would you draw up regarding the church's involvement in the politics of our culture?*

2. After the discussion explore with the group the ways the church responds to social issues. Explain the distinction between works of charity and work for social justice. In these or similar words point out that charity has to do with direct service to address immediate needs, such as, soup kitchens help with hunger. The work of social justice often involves systemic changes. As an example, charity means making sure homeless people have food while the work for social justice would ask the question why are there so many homeless and what ought we to do change the situation.

3. Research and provide for the group various examples in your state, city or parish of groups or individuals involved in works of charity and in the work of social justice. Suggestions of those doing works of charity might be soup kitchens, St. Vincent de Paul, day care centers. Examples of groups working for social justice might be community organizing efforts, legislative networks, congress writing campaigns. Examples of how the Catholic Church is involved in social justice at the diocesan level might include the state Catholic conference, Campaign for Human Development projects, diocesan offices of justice and peace.

Putting Faith Into Practice

Elicit responses from the group to the following questions. *In light of the readings from the scriptures, the presentation on social justice and charity, and the examples given, how do you believe the parish ought to respond to social issues in your area? What is the challenge for you personally?*

Prayer

Close with one of the following songs related to justice: "Voices that Challenge" (David Haas, 1990, GIA), "Let Justice Roll Like a River" (M. Haugen, 1991, GIA). Many other songs related to our work for justice could also be appropriate.

Twenty-sixth Sunday in Ordinary Time

The Word In Liturgy

Amos 6:1a, 4-7
Psalm 146:7, 8-9, 9-10
1 Timothy 6:11-16
Luke 16:19-31

"Woe to the complacent in Zion!" The words of the prophet Amos ring out in the church today, warning of the destruction that awaits those who ignore God's demand for justice. The wrath of God is raised, according to the prophet, by the callous self-indulgence of the wealthy. The rich are not depicted here as the cause of misfortune to the poor, as they are in the portrait of greed and corruption that was painted in last week's reading from Amos. Rather, they are called to task for their culpable *indifference* to the needs of others. "Joseph" here refers to those who suffer injustice in the kingdom of Israel. The complacent in Zion, who "are not made ill by the collapse of Joseph," are thus like Joseph's brothers, who threw him into a cistern to die, and then sat down to a meal (Genesis 37:18-35). Sated with wealth and pleasures, they have closed their hearts to compassion, and so have earned the destruction that will fall on them at the hands of the Assyrian invaders.

Psalm 146 continues to play on the theme of justice. It is a psalm of praise for God, who rescues the poor and the oppressed. God is presented both as Creator and Redeemer in this scene of liberation, shared abundance, and healing which accompany his reign.

Timothy, the young person to whom this letter was written, was regarded by Paul as a dear friend, as well as a promising Christian leader. Here we see how Timothy's calling is grounded in baptism. The writer of the letter makes a solemn charge to Timothy, calling him to courageous and faithful witness. He calls Timothy a "man of God"—a title used for Moses and the prophets. He praises Timothy's "noble profession of faith"—which most probably refers to his baptism.

(Jesus' "profession of faith" may indicate his words proclaiming his messianic identity before Pilate, or may simply refer to his crucifixion.) The "appearance" (epiphaneia) to which the passage refers is the parousia (the second coming of Christ).

In Luke's gospel, prior to the passage we hear today, some of the religious leaders have been characterized as "money-lovers." They have rejected Jesus' teaching about possessions and even mock him for it. The parable of the rich man and Lazarus speaks to such hardness of heart. In today's parable, unique to Luke, two men's lives and final destinies are contrasted. The rich man (sometimes called "Dives" in the tradition—*dives* means "rich" in Latin) feasts sumptuously every day, while the poor man, Lazarus, lies at his door starving. Lazarus is hungry, diseased, crippled and cries out for mercy, but he receives none from the rich man, who ignores him.

After death, the fortunes of the two are reversed. Lazarus rests "in the bosom of Abraham," i.e., close to the heart of great father of the Jewish people, while the rich man must endure the sufferings of the damned. Now it is he who must cry out for mercy. The scene as it is visualized in the parable would have been familiar to a Jewish audience. Belief in an afterlife did not come into Judaism until the second century B.C., but when it did, *sheol*, the abode of the dead, began to be imagined as having two separate compartments: one for the just, and one for the wicked. It was believed that one could see from one to the other, but not pass through the boundary between them.

The point of this parable is unmistakable. Care for the poor is a non-negotiable requirement of the covenant, attested by Moses and all the prophets. Those who choose to ignore this obligation will not fare well in the next life. Most chilling in the story is the specter of those whose hearts are so hardened that they will not listen "even if one should rise from the dead"—a clear allusion to those who will fail to be converted, even by the resurrection of Jesus.

Catholic Doctrine

Social Justice: Part II

Jesus uses a parable about a wealthy, indifferent man and a poor, needy beggar to teach compassion for others in this world before it is too late and we are judged in the next world. This gospel text relates to our Catholic social teaching on justice and the creation of right relationships in society. Sinful inequalities affect millions of women and men throughout the world. That these inequalities have existed throughout history and in every society does not excuse them. The Catholic Church insists that these unequal conditions between individuals openly contradict the gospel (CCC 1938).

The social teaching of modern popes has contributed to a quantum leap in the Catholic understanding of the role of individuals, groups and governments in promoting the common good (see Catholic Doctrine, 33 Sunday Ordinary Time, first paragraph, for a listing of this papal contribution). The Second Vatican Council also teaches, "Their equal dignity as persons demands that we strive for fairer and more humane conditions. Excessive economic and social disparity between individuals and peoples of the one human race is a source of scandal and militates against social justice, equity, human dignity, as well as social and international peace." (GS, 29)

But it is not merely a matter of material goods and their just distribution. It is also a matter of spreading spiritual goods of the faith by which the Church has, in turn, opened up new paths for the development of temporal goods. Pius XII wrote, "For two thousand years this sentiment has lived and endured in the soul of the Church, impelling souls then and now to the heroic charity of monastic farmers, liberators of slaves, healers of the sick, messengers of faith, civilization, and science to all generations capable of offering to everyone possible a life worthy of [the human person] and of a Christian." (Pius XII, Discourse, June 1, 1941)

John Paul II has made his own unique contribution to the Church's understanding of solidarity, not only in his stance towards his homeland of Poland under the former Soviet sphere, but in his encyclical which commemorated the twentieth anniversary of Paul VI's Populorum Progrssio. John Paul wrote, "Solidarity helps us to see the "other"— whether a person, people or nation—not just as some kind of instrument, with a work capacity and physical strength to be exploited at low cost and then discarded when no longer useful, but as our "neighbor," a "helper". . .to be made a sharer, on a par with ourselves, in the banquet of life to which all are equally invited by God." (SRS 39.5) He goes on to say, "Solidarity therefore must play its part in the realization of this divine plan, both on the level of individuals and on the level of national and international society. The "evil mechanism" and "structures of sin" of which we have spoken can be overcome only through the exercise of the human and Christian solidarity to which the Church calls us and which she tirelessly promotes. Only in this way can such positive energies be fully released for the benefit of development and peace." (SRS 40.4)

In 1991, on the anniversary of the ground breaking encyclical of Leo XIII, Rerum Novarum (1891), the U.S. Catholic bishops issued material that summarized the main themes of Catholic social teaching over the last one-hundred years. Those themes are: 1) the option for the poor and vulnerable, 2) the call to family, community and participation, 3) the life and dignity of the human person, 4) the rights and responsibilities of the human person, 5) the dignity of work and the rights of workers, and 6) solidarity.

The Catholic Church, in its social teaching on justice and human solidarity, witnesses to and works towards that vision of Jesus who never saw the distinctions between people, rich and poor, so much as he saw the distinctiveness of every child of God.

Catholic Culture

John Paul II has upheld St. Peter Claver as a model Christian witness to human solidarity. Peter Claver (1581-1654) was a Spanish Jesuit missionary. He became known as the "saint of the slaves," for at Cartagena, Colombia, his practice was to meet slave ships arriving from Africa and go into their holds, caring for the physical and spiritual good of those who were soon to be slaves. (Encyclopedia of Catholicism, p. 989)

Even the Catholic Church has a body of law which helps to direct "canonical discipline in fidelity to" Jesus Christ. The Code of Canon Law stipulates how right relationships are ordered within the organization of the Church. In part, it governs how sacraments are celebrated, worship is regulated, authority is wielded, teaching is promoted and the property of the Church is protected. When Pope John XXIII called for an ecumenical council, he also initiated a reform of the current Code of Canon Law. The project was not completed until after the Council and during the pontificate of John Paul II. On January 25, 1983 he promulgated the "new" Code which replaced the 1917 Code of Canon Law.

Dismissal Catechesis (30 min)

Getting Started

Before Mass, prepare the meeting space with a prayer environment and a place for the lectionary. Be sure that there are enough chairs for everyone and that the chairs are set up in a manner which facilitates group discussion. Upon dismissal, gather the catechumens and the candidates in a circle. Place the lectionary in a prominent place and invite the group to silence. Begin with a prayer of your own composition or the following:

> God of power,
> look upon these your servants
> as they deepen their understanding of the Gospel.
>
> Grant that they may come to know and love you
> and always heed your will
> with receptive minds and generous hearts.
>
> Teach them through this time of preparation
> and enfold them within your Church,
> so that they may share your holy mysteries
> both on earth and in heaven.
>
> We ask this through Christ our Lord. Amen.
> (from Blessings of the Catechumens in Rite of Christian Initiation of Adults, p. 49)

First Impressions

Recall for the group the Old Testament reading and the gospel, bringing out the strong words in both readings. God's word is very strong this Sunday. First, the woes of the Old Testament and then the gospel story seem to depict a lack of compassion on Abraham's part. As a large group invite the participants to respond to the following questions: *What do today's readings say to you? What strikes you?*

Making Connections

1. Point out that the readings are difficult for us to hear especially when we want the word of God to comfort us rather than challenge. Today's readings continue our discussion from last week about social justice. As pointed out in The Word in Liturgy section, the difference in the readings this week is that they refer not to the cause of misfortune to the poor but instead deal with the indifference to the needs of others. Invite the participants to get into small groups and discuss the following questions: *Are there any people, situations, misfortunes in the world, that you feel indifferent towards? What is indifference and why do we become indifferent?* After the small groups have finished, invite participants to share any responses with the large group.

2. Commenting briefly on the scriptures, highlight the challenge of the word of God to wake up to our indifference. Indifference can have several ramifications. First, we can become vulnerable to accepting other people or society's opinions about people and issues. Second, indifference can lead to guilt for one's indifference which can lead to anger. Even though it is difficult to "care about" every person and issue, developing principles or guides to help us appreciate situations can help us through the mire of social issues. As a large group ask the participants to share the values and principles that guide them in their lives. An example would be "the dignity of life."

Prayer

Together recite or sing the Responsorial Psalm.

Extended Catechesis

SESSION FOCUS: *Social Justice*

Gathering

A. Sunday:

Invite everyone to gather and welcome any new people to the group. Ask each person to name some of the causes of indifference or excuses we use in order to justify our indifference. Some examples include: *"I don't have enough time." "What can I do, I am only one person and the problem is too big."*

B. Weekday:

If you gather during the week for extended catechesis, be sure to begin with a Celebration of the Word such as the following:

- Gathering hymn, first few verses only
- Greeting and Gathering Prayer
- Read Amos 6:1a, 4-7
- Sing the Responsorial Psalm
- Read 1 Timothy 6:11-16
- Sing the Gospel Acclamation
- Read Luke 16:19-31
- Conclude with the final verse of the Gathering Hymn

The Word (30 min)

1. Using the Word in Liturgy, explore the background of the readings today. Emphasize that the readings today continue our discussion about social justice but instead of looking at the causes of misfortune, this week we look at the problem of indifference to the needs of others. This is especially pointed out in the reading from Amos. In small groups, invite the participants to respond to the following question: *What is challenging, comforting, or disturbing from the readings today?* After the discussion, surface some of their responses to be shared with the large group.

2. Reflecting on the gospel, explore the background of the text especially as it relates to indifference and hardness of heart. Explain that care for the poor and the outcasts of our society is a "non-negotiable requirement of the covenant." Be sure to include a comment that the covenant with Israel continues to be our covenant. In and through Jesus the covenant was made concise in the command to love. This

command is found throughout the gospels and also in the epistles. The challenge for us as Church is how are we to love in a way that cares for the poor and the outcasts.

3. Invite the participants to gather in small groups and respond to the following scenario: *Pretend that you are all bishops. You have decided (with permission of the pope) to draw up guidelines, guiding principles on how to live out of this covenant of love for all people. Come up with some guiding values or principles. No less than three and no more than ten. Example would be: We believe that all life has dignity.* Have them write out their responses on newsprint and hang them on the wall. Allow for time for each group to present their principles.

Catholic Teaching (30 min)

1. Remind the participants that last week we looked at the Church's concern for social justice, the foundation for Catholic social teachings, and the distinction between the work of charity and the work for justice. Referring to the work of the groups in The Word, and to the Catholic Doctrine section explore the six themes of Catholic social teaching. Present them in these or similar words helping the group to understand that each builds on the other. Ultimately the six themes articulate what helps an individual to become all he or she can become and what supports the common good of all God's people.

2. Focus on *the life and dignity of the human person*. Highlight that the foundation for all the Church's social teaching is the belief in the dignity of all life, womb to tomb. This is based on the belief that we are created in the image and likeness of God. Ask the group to respond to the following questions: *Where and how do you see the Church speaking out on the dignity of life? What is your personal response?*

3. Focus on the *rights and responsibilities of the human person*. Clarify that each person has basic rights to freedom, religious liberty, food, shelter, health, security, education, employment. We have a responsibility to assure these rights for each other. We also must take responsibility for our own lives. Invite discussion of the following questions: *What is your personal response to this principle? Do you agree or disagree?*

4. Focus on the *call to family, community and participation*. Explain that the Church believes we are social creatures and we need each other in family and community. We have the responsibility and the right to be involved in the broader community. Elicit responses to the following questions: *How do you see the Church involved in this principle? What is your personal response?*

5. Focus on the *dignity of work and the rights of workers*. Speak to the value that the Church places on work as our participation in creation. In addition, the Church speaks out for a living wage for people and the right of workers to organize to protect themselves. Invite participants to respond to the following questions: *How do you see the Church involved in this agenda? How do you respond?*

6. Focus on the *option for the poor*. The Church is very concerned for those who experience poverty, alienation, or oppression. They are often the voiceless in our society. Ask the group to respond to the following questions: *How do you see the Church involved in concern for the poor? Do you agree or disagree with the Church's action on behalf of the poor?*

7. Focus on *solidarity*. Explain to the group that the Church recognizes that we are all part of the human family throughout the earth. National boundaries and agendas are secondary in a concern for people. Encourage discussion on the following questions: *How do you see the Church involved in promoting solidarity of all the people of God? Do you agree or disagree with the action of the Church?*

Putting Faith Into Practice

1. There are many people in parishes who are often involved in some capacity in one of the above actions. Invite a person to come and speak about his or her work for justice and how people can become involved.

2. After the presentation invite the group to reflect in silence how they hear themselves affirmed and challenged by the teaching of the Church? How do they hear themselves called to respond? What will it cost them (time, energy, etc.) and are they willing to pay the price? Invite those who are interested to share some of their responses.

Prayer

Close the session with the song, "Voices that Challenge," by David Haas, or another selection with a social justice theme.

Twenty-seventh Sunday in Ordinary Time

Understanding this Sunday:

Background for Catechesis

The Word In Liturgy

Habakkuk 1:2-3; 2:2-4
Psalm 95:1-2, 6-7, 8-9
2 Timothy 1:6-8, 13-14
Luke 17:5-10

"In the gospel is revealed the justice of God, which begins and ends with faith; as Scripture says, 'the just... shall live by faith.'" So writes St. Paul at the outset of his great work on justification in his letter to the Romans (1:17). The scripture he quotes is from today's first reading: Habakkuk 1:2-3, 2:2-4. In this very brief book, written in 597 B.C., the prophet Habakkuk questions God's direction of the world. Why do the wicked flourish, and the just suffer? The first verses of the reading are the beginning of a chapter describing the woeful state of human affairs that Habakkuk experiences, including but not limited to the evils of the Babylonian invasion. The word "violence" for Habakkuk signifies every form of greed and lawlessness that tramples on human rights. At the beginning of the next chapter, in response to the prophet's heartfelt question, God instructs him to write down the vision he receives and to trust that it will be fulfilled in its own time. God's answer does not actually answer the prophet's question. Yet it presses him to a difficult yet certain place of truth: He must trust. He must endure. He must have faith.

Today's gospel is no less challenging. In each of the synoptics, the disciples ask Jesus to increase their faith. In Mark, it is in response to the call to prayer. In Matthew, it results from the disciples' disappointment at being unable to cast out demons. Here, in Luke, it follows upon several sayings concerning the demands of the moral life—specifically, the requirements of avoiding scandal and forgiving seventy times seven times. By using the image of the mustard seed, Jesus points out that it is not the quantity of one's faith that matters. His vigorous, Semitic expressions are not to be taken literally; the point is that even the smallest amount can enable one to do amazing, unimaginable deeds. The passage goes on to compare the disciples to servants or slaves, on whom their master has a legitimate claim. Should God be impressed if they avoid scandal, practice forgiveness, have faith? Even if they do all these things that are required of them, they have only done the minimum, the gospel asserts.

Today's reading from 2 Timothy in many ways is warm and nurturing, yet it, too, has a strong inner core that challenges the reader to a genuine embrace of the demands of faith. Timothy is presumed to be a younger contemporary of Paul, possessing the Spirit through his baptism and his ordination (through the laying on of hands) to serve the Christian community. The letter's author (who may or may not actually be Paul) encourages him to act in such a way that the Spirit he already possesses will increase in him and make him "strong, loving and wise." He is exhorted to bear hardships for the sake of the apostolate. He is also enjoined to make a clear and orthodox presentation of the faith. Possibly in opposition to Gnostic elements which called for adaptations that would compromise the apostolic character of the faith, the letter speaks from a firm position in favor of keeping the teachings of the apostles alive and intact.

Possessing the Spirit given to him by the laying on of hands, Timothy would serve the community of faith. Yet he himself needed to be encouraged to grow strong in the Spirit in various ways for the good of the whole community of disciples. Today's readings offer an opportunity for catechesis on the Sacrament of Holy Orders: a sacrament in service to communion in the church—especially to our communion as a people of faith.

Catholic Doctrine

The Sacrament of Holy Orders

The sacrament of Holy Orders consecrates one in Christ for service to the Church. As the Second Vatican Council teaches, "Those among the faithful who have received Holy Orders are appointed to nourish the Church with the word and grace of God in the name of Christ." (LG 11) Based on the example of Jesus who chose men as apostles to follow him and gave them authority to preach and heal in his name, the sacrament of Holy Orders is only conferred upon men. Three degrees constitutes Holy Orders in the Church: the episcopate, the presbyterate, and the diaconate (bishops, priests and deacons).

By Baptism and Confirmation, all the faithful share in the common priesthood of all believers. The priesthood of all believers is not the same as the special consecration received in the sacrament of Holy Orders. All the faithful share in the mission and worship of the Church. But the Second Vatican Council, relying on the ancient tradition of the Church, teaches that there is an essential difference between the priesthood of all believers and the ordained priesthood. Historically, even our forebears in faith, the people of Israel, who were set apart from all the nations by God, had from among their members, a particular group, the tribe of Levi, which exercised a priesthood. The function of the Levites prefigured the ordained priesthood of the New Covenant (CCC 1541).

Our Catholic understanding is that the bishop receives the fullness of Holy Orders. Bishops hold this chief office as the direct successors of the apostles. Thus, in ordaining a bishop, the Church believes that "by the laying on of hands which confers the sacrament of orders in its fullness, the apostles passed on the gift of the Holy Spirit which they themselves had received in Christ . . . [such that] by a succession of bishops unbroken from one generation to the next, the powers conferred in the beginning were handed down, and the work of the Savior lives and grows in our time." (*Roman Pontifical*, *Ordination of a Bishop*, *Homily*, n. 18.)

The fullness of Holy Orders received at episcopal consecration confers the threefold ministry of preaching and teaching, sanctifying and governing. Thus, the Catholic Church believes that bishops are constituted as true and authentic teachers of the faith. They are stewards of the mysteries of God. And they are to govern or lead by serving. The gospel images of Jesus which correspond to these ministries are teacher, priest and shepherd.

Bishops are entrusted with the care of a local Church (diocese) but they exercise their threefold ministry collegially, with all the other bishops and in union with the head of the college of bishops, the Pope (CCC 1560). Priests are co-workers associated with the bishop, who hands on to them in a subordinate way his own ministry, so that Christ's apostolic mission may be fulfilled (CCC 1562). Deacons assist bishops and priests in the celebration of the divine mysteries, in the distribution of Holy Communion, in blessing marriages, in the proclamation of the Gospel, in presiding over funerals and in the various ministries of charity (CCC 1570).

Holy Orders configures one to Christ as teacher, priest and pastor. In the Latin Rite, all ordained ministers remain celibate for life, with the exception of permanent deacons. Celibacy is the sign that the ordained give themselves to God and the service of others (CCC 1579).

This is, seemingly, a daunting role and identity within the community of the faithful. A young priest of the Church, St. Gregory of Nazianzus, thus exclaimed, "We must begin by purifying ourselves before purifying others; we must be instructed to be able to instruct, become light to illuminate, draw close to God to bring him close to others, be sanctified to sanctify, lead by the hand and counsel prudently. I know whose ministers we are, where we find ourselves, and to where we strive. I know God's greatness and [our] weakness, but also [our] potential. (St. Gregory of Nazianzus, *Oratio* 2, 71, 74, 73: PG 35, 480-81.)

Catholic Culture

Christ the Priest depicts Jesus with arms outstretched upon the cross (as if bestowing a blessing), fully robed in liturgical vestments.

A recent movie that illustrates the bishop as shepherd who is willing to lay down his life for his flock is *Romero*.

The essential rite during the ordination of a bishop is the laying on of hands and the prayer of consecration. But there are other rites which surround this and help to complete it: an anointing with sacred chrism, handing the book of the gospels to the newly ordained bishop, along with the ring, miter and crosier. These signify his ministry to proclaim the Word of God, his charge to be faithful to the Church, and his office of shepherd (CCC 1574).

Notes

Dismissal Catechesis (30 min)

Getting Started

1. Prepare the center table with a dish of mustard seeds, a lighted candle, and a place for the lectionary. Gather in a circle of chairs.

2. Have everyone sit in silence for a moment and become quiet. Pray: *God, you bring us together today. We are grateful for you and the many ways you nourish our hearts and spirits. Open us now to hear the word you want to speak within and among us. We are your humble servants, and pray through Christ and the Spirit. Amen.*

First Impressions

1. Recall a few phrases from scripture: *"Write down the vision—it will surely come; Stir into flame the gift of God; and We are useless servants. We have done no more than our duty."* Ask the participants to talk in pairs about this question: *What image or phrase caught your attention today?*

2. Have them regather as one group and share their responses. Call on each pair to encourage sharing. Briefly summarize the variety of responses.

Making Connections

1. Ask participants to discuss the following questions in pairs: *In what way do you need an increase in faith? In what way has your faith grown?* Give examples.

2. State: *In this passage of Luke's gospel, Jesus connects having greater faith with being of service.* Invite participants to discuss in the large group: *What is the connection between faith and service?* Give examples.

3. Conclude by asking participants to name something they want to take with them from God's word today. Go around the circle for this naming.

Prayer

1. Invite each participant to hold one of the tiny seeds representing the seed of faith in them.

2. Proclaim the second reading 2 Timothy 1:6-8, 13-14.

3. Pray: *Gracious God faith in you gives us all we need. We pray as the apostles did: Increase our faith. Make us your faithful servants in all that we do. We pray in Jesus' name. Amen.*

4. Sing the refrain of Psalm 95 used at today's Mass.

Extended Catechesis

SESSION FOCUS: *The Sacrament of Holy Orders*

Gathering

A. Sunday:

1. Welcome sponsors and additional participants. Have them sit in small groups.

2. Invite all into a moment of silence. Summarize the sharing from the dismissal catechesis.

3. Ask all to hold one of the seeds. Pause for a moment of quiet. Proclaim the Gospel, Luke 17:5-10.

B. Weekday:

1. As the group gathers in the circle, greet and welcome each person.

2. Invite everyone to take one of the tiny seeds. Ask the participants: *In what way have you experienced your faith since Sunday?* Invite a brief response in the large group.

3. Then lead this Celebration of the Word.
   - Hymn: We Walk by Faith
   - Second Reading: 2 Timothy 1:6-8,13-14
   - Silence
   - Sing: Alleluia
   - Gospel: Luke 17:5-10
   - Silence
   - Pray: *God, through your Spirit you light the flame of God's gift of faith in us. Make us your faithful servants. May we live in service of your gospel, until you reign in all parts of our city and world. We ask this through our Lord Jesus Christ, your Son, who lives and reigns with you in the unity of the Holy Spirit, One God for ever and ever. Amen.*
   - Hymn: The Servant Song

The Word (30 min)

1. Introduce the Gospel with these points:
   - Jesus uses an extreme example of the tiny seed of faith being able to uproot a very large tree with an extensive root system and transplant it in the sea.
   - Faith is a gift of a personal relationship with God that leads to cooperation with and response to God's action.
   - Luke puts together the apostles' request for an increase of faith and a teaching on being a servant.

Ask participants to reflect on these questions: *When have*

you felt like a servant? What was difficult for you? What was life-giving for you?* Participants may use the Participant Book (page 106) or the blackline handout. Invite small group sharing. Then, invite some large group sharing of a servant experience.

2. Given these different experiences of being servant, ask participants to discuss in small groups: *What do you feel about Jesus' statements that: So you also, when you have done all that you were ordered to do, say, "We are worthless slaves; we have done only what we ought to have done!"* Luke 17:10 *What do you think he is saying?*

3. Then, invite some sharing in the total group. Listen for and bring out the following understandings:

We belong to God.

All we have is from God.

When we are given all in love, we return all we have and are.

God is asking for a total commitment as a disciple of Christ.

4. Ask participants to do the following: Evaluate how you see yourself on a scale of 1 to 10, with 10 being high, in terms of total commitment as a disciple. Name one way God is asking you to give more of yourself over to him. They may use the reflection in the Participant Book (page 106) or on the blackline handout. Then allow some time for sharing in small groups. Ask for some summary responses in the total group.

Catholic Teaching (30 min)

1. Make the following points:

- *1 Peter 2:5 refers to the priesthood of all believers to which all the baptized belong.*

- *Vatican Council II describes the church as the body of Christ, the people of God, all joined to Christ by baptism with distinct roles and various ministries.*

In the large group ask participants to respond to this question: *In what ways do you and others in the parish minister as an expression of the meaning of your baptism?* Elicit examples of outreach as well as liturgical and various pastoral examples.

2. Present a teaching on the Sacrament of Holy Orders in these or your own words:

Out of the priesthood of all believers the church calls forth and ordains certain people to be stewards of the faith and shepherd of others. This ministry began with the apostles. A disciple is a learner, a follower. An apostle is a witness of the life, death, and resurrection of Christ who is sent out on mission to others. In the early church two

types of leadership emerged: that of leading through charismatic gifts given, as in the Corinthian church, and leading via an office given to them, as in the Roman church. The three forms of this ministry were already occurring within the early church: the episcopate, the presbyterate, and the diaconate. The Sacrament of Holy Orders pertains to bishops, priests, and deacons.

The bishop, in direct succession from the apostles, is given authority to nourish the church with grace and the word of God. The word cathedra from which cathedral comes, means a chair, a place of teaching with authority. Each cathedral has the bishops chair in a prominent place. Each country has a Conference of Bishops who present moral teaching on important societal issues. For example, in the U.S., bishops issued a letter on the economy, Economic Justice for All.

Priests share in the ministry of the bishop. Priests, though taking on many pastoral and administrative duties, by right of ordination preside at the Sacraments and Mass. Diocesan priests promise to live celibately and pledge obedience to the local ordinary (bishop). Priests in religious orders also take vows usually of poverty, celibacy, and obedience.

There are both transitional deacons, who will go on to ordination to the priesthood, and permanent deacons, who will remain deacons. Acts of the Apostles 6 records the choosing of the seven deacons needed for assistance.

The Sacrament of Holy Orders is conferred through a laying on of hands. The person is anointed with the oil of chrism, the same oil used in Confirmation.

3. Ask participants: *What bishops, priests, and deacons do you know or have you heard about?* List these in categories on newsprint.

Or . . .

Participants may use the reflection in the Participant Book (page 106) or on the blackline handout..

Putting Faith Into Practice

State that Christ calls all people to ministry as servant of others. Ask participants to respond to this question in small groups: *What is one way you will minister to another this week?*

Prayer

1. Lead into prayer saying: Open yourself prayerfully to God and place yourself in God's service.

2. Allow for a moment of quiet prayer.

3. Proclaim 2 Timothy 1:6-8, 13-14.

4. Sing: The Servant Song

Twenty-eighth Sunday in Ordinary Time

The Word In Liturgy

2 Kings 5:14-17
Psalm 98:1, 2-3, 3-4
2 Timothy 2:8-13
Luke 17:11-19

Written around the time of the destruction of Jerusalem by Babylonian invaders in 587 B.C., the books of Kings were composed to instruct and encourage the survivors of this terrible catastrophe. One of the three major themes of these books, exemplified in today's passage, is that the Word of God through prophets guides and directs the people. Today's passage tells of a foreigner who, having received a miraculous healing through the prophet Elisha, gives thanks to the prophet and acclaims the God of Israel. Naaman the Syrian, a military commander whose very presence caused alarm to Israel's king Jehoram because of the rather uncertain peace enjoyed between Israel and Syria, nonetheless is impelled by his illness to seek out Elisha for healing. (Leprosy could refer to a variety of skin diseases—some curable, some not.)

We pick up the narrative after Naaman has bathed and been cured, and learn of his gratitude and his faith. Because of the belief that deities could not be worshipped except on their own soil, and his recognition that Yahweh, though God of all, has a particular relationship to Israel, Namaan asks for two mule-loads of earth to bring home on which to build his own altar for offering sacrifices to the God of Israel. Psalm 98 rejoices in the saving works of God, revealed to the nations.

Although the overall authorship of 2 Timothy is questionable, verses 8-10 in today's reading are probably authentic to St. Paul. In his imprisonment, Paul retains confidence in the unstoppable power of God's word. The resurrection is a stronger reality than any obstacle that might be placed in the way of its proclamation. The second part of the passage is a quote from an early Christian hymn. The dying and rising to which the passage refers is not just experienced symbolically

in baptism, but also in the concrete physical sufferings and dangers demanded by carrying forth the message. The apparent contradiction of the last two lines: "if we deny him, he will deny us" and "if we are unfaithful, he remains faithful" can be resolved by understanding that the faithfulness or unfaithfulness identified here is to God. Jesus always remains faithful to his Father and to his mission. Our lapses do not interfere with his truth. Yet the hard fact that some may, in their freedom, choose to deny Jesus, is attested in the previous line. By choosing to deny Christ, some will bring upon themselves rejection.

Today's account of the ten lepers in unique to Luke's gospel. Leprosy—a blanket term for a variety of skin diseases—caused its sufferers to be separated from society and was associated with moral guilt as well. Here, as is usual in Luke's gospel, the performance of healing is a sign of God's kingdom. Luke frequently cites the openness of foreigners to the person and message of Jesus, as in this story where the sole leper to return and give thanks is a Samaritan. The Samaritan prostrates himself before Jesus—a gesture of recognition of overwhelming greatness and of adoration. His response of gratitude is the response of faith. He is "saved," not merely "cured." Jesus contrasts his reaction to those who did not return. Once again, ironically (as in 10:33), a Samaritan provides the example to follow.

In many respects the story is parallel to the account of Naaman the Syrian. The disease of leprosy is the same. A miraculous healing takes place in both cases. Gratitude is expressed. And the one who is healed is an outsider to the people of Israel. The stories attest to the universal scope of God's will to save and the presence of the gift of faith in unlikely people. They are likewise an eloquent witness to the appropriateness and necessity of giving thanks to God, which may be the subject of today's catechesis.

Catholic Doctrine

Prayer of Thanksgiving

Our Catholic tradition names five basic types of prayer: the prayer of blessing and adoration, the prayer of petition, the prayer of intercession, the prayer of thanksgiving and the prayer of praise. Any particular moment of prayer between an individual or group and God may very well move between these various types. For the sake of understanding, however, Catholic teaching clarifies these different types of prayer. The scriptures for this Sunday (Naaman's offer of a gift to God's prophet, the one leper who returned to give thanks to Jesus) vividly illustrate the prayer of thanksgiving.

All of life and creation is a gift from God. How much more is the gift given to us in Christ by which life and creation is redeemed and set free from sin and its wages. The whole stance of the Church, therefore, is one of thanksgiving for God's saving action in Jesus.

Eucharist, the very word we use to denote the table fellowship and the saving sacrifice of Jesus made present in the breaking of the bread and the sharing of the one cup, is derived from the Greek for "thanksgiving." The character of the Eucharistic banquet is a profound thanksgiving for the Church's experience of the gift of salvation in Christ (CCC 2637).

But the thanksgiving we render to God need not take place only when Eucharist is celebrated. Every moment and every need is potentially a springboard for thanking God (CCC 2638).

While the fullest form of our thanks to God is expressed in the Eucharist, this type of prayer was not unknown to our forebears in faith. Some of the earliest thanksgiving prayers rendered by our ancestors in faith are rendered by a servant of Abraham and by Jethro, the father-in-law of Moses. On finding Rebekah, the servant prays, "Blessed be the Lord, the God of my master Abraham, who has not let his constant kindness toward my master fail. As for myself also, the Lord has led me straight to the house of my master's brother." (Gn 24:27) Jethro prays, "Blessed be the Lord who has rescued his people from the hands of Pharaoh and the Egyptians. Now I know that the Lord is a deity great beyond any other; for he took occasion of their being dealt with insolently to deliver the people from the power of the Egyptians." (Exodus 18:10) In both instances, the formula is fixed, that is, there is a benediction and an "anamnesis" (a "remembering of God's deeds/gifts).

God's relationship to us is characterized over and over again by gift giving. The greatest gift is the life, ministry, suffering, and death of Jesus. There are many threads of continuity between our ancestors in faith and ourselves, but one of the strongest and deepest is our common prayer of thanksgiving for the graciousness of God.

St. Paul urges, "In all circumstances give thanks, for this is the will of God for you in Christ Jesus." And again, he writes, "Persevere in prayer, being watchful in it with thanksgiving . . ." (1 Thessalonians 5:18 and Colossians 4:2)

Catholic Culture

The Preface Dialogue that opens every liturgy of the eucharist begins with the exhortation to lift our hearts to God giving thanks, "Let us give thanks to our Lord our God. It is right to give him thanks and praise." (*Roman Missal*, The Order of Mass, Eucharistic Prayer.)

A poem by e.e. cummings expresses thanks to God:

> *i thank You God for most this amazing*
> *day: for the leaping greenly spirits of trees*
> *and a blue true dream of sky;and for everything*
> *which is natural which is infinite which is yes*
>
> *(i who have died am alive again today,*
> *and this is the sun's birthday;this is the birth*
> *day of life and of love and wings: and of the gay*
> *great happening illimitably earth)*
>
> *how should tasting touching hearing seeing*
> *breathing any-lifted from the no*
> *of all nothing-human merely being*
> *doubt unimaginable You?*
>
> *(now the ears of my ears awake and*
> *now the eyes of my eyes are opened)*

(E.E. Cummings, *Complete Poems 1913-1962,* A Harvest/HBJ Book, New York, 1963, p. 65.)

Notes

Dismissal Catechesis (30 min)

Getting Started

1. Prepare the space ahead of time with a table, a cornucopia that contains seasonal fruits, vegetables and nuts. Include also the parish directory and pictures of family members, a candle and place for the lectionary.

2. Invite the catechumens and candidates to be seated in a circle around the table on which rests the Lectionary, a lighted candle, a cornucopia and a the parish directory and pictures. Pray in these or similar words: *"O God, source of gifts, we give thanks and praise to you for the many blessings you have bestowed on us. Help us to never take you for granted. Open our minds and hearts to hear your message for us today. We ask this in the name of Jesus, our brother who lives and reigns with you in union with the Holy Spirit, one God forever and ever. Amen."*

First Impressions

1. Invite everyone to close their eyes and to take several deep breaths. Lead them through a recollection of the Liturgy of the Word just celebrated. Use the opening song and a few words or phrases from the prayer and each of the readings, including the responsorial psalm and the homily. After a few minutes of quiet, ask them to name words or phrases from the Liturgy that touched them.

2. In pairs, ask them to share on these or similar questions: *Whom does this Liturgy console? Whom does this Liturgy challenge?* After several minutes, elicit responses and comments in the large group. Summarize the discussion.

Making Connections

1. Focus on the table in the center. *What do the items there represent? What would you add to the table? Why? What would you take from the table? Why?*

2. Today's readings speak to us about saying thanks. Speak about the many times each of us has intended to say thank you but just never got around to it, or the times we said that we really want to get over to see so-and-so, but something happens and it's too late. A thank you means a lot to each one of us, whether it's from a child, a teenager, an adult, a member of the family or even a stranger. Discuss why the "thank you" means so much to us. When have you been surprised by a thank you and when have you been disappointed when a thank you never happened? Summarize the importance of saying thank you.

Prayer

Pray together the responsorial psalm.

Extended Catechesis

SESSION FOCUS: *Giving Thanks*

Gathering

A. Sunday:

Gather everyone in a circle and sing "We Gather Together" (Kremser: Translation from German by Theodore Baker, Oregon Catholic Press). Proclaim the gospel: Luke 17:11-19.

B. Weekday:

Welcome everyone. Begin with a Celebration of the Word, such as:

- Song: "We Praise You"
- Sign of the Cross and Greeting
- Reading: 2 Kings 5:14-17
- Quiet
- Alleluia
- Gospel Luke 17:11-19
- Alleluia

The Word (30 min)

1. Have the group in pairs examine their experience of having been taken for granted from two points of view: the one taken for granted and the who has done the taking. *What do our experiences teach us about being thankful and receiving thanks?*

2. Recall that Namaan, who returns to give thanks to Elisha, is instructed that such power to heal comes from the God and that Elisha does not use his spiritual gifts for his own gain. Namaan takes the two mule loads of dirt back to Syria where he builds an altar to give thanks to the God of the Israelites. Ask the group to imagine the response and surprise of the Syrians. Imagine also the response and surprise of the Israelites that a foreigner and an enemy is healed by their God. Have the group in pairs share their responses to the following question: *In what ways do we direct the recognition of good works to God, the giver of all gifts, and in what ways do we lay claim to such recognition as if it were our own power?*

3. Continue your input: Perhaps the words of Paul to Timothy also help us to reflect on our recognition of God's faithfulness. God is not limited by human standards or conditions or boundaries. God does not respond in the way humans sometimes respond. God is always faithful. God is always ready to forgive. God is always inviting us to be faithful but does not control us. In our freedom, we can choose to deny Jesus and in so doing bring rejection upon ourselves. Ask the group to reflect on the times in their life when they questioned God's presence, God's will, God's judgment, God's love.

Catholic Teaching (30 min)

1. Direct the participants to the Participant Book (page 109), or the blackline handout, or use a piece of paper to jot down the times and types of prayer they do. The Catholic tradition lists five basic types of prayer: the prayer of blessing and adoration, the prayer of petition, the prayer of intercession, the prayer of thanksgiving and the prayer of praise. Ask participants to look over the types of prayer they named. *Are all five types listed? Which one is named most? least?*

2. Continue your input: *Today's Gospel speaks directly about the prayer of thanksgiving. There are ten lepers healed and yet only one returned to Jesus to offer thanks. The one who returned is a Samaritan. He prostrates himself before Jesus—a posture of adoration and recognition of overwhelming greatness.* In pairs ask the group to enumerate the ways in which we say thank you today and to whom we give thanks. Summarize their sharing and ask them to think about the reality that in our society so much emphasis is placed upon individual rights and privileges that we forget God has given us everything. We think we deserve it, so why thank someone for what is already right-fully ours? Yet all is a gift from God.

3. Tell the group that the fullest form of our thanks to God is expressed in the Eucharist, a Greek word meaning thanks-giving. The Eucharistic celebration is a profound thanks-giving for the Church's experience of the gift of salvation in Christ. Our thanks need not take place only when Eucharist is celebrated, but every moment and every need is potentially a springboard for thanking God.

Putting Faith Into Practice

Encourage participants to create a place of prayer in their homes—perhaps a favorite chair or favorite room or favorite window. Suggest that they place on a nearby table a Bible, a candle, family album(s) and notebook, and each day take some time to sit quietly in prayer. Some days, they may want to make a list of people or things they want to talk to God about. They might look through the family album and simply thank God for their loved ones and the many wonderful family experiences represented in the pictures. Encourage them to begin and end each day with words of thankfulness and praise to God for the gifts they have been given.

Prayer

Invite everyone to close their eyes. Take a few deep breaths. Invite God into the quiet of your heart. Speak to God about all the things for which you are thankful. Sing "Now Thank We All Our God."

God, we give you thanks for the gift of life for the people who have nurtured our lives and helped us to know of your marvelous love; for all creation, the great and the small; for the gift of freedom which allows us to say yes to the gift of faith; for the gift of reconciliation which allows us to be generous in forgiving one another. God, you are the great gift of love. Thank you.

Twenty-ninth Sunday in Ordinary Time

Understanding this Sunday:

Background for Catechesis

The Word In Liturgy

Exodus 17:8-13
Psalm 121:1-2, 3-4, 5-6, 7-8
2 Timothy 3:14-4:2
Luke 18:1-8

The most fundamental theological point in the story of Exodus 17:8-13 is that the Israelites win the battle not through their own military prowess, but by the powerful intervention of their God. In the context of its proclamation in today's liturgy, however, our attention is drawn even more strongly to the way in which Israel obtains divine help. Moses' persistence in prayer, aided by his assistants, is revealed to be absolutely essential to securing the victory.

The Amalekites were an enemy tribe in southern Palestine whose name suggests descent from the tribe of Esau. They fight several times against Israel—in this instance to resist their approach to the promised land. The staff that Moses raises has been associated with the protection of Yahweh and wonder-working in the Exodus. In this incident at Rephidim, Moses is established as the mediator between the people of Israel and God, a role designated by later Christian typology as an image of Christ—the definitive mediator who intercedes for the human race before God.

Trust in God is the dominant theme of Psalm 121. The mountains to which the psalm refers may either be the mountains near Jerusalem, or the surrounding hills on which pagan sanctuaries were located. If the latter is the case, the answer to the question "From whence shall my help come?" implies a rejection of other gods in favor of Yahweh. The idea of turning to God for help connects the psalm strongly with the Exodus reading.

We saw the importance of Moses' persistence in the Exodus reading. Perseverance is a key element in the reading from 2 Timothy as well. One of the "Pastoral Epistles" this letter purports to be from Paul, but its authorship is somewhat

uncertain. The context of the letter is Paul's impending death, and thus the question of the continuation of the church beyond the life span of the apostles is a pressing one. In general, the letter emphasizes structure as they key to endurance. Today's passage praises the Scriptures (here meaning the Jewish scriptures) as a source of unfailing help and guidance, and is an exhortation to stay with the task of preaching the word, to remain faithful, and to never lose patience.

This week and next Sunday we hear a pair of parables unique to Luke, about prayer; the first is told to his disciples (affirming), the second to some of the religious leaders (condemning). Today's parable sets up a comparison between an unjust judge, and the just God in order to make emphatic the point of God's willingness to hear and respond to human petitions. Widows in the ancient world were severely disadvantaged because they lacked male protection and economic support in societies structured around men. The widow's persistence is her only resource.

The unjust judge finally gives in to her because she wears him down. The expression "she will end by doing me violence" is, literally in Greek, she will "give me a black eye," which suggests, as it does in English, both that she will cause him social embarrassment and that she may well sock him in the face! Rather than criticize the widow for such unseemly potential behavior, Jesus turns a challenge instead upon his listeners. Do they dare to be this insistent in calling upon God, who is a just judge? Do they have any faith? If they did they would persist in their petitions in prayer, and not lose heart. Indeed, the elect (*eklegoi*) "cry out to him night and day"—and God hears them.

Catholic Doctrine

Petition and Intercession in Prayer

Prayer can be characterized as blessing and adoring God, thanking God, praising God, and asking God. The vocabulary of asking for something in the New Testament scriptures is rich in its diversity: we beseech, plead, invoke, entreat, cry out and even struggle in prayer before God. Our Catholic tradition understands this richness in two basic forms of asking God for something: petitionary prayer (asking for oneself) and intercessory prayer (asking for another). We are created beings and know ourselves as such; we are not our own beginning or our own last end. In asking God for something in prayer we know we are going to the Creator because we are sinful, limited and in need of the love and goodness that only God can provide (CCC 2629).

Christian petition is kingdom-centered, that is, ultimately focused by the teaching and the message of Jesus Christ. In petitioning God we ask first for the kingdom to come, as in the Lord's Prayer itself, and secondarily, we ask for all that we need in order to welcome, prepare for and cooperate with its coming. Those who pray in this fashion, therefore, participate in the mission of Christ. Collaborating together in the Spirit, the mission of Jesus is now the object of the prayer of the apostolic community (CCC 2632).

Sharing together in God's saving love, awaiting the fullness of the kingdom, Catholics understand that every need can become the object of petition. The very first need of every individual is to be freed from sin. Asking forgiveness for our sins is our first priority in petitioning God in prayer.

Intercessory prayer is a special sort of petition which approaches God as did Jesus, that is, petitioning God on behalf of others. Thus, whenever one engages in intercessory prayer, one participates in Christ's prayer, for Jesus himself "intercedes for us. . .and intercedes for the saints according to the will of God" (Romans 8:26-27). Jesus Christ is the mediator who intercedes for us before the throne of God.

St. Augustine advises: "So that we might obtain the life of happiness, he who is true life itself taught us to pray, not in many words as though speaking longer could gain us a hearing. After all, we pray to one who, as the Lord himself tells us, knows what we need before we ask for it. Why he should ask us to pray, when he knows what we need . . .may perplex us if we do not realize that our Lord and God does not want to know what we want (for he cannot fail to know it) but wants us rather to exercise our desire through our prayers, so that we may be able to receive what [God] is preparing to give us. . . .The deeper our faith, the stronger our hope, the greater our desire, the larger will be our capacity to receive that gift, which is very great indeed." (St. Augustine, from a letter to Proba, *Epistulae*, 130, 8, 15. 17-19: CSEL 44, 56-7. 59-60 found in Liturgy of the Hours, v. IV, Twenty-Ninth Sunday in Ordinary Time, Office of Readings, p. 408).

Catholic Culture

Catholics believe that the ultimate end of all our praying is God. That prayer is offered through Christ, the one mediator. To emphasize that Christ alone is the mediator between God and humans, all our prayers at liturgy are made "through Christ our Lord."

But because of our understanding of the communion of saints, we have from the earliest of times also focused prayer through Mary and the saints. Mary is considered the perfect prayer and Mediatrix. And the saints, by their example, encourage us and give us hope in our prayer.

A popular form of prayer is the novena (Latin for "nine") which can be made publicly or privately and is a series of nine successive times in prayer, whether that is nine continuous days, nine specific weekdays (for example, nine Mondays) or nine specific days of the month (for example, nine first Fridays). Public novenas are specific prayers focused in a particular saint, in Mary or an image (for example, the Sacred Heart of Jesus), recited in common and sometimes followed by Benediction. Novenas are frequently prayed because of special intentions, where one is asking for something either for oneself or another. (*Encyclopedia of Catholicism*, McBrien, p. 922)

The General Instruction of the Roman Missal stipulates the categories for the General Intercessions (or prayer of the faithful) as follows: 1) for the needs of the Church, 2) for public authorities and the salvation of the world, 3) for those oppressed by any need, and 4) for the local community. (GIRM, n 45)

Notes

Dismissal Catechesis (30 min)

Getting Started

1. Prepare the space with a lighted candle and a place for the lectionary on the center table. Gather in a circle.

2. Invite participants to sit in silence for a moment and become aware of the prayer in their hearts. After a moment of quiet, invite them to hold their arms up in prayer, like Moses, and pray silently. Then pray: *God, we your people whom you gather bring our prayer to you this morning. Hear and respond to what we ask of you. We pray in love and in trust. Amen.*

First Impressions

1. Ask participants to share their experiences through this question: *What feelings were evoked in you as you prayed with outstretched arms?*

2. Recall the images from scripture of the Israelites winning as long as Moses kept his hands raised in prayer, of Paul's reminder to be faithful to what we have learned and believed, and of Jesus parable about the judge worn out by the widow's persistence. Ask participants to share with another person: *What did you hear God saying to you personally in today's liturgy?* Have them share their responses in the large group. Call on each pair to encourage sharing. Briefly summarize the variety of responses.

Making Connections

1. Invite the participants to share in the large group their response to the following question: *When you pray do you most often pray a prayer of petition and intercession, or do you spend more time sharing your thoughts and feelings with God?* Then ask: *Is this a change from a former way of praying? In what ways has your prayer changed?* Facilitate and encourage conversation.

2. Ask the participants to respond to this question: *How do you feel about asking for things from God in prayer?* Encourage them to give some examples of their experiences of intercessory prayer.

3. Ask the participants to respond to this question in the large group: *What do you want to remember from today's liturgy and sharing?* Highlight from their responses the importance of intercessory prayer.

Prayer

State: *For our prayer today I invite you to sit with open hands in front of you. Become aware of one thing you want to pray for, whether a quality such as patience, a health concern for someone, or a specific intention. We will go around the circle and name our prayer. After each naming, we will all respond, Lord, hear our prayer. Then begin the prayer. Conclude with: We ask all of this in the name of Jesus. Amen.*

Extended Catechesis

SESSION FOCUS: *Petition and Intercession*

Gathering

A. Sunday:

1. Welcome sponsors and other participants. Ask participants to sit in pairs.

2. Ask a catechumen or candidate to briefly summarize the dismissal sharing.

3. Invite all to become aware of their prayer, and then to pray this prayer in silence.

4. Sing : O God hear us (while raising arms), hear our prayer(while lowering arms). Sing this prayer with gesture three times.

5. Proclaim the Gospel, Luke 18:1-8

B. Weekday:

1. Welcome everyone.

2. Ask participants to share in the circle: Since Sunday, name some times you have asked God for something in prayer.

3. Lead a celebration of the Word.

   - Hymn: Make Me a Channel of your Peace
   - Sign of the Cross, Greeting
   - First Reading: Exodus 17:8-13
   - Psalm 121 (or one used at the Sunday liturgy)
   - Alleluia
   - Gospel: Luke 18:1-8
   - Silence

Invite participants to notice what they want to ask God for at this time in their lives, and pray for this in silence. Conclude by singing: "O God hear us" (while raising arms), "hear our prayer" (while lowering arms). Sing this three times with gesture.

The Word (30 min)

1. Make these statements about todays scriptures:

   - *The Exodus reading has a powerful image of God protecting the Israelites as long as Moses prayed.*
   - *The prayer posture of arms extended upward is one of dependence and petition.*
   - *The widow continually going to the judge and stating what she wanted.*

Ask participants to reflect on this question: *Describe some experiences you've had of asking for something more than once with a favorable result.* Participants may use the Participant Book (page 110) or the blackline handout. Then ask them to share their reflection in pairs. When they have finished invite some large group summaries.

2. Make the following points:

- Luke portrays a widow as the one who is asking for her rights.
- In Jewish culture the widow was powerless.
- The poor, referred to as the "anawim," included the oppressed, widows, and orphans, who were thought to have God's special protection.
- Scripture scholars believe this unjust judge was tired of the widow and literally afraid of a black eye.

Ask participants to discuss in pairs: *What do you think Luke is trying to say to you in using these two figures of an unjust judge and a poor widow?* When they are finished, invite some large group response. Highlight that we are as powerless as the widow when we ask God for something.

3. State the following points:

- At the beginning of this passage Jesus exhorts us to pray always.
- Jesus states God will grant justice to them, and quickly.

Proclaim the Gospel again. Ask participants to reflect on this question: *What happens in your relationship with God when you ask God for things?* Participants may use the Participant Book (page 110) or the blackline handout for this reflection. Then give some responses in the large group. If not stated, bring out these points:

- *Asking for things from God moves one into relationship, requires an openness, and out of this relationship God can and does respond.*

Allow time for conversation.

Catholic Teaching (30 min)

1. Ask participants to engage in this exercise: Stand, as Moses did, with arms outstretched and silently ask God for something you need. Have them sit down and ask: *What feeling does this posture evoke in you?* Elicit from them and mention the sense of openness, pleading, receptivity, and reliance on God.

2. Present the following teaching or use your own words:

Petition is one of the major forms of Christian prayer, which include thanksgiving, adoration, and praise. Petitioning God is part of the ongoing life of a Christian. St. Ignatius of Loyola, known for his Spiritual Exercises, believed that God actually places desires of the heart in people as a way of drawing them closer to God. Ignatius encouraged people to pray the desires of their heart. This belief counterbalances the feeling that some people have that they are bothersome to God when continually asking for something.

The posture of our body during prayer helps us experience our prayer. Recall your experience of praying with arms outstretched.

At times in intercessory prayer we receive what we ask for, and at other times, we do not. God forms people in the process of intercessory prayer. At times God seems present, and at times absent. Spiritual writers believe the experience of God's absence is an important time when God is waiting for a deeper opening in the person or inviting the person to a new level of faith or relationship. Especially in these dry or dark periods staying faithful in prayer is important.

As members of a community, we are asked to pray for the needs of other. At each Mass intercessions are prayed for the world, the global church, as well as needs of people who are present. Many parishes have prayer chains for people in special need. The community will often gather in prayer to support people in times of need.

3. Ask participants to discuss: *What are your beliefs about the power of prayer?*

OR . . .

Participants may use the reflective exercise about prayer in the Participant Book (page 110) or on the blackline handout..

OR . . .

Hold an evening of prayer to pray for special needs.

Putting Faith Into Practice

Ask participants to reflect on this question: *What is God inviting you to bring to prayer that you are willing to spend some time with this week?* Participants may want to write this action in the Participant Book (page 111) or on the blackline handout. Then ask the participants to share this commitment in pairs.

Prayer

1. Have each pair of participants pray together for what they have stated to one another.

2. Celebrate a minor exorcism E as stated in the ritual text (RCIA #94), making adaptations when candidates are present.

Thirtieth Sunday in Ordinary Time

Understanding this Sunday:

Background for Catechesis

The Word In Liturgy

Sirach 35:12-14, 16-18
Psalm 34:2-3, 17-18, 19, 23
2 Timothy 4:6-8, 16-18
Luke 18:9-14

The book of Sirach, also called Ecclesiasticus, was written in about 180 B.C. by Jesus ben Sira, a man of great love for wisdom and learning, who was well-traveled and in later life conducted a school in Jerusalem. The book explains Judaism, and enjoyed popular acceptance, but was never received into the Jewish canon, which was fixed by Pharisaic Jews—at least in part because of its affinities with the writings of the Sadduccees. Today's passage concerning prayer immediately follows a reminder that God cannot be bribed. It stresses the justice of God in hearing and answering sincere prayer, but also emphasizes the solicitude of God for the oppressed: the weak and powerless who have no one to take their part. In a male-dominated society such as Israel, widows and orphans were particularly vulnerable, and God is keenly responsive to them. God is judge and advocate for the lowly who cry out for help.

Psalm 34 further emphasizes God's openness to the prayers of the poor. Here the poor include all those who are "lowly," the just who "cry out," the "brokenhearted," and those "crushed in spirit." Paul, writing at the end of his Roman imprisonment is by his own account one such as the psalm assures in announcing: "When the just cry out, the Lord hears them, and from all their distress he rescues them." Totally abandoned by human help when his case came to court, Paul rejoices nevertheless that "The Lord stood by my side and gave me strength . . ."

Paul senses his coming martyrdom and expects his own blood to be shed (a libation is a liquid poured on the ground at a

sacrifice). Yet he is not despairing. Taking his metaphors from athletic events, he presents his life as a race that he has run, and his eternal reward from God as a "merited crown" (the wreath of victory awarded at contests) that will surely await him.

Today's gospel continues the theme of prayer with the story of the self-righteous Pharisee and, in contrast, the tax collector who addresses God with deep humility. The Pharisee prays "to himself" (a nuance present in the Greek original but not in our English translation)—possibly suggesting that his proud and boastful prayer is a self-motivated discourse not even truly directed to God at all! His virtuous behaviors, which he catalogues in the prayer, go well beyond Jewish law at the time concerning fasting and charitable giving, it is true. Yet they are combined with a kind of petty, mean-spiritedness that even while addressing God seeks self-aggrandizement by denigrating others.

In contrast, the tax collector is aware of his sinfulness and speaks directly to God from his grieving heart. He is not looking over his shoulder comparing himself to his neighbors, but is completely absorbed in pleading with God. He exemplifies a real (not theatrical) humility. Like the oppressed of the first reading and the poor of the psalm, his sincere prayer is heard and he "went home . . . justified"— that is, having won his suit, gotten what he was seeking: God's mercy. Humility before God in prayer, a theme seen in all of this Sunday's readings, may be the subject of today's catechesis.

Catholic Doctrine

Humility before God in Prayer

The mystery of faith is nurtured in a vibrant personal relationship with the living and true God. This relationship is called prayer. What is the fundamental stance of the believer who prays? St. Therese of Lisieux writes, "For me, prayer is a surge of the heart; it is a simple look turned toward heaven, it is a cry of recognition and of love, embracing both trial and joy." (*St. Therese, Manuscrits autobiographiques*, C 25r)

Prayer raises our mind and heart to God, but not as a self-centered enterprise. In other words, believers pray not out of pride or willfulness but from the depths of a contrite and humble heart. Humility (from the Latin humus, or "earth") is the foundation of and basic stance of prayer (CCC 2559). We are fashioned from the clay of earth, gifted, yet limited, mortal and in need of God.

In the gospel of John, Jesus exclaims to the Samaritan woman, "If you knew the gift of God!" (Jn 4:10) The amazing nature of authentic prayer is that God offers us everything we need in prayer. Indeed, the Lord seeks us out in prayer, thirsts for us. Prayer becomes the encounter of God's thirst with ours. The divine love of the Most High thirsts, that we may thirst, in turn, for God (CCC 2560). Humility enables one to approach the life-giving waters that God offers us in the sacrifice of Jesus who says to us, "I thirst." (Jn 19:28)

All forms of prayer are founded in humility before the awesome love of God. But it is in meditation and contemplation where the rich strains of our Catholic tradition affirms the absolute necessity of humility.

In meditation, one's attentiveness is focused through scripture texts and images, icons, liturgical texts and prayers, writings of the spiritual fathers, other spiritual works and the great "books" of creation and of history. Focusing one's meditation through these devices, one seeks to open up the book of life and to the extent that one is humble and faithful, discovers the movement and call of God as the heart is stirred (CCC 2706).

In contemplative prayer, one seeks God as one's lover. It is a silent, wordless communion that can only be received (not achieved). It is a gift given by God to the one who prays knowing that everything is provided to us by divine love. This type of praying requires a total and humble surrender to the loving will of God the Father in ever deepening union through the Spirit with the beloved Son, Jesus (CCC 2712).

False humility, that is, putting on a show of humility to please people or manipulate God, should not be confused with genuine humility before God. Likewise, the denial or suppression of true gifts, blessings and God-given goodness is far from the meaning of Christian humility.

Catholic Culture

The church of the Madonna dell'Orto in Trastevere, Rome, was founded in 1492 by the corporation of market gardeners. Built by Bernini, careful attention to light was exercised which only increases the power of the marble sculpture of the blessed Lodovica Albertoni. She is depicted laying supine, in mystical prayer, her flowing robes highlighted by the play of light and her hands set about her heart, her mouth open slightly as if in rapture. The statue clearly characterizes this humble mystic rapt in prayer, overcome by divine love.

The traditional postures for prayer are standing and kneeling. The former derives from our forebears in faith, the Jews who stood with hands outstretched as a sign of reverence and humility—their open hands contained nothing and were to be filled by God. The latter derives from the medieval court as a sign of respect and humility where one's hands were folded and placed within one's liege to whom faithfulness was pledged.

Another prayer posture is prostration (lying face down upon the floor). At the start of the Good Friday liturgy, the priest and ministers process in and prostrate themselves in silent prayer. This extremely humble physical posture, most likely originating in the oriental potentate's court, is stipulated in Catholic liturgy on Good Friday as the community recalls the passion of Christ and in a most formal way prays, making intercessions for the needs of the world and the Church.

In the pre-Vatican II liturgy, the ritual action of beating one's breast signified an acknowledgment of sinfulness and humility before God.

Caravaggio's painting, the Madonna of the Pilgrims also known as the Madonna of Loreto, which he painted for three years starting in 1603, portrays the Virgin as a Roman patrician holding the naked Christ. The beauty of Mary is heightened by "the tenderness of her silent dialogue with her humble admirers." The contrast between Mary and the poverty of the two praying peasants is striking. (*Rome*, Knopf Guides, Alfred A. Knopf, Inc., New York, 1994, p. 285)

On Ash Wednesday, as people come forward to be signed with the cross in ashes, the words are spoken, "Remember. . .you are dust and to dust you shall return." (RM, Ash Wednesday, Blessing and Giving of Ashes)

Notes

Dismissal Catechesis (30 min)

Getting Started

1. Place an arrangement of autumn leaves and flowers in the center of the circle, along with a lighted candle.

2. Invite the candidates and catechumens to gather in the circle of chairs.

3. Begin the session by asking all to stand for prayer. You may choose to begin the prayer time with a verse or two of the Gathering Hymn from the liturgy. Then proceed to pray in these or similar words:

   God of the autumn winds and colorful leaves, blow through us, now. May the Spirit, the wind that blows where it will, stir up our hearts and minds, opening them to your Word. May the Spirit, that is present in the colorful leaves, create in our imaginations, new insights into this living Word. May this same Spirit, felt in the brisk, cool air, touch our lives with compassion for the poor. Hear our prayer this day as we seek to know you and love you. Amen.

First Impressions

1. These past weeks have been focused on prayer. Based upon the past two sessions, invite the participants to recall and summarize their understanding of prayer.

2. After taking a few responses from the large group, ask them to move into smaller groups to share their ideas about today's readings. These questions will help stimulate the sharing time. *What new insights about prayer can you name from the scriptures at today's liturgy? Which characters in these passages can you identify with and why? What about these readings impressed you?*

3. In the large group, elicit some of the responses to these questions.

Making Connections

1. Explain the first reading from Sirach in these or similar words:

   The author, Jesus ben Sira, offers several insights into prayer in this passage. We are assured that God is fair and just in answering sincere prayer. The writer further explains that God has special concern for the poor, weak and lowly who cry out for help. The rich person's extravagant sacrifice does not merit more of God's attention, nor does the meager sacrifice of the poor merit less from God. Remember the poor widow who gave of what little she had? God, instead, looks at our inner disposition.

2. Gather the group into pairs. Invite them to share on these questions: *What inner attitudes make for sincere prayer? What can the poor teach us about our own prayer?*

3. Listen as the pairs share their responses with the whole group. Summarize their discussion and invite them to note one thing in the Participant Book (page 113) or on the blackline handout that they wish to remember from this session.

Prayer

Close this session with Psalm 34. As you pray 2 or 3 verses at a time, invite the group to respond: "I will bless the Lord at all times. God's praise shall be always in my mouth."

Extended Catechesis

SESSION FOCUS: *Humility before God in prayer*

Gathering

A. Sunday:

1. Offer those who are joining the group a sincere welcome. Invite them to join the circle. You may choose to play some background music as they enter.

2. Begin the prayer with the song, "The Lord Hears the Cry of the Poor." Proclaim the gospel. Pray the Collect from today's liturgy and celebrate the Blessing found in RCIA # 96, C or E (adapted if there are baptized candidates in the group).

B. Weekday:

1. Prepare a short liturgy of the Word, using a format similar to that offered below.

   - Opening Song: "The Cry of the Poor" (Foley)
   - First Reading: Sirach 35:12-14, 16-18
   - Silence
   - Second Reading: 2 Timothy 4:6-8, 16-18
   - Silence
   - Gospel: Luke 18:9-14 (Invite two members of the team to dramatize this passage)
   - Silence

The Word (30 min)

1. Offer a little background for the gospel reading.

   The Pharisee was a respected member of Jewish society. He even went beyond the prescriptions of the religious law. On the other hand, the tax collector was despised in the Jewish culture. Known for extorting money, he was shunned by his contemporaries. Two opposite extremes are presented by Luke to indicate Jesus' challenge to the society in which he lived. We, too, are challenged to uncover our deepest sentiments and beliefs about prayer, God and ourselves.

2. Invite the participants to answer the following questions in the large group: *Who was the Pharisee really praying to? What does this passage point out about comparing ourselves to others? What does the tax collector teach about sincerity in prayer?*

3. Ask the group to take time to reflect on the worksheet provided in the Participant Book (page 112) or on the blackline handout. Encourage the candidates and catechumens to share their responses with their sponsors and godparents during the coming week.

Catholic Teaching (30 min)

1. Using this meditation, invite the participants to center themselves and pray. To help them center, ask them to sit comfortably, begin to relax and become aware of their breathing and heart beat. As you move through this meditation, pause when it seems appropriate—slowly guide the prayer—feel free to improvise.

Close your eyes and move deep within yourself. God dwells within each person. God is at the center of your being. Move into that center where God dwells.

Imagine with me that you are on a hillside. It is the fall of the year. The breezes are tugging at your clothes and hair. The scent of the air is crisp. As you begin to walk up the hill, you notice a person sitting on a nearby rock. Moving closer, you are amazed to see that it is the Lord. Jesus beckons to you and invites you to sit down on a warm, smooth rock next to him.

You feel comfortable and full of peace. The warmth of the rock, the gentle presence of the Master surrounds you. Jesus gazes at you and asks, Why are you troubled?" You begin to tell him of your discoveries about your deep-seated attitudes. Your prejudices, your self-righteousness—all the list of weaknesses.

He looks at you tenderly. He accepts you, for who you are, with all your weaknesses, your faults, your misguided mindsets.

You find yourself closing your eyes. Comforted, content, you begin to pray with all your heart. You pray with sincerity and humility, praising God for all his goodness to you and asking God's mercy. As you open your eyes, you find you are alone on the hillside. But the words, "The Lord hears the cry of the poor," echo in your heart as you leave the hillside and return to this room.

2. Explain that this type of meditation, imaginatively using scripture, symbols and icons, is part of the Catholic tradition called "prayer of meditation." Encourage them to try this prayer form on their own.

3. In groups of three or four, invite the participants to share their prayer experience. *What did you feel as you prayed this meditation? What did you learn about your relationship to God in prayer? Having had this experience, how would you describe prayer before God that is characterized by humility?*

Putting Faith Into Practice

1. Explain the concept that our prayer takes on this quality of humility through our experiences with the poor and the marginalized. This might be a good example for today:

A contemporary Canadian Catholic, Jean Vanier has lived the prayer of humility through his profound experiences with persons with mental retardation and other disabilities. Vanier, a layman, chose to live with those who suffer rejection because of their disabilities, and established l'Arche communities, and Faith and Light communities worldwide. For Jean Vanier, prayer becomes authentic when we listen to and really see the poor and the outcasts of our society. By his very life he challenges all Christians to open our hearts to God in adoration and to open our hands to the poor in service.

2. Invite members of the group to share other examples of people who are humble in their prayer through their relationship with the poor and outcast.

Prayer

Pray this reflection taken from, "Be Not Afraid" by Jean Vanier (Paulist Press), pages 25 and 26.

Jesus is the One who walked between the two worlds
calling the poor to life
making the rich understand
that they are on the road
to death
for where else can he be heading
this man who shuts himself in things
and riches and ambition and power?

Jesus is the One who placed Himself between
Lazarus and the rich man
the Levite and the poor man
beaten by brigands lying half dead
not far from Jericho

Jesus placed Himself between
The poor man on his knees at the back of the temple
who wept and dared not even look before him
and the Pharisee up front who said to God,
"Look at me
You must be glad to think
You created someone
as beautiful as me."

Jesus is the One who wants to unite
these two worlds.
We must look at Him, and follow Him
between these two worlds.
yearning to love
hidden in the bosom of the Father
thirsting
thirsting to give life
He calls me to walk
between these two worlds
with Him, in Him
to give life
to give my life.

Thirty-first Sunday in Ordinary Time

Understanding this Sunday:
Background for Catechesis

The Word In Liturgy

Wisdom 11:22–12:2
Psalm 145:1-2, 8-9, 10-11, 13-14
2 Thessalonians 1:11-2:2
Luke 19:1-10

The book of Wisdom, attributed to Solomon, was in fact composed some time in the first half of the first century before Christ by an anonymous Jewish author in Alexandria, Egypt. It is thus the last of the Old Testament scriptures to be written. The book is an extended meditation and reflection on the distilled meaning of all the Old Testament writings that precede it. Today's passage is a digression in a section devoted to the Exodus, and it reflects on the ways of the all-powerful and all-merciful God, who out of love holds in being everything in creation. It is followed by Psalm 145, a hymn of praise to God. In today's liturgy, this all-inclusive love of God becomes the background for Jesus' announcement in the gospel that "The Son of Man has come to search out and save what was lost."

Today's passage from Paul's second letter to the Christian community at Thessalonica enjoins them to persevere in good works and in faith. Having received a high calling and a "gracious gift" from God, having in themselves honest intentions, and having embarked on "works of faith," members of the community now are challenged to realize their potential. They do not do this on their own, but, rather, Paul's prayer is that God will make them worthy, and through them give glory to Jesus. Although the second coming of Christ was believed to be near at the time of the writing of the first letter to the Thessalonians, by the second letter this expectation was receding. Here, Paul voices a pastoral concern that false rumors of Christ's immanent return are spreading agitation and fear. He urges the community to remain calm and resist such disturbances.

The story of Zaccheus, unique to Luke's gospel, is one of a pair of stories that respond to the question of Jesus' disciples in 18:26 "then who can be saved?" In the eyes of the people, Zaccheus is assumed to be doubly despicable: he is a chief tax-collector, and he is rich. When Jesus agrees to go to his home, not only the religious leaders but the whole crowd murmurs objections. Tax collectors were despised as collaborators with the Roman ruling elite, and suspected of extorting money from the people as a means of enriching themselves.

Zaccheus, however, whose name in Hebrew means "the pure or innocent one" stands his ground and states (in the present tense) that he shares his possessions with the poor, and that if he has defrauded anyone, he pays them back fourfold — the harsher penalty assigned by Jewish law. Often interpreted as a conversion story, in which Zaccheus *decides* as a result of his meeting with Jesus to repent of his sins and to begin to practice generosity, this passage upon careful reading is revealed to be something quite different. Zaccheus is an example of hidden goodness revealed by the encounter with Jesus and gathered up into the reign of God. Appearances deceive. But truth emerges in the encounter with Jesus. The little man climbs a tree in order to see Jesus. But more important is the fact that Jesus sees him.

The story of Zaccheus in Luke provides the reverse of the story of the rich young man in 18:18-23. Both Zaccheus and the young man are rich and powerful, but the rich young man has the appearance of uprightness in the community, whereas Zaccheus is rejected by the community as a sinner. The rich young man is unable to part with his possessions and goes away sad. Zaccheus however shares his wealth (always in Luke the use possessions reveal the disposition of the heart), and he welcomes Jesus "with great joy." He therefore is revealed to be justified before God—a true son of Abraham.

Both having faith and displaying the works of righteousness, he welcomes the Messiah with joy.

Catholic Doctrine

Justification

Our Catholic understanding is that justification is God's saving action in Jesus by the Holy Spirit which frees us from sin and renews us. Justification, in short, opens the way to salvation by good works through the community of the faithful, the church. Those who are justified are cleansed from sin and put in a right relationship with God. For us believers this happens in the gift of baptism (CCC 1987).

The Protestant reformers emphasized the universality of sin, the absolute gratuity of justification and insisted that human freedom was destroyed by original sin. The Council of Trent rejected this view. Instead, the Church proclaimed that it is possible to cooperate with God's grace and to be renewed inwardly. It is possible to grow in holiness as we practice the virtues of hope and love moving toward eternal life and increasing grace within ourselves by our good works. Unfortunately, the way in which the Catholic Church and the Reformation theologians initially spoke about justification only furthered the split in Christianity. Today, there is much closer agreement on the basic themes of justification: God justifies by grace alone, through the saving action of Jesus Christ, and individuals appropriate that justification by their faith-in-action.

Thus, in today's gospel passage, Zaccheus stands as an image of one who is justified, one who cooperates with God's grace in life and moves toward greater holiness and inward renewal by his good works. Jesus recognizes that Zaccheus is on the path of righteousness ("Today, salvation has come to this house, for this is what it means to be a son of Abraham.") Justification, from our Catholic viewpoint, detaches us from sin, which contradicts divine love and purifies us, making us members of the household of God. It reconciles us with heaven, heals us, and frees us from our slavery to sin (CCC 1990). In this way, justification puts us right with God; it is an acceptance of divine righteousness within us. Justification opens for us the avenue of faith, hope and love (CCC 1991).

We do not merit justification on our own. It is merited for us by the passion of Christ who offers himself on the cross, holy and pleasing to his heavenly Father. His blood becomes the atonement for the sins of all. Baptism bathes us in the blood of Christ and confers upon us justification and membership in the household of the faithful. In those saving waters, we know that original sin is removed, personal sins are forgiven and we are made totally new creatures, although the effects of sin in the world, such as sickness, death and proneness to further sin remain.

All of this is implied in the Catholic teaching of justification. We uphold the absolute sovereignty of God who alone saves us and justifies us. The reformers also spoke of inner change and outward works of love toward one's neighbor. The area in which we differ today is in our focus on God's saving activity through the Church and the sacraments as celebrated and lived.

Catholic Culture

Julian of Norwich (1342-1416), who devoted herself to strict solitude and penitential works, received a series of sixteen mystical visions in 1373. Her writings today have attracted new interest. She describes one of her visions in terms similar to today's reading from Wisdom. "And in this he showed me something small, no bigger than a hazelnut, lying in the palm of my hand, as it seemed to me, and it was as round as a ball. I looked at it with the eye of my understanding and thought: what can this be? I was amazed that it could last, for I thought that because of its littleness it would suddenly fallen into nothing. And I was answered in my under-standing: It lasts and always will because God loves it; and thus everything has being through the love of God." (*Julian of Norwich: Showings*, ed. Edmund Colledge, OSA and James Walsh, SJ, Paulist Press, New York, 1978, p. 183)

Catholic culture has tended to emphasize the unworthiness of humans to receive God's favor—a sentiment expressed in popular devotion through prayers and hymns such as "Lord, I am Not Worthy" (a favorite of the generation before Vatican II). At the same time, Catholics have always affirmed that real holiness is possible for human beings, and can be sought through prayer, good works and the sacraments.

Notes

Dismissal Catechesis (30 min)

Getting Started

Invite the group to form a circle. Light a candle and place the lectionary in a prominent place. After a moment of silence invite the group to reflect on the Sunday reading of Zaccheus.

First Impressions

Guide the group through a brief imagination experience using the following or similar words:

Imagine yourself standing at a corner near your home with a lot of other people, as in a parade. The word is out that Jesus is coming by. You see him coming in the distance and you are determined to see him. Go to a place where you can call out to him and he will notice you.

He passes near you; you call out and he turns and looks you straight in the eye, walks toward you, and then says: "Tonight I will have dinner in your home!" Discuss this guided imagery using the following questions: How do you feel about Jesus coming to dinner at your home? What's the first thing you think about? Allow participants to share any or their responses with the large group.

Making Connections

1. Using the responses shared in the large group discussion from First Impressions, point out ways that their experiences contain elements of the story of Zaccheus. Note to the group that Zaccheus did not hesitate and that when he was questioned he stood his ground. Be sure to also bring out that although Zaccheus positioned himself to see Jesus, the response by Jesus was almost as though he had been looking for Zaccheus.

2. Jesus looks for us, seeks us out. He wants to be invited into our homes. Ask the participants to reflect on the following question in small groups: *What would Jesus see if he was asked to enter into our homes, that is, our hearts and minds? Is there anything you would want to rearrange, fix up, hide, showcase? How would Jesus respond to the truth about your "home?"*

Prayer

1. Invite the group into silence and then have them privately respond in a journal or in quiet prayer to the following question:

Jesus waits to be invited into our "homes." Are you ready to receive him? Is there a risk in welcoming him into our lives?

2. Take a moment, and if you want, invite Jesus into your life.

3. Conclude prayer by singing together, "Take, Lord, Receive" (Foley, NALR, 1975).

Extended Catechesis

SESSION FOCUS: *Justification*

Gathering

A. Sunday:

Invite the group to gather and welcome any new people. Invite them to silence and then either sing or say the following song:

"Take, Lord, Receive" (Foley, NALR, 1975) Jesuit prayer of surrender.

Invite each person to share one word or phrase from the gospel or homily.

B. Weekday:

If you gather during the week for extended catechesis, begin with a Celebration of the Word such as the one below.

- Gathering Hymn
- Greeting and Gathering Prayer
- Read Wisdom 11:22-12:2
- Sing the Responsorial Psalm
- Read 2 Thessalonians 1:11-2:2
- Sing the Gospel Acclamation
- Read Luke 19:1-10
- Close with a prayer from the Preface for the Sundays in Ordinary Time

The Word (30 min)

1. In these or similar words point out to the group that the scriptures speak of God's love offered to all people. As with Zaccheus we are invited to accept the offer of God's love. In small groups or pairs, invite the group to reflect on the following: *Where and how is God offering love in their lives right now? Name the people, places, and events where the offer of love is being extended to you. How are you responding?* Ask for a few responses after the small group sharing.

2. Referring to the Word in Liturgy section give a commentary regarding the readings. Be sure to point out in these or similar words: *The focus of the Old Testament and the gospel readings is that God's offer of love is for all people. This love, God's grace, is a gift and not something we can earn. As with Zaccheus, who welcomed Jesus into his home, the offer of love calls for a response from us.* Ask the group to respond to the following question in small groups and then ask for large group feedback. *As we listen to the readings and to the small group sharing what do these readings have to say to us as church, as the people of God?*

Catholic Teaching (30 min)

1. Referring to the gospel reading about Zaccheus develop an understanding of justification. As the Catholic Doctrine section suggests, point out that Zaccheus stands as an image of one who is "justified" by cooperating with God's grace in life. This cooperation with God's grace moves one toward greater holiness and greater renewal through good works. Explore with the group what it means to cooperate with God's grace by asking them to discuss this in small groups. After the small group discussion surface some of the responses in the larger group.

2. Define and develop the Church's teaching on justification using the Catholic Doctrine section. Focus on God's saving love for us that sets us free from sin and renews us, on the fact that we do not have to merit this love, and on baptism which cleanses us from sin. Point out that this love which saves us and justifies us calls for a response in faith to God.

3. Ask the participants to move into small groups to reflect on the following questions: *What questions does this teaching on justification raise for you about your relationship with God? How does it affirm you and challenge you?* Afterward, invite any comments or responses to be shared with the large group.

Putting Faith Into Practice

Point out to the group that our response in faith to God's great love, the development of our relationship with God, and our desire for God to accomplish within us what is good requires on our part a commitment, surrender, and deeper trust in God. Ask the group to reflect quietly, to journal, and/or to share with other person the following question: *Are there any areas of your life where it is difficult to believe that God truly loves you? What do you need to be able to believe that you are loved, that God's grace is moving in your life, and that you are forgiven your sins?*

Prayer

The following adapted Rite of Blessing is suggested as a closing prayer. Invite the participants of the group to lay hands on each other.

Lord, form these people by the mysteries of our faith. Grant that they may come to know and love you and always heed your will with receptive minds and generous hearts. Help them to turn to you in all things, to desire only your will in their lives. We ask this through Christ our Lord. Amen.

Closing song: "Take, Lord, Receive"

Thirty-second Sunday in Ordinary Time

Understanding this Sunday:
Background for Catechesis

The Word In Liturgy

2 Maccabees 7:1-2, 9-14
Psalm 17:1, 5-6, 8, 15
2 Thessalonians 2:16-3:5
Luke 20:27-38 [or 20:27, 34-38]

The heroism of a family of seven brothers and their mother in the face of death is the subject of today's Old Testament reading. Under the Selucid dynasty, Palestinian Jews were being pressured to give up the mandates of their religion in favor of Hellenistic practices. This persecution ultimately led to the successful revolt of Judas Maccabeus in 167 B.C. that resulted in a treaty allowing Jews to follow their law. Resistance to the Hellenizing policies of the Selucids could cost pious Jews their lives, yet some did resist, as today's passage illustrates. These Jews were known as the Hasidim or "pious ones"—the Pharisees spoken of in the New Testament were possibly their successors. What is most significant for today's liturgy is the testimony of the last brother who professes faith in a resurrection from the dead. Belief in a personal resurrection or an afterlife did not appear in Judaism until about 200 B.C., and so, at this time, was a relatively novel idea. As it is presented here, the wicked will perish, and only the just will be raised.

The psalm that follows is the lament of one who is unjustly accused. The excerpts sung in today's liturgy both celebrate steadfastness in being faithful to the ways of God (such as the first reading illustrated), and express confidence in a future meeting with God. Probably the individual in the psalm expects to "wake" in God's presence because he has spent the night in the temple awaiting an answer to his prayer for justice, but in the context of today's liturgy we are plainly intended to read this as an allusion to the resurrection.

The second reading, from one of the earliest of the New Testament letters, is directed to the Christian community at Thessalonica and is warm and encouraging in tone. It consists of three short prayers: the first and third for the Thessalonian Christians, and the second for the author and

all those who are working to spread the good news. As is frequently the case in the lectionary, the second reading has few themes in common with the first and third, which this Sunday are steeped in conflict and controversy. Thus it appears in the liturgy as a peaceful, almost idyllic interlude of trusting prayer for one another in the first-generation Christian community, its only connection to the other readings being possibly the reference to the "eternal consolation and hope" given by the Father to those who follow Christ.

Today's gospel is one of a series of episodes in which spies of the enemies of Jesus are sent to trip him up—that is, to ask him questions seeking to discredit him with the people. In this passage, some Sadducees question Jesus about the resurrection. The Sadducees were a conservative group that accepted only the Torah, and no subsequent writings (such as the prophetic literature), and believed neither in angels nor in the resurrection of the dead. The question they pose to Jesus is a *reductio ad absurdam* of the question of marriage status in the next life. Mosaic law required a deceased man's brother to marry his widow in order to beget a child who would carry on his family line. The Sadducees who question Jesus posit a family of seven brothers, each marrying the same woman in sequence. Jesus' reply rebuts his antagonists on their own ground, arguing from the Torah in favor of belief in resurrection. It also skillfully turns the question from a legal riddle to a question of the identity and works of God himself. In this Sunday's liturgy, no less important is the substance of Jesus' affirmation of life after death, which may be the subject of today's catechesis.

Catholic Doctrine

Heaven and Hell

We believe that death is not an end, but a threshold, and it is over this threshold that we pass into a life beyond this earthly existence. Catholic teaching holds that there are three distinct modes of existence in the next life, and we identify the places where these modes are experienced as heaven, purgatory and hell. In this doctrine section for this Sunday heaven and hell are treated. Purgatory is treated in the doctrine section for the feast of All Souls.

Hell is the mode of existence for those who are eternally damned. We believe that we are united with God when we freely choose to love God and our neighbors. Jesus himself warns that if we do not meet the needs of the hungry and the thirsty, if we do not welcome the stranger, clothe the naked, care for the ill, and visit those imprisoned we will be excluded from his presence and be cast into the "eternal fire prepared for the devil and his angels" (Mt 25:41). The Catholic Church teaches that if one dies in a state of mortal sin without repentance we are then separated from God by our own free choice. This state of final and eternal self-exclusion from union with God is termed "hell." (CCC 1033)

No one is predestined to hell. Indeed, God is a loving God and acts to save all. But some choose not to be saved and to reject God. Hell is the inheritance of all who willfully turn away from divine love in a persistent state of deadly or mortal sin unto death. Thus the Church implores the mercy of God, "Father, accept this offering from your whole family. Grant us your peace in this life, save us from final damnation, and count us among those you have chosen." (*Roman Missal*, Eucharistic Prayer I)

Heaven is the mode of existence for those who are eternally blessed. We believe that those who die in the Lord, who die in grace and friendship with God and who are perfectly purified live for ever in the blessedness of the beatific vision. They see God as he is, "face to face" (1 Jn 3:2).

We proclaim that by his saving death and resurrection Christ has won for us new life and has opened the gates of heaven for us. The beatific vision, this total and complete union with God is accomplished by Christ who makes partners in his heavenly glory all those who believe in him and who have remained faithful. (CCC 1026)

This complete communion with God in heaven is a mystery that while we proclaim it defies exact description. And so, for example, Scripture uses images to convey this mystery: life, light, peace, wedding feast, wine of the kingdom, the Father's house, the heavenly Jerusalem and paradise. However much we grope to convey the reality of this mystery, it is beyond us, until that time when God opens up heaven to us and gives us the capacity to fully contemplate his glory. This beatific vision is the ultimate end and fulfillment of our deepest human longing and the supreme, definitive happiness. (CCC 1024 & 1028)

St. Cyprian exults in a letter, "How great will your glory and happiness be, to be allowed to see God, to be honored with sharing the joy of salvation and eternal light with Christ your Lord and God . . . .to delight in the joy of immortality in the Kingdom of heaven with the righteous and God's friends." (St. Cyprian of Carthage, *Epistulae*, 58, 10,1: CSEL 3/2, 665)

Catholic Culture

Nardo di Cione was active as an artist in Florence in the years 1343-66 and produced a painting of the *Last Judgment with Paradise and Hell*. It fills the walls of the Strozzi Chapel. While the painting depicting the last judgment is situated on the window wall behind the altarpiece, the side walls are given over to panoramas of heaven and hell. Paradise is depicted in stately fashion and contains an ordered beauty, row upon row of costumed figures—as if they are all in church. Hell, on the other hand, is an attempt to illustrate the punishments described by Dante in the *Inferno*. The torments are shown explicitly and in detail in separate sections corresponding to the circles described by Dante. There is a pandemonium and murderous intensity to Nardo di Cione's depiction of hell that contrasts with the stately, hierarchic beauty of heaven. (*History of Italian Renaissance Art*, 4th ed., Frederick Hartt, pps. 135-36).

Notes

Dismissal Catechesis (30 min)

Getting Started

Invite the candidates and catechumens to be seated in a circle around the table on which has been placed the Lectionary and a lighted candle. Pray in these or similar words:

"All good and gracious God, your Son, Jesus Christ, triumphed over the powers of death and prepared a place for us in heaven. Bless us who gather this day to give you thanks for his resurrection and bestow on us the gift that someday we may praise you with all the angels and saints in that glorious place called heaven where Jesus lives and reigns with you and the holy Spirit, one God forever and ever. Amen."

First Impressions

1. Ask everyone to close their eyes, take a few deep breaths and recall the Liturgy of the Word just celebrated. *What word or phrase touched you?* After a few moments of silence, invite them to open their eyes and to share their responses. Jot these down on paper or on a chalkboard.

2. Continue with the whole group asking what they found exciting or perplexing about the liturgy just celebrated. *What questions does this liturgy raise for you, or what stands out for you?* Record these also on large paper or chalkboard.

Making Connections

1. To enable the candidates and catechumens to connect these scriptures to their daily lives review with them the story of the seven brothers and their mother. Note that this family refused to break the laws of their faith. Discuss the courage they displayed. What does this demonstration tell us about their faith?

2. Ask the questions: *In your lives today, what would you be willing to die for? In what ways have we been tested? On a scale of 1 (low) to 10 (high), where would we mark the importance of our faith when faced with such a test? Would our faith be stronger if we knew our choice would lead to immediate death or do we find choosing to be faithful more difficult in the day-to-day living of faith? What does the example of the seven brothers and their mother teach us?* Discuss the promise made to those who choose to follow the law of God and what is promised to those who choose to be unfaithful to the law. In what ways does God's promise influence our decisions about how we live?

Prayer

Spend some time in quiet reflecting on the commandment of love that Jesus gave to us. Reflect also on how committed we are to making Christ and his commandment the goal of our lives. Conclude by praying the responsorial psalm from today's liturgy.

Extended Catechesis

SESSION FOCUS: *Heaven and Hell*

Gathering

A. Sunday:

Welcome the sponsors, team members and other companions. Invite everyone to stand in a circle and sing "Eye Has Not Seen" (Marty Haugen, GIA Publications).

B. Weekday:

Welcome everyone. Begin with a Celebration of the Word such as:

- Opening Song from Sunday's Liturgy
- Sign of the Cross and Greeting:
- Reading: 2 Maccabees 7:1-2, 9-14
- Quiet
- Alleluia
- Gospel Luke 20:27-38 [or 20:27, 34-38]
- Alleluia

The Word (30 min)

1. Using these or similar words explain the background of the first reading.

   The two books of Maccabees are in the Catholic Bible, and we regard them as sacred texts. The books reference the tumultuous times of the second century before Christ. Following the colonization by the Greeks of the known world surrounding the Mediterranean Sea, the Greek language, religion and culture dominated these regions. The century following the death of Alexander the Great witnessed the division of his empire and a family, Seleucids, ruled the Middle East. About 167 B.C., the Seleucid emperor, Anticohus Epiphanes, in an effort to strengthen his control over the conquered peoples, demanded that everyone adopt the Greek way of life. The story of the seven brothers and their mother enduring torture and scourging and even death demonstrates their great faith. The mother and brothers are examples for all Jews to follow. Their refusing to eat pork symbolizes their refusing to give up their faith.

2. Ask participants to discuss in pairs when Christians today are challenged to not give up their beliefs and to name the costs of being faithful to the teachings of faith.

3. Turn the discussion to a consideration of faith in the resurrection. Point out that what is most significant for us this Sunday in the first reading is the brother's profession of faith in a resurrection from the dead. This belief in a personal resurrection or an afterlife did not appear in Judaism until about 200 BC. As it is presented here, the wicked will perish, and only the just will be raised. State that the Gospel is also concerned about death and life. The Sadducees, a conservative group, accepted only the Torah, the first five books of the Bible, and did not believe in angels or the resurrection of the

dead. The question they pose to Jesus is their attempt to discredit him and his teachings. Jesus turns the question from a legal riddle to a question of the identity and works of God himself. This particular episode is one of a series that illustrates how the narrow conceptions of the Sadducees, and their concerns about progeny, clan and inheritance, prove inadequate to receiving the Messiah and his affirmation of life after death.

4. Ask participants to discuss the following question in pairs: *How are they consoled by these readings? How are they challenged by them? What questions do these readings raise for them?* After some time, elicit responses and comments with the whole group.

Catholic Teaching (30 min)

1. In groups of three or four, ask each person to complete the following statements: *The resurrection is . . . Heaven is . . . Hell is . . .* refer to the Participant Book (page 116) or the blackline handout. Discuss with the whole group how their ideas of resurrection, heaven and hell have changed or deepened in their understanding over the years. What or who has influenced their understanding?

2. Show several pictures or slides showing artistic depictions of heaven and hell. Artists and writers through the centuries have used their imagination to visualize heaven and hell. Invite the group to name what they would include or exclude in their descriptions of heaven and hell and why.

3. Describe and discuss the words that Catholics use to describe heaven: beatific vision, eternal banquet, paradise, eternal life, etc. Also define the words we use to describe hell; eternal damnation, fires of Gehenna, inferno. What do such words convey about heaven and hell?

4. Stress the free will of each person to choose either to accept God's loving offer of eternal life (heaven) or to reject that offer (hell). No one is predestined by God to hell. Heaven is the reward of all who are faithful to living a moral life, that is, practicing love of God and love of neighbor as found in the corporal and spiritual works of mercy. Hell is the punishment of all who willfully choose to completely sever their relationship with God.

5. Point out that God created all things good, as is proclaimed in the Book of Genesis. Sin entered the world through the free choice of Adam and Eve. Jesus Christ redeemed all of us for heaven but each person must freely choose to accept this redemption and to live their lives in accord with the teachings of Christ.

6. Invite them to complete the phrases again: *The resurrection is . . . Heaven is . . . Hell is . . .* Name an affirmation or insight gained in this session.

Putting Faith Into Practice

1. Go back to the first reading, 2 Maccabees 7:1-2, 9-14. Invite the group to ponder the faith of the brothers and their mother and their willingness to die rather than deny their God or the beliefs by which they live. They believed in the promise of everlasting life: heaven. They believed that this life is temporary. They believed that this life is but a threshold to everlasting happiness.

2. Spend some time this week recording your thoughts about your relationship with God, your faith. If put to the test would you be willing to die for it? Ponder also the many ways your faith is put to the test each and everyday. In what ways does your belief in heaven and hell make a difference in the moral decisions you make?

Prayer

Invite everyone to stand in a circle. Ask the sponsors, team members and other companions to stand behind and place their hand on the shoulder of a catechumens and candidates. After a few minutes of silence, celebrate Minor Exorcism, D (RCIA #94), adapted for the group. Conclude with the song, "Eye Has Not Seen."

God, creator of all the living, your son came to live among us to show us a life beyond the cares and burdens of this world. Help us not to become so mired in the day-to-day trials that we lose our way. Make us strong in mind and body to do your work on earth. Keep us focused on the ressurection and life eternal with you. We ask this through Jesus Christ who lives and reigns with you in union with the Holy Spirit, one God, forever and ever. Amen.

Thirty-third Sunday in Ordinary Time

Understanding this Sunday:
Background for Catechesis

The Word In Liturgy

Malachi 3:19-20a
Psalm 98:5-6, 7-8, 9
2 Thessalonians 3:7-12
Luke 21:5-19

As we near the end of the liturgical year, the readings call to mind the end times in various ways. Malachi, an anonymous prophet (mal'akki simply means "one who is sent") writing in the fifth century before Christ, encountered a great deal of moral laxity among the people during the tumultuous period after the return from the exile. In this passage he speaks of a coming "day of the Lord," which will bring judgment upon them, punishing the guilty and rewarding the just. The idea of the "day of the Lord" was, at the time this book was written, already a very old one. It had been used by the prophet Amos and others in the eighth century to arouse the moral consciences of those who enjoyed privilege at the expense of the poor. Here the symbol of the sun suggests that evildoers will be burnt and the righteous healed on the day when the Lord comes.

The psalm reaffirms the first reading's emphasis on God's justice, which is coming. Human beings and even inanimate created things—rocks, trees, hills and mountains—rejoice demonstrably at the coming of God to rule over them with justice. In today's world where ecological concerns have become more and more pressing, one may easily imagine the "joy" of rocks and trees at God's coming to reign over them with justice, which includes respect for the integrity of creation. The psalmist certainly attributes to the earth a responsiveness before God, weaving together motifs of creation and redemption in this song of joy.

The community at Thessalonica that Paul writes to in our second reading was in the throes of a practical problem probably brought on by the expectation that the end of the world was coming soon. A number of people stopped working (why work when the world may end at any time?), and the food ran short. In this passage Paul appeals to them using himself and the other apostles as examples, exhorting them to diligence and responsible action. Paul's teaching is not about "workfare" or the modern problems of unemployment in an industrial society. Rather, it is about the proper use of time and talents in a community of people who must depend on one another. His words are a reminder that in the absence of purposeful activity other problems, such as gossip, begin to thrive.

Today's gospel passage is taken from a longer apocalyptic passage (Luke 21:5-30) that began with admiration for the physical splendor of the temple. Jesus' terrifying prediction of the destruction of the temple is accompanied by more involved predictions of the end times, including those in today's reading. Events of cosmic or national significance are followed by descriptions of the persecutions that the Christian community will face, and the disasters that will befall individuals because of their faith. Believers will be upheld and triumph over their persecutors not by their own power, but through the words and wisdom of Jesus. Though death is predicted for some, even death will not be the end of life for them ("not a hair of your head will be harmed"). The passage ends with a counsel of patient endurance. In spite of the horrors predicted, the picture of the Christians that emerges is not that of helpless individuals swept away on the tide of events. Rather, believers have reason to trust and stand firm in their faith. In the face of overwhelming circumstances, Jesus will be present to them.

The focus of today's catechesis may therefore be on justice—justice which comes from God, is to be mirrored in human lives and communities and the whole created world, and will bring final vindication to those who trust in God.

Catholic Doctrine

Justice

Papal documents, beginning with Leo XIII's *Rerum Novarum* (1891), present Catholic teaching on social justice issues in the modern world. This first encyclical began the papal process of delineating a broad theological framework for addressing justice concerns. The progress of Catholic social teaching was continued in Pius XI's *Quadragesimo Anno* (1931), John XXIII's *Mater et Magistra* (1961) and *Pacem in Terris* (1963), Paul VI's *Populorum Progessio* (1967) and in John Paul II's *Laborem Exercens* (1981), *Sollicitudo Rei Socialis* (1988) and *Centesimus Annus* (1991).

We owe God and we owe one another. How we dispose of that which we owe God is sometimes described as the virtue of religion (CCC 1807). How we dispose of what is owed to our neighbor causes us to respect the rights of all and to work toward harmonious relations promoting equity and the common good.

The word "justice" is derived from a Latin root *ius,* which means "right." Pursuing justice means pursuing other's rights and the duties flowing from those rights. For example, the duty which obligates one to respect another's body flows from the other's right to the fullness of life. Pope John XXIII outlined basic human rights in *Pacem in Terris* (11 April 1963, n. 11-45) as the right to life and a worthwhile manner of living, the right which respects one's person regardless of sex, ethnic background, religion or nationality, the right to freely pursue and express the truth, the right to a basic education, the right to worship, the right to gainful work, decent working conditions and proper compensation, the right to meet and associate, and the right to emigrate (Richard P. McBrien, *Catholicism*, New Edition, Harper SanFrancisco, p. 944).

Justice, as envisioned here, is not meted out by our courtrooms and in civil proceedings. It is a quality of faithful persons who love God and therefore love their neighbor. It is not the retribution of the Old Testament scripture, taking an eye for an eye, but the "words and the wisdom" promised by Jesus to those who stand firmly and equitably in the midst of trying times (this Sunday's gospel passage).

Justice would not be needed if we were in heaven, or if the kingdom were totally established on earth and we experienced the God who is "all in all." In some sense, justice is necessary because it is the force or power regulating relations between those who are separate from one another, stranger to each other. In other words, if perfect love characterized our relationships and the workings of this world, there would be no need of justice.

This is the virtue that helps to enhance and refine the full development of the individual who lives in society, that is, among others. In the oft-quoted words of Pope Paul VI: "If you want peace, work for justice."

Catholic Culture

The virtue of justice has been symbolized in artwork by the convention of a woman, crowned and wearing a blindfold, holding scales or a sword or both. The scales are pre-Christian in origin, but the sword may well derive from the *Sol Justitiae*, that is, Christ with sword and scales as represented in an engraving by Durer dating from the late 1490s. A statue of a blindfolded woman, scales in one hand and sword in the other, can be seen standing above the dome of the Old Bailey, which houses the Royal Courts of Justice in London. (*The Oxford Companion to Christian Art and Architecture,* Peter and Linda Murray, Oxford University Press, 1996, p. 264.)

St. Joseph did not divorce Mary or have her stoned, upon hearing that she was pregnant, as he could have based on the Mosaic law. Instead, he continued to give to her what was owed to her: respect and love. After prompting by an angel in a dream, Joseph married her. Acting as he did toward her, the Church describes him as, ". . .that just man, that wise and loyal servant. . ." (*Roman Missal*, Preface for Joseph, Husband of Mary.) He is a model of justice in the kingdom.

Notes

Dismissal Catechesis (30 min)

Getting Started

Be sure that the meeting space has been prepared in advance with a prayer environment and a prominent place for the lectionary. Gather in a circle and invite the group to silence. Begin with the following prayer or one of your own composition.

Let us pray with hearts that long for peace.

God, all powerful, ever-living source of all that is good, from the beginning of time you promised your people salvation through the future coming of your Son, our Lord, Jesus Christ. Help us to drink of his truth ad expand our hearts with the joy of his promises, so that we may serve you in faith and in love and know for ever the joy of your presence. We ask this through Christ our Lord. Amen.

First Impressions

Before reading the gospel, invite the group to think about the following: *As you hear the gospel listen for what words, phrases or images speak to you.* Proclaim the gospel and then invite the group to form small groups to talk about their responses to the reading.

Ask the group to respond to the following: *The gospel paints a picture of the 'end times.' If you were to find out that the world was to end in a week what would you do now, and how would it be different from how you are living your life now?*

Making Connections

1. Note that the readings raise the question of how we would live our lives differently if we knew we didn't have long is not a new one. The issue for us is how as Christians we ought to live all the time. Referring to the Word in Liturgy speak about the theological term "the day of the Lord." Bring out and connect for the group the meaning of this phrase and the importance that every day be a day of the Lord. Discuss with them how being a Christian makes a difference in daily life. As the facilitator/catechist share a story that speaks of the role of faith in your own life.

2. Invite the group to reflect on how their faith provides strength for their daily lives, especially in the face of over-whelming circumstances. Ask the group to share stories of how and where they find support, encouragement and hope in life.

Prayer

As a closing, invite the group to share spontaneous prayers for one another. An example of a format might be:

Participant: *I ask for your prayers and support as I . . .*

Catechist/Presider: (at the closing of the prayer)
   May the Lord bless us, in the name of the Father, the Son, and the Holy Spirit. Amen.

Extended Catechesis

SESSION FOCUS: *Justice*

Gathering

A. Sunday:

Invite everyone to gather and welcome any new people. Take this moment to point out to the group that we are near the end of the liturgical year and that the readings focus our attention on the end times. Consequently, we will explore the meaning of the end times for our lives today. Ask each participant to share one of the ideas they held as a child about what the year 2000 would be like.

B. Weekday:

If you gather during the week for extended catechesis, begin with a Celebration of the Word such as:

- Gathering Hymn
- Greeting and Gathering Prayer
- Read Malachi 3:19-20a
- Sing the Responsorial Psalm
- Read 2 Thessalonians 3:7-12
- Sing the Gospel Acclamation
- Read Luke 21:5-19
- Conclude using a prayer text from the Preface for the Sundays in Ordinary Time

The Word (30 min)

1. As we come to the end of the millennium, there are many voices about the end times. The gospel provides one such scenario. Have the participants respond to the following question in small groups: *Do you believe there will be an end time? Describe it. Does the gospel picture influence your conception of the end time?* Explore comments to be shared with the large group.

2. Using the Word in Liturgy Section bring out the historical and religious background to the Old Testament and gospel readings. Give an explanation of the meaning of the day of the Lord pointing out that it was meant to be filled with hope. The Day of the Lord was understood to be a time when God would reign in justice. For a people often oppressed this would have been great words for rejoicing.

3. Another concept that reflects Israel's belief in God's justice has to do with the Year of Jubilee. In this year, all would be set right and just, the world and all within it would be in balance again, slaves set free, property restored, the goods of the earth shared evenly. This, too, was the day of the Lord.

4. The gospel, as well, focuses on the predicted horrors that await the end of time. Through it all, though, there is a sign of hope for those who trust and believe in God, who will always be present to them. God's reign will be one of justice for all people. Ask the participants to reflect on the meaning of the word for the Church as the people of God, and for the world.

Catholic Teaching (30 min)

1. The Catholic teaching on justice permeates every aspect of our lives as Christians. This Sunday is a good opportunity to focus on justice as a sign of the Kingdom of God. Referring to the Catholic Doctrine section, develop an understanding of the Church's concern for justice.

2. Explore the background for the concept of the kingdom as the desire of the Israelite people to be set free from oppressive and incompetent rulers. They longed for the day when God would rule for it would be a time of justice, love, forgiveness, and God's righteousness would rule. In fact, point out, that these are the very signs today of the in-breaking of the reign of God. When we love we experience the breaking in of the reign of God in our midst. When we forgive, there is a sign of the reign of God.

3. Invite the group to reflect on places, events, experiences of the in-breaking of God's reign in their lives. Using such words as *love, forgiveness, justice, hope,* have the participants in small groups describe how and where the reign of God is happening in their lives. After some discussion ask the groups to identify where the kingdom of God is breaking into our world. Have them share this in small groups and then as a large group.

Putting Faith Into Practice

Each of us is called to be an agent or a herald of the coming reign of God by our words and our deeds. Invite the group to reflect quietly and/or to journal on how they hear the call in their own lives to be agents or heralds of the coming reign of God. Ask for some people to share their responses with the larger group.

Prayer

As a closing prayer invite the group to recite or sing the Responsorial Psalm.

Thirty-fourth Sunday in Ordinary Time

CHRIST THE KING

Understanding this Sunday:
Background for Catechesis

The Word In Liturgy

2 Samuel 5:1-3
Psalm 122:1-2, 3-4, 4-5
Colossians 1:12-20
Luke 23:35-43

On this last Sunday of the liturgical year, the church celebrates the feast of Christ the King. Instituted by Pope Pius XI in 1925 to combat the growing secularism and atheism of his time, it is one of the so-called "idea feasts" that do not celebrate an event in the life of Jesus but rather some aspect of his identity. In it we recognize and honor Christ as ruler of all. The original feast of Christ the King is the Ascension, in which the church celebrates the exalted Christ, crowned with glory at the right hand of God. Today's celebration should remind us of that more important feast as the liturgical year comes to a close.

The readings will not allow us to take a shallow view of Christ's reign, confusing earthly power and prestige with the Savior's divine majesty and goodness. Instead, the feast fixes Christ's messianic kingship squarely in the mystery of the cross, stretching us uncomfortably on the crossbeam of a paradox. Our salvation is won by having our king die a horrible, ignominious death, betrayed by his friends and the people he came to save. In Luke's gospel, further paradoxes abound. A common criminal facing death alongside him is moved to confess faith in him. Despite themselves, his torturers acclaim him. Those who taunt him ironically announce the truth of his identity (the three taunts forming a parallel with Satan's three temptations in Luke 4:1-13). What kind of a king is this? Luke's account invites us to see that Christ is the king who cannot be overcome by the world, or by sin, or by death. His reign from the wood of the cross indeed brings salvation to the outcast and the sinner.

The first reading recalls a foundational event in the life of the chosen people: the act of anointing David king of Israel. David was Israel's first true king, and a towering figure in its

religious and political history. The Hebrew scriptures chronicle his rise to leadership through military victories and acclamation by the people. They also attest his selection by God through the prophet Samuel before he had done a single great deed. In today's passage from 2 Samuel, the accent falls on the human, political element in David's ascent to power. The leaders of the northern kingdom of Israel come to Jerusalem to acclaim David as king. By so doing, they unite two kingdoms in the person of king David: Judah in the south, and Israel in the north. The etymology of the Hebrew word *nagid* which here is translated "commander," may mean "one who is proclaimed" or "one who steps to the fore."

Psalm 122 sings of the joy of going to God's temple in Jerusalem. The city of Jerusalem is particularly David's city. From this stronghold he reigned over both Judah and Israel. Jerusalem is a center both of worship and of royal administration; in tones of awe and joy the psalmist describes all of Israel going there in pilgrimage.

In the letter to the Colossians, which contains an early Christian hymn concerning Christ's reign over the whole universe, the Colossians are urged to give thanks to God for having brought them into the kingdom of his "beloved Son." All things in heaven (the angelic hierarchy is named: thrones, dominations, etc.) and earth (including the church) are reigned over and reconciled in the person of Christ. The letter also links this kingdom with the forgiveness of sins—a theme found also in today's gospel passage. Christ the King is the image (icon) of God, and he enjoys a cosmic and eternal reign (Colossians). Yet he is also the saving, crucified Messiah, who reaches out to sinners even as he is dying on the cross (Luke). Christ as king may be the focus of today's catechesis.

Catholic Doctrine

Christ the King

In the prayer of blessing for a cross, the Church prays, "When his hour had come to return to you in glory, [Father,] the Lord Jesus, our King, our Priest, and our Teacher, freely mounted the scaffold of the cross and made it his royal throne, his altar of sacrifice, his pulpit of truth." (BB, Order for the Blessing of a New Cross for Public Veneration, n 1250). The vision of Christ the King which is presented in the gospel text for this Sunday contradicts all our worldly notions of what a king or ruler should be. He is not seated in comfort upon a throne. He is not accepting the adulation of the people or the acclaim of foreign dignitaries. It is a scene of violence and murder, a horrid event, which is transformed by the power of God into the venue of grace and the work of Christ for our salvation (CCC 312). Thus, truly the cross is the throne of Christ the King who is Lord and ruler over a dominion that confounds and overturns worldly calculations.

Catholic teaching asserts that Christ's lordship extends over all of human history (CCC 450) and that he reigns above every earthly power and principality (CCC 668). What does this mean? First, this means that Jesus Christ is the redeemer of all people. Past, present and future generations are offered salvation in the one who by his suffering, death and resurrection has achieved what we could never achieve on our own. Second, no earthly reality or person is above Jesus; he reigns supreme and everything and everyone is subject to the power of his saving love and goodness.

Jesus, the Lord, also reigns supreme over the Church, which considers Christ its head (CCC 792). The Second Vatican Council taught, "[T]he Church, endowed with the gifts of her founder and faithfully observing his precepts of charity, humility and self-denial, receives the mission of proclaiming and establishing among all peoples the kingdom of Christ and of God, and she is, on earth, the seed and the beginning of that kingdom. While she slowly grows to maturity, the Church longs for the completed kingdom and, with all her strength, hopes and desires to be united in glory with her king." (LG, 5) Thus, the Church is not to be confused with the kingdom. The Church, rather, serves the kingdom.

Because believers are in this world as pilgrims who are journeying toward the kingdom yet to come, there is a tension we experience. We are subject to human authority, and yet, our ultimate allegiance belongs to Christ alone. As the Second Vatican Council noted, "the earthly and the heavenly city penetrate one another" but in the mystery of human history,

the Church and its members serve to endow daily activity with a deeper meaning (GS, 40). That deeper meaning is the kingdom of Christ and the Lord of history's saving actions.

Christ the King acts to save us and raise us up, recreating us by the power of his sacrificial love. In that power and love he claims us for his own and offers us as a holy people to God, his heavenly Father. Thus, the Church prays on this feast which ends the liturgical year, "As king he claims dominion over all creation, that he may present to you, his almighty Father, an eternal and universal kingdom: a kingdom of truth and life, a kingdom of holiness and grace, a kingdom of justice, love and peace." (RM, Preface for Christ the King, P51)

Catholic Culture

St. Augustine's treatise the *City of God* was begun after the Vandals sacked Rome in 410 and was not finished until about the year 427. It is divided into twenty-two books and treats of creation, salvation and the ultimate return of all things to God. This influential work by an early Father of the Church insists that human culture was a preparation by God for the revelation of Christ and employs the image of the heavenly city and the earthly city.

The young Raphael's *Disputa* (or *Disputation over the Sacrament*) was painted from 1510-11 in the Vatican apartments in the Stanza della Segnatura, the highest papal tribunal while Michelangelo was at work on the Sistine Chapel. This painting shows the Virgin Mary and John the Baptist flanking an enthroned Christ surrounded by the heavenly panoply of patriarchs, prophets, angels and saints all presided over by God the Father. This court of heaven looks down upon the theological discussion regarding the doctrine of the Eucharist, with theologians, the pope (Julius II who commissioned the work), cardinals and people in fierce debate on either sides of an altar upon which is placed a monstrance displaying a Host—over which hovers the Holy Spirit. This entire complicated and yet masterfully balanced scene is dominated at its center by Christ the King, enthroned, but as the viewer looks closely at his outstretched hands, the wound marks are clearly visible as he blesses.

The familiar Catholic hymn "To Jesus Christ our Sov'reign King" (text, Msgr. Martin Hellriegel) expresses in its second verse the supremacy of Christ, "Your reign extend, O King benign, to ev'ry land and nation; for in your kingdom, Lord divine, alone we find salvation."

Notes

Dismissal Catechesis (30 min)

Getting Started

1. Prepare the space ahead of time. Have a candle, an icon, statue or picture of Christ the King arranged in the space.

2. Invite the candidates and catechumens to stand in a circle around the table. Light a candle. Chant "Jesus, Remember Me."

First Impressions

1. Invite everyone to be seated and to close their eyes; take a few deep breaths and to recall the Liturgy of the Word just celebrated. Ask them to reflect on a word or phrase from the Liturgy of the Word just celebrated or reflect on the mood of the Liturgy. After a few minutes elicit responses from them.

2. Situate this Sunday, the last of the liturgical year. With the whole group discuss the following: *What did they hear as the message of this Sunday's liturgy? What did you find surprising in these scriptures we have just heard?*

Making Connections

1. List on paper or chalkboard the qualities we associate with David, the King of the Israelites. List the qualities of Christ the King. List qualities we look for or admire in leaders today. *What are the common elements? What are the major differences? What is our response when leaders aren't always what they seem to be? How can we cultivate the qualities of good leadership?*

2. Discuss reasons why we celebrate the feast of Christ the King on the last Sunday of the liturgical year. Explore their response to naming Christ as king. *In what ways are we challenged to live our lives since Christ is our king? Is this a difficult idea for us to accept? Why or why not?*

Prayer

Invite everyone to stand and sing "To Jesus Christ our Sovereign King."

Extended Catechesis

SESSION FOCUS: *Christ the King*

Gathering

A. Sunday:

Welcome everyone and invite them to sit quietly in a circle. Have on the table in the center of the circle a lighted candle, the statue, picture or icon of Christus Rex. After some silence, chant "Jesus, Remember Me." Proclaim the gospel: Luke 23:35-43.

A. Weekday

1. Welcome everyone. Begin with a Celebration of the Word such as:

- Song: "Jesus, Remember Me"
- Prayer: Pray the Opening Prayer from Sunday's Liturgy
- Reading: 2 Samuel 5:1-3
- Quiet
- Colossians 1:12-20
- Quiet
- Alleluia
- Gospel Luke 23:35-43
- Song: "To Jesus Christ our Sovereign King

The Word (30 min)

1. Proclaim 2 Samuel 5:1-3, unless you have used Gathering B above. Lead participants to imagine a nation so united in its selection of a leader. Present the qualities and achievements of David which led the people to choose him. Continue with David's ability to unite people from two different kingdoms: Judah in the north and Israel in the south. Jerusalem becomes the center of leadership and the site of the great temple which Solomon, the son of David, would build.

2. Invite participants to use the Participant Book (page 120) or the blackline handout. Contrast the kingship of Christ with that of David's. The kingdom of Jesus Christ is not of this world. Explore the difficulties some of the Israelites had in accepting Jesus as King. What kind of king is this? They were desirous of a human king and all the benefits they would have enjoyed because of such a king. Jesus Christ is king of all; not an earthly king but a divine king.

3. Ask participants to think about ways that we, too, have difficulties accepting such a king. *Do we not want the benefits of loyal subjects to be granted to us in this life?* Ask for responses.

4. Continue by pointing out that Luke's account invites us to see that Christ is the king who cannot be overcome by the world, or by sin or by death. Our salvation is won by having our king die a horrible death on a cross. His reign from the wood of the cross indeed brings salvation to the outcast and the sinner. His kingdom is clearly not of this world.

5. Explain that the letter to the Colossians is an early Christian hymn concerning Christ's reign over the whole universe. The Colossians are urged to give thanks to God for having brought them into the kingdom of his "beloved Son." Invite everyone to close their eyes and to take a few deep breaths. Reread Colossians 1:12-20 (unless you have used Gathering B above), pausing frequently. After some silence invite everyone to open their eyes. In pairs, ask them to share the words, phrases or images they heard in the letter. In a few minutes, gather their responses in the large group. Conclude by stressing that Christ is the image of God and that Christ reigns over all things in heaven and earth. Christ is also the saving, crucified Messiah who reaches out to sinners even as he is dying on the cross.

Catholic Teaching (30 min)

1. Explore the origins of this feast. Include the following points:

   - It is a recently declared feast. Pope Pius XI named the feast of Christ the King on the 1600th anniversary of the Council of Nicaea, 325.

   - The Council of Nicaea clearly stated the divinity of Christ. (Consult the information of the 4th Sunday of Easter.)

   - The feast was originally celebrated on the last Sunday of October but was transferred to the last Sunday of the church year.

   - The feast of Christ the King clearly celebrates that heaven and earth are one in Christ.

   - In Christ's kingdom sinners and outcasts become saints.

   - Boundaries no longer exist and all are united under the kingship of Jesus Christ, a king who was willing to suffer, die and rise for us.

2. Explore the paradox of the cross and salvation that in dying on the cross Christ stretched out his arms to embrace all sinners. Invite participants to name life experiences that are both blessings and burdens such as losing one's job which causes a family to reevaluate its priorities or the death of loved which helps a family to take the time to say the important things to one another now rather than waiting till another time.

3. Elicit from participants their response to the dialogue between Jesus and the thieves who are crucified with him. The good thief of the Gospel helps us to realize that all sinners are forgiven who recognize Jesus Christ. Christ is approachable and responds even to convicted criminals. In the compassion of Christ all sins are forgiven. God's greatest gift is bringing us into the kingdom of heaven through Jesus Christ. Discuss in what ways the kingdom of Christ is a reality in our lives today.

Putting Faith Into Practice

Point out that the cross is central to our faith, and is the means of our salvation. Reflect on the challenges we face each day as the way in which embrace the cross. The cross has been trivialized in many ways yet it is key to our understanding of the reign of Jesus Christ. Spend some time now and during this coming week journaling on the importance of the cross and what it means to embrace the cross. Reflect and journal also by naming those who witnessed the crucifixion of Christ and what role each played and in what ways does each of us play those roles in our lives.

Prayer

Invite everyone to become quiet. Hold up the statue, picture or icon of the Christus Rex for all to see. Pray together responsorial psalm for the feast of Christ the King.

To Jesus Christ, our sovereign king, we give you thanks and praise. To you, all creation bows down in humble homage. In you, we place all our faith, all our hope, all our love. Empty our hearts of anger, bitterness and doubt. Fill them with the peace you alone can give. Make us eager to continue your work, that through it you will reign over the hearts of all people. Amen.

HOLY DAYS AND FEASTS

Immaculate Conception

DECEMBER 8

Understanding this Feast:
Background for Catechesis

The Word In Liturgy

Genesis 3:9-15, 20
Psalm 98:1, 2-3, 3-4
Ephesians 1:3-6, 11-12
Luke 1:26-38

The Advent season is a special time to remember Mary, the mother of Jesus. Her life, her witness, her role in the economy of salvation, and, today, her very nature, are the subject of our reflection and inform the church's prayer in the liturgy.

Since the eighth century in the East, and the eleventh century in the West, the Christian church has set aside a day to celebrate Mary's conception in the womb of her mother, Anne, thus indicating a reverence for Mary's whole person. The dogma of the immaculate conception was not defined by the church, however, until the mid-nineteenth century. The church of the United States, for whom Mary of the Immaculate Conception is its patron saint, holds this day in high esteem as one of its holy days of obligation.

The reading from Genesis sets the context for this feast in the sin of our first parents, with its far-reaching consequences. God's judgment upon the serpent, who, in the Christian tradition is identified with Satan, is cast in terms of an ongoing conflict with humanity. Eve, the mother of all the living, stands at the head of a perpetual struggle.

Mary's wholly exceptional exemption from the consequences of the sin of Adam and Eve is at the heart of the theological dogma of the Immaculate Conception. This point is not stated explicitly in the readings. It is known, however, by its effect — namely, Mary's free acceptance of the will of God in her life, expressed in the most extraordinary circumstances. This is, more directly, the subject of the gospel reading, which tells the story of the Annunciation.

That story is remarkable for its focus on Mary. In contrast to Matthew's gospel, in which Joseph is the more central figure,

Luke's account brings to light God's high regard for Mary. No particular marks of social status are hers. She has neither husband nor child, she does not share Joseph's Davidic ancestry, and she is not described as virtuous under the law, as was Zechariah in Luke's parallel story of the announcement of the birth of John the Baptist. Yet the Lord favors Mary, despite her youth, her poverty, and her womanhood in a society that gave preference to men. The angel greets her with an address that is both respectful and beautiful in the original Greek, and for which there is probably no adequate translation. Finally, the event that is about to take place in Mary's life is affirmed by a sign that takes place in someone else's life — the pregnancy of Elizabeth in her old age. This way of calling attention to God's faithfulness is found often in the Acts of the Apostles (also written by Luke).

Mary's freedom from original sin signifies more than her own blessedness, as "highly favored" of the Lord. The relevance of the immaculate conception extends to all people: Because of Mary's assent to God, the incarnation and thus the redemption of the world became possible.

Taken together, therefore, the first reading and the gospel embrace the whole drama of sin and redemption of the human race. The reading from Paul's letter to the Ephesians shows that this redemption was in the plan of God from the beginning.

Catholic Doctrine

The Immaculate Conception of the Blessed Virgin Mary

This feast celebrates that Mary was conceived without sin. In 1954 Pius XII articulated this understanding of Mary's immaculate conception: Mary was free from any stain of original sin from the moment of her conception. This article of faith, declared by the Pope, was expressed as an infallible dogma and was the result of years of reflection and consideration by the Church. Although not stated explicitly in the scriptures, it relies on a very ancient tradition concerning Mary.

What does this dogma mean for us? Paul VI in his *Guidelines for Devotion to the Blessed Virgin Mary* (1974) stipulates, "The ultimate purpose of devotion to the Blessed Virgin is to glorify God and lead Christians to commit themselves to a life which conforms absolutely to his will." Mary's assent to the invitation to become the mother of God not only gives her an esteemed place in salvation history but also provides for us the model of a true disciple of Jesus—conformity to the will of God.

Louis J. Cameli explains (in *Mary's Journey*, Sadlier, New York, 1982), that Mary is holy not because of her own merits and not because of something she did. She is holy because God loved her. She was drawn close to God by the action of God's grace in her life. "Since she received God's favor from 'the first moment of her conception,' there can be no doubt that the responsibility for who she was rested with God" (p. 60). Something similar happens in our lives, too. In terms of our faith, there are no self-made people. Everything depends on a gift from God.

We are born in need of a relationship with Jesus Christ who removes the alienation between God and ourselves. Mary needed the same redemption, but it was achieved in a unique way, by her being conceived immaculately.

The Catechism quotes St. Ireneus who wrote of Mary's role in the plan of salvation, "The knot of Eve's disobedience was untied by Mary's obedience: what the virgin Eve bound through her disbelief, Mary loosened by her faith. The Fathers of the early Church called Mary 'the Mother of the living' and coined the expression: 'Death through Eve, life through Mary.'" (CCC 494) Thus this holy day celebrates that Mary was conceived without sin, she is the model for all Christian disciples, and her "yes" opened the way for our redemption.

Catholic Culture

There are countless artistic depictions of the Annunciation. They include some iconographic devices: Mary is usually seated, sometimes with scripture in her lap or on a reading stand in front of her to show her devotion to God; a lily often appears to signify Mary's purity; and a dove is also sometimes pictured, representing the Holy Spirit who will overshadow her. Fra Angelico, a fifteenth century monk, portrays this scene in an illuminated missal with the dove suspended over Mary by God the Father who holds in his hand a book with the Greek letter alpha and omega (representing the eternal Word, Jesus Christ, the "beginning" and the "end.") See Jaroslav Pelikan, *Mary Through the Centuries*, Yale University Press, New Haven, 1996.

Throughout the world there are many Marian societies and religious communities. These groups are dedicated both to devotion to Mary and to promoting the following of Christ based on Mary as a model.

Notes

Dismissal Catechesis (30 min)

Getting Started

1. Prepare the space ahead of time with a circle of chairs around a lighted candle and an art piece of Mary's Immaculate Conception. A common work is Guido Reni's "The Immaculate Conception" in which Mary is standing in the heavens with two angels upon the crest of the moon. Another depiction of the Immaculate Conception is found on the Miraculous Medal and paintings of Mary's apparition to Catherine Laboure, who had a vision of Mary standing on a globe with rays of light streaming from her hands.

2. Invite the catechumens and candidates to be seated. Pause for a few minutes and then pray in these words:

   O God, source of all life, we give thanks and praise to you for the gift of Mary, mother of Jesus. You honored this woman from the moment of her conception with the favor of sinlessness. You offered the young maiden, Mary, the privilege to bear and conceive your beloved Son. Her 'yes' to your holy will opened the way for our salvation. Send your Spirit to be our guide as we reflect on the meaning of Mary's Immaculate Conception for us today. We ask this in the name of Jesus, your Son, who lives and reigns with you and the Holy Spirit now and forever. Amen.

First Impressions

1. Explain the meaning of holy days in these words.

   Holy days are special feasts, recalling important events in the life of Jesus or persons linked to him. Catholics celebrate these, during the course of the year through participation in the Eucharist and reflection on the meaning and implications of the feast for our lives. On this feast of the Immaculate Conception the church celebrated Mary's conception in the womb of her mother, Anne.

2. Read from Genesis 3:9-15, 20, inviting the participants to close their eyes and listen closely.

3. In the large group ask this question: *What image or phrase seemed to have importance for you?*

4. Gather the candidates and catechumens into small groups and invite them to discuss the following questions: *What is the significance of Adam's nakedness? Why is Eve named the 'mother of the living'? What can you discover about the perpetual struggle of humankind with evil from this story?*

Making Connections

1. Return the attention of the participants to the large group and invite them to share their insights as to the human struggle with evil.

2. Explain the pervasive state of this conflict in these words.

   Everything that God created was intrinsically good. Somehow humankind broke with God's goodness and unconditional love. The story of Adam and Eve's fall is an attempt to explain that breach, which the Catholic Church calls 'original sin.' Thus we are born fallen or wanting, into a world in which the presence of evil compromises our freedom to choose the good for which we were made.

3. Tell this story of the perpetual struggle of the presence of evil.

   Listen in to this typical breakfast scene in the average household. Dad was still groggy from his late-night bowling bash. He drank a little too much in celebrating his terrific score. At breakfast, perpetual motion, Ashley dumped her glass of grape juice as she jumped up from the table to retrieve her homework from the dog. Megan, the high school freshman, let out a wail as purple drops covered her crisp, white uniform blouse. Connor ignored the girls and played with his soggy cereal. Dad screamed an obscenity and pushed himself up from the table, banging out the side door. Everyone gasped when they heard the screech of the tires as he rolled out of the driveway. Mom held back her fury as she calmed Ashley, now in tears, and got out the iron to ready a clean blouse for Meg. She hurried Connor into his jacket just as the school bus horn sounded for the third time. When everyone finally left, she pulled her robe around her, settled on the sofa with the hidden half-gallon of Premiere Rocky Road Ice Cream.

   Imagine the rest of the day for these family members. The guilt, anger, and resentment brooded in their hearts, in spite of the fact that this was really a loving family. This story illustrates the perpetual human struggle with evil we call 'original sin.'

4. Invite the group to quietly think about the effects of original sin in their own lives. Encourage them by reminding them that God's promised salvation is ours through the redemption of Jesus.

Prayer

1. With these thoughts in mind, invite the participants to pray.

   Let us now pray for the grace to be open to this redeeming love of God in our lives and in our world. Creator God, you have made us in love and desire to hold us in the palm of your hand. You sent your Son to redeem us from our inner struggle with evil and our outward sinful actions. Help us to believe in Jesus coming to set us free. Empower us to open our hearts to your Holy Spirit that we may truly become a people blessed and holy.

2. Join together in one voice to proclaim the psalm of Christ's victory over sin and evil. Lead the group in praying Psalm 98 together. Have copies available for people and distribute them prior to the prayer.

Extended Catechesis

SESSION FOCUS: *Immaculate Conception of Mary*

Gathering

A. Sunday:

1. Greet and welcome the sponsors, team members and other participants as they arrive. Invite them to join the circle of catechumens and candidates. Ask the group to quietly reflect on the art image of Mary. Ask the team to share their understanding of this holy day with the catechumens and candidates.

2. Begin the prayer by inviting all to join in singing, "Immaculate Mary." Be sure to have songbooks on hand for everyone. Proclaim the gospel, Luke 1:26-38. After a short time of silence, ask all to pray Psalm 98 together.

B. Weekday:

1. As the participants gather in the circle, greet and welcome each person. Encourage the team members to introduce themselves to the catechumens and candidates. Ask everyone to reflect quietly on the art image of Mary. Invite team members to share their understanding of this feast.

2. Ask those assembled to share ways they have observed or experienced God's favor these past few days.

3. Then pray this celebration of the Word.
   - Song: "Immaculate Mary"
   - First Reading: Genesis 3:9-15, 20
   - Psalm, "Sing To the Lord," Balhoff, Ducote and Daigle (NALR, 1979)
   - Gospel: Luke 1:26-38
   - Silence

The Word (30 min)

1. Invite the candidates and catechumens to share a summary of their insights from the Dismissal Catechesis.

2. Explore the background to the readings with the participants:

   The context for this feast of the Immaculate Conception of Mary is set in the first reading from the Book of Genesis. The sin of our first parents has consequences for all of humanity. Eve, the mother of all the living, is at the head of this struggle. All of humankind comes into this world in need of God's grace, the redeeming relationship with Jesus, and the sanctification of the Holy Spirit.

   Mary's free acceptance of God's will and plan for her life is the effect of her freedom from the consequences of this first sin of Adam and Eve. The focus of Luke's gospel is Mary. Through no merit of her own, she is highly favored by God. The greeting of the angel signals God's highest regard for this lowly virgin. Through her willing 'yes' to God's announcement, the redemption of humanity is possible.

3. Gather the participants into small groups and ask them to share their insights on these questions: *What about the angel's message do you find consoling? How would you describe Mary's favor with God? What connections do you find between account of the fall and Mary's 'yes'?*

Catholic Teaching (30 min)

1. Invite the participants to share these connections in the large group. Continue with this explanation of the doctrine of the Immaculate Conception.

   This Church doctrine centers on God's grace, freely won through the victory of Christ over sin and death. All of humankind is born in need of this relationship with Jesus, who removed the alienation between God and us. Mary needed the same redemption, but it was achieved in a unique way, in that she was conceived without sin, that is, immaculately. Mary's holiness did not come a result of her own merit, but because of God's love for her and through her, all of humanity. This dogma celebrates Mary's original sinlessness because through her existence, God's victory over sin and evil became possible. The Church believes that it is fitting that grace be freely given her from the moment of her conception because of her vital role in the drama of salvation.

2. Invite the participants into small groups to share these questions: *What is the importance of the Immaculate Conception for you and all of humanity? What about Mary's place of privilege is cause for us to glorify God? How have you been 'favored' by God?*

3. Draw the attention of the participants back to the large group. Invite them to share signs of God's favor in Mary's life. Record these on one column on a large poster. Continue by asking the group to share the ways they have been 'favored' by God. Record these in a second column on the same large paper.

Putting Faith Into Practice

1. Read Mary's response to the favor of God from Luke 1:46-55, the "Magnificat." Point out that this prayer names Mary's praise of God and lists all the wonderful things God has done for her and for us through her.

2. Invite everyone to turn to the Participant Book (page 124) or to the blackline handout to write their own Magnificat in response to God's favor. Encourage them to use the list, indicating God's favor to Mary and us, as a catalyst in writing their prayer. Allow enough time for them to compose their prayer.

Prayer

Focus the group for prayer by playing a recording of "Ave Maria." Invite the participants to gather in pairs, encouraging sponsors to join with their candidate or catechumen. Encourage them to quietly share their "Magnificat" with one another. All will be praying at the same time. Conclude by singing, "The Magnificat," *Worship*, p. 173.

Solemnity of Mary, Mother of God

JANUARY 1

Understanding this Feast:
Background for Catechesis

The Word In Liturgy

Numbers 6:22-27
Psalm 67:2-3, 5, 6, 8
Galatians 4:4-7
Luke 2:16-21

Today's celebration reflects the several liturgical traditions associated with this day over the centuries: the Holy Name of Jesus, the Circumcision, the Octave of Christmas and Mary, Mother of God. The common denominator for all of these feasts, of course, is that each in its own way expresses some aspect of the mystery of the Incarnation. Modern-day Popes have also designated January 1 as a World Day of Prayer for Peace, although there is only tenuous connection between that prayer intention and today's readings (cf. Nm. 6:26). Today's celebration is the most ancient Marian feast indigenous to Rome, and the calendar reform of 1969 has given it a place of prominence as a solemnity of Mary.

The most solemn benediction in the Jewish scriptures is found in the Book of Numbers, today's first reading, in which the "name" of God is invoked on the people. For the ancient Jews, to invoke God's name on someone was equivalent to rendering present the Almighty. This Aaronic blessing was prayed over the people by the priests at the conclusion of prayer and eventually became incorporated into the daily prayer of the Temple in Jerusalem. Our current Sacramentary has guaranteed its continued use in Christian worship by including it as one of solemn blessing prayers at the end of Mass. The prayer's three-fold repetition is a Hebrew way of intensifying the sentiment expressed This text seems unrelated to the Marian character of the celebration. Rather, it reminds us that the Christmas season is always about the blessing of God's saving grace that has been "invoked" on us in the birth of Jesus (a name which means "Yahweh is salvation").

In his letter to the Galatians, Paul is very concerned to explain that salvation comes to Jew and Gentile alike as a result of what God has done in Jesus, not from our own efforts to observe the Mosaic Law. Here, his reference to God's son, "born of a woman," (v. 4) has deep consequences for Christian belief in the full humanity and full divinity of Jesus, as well as for Mary's role in the accomplishment of God's saving plan. Christian consciousness early on recognized that authentic faith in Jesus as true God and true man demanded the proclamation that Mary is the Mother of God, just as surely as she is the mother of his full humanity. There are saving implications of what theology describes as this union of two natures in one person, achieved in the womb of the Virgin Mary. As St. Thomas Aquinas has said, Jesus took on our human nature, "so that he, made man, might make men gods" (Opusc. 57:1-4). Paul points to the link between the human birth of Jesus and our adoption as God's children (v. 7).

Mary's role in this divine plan is proclaimed in the Gospel. The infancy narratives are always christological assertions, even when they seem merely to dwell on quaint details of Jesus' birth and early childhood. Mary's role in the salvation won by Christ is presented here, first, as she is greeted by the shepherds with her newborn child in the manger and, then, as she faithfully fulfills the prescriptions of the Law regarding circumcision, naming her child Jesus, in accord with his divine destiny. Mary, as she "treasured all these words and pondered them in her heart," is an image of how every believer can be part of God's saving plan—by contemplating and cooperating with the mystery of a God who, by virtue of his birth of Mary, has become completely one with our human condition. Mary's motherhood assures us of the full humanity of Jesus. The Christ is God incarnate, in order to "redeem those who were under the law. . .[thus, we are] no longer a slave but a child, and if a child then also an heir" (Gal. 4:5, 7).

Catholic Doctrine

He was born of the Virgin Mary and became man.

The Council of Ephesus (431) proclaimed that Mary is truly the Mother of God (*theotokos*). On the first day of the new calendar year the Church celebrates the mother who has borne into this world the 'new day' of Christ our Savior.

The Catechism notes, "In the liturgical year the various aspects of the one Paschal Mystery unfold. This is also the case with the cycle of feasts surrounding the mystery of the incarnation (Annunciation, Christmas, Epiphany). They commemorate the beginning of our salvation and communicate to us the first fruits of the Paschal mystery." (CCC 1171) On this first day of January, between Christmas and Epiphany, the Church gathers to contemplate the Paschal Mystery through this celebration focused on Mary, Mother of God.

The Second Vatican Council observed that "In celebrating this annual cycle of the mysteries of Christ, Holy Church honors the Blessed Mary, Mother of God, with a special love. She is inseparably linked with the saving work of her Son. In her the Church admires and exults the most excellent fruit of redemption and joyfully contemplates, as in a faultless image, that which she herself desires and hopes wholly to be." (SC 103)

She is thus linked to the saving work of Jesus because she is not merely passively engaged by God. Mary freely cooperates in the work of our salvation through faith and obedience (LG 56). Refer also to the materials presented in the doctrine section on the Immaculate Conception.

The prayers for this feast express in poetic fashion the sentiment of the Church on this day, for example, "Father, source of light in every age, the virgin conceived and bore your Son who is called Wonderful God, Prince of Peace. May her prayer, the gift of a mother's love, be your people's joy through all the ages. May her response, born of a humble heart, draw your Spirit to rest on your people." (*Roman Missal*, Solemnity of Mary, Mother of God, January 1.)

Catholic Culture

While we celebrate Mary, Mother of God on this day, the Lutheran and Episcopalian churches celebrate the Holy Name of Jesus. The Byzantine calendar marks this as the feast of the Circumcision of Jesus. Pope Paul VI also asked "all people of good will" to observe the World Day of Peace on January l without changing or ignoring the designation of this day as celebrating Mary, Mother of God (DOL 497). Praying for peace on this day is fitting, given the third invocation in the Book of Numbers (first reading). The prayer of St. Francis expresses the desire for peace-making.

The *theotokos*, the Mother of God, is portrayed in traditional iconography with the infant Jesus seated on the lap of Mary. Her lap becomes his throne. In our tradition, the rosary is a fitting way of meditating on Christological doctrine by focusing on Mary. This is precisely what the Church does on this feast of Mary, Mother of God.

Notes

Presentation of the Lord

FEBRUARY 2

Understanding this Feast:
Background for Catechesis

The Word In Liturgy

Malachi 3:1-4
Psalm 24:7, 8, 9, 10
Hebrews 2:14-18
Luke 2:22-40 [or 2:22-32]

The feast of the Presentation, which had for some centuries in the Latin church been known as the feast of the Purification of Mary, was restored to its original meaning as a Christological feast by the Second Vatican Council. Originating in fourth-century Jerusalem as a celebration of the meeting of the old and new dispensations, the feast of the Presentation by the eighth century also came to be associated with the blessing of candles for liturgical use—an association it has kept to the present day—because of Simeon's canticle in today's gospel reading, which proclaims Christ as the light to the Gentiles.

All of today's readings involve the temple in some way. Today's first reading is from the prophet Malachi, who preached in about 460 BC. A staunch upholder of Judaism, the prophet was critical of the corrupt and ignorant priesthood of his day, as well as of abuses in the temple that Ezra and Nehemiah were later to correct. Today's reading comes from his fourth oracle, in which a sudden visitation of God to the temple results in the purification of its sacrifices and its ministers. The "messenger of the covenant" was not originally thought of as a messianic figure, but later the image was associated with the messiah or the precursor of the messiah (as for example John the Baptist, in Matthew 11:10). In the context of today's celebration, a messianic interpretation is very appropriate.

Psalm 24 is a procession hymn, describing the triumphant entrance of the king into the temple. The king is described in terms used for the ark of the covenant; he is the war-hero of Israel.

Today's reading from Hebrews celebrates Christ's sharing in

the frailty of human flesh and blood. Christ is the compassionate and faithful high priest (a central theme of the letter). Although the notion of the faithful high priest has many precedents in Judaism, the element of compassion is a new one to be associated with that role, and is taken no doubt from the actual experience of Jesus' life.

Luke's narrative in today's gospel makes it clear that Jesus comes into a family and a society within Judaism that is deeply ingrained with piety and lives in expectancy of the fulfillment of divine promises. The humble eloquence of Simeon, the profound piety of the elderly prophetess Anna, and even the simple poverty of the holy family (a pair of turtledoves was the sacrifice of the poor—those with greater means offered a lamb as well) combine to form a touching portrait of the manifestation of God's Son to the faithful of Israel. Simeon's canticle, like those of Mary and Zechariah, transforms a personal gift into a broad proclamation to the world. Mary here, as elsewhere, personifies Israel. The passage does not shy away from the prediction that Jesus will cause conflict and division within Israel (the sword that will pierce Mary's heart), but does at the same time proclaim that his coming is Israel's glory.

By restoring its christological focus, the church invites us to reflect on this feast as a celebration of Jesus the Christ. Today's readings bring to our attention the humanity of Christ, who was born subject to the law (Luke), and who is our compassionate high priest and messianic mediator (Hebrews). It also proclaims his coming as the very visitation of God (Malachi), offering salvation and light to all nations (Simeon's canticle).

Catholic Doctrine

The Two Natures

The Catholic Church confesses the belief that Jesus possesses two natures: Jesus Christ is fully human and fully divine. While this belief is based in the apostles' experience of him and is asserted by Scripture, the theological understanding of this doctrine was first addressed by the Council of Chalcedon in 451 due to the Monophysite controversy (or heresy). The Monophysites charged that the human nature of Christ ceased to exist when the divine person of the Son of God assumed it. (The doctrine section for the Fourth Sunday of Easter treats of the divinity of Christ.)

The Council of Chalcedon proclaimed, "Following the holy Father, we unanimously teach and confess one and the same Son, our Lord Jesus Christ: the same perfect in divinity and perfect in humanity, the same truly God and truly man, composed of rational soul and body; consubstantial with the Father as to his divinity and consubstantial with us as to his humanity; 'like us in all things but sin.'" The Council then answered the Monophysites and asserted, "We confess that one and the same Christ. . .is to be acknowledged in two natures without confusion, change, division, or separation. The distinction between the natures was never abolished by their union, but rather the character proper to each of the two natures was preserved as they came together in one person. . ." (Council of Chalcedon, DS 301-02)

Another way the Church expresses this is to assert that Jesus is both the Son of God and the Son of the Virgin Mary (CCC 724). The two natures of Christ, one divine and one human, are not confused, but united. They are united in the one person of Jesus Christ (CCC 481). This union does not cease (CCC 469).

St. Sophronius, a bishop of the early Church preached on the feast of the Presentation, "In honor of the divine mystery that we celebrate today, let us all hasten to meet Christ. Everyone should be eager to join the procession and carry a light. Our lighted candles are a sign of the divine splendor of the one who comes to expel the dark shadows of evil and to make the whole universe radiant with the brilliance of his eternal light. Our candles also show how bright our souls should be when we go to meet Christ. . . .Our eyes have seen the God incarnate, and because we have seen him present among us and have mentally received him into our arms, we are called the new Israel. Never shall we forget his presence; every year we keep a feast in its honor." (*Orat.3 de Hypapante* 6.7: PG 87, 3, 3291-93; LH v. III, Presentation of the Lord, Office of Readings, p 1350-51)

Thus, the feast of the Presentation celebrates that Jesus, the light of all peoples, is the only Messiah, "destined to be the downfall and rising of many." The Son of God is the only mediator between the Most High and humanity. How else could this be? If Jesus is not fully and truly human, how can he understand and identify totally with us? And if Jesus is not fully and truly divine, how can he ever assist us and transform us? The Council of Chalcedon and generations of faithful afterwards have answered, confessing belief in the two natures of Christ.

Catholic Culture

In the Northern hemisphere, this feast is celebrated in the dead of winter darkness. The assembly gathers prior to the liturgy outside the church and candles are blessed. As these blessed candles are lit, the people process into church singing and the Mass of the Presentation of the Lord is celebrated. Customarily, enough candles are blessed on this day in order to last through the year. Thus this feast also goes by the name "Candlemas."

A prayer which comes to us directly from the text of Scripture, the "Nunc Dimittis" (Latin for "now you are dismissing") from Simeon's exclamation found in Luke 2:29-32 is prayed by Catholics in the Liturgy of the Hours at Night Prayer to close the activities of the day and retire to bed. The accompanying antiphon petitions, "Protect us, Lord, as we stay awake; watch over us as we sleep, that awake, we may keep watch with Christ, and asleep, rest in his peace." (LH, Night Prayer)

Notes

Dismissal Catechesis (30 min)

Getting Started

1. Prepare the space ahead of time with a circle of chairs around a table covered with a white cloth.

2. In the dismissal, include a line about the candidates and catechumens going off to meet the light of Christ in the Word. Lead the procession of candidates and catechumens, carrying a lighted Christ candle. They can follow carrying lighted glass votives and singing "The King of Glory"or "Psalm 24: We Long to See Your Face" (Kevin Keil, GIA Publications, 1993.)

3. Place a lighted candle on the table in the center of the circle. Pause for a time to allow the effect of the lighted candles to affect the group. Pray in these or your own words:

Christ our Light, you have come to expel the dark shadows of sin and death. Your presence in our midst makes the whole universe radiant with the brilliance of your eternal light. You have come to refine us like gold that we might offer to God an appropriate sacrifice. May your revealing light bring light to our hearts as we prepare to open your Word today. Open the portals of our minds that the King of Glory might enter and dwell among us. Amen.

First Impressions

1. Ask the group to discuss insights about the significance of light. Explain that this feast celebrates the Presentation of the child Jesus in the temple. Invite them to share: *What did you notice that was different in today's liturgy?* If the blessing of candles was part of your parish celebration, clarify the significance of this blessing in these or your own words:

Since the eighth century, the blessing of candles to be used in the liturgy for the following year, has been part of this feast. In today's gospel, Simeon's prayer proclaims Christ as the light to the Gentiles. It is appropriate that we celebrate this joyous feast with the blessing and procession of lighted candles.

2. Invite the group to close their eyes as you recall some of the images from the first reading from the prophet Malachi 3:1-4. Slowly read these lines from this passage, allowing time for them to affect the participants.

"Lo, I am sending my messenger to prepare the way before me;"

"For he is like the refiners fire or like the fullers lye."

"He will purify the sons of Levi, refining them like gold or silver that they might offer due sacrifice to the Lord."

3. Direct the attention of the participants to small groups, asking them to discuss these questions: *What about this passage is consoling? Who is this messenger for you? Why is the messenger's refining/purifying mission so important?*

4. In the large group gather a few insights from the small group discussion.

Making Connections

1. Then ask the whole group: *What do we mean when we call Christ our "light?"* As they respond, write their insights on a large poster board or paper. Encourage them to think about Christ as illuminator of all darkness, the fire of Christ's love igniting our faith and fervor and Christ purifying us with the refiner's fire.

2. In small groups ask them to share: *When have you experienced the light of Christ in one of the ways described by the group?*

3. Invite the response of a few and summarize today's session in a few sentences. Ask each person to think of one way they could celebrate the feast of the Presentation by sharing the light of Christ to someone in darkness.

Prayer

Invite everyone to center their minds and hearts on Jesus our Light by pausing to look once again at the lighted candles. Ask all to stand and sing "The Light Shines On," (Carey Landry, NALR, 1985). Pray the Collect for today's feast and close by leading the following, ' Litany of Light,' asking all to respond: **"Christ You are our Light."**

Our hearts our grateful for all those times you shone your light in our darkness . . . Response

We are thankful for the ways you have purified our motives and refined our thoughts . . . Response

We stand in humble awe before the fire of your love . . . Response

King of Glory, enter our minds and hearts as we journey toward full initiation into your community of love, for this we pray. Amen.

Extended Catechesis

SESSION FOCUS: *Jesus is fully human and fully divine.*

Gathering

A. Sunday:

1. Welcome and greet the team, sponsors and other participants as they arrive. Invite them to join the circle around the table of lighted votive candles surrounding the lit Christ candle. Allow a time of silent reflection, with instrumental music, such as a piece from Handel's "Messiah" playing softly in the background.

2. Ask the new arrivals to share their impressions of the significance of today's feast of the Presentation of the Lord.

3. Begin the prayer by inviting all to stand and join in singing the Gathering Hymn from today's liturgy. Continue by asking one of the sponsors to proclaim the

gospel from Luke 2:22-40. Indicate to the group that they sit in silence to reflect upon the meaning of this passage. Close by inviting all to stand and sing the "Canticle of Isaiah" by John Foley.

B. Weekday:

1. Greet and welcome the participants as they arrive. Invite them to join the circle around the table of lighted votive candles, surrounding the lit Christ candle. Allow a time of silent reflection, with instrumental music, such as a piece from Handel's "Messiah" playing softly in the background.

2. Ask the group to share how the light of Christ has affected their experiences these past few days.

3. Lead this celebration of the Word:
   - Song: Gathering Hymn from the liturgy of the feast
   - First Reading: Malachi 3:1-4
   - Sing Psalm 24
   - Second Reading: Hebrews 2:14-18
   - Silence
   - Gospel: Luke 2:22-40 [or 2:22-23]
   - Song: "Canticle of Isaiah"

The Word (30 min)

1. Invite the candidates and catechumens to share their insights on the "Light of Christ" from the Dismissal session.

2. Explain the background for the scriptures in these words:

   The scriptures for this feast revolve around the temple. In the first reading from Malachi, the prophet calls for reform and restoration of the cult of the temple and the priesthood. He describes God's intervention first as the 'messenger' who would prepare the Lord's way, and secondly, the Lord would come in person to refine and purify the sons of Levi—the priestly tribe. In retrospect, Christians have traditionally thought of the messenger as the messiah or the precursor of the messiah, that is, John the Baptist. The second reading from Hebrews celebrates Christ as the compassionate and faithful high priest. The Presentation of Jesus in the temple is proclaimed in today's gospel from Luke. Both the Presentation of Jesus in the temple and his later cleansing of the temple are viewed as Jesus' action of purifying the temple, according to the promise of Malachi. Thus, this narrative is considered a messianic statement, that is, Jesus came to fulfill both the law and the prophets. This messianic call infiltrated the dialogue between his parents and Anna and Simeon. The object of Simeon's long wait has now been realized as he, inspired by the Spirit, declares, "my eyes have witnessed your saving deed . . . a revealing light to the Gentiles, the gory of your people Israel." The pious widow, Anna, gave thanks to God and spoke, "about this child to all who looked forward to the deliverance of Jerusalem."

3. Ask the participants to spend some time reflecting on the meaning of these scriptures in their own lives by turning to the Participant Book (page 128) or to the blackline handout.

4. Ask the participants to share their insights as to the meaning of Jesus in their lives in pairs. Sponsors and candidates or catechumens will want to gather together.

Catholic Teaching (30 min)

1. Invite the participants to share a few insights on the meaning of Jesus in their lives in the large group.

2. Explain the Catholic Teaching on the two natures of Christ making the following points. The Catholic Doctrine section of Understanding this Sunday will be helpful in your preparation.

   - The Council of Chalcedon in 451 confessed the belief that Jesus is fully human and fully divine in response to the Monophysite heresy. This controversy in the early church charged that the human nature of Christ ceased to exist when the divine person of the Son of God assumed it.

   - The teaching consists in this statement: "We unanimously teach and confess one and the same Son, our Lord Jesus Christ: at the same perfect in divinity and perfect in humanity, the same truly God and truly man, composed of rational soul and body; consubstantial with the Father as to his divinity and consubstantial with us as to his humanity; 'like us in all things but sin.'"

   - The two natures of Christ are united in the one person of Jesus Christ.

3. Invite the participants to gather into small groups to discuss these questions: *What qualities of Jesus are manifest in his human nature? What qualities exist in Jesus as truly divine?* Ask each group to record their discussion on paper with markers, writing large enough for all to read.

Prayer

Gather the group back to the circle surrounding the lighted candles. Invite them to silence as they keep the person with whom they wish to share the Good News of Jesus. Begin the prayer with inviting all to stand and sing, "The Light Shines On." Indicate that everyone be seated. Invite the participants to bring to the center of the circle those with whom they will share the Good News by prayerfully saying their first name. When all have finished close with this prayer:

Jesus, we desire to be messengers of your Good News. There are many in this world who need to hear the message of your human and divine presence with us. In your humanity, you have walked with us, felt the pains and joys of living and have loved much. In your divinity, you are our source of sustenance and transformation. We raise up to you not only ourselves, but those whose names be presented to this circle of prayer. You, who promised to be with us as we gather, have heard our cry. Give us the courage to share all that you have come to mean in our lives. Give us the words to speak the glory of your presence and promise—Son of God and Child of Mary. Prepare the hearts of those we bring before you that they might hear all that you have accomplished in your living, dying and rising. Amen.

The Ascension of the Lord

Understanding this Feast:
Background for Catechesis

The Word In Liturgy

Acts 1:1-11
Psalm 47:2-3, 6-7, 8-9
Hebrews 9:24-28; 10:19-23 [or Ephesians 1:17-23]
Luke 24:46-53

The earliest scriptural traditions did not distinguish the resurrection of Jesus and his ascension as two separate events. It is in the later gospel accounts—those of Luke and John—that we find these two dimensions of the paschal mystery most clearly described as separate chronological events. So, too, in the liturgical year, it was not until the fourth and fifth centuries that a separate feast of the ascension, celebrated forty days after the resurrection in accord with Luke's chronology in Acts, became commonplace.

All three years of the lectionary cycle use today's reading from Acts to introduce the notion of Christ's ascension. Luke's description is a carefully constructed narrative, meant to be understood in light of the parallel beginning of his Gospel (compare Luke 1:1-4 and Acts 1:1-2), as well as the many key themes found here and woven throughout his two-volume work. The Gospel's description of John's baptism in chapter 3 is alluded to in this passage as being surpassed by the disciples' forthcoming baptism with the Holy Spirit; Jesus' forty days (always a symbolic number in Luke) in the desert are balanced here by mention of the forty days during which he appeared to the disciples after his resurrection; the conclusion of the Gospel, in which Jesus commands the disciples to be his witnesses to all nations, is matched here with a similar command in virtually identical language. It is clear that the ascension, for Luke, is much more a proclamation of theological truth than mere historical remembrance. The thrust of that proclamation is captured effectively in the psalm refrain ("God mounts his throne to shouts of joy; a blare of trumpets to the Lord"). Psalm 47 is considered by scholars to be one of the so-called "enthronement psalms," presumably sung at an annual celebration marking Yahweh's kingship, which was symbolized in the reign of Israel's sovereign.

Today's reading from Ephesians reflects the sort of evolved theological understanding of the ascension which underlies Luke's deceptively simple description. Scholars suspect that the Pauline disciple who penned this letter very likely may have borrowed the opening prayer, from which our reading is taken, from an early liturgical hymn. The mention of Christ as head of the church recalls Paul's body metaphor in 1 Corinthians 12, but here the church is also called the "fullness" of Christ. To be noted is the fact that although Christ is described as reigning over all creation at God's right hand, he is still intimately present to and active in the church. The ascension is not about the removal of Christ from the church; rather, it is about a new form of his presence, a presence that is in many ways even more powerful and significant than was his earthly existence with the disciples.

The Gospel reading reiterates a number of important Lucan themes: that the Messiah had to suffer (cf. the similar explanation given to the disciples on the road to Emmaus), and that the disciples are to be witnesses to the ends of the earth, but beginning their mission from Jerusalem. Jerusalem is the epicenter of Luke's understanding of salvation history, the place where the paschal mystery of Jesus' death, resurrection and gift of the Spirit all occur. This description of the ascension is clearly earlier and less developed than the account in the Acts which follows.

Catholic Doctrine

"He ascended into heaven and is seated at the right hand of the Father" (Nicene Creed)

Our Catholic belief in the ascension could appear as nothing more than an historical remembrance of Jesus' final departure from this earthly existence. As such, its relevance to our lives today might seem marginal at best. Nothing could be farther from the truth. In fact, the ascension is a crucial dimension of the saving plan of God which we refer to as the Paschal Mystery. Theologically, the ascension is expressive of our conviction that Christ's death has saving ramifications for us. Moreover, it explains how it is that we can and must experience Christ's presence to and in the Church in a totally new way in the post-resurrection era.

In a famous sermon of St. Leo the Great [*Sermo 73*, 4 (CCL 138A:453), quoted in *The Liturgical Year*, vol. 3, by Adrian Nocent, trans. Matthew J. O'Connell, Collegeville: Liturgical Press, 1977, pg. 233], the doctrinal significance of this feast is succinctly captured: "The ascension of Christ thus means our own elevation as well; where the glorious Head has gone before, the Body is called to follow in hope. Let us therefore exult, beloved . . . For on this day not only have we been confirmed in our possession of paradise, but we have even entered heaven in the person of Christ . . . " The preface for today's Mass captures the same thought in the simple phrase, "where he has gone, we hope to follow." The CCC explains this teaching in detail in section 659. The ascension is all about our own triumph over sin, in the person of Christ the redeemer, enthroned at God's right hand.

A second sermon of Leo [*Sermo 74*, 2 (CCL 138A:455-57), ibid., pg. 234], equally noteworthy, goes even further in explaining the importance of the ascension for our lives today: "Thus what formerly had been visible in our Redeemer now took the form of sacred rites; and in order that faith might be purer and stronger, bodily vision was replaced by teaching . . . " In other words, in order that people of every time and place might have access to the saving presence of Christ, it is necessary that the earthly body of Jesus, limited to time and space, be replaced by his sacramental presence. And it is precisely the ascension that makes possible the gift of Christ's Spirit in the sacraments, the "sacred rites" of which St. Leo spoke.

Catholic Culture

The ascension is one of the glorious mysteries of the rosary. Belief in the ascension is professed in both the Apostles' Creed and the Nicene Creed.

Because of its central importance in the life of Christ, artistic representations of the ascension are frequently seen in churches. Two examples that have acquired a special place in the history of art are: the sculpture of the ascension in the tympanum of the west portal of Chartres Cathedral (c. 1145) in France, and a painting of the ascension by Giotto (d. 1336) in the Arena chapel in Italy. The oldest stained glass window in the magnificent cathedral of Le Mans, France, is an unassuming Romanesque depiction of the ascension, damaged during the French revolution (along with other parts of the cathedral) by a rioting mob who mistook the figure of Christ for an earthly king.

Notes

SESSION PLAN: The Ascension of the Lord

Dismissal Catechesis (30 min)

Getting Started

1. Prepare the space ahead of time. Provide a prominent place for the lectionary and a candle.

2. Ask the catechumens and candidates to gather in a circle and to pause in silence. After a moment of silence light the candle.

First Impressions

Invite the group to gather into small groups and react to the readings and the homily. Use these questions as a guide for the discussion:

What images did the readings present to you today? How did they speak to you and what meaning do they have for your life?

Making Connections

1. Begin by exploring the meaning of the Feast of Ascension. Bring out the following points:

   • That after the resurrection the risen Christ appeared to his disciples for 40 days, reminiscent of the 40 days in the desert.

   • That we believe that Christ, raised from the dead, ascended to the Father, and now comes to us through the Holy Spirit.

   • Move them to an understanding that Jesus, once bound historically, now resurrected and ascended, knows no bounds. Christ comes to us in a new way, forever.

   • Ask the group to discuss the following questions: Knowing that Jesus comes to us in new ways and that as Christ he is not bound by time and history, what does this mean for them? How, then are they called to live their lives?

Prayer

Using the refrain "God mounts his throne to shouts of joy; a blare of trumpets to the Lord" recite or sing Psalm 47 from the liturgy.

Extended Catechesis

SESSION FOCUS:
Christ has died, Christ has risen, Christ will come again

Gathering

A. Sunday:

1. Welcome any new people to the gathering. Invite silence and ask the group to recall the readings from the liturgy.

2. Begin with following refrain:

   *We remember how you loved us to your death, and still we celebrate, for you are with us here; and we believe that we will see you when you come in your glory, Lord.
   We remember, we celebrate, we believe.*

   Marty Haugen, (1980, GIA)

3. Lead into the following or similar prayer:

   Let us pray

   *God, our Father,
   We remember how through your son's death, resurrection and ascension, you revealed to us the fulfillment of your promise of salvation. We know we are blessed with your presence and that full happiness will come when we can be with you forever. Guide us in your ways, shows us the way to fullness of life in you. We ask this through Christ our Lord, Amen.*

B. Weekday:

1. Welcome everyone to the gathering. Invite the people to silence and begin with the refrain indicated above: "We Remember." Offer a prayer such as the one above and then proclaim the Sunday readings.

   • Read Acts 1:1-11
   • Responsorial Psalm 47
   • Hebrews 9:24-28, 10:19-23 [or Ephesians 1:17-23]
   • Luke 24: 46-53

The Word (30 min)

1. Invite the group to reflect on the experience of the disciple's after the death of Jesus. Help them to imagine what it would have been like to have followed Jesus, lived with him, ate with him, and now he was gone. Ask the group to move into small groups and to reflect on the following question:

   He is not here anymore. How does that make you feel? What are you going to do now?

2. After the discussion explore with the group how the gospel speaks about the disciples. Ask the larger group to respond to the question:

   How are the disciples different from after the death of Jesus and now at the ascension? Why are they different?

3. Using the Word in liturgy explore with the group how this event, the Ascension of Christ, makes the disciples different, how they are changed, and what action results from the change. Bring out that the readings express that because of the Ascension, Christ was now present to them in a new way. The Ascension is about Christ new presence that is more powerful a sign than his earthly existence. Their response was to go out and witness to the world.

4. Ask the group to gather in small groups and respond to the following questions:

   Christ is here. What are you going to do?

Catholic Teaching (30 min)

1. Begin by singing the refrain from "We Remember."

2. Help the participants to understand the importance of the Feast of the Ascension by pointing out that the refrain we sing can be used for the Memorial Acclamation of the Mass. Explain that the Memorial Acclamation is a statement of our faith, expression our belief that Christ died for us, was raised from the dead and will come again.

   Also point out to them that in the Creed of the church, we state that Christ "ascended into heaven and is seated at the right hand of the Father." Both the memorial acclamation and the creed express the fullness of the paschal mystery.

3. Develop with the group the following points:

   - Christ died. The messiah suffered, died and was buried. This death was a death for our salvation

   - Christ is risen. For the disciples the resurrection vindicated Christ's life and revealed to them the fulfillment of God's promised kingdom.

   - Christ will come again. Because of the Ascension Christ was not longer bound to early existence. Christ comes now in a new way and with him is the dawning of a new age, the final age promised by God. The new age we speak about is characterized by renewal, by God's presence through the Spirit.

4. Help the participants to appreciate that we live in the hope of living with God forever. The Ascension celebrates the beginning of the fulfillment of God's kingdom which is here but not completely.

5. Preparing them for the coming Sundays of the Easter Season, suggest to the participants that Ascension points to Pentecost with the coming of the gift of the Paraclete.

6. Ask the participants to reflect on the following question as a large group and write their responses on a board for all to see:

   What are the signs of God's presence now in our world, in our cities, in our neighborhoods?

Putting Faith Into Practice

1. Ask the catechumens and candidates to respond to the three questions in the Participant Book (page 130) or on the blackline handout.

2. Continue questioning that invites responses to the following. Have them share their responses with one other person.

   The disciples experience led them to action even in a time of waiting for the return of the Lord. How are you called to wait for God's fullness in your life? How do you hear yourself called to act?

Prayer

Sing together "We Remember" as a closing prayer.

Trinity Sunday

Understanding this Feast:
Background for Catechesis

The Word In Liturgy

Proverbs 8:22–31
Psalm 8:4–5, 6–7, 8–9
Romans 5:1–5
John 16:12–15

The Feast of the Holy Trinity was included in the universal calendar of the Church in 1334 by Pope John XXII. Before that, its origins can be traced to the middle of the fourth century, when the Preface of the Holy Trinity was composed, and to the start of the ninth century, when a votive Mass of the Trinity was first composed. The liturgy's celebration of the Trinity arose as a response to the fourth century heresy of Arianism, which denied the divinity of Christ, and gave rise to the formulation of the Creed we still recite at Mass every Sunday.

The Book of Wisdom, although it contains material that is much older, dates in its present form to the fifth century before Christ. The author seeks to reassure post-exilic Judaism of the abiding presence and desire of God to offer guidance to the people of the Covenant—a guidance that would be on a par with the "wisdom" available among the pagan nations. Previous generations had found in the Davidic dynasty such a guarantee, but the events of the exile had shaken the faith of many. Wisdom is offered here as a source of comfort for a nation still seeking to regain confidence in it own future. In this passage divine Wisdom is personified, a rather daring poetic license for the sacred author in the aggressively monotheistic milieu of Judaism. Wisdom describes herself as present with God before and during creation. The suggestion being made, of course, is that if she was there at creation she must surely know the "secrets" of the universe. Christian faith was quick to see in this passage a foreshadowing of Christ, whom Paul calls the very "wisdom of God" (1 Cor. 1:24).

The letter to the Hebrews (2:5–9) identifies the "man" referred to in verse five of today's psalm as Jesus. The liturgical

context of today's celebration suggests a christological application for other verses of the psalm as well, particularly its description of Christ's "rule over" the works of creation.

Christian theologians seeking to understand more deeply the inner nature of the Trinity have often taken as their point of departure the fundamental Christian experience described today in this section of Paul's letter to the Romans. He reminds the Christians of Rome that we have come to know "the grace in which we now stand" through "our Lord Jesus Christ." That love of God, Paul asserts, has come to us "through the Holy Spirit" which we have received as gift. Paul is not engaging in abstract speculation on the Trinity in this passage. Rather, he is writing to a community that had experienced first-hand the sort of "afflictions" to which he refers, afflictions that have made for "endurance, and endurance for tested virtue, and tested virtue for hope." In the midst of their trials, the Roman community had experienced the presence and saving action of a God to whom, as the gospel acclamation today sings, they offer glory as "the Father, the Son and the Holy Spirit."

Underneath the carefully constructed Johannine Last Supper discourse are similar traces of the lived experience of the early Christian community. They had come to recognize the Spirt of Jesus as an abiding source of truth, comfort and guidance. After the death and resurrection of Jesus, his disciples came to a deeper and fuller understanding of all that he had revealed to them during his ministry (see John 15:15: "I revealed to you everything I heard from my Father"). The disciples came to understand that the promised Spirit was the source of that deeper understanding, the one who would guide them "to all truth." In the setting of the

Last Supper, Jesus promises that the Spirit will come. By the time John's Gospel was written, the community had long since recognized in their own experience the fulfillment of Jesus' promise. Once again, we see how today's scriptures testify to the doctrine of the Trinity by revealing the lived experience of the Christian community, an experience that only later came to be formulated in more abstract fashion as a dogma of faith.

Catholic Doctrine

The Holy Trinity

One enters into the salvation offered by God being baptized in the name of the Father, and of the Son and of the Holy Spirit. Our faith as followers of Jesus, as Christians, rests upon the foundation of the Trinity. It is important to note that at baptism we are baptized in the name, not the "names," for we hold that there is only one God, the Father, his beloved Son and the Holy Spirit: the Most Holy Trinity (CCC 232)

Catholic teaching describes the Trinity as the central mystery of our Christian faith and life because it is the mystery of God's very self. It is, therefore, the fount of all the other mysteries of faith, the doctrine which underpins all the rest (CCC 234).

While our Catholic articulation of this doctrine evolved in response to misunderstandings and heretical movements, it evolved fairly quickly, being fixed within the first four centuries of the Church—and rests upon not only our conviction but our experience of God as Father, Son and Holy Spirit, one God, three divine persons (CCC 250). This experience was expressed, from the beginning, in the baptismal formula, in scripture (for example, 2 Cor 13:13 and Eph 4:4-6), in preaching, catechesis and the prayer of the Church (CCC 249).

There is some specific doctrinal terminology associated with explanations of the Trinity: the word "substance" (also "essence" or "nature") indicates the divine being in its unity; the term "person" (also "hypostasis") designates the Father, Son and Spirit in the real distinction among them; and the word "relation" indicates that their distinction lies in the relationship of each to the others. In using this terminology, the Church clarifies important aspects of the teaching on the Trinity. First, the Trinity is One. We do not believe in three Gods, but one God in three persons, that is, the divinity is not divided between the three. Each of the persons of the Trinity is God, whole and complete, such that each of them is that same reality of divine substance, essence or nature. Second, the divine persons of the Trinity are really distinct from one another, that is, God is truly one but not solitary. Thus, the person of the Father is distinct from that of the Son, the Son distinct from the Father, and the Spirit is distinct from Father and Son. Third, the divine persons of the Trinity are relative to one another. Because the divine unity is not divided by the persons, the distinction between them arises solely from the relationships which relate them to one another (CCC 252-53).

This mystery is reflected in the way in which the Church prays. All of the longer endings of the formal prayers in the Sacramentary, after being addressed to the Father, conclude with "We ask this through our Lord Jesus Christ, your Son, who lives and reigns with you and the Holy Spirit, one God, for ever and ever." We begin Mass in the name of the Father, Son and Holy Spirit. The Church proclaims, "Father. . . .we joyfully proclaim our faith in the mystery of your Godhead. You have revealed your glory as the glory also of your Son and of the Holy Spirit: three Persons equal in majesty, undivided in splendor, yet one Lord, one God, ever to be adored in your everlasting glory." (*Roman Missal*, Preface for Holy Trinity, p. 43)

Catholic Culture

In 1551 the Russian monk Andrei Rublev, after prayer and contemplation, treated the theme of the Holy Trinity and completed his icon depicting this mystery of the faith. Three "angels" or divine beings are seated at a table, in their midst, a chalice. The icon is described thus: "The movement which animates the entire composition proceeds from the angel on the right, is conveyed further by the inclination of the center angel, and, gathered in by the third angel, flows anew towards the right to conclude and perpetuate its ceaseless circular motion. Because they do not meet, the gazes of the three angels leave the interior space open to signify that the perpetual exchange and the communication of love between the Three Persons is a mystery of total interiority. But something unforeseen happens precisely in the returning motion of the angel on the left: already pushed forward by the angel's erect position, the arch of the circle formed by the three heads is further expanded by the lines of the seats and the footrests which converge towards a point outside the icon, where the viewer is standing. And thus the closed sphere of the Three is dis-closed, and the mystery of their superabundant Life is manifested to the one who contemplates as infinite Love the large chalice formed by the side angels, and as Love bestowed, the cup which rests on the table." (Maria G.Muzj, *Transfiguration*, Introduction to the Contemplation of Icons, St. Paul Books and Media, Boston, 1987, p. 165-66)

St. Patrick (c. 390-461), appointed bishop of Ireland and considered the "Apostle to the Irish" endured great hardships in spreading the faith to this country. Although not a monk himself, he encouraged monasticism. Two Latin works survive in his own handwriting, *Confessio* (an autobiographic statement) and *Letter to Coroticus* (protesting the British slave trade). A traditional folk tale ascribes to St. Patrick the famous instruction on the Trinity using the three-leaf clover.

Dismissal Catechesis (30 min)

Getting Started

1. Prepare the space with a cloth, lighted candle, and place for the lectionary on the center table.

2. Welcome the catechumens and candidates and gather in a circle of chairs.

3. Invite participants into a moment of silent prayer. Pray in these or similar words:

   Gracious God, today we celebrate your feast. You are revealed to us in Christ, and draw us into your love by the Holy Spirit. Teach us your wisdom. Grant this through Jesus Christ, who lives and reigns with you and the Holy Spirit, one God, for ever and ever. Amen.

First Impressions

1. Ask participants to recall their experience at the liturgy, from their awareness as they gathered with the community, to the hymn, collect, readings, sung psalm, homily, and dismissal.

2. After a moment of reflection, invite them to go around the circle and share something that stood out to them.

Making Connections

1. Point out that this feast of the Holy Trinity is celebrated yearly on the Sunday after Pentecost. State that the early church, who experienced God is these different manifestations, formulated the belief of three persons in one God. This feast came to be celebrated in the middle ages.

2. Comment on any of their statements of awareness as appropriate, such as the liturgical color white for this feast, the Proverbs reading about personified Wisdom who was with God before creation, or something specific from their experience.

3. Ask participants to talk about their experience of the Trinity, e.g., whether they think of the three persons, whether this is new for them, whether they relate more to one person of the trinity than another. Invite this sharing in the large group. As they share, comment briefly and invite further discussion from others.

4. Invite participants to notice something they wonder about the Trinity. Invite their expression of these statements in the large group.

Prayer

Invite participants to imagine the three persons of God present in this room as they pray. Take a moment to sense Yahweh God who created everything and was part of the experience of the people of Old Testament times; Jesus the Christ through whom everything was made, the revelation of God to us in his life, death, and resurrection, and who will come again; and the Spirit, the breath of God present at the time of creation, who now as the Spirit of Jesus continues to blow where it will to bring about the mission of Jesus. Then pray:

God, we experience you as creator, as Lord, as Spirit of peace and love. Open us to the fullness of your presence with us. We praise You, our loving God, now and forever. Amen.

Extended Catechesis

SESSION FOCUS: *One God, a Trinity of Persons*

Gathering

A. Sunday:

Welcome sponsors, spouses, fiancees, and team members. Ask them to sit in pairs, with sponsors and catechumen or candidate together. Additional persons also form pairs. Invite everyone into a moment of silence. Briefly summarize the dismissal catechesis. Pray today's opening prayer from the liturgy:

God, we praise you: Father all-powerful, Christ Lord and Savior, Spirit of love. You reveal yourself in the depths of our being, drawing us to share in your life and your love. One God, three Persons, be near to the people formed in your image, close to the world your love brings to life. We ask you this, Father, Son, and Holy Spirit, one God, true and living, for ever and ever. Amen. Proclaim the Gospel from the lectionary.

B. Weekday:

Ask each participant to name the person of the Trinity they have been present to the most since Sunday. Then pray this Celebration of the Word or use your own design.

- Sing: Holy God, We Praise Thy Name
- Sign of the Cross, Greeting
- Proclaim: Proverbs 8:22-31
- Sing: Psalm 8
- Proclaim: Romans 5:1-5
- Sing: Alleluia
- Proclaim: John 16:12-15
- Silence
- Pray: Use the prayer from the Sacramentary as stated in A. Gathering on Sunday

The Word (30 min)

1. Point out that in this Gospel passage from John Jesus talks about the close connection between the Father and himself, and between the Spirit and himself. Ask participants to talk in pairs about their experience of each of the persons of the trinity. Then invite a large group summary.

2. Ask participants to share in the large group about their sense of the significance of God being three persons. Bring out the awareness that God is a God of love, and love needs to be shared. Indicate that before the world was made, God's love was shared with other persons of the Trinity. State that God's love is shared by all of God's people. Note that believing in a God who is a community of three persons in whose image humans are made, implies that humans are communal beings. Ask participants to talk in the large group further about what it means to them that God is a trinity of persons.

3. Recall for the participants the beginning and end of the Romans reading, and the gospel. Ask participants to name in pairs what these readings tell them about who God is and how God acts. Then ask participants to name these insights in the large group. Highlight the different awarenesses such as God acts through Jesus, the Spirit pours out God's love in us, the Spirit guides us to truth, etc.

Catholic Teaching (30 min)

1. Have several sheets of paper available. Ask participants to focus on each person of the Trinity and give names or qualities the church attributes to each. Invite participants to think of each of the persons from before time, from Old Testament times, from New Testament times, and from the end of the bible to the present. Begin with Yahweh and put awarenesses on paper. Then proceed to Jesus. Conclude with the Holy Spirit. (Focus on one person at a time.)

2. Bring out the information in the next few paragraphs in an interactive way, referring to content from their brainstorming and inviting further responses. State that God always existed without beginning. Note that God, who created the world, began to be known by people in Old Testament times. Bring out the movement of people from having many gods to one God, and from knowing God as a transcendent and powerful to knowing a God of close personal relationship who acted in their lives. Note that this communal God brought the Israelites into relationship as a community as well as personally.

3. State that the second person of the Trinity always existed but took on a human nature at a given point in time through the Holy Spirit. Point out that the church views creation as having occurred through the second person of the Trinity. See John 1:1-3. State that the church sees the world under the reign of Christ at the fullness of time, at the end of the world. Note that Jesus, the Word of God, is the full revelation in human form of God.

4. Talk about the Spirit as always having existed, and as being part of the creative process. Note the reference to the wind over the waters in Genesis 1:2. Talk about the Spirit's activity through the prophets. Point out that with Jesus presence on earth, the Spirit began to be called the Spirit of Jesus. Note references to me Spirit as the advocate, consoler, spirit of love, truth, peace. Talk about the role of the Spirit in continuing the mission of Christ.

5. Note that the Apostles Creed, which was formulated very early, and the Nicene Creed formulated in 325 named the belief in a God of three equal persons, who had no beginning. Note the terms used begotten applied to Jesus and proceeds when referring to the Holy Spirit. Include a statement that the three are worshipped. Teach this prayer, a doxology, which gives praise to the Trinity.

   Glory to the Father, and to the Son, and to the Holy Spirit: as it was in the beginning, is now, and will be forever. Amen.

Putting Faith Into Practice

Ask participants to name in their pairs a concrete way they can witness to a loving, triune God by bringing this love about with some of God's people this week. Ask them to commit themselves to this action this week.

Prayer

Pray together the prayer: Glory to the Father, . . . Sing: Holy God We Praise Thy Name, vs 3.

The Body and Blood of Christ

The Word In Liturgy

Genesis 14:18-20
Psalm 110:1, 2, 3, 4
1 Corinthians 11:23-26
Luke 9:11b-17

Reverence for the Lord's presence in the Eucharist dates from the earliest generations of Christians, as is clear from the "bread of life" discourses in John and the many meal narratives with eucharistic overtones found in Luke and the other Gospel writers. But early Christian piety focused more on Christ's presence within the eucharistic action than in the reserved species. It was not until the 10th and 11th centuries that devotion to the Blessed Sacrament as an object of prayerful adoration developed extensively among the Christian faithful. A feast of the Blessed Sacrament was first celebrated in 1246, and within a hundred years the obser-vance had spread throughout the Christian world. Pope Urban IV commissioned St. Thomas Aquinas in 1264 to compose the formularies for a Mass that he ordered extended to the universal Church. Those texts are still used today as the opening prayer, the prayer over the gifts and the prayer after Communion in the Roman Missal.

The origins and even the purpose of the narrative in Genesis about Melchizedek are shrouded in mystery. Scholars speculate that the author of Genesis may have used this ancient tradition of David's ancestor, Abraham, meeting the priest-king associated with Jerusalem ("king of Salem") in order to legitimize the Davidic dynasty centered in Jerusalem. The Israelites would have considered the blessing of victory over enemies that is bestowed on Abram in this passage to have been passed down to all subsequent rulers on the throne of David. The significance of the bread and wine that is offered is most likely connected to Abraham's covenant with the Lord, but its exact relevance cannot be determined. The Roman Canon's allusion to "the bread and wine offered by your priest Melchizedek" is a witness to how early Christians

understood this scene as a foreshadowing of the eucharistic mystery. Psalm 110 testifies to the way the Jerusalem monarchy capitalized on the tradition of Melchizedek to interpret the ruler as having both a priestly and a royal status.

The problems within the Corinthian community that prompted Paul to write to them resulted in this text, our earliest example of Christian theological reflection on the meaning of the Eucharist. The larger context of this passage is Paul's concern over misconduct at their communal meals, where some were indulging to the point of excess, while the poor were allowed to go hungry. The factions that had divided the community in other ways (e.g., over which charismatic gifts were more important and whether Paul's or Apollos' disciples held more prestige) now seem to be infecting even their eucharistic gatherings. In technical language ("I received . . . handed on") designed to reinforce the importance of his teaching, Paul reminds the Corinthian community of the sacrificial meaning of their gathering. The death of the Lord was redemptive, a "new covenant" evocative of the Sinai covenant that also had been sealed with the blood of a sacrifice (Exodus 24:8). Not only do they gather "in remembrance" of the Lord's saving death; in addition, they do so with an eye to the future, as they "proclaim . . . until he comes." This eschatological perspective is an important basis for the ethical injunctions which are so prominent in this intervention by Paul into the life of the Corinthian community. Their reverence for the Body of Christ present in the Eucharist must be matched by their reverence for the Body of Christ that they recognize in one another.

The multiplication of the loaves and fishes is the only

miracle found in all four Gospels. Its eucharistic significance is clear from the precise and consistent language that is used in all of the Gospels ("taking . . . raised his eyes . . . pronounced a blessing . . . broke . . . gave"). The miracle would have reminded Jesus' contemporaries of a similar story in 2 Kings of Elisha and would have been perceived in a messianic context. The abundance of the leftovers were a sign of the lavish abundance of the messianic banquet. And, the prediction of the passion which Luke places immediately after this narrative occurs in all of the Gospels as a correction to the disciples' misunderstanding of the nature of Jesus' messiahship.

Catholic Doctrine

The Real Presence

On this feast when the Church contemplates the eucharistic banquet of the Lord, we proclaim our belief that "when we eat this bread and drink this cup we proclaim your death, Lord Jesus, until you come in glory." (*Roman Missal*, Memorial Acclamation, Eucharistic Prayer) As followers of Jesus, we carry out his command to "do this in remembrance of me" (1 Cor 1:24-25). What we remember is the sacrifice of the Lord, which in the Eucharist we offer again to the Father through the gifts of bread and wine through the power of the Holy Spirit and the words of Christ (CCC 1357).

The assembly gathers in faith, and God makes present Jesus, his body and blood, in the sacred species, the bread and wine offered in the Eucharist. This sacrament is "the source and summit of the Christian life," extolled by the Second Vatican Council (LG 11). It is a memorial of Jesus' death and resurrection, a sacrament of love, a sign of unity, a bond of charity, a Paschal banquet "in which Christ is consumed, the mind is filled with grace, and a pledge of future glory is given to us." (SC 47)

The emphatic proclamation of this awesome mystery is only possible because from the earliest times the Church has experienced in this sacred meal the real presence of Jesus Christ. This means that when we eat this bread and drink this cup although we taste the fruits of the earth and our human hands (bread and wine) we experience in faith the body and blood of our Lord and Savior who sacrificed himself on our behalf. Thus, St. Ignatius describes this sacred meal as "bread of angels, bread from heaven, medicine of immortality." (St. Ignatius of Antioch, *Epistula ad Ephesios*, 20,2: SCh 10, 76)

We believe that when the Church gathers, Mass is celebrated with the Liturgy of the Word and the Liturgy of the Eucharist, and within the Eucharist, bread and wine are presented and prayed over, the Spirit of God descends and makes those elements into the body and blood of Jesus Christ. The Church has insisted from the earliest times that this is the "real presence" of Christ, that is, real in the fullest sense a substantial presence by which Christ, both God and man, makes himself wholly and entirely present (CCC 1374). Why? Most especially because Jesus himself promised this and secondarily because the apostles and those who have followed in this Church have experienced it to be so.

A substantial change takes place within the elements of bread and wine. Indeed, the term in our tradition for the change which takes place is "transubstantiation" (CCC 1376). St. Ambrose says of this change, "Be convinced that this is not what nature has formed, but what the blessing has consecrated. The power of the blessing prevails over that of nature, because by the blessing nature itself is changed. . . Could not Christ's word, which can make from nothing what did not exist, change existing things into what they were not before? It is no less a feat to give things their original nature than to change their nature." (St. Ambrose, *De mysteriis* 9, 50; 52: PL 16, 405-07)

The presence of Christ in the Eucharist continues as long as the eucharistic species (the bread and wine) subsist. We also believe that the real presence of Jesus exists wholly and totally in each of the elements, such that while an individual consumes only the eucharistic bread both body and blood are received and if only the eucharistic wine is consumed both body and blood of Christ are received (CCC 1377).

Catholic Culture

Benediction (from the Latin for "blessing") is a liturgical service wherein the consecrated host, the Body of Christ, is displayed in a special container called a monstrance (from Latin, *demonstrare*, to show) or ostensorium. Catholics pray before and adore the sacred species—based on our belief that the consecrated bread is no longer merely bread but the Body of Christ.

St. Thomas Aquinas, toward the end of his life, after completing his great theological work, the *Summa Theologica*, was said to have insisted that the mystery of God cannot be contained in the logical and rational dispositions of theology. The hymn which we Catholics traditionally use at Benediction services is attributed to St. Thomas Aquinas:

> *Godhead here in hiding, whom I do adore*
> *Masked by these bare shadows, shape and nothing more,*
> *See, Lord, at thy service low lies here a heart*
> *Lost, all in wonder at the God thou art.*
>
> *Seeing, touching, tasting are in thee deceived;*
> *How says trusty hearing? that shall be believed;*
> *What God's son has told me, take for truth I do;*
> *Truth himself speaks truly or there's nothing true.*
> (Thomas Aquinas, *Adore te devote*, trs. Gerard M. Hopkins)

Dismissal Catechesis (30 min)

Getting Started

1. Prepare the center of the circle before the gathering with a loaf of bread and a cluster of grapes.

2. Greet and welcome the catechumens and candidates as they enter the room and invite them to sit in the circle.

3. Ask the participants why this centerpiece was chosen. After a brief discussion, begin with prayer by singing the Gathering Hymn and the Gloria used at today's liturgy.

First Impressions

1. Invite the whole group to discuss these or similar questions: *What about today's liturgy was festive? From listening to the proclamation of the Word, what would you say is the predominant theme this Sunday?*

2. Explain to the participants a little about the feast celebrated at today's liturgy in these or similar words:

   The name of this feast is "The Body and Blood of Christ," or in Latin, "Corpus Christi." Today we celebrate the sacrament of the Eucharist, that is, the body of Christ blessed, broken, proclaimed and remembered.

3. Invite them to gather into smaller groups of about three or four. When they have settled down ask them to discuss the following: *What is the common thread in the readings, the story of Abram and Melchizedek; Jesus feeding the multitudes and Paul admonishing the Corinthians? What do you understand as the Catholic teaching about Eucharist? (For those who are from other Christian traditions) What beliefs do these traditions have about the Eucharist?* When the discussion is winding down, ask the whole group to share their responses.

Making Connections

1. Continue the large group sharing on the gospel by means of the following questions: *What is the source of abundance in the feeding story? How does this story expand your notion of God?*

2. In the small groups invite the participants to share their hunger for God and how that hunger is satisfied. Ask them to recall a time when they felt empty or dissatisfied. Then ask, *How did God 'feed' you?* Allow enough time in the small groups for each person to share their story.

3. After this sharing time, turn the attention of the participants back to the large group. Invite them to share the following: *From telling your story, what did you learn about God's desire to fill and satisfy you?* Summarize their insights and ask them to write one thing they wish to remember from this session in the Participant Book (page 135) or on the blackline handout.

Prayer

Prepare copies of Psalm 110 for everyone prior to the gathering. Begin the prayer with the Collect from today's liturgy. Then read, once again, the Gospel, Luke 9:11b-17. Close the prayer with everyone praying Psalm 110 together.

Extended Catechesis

SESSION FOCUS:
The Real Presence of Jesus in the Eucharist

Gathering

A. Sunday:

1. Greet the newcomers and invite them to join the circle. Ask them to share their insights into this feast, referring to the symbols in the circle's center.

2. After a short sharing, begin the prayer time by inviting all to sing two or three verses of the Communion Hymn used at the liturgy. Follow that with the prayer, attributed to St. Thomas Aquinas, "Adore te devote"; found in the Catholic Culture section of Understanding This Sunday. Ask a team member to proclaim the gospel, Luke 9:11-17. Close the prayer time with the Preface for today's liturgy.

B. Weekday:

1. Welcome and greet each person as he or she arrives. Invite them to gather in the circle to spend a short time in silence reflecting on the symbols of bread and grapes.

2. Encourage the participants to share their experience of Jesus presence in their lives over the past few days.

   - Lead this celebration of the Word.
   - Song: "We Are Many Parts" (Marty Haugen)
   - First Reading: Genesis 14:18-20
   - Psalm 110: Using the copies from the Dismissal Catechesis, recite together.
   - Second Reading: 1 Corinthians 11:23-26
   - Silence
   - Gospel: Luke 9:11b-17
   - Sing the Gloria

The Word (30 min)

1. Invite the participants to offer a line or phrase describing their understanding of the meaning of Eucharist. These can be recorded on paper or a poster large enough for everyone to read.

2. Explain the background for the first reading and the gospel in these words:

   While this particular passage from the Book of Genesis is shrouded in mystery, it has long been believed that the bread and wine offered by Melchizedek as a foreshadowing of the Eucharistic meal. Christians have traditionally looked upon this offering as prefiguring the perfect sacrifice that Jesus would offer to the Father. The significance of the bread and wine that is offered is a commemoration of Abraham's covenant with Yahweh.

The gospel account of the multiplication of the loaves and fishes is significant in that it is the only miracle found in all four gospels, Matthew, Mark, Luke and John and it is found six times in the New Testament. The importance of this account lies in the consistent language used in all four gospels. "Then **taking** the five loaves and the two fish, and **looking up to heaven** said the **blessing** over them, **broke** them, and **gave** them to his disciples to set before the crowd." (Luke 9:16) From earliest times Christians attached a Eucharistic significance to Jesus' actions and gestures. The meals Jesus shared with his followers and the meals shared after his resurrection and these accounts of abundant feeding all offer a greater understanding of the Eucharist we celebrate today.

3. Ask the participants to share in small groups: *What can we say about the Eucharist from these two passages?* Allow a few minutes for this discussion and then ask the participants to name one thing they have learned about Eucharist from these two passages. Add these responses to the paper, writing large enough for everyone to see.

4. Continue to expand the meaning of the second reading from 1 Corinthians.

In the second reading taken from 1 Corinthians it is important that we understand the context of Paul's admonition. This early Christian community was having difficulty when they gathered for the Eucharist. Eucharist was celebrated in the context of a meal at the homes of these early followers of Christ. They brought food to share and eat. Some of the wealthier members, indulged to the point of excess, while the poorer members went hungry. By the time the sacramental part of the meal arrived, some were in no condition to recognize that they were participating in the saving meal of the Lord's body and blood. Paul uses this portion of his letter to deal with these issues. Paul reminds the Corinthians and us that the death of the Lord redeems all and that the sacrifice of bread and wine, now the body and blood of Christ, seals the covenant of union with God.

5. Remind the group to look back at their initial expressions of the meaning of Eucharist. (These are recorded on the paper.) In small groups ask them to discuss one or more of the following questions: *When Jesus says, "Do this in remembrance of me," what is it that he asks us to do? How is the sacrament of the Eucharist a way of celebrating our covenant with one another and with God? What does it mean to 'take' and 'eat' the body and blood of Christ?*

Catholic Teaching (30 min)

1. Continue the discussion on Eucharist, with this summary, taken from the Catholic Doctrine section of Understanding This Sunday.

Eucharist, one of the seven sacraments, is called the "source and summit of the Christian life." In celebrating Eucharist we remember Jesus' death and resurrection; we celebrate our union with one another and God; and we are nourished to live the Christian life and be the presence of Christ in the world.

The Catholic Church believed from its beginnings that Christ is really present—both God and man—in the consecrated bread and wine. We believe that the bread and wine is substantially changed into the Body and Blood of Christ first, because Jesus promised this and second, because the apostles and those who have followed in the Church have experienced it to be so. Indeed, Eucharist makes us who we are—the Church. As we eat and drink of the Body of Christ, we continue to witness to and work on behalf of the Lord's kingdom for the life of the world. We become the presence of Christ for others.

2. Gather the participants in pairs to share on these questions: *What can we say about a church that has a meal at the center of its faith? What response does the real presence of Jesus at the Eucharistic meal evoke in you?*

3. In the large group invite the participants' reactions and questions regarding the real presence of Jesus.

4. Ask the participants to turn to the Participant Book (page 134) or the blackline handout to compose their own prayer and respond to the questions provided.

Putting Faith Into Practice

Explain some of the practices that are part of the Catholic tradition which honor Jesus' presence in the Eucharist: Genuflection, tabernacle, the red sanctuary light, Eucharistic adoration, bringing Eucharist to the sick and homebound. This might be a good time to take them into the church to see some of the sacred vessels and the tabernacle.

Prayer

Invite the participants to gather in pairs and pray the prayer they composed with a partner. Close with the song, "Bread, Blessed and Broken."

Birth of John the Baptist

JUNE 24

The Word In Liturgy

Isaiah 49:1-6
Psalm 139:1-3, 13-14, 14-15
Acts 13:22-26
Luke 1:57-66, 80

Our earliest record of a feast celebrating the birth of Jesus stems from the fourth century. Not long afterward, Christians began to mark the day of John the Baptist's birth as well. It is surely not coincidental that the date assigned for Christ's birth was the winter solstice—the "birth" of the sun—while the date observed for John's birth was the summer solstice six months earlier. The Church celebrates the feast of most saints on the day of their *death*, when they entered heaven. We celebrate the *birth* of only two saints, however: the Blessed Virgin Mary and John the Baptist. Mary, by virtue of her immaculate conception, entered the world sinless at her birth. Tradition has suggested that John was also freed from original sin when he "leaped for joy" in his mother's womb upon meeting the Savior (Luke 1:41, 44); and so he, too, is regarded as having entered sinless into the world at his birth.

The liturgy chooses Isaiah's second Suffering Servant Song to be read at the Mass during the day. (The Vigil Mass also has a text from Jeremiah about being called before birth.) Scholars debate the exact origin and reference intended by this collection of poems in the Book of Isaiah that speak of a mysterious figure who will redeem his people through vicarious suffering. Most often, Christians have used the Suffering Servant Songs to understand more deeply the identity and mission of Jesus. Here, however, the vocation of the precursor of Jesus is highlighted. The application of this text to John seems dictated especially by its emphasis on the prophet being chosen from the womb ("from my mother's womb he gave me my name"), an emphasis found also in today's psalm ("you knit me in my mother's womb").

The reading from the Acts of the Apostles is taken from a sermon preached by Paul to the Jews of Antioch in Pisidia during his first missionary journey. Paul first offers a quick recapitulation of God's saving history of the chosen people, down to the choice of David as king, from whose descendants God has brought forth "Jesus, a savior for Israel." He then describes the important role played by John in announcing the coming Messiah through his preaching of a "baptism of repentance" and by the way he pointed to the one who would come after him. Here as elsewhere in the New Testament, the sacred author goes to the trouble of including John's explicit statement that he was not the Messiah, only the precursor. Scholars point out that the background to these statements must have been a flourishing cult of the Baptist who refused to acknowledge the superior role of Jesus in the plan of salvation. Authentic Christian faith, while recognizing John's role as secondary to Jesus, nonetheless sees in him the greatest of the prophets.

The key to a proper interpretation of Luke's infancy narratives is to remember that everything he has written in his Gospel is ultimately about the identity of Jesus as the Christ, Lord and Savior. Hence, Luke's description of the miraculous events surrounding the birth of John the Baptist is meant to contribute to the reader's conviction that a divine destiny is unfolding in this elaborate choreography. The intricately interwoven narratives of the birth of Jesus and of John reveal the links between their destinies as part of a single divine plan ("Was not the hand of the Lord upon him?"). Today's reading gives only a portion of the Lucan material on John, but enough for us to sense the significance of his birth as an essential step preparing for his role in announcing Jesus. John will later announce to his contemporaries what the angels proclaim at Bethlehem: ". . . a savior . . . who is Messiah and Lord." (Luke 2:11)

Catholic Doctrine

Human Cooperation with Divine Grace

The portrayal of John the Baptist's birth and his ministry in the gospel exemplifies how grace and human freedom intersect to unfold the divine plan of salvation. The birth of John emphasizes divine initiative. John's ministry represents the response of freedom.

We Catholics understand grace to be the favor of God, the free, undeserved assistance that the divine imparts to us in order that we might respond to his invitation to become adopted children of the Most High, to partake in the divine nature and eternal life (CCC 1996). In a word, grace is a gift from God. And this gift is manifold. It enables us to participate in the Trinitarian life. By baptism we are incorporated into Christ and therefore as adopted children can call God our "Father," in union with the Son. In baptism we are also gifted with the life of the Spirit who breathes charity in us and who forms the Church.

Significant in an understanding of the Catholic perspective on grace is the notion that the very preparation for receiving God's favor is already the work of grace. God is the author who brings to completion the good work already begun in us (CCC 2001). St. Augustine informs us, "Indeed we also work, but we are only collaborating with God who works, for his mercy has gone before us. It has gone before us so that we may be healed, and follows us so that once healed, we may be given life; it goes before us so that we may be called, and follows us so that we may be glorified; it goes before us so that we may live devoutly, and follows us so that we may always live with God: for without him we can do nothing." (*De natura et gratia*, 31: PL 44, 264)

Thus, God reaches out to us. God acts. And that action of love toward us by God invites a response.

It is interesting that while the Catechism treats grace extensively in the latter part (around paragraph 2000), the very first paragraph of the entire work first refers to the calling or invitation of God whose purpose is that we might seek God out, know God, and love God with all our strength (CCC 1). In other words, the first words of our Catholic compendium of teaching refer to our vocation in God. The initiative of God invites our free response to collaborate in the divine plan of salvation for this world. This divine drama is illustrated in capsule by the birth and ministry of John the Baptist. St. Augustine instructs, "The Church observes the birth of John as a hallowed event. We have no such commemoration for any other fathers; but it is significant that we celebrate the birthdays of John and Jesus. This day cannot be passed by. . . John was born of a woman too old for childbirth; Christ was born of a youthful virgin. The news of John's birth was met with incredulity, and his father was struck dumb. Christ's birth was believed, and he was conceived through faith. . . Thus [John] represents times past and is the herald of the new era to come. As a representative of the past, he is born of aged parents; as a herald of the new era, he is declared to be a prophet while still in his mother's womb. For when yet unborn, he leapt in his mother's womb at the arrival of blessed Mary. . . .even before he was born; it was revealed that he was to be Christ's precursor. . . . these are divine happenings, going beyond the limits of our human frailty." (*Sermo* 293, 1-3: PL 38, 1327-1328 found in LH, vol. 3, Birth of John the Baptist, Office of Readings, p 1487)

Catholic Culture

A splendid early mosaic depiction of John the Baptist can be found in dome of the Arian Baptistry at Ravenna. The very center of the dome is dominated by Jesus' baptism by John as the Spirit in the form of dove hovers over Christ's head and the bearded Father sits opposite the Baptist, looking on. This center scene is circled by the Apostles who move in stately procession with garland crowns toward a throne upon which sits a jeweled cross. (John Beckwith, *Early Christian and Byzantine Art*, Yale University Press, New Haven, 1979, p 111)

An extremely detailed silver altar frontal which shows scenes from the life of the Baptist is found in the St. John the Baptist Baptistry, Florence. Commissioned in 1367 it was not finished until 1477. On the feast day of St. John, relics were displayed on this altar. The Baptist is the patron saint of the city of Florence and was considered an important civic symbol. Evelyn Welch, *Art and Society in Italy 1350-1500*, Oxford University Press, New York, 1997, 47-8)

John the Baptist is the patron saint of Puerto Rico, and the feast of his birth is a festive occasion for Puerto Rican Catholics. The capital, San Juan, is named for John the Baptist.

Notes

Dismissal Catechesis (30 min)

Getting Started

1. Prepare the space with a cloth, lighted candle, and place for the lectionary on the center table. Gather in a circle of chairs.

2. Invite participants into a moment of silent prayer. Sing "You Are Near" (Schutte) or another version of today's Psalm 139. Pray in these or similar words:

   God, today we celebrate the feast of John the Baptist whose voice announces the coming of your reign. May we today hear your voice and live more fully in your kingdom. We pray through Christ, the true light of the world. Amen.

First Impressions

Have participants recall their experience at the liturgy, from their awareness as they gathered with the community, to the hymn, collect, readings, sung psalm, homily, and dismissal. After a moment of reflection, invite them to go around the circle and share something that was meaningful for them.

Making Connections

1. Ask participants to name what they sense God was saying to them personally in the liturgy today. After a moment of reflection, have them share this in pairs.

2. Ask each pair to express some of their sharing in the large group. Highlight any observations about John the Baptist that are mentioned, and relate them to Christian life today.

3. State that today's words in Isaiah 49 talk of the experience of being called from birth and named in "my mother's womb" to be not only God's servant, but "a light to the nations." Invite participants to sense themselves as being formed in their mother's womb and named by God. Suggest to the participants that God has been leading them from the time in their mother's womb through all of their life experiences to be God's servant and voice. Ask participants to talk in pairs about what it's like to be aware of God's forming, naming, leading, and sending them personally. Then invite some large group sharing.

4. Conclude by asking participants to name something they want to take with them from today's liturgy and sharing. Go around the circle for this discussion.

Prayer

Invite participants to look inside themselves and become aware of the God who has made them. After a moment of quiet, proclaim Isaiah 49:1-6. Sing the refrain of "You Are Near" or Psalm 139.

Extended Catechesis

SESSION FOCUS:
John the Baptist gave his life to preparing the way for Christ.

Gathering

A. Sunday:
Welcome sponsors, spouses, fiancees, and team members. Ask them to form groups of four, with two sponsor/catechumen or sponsor/candidate pairs in a group. Additional people also form groups of four. Invite everyone into a moment of silence. Briefly share the content of the dismissal catechesis. Sing: You Are Near. Proclaim the Gospel from the lectionary.

B. Weekday:
Ask each participant to name a time since Sunday when they in some way pointed another person to God and God's reign. Go around the circle for this naming. Then pray this Celebration of the Word or use your own design.

- Sing: You Are Near
- Sign of the Cross, Greeting
- Proclaim: Isaiah 49:1-6
- Sing: Psalm 139
- Proclaim Luke 1:57-66,80
- Pray : *God, John the Baptist challenges us to repent and follow Christ. May our ears and hearts hear his message. Guide us to the way of salvation and peace. We ask this through Christ, the light of the world. Amen.*

The Word (30 min)

1. Give some background of the setting of today's Gospel. State that Elizabeth and Zechariah, like Abraham and Sarah, were elderly. Note that as with Mary, an angel came and announced to Zechariah that they would have a child. Add that the angel's greeting was also, "Do not be afraid," but when Zechariah asked how this would be, he was struck mute. State that the angel said the child's name was to be "John," which means "Yahweh has shown favor." Note that people were in disbelief of Elizabeth as she named the child John because usually a male child was named after the father or some other male in the family, which was not the present situation. State that the stories surrounding John's birth, as that of Jesus, are wonderful in themselves. Ask participants to recall any feelings about God's action or important stories about a birth of a child in their own family. Invite some small group sharing. Invite some response in the large group.

2. Invite participants to hear the Gospel again and notice what happened in people as a result of this amazing story, especially in seeing Zechariah being struck mute, and then speaking at the time of the child's naming. Invite some

large group response. Bring out from the participants' sharing the praise of God, fear, a sense that something new is happening and that God's hand is active in this child.

3. Then ask participants to share in their small groups their experiences of sensing that God was doing something in their lives. Invite some large group response. Highlight the awakening to and anticipation of God's action. Point out that John the Baptist is a pivotal character in scripture, a transition as a prophet before Christ who makes Christ known. Note that this uniqueness is reflected in the church's liturgical calendar that celebrates only three births, that of Jesus, Mary, and John the Baptist. State that other saints are remembered on the day of their death, their "birth" into eternal life.

4. Ask participants to become aware of this present moment in their lives as a time when something new is happening at God's hand. Besides the general sense of becoming Catholic, invite participants to notice in a concrete way the newness of what God is doing in them. Have them share this in small groups.

Catholic Teaching (30 min)

1. Invite participants to brainstorm everything they know about John the Baptist. Prepare a time line of his life, from conception to his beheading. Fill in events on paper as participants name them. Include the Visitation with the moments between his conception and naming in the temple. Note to the participants the familial relationship between John the Baptist and Jesus. Point out that little is known about John the Baptist's life from this time in the temple until his public appearance preaching repentance and announcing that God's reign is here.

2. State that scholars believe John was an ascetic and probably associated with the Essene community near Qumran. Note that John wore camel's hair clothing and ate locusts and wild honey (Matthew 3:4). State that John spoke with fierce passion ("You brood of vipers!" Luke 3:7) and preached repentance of sins. Talk about John's role in announcing the good news that God's reign is here now. Note the images John used from Isaiah 40:3 ff. Point out that as a result of his preaching, people were baptized (hence his name of "Baptist"), but that this baptism is different from Christian baptism. Ask participants what kinds of words, e.g., strong, fearsome, comforting, usually move them to change. Invite some small and large group sharing.

3. State that John was utterly important as the messenger of Jesus who prepared the way for him. Note Jesus' words that "among those born of women no one is greater than John; yet the least in the kingdom of God is greater than he." (Luke 7:28) Also bring out the sense in the prologue of John's gospel that John has come as a witness to the light. Ask participants who for them today are messengers that remind them that God's kingdom is now, or who are witnesses to the light of Christ. Invite some large group sharing.

Putting Faith Into Practice

Ask participants to name in their small group a concrete way they sense God is calling them to be a messenger to someone that God's reign is now. Encourage their commitment to an action this week.

Prayer

Invite participants to focus their eyes on the lighted candle, and recall that God, who has created and formed them, sends them into the world as a witness to the light of Christ. Ask each person to pray in their hearts for the grace they need to do this. Then pray:

God, use us as you did John the Baptist to announce the presence of Christ to the world. Make our voices strong. Guide us in your truth. We pray through Christ, the light of the world. Amen.

Sing: "Prepare the Way of the Lord."

Peter and Paul, Apostles

JUNE 29

Understanding this Feast:
Background for Catechesis

The Word In Liturgy

Acts 12:1-11
Psalm 34:2-3, 4-5, 6-7, 8-9
2 Timothy 4:6-8, 17-18
Matthew 16:13-19

This solemnity honors two great saints who, between them, represent the church's mission to both Jews (Peter's leadership was exercised from the Jerusalem church) and Gentiles (Paul is known as the "apostle to the Gentiles"). Saint Peter, who is called by Jesus "rock," and who is revered by Catholics as the progenitor of the Petrine ministry which has endured through the centuries, enjoys first place among the apostles and has a profound significance for the church. Saint Paul is likewise a towering figure, whose theological genius, evangelical fervor, and tireless pastoral ministry were so instrumental in the founding of the Christian religion. When we honor Peter and Paul, in truth we honor the church as well, for their contributions have forever marked the faith and life of God's people.

The first reading from Acts details Peter's miraculous escape from prison, where he had been placed by Herod Antipas after the beheading of James the apostle. The role of the angelic messenger, plus the dreamlike effortlessness with which Peter evades multiple guards, is freed from chains, and walks through open iron gates, accentuate the element of divine intervention. The significant mention of the fervent prayer of the Christian community during this crisis makes the further point that the power of prayer outstrips that of tyrants. The wisdom psalm which follows (Ps. 34) celebrates a faith response suitable to the crisis represented by the first reading. After a hymnic introduction and reference to deliverance, the portion of the psalm included in today's liturgy consists of injunctions to trust and fear the LORD.

It is fitting that the second reading, which relates to Paul, is not a narrative, but speaks in the apostle's own voice—since most of what we know about Paul is learned through his letters. Here, speaking from prison, he reflects on his suffering and immanent death. He uses three metaphors to express the significance of his life. He calls it "a libation," that is being poured out. A cup of wine or oil poured on the ground at Jewish sacrifices, the libation suggests that Paul sees his death as sacrificial. The "dissolution" he speaks of (in Greek *analusis*) can refer to the unyoking of an animal from a harness. It further suggests that his death will be a release from the labors he has undertaken for the sake of the gospel. Last of all, the metaphor of the athletic contest ("fight" and "race" refer to the striving necessary to life; the "crown" a laurel wreath worn by a victorious athlete) suggests a purposeful life and death, made glorious by an everlasting reward in heaven. Paul confesses God's saving presence in his trials, and the passage ends with a prayer of praise—also characteristic of Paul's letters, which are frequently filled with prayer.

The gospel is Matthew's account of the confession at Caeserea Philippi, in which Peter identifies Jesus as the Messiah and Son of God, and is in turn acclaimed by Jesus. Given a new title ("rock" was not a known personal name at that time) and a mission of teaching authority through the passing of the "keys" and the power of binding and loosing, Peter is thus established by Jesus in a special role because of his confession. In the context of today's celebration, the central importance of Peter's ability to proclaim the true identity of Jesus stands out as the key element of the passage. Peter is the one who names Jesus the Messiah, and is thus named by him "the rock" on which he will build his church.

Catholic Doctrine

The Papacy and Collegiality

Peter is described as the church's foundation, echoing this feast's gospel image of the "rock." Peter confesses his faith in Jesus as the Christ, the Son of God, the anointed Messiah. Paul takes up this theme immediately after his conversion and at the start of his own ministry (CCC 442).

This profession forms the centerpiece of apostolic faith embodied in the Twelve, in which the primary place is given to Peter (as the church understands this gospel text). His mission is to ensure that this profession of faith does not waver among the college of the Twelve, that they do not lapse from it, and that they remain strong in it (CCC 552).

Tradition holds that because both Peter and Paul, the two major leaders of the apostolic Church, were martyred in Rome, the responsibility for continuing to ensure the profession of the faith has been handed on to the bishop of the local church of Rome. We believe that the charge of shepherding the Church has passed down from Peter to successive holders of the office of bishop of Rome (CCC 862).

Although the occupant of the Chair of Peter presides over the whole Church in charity, responsibility for shepherding does not rest with this bishop alone. Jesus called to himself Twelve, and this apostolic witness and function in the Church is given to all the bishops who together with their head, the Pope, exercise their office collegially.

In recent times, Vatican II saw the collegial exercise of their apostolic office by the Pope and bishops as deriving from the font of the Church, the Trinity, which is a community of love. It also understood that this collegial concept was based in its teaching that the People of God constitute the church. Finally, the Council, in describing the pastoral office of bishop, insisted that the bishops cannot make decisions without listening and responding to people. All of this served as background to the Second Vatican Council's delineation of collegial exercise of apostolic authority.

The Second Vatican Council asserts, "Just as, in accordance with the Lord's decree, St. Peter and the rest of the apostles constitute a unique apostolic college, so in like fashion the Roman Pontiff, Peter's successor, and the bishops, the successors of the apostles, are related with and united to one another. . . .This college, in so far as it is composed of many members, is the expression of the multifariousness and universality of the People of God; and of the unity of the flock of Christ, in so far as it is assembled under one head." Thus, episcopacy (the office of bishop) is not just a juridical concept of the papacy. Bishops are the result of the real communion of the Church and the nature of ordination for service to the People of God."

The Catholic Church asserts that the Pope "holds supreme and full authority over the universal Church" (LG, 22). But in the exercise of this unique ministry of charity, the whole body of bishops have collaborated. One example of such collaboration is ecumenical councils. Twenty-one councils have been held since the first apostles met in Jerusalem to resolve the issue of Gentile converts to Christianity. The most recent was the Second Vatican Council (1962-65), called by Pope John XXIII. In addition, since Vatican II, the Synod of Bishops has met periodically to advise the Pope on certain issues and topics. Some recent topics have been priesthood and justice (1971), evangelization (1974), catechesis (1977), the Christian family (1980), reconciliation (1983), the laity (1987), and religious life (1994).

Catholic Culture

A little over a generation ago, Catholics thrilled to the sight of bishops thronging Rome for the Second Vatican Council as images were telecast around the globe and reports filled the airwaves, newspapers and magazines. Although the First Vatican Council had been held prior to the turn of the century (1869-70), no one anticipated John XXIII, elected at age seventy-seven, to convoke such an undertaking. This exercise in collegiality was completed by Paul VI. Today, the Church continues to reflect upon and deepen its understanding of this monumental event in the history of the contemporary Church.

The *ad limina* (Latin for "to the threshold") visit is required of every diocesan bishop who visits the Pope to report regularly on the status of the diocese and to go "to the threshold" of the tombs of the apostles Peter and Paul and pray. This visit is seen as one way that the bond of communion between the Pope and the bishops is maintained.

The Italian artist Perugino (whose real name was Pietro Vannucci, c. 1445-1523) created a fresco of *Christ Giving the Keys to St. Peter* found in the Sistine Chapel. It is composed of brilliant colors. In the foreground Jesus is handing a kneeling Peter the keys to heaven and earth while the disciples and others watch. Behind this grouping, an enormous piazza stretches (and in it can be discerned two other gospel scenes: Jesus teaching give to Caesar what belongs to Caesar and the attempting stoning of Jesus who passes through the crowd). In the far background of the piazza stand two triumphal arches modeled on those of Imperial Rome and at the fresco's vanishing point, a beautiful domed church. Thus, one's eyes are drawn to the sides of this "infinite" piazza that have no buildings. Is this the artist's attempt to symbolize the all-encompassing papal authority? (Hartt, *History of Italian Renaissance Art,* fourth edition, p. 367-68)

Dismissal Catechesis (30 min)

Getting Started

1. Prepare the center table with a red cloth, a large rock that is able to be passed around, a lighted candle, and a place for the lectionary. Gather in a circle of chairs.

2. Invite participants to sense the presence of Peter and Paul, strong apostles and martyrs. Pray in these or similar words:

   God, we praise you today as we honor Peter and Paul, who with deep faith in you proclaimed your gospel without fear even of death. Strengthen us in this same faith and that we may proclaim your gospel to others. We ask this through Christ, our Lord. Amen.

First Impressions

1. Ask participants to share in pairs something that caught their attention from the liturgy today.

2. Invite sharing in the large group. Facilitate conversation around what each person brings forth. Comment on the liturgical color red used for the feasts of apostles and martyrs.

3. Ask participants to brainstorm about all they know about Peter and Paul. Bring out the awareness that Peter, our first leader in the faith, spread the faith to the people of Israel, and Paul, who was converted, taught the faith to the Gentiles from various nations. Note that both Peter and Paul received new names from God.

4. Invite participants to reflect and then name who the apostles of the faith have been for them in their lives, either by what they have experienced personally or by what they have observed. After the names are shared, ask participants to talk about ways the faith has spread to them.

5. Then ask participants to formulate one sentence about what celebrating this feast of Peter and Paul means to them. Go around the circle for this naming.

Prayer

Invite participants to name something they need to be a stronger apostle of the faith. Then pray: *God, you both give us the gift of faith and call us to share the faith we have been given with others. Give us what we need to be your apostles in all dimensions of our lives. We pray in Jesus' name. Amen.*

Extended Catechesis

SESSION FOCUS:

The ministry of the papacy and college of bishops unfolds from the faith rooted in Christ and spread by Peter and Paul.

Gathering

A. Sunday:

Welcome sponsors, spouses, fiancees, and team members. Have them sit in groups of four with two sponsor/cate-chumen or sponsor/candidate pairs in a group. Additional people also form groups of four. Ask a participant to give a brief summary of the dismissal sharing. Sing: "We Are Called," (David Haas, GIA Publications). Ask participants to sense the faith of Peter and Paul, and the long tradition of the handing down and spreading of faith begun in them. Pass around the rock and invite participants to sense the meaning of Jesus calling Simon "rock." Proclaim the Gospel from the lectionary.

B. Weekday:

Prepare the space as in the dismissal catechesis. Pass the rock from one person to the next, inviting them to sense the meaning of our faith being handed down from Christ through the centuries. Ask participants to name while holding the rock a way since Sunday they did something to spread the faith or a way their own faith was strengthened by another. Then conduct a Celebration of the Word.

- Sing: We Are Called
- Sign of the Cross, Greeting
- Proclaim: Acts 2:12-11
- Sing: Psalm 34
- Proclaim: 2 Timothy 4:6-8,17-18
- Sing: Alleluia
- Proclaim : Matthew 16:13-19
- Silence
- Pray: *Through the prayers of the apostles Peter and Paul, may we who received faith through their preaching share their joy in following the Lord and spreading the faith of the church. We pray in the name of Jesus. Amen.*

The Word (30 min)

1. State that this event of Jesus asking his disciples who people say that he is is found in Matthew, Mark, and Luke. Note that Matthew's Gospel adds Jeremiah, an important prophet in the Jewish community, as one of the responses. State that Peter, as the rock or foundation of the church, gave his life to spread the faith and eventually was martyred. Ask participants to share in their small groups what they think it might have been like for Peter to be called "rock," to have the keys entrusted to him, and to live this out in his life. Then invite some large group sharing.

2. Recall for the participants that in the reading from Acts, James had just been beheaded when Peter was taken into custody. Note that Acts says the church, meaning the community of believers, was praying fervently for people. Bring to mind the wondrous activity of the angels who freed Peter. Note also that Paul was rescued from the lion's mouth. Note that this was a time of great faith in the church. Ask participants to name and share in their groups times in their own lives they experienced the presence of great faith. Then invite some large group response.

3. Note the image in the Timothy reading of Paul's assurance of receiving a crown of victory, running a good race and keeping faith. Given the scriptural images of the church at prayer, an angel freeing Peter from prison, running the race, a crown, the rock, and the keys, ask participants to note their own images of faith as they live. Give time for small group sharing. Then ask participants to simply call out some of their images of faith.

4. State that Peter and Paul were both on fire with their faith in Christ and gave their lives to the spread of the Gospel. Ask participants to name a concrete way they are being invited to give themselves over more fully to their faith in Christ. Suggest that as they do this the faith will necessarily spread to others. Give time for some small group sharing.

Catholic Teaching (30 min)

1. State that the faith was spread to both Jews and Gentiles through the activity of Peter and Paul. Note that as stated in Matthew 16:18 and 19, Jesus handed on to Peter authority for the foundation of a church. Note that the entrusting of the keys of the kingdom of heaven to Peter is a handing on of authority. Point out that Jesus gives the power to bind and loose, which is viewed as a teaching authority. Note that as the rock of the church after Christ, Peter has come to be thought of as the first pope, and that all popes are successors of Peter. Ask participants to name the present pope, when he became pope, and any other popes and what they are noted for. You may want to specifically mention John XXIII calling Vatican Council II. Note that the pope is the Bishop of Rome, and is seen as the foundation of unity in the church. Talk about the teaching authority of the papacy.

2. State that the pope governs the church along with the college of bishops. Talk about the college of bishops as sharing authority for the church in accord with the pope. Note that the college of bishops acts powerfully at the time of an ecumenical (worldwide) council, such as Vatican Council II. Ask participants to share anything they remember about Vatican Council II. Point out that the pope both shares his authority for the church, and is always the final voice in the church's governance. See the Catholic Doctrine section.

3. Mention that each country has a conference of bishops that makes recommendations to the pope about matters pertaining to the local church they shepherd. Elicit names of local bishops, and of other well known bishops. Give examples of some of the work of the bishops' conference such as pastoral letters in the area of faith and morals, and liturgical concerns.

Putting Faith into Practice

Ask participants to name in their small group something they will do this week to share their faith with another.

Prayer

Celebrate the Minor Exorcism J indicated in RCIA #94. When candidates are present, the language needs to be adapted to reflect their baptismal status. Then pray: *God has built the church upon the rock of Peter's faith. May God bless us with a solid faith. Paul's labors and preaching were undaunted in times of trial. May Paul's example inspire us to proclaim our faith. May Peter and Paul's untiring witness and prayers lead us to full life with Christ. We ask this through Christ our Lord. Amen.*

The Transfiguration of the Lord

AUGUST 6

Understanding this Feast:
Background for Catechesis

The Word In Liturgy

Daniel 7:9-10, 13-14
Psalm 97:1-2, 5-6, 9
2 Peter 1:16-19
Luke 9:28b-36

The Transfiguration celebrates an event in the life of the Lord, and thus draws the church into a deeper appreciation of his identity and mission. When the church proclaims the story of the transfiguration on the second Sunday of Lent, as it does each year, it looks toward the specific ways in which that event prefigures the glory of Easter, and leads the faithful to a renewal of their baptism during the Lenten season. Here, the focus is rather on the glory of God seen in Jesus. We behold God's glory through the apocalyptic vision of the prophet Daniel, we celebrate it through the psalm, we are dazzled by it along with the apostles as we behold the face of Jesus on the high mountaintop, and we affirm it along with the second letter of Peter as a promise of the Second Coming.

The book of Daniel, written in the mid-second century B.C., is a combination of edifying stories and apocalyptic literature. The book promotes faithfulness to Judaism and resistance to Hellenizing influences. In it the God of Israel is presented as the Lord of all human history. Today's reading is part of an apocalyptic vision in which the Son of Man, who represents the kingdom of the holy ones of God, comes down from heaven and is given dominion by the "Ancient One" who represents God. The Son of Man in the passage was later taken to be a messianic figure. When "Son of Man" became the preferred title of Jesus, the church interpreted this passage to point to him, and combined this apocalyptic vision with the notion of suffering. God is presented here, as in the psalm, with the typical features of a theophany (appearance of God to human beings), such as fire, and light. Psalm 97 is a hymn of praise to Yahweh as king. It proclaims God, describes a theophany, and closes with a response of joy.

The second letter of Peter, written near the end of the first century of the beginning of the second, uses the name of Peter, but is too late to have been written by Peter himself. (Later authors used the name of an authoritative witness to indicate the importance of the content of the letter.) The purpose of this letter is mainly to warn against the dangers of false teachers. Thus it reveals the continuing concerns of the early church in the period after the death of the first apostles. Today's passage encourages the community to expect the *parousia* (second coming of Christ) because of what had been seen by the apostles in the transfiguration.

In the larger context of Luke's Gospel, the Tranfiguration scene occurs just after Peter's confession of faith and between the two predictions of the Passion. Jesus is portrayed speaking with Moses (representing the Law) and Elijah (the Prophets) about his "passage" (the Greek word is "exodus"), by which Luke understands the suffering, death and resurrection Jesus was about to undergo in Jerusalem. The message of the voice from heaven is clearly directed to the early Christian community, affirming that Jesus is God's Son, the Chosen One, and insisting that they "listen to him," in similar times of prayer. Coming to know Jesus in this way involves a recognition of his messianic, divine identity, as well as a willingness to follow him along the path of suffering to glory.

Significant visions of the glory of God have caused apostles, saints, and holy people throughout the centuries to experience religious awe, know their own frailty, and glimpse a future that inspires hope. The feast of the Transfiguration— that vision of Jesus that foreshadowed the resurrection—is an appropriate occasion to reflect on God's immediate and personal revelation to human beings, which may be the subject of today's catechesis.

Catholic Doctrine

Visions and Private Revelations

The starting point for our stance on visions and private revelations can be found in what we believe Jesus himself reveals. The Catholic Church teaches that Jesus Christ alone offers the fullness of God's revelation to us. The mystery of Christ illuminates the mystery of creation (CCC 280). Indeed, in his life, his mission, his suffering, death, resurrection and ascension God's Son reveals to us the love of the Father through the Holy Spirit. The apostles witnessed to the truth of the resurrection and, in time, the gospels were set down in writing. Together, Scripture and Tradition form one single deposit of revelation which the Church preserves, preaches from and interprets in the light of present day needs. [This subject is treated at greater length in the Fifth Sunday of Ordinary Time, Year C.] Thus, the Second Vatican Council, citing 1 Timothy 6:14 and Titus 2:13, taught, "The Christian economy, therefore, since it is the new and definitive covenant, will never pas away; and no new public revelation is to be expected before the glorious manifestation of our Lord Jesus Christ." (DV, 4)

In other words, the Council teaches that everything that God chooses to communicate to us for our salvation has been done so in Jesus and that no new "public" revelation will be given before Christ comes a second time in glory to this world of ours. This does not mean that the content of revelation as given in Jesus cannot be understood anew or interpreted freshly given the situation of the world. It simply means that nothing will be added.

In the history of Christian mysticism there are many examples of individual mystics who have claimed a private experience which communicates or reveals the activity of God. This extraordinary phenomenon may be comprised of images, ideas, or words. This communication of God to the mystic may result in physical, psychological or intellectual manifestations. The appearances of Mary at Lourdes and Fatima fall into this category of private revelation. Approved by the Church as credible, these apparitions are nonetheless not held by the Church to be part of the content of doctrine or teaching. The approval is stated in the negative, that there is nothing there which would harm the faith. As for the recent Marian apparitions at Medjugorje, the Church has not yet con-cluded its investigation, although many pilgrims have visited this site and found solace and encouragement to their faith.

As with any image or artistic rendering of the mystery of God's self-revelation to us in Jesus, none of these apparitions or mystical experiences and visions can supersede the Christ event. In that sense, both in art and in these visions, that which is communicated enhances and draws out the meaning conveyed by Jesus Christ, eternal Word of God.

Although it is difficult to precisely define mysticism, some mystics who have related in their writings or preaching the direct experiences of the divine in their personal prayer and contemplation are St. Bernard of Clairvaux (d. 1153), St.Francis of Assisi (d. 1226), Meister Eckhart (d. 1327), St. Bridget of Sweden (d. 1373), St.Catherine of Siena (d. 1380), Julian of Norwich (d. 1420), St. Joan of Arc (d. 1431), St. Teresa of Avila (d. 1582), St. John of the Cross (d. 1591), and St. Ignatius Loyola (d. 1556).

Perhaps St. John of the Cross speaks for all of the mystics down through the ages when he writes, "In giving us his son, his only Word (for he possesses no other), he spoke everything to us at once in this sole Word—and he has no more to say. . .because what he spoke before to the prophets in parts, he has now spoken all at once by giving us the All Who is His Son. Any person questioning God or desiring some vision or revelation would be guilty not only of foolish behavior but also of offending him, by not fixing [their] eyes entirely upon Christ and by living with the desire for some other novelty." (*The Ascent of Mount Carmel*, 2, 22, 3-5, in *The Collected Works*, trs. K. Kavanaugh, OCD and O. Rodriguez, OCD, Institute of Carmelite Studies, Washington D.C., 1979, p. 179-80, or LH, Second Week of Advent, Office of Readings)

Catholic Culture

St. Bridget of Sweden, born into a noble family, married and had eight children, one of whom was St. Catherine of Sweden. She made a pilgrimage to St. James at Compostela, Spain, and upon her husband's death she entered religious life, eventually establishing a monastery for nuns and monks. Making further pilgrimages to the Holy Land she claimed to have visions of the nativity and the passion from the Virgin herself. These visions were recorded and became the basis for paintings, especially of the nativity, which show Mary dressed in white, kneeling on the ground, with her cloak and shoes beside her and the naked child Jesus from which a brilliant light shines forth overpowering the candle held by Joseph. Grunewald's Isenheim altarpiece panel of the *Virgin and Child* is also associated with her visions. (*Oxford Companion to Christian Art and Architecture*, p. 66).

Notes

Dismissal Catechesis (30 min)

Getting Started

1. Prepare the center of the circle with a lit candle and an icon of the Transfiguration (early 15th century, Novgorod School found in *Festal Icons of the Lord*, Sr. Helen Weier (The Liturgical Press) before the gathering.

2. Invite all to join the circle as you welcome and greet the catechumens and candidates. Have soft instrumental music, for example, the Gregorian chant, playing in the background. Allow some time for the participants to gaze at the icon and pray in quiet.

3. Close the prayer time with the short passage from Daniel 7:9-10, 13-14 used as the first reading in today's liturgy.

First Impressions

1. Invite the group to offer their insights from the liturgy of the word and the quiet prayer time with this question: *What is the motif of today's feast?* Listen carefully to their ideas.

2. Continue the discussion of today's feast in small groups. These or similar questions may be used: *What images from today's scriptures are particularly meaningful for you? Where was there consolation and reassurance in these passages? What did you find confusing or difficult to understand?*

Making Connections

1. Continue the conversation in the small groups with these questions: *What do you find troubling in your own journey of faith? Have you ever experienced doubts raised by 'false teachers,' as did the community to whom Peter's second letter is addressed? Have you felt that God took a long time to 'appear' when you needed God's consolation or God's presence?* Encourage the participants to share their experiences of doubt or waiting with one another.

2. Invite the participants to share a few stories of discouragement in the large group. Don't force the sharing, just allow those who are willing and open a short time to share.

Prayer

Close the section by praying Psalm 97. The response of the group after the leader prays 2 or 3 verses is: "The Lord is King; let the earth rejoice."

Extended Catechesis

SESSION FOCUS: *Visions and private revelations*

Gathering

A. Sunday:

1. Welcome and greet the new arrivals as they join the circle. Begin this time of prayer with the song, "The Heavens Proclaim the Glory of God." Allow a time of silence for all to view the icon of the Transfiguration. Proclaim the gospel.

2. Continue to pray in these or your own words:

God of glory and awe, you created all people out of love. You redeemed us by sending your Son Jesus, in whom both the law and the prophets found fulfillment. You sanctify us and remain constantly with us through your Spirit. Let the cloud of your presence continue to overshadow and lead us as it did when it led the Israelites through the desert. Let us never falter or lose hope, but trust that you shall come again in glory to bring your reign to fullness in the Risen Lord. Amen.

B. Weekday:

Lead the Liturgy of the Word outlined below.

- Song: Gathering Hymn from the feast day liturgy
- First Reading: Daniel 7:9-10, 13-14
- Psalm 97: Prayed with the same response found in the
- Dismissal Catechesis
- Second Reading: 2 Peter 1:16-19
- Alleluia sung
- Gospel: Luke 9:28b-29
- Close with the song "Gloria"

The Word (30 min)

1. Continue in the same prayerful mode with this centering meditation:

Invite the group to close their eyes, remain quiet, and gradually sink into the depths of their beings, where God dwells. Take time to allow each person to become aware of their breathing, their heart beat and move inward. Then begin this imaginative scene, reading slowly and allowing for the meditation to unfold.

You are part of the close-knit group that follows Jesus. Are you Peter . . . James . . . John? On a bright, warm day, Jesus beckons you to follow him. Your heart beats with excitement. You have been singled out from all the rest. Curious, you walk with him, climbing to the top of the highest mountain. Sweaty and hot, you rush to keep up with the Lord, who is ahead. When you and the others reach the top, you are tired and flushed. Just as you sit to listen to the Master, he is transfigured before your eyes. You are dazzled by the brightness of the light radiating from his whole being. In the bright light you also see Moses and Elijah, who appear to be talking with Jesus. Peter wants to set up the festival tents, but as he speaks a cloud wraps around you and the others. You are transfixed as you hear a voice declare, "This is my beloved Son, with whom I am well pleased, listen to him." Your mind is racing, you feel . . . ? You tumble to the ground, prostrate. You are awed and filled with . . . ? Then Jesus reassures you and you stand up to discover Jesus alone. You leave the mountain, returning to this room, and taking up your book begin to journal your experience.

2. Gently invite the participants to remain silent as they take up their Participant Book (page 146) or the blackline handout, turn to the corresponding section, and begin to write their experience and feelings precipitated by the meditation.

3. Continue by presenting the background to the readings for this feast day.

The intention of the Book of Daniel is to encourage the Jews to remain faithful to their faith and traditions amidst growing persecution from the Hellenistic culture. Today's passage is part of an apocalyptic vision in which the Son of Man, who represents the kingdom of the holy ones of God, comes down from heaven and is given dominion by the 'Ancient One' who represents God. An apocalyptic vision is a revelation about heaven or other hidden regions of the cosmos, not normally accessible to humans. In this first reading the Jewish community is consoled and sustained by the promise that the Son of Man will share future glory with God's holy ones. In the same vein the author of second Peter reassures the early Christian community that Christ will come again in glory. In the light of their confusion caused by false teachers, the community is encouraged by the eyewitness account of Jesus' glory at the transfiguration. In the gospel, the glory of God is seen in the transfigured form of Jesus on the mountain, as an encouragement to his apostles and us.

4. Invite the group to discuss their reaction to these passages, in small groups, with the following questions: *What about these readings do you find encouraging? What does it mean when we speak of God's glory? How do you imagine God's holy ones will share in God's glory?*

Catholic Teaching (30 min)

1. Continue to share with the large group the concepts found in the Catholic Teaching section of Understanding This Feast on visions and private revelations. Use the script provided to prepare your own prior to the session.

God is fully revealed to us in the life, ministry, teaching, death and resurrection of Jesus. We can come to understand God through the Scripture and Tradition of the Church as the primary means of revelation. In other words, everything that God chooses to communicate to us for our salvation has been done so in Jesus and no new 'public' revelation will be given before Christ comes a second time in glory. However, the content of that revelation, given in the person of Jesus, can be understood anew or be freshly interpreted in the context of the world.

Throughout the history of the church, Christian mystics have claimed private experiences which reveal the activity of God.

2. Invite the participants to share any stories from the Lives of the Saints or the Marian tradition which include private revelation or visions.

3. Take some time to present a few criteria for authenticating visions. These include: 1) The vision or private revelation may not contradict anything in Scripture or the Catholic

Tradition; 2) The message of the vision does not add to revelation, but enhances it; 3) It usually leads to some common good or builds up God's people, for example, the continued healing at Lourdes.

Putting Faith Into Practice

1. Tell the story of Hildegard of Bingen. This summary will be helpful. Further reading on Hildegard can be found in Gloria Durka's *Praying with Hildegard of Bingen* (St. Mary's Press) and *Hildegard of Bingen: Scivias, The Classics of Western Spirituality* (Paulist Press).

Hildegard had a deep spiritual awareness from her early childhood. A vision of a dazzling light came to her at the age of three and continued throughout her lifetime. But she only revealed them to Jutta, her childhood tutor, to whom her parents entrusted Hildegard from the age of eight. When she was forty-three, Hildegard received a prophetic call from God telling her to say and write what she saw and heard. Thus, today we have a record of her visions, poetry, music, and drawings in the book known as Scivias (Know the ways). Most of the figures who appeared in Hildegard's visions were images from the Hebrew Scriptures. Each vision was interpreted with help from a voice from heaven.

2. Invite the group to listen to this description of one of her visions:

"It happened that, in the eleven hundred and forty-first year of the Incarnation of the Son of God, Jesus Christ, when I was forty-two years and seven months old, Heaven was opened and a fiery light of exceeding brilliance came and permeated my whole breast, not like a burning but like a warming flame, as the sun warms anything its rays touch. And immediately I knew the meaning of the exposition of the Scriptures . . . I had sensed in myself wonderfully the power and mystery of secret and admirable visions from my childhood—that is, from the age of five—up to that time, as I do now. This, however, I showed to no one except a few religious persons who were living in the same manner as I." [*Hildegard of Bingen, Scivias,* tr. by Mother Columba Hart and Jane Bishop (Mahwah, NJ: Paulist Press, 1990), p. 59-60.]

3. Ask the participants to pause and reflect on this question: *When have you experienced God as a warm, revealing light?*

Prayer

While the group is quietly reflecting you may choose to play one of Hildegard's compositions, found on the popular cassette or CD, *Visions.* Close with this prayer excerpt from "Meditations with Hildegard of Bingen."

The soul is kissed by God
in its innermost regions.

With interior yearning,
grace and blessing
are bestowed.

It is a yearning to take on God's
gentle yoke,
it is a yearning to give one's self

Assumption

AUGUST 15

The Word In Liturgy

Revelation 11:19a; 12:1-6a, 10ab
Psalm 45:10, 11, 12, 16
1 Corinthians 15:20-27
Luke 1:39-56

The cult of the saints developed gradually in the early Christian centuries. The earliest expressions of devotion to the saints were directed towards martyrs who had shed their blood for the faith. Later, confessors, virgins and other ascetics gradually were included among those receiving special honor. The definition of the Council of Ephesus (431) that Mary is *Theotokos*, Mother of God, seems to have been a major impetus for the Church's Marian devotion. Today's feast grew up in Jerusalem in the fifth century and was originally called the Dormition (falling asleep) of the Virgin. The feast was universally observed by the end of the sixth century in the East and the seventh in the West, where it came to be called the Assumption. On November 1, 1950, Pius XII defined the Dogma of the Assumption as an article of Catholic belief.

The Book of Revelation was written to encourage the early Christian community during a time of persecution. Its exotic language and imagery were a deliberate attempt to hide from the uninitiated the full meaning of its teaching. The section read today starts with a vision of the ark of the covenant in heaven, and then shifts immediately to a woman "clothed with the sun." The ark, kept in the holy of holies of the Temple, had been lost when Jerusalem was destroyed in 587 B.C. As a symbol of God's abiding presence, it is replaced here by the woman, who gives birth to a child who is acclaimed God's "Anointed One." The imagery of a dragon attempting to snatch the child at its birth is borrowed from the Greek myth of Apollo, pursued by Python but rescued by Zeus. For the Roman authorities persecuting the Christian community, these visions are no more remarkable than their own myths of the gods. For the Christian reader, this was a coded tale of

God's ultimate triumph over the demonic forces at work in the world, especially the forces of the Roman state that were persecuting the Christian community. The woman in labor may be Israel, giving birth to the Messiah, or perhaps Mary, the Messiah's physical mother, or even Holy Mother Church, giving birth to offspring that form the Body of Christ. The responsorial psalm, originally composed for a royal wedding, becomes in the context of today's liturgy a song about the royal nuptials between Christ and his bride, the Church.

In Chapter 15 of Paul's first letter to the Corinthians, he addresses a number of questions that were being posed about the resurrection of the dead. He is concerned to teach clearly two crucial truths: First, Christ has risen from the dead. In the verses immediately preceding today's reading, he has shown the consequences of a denial of Christ's resurrection. Here, he states positively the truth that Christ lives and reigns now "until God has put all enemies under his feet." Second, Paul asserts that those who die in Christ will also share in his resurrection. He uses the image of first fruits to imply that others will follow Christ's lead. And, using the notion of inherited destiny found in traditional Jewish understandings of Adam, he draws a parallel between Adam and Christ, who will bring to life "all those who belong to him." The use of this text to celebrate today's feast is an obvious choice, given the Church's understanding of the Dogma of the Assumption as Mary's experience of being "more fully conformed to her Son . . . conqueror of . . . death" (*Munificentissimus Deus*, 43).

Scholars are in agreement that the infancy narratives in Luke's Gospel are profound theological reflections on the identity and mission of Jesus, not mere historical remembrances. The reading chosen for today's feast casts the spotlight on the great blessings enjoyed by Mary by virtue of the identity of her offspring. Hers is a reflected glory, but a glory nonetheless. The "greatness of the Lord" proclaimed in her being is the source of the extraordinary blessings she received—including her assumption, the subject of today's feast. The phrase, "[God] has . . . raised the lowly to high places" may be interpreted as a poetic description of the deep truth contained in the imagery of Mary's assumption body and soul into heaven. Ultimately, what we celebrate today in Mary is a proclamation of our faith in "God who is mighty [and who] has done great things."

Catholic Doctrine

The Assumption of Mary

This feast celebrates a long-held belief of the church, which was not officially defined however until recent times. In his apostolic constitution of 1950, Pius XII declared as an article of faith that: ". . . [T]he Immaculate Virgin, preserved free from all stain of original sin, when the course of her earthly life was finished, was taken up body and soul into heavenly glory, and exalted by the Lord as Queen over all things, so that she might be the more fully conformed to her Son, the Lord of lords and conqueror of sin and death." (*Munificentissimus Deus*, 1 November 1950 n. 43; AAS 42, 1950; DS 3903).

In the Western church we generally refer to this feast and the doctrine involved as "the assumption" of Mary. In common parlance, however, "to assume" means "to put on" or "to take upon oneself" or simply "to take for granted." As the Church uses it in describing this feast and this doctrine "assumption" means being "taken up" into heaven by God.

What is the meaning of this feast? We believe that Mary's assumption is a unique participation in Christ's resurrection (CCC 966). This doctrine declares that the resurrection we hope for Mary now enjoys completely. The Mother of God anticipates that which will be our destiny—she has been taken up fully into the life of God which awaits us all. In a sense, this teaching of the Church says that one of us has made it and is therefore a sign for us.

This doctrine is also related to our belief that at the end of Mary's earthly life she did not cease being an intercessor for us (CCC 969). The Second Vatican Council asserted, "This motherhood of Mary in the order of grace continues uninterruptedly from the consent which she loyally gave at the Annunciation and which she sustained without wavering beneath the cross, until the eternal fulfillment of all the elect. Taken up to heaven she did not lay aside this saving office but by her manifold intercession continues to bring us the gifts of eternal salvation. . . .Therefore the Blessed Virgin is invoked in the Church under the titles of Advocate, Helper, Benefactress, and Mediatrix." (LG, 62) And yet this role of intercessor and the doctrine of the assumption does not supercede in importance Christ, but flows from the Lord. Thus the verse and response that concludes the Litany of the Blessed Virgin Mary begs, "Pray for us, holy Mother of God/That we may become worthy of the promises of Christ.

The Preface for this Mass sums up our belief which we celebrate today, "Father. . . . Today the virgin Mother of God was taken up into heaven to be the beginning and the pattern of the Church in its perfection, and a sign of hope and comfort for your people on their pilgrim way. You would not allow decay to touch her body, for she had given birth to your Son, the Lord of all life, in the glory of the incarnation." (*Roman Missal*, Preface for the Assumption, p. 59)

Catholic Culture

A fresco dating from the ninth century found in the church of San Clemente, Rome, depicts the assumption. On the north side of the cathedral of Florence there is a door known as the Porta della Mandorla (Italian for "almond") due to the almond shaped oval framing or enclosing the *Virgin in Glory* above the prophets, a joint work by Antonio di Banco, his son Nanni, and Donatello (c. 1414). The mandorla is an artistic device frequently used to highlight a figure in heavenly splendor and glory.

Zermatt, Switzerland, high in the Alps and tucked in the shadow of the Matterhorn, annually holds a gigantic festival parade on the Feast of the Assumption that starts with Mass and ends about three hours later. All of the surrounding cantons are invited to send representative bands, floats, and performers. Zermatt does not allow any gas fueled conveyances within the town limits. The parade is particularly quaint and colorful and draws tourists worldwide on this day honoring Mary.

Notes

Dismissal Catechesis (30 min)

Getting Started

1. Prepare the space with a cloth, plant, an icon of Mary's dormition or a statue of Mary, lighted candle, and place for the lectionary on the center table. Gather in a circle of chairs.

2. Invite participants to imagine Mary and sense their feelings toward her and relationship with her. Sing a version of the Magnificat.

First Impressions

Today's feast of the Assumption celebrates that upon Mary's death she was assumed both body and soul into heaven. Have participants recall the gathering hymn, the various readings, homily and dismissal. Ask them to state something that speaks to them or catches their attention. Invite sharing in pairs. Then ask each pair to give input to the large group.

Making Connections

1. Ask participants to name what they know about Mary, about her life and death, and about the church's view of her. Invite large group sharing. With this input, pull together some of the basic facts about Mary's life as recorded in scripture. Then ask participants to name how they think of Mary, and who she is for them. Again invite a large group sharing. Be aware that, for some participants, relationship with Mary will be new or somewhat unfamiliar, and possibly uncomfortable. Invite some discussion about Mary and her role in the life of the church.

   Then ask participants to name what images of Mary they have seen portrayed in icons, statues, or paintings. Invite them to name images that appeal to them. Note the well-known image of Mary presented in Revelation 12:1 of a heavenly woman clothed with the sun, with the moon under her feet and a crown of twelve stars on her head.

2. Conclude by inviting participants to name something they want to remember from today's liturgy. Go around the circle for this discussion.

3. Provide copies of the prayer, the Hail Mary, for participants. Point out that the second part of the prayer, "Blessed are you among women, and blessed is the fruit of your womb," comes from today's gospel from Luke at the time of Mary's visitation to Elizabeth. Note that on this feast of Mary assumed into heaven, she who is with God is asked in this prayer to "pray for us at the hour of our death."

Prayer

Pray the Hail Mary aloud together.

Extended Catechesis

SESSION FOCUS:
Mary's Assumption: Sign of Hope for the Church.

Gathering

A. Sunday:

Welcome sponsors, spouses, fiancees, and team members. Ask them to form groups of four, with two sponsor/catechumen or sponsor/candidate pairs in a group. Additional people also form groups of four. Invite everyone into a moment of silence. Briefly share the content of the dismissal catechesis. Sing a version of the Magnificat. Proclaim the Gospel from the lectionary.

B. Weekday:

Prepare the space as suggested in the dismissal sessions. Ask each participant to name a time when they thought about Mary or prayed to Mary since Sunday. Then lead this Celebration of the Word or use your own design.

- Sing: a version of the Magnificat
- Sign of the Cross, Greeting
- Proclaim: Revelation 11:19a, 12:1-6a, 10ab
- Sing: Psalm 45
- Proclaim: 1 Corinthians 15: 20-27
- Sing: Alleluia
- Proclaim: Luke 1:39-56
- Silence

Conclude with the following words (from the introductory rite at Mass):

Let us rejoice in the Lord and celebrate this feast in honor of the Virgin Mary, at whose assumption the angels rejoice, giving praise to the Son of God. Let us pray the Hail Mary together. Hail Mary,. . . etc.

The Word (30 min)

1. State that this Gospel passage from Luke presents the well-known scene of Mary's visit to Elizabeth. Note especially Mary's statement which has come to be known as the "Magnificat." State that many of the words of the Magnificat are found earlier in scripture in Hannah's words in 1 Samuel 2:1-11. Ask participants to share in their small groups what this scene of the visitation and these words of the Magnificat tell them about what kind of a woman Mary was. Then invite some large group sharing.

2. Before proclaiming the Gospel again, ask participants to listen for a word of phrase that stands out to them. After proclaiming the Gospel, invite participants to go around the room and simply call out the word or phrase, forming a sort of litany of verses. Then ask participants what they hear God speaking to them through these words. Allow time for some small group sharing. Then elicit some responses in the large group.

3. Recall for the participants the Revelation reading that pictures a sign of Mary, clothed with the sun. Note that the visitation portrays a young Mary pregnant with Jesus and already faithful to God. Point out that the Corinthians reading talks about all who die being raised with Christ. Ask the participants to name what they hear in joining these readings together for the celebration of Mary's being assumed body and soul into heaven. Invite large group sharing.

4. Given the various images of Mary from today's scripture and today's feast of the Assumption, ask participants to name an image of Mary they want to carry with them. Ask this in the large group.

Catholic Teaching (30 min)

1. Ask participants to name their understanding of who Mary is for the church. With their sharing, interweave some of the historical content of this feast. Recall that, on the cross, Jesus said to Mary, "Behold your son," and to John, "Behold your mother." The church sees in this exchange a relationship established between Mary and the church. Note that scholars believe that Mary went with John to Ephesus and lived her final years there. Point out that Mary's death is often referred to as her "dormition," that is, her falling asleep—a once familiar way of referring to death. Note the existence of icons of Mary's dormition.

2. State that as the church struggled to identify Mary's role, the tradition of Mary's assumption body and soul into heaven existed from early in the church's history. Note that the liturgical remembrance of this feast on August 15 has been celebrated since the thirteenth century. Point out that the Assumption of Mary was officially promulgated as a dogma of the church by Pius XII on November 1, 1950.

3. For the church this feast is both a statement of Mary's honored status at God's side and a promise of what is to come for all of God's faithful people. Note that the church sees this assumption of Mary's body as well as her soul into heaven as a special honor given to God's mother. Note that from this privileged place Mary is seen as one who is able to intercede for the church, her children. Ask participants to talk about how they view prayer to Mary. Talk about Mary's role as intercessor and mediatrix.

Ask participants to state ways this feast gives hope for our future with God. Elicit various statements from the participants of this hope for living daily a faith-filled life, for living in union with Christ who has conquered all sin and death, for being fully united with God after death. Invite participants to imagine all of God's people one day joined together with God and Mary.

Putting Faith Into Practice

Ask participants to name something they are able to do this week to live life more fully in union with God. Ask them to share this and their commitment to this action in their small groups.

Prayer

Pray the prayer from the sacramentary:

Let us pray. Father in heaven, all creation rightly gives you praise, for all life and all holiness come from you. In the plan of your wisdom she who bore the Christ in her womb was raised body and soul in glory to be with him in heaven. May we follow her example in reflecting your holiness and join in her hymn of endless life and praise. We ask this through Christ our Lord. Amen.

Sing "Hail Mary: Gentle Woman" (Landry).

The Exaltation of the Cross

SEPTEMBER 14

Understanding this Feast:
Background for Catechesis

The Word In Liturgy

Numbers 21:4b-9
Psalm 78:1-2, 34-35, 36-37, 38
Philippians 2:6-11
John 3:13-17

Two historical events in Jerusalem stand in the background of this feast. The first is the dedication of the basilica of the Holy Sepulchre in the fifth century (on September 14). The second is the recovery of the true cross from the Persians in the seventh century. The readings of the day do not dwell on the sufferings of Christ, as one might expect, but, rather, celebrate the cross as a focus of healing and redemption.

The first reading presents a wonder worked by God through the prophet Moses to save the Israelites from illness caused by a plague of serpents. Because their bite caused inflammation, the serpents who attacked the Israelites were called "sarap," which means "fiery." Set in a moral context—the people repent of their sin of complaining bitterly (in Hebrew, the expression is: their spirits "loath" God and Moses)—the miraculous cure through the bronze serpent is shown to be a work of divine mercy. It is God who punishes and God who cures.

The psalm which follows is a historical psalm written in a hymn style. Most of the psalm that is included in today's liturgy pertains to the infidelity of Israel during the forty-year wandering in the wilderness, thus accentuating the background of sin and rebellion that provides the context for our redemption through the cross.

The early Christian hymn proclaimed in today's second reading from Paul's letter to the Philippians contains a beautiful and profound theology of the incarnation, centering on the cross. The *"kenosis,"* or self-emptying of

Jesus, is a voluntary and intentional renunciation of divine power and majesty for the sake of identification with human beings. The hymn is perfectly balanced between the downward movement leading to Jesus' death on a cross, and the upward movement of his glorification by God and the whole cosmos. The hymn's context in the letter makes it clear that the self-emptying of Christ, which leads to the cross—and through the cross to glory—is the paradigm of the Christian life.

Although contemporary Christians tend to refer to the cross and resurrection as separate events, the early church did not maintain such a rigid distinction, but viewed them as a single mystery to be proclaimed and lived. When today's gospel refers to Jesus being "lifted up," this same rich ambiguity is evident. Jesus is lifted up in his crucifixion. He is also lifted up in the resurrection and ascension which completes the process of his glorification. The monologue of Jesus, of which today's reading is a part, begins with a question from Nicodemus concerning Jesus' *ascension*.

To illustrate God's saving work in Jesus, John makes reference to the incident in Numbers that was the subject of the first reading. Just as looking upon the serpent brought healing to the Israelites, so looking upon Jesus will bring salvation to all who see him "lifted up." The passage closes with an affirmation of the overpowering love of God that grounds the whole mystery of Christ's self-giving, and leads to the human person to faith.

Catholic Doctrine

The Atonement (Sacrifice of the Cross)

The atonement represents our Catholic understanding that the suffering and death of Jesus achieves the forgiveness of sin and expiates our human guilt, thus reconciling us to God. Jesus' violent death was not an accident of history or some coincidence of fate, but was part of God's plan to save us (CCC 599). Because the crucifixion occurred at the time of the Jewish Passover, early Christians recognized Christ as the Paschal Lamb sacrificed on our behalf (1 Cor 5:7). In addition, relating Jesus' death to another Jewish feast, the Day of Atonement, they saw in the Christ the high priest and victim whose singular self-sacrifice ultimately expiated sins and restored humanity to a right relationship with the divine (Heb 4:14-10:39).

It must be emphasized, however, that atonement, in our Catholic viewpoint, did not take place because God is a vengeful or bloodthirsty divinity who delights in suffering and death. It is not as if an angry God needed to invest Jesus with all the sins of humanity in order to be appeased or propitiated by the blood shed upon the cross. To the contrary, Jesus freely takes up his cross, filled with divine love, utterly faithful to the course of his entire mission which is one of "good news:" God loves us, forgives us, and calls us back to himself. The cross, death and resurrection of Jesus thus fulfill his mission.

St. Athanasius (d. 373), in his treatise *De Incarnatione Verbi*, asserted that through human weakness sin entered the world, but through the divine initiative of incarnation and self-sacrifice we were recreated. This theme is expanded upon by Anselm of Canterbury (d. 1109) in *Cur Deu Homo*, the teaching of the Council of Trent (1545-63) and in the work of St. Thomas Aquinas (d. 1274). This body of Catholic theology all nuances the same theme, which is that Christ freely accepted suffering in this world not because of an angry God but out of a love which then purified and repaired a moral order defiled by sin.

Thus, the Church prays ". . . Lord God. . . . When his hour had come to return to you in glory, the Lord Jesus, our King, our Priest, and our Teacher, freely mounted the scaffold of the cross and made it his royal throne, his altar of sacrifice, his pulpit of truth. On the cross, lifted above the earth, he triumphed over our age-old enemy. Cloaked in his own blood, he drew all things to himself. On the cross, he opened out his arms and offered you his life: the sacrifice of the New Law that gives to the sacraments their saving power. . . . May our sins be nailed to his cross, the power of life released, pride conquered, and weakness turned to strength. May the cross be our comfort in trouble, our refuge in the face of danger, our safeguard on life's journey, until you welcome us to our heavenly home." (BB, Order for the Blessing of a New Cross for Public Veneration, 1250)

St. Rose of Lima (1586-1617) wrote, "Apart from the cross there is no ladder by which we may get to heaven." (St. Rose of Lima, cf. P. Hansen, *Vita Mirabilis*, Louvain, 1668)

Catholic Culture

Christian art and iconography depicts the cross in various forms, from the Greek tau (shaped like the letter T), and the St. Andrew's cross shaped like an X, shapes ornamented in different styles including the Maltese cross, the Crusader's cross, the Celtic cross or the ancient Chi/Rho cross.

The practice of signing oneself with the cross is mentioned as far back as Tertullian (c. 160).

Helena, the mother of Constantine, is reputed to have discovered the true cross of Christ in about 326. Relics of the true cross were then distributed throughout Christendom. Gentile Bellini's painting on canvas depicts a *Procession of the Relic of the True Cross* (1496) a gigantic and detailed panorama set in the Piazza San Marco for the Scuola di San Giovanni Evangelista of Venice. The *scuole* of Venice were confraternities dedicated to good works and the pride of this particular confraternity was possession of a relic of the true cross. (Hartt, *History of Italian Renaissance Art*, 395-6)

G.K. Chesterton writes, "As we have taken the circle as the symbol of reason and madness, we may very well take the cross as the symbol at once of mystery and health. . . . For the circle is perfect and infinite in its nature; but it is fixed forever in its size; it can never be larger or smaller. But the cross, though it has at its heart a collision and a contradiction, can extend its four arms forever without altering its shape. Because it has a paradox at its centre it can grow without changing. The circle returns upon itself and is bound. The cross opens its arms to the four winds; it is a signpost for free travelers." (G.K. Chesterton, *Orthodoxy*, Image Books, Garden City, NY, p 28-9).

The practice of venerating the cross on Good Friday originated with venerating relics of the true cross. That is why we Catholics venerate the wood of the cross, rather than the corpus. This is also why Stations of the Cross must at least partially be made of wood.

Some Christians in the Philippines voluntarily undergo crucifixion for a short time as a penitential practice.

Patristic texts contrast the "tree of life," the cross, to the tree in the garden of Eden. The tree in Eden, which was the means of the first human sin, through which death came into the world, is the tree of death. The cross is the tree of life.

Dismissal Catechesis (30 min)

Getting Started

1. Prepare the space with a large cross in the center, perhaps with a green plant at its base. Place a red cloth and a lighted candle on the center table with a place for the lectionary.

2. Invite all to simply gaze at the cross in silence for a moment. Then invite all to slowly and deliberately trace the cross on their whole body, head to toe, shoulder to shoulder.

First Impressions

1. State that today's feast, the Triumph of the Cross, is always on September 14 and replaces the Ordinary Time Sunday because of its significance for our Christian faith.

2. Recall for the participants a few images from the hymn and readings. Ask them to share in pairs what stood out for them at the liturgy.

3. Have them come back together in a large group and share their responses. Call on each pair to encourage sharing. Comment that the color red used for this feast symbolizes the blood of Christ. Red is also used for the feast of martyrs, who in imitation of Christ, shed their blood.

Making Connections

1. If they have not mentioned it, ask participants to recall the Rite of Acceptance into the Order of Catechumens/Welcoming, and the signations with the Cross. Ask them to talk about what the cross has meant to them since this rite. Have them share this in pairs, then in the large group. Facilitate the conversation and summarize what is said.

2. Invite participants to discuss how God spoke to them personally about the cross at today's liturgy. Ask them to share this first in pairs, then in the large group.

3. Move this awareness to prayer by asking each participant to name in a phrase or sentence what they need to embrace the cross in their lives. Go around the circle for this discussion.

Prayer

Invite participants to hold their hands open before them. Pray:

Loving and gracious God, through Christ you teach us that the cross is not only a means of suffering, but also a cross of triumph. We place the crosses be bear in your hands. Through bearing our crosses with Christ, may we one day share in his glorious resurrection. We ask this through Christ, our Lord. Amen.

Extended Catechesis

SESSION FOCUS: *Christ saved us through the cross.*

Gathering

A. Sunday:

Welcome sponsors, spouses, fiancees, and team members. Have them sit in groups of four with two sponsor/catechumen or sponsor/candidate pairs in a group. Additional people also form groups of four. Invite all into a moment of silence. Summarize the sharing from the dismissal catechesis. Sing: "Lift High the Cross." Proclaim the Gospel from the lectionary.

B. Weekday:

Prepare the environment as in the dismissal catechesis. Ask each person to name a situation where they have noticed the cross since last Sunday. Then lead this Celebration of the Word or use your own design.

- Sing: Lift High the Cross, vs. 1-3
- Invite people to slowly trace the sign of the cross on their body.
- Greeting
- Proclaim: Numbers 21:4b-9
- Sing: Psalm 78
- Proclaim: Philippians 2:6-11
- Sing: Alleluia
- Proclaim: John 3:13-17
- Silence
- Sing: Lift High the Cross, vs. 4-5

The Word (30 min)

1. State that the serpent is often used symbolically as both a symbol of evil, and of healing. Call to mind for the participants that the caduceus, the symbol of modern medicine, is that of a serpent entwining a staff. Note that in the Numbers reading the serpent mortally wounds people, and God saves people who look at the image of the serpent.

2. Note that the Gospel passage from John connects the lifting up of the serpent with the lifting up of Christ. State that in contrast to the serpent who is not the one who heals, it is Jesus who saves us. Ask participants to talk in their small groups about ways they have been lifted up, ways they have found life through the cross. After this sharing, invite some response in the large group.

3. Note that the writers of John's gospel are concerned that people come to belief in Jesus. State that the hope of people coming to believe is stated in several of the encounters Jesus has with people, as well as at the end of the passion

narrative and at the first ending of the Gospel in Chapter 20. Proclaim the Gospel again. Ask participants to talk about, given the context of Jesus being lifted up as the serpent in the desert, what is meant by believing in Jesus. Give some time for small group sharing. Then invite responses in the large group. Elicit an awareness that believing in Jesus, more than an intellectual or even personal relationship, includes dying and rising with Christ through life's experiences. State that the scripture points out that we are able to comprehend this great mystery in the light of God's love.

4. Ask participants to name in their small group what cross they are embracing at this time that they believe through, with, and in Christ will lead to fuller life. After about five minutes, invite participants to pray for and with one another in whatever way their group chooses. Allow a few minutes for this prayer.

Catholic Teaching (30 min)

1. State that the feast of the triumph of the cross celebrates the profound mystery of Christ's bringing about new life for all people through the cross. Note that this feast highlights Christ's mission as savior of all people. Note that the saving mission of Christ is understood in various ways. Ask participants to brainstorm all the ways they sense Christ is savior. Have them do this in small groups, with someone recording responses. Then as the responses are shared in the large group put the responses on paper.

2. Recall for the participants Jesus' statement of his understanding of his mission in Luke 4:18-19 of being a liberator, of bringing good news, of giving sight, of freeing the oppressed, and of proclaiming a year of favor. Add these to the newsprint if they have not been named. Include Christ's ministry of forgiving and healing, if not already mentioned.

3. Then state that "Savior" is a title with a theological meaning. Ask participants to name other titles the church has given to Jesus. Elicit from them the titles of redeemer, liberator, anointed one, messiah, etc. Begin talking about an understanding of Christ the redeemer as one who "atones" for sins. Point out that as noted in scripture the early church came to an understanding that Christ died for people's sin, the sin of the world. Recall for the participants some of the images of the suffering servant described by Isaiah, especially in Chapter 53. State that this scripture describing the innocent lamb who was slaughtered for human offenses provided a transition to understanding Christ as atoning for the sin of all. Note the well-known statement in Isaiah 53:5: "by his wounds we are healed."

4. Write the word "atonement" on the paper. Separate the word, drawing a line after the first "t," and after the first "e." Note the words formed, "at-one-ment" is what the root of the word "atonement" means. "Atonement" means at

one, making one, uniting, reconciling. The church often names and prays to Christ as one who has reconciled the world to himself. State the words of the "Lamb of God" litany from the Mass as an example of how this understanding is part of the church's liturgy.

5. Note that the mystery of the cross as the way to new life is core to the Catholic way of life. Point out that the church continues to share in Christ's freedom from sin and death in the cross. Invite participants to give examples of how the church (of which they are a part) find true life through the cross.

Putting Faith Into Practice

Ask participants to name a way they are invited and will commit themselves to share in the mystery of the cross with Christ this week. Have them share this in the small groups.

Prayer

Invite all to come forward in silence and touch the cross. Proclaim Philippians 2:6-11. Celebrate Minor Exorcism G as indicated in the ritual text, RCIA #94. Sing: Lift High the Cross.

All Saints

NOVEMBER 1

The Word In Liturgy

Revelation 7:2-4, 9-14
Psalm 24:1-2, 3-4, 5-6
1 John 3:1-3
Matthew 5:1-12a

The remote origins of this feast are found in the honor that early Christians paid to the martyrs, remembering them on the anniversary of their death, often at the very place of their martyrdom. After the age of persecution had ended, other holy individuals were gradually added to the list of those commemorated annually. In the fourth century, saints were named in the Eucharistic Prayer. By the fifth century, a feast of All Saints was celebrated in certain churches of the Christian East. When Pope Boniface (d. 615) transformed the Roman pantheon into a Christian church on May 13, 610, he designated that day as a feast of all saints. It was under Gregory IV (d. 844) that the feast was moved to November 1, and thenceforth the observance spread throughout the West.

Today's reading from the Book of Revelation contains excerpts from two visions, each portraying in vivid imagery the salvation of the just. In the first, an angel comes from the east (the place from which the messiah was expected to come) "holding the seal of the living God." In the ancient world, a sovereign's seal was a sign both of ownership and of protection. Thus, the angel's placing of the seal on the forehead of God's servants affords them protection in the time of trial. The number 144,000 is symbolic of a vast, all-inclusive throng (the perfect number twelve squared, times one thousand). In the second vision, the survivors of the time of trial (i.e., the Roman persecutions under Domitian, 81-96) are revealed in glory, an obvious appeal to those still undergoing persecution to persevere. Their white robes are reminiscent of their baptismal garments as well as symbolic of the "washing" they have undergone in the blood of the Lamb, both references are expressive of the saving action of Christ on behalf of his faithful followers.

Scholars have helped us understand the internal struggles within the Johannine community that prompted the writing of this letter. Apparently, a split had developed to the point of some members leaving the community (see 1 John 2:19). The author warns his followers against the errors of those who have left, and reiterates key points of his own teaching. He insists here that the transformation of the believers under the power of Christ's grace is real ("children of God . . . is what we are"). But that transformation is a progressive, ongoing reality, not something that happened once and for all, freeing a person to disregard all further ethical concerns ("what we shall later be has not yet come to light"). The letter offers a classic description of what it means to be a saint, what true holiness consists in: " . . . we shall be like him [Christ]."

Matthew uses various subtle cues to underline the tremendous importance of Jesus' teaching contained in the Beatitudes. Like Moses, he ascends a mountain to proclaim the law of the (new) covenant. Unlike Moses, he speaks words on his own authority. What he says describes not only who is a member of God's Kingdom; he also prescribes how those who wish to belong in that Kingdom must act. The nature of Christian holiness is summed up in these idealistic yet demanding pronouncements of who is "blessed" in God's Kingdom. The suffering and persecution of the "little ones" are recognized as a source of holiness; so, too, is action aimed at transforming the world to make it conform to the Kingdom which Jesus announced.

Catholic Doctrine

The Communion of Saints

All Christians who follow in the way of Jesus are called to a life of holiness and witness on behalf of the kingdom of God. The Second Vatican Council stated, "It is therefore quite clear that all Christians in any state or walk of life are called to the fullness of Christian life and to the perfection of love, and by this holiness a more human manner of life is fostered also in earthly society." (LG, 40) Using the strength which Christ provides, we who confess his name are given the grace to follow in his footsteps and conform ourselves more closely to the image of Jesus. Thus, we are able to devote ourselves wholeheartedly to the glory of God and serve our neighbor. The holiness which is fostered among the People of God by the grace of Christ will grow in fruitful abundance "as is clearly shown in the history of the Church through the life of so many saints." (LG, 40)

The title of saint (from Latin *sanctus* for "holy') was initially attributed to certain individuals by popular devotion, but since about the 10th century there has been a formal papal procedure for bestowing this honor. Prior to the development of the formal procedure, in about the third century, the holy men and women understood as saints were considered as intercessors before God. Tertullian, Origen and Cyprian supported this view in their writings and preaching. (W. Beinert & F.S. Fiorenza, *Handbook of Catholic Theology*, p. 637)

Contemporary Catholic teaching asserts that we assimilate the teachings of Christ from the Word of God and obtain grace from the celebration of the sacraments, and in communion with the whole Church, the Christian vocation is fulfilled. It is from the Church that one learns the example of holiness and recognizes its model in the Virgin Mary, the Mother of God and discovers it in the spiritual tradition and long history of the saints.

One of the credal affirmations is belief in the "communion of saints." What is meant by this phrase? The Catechism asserts quite simply and clearly that the communion of saints is the Church. The Church forms one body, with Christ as its head, who shares his riches with all the members through the sacraments. Those riches, governed by one and the same Spirit throughout all the members, are considered as one common fund (CCC 947). The term *communis in sacris*, therefore, indicates both a sharing in holy things (the riches of Christ) and a sharing among a holy people (we who are claimed for God in Christ).

Thus, in the New Testament, "the saints" refers to the whole body of believers, the Church. But, in terms of the formal, ecclesial procedure for the recognition of saints (canonization), the term refers to those men and women who throughout our Christian history who have been outstanding in holiness, sometimes heroic in their efforts to witness to the kingdom of God.

In Catholic teaching the saints are variously described as our companions in prayer, as patrons for those individuals who take their names or who are in certain walks of life, and as intercessors for us before the throne of God (although Christ is the One mediator between God and humanity). Because of this, Catholics hold that to God alone is due our worship (Latin, *latria*), and that the saints deserve veneration (Latin, *dulia*), which is different. The Second Vatican Council teaches, "The Church has always believed that the apostles and Christ's martyrs, who gave the supreme witness of faith and charity by the shedding of their blood, are closely united with us in Christ; she has always venerated them, together with the Blessed Virgin Mary and the holy angels, with a special love, and has piously for the help of their intercession. Soon there were added to these others who had chosen to imitate more closely the virginity and poverty of Christ, and still others whom the outstanding practice of the Christian virtues and the wonderful graces of God recommended to the pious devotion and imitation of the faithful." (LG, 50)

Catholic Culture

The Litany of Saints is prayed in Masses where churches are dedicated, at Ordinations, at Confirmations, at the Easter Vigil, at Baptisms and as one form of the commendation of the dying.

Catholic churches are often filled with images of the Virgin Mary and of the saints, in paintings, mosaics, stained glass, murals, and statues. The type of medium is restricted only by the genius of the artists and materials involved. The purpose of these representations is not to compete with our worship of God but to inspire us with the example of these holy men and women who have gone before us and who are yet part of the communion of all saints of the household of God.

An ancient Martyrology dates to the sixth century, the "Hieronymian" (attributed to St. Jerome, in error). Pope Gregory XIII promulgated the Roman Martyrology in 1584. The last "typical" or official edition was published in 1919 and later revised in 1921. Since the seventeenth century a group of Jesuits located in Brussels, the "Bollandists" (the first was Jean Bolland, 1596-1665), have dedicated themselves to critically studying documents related to the lives of the saints. They publish the Acta Sanctorum or the "Acts of the Saints." (*Days of the Lord*, v 7, The Liturgical Press, Collegeville, MN, 1994, p. 376, footnote 3).

Notes

Dismissal Catechesis (30 min)

Getting Started

1. Prepare the space ahead of time with a circle of chairs and various statues and art works depicting a variety of saints around the room. Place a statue or icon of Mary and a candle on a table with a white cloth in the middle of the circle. You will also need printed copies of Psalm 24, indicating the antiphonal order—right and left—which you will use for the opening prayer.

2. Greet and welcome the candidates and catechumens as they enter the space. Invite them to look at the various statues and art works before they are seated in the circle.

3. Begin the prayer by singing the Gathering Hymn used at today's liturgy. Ask all to pray Psalm 24, indicating the right and left sides of the room.

First Impressions

1. Invite the participants to share their experience of today's liturgy in the large group asking: *What did you notice today? What did we celebrate?* Explain the concept of Holy Days if this is the first time you are gathering on this type of church feast.

2. Name the following images to help the group recall the Scriptures. Invite the participants to close their eyes as you read the list slowly and prayerfully.

   "put the seal on the foreheads of the servants of our God"
   "wearing white robes and holding palm branches"
   "white in the blood of the Lamb"
   "called the children of God"
   "he went up the mountain"
   "blessed are . . ."
   "theirs is the kingdom of heaven"

3. Gather the participants into small groups and ask them to discuss the following: *What about these passages did you find inspiring? What image is empowering for you? Why?*

Making Connections

1. When they have finished, turn their attention back to the large group and ask: *From these readings, how would you describe 'holiness?'* Prepare ahead of time a poster with the word HOLINESS in the center with radiating lines from the word. On these lines write those qualities of holiness named by the participants.

2. Continue the discussion in small groups, using these questions: *What are the challenges to holiness presented in these Scriptures? From these passages, how is holiness possible?*

3. Ask the small groups to share one thing they discussed. Summarize their comments to close the session.

Prayer

1. Prepare for prayer with a moment of quiet. Invite all to join in singing, "Come to the Water" (Weston Priory). Be sure to have songbooks available. Continue to pray in these or similar words:

   Holy God, we praise you today for setting before us the witness of so many who have gone before us in faith: all the martyrs, virgins, widows, teachers and holy men and women known for their actions on behalf of your kingdom. We join with them as they cry out, "Salvation comes from our God, who is seated on the throne, and from the Lamb." (Rev. 7:19) *"Amen, Blessing and glory, wisdom and thanksgiving, honor, power and might be to our God forever and ever. Amen."* (Rev. 7:12)

2. Close by singing together, "Holy, Holy, Holy."

Extended Catechesis

SESSION FOCUS: *Communion of Saints*

Gathering

A. Sunday:

1. Extend a welcome to the sponsors and other participants as they join the circle. Invite them to look around at the statues and art pieces of the various saints.

2. When all have joined the circle, begin the prayer by inviting all to sing, "Blest are They" (David Haas). You will need to have songbooks available at this session. Continue the prayer with the proclamation of the Gospel, Matthew 5:1-12a and close with the following Prayer for Holiness:

   Let us cry out with the assembly of white robed saints as we respond:

   "Salvation comes from our God, who is seated on the throne, and from the Lamb"
   Wash us in the blood of the Lamb . . . Response
   Clothe us in your white garment of grace . . .
   Response
   Protect us with the seal of you Kingship . . . Response
   Call us your children, for that is what we are . . .
   Response
   Purify our hearts and comfort our mourning . . .
   Response
   Fill our hungering, thirsting and longing . . .
   Response
   Bless us when we suffer for the sake of your kingdom . . . Response

B. Weekday:

1. As the participants assemble, encourage them to join the circle with warm greetings of welcome. Prepare the space in the manner described for the Dismissal catechesis.

2. Invite all to consider the following question and then respond in the large group: *What glimmers of holiness did you observe this past week?*

- Lead this celebration of the Word
- Song: "Blest are They" (Haas)
- First reading: Revelation 7:2-4, 9-14
- Psalm 24:1-2, 3-4, 5-6
- Second Reading: 1 John 3:1-3
- Direct the group to pause in silence and consider what it to be a child of God.
- Gospel: Matthew 5:1-12a
- Prayer for Holiness (as above)

The Word (30 min)

1. Ask the participants to respond to these questions, after having looked at the various art works depicting the lives of the saints: *How would you describe a saint? What saints are particularly important for you? Why?* Note for the group that St. Paul referred to all the baptized as 'saints.'

2. Present this background to the scriptures to the whole group:

Today's feast celebrates our present process of conversion as we aspire toward holiness and the future realization of our sainthood. The first reading from the Book of Revelation presents two visions that describe symbolically our progress toward sanctity. First, we are all sealed on the forehead; that is, we are under God's protection. We belong to God as the second reading from 1 John 3:1-3 so emphatically states. We are truly God's own children. In the second vision those who persevered through trials and persecution are revealed in the glory of white robes, washed in the blood of the Lamb. These saints embody the inner attitude and moral behavior that we are challenged to live in the present time. They have entered into glory because of their conversion to Christ and their actions on behalf of the kingdom.

Actions on behalf of the kingdom are described in Jesus' proclamation of the beatitudes on the mountain. The heart of today's gospel, from Matthew 5:1-12a, is the beatitudes, which offer all believers the attitudes that are normative guides for holiness. The first four beatitudes inform us of the spiritual posture or inner attitude we are to acquire. That is, they describe the openness and simplicity of the anawim—the little ones of the scriptures. The last four beatitudes hold up the moral actions for justice that need to be enacted by all who would build God's kingdom in union with all the saints.

3. Ask the participants to turn to the Participant Book (page 146) or to the blackline handout, and reflect on the Beatitudes and respond to the questions. When they have finished, gather them into small groups to share their insights into the questions.

Catholic Teaching (30 min)

1. Listen to some of the responses from the small group discussion, particularly the last question in the Participant Book (page 146) or the blackline handout, *What makes this impossible challenge a lived reality for us?* If they have trouble with this question mention: *Christ's saving action,*

the witness of the saints and God's protection as possibilities.

2. Offer the following points in a short teaching on the communion of saints.

- All Christians are called to a life of holiness, that is, to conform ourselves to the image of Christ.
- Saints (the word is derived from the Latin word for holy) are considered to be intercessors before God. They are not worshipped but venerated for the model of holiness that they offer to those of us still on earth.
- The Virgin Mary is venerated, with all the saints, for her witness of holiness and her constant 'fiat,' that is her 'yes' to God's will in seemingly impossible circumstances.
- The Communion of Saints celebrates the one body of the church, with Christ as its head. Those who have gone before us, those still on earth and those yet to come all share in the holiness of Christ as a holy people, sealed in the blood of the Lamb.

3. Invite the participants to listen to the personal story below, or one of your own, that may enhance their understanding of the church's doctrine of the Communion of Saints.

The following is a true story of one person's experience of coming to believe more deeply in the church's doctrine of the Communion of Saints. There are many such stories. Listen:

"As my mother-in-law flitted in and out of a coma, dying of cancer, friends and family visited her bedside. Hour by hour they came to pray, sing and hold her limp hands. I observed this phenomena over the course of four days and nights. The vigil at her bed still remains etched in my heart. There, I became acutely aware of the union we all share in the Body of Christ. I felt all her dead loved ones were meeting her to offer welcome into the kingdom. The presence of the Virgin Mary was almost palpable. The saints prayed with all those who gathered to open the gateway for a peaceful crossing over into new life. This beautiful experience of dying has convinced me of the depths of the union among the living and the dead—the Communion of Saints."

Putting Faith Into Practice

1. Invite the participants to gather in sponsor/catechumen, and sponsor/candidate pairs to share their own stories, by instructing them to describe their own experience of the Communion of Saints. When they have finished sharing ask, *What has this meant in your life as you struggle to grow in holiness?*

2. Invite two or three team members to describe the 'beatitudes' as present or modeled in the life of one of their favorite saints. Encourage all to learn more about these holy ones, suggesting several books they might wish to become familiar with, such as *Butler's Lives of the Saints.*

Prayer

Close with the Litany of the Saints, found in the Rite of Christian Initiation for Adults, #221, in the Easter Vigil Liturgy.

All Souls

**Understanding this Feast:
Background for Catechesis**

The Word In Liturgy

See Lectionary, n. 789-793

Readings for the feast of All Souls may be taken from any of the Masses for the dead. The choices can be found in the Lectionary, from n. 789-793. In view of the great number of possible readings (52 in all), we will not supply a scripture commentary here. Nevertheless, the scripture readings chosen for and proclaimed in your liturgy remain the foundation for catechesis. The catechist should reflect on the readings with the help of a bible commentary, and invite the catechumens and candidates into prayerful reflection on the readings in a way similar to the method that has been used on other Sundays: first in the Dismissal Catechesis, and then in the Word section of the Extended Catechesis.

What follows is an essay on an appropriate doctrinal focus for this feast of All Souls: the church's teaching concerning purgatory. The catechetical session gives a general outline of the catechesis based on the Sunday readings, and further attention to catechizing upon the church teaching that is described here.

Catholic Doctrine

Purgatory

In our Catholic understanding, purgatory is a state of purification between death and heaven whereby the remaining obstacles to the full enjoyment of one's personal and eternal union with God are removed. For those justified and reconciled in Christ, this purification completes the process of sanctification such that one can enter into union with the triune God (CCC 1030).

The obstacles which are removed are venial sins not repented at the time of death and any remaining effects or consequences to one's person of repented and forgiven mortal or deadly sins committed during one's earthly life. In our Catholic understanding, purgatory is not an opportunity to reverse the course of one's earthly life. Conversion is not possible in purgatory if conversion did not take place in life before death. Since an individual judgment follows immediately upon death, purgatory is that interval after death that erases conditions preventing persons from enjoying full fellowship with God.

It is important to note that while Scripture refers to a cleansing fire (1 Cor 3:15; 1 Pt 1:7) and burning flames figure in some artistic depictions of purgatory, the operative notion in Catholic doctrine and theology on purgatory is that it is a state of purification not punishment (CCC 1031). This state may even last only an instant, as we count time. What the doctrine upholds is that purgatory is a transitional state which makes one ready for the experience of the beatific vision.

It is also important to note that the doctrine of purgatory upholds an unbroken liturgical practice in our Church to making intercessory prayers for the dead (CCC 1032). The Councils of Florence (1439), and Trent (1563) refer to this venerable practice which dates from the earliest times of the Church. And the Second Vatican Council observes, "In full consciousness of this communion of the whole Mystical Body of Jesus Christ, the Church in its pilgrim members, from the very earliest days of the Christian religion, has honored with great respect the memory of the dead; and, 'because it is a holy and a wholesome thought to pray for the dead that they may be loosed from their sins' (2 Mac 12:46) she offers her suffrages for them." (LG, 50).

Thus, in the Eucharistic Prayer we pray for the dead, a practice originating in the third century. "Remember, Lord, those who have died and have gone before us marked with the sign of faith, especially those for whom we now pray. . ." and at this point in Eucharistic Prayer I names of the deceased may be inserted into the prayer. (*Roman Missal*, EP I) The instruction for a blessing of a cemetery quotes Eucharistic Prayer IV, saying that "Christians therefore offer prayers to the heavenly Father for all and when they pray to him they include all, both those 'who have died in the peace of Christ and all the dead whose faith is known to God alone.'" (*Book of Blessings*, *Order for the Blessing of a Cemetery*, n. 1418) Indeed, there is also the generally accepted practice of offering Mass for the deceased in the firm conviction that, as part of the communion of saints, we may "assist" them by our prayers. (Order of Christian Funerals, Rite of Committal, n. 216)

St. Catherine of Genoa (1347-80) meditates, "There is no joy save that in paradise to be compared to the joy of the souls in purgatory. This joy increases day by day because of the way in which the love of God corresponds to the love of the soul, since the impediment to that love is worn away daily. This impediment is the rust of sin. As it is consumed, the soul is more and more open to God's love." (from *Catherine of Genoa: Purgation and Purgatory, the Spiritual Dialogue*, trs. Serge Hughes, Paulist Press, New York, 1979, p. 72)

Catholic Culture

The idea that the prayers of the living could assist the dead gave rise to Chantry chapels where Masses were said for the repose of the souls of deceased family members or members of corporations and guilds. Henry VII's chapel in Westminster Abbey is one example as is Michelangelo's Medici chapel in San Lorenzo, Florence. Work on the Medici chapel was interrupted by the sack of Rome, and it was never totally completed. Yet it is a masterpiece whose every detail contributes to the whole. On and off construction continued from 1519 through 1534. It houses the tombs of Giuliano and Lorenzo de Medici. Michelangelo deliberately placed the windows so that the entire chapel would be bathed in a pearly radiance, meant to suggest the perpetual light shining upon the dukes in death. Masses of the Dead were still being celebrated four times daily well into the seventeenth century.

Botticelli's series of drawings illustrating Dante's Divina Commedia attempts to depict the particular images of purgatory as found in those poems.

On this feast day, many Catholics visit the graves of loved ones and leave mementos and flowers. This is a significant day for Latinos. On *el dia de los muertos* food is left out on a table in the house and on the table are displayed skulls made of sugar with the names of deceased ones on the forehead of the skull. Candles are lit so that the deceased can "see" the food when they visit during the night. On this day, it is also an Hispanic custom to visit cemeteries with flowers and music to hold a picnic at the gravesites of family members and friends.

Notes

Dismissal Catechesis (30 min)

Getting Started

Have a table prepared with white cloth on which is placed the parish's Book of the Dead or Book of Remembrance, a lighted candle and a plant. Invite everyone to be seated in a circle around the table. Pray in these or similar words:

"O God, giver of all life, we gather today to give thanks and praise for all those who have gone before us. We remember in a special way those members of our own families, friends and members of this parish who have died. Bless them with the gift of eternal life, console their families. Help us to be prepared when the hour of our death is upon us. We ask this in the name of Jesus Christ, your son, who lives and reigns with you in unity with the Holy Spirit, now and forever. Amen."

First Impressions

Recall words and phrases from the Liturgy of the Word. Include phrases from the songs and prayers as well as the readings. Spend a few minutes in quiet. Discuss with the catechumens and candidates the mood or feelings expressed in this liturgy. *How is it different; how is the same as other liturgies? What surprised or puzzled them about today's feast?*

Making Connections

1. Elicit their remembrances of loved ones who have died. Suggest such activities as remembering anniversaries, Memorial Day, family albums, genealogy charts and family gatherings during which stories are told. Often in families as children are growing up, adults will make comments comparing the child's behavior, looks, personality to that of someone who has died. Progeny perpetuate the family name and story.

2. Ask participants whether they have been to a Catholic funeral. Have displayed a funeral pall, the Paschal candle, and incense, and explain their symbolism. Discuss the three movements of a funeral liturgy: vigil, Mass of Resurrection and committal rite. Explain that the white vestment—a sign of resurrection and Easter—is worn on All Souls Day and at every funeral.

3. What does each of us believe about death and what happens to the person who has died? Proclaim 2 Maccabees 12:46. What does this reading say about death and remembering those who have died?

Prayer

Teach the prayer: *Eternal rest grant unto them, O Lord. And let perpetual light shine upon them. May their soul and all the souls of the faithful departed rest in peace. Amen.*

Extended Catechesis

SESSION FOCUS: *Purgatory*

Gathering

A. Sunday:

Welcome everyone and invite them to be seated in groups of three or four. Invite everyone to recall a loved one who has died. After a moment of silence, pray the following prayer from the funeral liturgy:

"May the angels lead you into paradise, and the martyrs come to welcome you, and lead you into the holy city, the new and eternal Jerusalem."

Offer each person the opportunity to speak the name of a loved one who has died and direct everyone to respond with the words, *"Rest in peace."*

B. Weekday:

Welcome everyone. Begin with a Celebration of the Word, such as:

- Song: "I Am the Bread of Life" (Toolan)
- Sign of the Cross and Greeting
- Reading: 1st Reading proclaimed on the feast
- Quiet
- Alleluia
- Gospel Proclaimed on the feast
- Alleluia

The Word (30 min)

Reflect with the group on the readings that have been proclaimed, consulting a Bible commentary, such as the Collegeville commentary, for any points that are unclear to you.

Catholic Teaching (30 min)

1. Direct people to list their ideas of purgatory, include ideas they have heard as well as questions that they want to explore further regarding purgatory. Have one person from each group report key comments, observations and questions to the whole group.

2. Delve into the common perception of purgatory as fire. Refer to 1 Corinthians 3:15 and 1 Peter 1:7. Explain that the operative notion in our Catholic doctrine and theology on purgatory is that it is a state of purification not punishment. This state may even last only an instant, as we count time. What the doctrine upholds is that purgatory is a transitional state which makes one ready for the experience of the beatific vision.

3. Point out that purgatory is a state of purification between death and heaven whereby the remaining obstacles to the full enjoyment of one's personal and eternal union with God are removed. For those justified and reconciled in Christ, this

purification completes the process of sanctification so that one can enter into union with the triune God.

4. Tell the group of the unbroken liturgical practice in our Church of making intercessory prayers for the dead. This practice dates to the earliest times of the Church: Tertullian, about 160 AD; St. Cyprian, Bishop of Carthage, about 250 AD; St. Cyril of Jerusalem about 315 AD just to name a few. In the Eucharistic Prayer, we pray for the dead. There is also the generally accepted practice of offering Mass for the deceased in the firm conviction that, as part of the communion of saints, we may "assist" them by our prayers.

5. Read to them the quote of St. Catherine of Genoa found in Understanding This Sunday.

Invite them to discuss this quote.

6. Gather from the whole group insights and clarifications gained from this session. Mention any remaining questions or comments.

Putting Faith Into Practice

1. Discuss with them customs for remembering the dead such as visiting the cemetery, planting flowers, requesting a Mass of Remembrance for a loved one, memorials, as well as other cultural practices.

2. Show them the Book of the Dead or the Book of Remembrance. Invite them to write in the Book of Remembrance names family members and friends that they would like to add.

Prayer

Gather as a large group standing around the Book of Remembrance. Spend a few moments again recalling people who have died. Sing "On Eagles Wings" (Joncas).

Dedication of St. John Lateran

NOVEMBER 9

The Word In Liturgy

Ezekiel 47:1-2, 8-9, 12
1 Corinthians 3:9c-11, 16-17
Psalm 84:3-6, 8, 11
John 2:13-22

The feast of the Dedication of St. John Lateran celebrates the founding of the cathedral of the bishop of Rome. Just as in each diocese the diocesan cathedral is considered the mother church of all the parish churches, so the pope's cathedral, St. John Lateran, is considered the mother and head church of the city of Rome and all the Roman Catholic communities in the world *(Omnium urbis et orbis Ecclesiarum Mater et Caput)*. It was the first Christian basilica to be erected in Rome, by the emperor Constantine in about 314-318 A.D., and it became the model of all subsequent Christian churches. It was dedicated to the Redeemer and later to Saints John the Evangelist and John the Baptist. Its magnificent baptistry is likewise dedicated to St. John the Baptist. Over the centuries, the church was several times destroyed (by invaders, earthquake, and fire) and rebuilt. Its importance in the history of the Church is great. Until 1870, popes were crowned there, and it was the site of five Councils between 1123 and 1512.

The spiritual significance of this feast is explored in various ways through the readings, all of which are taken from selections that may be used at the dedication of any church. The first reading, from Ezekiel, describes a wonderful vision in which the prophet sees a new temple that is the source of life and abundance for all who gather at the streams which flow from it. Speaking from the context of exile and deprivation, Ezekiel voices a prophetic promise that gave hope to his hearers. In this vision, the temple's life flows out as water, and irrigates the surrounding land. The connection with today's feast is unmistakable, as we see the many communities of faith all over the world which have flowed out of the Church at Rome and continue to produce fruit and flourish

in connection with their center. To Christian readers, the water also may suggest the new life of baptism, which flows from God through the Church and brings abundant life and lasting growth.

The second reading, from St. Paul's first letter to the Corinthians, again uses the image of the temple, but in a different way. There are two main points here. Christ is the foundation stone upon which the temple is built. No other foundation can be claimed. This point is essential for our celebration of the feast, lest we begin to think that what we commemorate is no more than bricks and mortar. The living Christ is the foundation of the Church, and to celebrate the dedication of St. John Lateran is to see in that venerable building a touchstone for the mystery of the Church's unity in Christ as it goes on its pilgrimage through history. The second point to observe is that Paul is referring to the community when he says "you are God's temple." In this passage he is speaking not of the indwelling Spirit in each individual believer, but of the mystery of the Spirit in the community of the Church. "You" is plural. Thus, the reading directs us to the heart of the feast we celebrate: the action of Christ and the Spirit sustaining the worldwide community of the Church.

John's gospel presents us with an image of Jesus filled with prophetic zeal (see *Catechist's Manual, Year B, Third Sunday of Lent)*. His actions recall and fulfill the prophetic expectation that when the Messiah comes he will purify the temple. His words also call attention to "temple" as a description of his own body—to be destroyed by death but raised up again in three days. In the context of today's liturgy the accent may appropriately fall either on Christ's role in purifying the temple or on the prediction of his paschal mystery. In the first instance, purification recalls the need for vigilance and reform in the Church. According to the Second Vatican Council, the Church is always called to reform (*ecclesia semper reformanda*). Christ is not only the foundation, supporting the Church, but also its Lord who comes in sovereign freedom to apply to it the refiner's fire of judgment. The passage keeps us from an overly domesticated view of the Church, which treats Christ as a tolerant absentee landlord. It reminds us that Christ will not bear with corruption or the neglect of true worship. In the second instance, we may reflect on the "zeal for God's house" which consumed Jesus, and led to his suffering, death and resurrection. The Church is no mere human project, but is born out of the paschal mystery of Jesus. The temple he erects is his risen body. If we belong to that risen body of Christ, we too must be zealous for the life of the Church, its unity, its right worship, its holiness, its apostolic fervor. Our doctrinal focus today therefore is on the four marks of the Church: the Church is one, holy, catholic, and apostolic.

Catholic Doctrine

The Four Marks of the Church

The feast we celebrate today observes the anniversary of the dedication of the cathedral church of Rome. When the Emperor Constantine officially recognized Christianity, he made generous gifts to the Church, one of which was a palace and grounds formerly belonging to the Laterani family. In 324 he added a large church on the grounds named the Basilica of the Savior. Legend has it that the basilica was dedicated on November 9 that year. Later a baptistry was added and dedicated to St. John the Baptist. In subsequent years the entire edifice became known as St. John of the Lateran. Because it is the cathedral church of the bishop of Rome, the feast, at first observed only in Rome, was later extended to the whole Church as a sign of devotion to and of unity with the Chair of Peter.

Thus, while this feast originates in a particular edifice in a particular place, it truly celebrates the universal Church which is apostolic, catholic, holy and one. The following is a brief summary of each of these characteristics.

We believe the Church is apostolic because it is founded upon the apostles, those chosen witnesses who were sent out on mission by the Lord himself and who later testified to the saving plan of God in Christ (CCC 857). Through the agency of the Holy Spirit the Church is entrusted to keep and to hand on the teaching of the apostles. Down through the ages the Church continues to be nourished in the teaching of the apostles by their successors, the college of bishops "assisted by priests, and one which [the bishops] share with the successor of St. Peter, the supreme pastor of the Church. . ." (Second Vatican Council, *Ad Gentes*, 7 November 1965, n 5)

We believe the Church is catholic or universal because Christ is its head. The body, the Church, is in union with its head who has provided "the fullness of the means of salvation" to us. (Second Vatican Council, *Unitatis Redintegratio*, 21 November 1964, n 3) This fullness of the means of salvation is to be found in a correct and complete confession of faith, sacramental life and ordained ministry in apostolic succession (CCC 830). The Church is also catholic in the sense that its mission is to the whole world. This universal Church is truly present in each local or particular church, a diocese or eparchy, that is legitimately organized around its pastor who is in communion with the Church of Rome (CCC 832-34).

We believe the Church is holy because Jesus, the Son of God, with the Father and the Spirit, is acknowledged as the Holy One and loved the Church so much that he sacrificed himself in order to sanctify his ecclesial body (CCC 823). Thus, the Church is called the "holy people of God" and her members "saints" (Acts 9:13; 1 Cor 6:l; 16:1). This holiness with which the earthly Church is endowed is real but also imperfect. Every individual within the Church, including ordained ministers, acknowledge that they are sinners. Pope Paul VI wrote, "The Church is therefore holy, though having sinners in her midst, because she herself has no other life but the life of grace." (Paul VI, *Credo of the People of God: Solemn Profession of Faith*, 30 June 1968, 19; quoted in CCC 827)

We believe the Church is one because of its source, the divinity, who is the supreme example of unity: the God who is three-in-one (CCC 813). The Second Vatican Council, in different documents, also asserts that the Church is one because of its founder, Jesus, the Word made flesh, who by his saving action restores unity in "one people and one body" (GS, 78) and that the Church is one because of the Holy Spirit, "the principle of the Church's unity." (UR, 2)

These four characteristics, which we profess in the Creed, indicate essential elements or qualities of the Church and its mission. In and of itself, the Church does not possess these elements. They are gifts given by Christ and, simultaneously, a challenge. For the Church is called to realize, appropriate and work with this endowment.

Catholic Culture

The Lateran basilica is filled with venerable relics. The high altar itself is constructed over a wooden table which, as legend has it, St. Peter celebrated the Eucharist with the ancient Christians of Rome. (Mary Ellen Hynes, *Companion to the Calendar*, LTP, Archdiocese of Chicago, 1993, p 166)

The famous Lateran Treaty or "Concordat" agreed upon between the Vatican and Mussolini was finalized and signed at the Lateran Palace. The agreement stipulates that the Lateran grounds are also considered part of Vatican City State.

Dismissal Catechesis (30 min)

Getting Started

1. Before the session, prepare the meeting space with a prayer environment and enough chairs. Be sure that the room is set in a manner conducive to group discussion.

2. Gather the group and place the lectionary in a prominent place. Invite the participants to join you in beginning with a prayer. You may use the following prayer or one of your own composition. The following prayer is from the Common of the Dedication of a Church.

   Father,
   each year we recall the dedication of this church
   to your service.
   Let our worship always be sincere
   and help us to find your saving love in this church.

   Grant this through Jesus Christ, your Son,
   who lives and reigns with you and the Holy Spirit,
   one God, for ever and ever.

First Impressions

1. Explain to the group that the Church is celebrating the feast of St. John Lateran. Share with them the significance of the basilica of St. John Lateran as a symbol of the universal church. You may use the following words from the Catholic Doctrine section or summarize the teaching in your own words.

   The feast we celebrate today observes the anniversary of the dedication of the cathedral church of Rome. When the Emperor Constantine officially recognized Christianity, he made generous gifts to the Church, one of which was a palace and grounds formerly belonging to the Laterani family. In 324 he added a large church on the grounds named the Basilica of the Savior. Legend has it that the basilica was dedicated on November 9 that year. Later a baptistry was added and dedicated to St. John the Baptist. In subsequent years the entire edifice became known as St. John of the Lateran. Because it is the cathedral church of the bishop of Rome, the feast, at first observed only in Rome, was later extended to the whole Church as a sign of devotion to and of unity with the Chair of Peter.

2. Invite the group to reflect on how they feel about becoming a member of a universal Church. Ask them what hesitations, concerns, or questions they have. Depending on the size of your group, you might offer the group an opportunity to discuss in small groups before sharing with the large group.

Making Connections

1. Share with the group what it means for you to be a member of a universal Church. Include in your sharing any questions it has raised for you and the blessings it has held for you as a Catholic.

2. Explore how the Church's universal dimension impacts the life of Catholics throughout the world. A simple example would be the liturgy and how it is the same throughout the world, but at the same time culturally adapted to the people. Another example would be the hierarchical structure of the Pope and bishops. Explain to the group that even with a universal dimension that allows for diversity it is called to be one Church. This unity is a gift, a charism of God in Jesus Christ.

3. Invite participants to gather in small groups to discuss the following questions: In light of the discussion, how are you challenged? What gift does being part of a universal church offer to you? Afterward, elicit any comments or responses from the group.

Prayer

Conclude with spontaneous prayers for the Church, such as the following:

Let us pray.
Loving God, You desire that all your people throughout the world come to know the glorious joy of your salvation. Hear our prayers for your people:

For the Church, the people of God, throughout the world, may they grow in their witness of God's love for all people. We pray to the Lord.
Response: *Lord, hear our prayer.*

For the Pope, may he grow in wisdom. We pray to the Lord.
Response: *Lord, hear our prayer.*

For our Bishop (name), may he be faithful in his proclamation of the gospel. We pray to the Lord.
Response: *Lord, hear our prayer.*

For our parish, may we grow in our witness, in God's wisdom, and in our faithful action to proclaim the gospel. We pray to the Lord.
Response: *Lord, hear our prayer.*

(Invite the group to offer their own prayers and then conclude with the following:)

Lord, we know that you hear our prayers and we thank you for all that you are doing in our lives. We ask these prayers in Jesus' name. Amen.

Extended Catechesis

SESSION FOCUS: *The Four Marks of the Church*

Gathering

A. Sunday:

Welcome the sponsors and team members to the expanded group. Ask the group to respond to the following question: *When God established the Church through Jesus Christ, what characteristics do you believe God intended the Church to exemplify?*

B. Weekday:

If you gather for extended catechesis during the week, be sure to begin with a Celebration of the Word. For this feast day, there are 22 possible scripture tests. Select readings to use with the a prayer format such as:

- Gathering Hymn
- Greeting and Gathering Prayer
- Proclaim: Ezekiel 47:1-2, 8-9, 12
- Sing the Responsorial Psalm (See Lectionary #703)
- Proclaim: 1 Corinthians 3:9c-11, 16-17
- Sing the Gospel Acclamation
- Proclaim: John 2:13-22
- Pray using a prayer text from the Common Dedication of a Church

The Word (30 min)

1. Prepare for catechesis with the help of the Word in Liturgy commentary and invite the catechumens and candidates into prayerful reflection on the readings in a way similar to the method that has been used on other Sundays.

2. The following questions may be helpful: *What word or phrase spoke to you from the liturgy? What meaning did it have for you?* Continue with further discussion about the meaning of the scriptures or their lives. Conclude by asking: *In light of the liturgy, the scriptures, and our discussion, how do you hear yourself being called to respond to the word in the coming week?*

Catholic Teaching (30 min)

1. Remind the group that we are celebrating the Feast of St. John Lateran. Explain to the group, using the Catholic Doctrine section, that we are not just celebrating a particular place in Rome. Rather, the Feast of St. John Lateran provides an opportunity to celebrate the universal Church which is one, holy, catholic, and apostolic.

   As a prelude to a discussion of the four marks of the Church, recite the section of the Nicene Creed that professes our belief in one, holy, catholic, and apostolic Church. Explain to the group that these marks do not belong exclusively to the Roman Catholic Church. They are marks of the church as the body of Christ with Christ as the head. They are gifts given by Christ to the church already present but not complete. We are challenged to fully realize, appropriate, and work toward the fullness of a church which is one, holy, catholic, and apostolic.

2. Focus on the church as one. Ask the participants who have been baptized in another tradition to share their own experiences of being baptized. Ask: *What was it like and what does it mean to you?* After sharing, ask the group why we do not re-baptize people who have already been baptized in a Christian tradition? Be sure that the group understands that the Church recognizes the baptism of other Christian churches. In spite of the plurality of churches, we are one in our baptism and the source of our being one is the Trinity. Conclude by discussing the following question: *How are we called individually and as a community to work for unity among the churches?*

3. Focus on the church's mark of holiness. Ask the group: *What does it mean to be holy?* Explain to the group that all people of the church are called to holiness and that the source of this holiness is Christ. Using the Catholic Doctrine section, share how the church shares in the holiness of Christ, albeit imperfectly because of sin. Through God's grace we are made holy. Ask the participants to share in pairs how they believe they are called to holiness.

4. Focus on the church as catholic. Point out to the group that catholic does not refer to Roman Catholic. Rather, this mark indicates that the church is to be universal, which is the meaning of catholic. The source of its universality is Christ. The church is in union with Christ, who has provided the fullness of the means to salvation for us. Explain to the group that the church's mission is to proclaim the good news of salvation to all the world. The universal proclamation of God's good news is to be adapted to the situations and circumstances of the world. Share how the church proclaims the good news through the work of missionaries or agencies such as Catholic Relief Services or Catholic Charities.

5. Focus on the church as apostolic. Develop a definition of apostle as one who is sent by Jesus Christ and who is faithful to his message of salvation. As the early apostles were faithful, so the church is called to be faithful to Christ. Bring out that since the earliest days, the church, in its desire to be faithful, has entrusted the teachings of the gospel to its bishops. Ask the group to share in pairs the ways they believe they are called to be faithful to Jesus Christ.

Putting Faith Into Practice

Ask the group to respond to the following questions with one other person: *In light of the discussion and reflection, how are you challenged? How are you hopeful?* After the pairs have finished, invite any comments or responses to be shared with the large group.

Prayer

Conclude the session with an adaptation of the reading from Ephesians 1:15-19.

Listen to the words of St. Paul's letter to the Ephesians as if they were addressed to you personally. For they are intended for you, as they are for every generation of believers.

For my part, from the time I first heard of your faith in the Lord Jesus and your love for all the members of the church, I have never stopped thanking God for you and recommending you in my prayers. May the God of our Lord Jesus Christ, the Father of glory, grant you a spirit of wisdom and insight to know him clearly. May he enlighten your innermost vision that you may know the great hope to which he has called you, the wealth of his glorious heritage to be distributed among members of the church, and the immeasurable scope of his power in us who believe.

This is asked in the name of our Lord, Jesus Christ. Amen.

Index

Index of Doctrinal Themes

SUNDAY/FEAST	DOCTRINAL FOCUS

Advent 1

The Second Coming of Christ
Nicene Creed: "He will come again in glory"
kingdom of God: already here, not yet fully manifested
Eucharistic banquet as a pledge of the fullness of the kingdom
fervent prayer of Christians: "maranatha" ("come, Lord Jesus")
actively working for the kingdom in this world
false expectations: secularism and millenarianism

Advent 2

Hope for salvation
function of prophets: to educate us in hope
John the Baptist points the way to Jesus Christ
waiting for salvation in faith

Advent 3

Moral conversion prepares for the coming of Christ
humans created with an innate sense of goodness
moral conversion an imperative for all
daily living and conversion to Christ
cardinal virtues (prudence, justice, fortitude and temperance)

Advent 4

The coming of Christ in the flesh
the Messiah born into the world
Jesus Christ, fully human and fully divine
the revelation of God to us in Jesus
sacredness of life from the womb & role of the unborn

Christmas Day

Christ came for our salvation
Incarnation of the eternal Word in Jesus Christ
Incarnation as unmerited grace of God to us
"invisible God made visible" in Jesus Christ

Holy Family

The family as the domestic church
role of the family as the "domestic church"
family as the primary cell of society
the communion of persons found in the Christian family

Epiphany

Christ is the light of all nations
all find radiance in God's light, in Christ
significance of epiphany, which means, "showing forth"
the Church's missionary impulse

Baptism of the Lord

One Baptism for the forgiveness of sins
purification from sin and new birth in the Spirit
Original sin and personal sin and Baptism
womb of Baptism and font of the household of God
handing on faith through Baptism

Lent 1

Divine election
God's initiative in choosing a people
Historical events reveal God's choice
The Chosen One, Jesus Christ, elect of God
Jesus' humble submission to the will of the Father
Catholic Church and its inheritance of Israel's election

Lent 2

Contemplative prayer
types of prayer: spoken, meditative and contemplative
the gift of contemplative prayer
mystics and contemplative prayer in the life of Christians

Lent 3

God is kind and merciful
Jesus, the full revelation of the God who saves us
the mercy of God

Lent 4

Conversion
the Lenten invitation to turn away from sin
the human tendency to concupiscence
newness of life in Baptism
life-long conversion for individuals and for the Church
inner conversion signaled by outer "good works"

Lent 5

Reconciliation
God's unconditional love
Jesus, the primordial sacrament of reconciliation
Believers freed from the slavery of sin by the action of Jesus Christ
sins after Baptism and sacrament of Reconciliation

Passion Sunday

The meaning of suffering
salvation accomplished by the paschal mystery of Jesus
uniting human experience to the paschal mystery
the compassion of God revealed in the suffering of Jesus
the sacrament of the Anointing of the Sick

Easter Sunday

The resurrection of Jesus Christ
death of Jesus does not exhaust the love of God for us
divine love and the paschal mystery
resurrected, glorified body of Jesus not a ghost
resurrection, an actual, historical event
resurrection ratifies the whole life and teaching of Jesus

Easter 2

Faith
faith and the invitation of a relationship of love with God
Hebrew and Greek scriptural terms for "faith"
the community that hands on the gift of faith to the individual
doubt and struggling with belief in the face of human experience
Baptism and being born into a community of faith

Easter 3

Eucharist calls us to mission
discipleship, Eucharist and evangelization
the perfection of all our gifts in the Eucharist
Mass sends us forth to put our gifts in service to God's reign

Easter 4

The divinity of Christ
the Arian controversy
Council of Nicea and articulation of the full divinity of Christ
the Trinity: One God in three persons
early Church fathers and creating a vocabulary for God's mystery

Easter 5

The new commandment to love one another
the covenant of God with Israel and the Law
new commandment of Jesus based in the old covenant
perfection of the old covenant in new covenant
God exemplified in Jesus who loved others

Easter 6

Peace
Hebrew understanding of "shalom"
challenge of peace for followers of Jesus Christ
peace is not an optional commitment for disciples

Easter 7

Christian unity
ecumenical movement and the universal Catholic Church
Catholic Church founded by Jesus
other Christian churches and the one Church of Jesus
Christians joining together in prayer, good works, study and dialogue
the prayer of Jesus that all may be one

Pentecost

The gifts of the Spirit and the sacrament of Confirmation
believers sealed with the gift of the Holy Spirit
purpose of this sealing: witness
the designation "Christian" which means "anointed"

Ordinary Time 2

Sacrament of Marriage
Marriage, human institution and part of God's plan
ends of marriage: children and the unity of the couple
Marriage as a covenant (not a contract) between husband and wife
indissolubility of marriage
unions lacking what is necessary for the sacrament and annulments

Ordinary Time 3

Sacred scripture
the eternal Word of God: Jesus Christ
Scripture and tradition flow from the one source of divine revelation
the inspiration of scripture and God's truth conveyed
ministries of the Word
conversion and the challenge of scripture

Ordinary Time 4

The Christian call to prophecy
seeing life from the perspective of God and speaking the Word
one aspect of the identity of Jesus: prophet
believers share in the identity of Jesus the prophet by Baptism
mission and witness of Christians

Ordinary Time 5

Tradition
the God of revelation who continually engages believers
teaching authority of the bishops and the sacred deposit of the faith
Tradition, a process and a content, that builds up the body of the Church

Ordinary Time 31	**Justification** God's saving action in Jesus that frees us from sin and renews us Protestant reformation and Council of Trent and justification justification merited for us through passion of Christ absolute sovereignty of God who saves us
Ordinary Time 32	**Heaven and Hell** death is a threshold to a life beyond this one hell and eternal separation from God as consequence of mortal sin heaven and beatific vision (union with God) as consequence of grace
Ordinary Time 33	**Justice** richness of modern Catholic social teaching religion and what we owe God, justice and what we owe others justice as a quality of faithful persons social beings living in an imperfect world as necessity of justice
Ordinary Time 34	**Christ the King** Christ's cross as royal throne and altar of sacrifice Kingship of Christ confounds and overturns worldly calculations Lordship of Christ over all of human history Lordship of Christ over the Church our ultimate allegiance belongs to Christ alone the eternal and universal kingdom
Immac Conception	**Immaculate Conception of the Blessed Virgin Mary** Pius XII and articulation of this dogma Paul VI: devotion to Mary leads us to glorify God Mary, model disciple and Mother of God holiness of Mary due to God's love of her and God's grace Mary's redemption achieved in unique way: immaculate conception Mary's yes to God
Mary, Mother of God	**"He was born of the Virgin Mary and Became Man"** Council of Ephesus and declaration of Mary as Mother of God Mary linked to the work of the Son, Jesus start of the calendar year, honoring Mary, contemplating paschal mystery Mary's free cooperation with plan of God
Presentation of the Lord	**The Two Natures of Jesus Christ** Jesus Christ: fully human, fully divine Council of Chalcedon and formulation of this doctrine Jesus, Son of God and Son of Mary this feast day and going to meet the Lord with lighted candles Jesus Christ: the light of all peoples
Ascension of the Lord	**"He Ascended into Heaven and is Seated at the Right Hand of the Father"** the ascension of Christ as part of the paschal mystery salvation in Christ Christ's presence to and in the Church in post-resurrection era Christ's ascension and our call to follow in hope ascension and Christ's Spirit in the gift of the sacraments
Birth of John the Baptist	**Human Cooperation with Divine Grace** grace and human freedom grace as a gift from God preparation to receive grace is also a gift from God God reaches out to us; we are invited to respond our vocation in God: illustrated by life of John the Baptist
Peter and Paul	**Collegiality** essential element in ministry of bishop college of bishops in union with pope examples of collegiality collegiality expressive of universality of Church **analogy of the human body**
Transfiguration	**Visions and Private Revelations** Jesus Christ alone is the fullness of God's revelation the mystery of Christ and the mystery of creation scripture and tradition and the deposit of revelation no new public revelation until the second coming of Christ mysticism and revelation manifestation of Mary at Lourdes and Fatima enhances the meaning of Christ God "speaking" everything to us in his Word, Jesus Christ
Assumption	**The Assumption of Mary** based in ancient Church tradition Pius XII and articulation of this doctrine the assumption and Mary's unique participation in Christ's resurrection Vatican II on Mary: her work as intercessor continues
Triumph of the Cross	**Redemption** passion and death of Jesus is triumph of his love self-offering of Jesus in love to God the Father Jesus, the redeemer who liberates us from sin and death work of redemption continued in the Church effects of redemption extend to human history and creation gift of redemption: removes estrangement, offers us a "center"
All Saints	**The Communion of Saints** all Christians called to holiness of life exemplary Christians, the saints saints, intercessors before God and companions in prayer, modeled on Mary the communion of saints and the Church distinction between worship (God) and veneration (saints) apostles, martyrs and supreme witness of shedding blood for faith Blessed Virgin Mary, angels and saints
All Souls	**Purgatory** state of purification (not punishment) between death and heaven removal of obstacles (venial sins) to union with God beatific vision purgatory and tradition in our Church of interceding in prayer for the dead communion of saints and praying for dead Eucharistic Prayer and praying for dead offering Mass for the dead
Dedication of John Lateran	**The Four Marks of the Church** John Lateran, the cathedral church of Rome this feast celebrates the "whole Church" Church: one, holy, catholic, and apostolic these characteristics flow from Jesus and professed in the Creed these characteristics an endowment that challenges entire Church

---

LITURGY:

Book of Blessings. Prepared by International Commission on English in the Liturgy, Approved for use in the Dioceses of the United States of America by the National Conference of Catholic Bishops and confirmed by the Apostolic See. The Order of St. Benedict, Inc., The Liturgical Press, Collegeville, Minnesota, ©1989.

General Instruction of the Roman Missal, Fourth Edition, 27 March 1975, The Roman Missal, The Sacramentary. English translation prepared by the international Commission on English in the Liturgy, Approved for Use in the Dioceses of the United States of America by the National Conference of Catholic Bishops and confirmed by the Apostolic See. Catholic Book Publishing Co., New York ©1985.

Liturgy of the Hours, The, According to the Roman Rite. English Translation prepared by the International Commission on English in the Liturgy, Catholic Book Publishing Company, New York, 1975.

Order of Christian Funerals. Prepared by International Commission on English in the Liturgy, Liturgy Training Publications 1800 North Hermitage Avenue, Chicago, IL 60622-1101 ©1989, Archdiocese of Chicago.

Rite of Anointing and Pastoral Care of the Sick. The Rites of the Catholic Church, English translation prepared by The International Commission on English in the Liturgy ©1976. Pueblo Publishing Company, Inc., 1860 Broadway, New York, NY 10023 ©1976.

Rite of Baptism for Children. The Rites of the Catholic Church, English translation prepared by The International Commission on English in the Liturgy ©1976. Pueblo Publishing Company, Inc., 1860 Broadway, New York, NY 10023 ©1976.

Rite of Christian Initiation of Adults. The Rites of the Catholic Church, English translation prepared by The International Commission on English in the Liturgy ©1976. Pueblo Publishing Company, Inc., 1860 Broadway, New York, NY 10023 ©1976.

Rite of Ordination of a Bishop. The Rites of the Catholic Church, Volume Two, English translation prepared by The International Commission on English in the Liturgy ©1969, Pueblo Publishing Company, Inc., 1860 Broadway, New York, NY 10023, 1980.

Rite of Penance. The Rites of the Catholic Church, English translation prepared by The International Commission on English in the Liturgy ©1976. Pueblo Publishing Company, Inc., 1860 Broadway, New York, NY 10023 ©1976.

The Roman Missal, The Sacramentary. English translation prepared by the international Commission on English in the Liturgy, Approved for Use in the Dioceses of the United States of America by the National Conference of Catholic Bishops and confirmed by the Apostolic See. Catholic Book Publishing Co., New York ©1985.

DOCUMENTARY RESOURCES:

Acta Apostolicae Sedis

Documents on the Liturgy 1963-1979. Conciliar, Papal, and Curial Texts, International Commission on English in the Liturgy, The Liturgical Press, Collegeville, Minnesota, ©1982.

SECOND VATICAN COUNCIL:

*Note: These documents are found in: Vatican Council II, Volume 1 The Conciliar and Postconciliar Documents, New Revised Edition, Austin Flannery, O.P. General Editor, Costello Publishing Company, P. O. Box 9, Northport, New York 11768, ©1996.

Ad Gentes Divinitus, 7 December 1965

Apostolicam Actuositatem, 18 November 1965

Dei Verbum, 18 November 1965

Dignitatis Humanae, 7 December 1965

Gaudium et Spes, 7 December 1965

Lumen Gentium, 21 November 1964

Presbyterorum Ordinis, 7 December 1965

Sacrosanctum Concilium, 4 December 1963

ECCLESIASTICAL DOCUMENTS/CONGREGATIONS:

Bishops' Committee on the Liturgy, National Conference of Catholic Bishops, Order for the Solemn Exposition of the Holy Eucharist. The Liturgical Press, The Order of St. Benedict, Inc., Collegeville, Minnesota, 1993.

Sacred Congregation for the Clergy, *General Catechetical Directory*, The Catechetical Documents A Parish Resource. Martin Connell, Editor, Archdiocese of Chicago: Liturgy Training Publications, 1800 North Hermitage Avenue, Chicago, IL 60622-1011 ©1996.

ECCLESIASTICAL WRITERS:

Ambrose, St.:
  De sacramentis
  De mysteriis

Augustine of Hippo, St.:
  De civitate Dei
  Enarrationes in Psalmos
  In evangelium Johannis tractatus
  Sermones

Bonaventure, St.:
  Breviloquium, Prologue

Gregory of Nazianzus, St.:
  Orationes

Irenaeus of Lyons, St.:
  Adversus haereses

Leo the Great, St.:
  Sermones

Newman, John Henry, Cardinal:
  Letter to the Duke of Norfolk, 5

Thomas Aquinas, St.:
  Collationes in decem praeceptis
  Summa theologiae

PAPAL WRITING:

Paul VI:

  Evangelii Nuntiandi, 1975, The Catechetical Documents A Parish Resource. Martin Connell, Editor, Archdiocese of Chicago: Liturgy Training Publications, 1800 North Hermitage Avenue, Chicago, IL 60622-1011 ©1996.

John Paul II:

Dives in Misericordia, 1980, <u>The Encyclicals of John Paul II</u>, Edited by J. Michael Miller, C.S.B., Our Sunday Visitor Publishing Division, Our Sunday Visitor, Inc. 200 Noll Plaza, Huntington, Indiana 46750, ©1996.

Evangelium Vitae, 25 March 1995, <u>The Encyclicals of John Paul II</u>, Edited by J. Michael Miller, C.S.B., Our Sunday Visitor Publishing Division, Our Sunday Visitor, Inc. 200 Noll Plaza, Huntington, Indiana 46750, ©1996.

Familiaris consortio, 22 November 1981, an Apostolic Exhortation

Reconciliatio et Paenitentia, 2 December 1984 <u>Reconciliation and Penance</u>, In the Mission of the Church Today. Post-Synodal Apostolic Exhortation of His Holiness Pope John Paul II. Printed and published by Pauline Books & Media, 50 St. Paul's Avenue, Boston, MA 02130.

Redemptoris Missio, 7 December 1990, <u>The Encyclicals of John Paul II</u>, Edited by J. Michael Miller, C.S.B., Our Sunday Visitor Publishing Division, Our Sunday Visitor, Inc. 200 Noll Plaza, Huntington, Indiana 46750, ©1996.

Salvifici Doloris, 11 February 1984, <u>On the Christian Meaning of Human Suffering</u>, Apostolic Letter of John Paul II, Printed and published by Pauline Books & Media, 50 St. Paul's Avenue, Boston, MA 02130.

Solicitudo Rei Socialis, 19 February 1988, <u>The Encyclicals of John Paul II</u>, Edited by J. Michael Miller, C.S.B., Our Sunday Visitor Publishing Division, Our Sunday Visitor, Inc. 200 Noll Plaza, Huntington, Indiana 46750, ©1996.

Ut Unum Sint, 25 May 1995, <u>The Encyclicals of John Paul II</u>, Edited by J. Michael Miller, C.S.B., Our Sunday Visitor Publishing Division, Our Sunday Visitor, Inc. 200 Noll Plaza, Huntington, Indiana 46750, ©1996.

OTHERS:

Beinert, Wolfgang and Fiorenza, Francis Schussler, Editors:
<u>Handbook of Catholic Theology</u>. The Crossroad Publishing Company, 370 Lexington Avenue, New York, NY 10017, ©1995.

Bishops' Committee on the Liturgy:
<u>Catholic Household Blessings & Prayers</u>. National Conference of Catholic Bishops, United States Catholic Conference, Inc., Washington, D.C. ©1988.

Cameli, Louis J.:
<u>Mary's Journey</u>. William H. Sadlier, Inc., 11 Park Place, New York, NY 10007, ©1982.

Catherine of Genoa:
<u>Purgation and Purgatory, the Spiritual Dialogue</u>. translation by S. Hughes, Paulist Press, New York, 1979.

Chesterton, Gilbert. K.:
<u>Orthodoxy</u>. Image Books, Div. of Doubleday & Company, Inc., Garden City, New York, 1959.

Colledge, Edward and Walsh, James:
<u>Julian of Norwich: Showings</u>. Paulist Press, New York, ©1988.

Cummings, E. E.:
<u>Complete Poems 1913-1962</u>. Harcourt Brace Jovanovich, Publishers, New York, 1980.

Ferrone, Rita:
<u>Forum Essays: On the Rite of Election</u>. Archdiocese of Chicago: Liturgy Training Publications, 1800 North Hermitage Avenue, Chicago, IL 60622-1101, ©1994.

Foster, Richard J.
<u>Prayer: Finding the Heart's True Home</u>. ©1992 Richard J. Foster, Harper, Collins Publishers, San Francisco, 1992.

Hynes, Mary Ellen:
<u>Companion to the Calendar</u>. Archdiocese of Chicago, Liturgy Training Publications, 1800 North Hermitage Avenue, Chicago, IL 60622-1101, ©1993.

Jurgens, William A.:
<u>The Faith of the Early Fathers</u>, Volume I, The Liturgical Press, The Order of St. Benedict, Inc., Collegeville, Minnesota, 1970.

Mottola, A. translator:
<u>The Spiritual Exercises of St. Ignatius</u>. Image Books

Peschke, S.V.D., C. Henry:
<u>Christian Ethics</u>, Volume II. C. Goodliffe Neale, Dublin, ©1978.

ART AND CULTURE:

Batastini, Robert J. and Cymbala, Michael A., Editors:
<u>Gather Comprehensive</u>. GIA Publications, Inc., 7404 South Mason Avenue, Chicago, IL 60638, ©1994.

Batastini, Robert J., Editor:
<u>Worship</u>. GIA Publications, Inc., 7404 South Mason Avenue, Chicago, IL 60638, ©1986.

Beckwith, John
<u>Early Christian and Byzantine Art</u>. Yale University Press, New Haven, CT ©1993.

Hartt, Frederick:
<u>History of Italian Renaissance Art, Painting, Sculpture, Architecture</u>. Fourth Edition, Revised by David G. Wilkins, Harry N. Abrams, Inc., Publishers, New York, ©1994.

Janson, H. W.:
<u>History of Art</u>, Fourth Edition, Revised and expanded by Anthony F. Janson. Harry N. Abrams, Inc., Publisher, New York, ©1991.

Marcelin-Rice, Louis and Newton, Kate, Translators:
<u>Rome</u>. Knopf Guides, Alfred A. Knopf, Inc., New York, ©1994.

Murray, Peter and Linda:
<u>The Oxford Companion to Christian Art and Architecture</u>. Oxford University Press, New York, ©1996.

Muzj, Maria Giovanna:
<u>Transfiguration</u>, Introduction to the Contemplation of Icons, St. Paul Books & Media, 50 St. Paul's Avenue, Boston, MA 02130, ©1991.

Pelikan, Jaroslav:
<u>Mary Through the Centuries</u>. Yale University Press, New Haven, CT, ©1996.

Welch, Evelyn:
<u>Art and Society in Italy 1350-1500</u>. Oxford University Press, New York, 1997.